D1420470

Massine

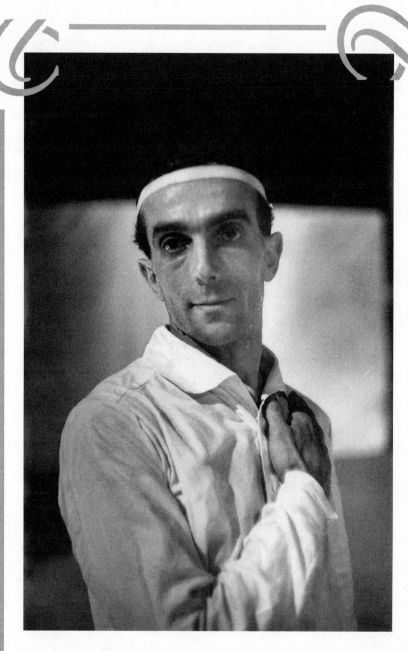

Massine rehearsing the role of Saint Francis in Nobilissima Visione, *1938*

Massine

A BIOGRAPHY

Vicente García-Márquez

NICK HERN BOOKS · LONDON 1996

A NICK HERN BOOK

Massine *first published in Great Britain in 1996 by Nick Hern Books Ltd, 14 Larden Road, London W3 7ST, by arrangement with Alfred A. Knopf, Inc., New York.*

Owing to limitations of space, acknowledgments for permission to reprint previously published material may be found on page 445.

Printed and bound in the United States of America

British Library Cataloguing-in-Publication Data A catalogue record for this book is available from the British Library
ISBN 1 85459 224 6

Contents

PART THREE

The 1920s

PART FOUR

Years of Transition: The Symphonic Ballets

CONTENTS

ACKNOWLEDGMENTS

I OFFER SPECIAL THANKS to the following persons who have assisted me since the inception of this book: Youly Algeroff, Alicia Alonso, Antonio, the late Sir Frederick Ashton, Vladimir Augenblick, Jean Babilée, Nancy van Norman Baer, Irina Baronova, André Beaurepaire, Anne Bertrand, Dinko Bogdanie, Richard Buckle, Jan Garden Castro, the late Lucia Chase, Ariane Csonka, Alexandra Danilova, Olga de Basil, Lila de Nobili, Guillermo de Osma, Dame Ninette de Valois, Mary Ann de Vlieg, Robert Descharnes, Eugenia Delarova Doll, the late Sir Anton Dolin, François Duplat, the late Parmenia Migel Ekstrom, the late Luis Escobar (Marqués de las Marismas del Guadalquivir), Ricardo España, Tamara Finch, Frederic Franklin, Lynn Garafola, Daniel Garbade Lachenal, Robert Gaston-Cottin, the late Ettore Giannini, Julio González, Alexander Grant, Tamara Grigorieva, Louisa Horton Hill, the late Jean Hugo, the late Roman Jasinski, the late Robert Joffrey, Valentina Kachuba, the late Boris Kochno, Josseline Le Bourhis, Tatiana Leskova, Irène Lidova, the late Eugene Loring, Felix Lorenzo, Mariemma, Fred and Elena Maroth, Tatiana Massine, Alejandro Medina, Madeleine Milhaud, Curtis Millner, Bruce Nalezny, Ricardo Naymanovich, José Manuel Pacheco, Jean-Pierre Pastori, Duarte Pinto-Coelho, the late Michael Powell, Thelma Schoonmaker Powell, Tatiana Riabouchinska, Marie-Thérèse Rose, Roger Salas, Henri Sauguet, Moira Shearer, Irene Skoric, Vassili Sulich, Ludmilla Tcherina, Tamara Toumanova, Alexandre Vassiliev, Nina Verchinina, Baron Tilo von Watzdorff, Igor Youskevitch, and George Zoritch.

And to the following individuals and institutions: María Isabel de Falla and Elena García de Paredes and the Fundación Archivo Manuel de Falla; Madeleine Nichols and the Dance Collection of the Library of the Performing Arts, New York Public Library; Martine Kahane and the Bibliothèque de l'Opéra de Paris; Brigitte Léal and the Musée Picasso; Ornella Volta and the Fondation Erik Satie; Patrick Bensard and the Cinémathèque Française de la Danse.

I am indebted to Lorca Massine, Peter Massine, and Theodor Massine, with particular gratitude to Tatiana Massine Weinbaum.

I would also like to thank Lynn von Kersting for providing me with a paradisiac retreat while proofreading the text; Kevin Boynton, who typed the first copy of the manuscript and whose editorial work was most valuable; Elizabeth Souritz, who conducted research in Moscow on Massine's early years; Jean Bromage, who devoted many long hours to the final research for this book in the Dance and Theater Collections of the New York Public Library; and Ivan Webster, who typed the final manuscript and whose editorial work on the text was essential. Lastly, my gratitude to Robert Gottlieb and to my editor, Susan Ralston, for her wholehearted support.

INTRODUCTION

MY FIRST ENCOUNTER with Léonide Massine took place in 1978 at Los Angeles International Airport. He had been invited by Tatiana Riabouchinska and me to attend the opening performance of the Southern California Ballet at UCLA. As I waited for him to emerge from the plane, I was filled with anticipation and expectation, for in minutes I was to meet one of the indisputable titans of twentieth-century dance.

Until that day, Massine had been for me a bit of an abstraction, a mythic figure. For years he had been regarded in the dance community as a legendary personality from times gone by. In recent years his activities in the United States had been minimal: he had conducted some master classes and, most importantly, had painstakingly staged revivals of his work for the Joffrey Ballet and, later, the Oakland Ballet.

The wait at the airport seemed endless. After a considerable passage of time—everyone seemed to have deplaned—I grew concerned, fearing that Massine might have missed his flight. Anxiously approaching an attendant to ask if any passengers were still on board the aircraft, I saw emerging through the empty aisle a small, gaunt figure of a man. His presence was authoritative; his eyes, even at a distance, were piercing; he looked like an ascetic monk or a wise, aged philosopher. He was accompanied by an attractive young woman—his assistant, Mary Ann de Vlieg. They made an imposing couple, both studiedly unapproachable. I introduced myself and we exchanged civilities. Massine hardly spoke—only later, in the car, was he the least bit expansive, and then it was to pay a compliment to Ms. de Vlieg. His gaze was disturbing and impenetrable, suggesting the insight of the sage unprepared to divulge any secrets.

The three days Massine spent in Los Angeles were filled with activity. He attended two performances of the company, and after the premiere spoke publicly in praise of the dancers. His master class at Riabouchinska's studio was packed with students and balletomanes eager for a closer glimpse of the legend. The class ended poignantly, and unexpectedly, with Riabouchinska and Massine dancing the opening section of their famous mazurka from *Le Beau Danube*.

My memory of their reunion is still unusually emotional. Their encounter was warm yet somehow distanced, bordering on awkwardness, with an almost total lack of verbal communication; words between them seemed unnecessary, and talk of the past was irrelevant for two people whose lives were linked by the sharing of a common history in the making of dance, perhaps the most ephemeral of the arts. During the first bars of the mazurka their complicity was palpable, when, oblivious to the world around them, they immersed themselves in each other's eyes, perhaps recapturing long-past memories and reasserting the profound bond that, in spite of years of silence, united them.

At the time Massine visited Los Angeles I was already conducting research for my Ballets Russes book. I took advantage of his stay there to discuss with him, whenever possible, his early symphonic ballets. In spite of his apparent aloofness and inaccessibility, which sometimes intimidated me, he was ingratiating, and conscientiously answered my questions. To my surprise he invited me to join him in France, where, later in the summer, he was to teach a choreography workshop in Rennes. I accepted on the spot, without thinking of dates or my own availability.

In Rennes I attended some of his lecture-demonstrations, and we spent time together at lunch and, after class, in the afternoons. Our conversations took in his work from the past and, above all, the new ideas he had for future work. He was particularly keen on creating a ballet where dancers never entered or exited the stage, but metamorphosed themselves continuously, in a different kind of evolution of movement. Despite his laconic manner and elusiveness, I felt a special bond being established between us. Again to my surprise, he invited me to visit him later in the summer on his private islands in the Gulf of Salerno.

If Isole dei Galli are full of timeless legends dating back to the mythical sirens' islands of Ulysses, they are no less legendary as Massine's hermitic retreat for more than fifty years; a refuge for work and rest which had been visited only by some of his closest friends and collaborators: Stravinsky, Hindemith, Reinhardt, Powell, Markevitch, and once, even, the king of Italy. On the island, life was monastic, dominated by Massine's methodical, almost obsessive, regime: swimming at 7:00 a.m., breakfast afterwards, then a walk around the steeply rocky surrounding hills, followed by work in the library until lunchtime, when we assessed his ballets and pored over the many notebooks in which, for decades, he had annotated his choreography. Any question of mine that hinted at a personal dimension, or might call for a personal opinion about anyone at all, was simply disregarded, as he continued analyzing his work. After lunch he would disappear into his private rooms, from which he would not emerge until sunset, when he sat with his entourage and visitors—no words were exchanged—on a terrace outside the tower, contemplating the resplendent sun's slow fall into the southern Mediterranean. It was a time of introspection and meditation. When I left the island several weeks later, Massine insisted on accompanying me to the mainland. In a motorboat so tiny I feared for our safety, he lay on the deck impassively, his hat covering his face, as we lurched through the choppy waves and the coastline gradually grew closer. We made plans to meet in New York in the winter. I was never to see him again.

The case for a biography of Massine is at once burning and close to impossible; the artistic giant is so often outfoxed by the man cloaked in mystery. My approach has been essentially historical rather than internal, since time after time the inner man simply could not be coaxed to the surface. If his creative work is well documented by prominent writers, critics, and witnesses of his time, Massine, the man of flesh and bone, remains forever an enigma. As a biographical subject he is in many ways ideal, for in studying his work within the context of the era that produced it, he serves as a unifying thread through decades of the development of art in the West. He was, above all, a man who not only remained for years at the vanguard of dance but was an integral part of the cultural history of our century. Through an amalgam of poetic, aesthetic, and philosophical tendencies he revitalized ballet and validated himself as an artist.

Documenting his body of work was an arduous but fascinating task. Trying to capture the persona, the man's inner life, turned into a quite misbegotten, though endlessly fascinating, crusade. His introspective stance throughout his life became a device and medium for abstracting himself, for withdrawing from the world around him, perhaps, as Jung would put it, "to prevent the object from gaining power over him." For Massine, the creative process, in tandem with theoretical observation, dominated his contribution to the world; and thus, particularly in his case, the creative act constitutes the involuntary biography of his soul. To look for any other clues to his inner self—even from those closest to him—is an insurmountable task. There are glimpses here and there of the essence, but he eludes us constantly, becoming ever more baffling.

PART ONE

Moscow

What the soul cannot reflect makes no
impact on it; but since the willpower can
control whether the soul reflects something
or not, the soul meets only what it wants
to meet. . . . But one of the soul's strongest
impulses is greed for the new, an
inclination towards the unfamiliar. . . .

—NIETZSCHE

Miassine with his sister, brothers, and parents, circa 1900

CHAPTER 1

Moscow, July 1895–November 1913

LEONID FEDOROVICH MIASSINE* was born in Moscow on July 27, 1895 (August 8 in the Western calendar), and christened at the St. Pimen Church.[1] His father, Fedor Aphanasievich, was a native of Simbirsk on the Volga River; his mother, Eugenia Nikolaevna Gladkova, came from Kharkov in the Ukraine.

Some years earlier his parents had settled in Moscow, where at the time of Leonid's birth both were employed at the Imperial Theater. Mrs. Miassine (under the name of Miassina) had sung soprano in the Bolshoi Theater Chorus since September 1884. Since September 1891 Mr. Mias-

---

* The spelling was changed to "Léonide Massine" early in his professional career. See page 60.

3

sine had played the French horn in the Bolshoi Orchestra.² The household included the couple's five children, Mikhail, Gregori, Konstantin, Raissa, and Leonid, as well as a housekeeper the children came to call Aunt Feodosia, and her three children, Maria, Irina, and Philip.

With his calm and implacable manner, Mr. Miassine was the family bulwark, the ultimate parental authority. Mrs. Miassine's warmth, vivaciousness, and optimism—"without the stubbornness"³ Massine would later describe as typical of the Ukrainian temperament—held the family together. She controlled the family purse strings, saw to the children's education, and ran the Miassine household.

Firstborn Mikhail was twelve years older than Leonid. As a young man, after completing his engineering studies at Moscow's School of Engineering, he enlisted in the army. In 1904 he was wounded opposing the Japanese incursion into Manchuria. He recovered from his injuries and was awarded the St. Vladimir Medal for military bravery. Afterwards his family took unabashed pride in this honor; and Mikhail's courage under fire deeply awed little Leonid, who idolized his eldest brother. When Mikhail returned home after long tours of duty, what most indelibly impressed Leonid was his brother's remoteness as he stood in his uniform, gleamingly handsome and altogether unapproachable.

Gregori, second-born and ten years older than Leonid, was, Massine wrote, "impulsive and emotional,"⁴ the family romantic, which might account for his tendency to run afoul of his father's strict notions of proper conduct. Once, while Gregori was an engineering student (at the same school Konstantin attended), his father learned that he was cutting classes to be with his girlfriend. Mr. Miassine would not abide such breaches of discipline. Gregori was no longer allowed in the house. During this period of estrangement he found temporary employment with the railroad, and dared visit his mother only when his father was not at home. Not long afterward, however, he completed his engineering studies and joined the military, and he soon was stationed in Chelyabinsk, Siberia, as a military construction engineer. Leonid was bewildered by Gregori's retracing of Mikhail's footsteps into the army. The impassioned, gentle Gregori seemed to Leonid a poor choice for the military. And here was another brother gone far away.

Konstantin, the third child, eight years Leonid's senior, was the brother closest to him in age and a tender mentor. Konstantin lavished attention on the baby of the family. He patiently drilled Leonid in the principles of geometry and taught him a healthy respect for skilled marksmanship. Konstantin was a lighthearted taskmaster, and Leonid delighted in his company, even when the two of them were detailed to shovel snow in the deep Russian winter. While Mikhail and Gregori pursued their military careers far from home, Konstantin served as Leonid's loyal male comrade during his formative years.

Leonid's sister, Raissa, was nearest in age to him, and in their combustible rivalry for attention they apparently quarreled often. Raissa poked fun at her brother's solitary dancing, nicknaming him "the circus dancer," while Leonid taunted her as "Baba Yaga," the old witch of Russian folklore.[5]

The Miassines lived on the ground floor of a narrow stone building on Schemilovsky Street, a row of low-roofed dwellings adjacent to a mews in the Sushchevsky Quarter of Moscow, near the imperial stables. On the floor above, the jeweler Sergei Sergeivitch Gagolin kept his workshop, a source of wonder for the young Leonid.

The days in Schemilovsky Street were tranquil. From within the secluded, walled-in courtyard that faced the Miassine house one could hear neighborhood children at play. Often Mrs. Miassine spent most of her day rehearsing at the Bolshoi Theater. While she was away the household ran smoothly, and by late afternoon the "large, high-ceilinged flat was always bursting with activity. The kitchen would be full of women— Aunt Tekla [Mrs. Miassine's closest friend], Aunt Feodosia, her daughters Maria and Irina, my sister Raissa—all helping to prepare our big main meal. In the dining room my elder brothers, Gregori and Konstantin . . . sat working at their higher mathematics, while I wandered from room to room, chatting with the women in the kitchen, listening to my father practicing in the living room, and peering at my brother's geometrical drawings, which looked to me like some strange hieroglyphic language."[6] And Leonid's "great moment" of the day was when he heard "the horse-drawn coach"[7] that brought his mother home from the theater. In the early evening, listening to his father practice his French horn, Leonid would sit transfixed with joy, especially when he was permitted to request his favorite selection, Beethoven's Overture to *Fidelio*.

The year Leonid turned seven, he and the family spent the first of what would become annual summer respites in Zvenigorod-Moskovsky, about forty miles from Moscow. Here the Miassine family built (with financial help from Mr. Miassine's brother Vasili) a wooden dacha on a hill overlooking the Moscow River. The senior Miassines did much of the building and carpentry in and around the house, including bookshelves, cupboards, and an outside fence. The children joined in, and little Leonid helped paint the walls burgundy red and the roof dark forest-green.

Massine

These summers in Zvenigorod-Moskovsky were idyllic, with the family blissfully adrift in what Chekhov, in *The Sea Gull,* called Russia's "charming country dullness." They would arrive at the dacha in July, after the elder Miassines had finished their freelance summer engagements during the Bolshoi Theater's off-season. With Mikhail and Gregori away, the summer household consisted of the parents, Konstantin, Raissa, Leonid, and Aunt Feodosia and her children. Mr. Miassine looked after the vegetable garden with his wife, who was also in charge of the flower garden in front of the house. She shared household duties with Aunt Feodosia. Raissa spent most of her free time reading French and Russian novels.

Leonid and Konstantin would escape into the nearby pine forest to hunt partridge and guinea fowl. Leonid relished the athletic Konstantin's company, but even at this early age he began to prefer solitude. He particularly enjoyed rising at dawn to wander alone through the woods to pick wild strawberries and mushrooms for his mother. The singing of the birds or a long swim in the cool river transported him to his own world. He would spend entire days alone fishing and eating handfuls of strawberries before returning home at sunset. Thus, though there were moments at the house when he joined his sister and village children in games, singing old rhymes and learning village dances, such as the *Khorovod,* in his autobiography he reveals that these summer interludes at the dacha endowed him with a critical, secretly longed-for opportunity to commune with nature and learn to stand alone.

Teatime at the dacha was warmly sociable, an occasion for affable village neighbors to come calling. They often included the family's closest friend, a basso named Unitzky who sang in the Bolshoi Theater chorus. The traditional samovar was set out on a wooden table beneath the lilac tree, and on it Aunt Feodosia would arrange freshly baked bread and homemade jam. Mr. Unitzky and Mrs. Miassine delighted everyone with Ukrainian songs. At such moments, Massine recalled, "I would lean back in my chair meditatively sipping my tea and caressing Miltoshka [the family dog], and let myself be lulled by their voices into a waking dream."[8]

During one of the first summers at the dacha, Mr. Miassine took his youngest son to the nearby monastery of St. Saavo. As Leonid gazed upon the onion-domed cupola, the measured peals of its eleventh-century iron and silver bells moved outward in layers of sound, gently caressing the surrounding countryside. Leonid's Russian Orthodox religious upbringing had never been strict, but now, holding his father's hand as he entered the monastery and began wandering its cloisters, he felt a consuming spiritual identification with the chapel's air of sacred mystery and ancient mysticism. The dimly lit space and the candles flickering before the icons worked deeply on the introspective and meditative boy. He had studied the life of Saint Saavo, whose retreat to a hermitage atop a nearby hill had symbolized his rejection of all worldly vanity. Viewing the saint's mortal remains displayed under glass in the chapel, Leonid felt "his presence pervading the building, and in my boyish way I understood his renunciation of the material world, and his search for a contemplative, spiritual life. Sitting in the chapel, gazing at the frescoes and icons there, I felt for the first time a sense of peace and exaltation. . . ." Sixty years later, he would write in his autobiography that "some pattern or pervasive theme in my future creative life began to take shape on that morning. . . ."[9]

Leonid's education began at home, when he was five. His mother and, especially, his Aunt Tekla taught him to read and write and laid out the basic principles of religion, zoology, and mineralogy. With help from his father and Konstantin he tackled geography, geometry, and history. At age eight his home tutoring ceased. At the suggestion of Mme Chernova, a friend of Mrs. Miassine's from the Bolshoi chorus, he was registered to take the entrance exams at the Moscow Imperial Theater School. During her many visits to the Miassine home, Mme Chernova had noticed how charmingly little Leonid played his mouth organ and danced. She wanted these rudimentary artistic inclinations to flourish. Though his parents stressed the importance of an academic education (curiously, music had not been included in their home curriculum), Mme Chernova's persistence and their son's boundless enthusiasm won them over.

Their hesitation seems odd. Music and theater were an integral part of the family environment, and discussion of their work at the Bolshoi no doubt occurred daily. When he was six years old, Leonid had accompanied his mother to a theater in central Moscow where she sang during the summer operetta season. Fascinated, he left her dressing room and roamed backstage, where "all was in semi-darkness, and the curtains and backcloths hung over me like black clouds. As I made my way through the jumble of gilded stairways and papier-mâché hedges, I felt as though I were entering a dream world."[10] Perhaps one can say that at this moment Miassine, gazing from the dimly lit stage at his first empty auditorium, took his initial step toward making ballet history.

Each year after the Bolshoi season ended, Mr. Miassine would obtain part-time jobs playing in open-air concerts at genteel summer resorts. (Although he was in good health, these travels also gave him the chance to take a cure in some of Russia's fashionable spas.) Leonid would sometimes accompany him, once to Pyatigorsk at the foot of Mount Beshtaou, and another summer to Zheleznovodsk (the City of Iron Water), with its promenades, gardens, and grand hotels, where the surrounding mountains included Elbrus and mighty Kazbek, the highest peak in the Caucasus.

Leonid loved attending the orchestra rehearsals. He found himself captivated by the conductor, who, like a magician, appeared to dominate a stage full of musicians by a simple wave of the baton. He delighted in seeing his father play at a nod from the maestro. In rehearsal his father seemed "stronger and more serious" than the other players. While Leonid's tiny feet tapped along to the music of Rimsky-Korsakov, he beamed at his father from where he sat. "But father never smiled back,"[11] so the child's plea for recognition went unanswered. Apparently the pattern persisted. Toward the end of his life he said: "I was the last one in the family, and almost forgotten. I was the freak. They did not know what to do with the little chap."[12]

On examination day at the Imperial Theater School Leonid was filled with anticipation and fear:

I could hardly eat my breakfast when the morning came for Father to take me to the school. Once there, I sat in the bare waiting-room, holding his hand, until my name was called out and I was shown into a cramped cubicle, where an aggressive little doctor named Kazansky peered at me through rimless spectacles which made his eyes look as large and round as an owl's. He told me to take off my clothes, and there I stood, completely naked, surrounded by white-coated attendants, while he examined my arms, legs, neck and spine, to see if I had the physique necessary for a dancer. As he hammered my knees for reflexes and carefully tested my joints and muscles, I became more and more convinced that I would never pass the test. I felt that I had no talent at all, and that my puny body could never meet the requirements of the Theater School.[13]

Leonid took the entrance examinations for the ballet department of the Theater School, which included religion, Russian language, and arithmetic, and proved competent, earning grades of 4+, 4, and 4, respectively (4 being equivalent to a B in the American system).[14] To his enormous gratification, he was accepted for the regular trial period of one year.

The most important Russian theatrical institution of the nineteenth century was the Imperial Theaters, which included St. Petersburg's Maryinsky Theater (opera and ballet) and Alexandrinsky Theater (drama) as well as Moscow's Bolshoi Theater (opera and ballet) and Maly Theater (drama). These theaters were wholly subsidized by the state. Their recruits came mainly from the Imperial Theater Schools in St. Petersburg and Moscow, which were then the most prestigious institutions of ballet, drama, and opera education and training in Russia. The Moscow school dates from 1773, when a Moscow orphanage, the Vospitatel'nyi Dom, hired instructors to train the inmates as professional singers, actors, and dancers. Part of the school's curriculum required students to participate in theater performances. Systematic instruction began in 1773, at the same time that the orphanage was handed over to the Petrovsky Theater, where the Bolshoi itself has stood since 1825. Throughout the nineteenth century some of Europe's most renowned ballet masters came to work in Moscow. Although during the century's closing decades the Bolshoi Ballet was at something of a creative standstill, its artistic renewal was in fact under way when Leonid entered the Imperial Theater School in 1904.[15]

In St. Petersburg, the ballet classicism of Marius Petipa and Lev Ivanov had reached its peak. In Moscow, the Bolshoi was more restive. Since 1900 Alexander Gorsky had been leading it in new directions, emphasizing a dance-drama approach opposed to the conventions of academic ballet. Before arriving at the Bolshoi, Gorsky had been a pupil of Petipa's, a dancer with the Maryinsky Theater, and a teacher of Vladimir Stepanov's choreographic notation theory (which he later revised) at the Imperial Theater School in St. Petersburg. In 1898 he was invited to stage *The Sleeping Beauty* for the Bolshoi, and in 1900 he was officially transferred there. The artistic renewal Gorsky set in motion at the Bolshoi was in reality part of the modernist movement that was advancing on fin-de-siècle Moscow, a pivotal shift toward bold Russian innovation and experimentation in the arts.[16]

Consequently, though the organizational structure of the Imperial Theaters did not easily accommodate change, it could not remain untouched by the artistic upheaval taking place in Moscow. At the Bolshoi, Gorsky's attraction to the novel theatrical ideas of Konstantin Stanislavsky[17] generated renewed interest in the mise-en-scène as an element that gave added cohesiveness to a ballet production. Breaking from the traditional classical symmetry, Gorsky made the corps de ballet integral to a work's dramatic development. He also introduced character dance steps to the ballet vocabulary, to make it less technical and more expressive. Dance historian Elizabeth Souritz writes: "Gorsky considered that ballet could survive only if it became an art of its time. He felt keenly the need to renew its themes and its language."[18] During his tenure as teacher and choreographer at the Bolshoi, Gorsky made dancers study the expressiveness of the body (torso and arms) and emphasized the fundamental principle that if movement is to have any emotional content, it can come only from the specific context in which the steps are performed. One important result was that the dancers began to rely on acting to enliven their characterizations. Among the generation who exemplified the new Gorsky style were Mikhail Mordkin, Sofia Fedorova, and Yekaterina Geltzer, all of whom personified the dynamism and brio that became the hallmark of the twentieth-century Bolshoi Ballet.

Soon after his acceptance Leonid found himself in the high-ceilinged rehearsal rooms of the Imperial Theater School, where basic ballet class (for six male and six female students) was taught by Nikolai Petrovitch Domachov. This class consumed the morning.[19] The afternoon included lessons in arithmetic, geography, Russian history, literature, and French. Leonid, already the deeply private person he was to remain for the rest of his life, must have found it a blessing to be a day student rather than a boarder. As it was, his daily classes must have made him yearn for the security of home. But he quickly fell in with the school's highly disciplined schedule. Uniforms were mandatory. Boys wore blue jackets with Russian-style, stand-up velvet collars to which were pinned two miniature lyres. Girls wore dark red uniforms and white aprons. On Sunday all students attended mass in the upstairs chapel over the classrooms.

During his year-long trial, Leonid got his first taste of the theatrical world at work. Once, he and a group of students were taken across from the school to the Maly Theater, where they watched a rehearsal of a scene from Gogol's *The Government Inspector*. This first exposure left Leonid "enthralled by the wonderful voices and the expressive gestures." He was so taken by the experience that he felt he "would never be happy until I too could appear on the stage."[20] The experience would focus him in the next few years on acting more than dancing, though when he played with Raissa and their neighbors the Panshin children, he still enjoyed showing off dance steps he had learned in school and dreaming up brief, simple routines with them on the spot.

Once the first-year trial period was completed, a second student examination was required for final acceptance into the school, "this time in

Miassine in the uniform of the Imperial Theater School

an enormous mirrored hall where I was surrounded by flinty-faced examiners staring at me from their benches. Standing alone in the center of the room, I was asked to demonstrate the first five basic positions of the dance. For one moment I felt completely paralysed, and was sure I would not be able to move a muscle. Somehow, as if in a dream, I took a deep breath and found myself moving across the room demonstrating the positions and several dance steps." [21]

How well he did turned out to be irrelevant for a while. Soon after the first-year trial period ended, the school was closed due to the political turmoil that led to the 1905 revolution.

Nineteen hundred five was a momentous year in Russian history; its aborted January revolution in the "Bloody Sunday" massacre at the Winter Palace shocked the world. As the rebellion roiled through Moscow's streets, anxiety permeated the Miassine household. The family remained barricaded in their flat; the only sounds that reached them were screams, gunshots, and, from the nearby imperial stables, the loud galloping of the Cossacks' horses. The commotion terrified Leonid, who suffered recurring nightmares of Cossacks galloping into the courtyard. To allay his little brother's fears, Konstantin read to him and played games with him, but he found that Leonid was most soothed by a miniature theater he had built for him:

> *I [Leonid] helped him to cut out the characters from cardboard. Then, by tying strings to them, we made them glide smoothly across the little stage in front of the footlights. The music for our productions was provided by a friend, Yuri Ziman, who lived in our block of flats. He had a guitar on which he could play two tunes: Strauss's "Vienna, always Vienna" and one of Liszt's Hungarian Rhapsodies. We choreographed the Viennese waltz by pulling two strings in different directions, and so making our characters dance together with jerky, rhythmic movements. Our most ambitious effort was a midnight scene in a wood, lit by one small candle and accompanied by the Hungarian Rhapsody played very slowly. For this we cut out several witches from sheets of paper, and attached them to threads which I manipulated with both hands. But whenever I tried to make them fly, the threads got entangled, and the witches hung in a motionless cluster.*
>
> *I got a curious sense of satisfaction out of manoeuvring my little cardboard characters, making patterns of movement which corresponded to Yuri's music. And the sight of them on the stage, lit only by wavering candlelight, made an impression on me which has remained one of my most vivid childhood memories.*[22]

Escape from an oppressive reality into theatrical fantasy: the rest of Massine's life would be punctuated by precisely this need to grab for security amidst bewildering uncertainty.

When the worst of the street fighting subsided, Mr. Miassine, Konstantin, and Leonid emerged from the house. They were stunned. Leonid, walking between his father and brother and clutching their hands, saw streets with dead bodies sprawled among the remains of barricades, surely a devastating sight for a ten-year-old. The effect on Leonid was to be lasting. For the first time death on a massive scale brought home to his child's world the unpredictable fragility of life. As he later described the scene's impact:

> *Twisted and contorted, their limbs had stiffened into every conceivable position of suffering. Rows of outstretched arms, torsos, and staring faces passed before my eyes as we searched among the dead for people we had known. I felt a gnawing ache in the pit of my stomach, and by the time we left the scene I was weak and feverish. On my way home I saw a group of children playing among the debris of one of the barricades. Listening to*

their gay, carefree voices, I felt a sudden sense of detachment from their childhood world of innocence. Suddenly I let go of my father's hand, and walked home on my own.[23]

Somehow, life in Moscow soon returned to normal. Although threats to close down the Imperial Theater School permanently never materialized, no new students were accepted between 1906 and 1910.[24] Leonid was thrilled to be back in school. Now, for the first time he thoroughly enjoyed his dance lessons, and he especially relished his literature classes. Here he was exposed to the works of Lermontov, Pushkin, Fet, and Nikolai Nekrasov. He took particular delight in the Nekrasov poems that dealt with country life, memorizing them and reciting them often.

Leonid proved such a diligent and hard-working pupil that on May 10, 1906, along with his classmate Margarita Kandaurova, he was allowed to advance to the second year of the seniors' department of class 1, although he was younger than the required age. On November 13, 1907, he became a "half-pensionary" (a half-scholarship student), at public cost. His school records make no mention of any disciplinary infractions.[25]

In time the curriculum expanded to include elementary physics, drama (dropped from the curriculum in 1910), and dance notation, in which Leonid excelled. (In her unpublished memoirs, Maria Gorshkova, his dance notation teacher from 1910 to 1912, calls him her best student.)[26]

All students were required to participate in Bolshoi and Maly productions. Some ballets were a special treat for them, especially Gorsky's *The Little Humpbacked Horse,* where the apprentices joined the corps de ballet in all three acts plus the finale. Students also got to see famous performers at work. Leonid noticed how meticulously Gorsky coached his dancers during Bolshoi rehearsals. Among the dancers he admired were Maximilian Froman, Vladimir Riabtzev, and Geltzer. (Leonid was deeply amused when, offstage, Mikhail Mordkin sported the ten-gallon hat and raccoon coat he had bought during an American tour.)

The ballerina Margarita Vassilieva's description of Gorsky at work shows how he mapped out his ballets before beginning rehearsals, methods that Massine would later draw on. "[Gorsky] always arrived at rehearsals with the score under his arm, with every scene quite ready and worked out, with sketches for separate dances and a complete plan of the whole production. And when work actually started, one only had to see his burning eyes, the state of creative fervor that seemed to possess him completely, to the oblivion of everything else."[27] There was a flurry

Ballet class at the Theater School; Miassine is third from right.

Miassine partnering Margarita Kandaurova, who became one of the
Bolshoi's leading dancers in the 1920s

of excitement when it was announced that the Bolshoi's régisseur would be visiting the school to select a small, dark student to play the role of the dwarf Chernomor in a new production of Glinka's *Ruslan and Ludmilla*. To Leonid's surprise, he was chosen. Not only was this, at an early age, his first solo character role; but, as it turned out, it was also an opportunity that helped set his future artistic course. "I . . . was amazed to discover," he wrote later, "that I had to march on to the stage wearing a heavy turban, a long brocade robe and an even longer white beard, which had to be carried on two cushions by several attendants. Weighed

Ten-year-old Miassine in Ostrovsky's play Poverty Is Not a Crime, *at the Maly Theater*

down by all this, I had practically nothing to do but scowl, look forbidding, wave my arms and cast a spell over the lovely heroine. I was overwhelmed by the splendour of my exotic costume, and became so involved in my part that I was oblivious of the audience and of the rest of the company." The role of Chernomor reignited in the young Leonid his youthful fancy of becoming an actor, and he believed that now "the theater offered me a greater opportunity to express myself and to project my own personality than dancing."[28]

Leonid's portrayal of Chernomor must have been a considerable accomplishment, for he would go on to be cast in a series of character parts at the Bolshoi and Maly theaters. His next assignment at the Maly came in 1908, as Egorka in Alexander Ostrovsky's *Poverty Is Not a Crime.* In 1909 there were two more roles at the Maly: Dobrotvorsky's Boy in Ostrovsky's *Poor Bride* and Mishka in Gogol's *Government Inspector.* In all of these plays Leonid shared the stage with the Maly's leading performers. His commitments as a juvenile actor meant that he began to spend precious hours in the theater, rehearsing and performing. During the run of *The Government Inspector* he stood

> enthralled at the side of the stage, watching Konstantin Nikolaevich Rybakov, with his grand sweeping gestures and resonant voice, portray the corrupt old mayor who was trying to present an acceptable image of himself as a benign elderly official. I was equally impressed by the acting of Padarin, a tall distinguished-looking actor playing the part of the Government Inspector's old servant who humbles himself for his master's sake. It was exciting, too, to watch Ostujev's strong, decisive performance as Khlestakov, the adventurer who passes himself off as the Government Inspector, a forthright hero who represents a younger generation seeking to rid Russia of political corruption.[29]

Leonid's introspective, meditative bent and his penchant for daydreaming had found an appropriate outlet in the make-believe world of the theater. His acting permitted him to venture out into the world; yet once the applause ended he could quickly retreat to his inner reality. He was an avid observer of the actor's craft, of the "manners, voices and gestures" that are the medium of the actor. No doubt his fascination with acting was part of his adolescent search for a more secure identity. But acting had cast a profound spell over him. He found that on his way home from the theater each day he was "still going over the scenes from the play. At home I would repeat Ostujev's lines in exactly his tone of voice." Or he would deliver Rybakov's lines to Aunt Feodosia and her family, mimicking the older actor's movements and gestures. Caught up in his newfound power to move and impress, he also probably affected some of the arrogant offstage posturing of the actors, for he had to be reminded (probably by his mother and Aunt Feodosia) that his dramatic education was not complete and he "was not yet a famous actor."[30] In his autobiography he remembers a visit to his brother Mikhail, who by then was married and living in Helsinki, commanding a military radio station. Upon his departure he waved at the couple from the boat, decked out in his gifts from Mikhail, a new coat and hat, "the latter with its brim turned down at a rakish angle, which I thought very suitable for a promising young actor."[31]

In 1909 Leonid would undergo his first experience of grief at the loss of a loved one. When the family returned to Moscow from Zvenigorod-Moskovsky in September, his brother Konstantin remained behind at the dacha to go hunting with a friend during their expedition and accidentally was shot and killed. He was twenty-one years old and had just graduated with high honors from engineering school; the family was "confident he had a brilliant future before him."[32] Word of his death arrived in a telegram from the family's neighbor and friend Unitzky. Mme Miassine at first refused to believe the horrible news. And in spite of its weeping, the whole family was clearly in a state of shock. Miassine remembered that he

suddenly felt that I must go and tell some of Konstantin's friends what had happened. I ran out of the house, down the street, past the livery stables, and on to the main boulevard. With only a vague idea of where they lived, I searched for his friends in the back streets and courtyards, but found no one. Driven by an overwhelming feeling of horror, I continued to run through the city, along the boulevards, through parks and squares, until I finally collapsed from exhaustion in an unfamiliar road on the outskirts of Moscow. I lay there for what seemed like hours, until the initial shock of the news had worn off. In the evening I arrived back home, weak and shaken.[33]

Massine fills three pages of his autobiography with his account of the tragic death of his brother and the funeral in Zvenigorod-Moskovsky, which he attended with Raissa and their parents. Konstantin's death left "an ineffaceable scar."[34] And while time seemed to heal the tragedy for the rest of the family, Mr. Miassine would never quite recover from his son's death.

Leonid returned to his young artist's life. With help from a Bolshoi Orchestra colleague of his father's, he began to study the violin. For five years he worked with "great concentration" at mastering the instrument, in order to "enlarge my understanding of serious music."[35] He also enjoyed playing the balalaika, especially during the weekends he spent with his godmother, Alexandra Alexandrovna Puskova, a dramatic soprano with the Bolshoi and one of his mother's most beloved friends.[36]

He seemed to prefer acting more than ever. He writes in his memoirs:

By the time I was fifteen I had definitely decided that I would be an actor. The theater, to me, was far more stimulating and challenging than the bal-

let, and apart from the fact that the plays I had appeared in held greater interest for me than any of the Bolshoi productions, I found actors more intelligent and articulate than most of the dancers I knew. In comparison with the Maly productions, the ballet was a mediocre form of light entertainment. Except for the ballets of Tchaikovsky, the music was mostly on the level of Pugni and Minkus. Yet I realized too how much of my ballet training had helped me in my acting. Physical control and an understanding of movement were invaluable assets when it came to character interpretation and projection on the legitimate stage. In fact both halves of my education complemented each other. My acting improved through my knowledge of movement, and my experience in the theater helped me to create vivid characterizations in my dancing.[37]

Already by 1912 Leonid appears in the registry of the Moscow Imperial Theaters as the recipient of a six-hundred-ruble scholarship. Beginning in 1911 his acting responsibilities at the Maly had expanded; in a Maly Theater report on the 1911–12 season he is named as performing six roles, three of which were new assignments.

One of these, Mitya in Persianinova's *The Big Ones and the Small Ones*, marked a turning point in Leonid's acting career. The play was premiered in December 1911 as a benefit performance for the acclaimed actress Nadezhda Nikulina (one of Ostrovsky's favorites), who was celebrating fifty years on the Maly stage. The production included some of the Maly's most prestigious actors. That Leonid shared the stage with these luminaries on such an auspicious occasion testifies to his status as the Maly's up-and-coming young actor. The press notices also must have pleased him. According to *Theatre*, "the most interesting among the male performers was Mitya, [played by] the student Miassine . . . ,"[38] and a later review called his performance "excellent."[39] *Season News* glowed: "The boy Miassine who is graduating this year from the Ballet School attracted attention. His performance of the role of the young hero was captivating, youthful and interesting. There was no false note, and such humor and pathos—all was very good. One can predict a great future for this sixteen-year-old actor."[40]

Leonid continued to perform in ballet productions at the Bolshoi: as the Monkey in *Pharaoh's Daughter*, in the Khan's suite in *The Little Humpbacked Horse*, and as Prince Avenan in *The Sleeping Beauty*, all choreographed by Gorsky. As the Monkey he had to "swing down from the branch of an exotic tree, perform a short solo on all fours, and return to my tree without once standing erect. It was a great strain to do this on

Miassine in The Big Ones and the Small Ones, *with actress
Nadezhda Nikulina, Maly Theater, 1911*

The Big Ones and the Small Ones, *Maly Theater, 1911;
Miassine is on the extreme left.*

the steeply raked stage of the Bolshoi, and afterwards I would be physically exhausted."[41]

Leonid was encouraged by some of the Maly's most prestigious performers to pursue an acting career. Once, during a rehearsal, Mikhail Provich Sadovsky, son of the famous Prov Sadovsky, ostentatiously pointed at Miassine and proclaimed: "There is a boy who has God's spark!"

Leonid's friend Nicholas Zverev, seven years older and a member of the Zimin Theater corps de ballet, also encouraged him, but in another direction. Zverev took Leonid to the studio of the forty-two-year-old Anatoli Petrovich Bolchakov, whose private art school at 4 Miasnitsky Lane attracted a number of male dancers.[42] During 1912 and 1913 Leonid studied drawing and painting under the tutelage of Bolchakov, whom he described as "a friendly, disheveled young man wearing a long white linen smock." According to Bolchakov's widow, Leonid was very keen on drawing and painting and, like the other students, loved the teacher for the genuine interest he took in their lives and careers. It was in this warmly supportive environment that he began to familiarize himself with the works of such artists as van Gogh, Degas, and Toulouse-Lautrec: "Although the reproductions [Bolchakov] showed us were drab and muddy, he had a way of generating enthusiasm as he talked. Until then I had never thought seriously about art, but now I was puzzled and intrigued by such things as the curious angles and positions of the dancers in Degas's pictures, and by the grotesque characterizations in Toulouse-Lautrec's posters. When I stayed on after classes to talk to Bolchakov I found him more like a friend than a teacher."[43]

Leonid's relationship with Anatoli Petrovich became crucial to his growth as man and artist. Their enduring friendship, which began on mentor-pupil terms, without question became Leonid's deepest emotional liaison outside of his family. This was especially true when, after Mr. Miassine's retirement from the Bolshoi in 1911, the family settled permanently at the dacha, making it necessary for Leonid to rent a room near the Theater School. In a 1914 letter to Bolchakov Leonid would acknowledge that it was Anatoli Petrovich who had taught him to love and to live.[44] The relationship was driven by Leonid's thirst for knowledge. The dialectical flow of ideas between them engendered within the young man a firmer sense of mission. He had received only a limited education in the arts and humanities from the Imperial Theater school system. "It was he," Leonid would later write, "who had first aroused my interest in art."[45] As their emotionally charged friendship deepened, Miassine came to discover and appreciate art of a higher order. His exposure to new aesthetic developments enriched his artistic consciousness. The principles underlying the Italian Renaissance and impressionism became freshly available to him, like newfound wisdom. Bolchakov instilled in Miassine an early love for Italy, especially Rome. He showed Leonid "books containing illustrations of Italian cathedrals and of the frescoes and other works of art contained in them. . . . Bolchakov had never been outside Russia, but he could describe the treasures of Tuscany and the paintings in the Louvre as vividly as the most experienced traveller." [46]

In Leonid's letters to Anatoli Petrovich after the dancer's departure from Moscow, their discussions ranged from the early Christian churches and Byzantine mosaics to the contemporary work of Michel Larionov. Anatoli Petrovich prompted Leonid to visit the Tretiakov National Gallery, even though he would later confess that "at the time my taste was not sufficiently developed, and the academic portraits and landscapes I saw there made practically no impression on me." [47]

Anatoli Petrovich's study, with its hodgepodge of easels and plants, provided Miassine with an unfettered and genial setting in which he could meet young artists and students outside the more restrictive environment of the Imperial Theaters. Under their teacher's watchful eye, the young students engaged in intense discussions about art and current affairs. In addition to Zverev and fellow dancer Dmitri Kostrovsky, Leonid also befriended three female classmates, Elena Domiavnova, Elizabeta Stepanovna, and Elena Egorovna. [48]

Leonid graduated in August 1912 and was promptly accepted into the Bolshoi ballet company with a yearly salary of six hundred rubles, plus the customary hundred extra for "équipement." [49] The next year was filled with hard work and achievement.

He danced in ten ballets, including new roles in *Swan Lake* (the Tarantella), *Don Quixote* (the Knight of the Silver Moon and Carasco), and *Le Corsaire* (in the Oriental dream scene). He also appeared in thirteen opera ballets, including those in *The Snow Maiden, The Queen of Spades, Faust, Sadko, Eugene Onegin,* and *Les Pêcheurs de perles,* all choreographed by Gorsky. Leonid also danced a menuet and an écossaise in the comedy-divertissement *Assemblée.*

With his new solo parts at the Bolshoi multiplying, his position in the company was solidifying. When Alexander Yuzhin, manager of the Maly drama company, solicited special permission for Leonid's participation as Kolya in C. S. Palynov's play *Ring of Fire,* [50] the Bolshoi's régisseur, A. Bulgakov, replied: "Mr. Miassine distinguished himself during this sea-

Miassine (standing, left) with friends in Moscow, circa 1912

son; I even entrusted him with solo performances; therefore, his absence would be very noticeable. However, I do not have the right to keep him from participating in drama performances, because it is undoubtedly beneficial for his artistic development."⁵¹ Among the other new acting roles Leonid undertook at the Maly were Sergei in Leonid Andreyev's *Professor Storytsyn* and Tsarevich Mikhail Feodorovitch in *1613*. For his role as the tsarevich, Leonid

> had to learn to employ noble gestures and a grand manner, particularly in
> the dramatic scene before the young Tsar's coronation when, clad in my
> sumptuous robes, I confronted my mother, the Tsaritza, played by that

great actress Alexandra Alexandrovna Yablochkina. This was an impor-
tant part for me, and one in which I gained invaluable experience. After
playing it I felt much more confident on stage, and ready to accept any new
part which was offered me.[52]

His professional schedule during the 1912–13 season was so hectic
that he performed 176 times in ballets, dramas, and operas.

Gorsky's realistic approach to ballet undoubtedly had a substantial
influence on Leonid during his formative years at the Bolshoi, where
he absorbed both the classical academic tradition and Gorsky's determination to revitalize it. As a reformer, Gorsky "pierced the performance
with a clear line of action, dramatized the dance, saturated the ensemble
scenes with playful moments, and introduced details from everyday
life. . . ." This markedly dramatic approach was evident in both his new
ballets and his reworking of the classics. About his version of *Don
Quixote* Souritz writes: "Gorsky added new integrity and meaning to
Petipa's Don Quixote, which had previously been rather eclectic
and amorphous, and in so doing made it more viable."[53] In this work
Gorsky tried "for the first time to break with the clichés of 'balletic-
pseudo Spain.' His major success . . . was the fact that the dancing
was born 'from emotional states that kindled a consuming need for
dance.' "[54] In his 1912 production of *Swan Lake* (in which Leonid
danced) Gorsky "did away with the sedate formation of straight frontal
lines and added character dancing, ending [Act I] with a vigorous, somewhat medieval-looking farandole with torches in the dancers' hands."[55]
According to critic André Levinson, "the finale of the first act of
Swan Lake, listless and sloppy in the St. Petersburg production, in
Gorsky's version has become an artistic, vigorous torch procession of
medieval *fantoccini*."[56] Interestingly, Leonid was more impressed by
Gorsky's

personality than by his artistic creations. It was enchanting to watch him
glide 'round the stage, demonstrating phrases of movement with an ethe-
real grace which few of his dancers could equal. In Don Quixote he
began to break away from the old academic tradition of rigid rows of
dancers stepping forward at specified moments to perform their set pieces,
attempting to replace this formality by integrated ensembles forming flow-
ing patterns of movement. But it struck me that he was an inventive artist
who could never quite transmit his ideas to his dancers. He lacked the abil-

ity to manipulate large groups on stage, and so his inventions remained only half-realized.[57]

Leonid's favorite work by Gorsky was *Schubertiana*, which he considered "charming, graceful and well composed."[58]

It would be a mistake, however, to undervalue in Massine's future choreographic essays the influence of Gorsky's dramatic expressiveness, his integration of character dance into academic ballet, and his stress on plasticity of movement.

WHAT DIRECTION HAD Leonid's acting training taken after 1910, when drama courses were dropped from the curriculum at the Theater School? How aware was he of Stanislavsky's reforms? Massine does not discuss Stanislavsky in his autobiography, but it seems inconceivable that any serious aspiring actor in Moscow would not have come into contact with the ideas of a man who by 1910 had become a theatrical institution. Stanislavsky's efforts to revolutionize the theater already were being debated during his days with his amateur troupes, the Alexeyev Circle (his family name was Alexeyev) and the Society of Art and Literature, in the 1880s and early 1890s, well before he founded the Art Theater in 1898. And from the early years of the Art Theater, his reforms had had an impact on the Maly. Not only did he enjoy a frank rapport with the Maly actors, who he believed were the strongest spiritual influence on his development; but two of the Maly's most revered teachers, Alexander Lensky (1847–1908) and Alexander Yuzhin (1857–1927), had championed his ideas. Yuzhin (Prince Sumbatov), one of Moscow's most important dramatic coaches, was greatly admired by Stanislavsky, and vice versa: Yuzhin once declared that the Maly should have been taken over by Stanislavsky. Undoubtedly Leonid's acting training from 1908 on had been primarily in Yuzhin's hands, and it was probably Yuzhin who directed him in most of his roles at the Maly. Yuzhin was a thorough director, according to the actress N. L. Tiraspolskaya: "He was able to give very wise and useful advice about principles. He analyzed a play profoundly and cleverly ridiculed the false pathos and the overworked posing of the student. His illustrations glowed with a magnificent skill."[59]

In January 1913, Stanislavsky established the First Art Theater Studio for the purpose of training actors according to his own method. In various interviews, Massine has mentioned meeting Stanislavsky for the first time in the flat of the famous Maly actress Olga Gosvskaya, who joined the Art Theater in 1910.[60] (At the time of the meeting, she and Leonid were working together on Shakespeare's *Antony and Cleopatra.*) And though he himself was never involved with the Art Theater, in conversations with the author, Massine stated that he had been familiar with Stanislavsky's theories and that before leaving Moscow at the beginning of 1914 he had discussed with Stanislavsky himself the possibility of working with him.

PART TWO

Diaghilev

*A drive towards unity, reaching beyond
personality, the quotidian, society,
across the chasm of transitoriness: an
impassioned and painful overflowing into
darker, fuller, more buoyant states; an
ecstatic affirmation of the totality of life
[or art] is what remains constant . . . the
eternal will for regeneration, fruitfulness,
recurrence; the awareness that creation
and destruction are inseparable.*

—NIETZSCHE

Miassine at the time he joined the Diaghilev company, Moscow, 1914

CHAPTER 2

Moscow, December 1913–Paris, August 1914

THE WINTER SEASON at the Bolshoi Theater proved to be a turning point for Miassine. At the beginning of December he danced again in *Don Quixote* and *Swan Lake,* and at one of these performances Serge Diaghilev was in the audience.

Serge Pavlovich Diaghilev, born in 1872, held a prominent place in the Russian renaissance at the turn of the century. In 1898 he founded the influential St. Petersburg art and literary journal *The World of Art* (*Mir iskusstva*), which appeared in twelve numbers from 1898 to 1904. Among his associates were the painters Alexandre Benois (who co-edited the magazine with him), Leon Bakst, and Konstantin Somov and Diaghilev's journalist cousin and lover, Dmitri Filosofov.[1] *The World of Art* was a major force in the rise of Russian modernism. Its objectives, fostered also by the important art exhibits it mounted, were to disseminate the tenets of emerging artistic trends in Europe and Russia and to revitalize an interest in the heritage of Russian art. In its first two years the journal paid particular attention to the growth of art nouveau in Europe; later issues focused interest on postimpressionist painters, especially Gauguin and van Gogh. The symbolist poets found a platform in *The World of Art* from which to express their aesthetic principles. In a recent re-evaluation of the journal the Soviet historian Alla Gusarova has observed, "For us *The World of Art* is not only drawings, paintings, books, the embodiment of mental grace, the mind, the high culture of its creators, the reverential love of nature and art. It is a noble enthusiasm for the study of Russian antiquity, a discovery of entire sections of Russian art, almost unknown before. It is examples of artistic criticism, intelligent, sensitive and tolerant of the searchings of their young contemporaries, even those alien in spirit."[2]

Nearly a year after the first issue appeared, Prince Serge Volkonsky, director of the St. Petersburg Imperial Theaters, retained Diaghilev as a coordinator of special projects, a position he held from 1899 to 1901. During this period, Diaghilev edited the Imperial Theaters' yearbook and, later, was entrusted with the production of the ballet *Sylvia*, which led to intrigue and a series of complications that unfortunately resulted in his dismissal.[3]

But neither reversals nor commotion ever stopped Diaghilev; with time, all was made to bend to his indefatigable will. In the midst of the turmoil caused by the abortive 1905 revolution, for example, Diaghilev organized the Russian Historical Portrait Exhibition in St. Petersburg. In 1906, also in St. Petersburg, he mounted a retrospective exhibition of Russian painting, which went on to Paris, where it was presented at the Salon d'Automne.[4] The show was magnificent, surveying everything from fifteenth-century icons to the works of the young artists of the School of Moscow. With the 1906 Paris exhibition of Russian art, Diaghilev began what Alexandre Benois called his "export campaign of Russian art."[5] Setting his sights on Western Europe, Diaghilev in 1907 brought to Paris a series of concerts featuring Russian music, and the following year he presented Mussorgsky's *Boris Godunov* with Chaliapin in the title role.[6]

By 1909 Diaghilev was committing his organizational talents to ballet, introducing to the West the finest fruits of Russian training as exemplified by the dancing of Anna Pavlova, Tamara Karsavina, and Vaslav Nijinsky. Through his efforts Western Europe would witness the revolutionary choreography of Michel Fokine, whose work reflected a shift away from acrobatic virtuosity and Petipa-inspired classicism toward a more naturalistic style. At the same time, stage design and costuming by such artists as Benois and Bakst took on a new fluidity and richness of color. Diaghilev's productions of *Les Sylphides, Firebird, Petrouchka, L'Après-midi d'un faune,* and *Le Sacre du printemps* gave a new beginning to ballet, while in *Firebird, Petrouchka,* and *Le Sacre du printemps* the music of Igor Stravinsky took the theater world by storm.[7]

In the winter of 1913 Diaghilev was in Moscow to recruit a leading dancer for his forthcoming production of Richard Strauss's biblical ballet *The Legend of Joseph,* a work with a libretto by Hugo von Hofmannsthal and Count Harry Kessler, costumes by Bakst, and a sumptuous decor in the Renaissance style of Veronese by José María Sert.[8] When the ballet first was planned in 1912, it was intended that Nijinsky would choreograph and dance the title role, but later events changed everything: Nijinsky's unexpected marriage to Romola de Pulszky in September 1913 led Diaghilev to terminate his association with the dancer, both as his lover and as the company's leading dancer-choreographer.

Diaghilev went to Russia. First he stopped in St. Petersburg to see Fokine, who had left the Ballets Russes once Nijinsky was launched as a choreographer, and persuaded him to take charge of the Strauss ballet. He then traveled to Moscow to meet with the artist Natalia Gontcharova, whom he hoped to engage as the designer for his upcoming production of Rimsky-Korsakov's opera *Le Coq d'or.*[9] Gontcharova and her companion, the artist Michel Larionov, were leaders in the Russian avant-garde art movement, and Diaghilev had much admired their work ever since he had exhibited some of their paintings in his 1906 exhibition. When he arrived in Moscow, she was enjoying great success with a retrospective of nearly eight hundred paintings.[10]

Diaghilev attended ballet performances at the Bolshoi Theater and was captivated by the young Miassine's charismatic presence, his piercing eyes and Byzantine looks, as he danced the Knight of the Silver Moon in *Don Quixote* and the tarantella in *Swan Lake.* Not only had the impresario found his ideal Joseph; he also must have sensed the youth's potential, his pliant sensibility, and his remarkable individuality, for he immediately enlisted Mikhail Savitsky, a Bolshoi dancer who had just joined the Ballets Russes, to arrange a meeting.

The prospect of being sought after by a man of Diaghilev's artistic prominence, international achievements, and personal notoriety must have filled Leonid with high anticipation. He soon found himself visiting the impresario at the Metropole Hotel, located on Theater Square across from the Bolshoi, Maly, and Nezlobin theaters. Massine writes:

> When I walked into the orange, gilded lobby I felt as though I were entering a larger-than-life world of fantasy. Timidly I made my way through rows of potted palms and porters in gold braid. When I asked for Diaghilev at the reception desk, I was shown into the lift and a few moments later was knocking at his door. It was opened by a young Italian with curly black hair and beady eyes. He smiled when I gave him my name, and showed me into a formal little sitting room. "Monsieur Diaghilev will be with you in a moment," he told me.
>
> I sat down stiffly on a plush sofa. The Italian disappeared into another room, and I heard him say, "Signor Baron, Signor Miassine is here to see you." A moment later Diaghilev appeared in a dressing gown. At first glance he appeared tall and imposing, but when I stood up I realized that he was only of medium height, but that he had an unusually large head and broad shoulders. The next thing I noticed was the streak of silver-white hair, like a feather, over his forehead. Peering at me through his monocle, he looked at me like a creature from another planet.[11]

Once the interview was completed, a "dazed and bewildered" Miassine visited the Theater School to tell his friends about Diaghilev's proposal to join his ballet company and to undertake the role of Joseph. His friends counseled against it, contending that it was unwise for him to leave Moscow when in the upcoming *Romeo and Juliet* at the Maly he was being considered for Romeo, a role that could launch him on a serious career as a leading actor.[12]

Days of "restless indecision" followed. Diaghilev clearly represented the potential for artistic recognition on an international scale. For the dreamer that Miassine was, for the child so adept at losing himself in daydreams, for the ambitious young artist he was fast becoming, the choice was between the predictable—the Maly Theater—and the fantastic. Diaghilev appeared like the fairy-tale godfather who could, with the touch of his magic wand, change dreams into reality. But how ready was Leonid for Diaghilev? Was their meeting the act of providence he had been waiting for? Could the impresario catapult him out of his daily routine?

There is no doubt that after his visit to the Metropole Hotel the young man was torn between the security that Moscow provided and his fear of the unknown, a fear magnified by the prospect of replacing Nijinsky in *The Legend of Joseph*. But the actress Masoritznova's oft-repeated tales of Diaghilev's triumphant Parisian premieres[13] continued to grip his imagination; and coupled with Diaghilev's spellbinding personality, they would eventually dispel any doubts. Certainly it was a meeting of two extraordinary men—both narcissistic, gifted, and driven—the younger one discovering his first faith in his talent, the older one always conscious of the indelible stamp he had already left on an art form.

Miassine returned to the Metropole Hotel determined to refuse Diaghilev's offer, reiterating to himself his reasons. But: "I walked in, he peered at me through his monocle, smiled and waited for me to speak. I was just about to tell him that I could not accept his offer when, almost without realizing it, I heard myself say, 'Yes, I shall be delighted to join your company.' "[14]

Miassine and Diaghilev left Moscow on the night train to St. Petersburg.[15] Their first trip together marked the beginning of Diaghilev's tutorship of Miassine. He made clear to his young charge what must be understood above all: the twentieth century was witnessing a radical artistic transition. While Diaghilev talked, Miassine surely only listened. He later wrote that their discussions centered around "an entirely new concept of ballet" that would supersede an "old academic tradition" whose usefulness had been outlived. Diaghilev believed that in the fusion of music, dance, painting, poetry, and drama, in accordance with the examples of Greek and Wagnerian theater, a more complete and cohesive artistic expression might be achieved.

Once they arrived in St. Petersburg, preparations to launch the young dancer began. Miassine's final acceptance into the company was subject to Fokine's approval, so Diaghilev set up an audition with the choreographer. At Fokine's apartment Miassine was asked to reproduce the positions of the figures in a Roman mural and to perform a quick leap over a chair in the center of the room.[16] Once Fokine had accepted the new recruit, Miassine was sent to a photography session at Boissonan and Eggler, which actually provided him with an introductory study of the character of Joseph. Donning the shepherd's costume designed by Bakst, and following Fokine's instructions for the poses, Miassine tried to immerse himself in the character by assuming the expressions he thought appropriate to the role. His anxiety in a new and unfamiliar world, as well as his apprehension about the future, were channeled into an almost Stanislavskian "inner technique." He later wrote: "For a moment, as I shifted my position awkwardly under the glare of the photographer's lights, I had a glimpse of Joseph's character, and felt I could understand his fear and uncertainty when brought before Potiphar."[17] Once more Miassine evinced a tendency and ability to copy and reproduce the feelings and attitudes of others; a technical strength as well as a survival scheme, it apparently allowed him to work through some of his own internal struggles.

While Diaghilev stayed on in St. Petersburg, Miassine returned to Moscow alone, to make arrangements for his departure. At some point early in December he petitioned the Office of the Imperial Theaters for a leave of absence without salary for one year, beginning on January 14, 1914, due to family circumstances. The petition was denied.[18] By December 15, Diaghilev had sent Hofmannsthal a set of photographs of Miassine, and the librettist, in a letter to Richard Strauss, expressed his enthusiasm for the new Joseph, promising that Miassine's portrayal "will be the real thing—it has just that quality of purity which is the antithesis of the female character."[19] Diaghilev also wrote Miassine in Moscow setting forth the terms of their contract. On December 19 the dancer asked the Imperial Theaters to discharge him as of January 1, 1914, again citing family circumstances.[20] He was issued a passport on January 4, after which he traveled to St. Petersburg to join Diaghilev, who took him to the Hermitage before they left for Cologne to join the company. En route, the two men discussed *The Legend of Joseph* in greater detail. The impresario must have been quite pleased with his discovery, for despite their brief association, already by January 22 Diaghilev was extending the initial length of Miassine's engagement.[21]

As their intimacy deepened, Diaghilev revealed himself to be a fascinating human being. Miassine found in him "an underlying humanity and integrity which, I felt, derived from his total commitment to his art." In the presence of his companion Miassine began to feel that "all my past experience had been negligible, and that I was now embarking on an entirely new career." His first impression of the older man as "fantastic" and "unreal" began to dissipate, and "by the end of the journey I had begun to feel more at ease with Diaghilev."[22] The impresario had opened to the young man an unknown world, one of unlimited possibilities, where every moment was imbued with brilliant conversation about bold projects to come and the stimulation and excitement of new places. Diaghilev the magician began to cast his spell, and as Miassine's hunger for knowledge and for the new became consuming, he found himself enchanted by his ever-persuasive companion and steadily drawn into Diaghilev's dreamlike reality. Indeed, Miassine began to erect a near-heroic image of the impresario—doubtless to offset his virtually total dependence. Sexual dominance of the younger man completed Diaghilev's conquest.

In Cologne they stayed at the Domhof Hotel. Miassine was overwhelmed by the luxury of his surroundings; he regarded the hotel as "fairly decadent, completely out of my world," and "felt guilty about being" there. At bottom, he admitted, was the fact that "the hotel merely intensified all the fears and uncertainties which I felt about my new venture."[23]

Being integrated into the company must have been difficult for Miassine. Private and reclusive by nature, he was now thrust into prominence day after day both as Diaghilev's lover and as the center of the impresario's nomadic community. According to the Diaghilev ballerina Lydia Sokolova, Miassine's "impenetrability" was apparent from the beginning; she remembers him as "remarkably like a medical student. . . . He must have been scared. His eyes were so enormous that they seemed to swamp his little pale face, yet when he looked at you they remained completely blank, as if there was a shutter at the back of them. Miassine would stare straight at you, but his eyes never smiled. . . . There was no way of telling what thoughts were in his head."[24]

Nevertheless, Miassine found the company's collective spirit exhilarating, and also came to see how radically different its aesthetic approach was from the academicism of the Bolshoi. He was soon assigned the role of the Night Watchman in *Petrouchka* so that he might observe and understand Fokine's style. This 1911 ballet had a powerful impact on him; he found in it evidence of the "synthesis of elements" of which Diaghilev had spoken so enthusiastically. He marveled at *Petrouchka*'s integration of drama, music, painting, and dance, and saw that a whole new grammar of art had opened up to him. Moreover, he now saw that this choreographic style was "universal in its depth and intensity." In Fokine's choreography Miassine came to admire the intricate ensembles that dispensed with the "convenient academic groupings"; he found in them a "sharply observed, realistically interpreted interplay" between the characters even while "all the movements were held together by a sustaining and unifying rhythm."[25] Thus, gradually, his understanding of Fokine's conception deepened. He began to see in *Petrouchka* not only "a statement of the dramatic human contrast to the world of puppets," but also the ballet's inner truth in the "profoundly human character" of Petrouchka, a "tragic figure, symbolizing innocence caught up in a world of corruption."[26] (Fokine himself danced Petrouchka in these performances, with Karsavina as the Ballerina.)

Massine

Miassine received his first taste of the Ballets Russes' creative process during rehearsals for *The Legend of Joseph*, which already had begun. Working with Fokine was stimulating but strenuous:

> I was fascinated by the flowing, rounded movements which Fokine had devised for me, but when I tried to execute them I found that I was restricted by the stiff academic positions in which I had for so long been drilled. During the first week of rehearsals I struggled to readjust my body so as to achieve the effortless rhythm which Fokine demanded. He remained noncommittal about my progress, and although Diaghilev did all he could to bolster up my confidence, I remained convinced that I had undertaken a task which was beyond me.
>
> In my first dance Fokine's typically free and flowing movements, in which big elevation steps were followed by poses on one knee, evolution of the arms during fast running steps and occasional broad arm and body movements in a small spatial area, created a perfect visual equilibrium between movement and immobility. I found it very taxing, while under such a great physical strain, to maintain for so long the illusion that my movements were spontaneous and effortless, and I was exhausted long before the end of the dance.[27]

Miassine with Michel Georges-Michel and Diaghilev near Nice, 1914

By the time they came to rehearse the second scene, Miassine felt more comfortable. For the mime, he drew on his acting experience. Moreover, Fokine was a thorough and meticulous choreographer, offering descriptive images to help the dancer form his image of the shepherd. Now, in true Stanislavskian fashion, Miassine identified the qualities that linked him to the character, devising a convincingly acted interpretation. For instance, in visualizing the conflict with Potiphar's Wife as the embodiment of his inner anxiety, he found that "each time I struggled with her, I seemed to project into my acting all my own anguish and heartbreak at having left Russia to take on the incredibly taxing part." And "when Froman, who was playing the part of the Archangel, finally rescued me from Potiphar's cruelties and led me away with a firm and kindly handclasp, I almost felt that I was in truth being delivered from my own fears and uncertainties."[28]

Rehearsals for *The Legend of Joseph* were conducted throughout the German tour, but the schedule was intensified while the company was in Berlin. Leon Bakst arrived from Paris and sent back an enthusiastic telegram to Misia Edwards, Diaghilev's close friend and staunchest supporter: "Miassine marvelous and astonishing with sincerity, fluency of movement, fantastic figure, great art."[29]

After engagements in Hamburg, Leipzig, Hanover, Breslau, Berlin, and Zurich, the Ballets Russes arrived in Monte Carlo for a spring season from April 6 to May 6. Miassine was dazzled by Monte Carlo's "pink-painted hotels, outdoor cafés and whimsical houses," and "curved balconies"; it was like a "make-believe city, a set for a pretty operetta."[30] He and Diaghilev embarked upon a public social life. There were dinners with Misia and her lover José María Sert, the Spanish painter who was designing the sets for *Joseph*. They approved of Diaghilev's new companion, and helped Miassine to feel more at ease and less inadequate in his new environment. At a party at the Hôtel de Paris, the young dancer met and waltzed with the legendary Isadora Duncan. She reminded him of a figure on a Greek vase; he was struck by her harmonious gestures and by her "extraordinary freedom and expressiveness of movement."[31]

But mostly Miassine concentrated on *Joseph*. The celebrated teacher Enrico Cecchetti, who had worked with the greatest dancers of his time, gave him intensive private classes to strengthen his technique, and he continued to do so in Paris when the Ballets Russes moved there for a season at the Opéra.

Paris, the city that since the turn of the century had been fertile ground for a host of movements in modern art, exceeded all Miassine's expectations. He took in the broad, beautifully designed parks, strolled about the area around the Champs-Elysées, and leisurely ambled across the place Vendôme and the Faubourg-Saint-Honoré. All too aware of the differences between France and Russia, he puzzled over the social pastime of café conversation; though he admired Paris, he felt "very out of place, very much the oafish stranger in this elegant city."[32]

Miassine's schedule soon became hectic. Although he had time for a few visits to the Louvre, life centered around the forthcoming premiere. Cecchetti continued to coach him both privately and in his public class at the Opéra, a class also attended by Nijinsky, whom Diaghilev wanted Miassine to observe at work.

Excitement pervaded the Opéra stage. Diaghilev was surrounded by his collaborators, such artistic luminaries as Strauss, Hofmannsthal, Kessler, Fokine, Bakst, and Sert. Miassine began to comprehend the sources of the admiration, respect, and authority Diaghilev commanded when, during rehearsal, the impresario remarked that one musical passage was too long, and unnecessary besides. Strauss took his pencil and, following Diaghilev's suggestion, deleted about ten pages from the score.[33] Stravinsky also attended the rehearsals, and Miassine met the composer for the first time. At another session he was introduced to the poet Jean Cocteau and to the exquisite young artist Valentine Gross, a friend of Marcel Proust and a well-known personality in Parisian intellectual and artistic circles. (At one of these rehearsals Kessler introduced Cocteau to Gross—a meeting that would have major repercussions in the poet's life and, indirectly, for Miassine and the Ballets Russes.)[34] The keen interest aroused by the new discovery prompted Gross to seek, through the publisher Jacques de Brunhoff, Diaghilev's permission to draw Miassine. Probably still smarting from the outcome of his relationship with Nijinsky, Diaghilev denied the request. (The impresario's characteristic possessiveness was always apparent in his relationships with lovers and friends, and even in his dealings with his collaborators.)

Miassine's only concern, however, was the new ballet; he was particularly worried about the Opéra's stage, which was so steeply raked that he had difficulty keeping his balance. On May 14 the ballet had its *répétition générale,* with the striking Russian soprano Maria Kuznetsova as Potiphar's Wife, a mime role. For Miassine, life and art were once again intertwined, as he utilized his existential experience in the service of the theatrical one. He describes his mental state during that first performance:

By the time the curtain went up I was in a pitiable state of nervous tension. As I was carried on stage in my hammock I kept my eyes tightly shut, and when I finally opened them the glare of the footlights nearly blinded me. Struggling to retain my balance on the huge sloping stage during my solo dance, I felt my ordeal was far worse than anything that Joseph had been called upon to endure. During a long stretch of almost uninterrupted movement I became increasingly dizzy, but fortunately Joseph's brothers stepped forward to support me, and after a momentary respite I was able to finish the rest of the dance. After the agony of the opening scene the rest of the performance passed off easily enough, though my own buried fears nearly got the upper hand of me again during my struggles with Potiphar's wife, and by the time the final curtain came down I was almost fainting with exhaustion. As I lay sweating on the sofa in my dressing room, Diaghilev, Strauss and Benois came 'round to congratulate me. To my dazed mind they seemed as unreal as the imposing figures of Potiphar and his wife.[35]

Relying more on Miassine's physical appearance and his acting ability than on his ballet technique, Fokine had tailored the role of Joseph to exploit the best qualities of the young dancer. Miassine's lambskin costume, designed by Benois (his only contribution to this ballet) to personify youthful innocence and vulnerability, was so scanty (for its day) that the press dubbed the ballet *Les Jambes de Joseph,* or *Joseph's Legs.* Despite insinuations in the press that his dancing posed no threat to Nijinsky (who attended the premiere), Miassine was praised for his sensitive portrayal.

After Paris, the company began a London season at the Drury Lane Theatre on June 8. Anticipation ran high for *The Legend of Joseph,* and the press covered the preparations for the local premiere as thoroughly as they had in Paris. Strauss was undoubtedly one of the major attractions. One reporter wrote: "Seldom has a musical event provoked such interest in London beforehand as that which Dr. Strauss's ballet was able to command. When the great night arrived Drury Lane was packed, and literally humming with anticipation."[36] Strauss received a thunderous ovation when he appeared on the podium.

After a dress rehearsal attended by London society, Miassine made his British debut on June 23. Reviewers complimented him on his appearance and stage presence even as they acknowledged his lack of technical command. The *Sunday Times* wrote: "M. Miassine is not a very experienced dancer, but his youthful, ingenuous appearance was a great

Four studio portraits of Miassine in
The Legend of Joseph,
wearing the lambskin tunic
designed by Benois

asset." [37] This time Karsavina took the part of Potiphar's Wife. She thought Miassine was "quite remarkable" as Joseph; his "lack of virtuosity in those days lent pathos to the image he created." [38]

Life in London was more settled than in Paris. Diaghilev arranged for a tutor to provide Miassine with English lessons; and there were leisurely visits to the National Gallery, the Tate, and the Wallace Collection, where Diaghilev pointed out the works of Fra Angelico, Giotto, Uccello, and Mantegna, probably in preparation for Miassine's forthcoming Italian sojourn.

Since leaving Russia Miassine had maintained a close correspondence with his family and with his former art teacher, Anatoli Petrovich Bolchakov. His frequent letters to Anatoli Petrovich, which seem to have stopped at the outbreak of the revolution, [39] are permeated with Miassine's sincere love and affection and his emotional commitment to friendship. In June he wrote from London:

I miss [art] school, Anatoli Petrovich. At times I feel such an urge to start working again, with new strength and love. How could one find a model class here? It was possible in Paris, but I did not have time. Here I am not so busy, I work only in Joseph.

Now I take walks in London, and I was in the museum. How many interesting things there are in the British Museum and also in the National Gallery.

In the company, of course, there are many hostile people. Our group [the contingent of Moscow dancers who knew Bolchakov] is well disposed. Tarasov was helping me for some time. I have a close relationship with Matveich [Nicholas Zverev]. He is the kind of person I imagine him to be.

What can I say about the Fokines? They have their own world and their own life. He is indifferent to me, same as she. The fact is that he does not recognize anyone else but himself. When he wanted to get by without Nijinsky—whose name he does not want to hear—he started to work with me and in three months, even less, he made something out of me. In his creative work he has become labored and somehow sugared. Vera is ruining him.

Now I am working diligently at Cecchetti's almost every day. It seems that I am making progress. . . . Dancing is my weak side and now I am trying to work seriously.

Kolya [Nikolai Kremev] is studying every day. Sometimes during performances I can see him jumping somewhere offstage. A very hardworking fellow. I see him seldom, but we feel close. And his English lady [Lydia

Sokolova, née Hilda Munnings] is a very fine person; they are such a good match, it really surprises me.

I have met Nijinsky, but did not see his works yet. He will be here for four performances. When Fokine is here, I suppose Nijinsky is not going to be here. Fokine will not allow that. . . .

Is it really true that after all your work you cannot allow yourself to have a vacation in Italy?[40]

By July 28, Diaghilev and Miassine were back in Paris. That night, at Misia's apartment, they listened to Erik Satie and the Spanish pianist Ricardo Viñes play Satie's *Trois Morceaux en forme de poire*. To everyone's consternation, a friend arrived to announce that Austria-Hungary had declared war on Serbia. On August 1, Germany declared war on Russia. On the third, the two men left for Italy. When they crossed the border the following day, Germany had declared war on France and invaded Belgium.

Italy, summer 1914

CHAPTER 3

Italy, August 1914–United States, April 1916

ON AUGUST 4 Diaghilev and Miassine arrived in Milan to begin their holiday.[1] They planned to reassemble the company in Berlin by October 1; but once in Milan they realized that events in Europe were taking a much more serious turn than they had imagined. Miassine's impulse was to return to Russia to share in her destiny; but, as he explains in his autobiography, he was reluctant to walk away from what promised to be a brilliant future. Overcome with guilt and very much yearning for his family's approval, he wrote to them and to Anatoli Petrovich explaining his predicament. They supported him, urging him to pursue the artistic possibilities and to take advantage of the rare chance he had been given.

After a round of sightseeing in an oppressively hot Milan, Diaghilev and Miassine left for the much cooler seaside resort of Viareggio. The

Cecchettis joined them there, and the maestro resumed his daily regimen with the dancer. Miassine also enjoyed the city's open-air Marionette Theater, where he intently watched commedia dell'arte characters for hours at a time.[2] Pulcinella, Pimpinella, Capitano Spavento, and the other characters soon held him spellbound; he was "intrigued by their grotesque masks and their jerky, loose-limbed movements."[3] Their influence would soon be felt in his own work.

From Viareggio Miassine and Diaghilev drove to Pisa to visit its ancient cemetery, the Campo Santo, and then to San Gimignano and Monte Oliveto Maggiore. They went on to Siena,[4] and reached Florence at the end of September. There they took lodgings in a spacious flat at 4 Viale Toricelli. Despite the beauty that surrounded him, a lonely Miassine pined for his loved ones, and the theater, back home. He wrote to Anatoli Petrovich: "I recollect the time of work and love, for that you taught me, how to love, and I feel again as if I was burdening you, my dear Anatoli Petrovich. . . . What is going on at your place; who is working and where is Kolya Zverev? I will be here until times get better. Now it is rather difficult and sad. If you have a moment write about the theater in Moscow."[5]

As matters turned out, the Tuscan city was their base for the next month and a half. From there they made trips to Pistoia, Pescia, Lucca, and Ravenna. Miassine's artistic education continued in earnest now as Diaghilev patiently showed him the glories of Florence.[6] Under Diaghilev's tutelage, Miassine studied mosaics, frescoes, paintings, sculpture, and architecture and learned to appreciate the Byzantine, Gothic, Renaissance, and baroque styles. Among the painters he came to admire were Cimabue, Duccio, Donatello, Fra Angelico, Pietro Lorenzelli, Fra Filippo Lippi, Tintoretto, and Michelangelo.[7] For Miassine, "it was not merely the stylistic achievements of these early painters which affected me: it was their spiritual beauty and mysticism."[8]

Miassine was most deeply impressed by paintings whose theme was sacrifice, especially as portrayed in the figure of the grieving Christ. Such works as Cimabue's *Crucifixion,* Duccio's *Rucellai Madonna,* Berlinghieri's *Stigmata of St. Francis* and his triptych titled *Virgin and Child, Saints and Crucifixion,* along with the anonymous *Crucifixion* in the cathedral of Pistoia, he came to regard as lucid symbols of "innocence and humility."[9]

In Ravenna he found much to admire in the sixteenth-century Byzantine mosaics in the church of Sant' Apollinare Nuovo. He was particularly taken by the "beautiful depiction of the miracle of the loaves and fishes, with its gleaming golden background, and the stylized groupings of Christ, and the four disciples tightly placed together with the stylized arm and torso movements."[10] Once more, however, it was the figure of Christ that most moved Miassine: "What gives the mosaic its hypnotic power is the figure of Christ himself, presented as a young man in a purple robe, His arms extended to receive the loaves and fishes. . . . His compassionate, penetrating expression haunted my imagination."[11]

Miassine's Florentine experience reconfirmed the religious longings to which he had been prone since childhood. Now, as he walked through "the churches and museums of Florence I felt again the sense of peace and exaltation which I had experienced as a child of eight, and I could remember vividly my feelings when I had first seen, preserved under glass, the mortal remains of the monastery's patron saint, who had renounced the world in favor of a contemplative life. Perhaps it had been an unconscious identification of myself with St. Saavo which had stirred my youthful emotions."[12] The more absorbed in the sacred subject matter of these works he became, the more he felt "my response to these primitive paintings derived from the same longing for a contemplative, spiritual life."[13] This was an early sign of the growing spirituality that would lead Miassine toward the sanctification of art and his later asceticism.

These affirmations of religious fervor were a natural outgrowth of Miassine's personality, characterized since childhood by longings that would eventually lead him to seek a personal, transcendent meaning to existence. He had avidly read Dostoevsky and Lermontov before leaving Moscow,[14] and one can see a clear relationship between Dostoevsky's profound dismay at man's alienation from his spiritual world and the mature Miassine's sense of the tragedy of human existence. Miassine's fascination with the figure of Christ, bordering on quasi-identification, suggests either a messianic streak in his makeup ("I am the way, the truth, and the life") or an intuitive conviction that self-sacrifice would lead to redemption, a harmonious fusion of spirit and flesh.

Florence unquestionably nourished Miassine's spiritual side, while at the same time Diaghilev concentrated on giving his young charge a practical education in the arts. The impresario believed that meticulous analysis of paintings could teach a choreographer invaluable lessons in perspective, an understanding that he must have in order to place and configure dancers expressively on stage: "In the classical ballet," Miassine elaborated further,

> *dancers mostly dance in a 180-degree contact with the audience. This eye-to-eye contact destroyed the scenic illusion. The study of paintings pro-*

vided a concept of construction, bringing to the attention the focus of the scene. By studying the different painters it is possible to have a better understanding of how they used angles, perspective, and how they manipulated the stage to develop the subject. In painting all space is utilized. Paintings were also an example of how one could realistically and harmoniously conceive the arrangement of a scene. They also served as a guide to human behavior in order to convincingly create a character in his or her idiosyncratic gestures and in interaction with other characters.[15]

Diaghilev rounded out his teaching with improvisational exercises, calling on Miassine to reproduce poses from the paintings he had studied. And then, Miassine remembered:

One afternoon in the Uffizi, while I was looking up at Fra Filippo Lippi's Madonna and Child, *Diaghilev said to me, "Do you think you could compose a ballet?" "No," I answered without thinking, "I'm sure I never could." Then, as we passed on into another room I was suddenly aware of the luminous colors of Simone Martini's* Annunciation. *As I looked at the delicate postures of Gabriel and the Virgin Mary, I felt as if everything I had seen in Florence had finally culminated in this painting. It seemed to be offering me the key to an unknown world, beckoning me along a path which I knew I must follow to the end. "Yes," I said to Diaghilev, "I think I can create a ballet. Not only one, but a hundred, I promise you."*[16]

In this mystical way, Miassine's creative path was revealed to him. The opportunity for artistic fulfillment had arrived, and he knew it. Now his life had direction: he would try to synthesize the contrasting realities of the material world and the mysterious world of the spirit. And his idealism was total. He believed that his efforts, if solemnly undertaken, should lead to moments of divine exaltation and religious ecstasy. From now on his life would be a ceaseless striving after greater spiritual and artistic development.

The two men left Florence for Rome, where on November 10 they took up residence at the Grand Hotel.[17] Dazzled by the ancient city's beauty and vitality, Miassine wrote Anatoli Petrovich to sing the praises of Roman life and the Italian countryside. This letter clearly shows Diaghilev's overmastering influence. His perceptions are appropriated by Miassine; the younger man's insights and grasp of the world are mediated by the older man's:

It is impossible to visit Rome without thinking of you. I know you would be happy here, and I wish you could be with me. What sun, sky, air! The spirit of God is everywhere in this city.

I have just had the most beautiful trip. Starting from Viareggio, I drove with friends through Tuscany and the Campania. I have never seen such incredibly rich yet simple landscapes—everywhere deep green cypresses set against a rolling backcloth of golden fields. At sunset the Tuscan hills were a burning amber, their gentle silhouettes etched against a rosy sky. It was the landscape of all the Renaissance artists who have glorified Madonnas and sunsets! For me the beauty of their painting took on a new reality. After this trip I can understand the truth of their Tuscan coloring. . . . Traveling by car is much more exciting than going by train, for one can see the landscape unfolding all 'round you as you speed along the winding roads. There is a certain moment, just before twilight, when the country-side takes on its purest coloring and everything becomes more intense and more clearly defined. In the slowly fading light you can feel the landscape enveloping and penetrating into your soul.

For me those Tuscan sunsets transcended all earthly beauty and achieved a mystical tranquility of their own. I know that I have been very fortunate, for it is rare that one comes so close to this blessed land. I am writing this to you, Anatoli Petrovich, because I know that Italy means as much to you as it does to me. Truly this country is, as Dostoevski described it, a "cemetery of miracles."[18]

In the eternal city they visited archaeological sites as well as museums, monuments, and churches. (They were particularly astonished by the underground churches dating from the first century.) Miassine also managed to keep working at his drawing. He wrote to Anatoli Petrovich: "You know, I am working on drawing rather seriously. I work two hours daily and I am extremely happy."[19] Two days later he again told his old art teacher: "I continue to draw; my sight has become keener and [the result is] most interesting. I remember the precepts of the school and I keep them in order not to go astray."[20]

Florence had been devoted to the study of history. In Rome Mias-sine and Diaghilev were caught up in the intense fermentation and multi-form experimentation of futurism, a movement conceived by the Italian poet Filippo Tommaso Marinetti and announced by him in a manifesto published on the front page of *Le Figaro* on February 20, 1909. He pro-claimed the end of the art of the past and the birth of an art for the fu-ture. Futurism hailed modernity, revolution, electricity, speed, and

scientific advance, and aimed to alter man's mentality not only by revitalizing the arts but by creating a new language that would incorporate the
experiences of modern man. Marinetti gathered around himself a group
of prominent Italian artists, including Umberto Boccioni, Carlo Carrà,
Luigi Russolo, Giacomo Balla, and Gino Severini. Soon the futurists were
producing other manifestos, using the 1909 document as a model, treating in turn painting, architecture, language, theater, and film.

Diaghilev and Miassine witnessed the experimental efforts of the
futurists at close hand. They attended many *serate futuriste,* or futurist
evenings, which took place mostly in theaters. These manifesto readings
combined with theater, concert, and political assembly inevitably ended
in riot or scandal.[21] By 1914 the *serate* had become primarily a forum for
theatrical experiments governed by Marinetti's "Dynamic and Synoptic
Declamations"—poetry readings that integrated onomatopoeia with the
principles of one art form or another. The new theatrical language of the
futurists also demanded audience participation. One of the most talked-
about *serate* took place in Rome in March 1914, at Giuseppe Sproviere's
gallery. A reading of Francesco Cangiullo's poem "Piedigrotta," complete with costumes, scenery, and lighting designed by Balla, was accompanied by onomatopoeic instruments.[22] Diaghilev and Miassine attended
one of the subsequent performances the following autumn, and
Diaghilev became interested enough to discuss with Cangiullo the possibility of adapting the poem into a ballet with music by the futurist composer Francesco Balilla Pratella.[23]

But even more absorbing than their involvement with this artistic
movement was Miassine's first choreographic essay and the preparations
for it. In view of Miassine's Florentine experience, Diaghilev encouraged
him to create a ballet on a religious theme. He asked Ivan Meštrović, the
Serbian sculptor, then living in Rome, to design it. Diaghilev wrote to
Stravinsky: "I cannot tell you about the subject in any detail, but let me
say that what I have in mind is a performance of the mass in six or seven
short scenes. The epoch will be Byzantine, which Meštrović will arrange
in his own way. The music, a series of a cappella sacred choruses, should
perhaps be inspired by Gregorian chant, but of that more later."[24] He
would later decide that the work was to have no music and that Orthodox chants would be heard during the intervals.

As always, Diaghilev and Miassine found time to enter into the hectic social whirl, even in the midst of work. Among the people they saw
frequently were Gerald Tyrwhitt (later Lord Berners) of the British embassy and Vasily Khvoshchinsky, from the Russian embassy, with his wife.

The highly cultured Khvoshchinskys were prominent figures in Roman diplomatic and artistic circles. He wrote extensively about Tuscan painters, and together they founded a string quartet in Rome. The young and attractive Mme Khvoshchinsky befriended Stravinsky; their correspondence is unusually affectionate. It was at the Khvoshchinskys' flat that Miassine met Rodin, who was in Rome working on a commission for a statue of the Pope.

As the new year arrived, Rome was jolted by an earthquake, which Miassine found unnerving. "The new year came in a strange and frightful manner," he writes to Anatoli Petrovich:

I am still feverish. It was an unforgettable day and morning. In those seconds that brought death to so many people, I felt my worthlessness and pitiful helplessness. The shocks were so strong that it seemed that two or three seconds longer and everything would be finished. Afterwards it was pleasant and joyful, the sunshine and a perfect sky. It all ended like a fairy tale; where the ground broke a huge lake was formed. If it were not for the newspapers and processions with stretchers it would be like the fifth act of a nightmarish fairy-play.[25]

At this time Diaghilev decided that since the war would seriously restrict activities in Paris, he would send for Stravinsky, who was in Switzerland, and present the composer to Italian artistic circles. He channeled a great deal of energy into organizing this visit, and finally, on February 8, the composer arrived. In his honor Diaghilev put together a musical soirée at the Grand Hotel. The program featured the four-handed piano version of *The Rite of Spring,* performed by Stravinsky and the Italian composer Alfredo Casella, and excerpts from *The Firebird* played by Stravinsky, who also accompanied the singer Mayra Freund in a selection of his songs. On the following evening Casella conducted *Petrouchka* at the Augusteo Theater in the presence of the Roman intelligentsia.[26]

On March 3 Diaghilev's Russian compatriot Sergei Prokofiev arrived in Rome to discuss the possibility of collaboration. On the seventh he gave a recital, conducted by Bernardino Molinari in the Santa Cecilia Conservatory, in which he was the soloist in his Second Piano Concerto. Miassine found Prokofiev's company delightful.

Miassine and Diaghilev next spent a week and a half in Naples and Palermo, then returned to Rome, where they accepted Marinetti's invitation to visit him in Milan at the beginning of April. The visit was being arranged so that Diaghilev, Miassine, and Stravinsky, who was to join them, could attend a performance of Luigi Russolo's *intuonarumori,* or noise intoners. These were boxes of different sizes that projected a variety of sounds from individual speakers attached to each box; the aim was to explore noise as a new dimension of music. These "sounds" might well find their way into Miassine's new ballet. Diaghilev wrote to Stravinsky:

> *After 32 rehearsals* for* Liturgie, *we have concluded that absolute silence is Death, and that there is and can be no absolute silence in any air space. Thus the action must have some accompaniment, not musical accompaniment but, rather, sounds. The source of the sounds must not be revealed, and the passage from one to another must not be noticeable to the ear, i.e., they must flow into each other. No rhythm should exist at all, because the beginning and the end of sound should be imperceptible. The proposed instruments are guzli (psalters), bells with tongues wrapped in felt, aeolian harps, sirens, tops, and so on. Of course, this all has to be worked over. Marinetti urges us to plan a meeting in Milan, if just for a day, in order to discuss matters with the orchestra's representatives and to examine all of their instruments. In addition, he is going to send Pratella to Milan to acquaint us with his latest works, which are, as he puts it, stunning.* [27]

The demonstration in Milan took place in Marinetti's home and was attended by Diaghilev, Miassine, Stravinsky, and the futurists Pratella, Boccioni, Carrà, Cangiullo, and the Viscount of Madrone, among others. Cangiullo later wrote:

> *A Cracker crackled and sent up a thousand sparks like a gloom torrent. Stravinsky leapt from the divan like an exploding bedspring, with a whistle of overjoyed excitement. At this time a Rustler rustled like silk skirts, or like new leaves in April. The frenetic composer hurled himself on the piano in an attempt to find the prodigious onomatopoeic sound, but in vain did his avid fingers explore all the semitones. Meanwhile, the male dancer [Miassine] swung his professional legs, Diaghilev went ah, ah, like a startled quail, and that for him was the highest sign of approval. By moving his legs the dancer was trying to say that this strange symphony*

---

* Diaghilev must mean thirty-two working sessions with Massine, since the company was not in Rome.

was danceable, while Marinetti, happier than ever, ordered tea, cakes and
liqueurs. Boccioni whispered to Carrà that the guests were won over.[28]

Much talk about possible joint ventures between the futurists and
the Ballets Russes followed, though no actual collaboration took place
until 1916. At the time of the demonstration in Milan, Diaghilev was negotiating a tour of North America with Otto Kahn, chairman of the
board of the Metropolitan Opera. He decided to have his collaborators
and the company meet together in Switzerland, where they would begin
making preparations for the tour, which eventually got under way in January 1916.

Diaghilev and Miassine returned to Rome and met up with Misia
and Sert, and at the end of April the foursome left for Switzerland. They
drove north via Milan and Montreux (where they stayed at the Palace
Hotel) to the outskirts of Lausanne, where Diaghilev had rented a villa
called Bellerive, in Ouchy, on Lake Geneva. Here began one of the most
peaceful intervals in the history of the Ballets Russes, a period when the
company lived and worked with a hopeful sense of artistic community.

Diaghilev, who had grown dissatisfied with the work Meštrović had
done on *Liturgie*, considered asking Gontcharova to design the ballet.
Her expertise in adapting the style of Byzantine religious art and her
deep knowledge of Russian icons made her an ideal choice. Diaghilev invited her to Ouchy, but his cables went unanswered until he extended an
invitation to her companion, the painter Michel Larionov.[29] When the
couple arrived on July 16, he set them up in a studio in the garden of
Bellerive. He enjoyed their company. The brunet Gontcharova, a born
aristocrat, was brilliant, subdued, and tranquil, while Larionov, tall and
blond with slanted blue eyes, possessed a witty, volatile disposition.
Diaghilev would develop a close association with them in his deliberate
move toward modern Russian painting and away from the decorative
theatrical designs of his early period, dominated by Benois and Bakst.
The conservative Benois (along with another *World of Art* painter,
Somov) had been inclined to identify himself with the West and had
written articles in his native country denouncing the Russian avant-
garde.[30]

Soon dancers began arriving in Lausanne. Some were original
members of the Ballets Russes who had scattered once the war broke
out; others had been recruited in Russia and Poland by régisseur Serge
Grigoriev. They settled in pensions around Ouchy. Cecchetti taught three
classes: nine a.m. for the corps de ballet, ten for the soloists, eleven for

Natalia Gontcharova at Bellerive,
Lausanne, 1915

Miassine's private instruction. After lunch came rehearsals. Some were conducted in a market (used only in the early morning) at the top of a hill. Others took place at Bellerive. Many of them lasted for up to six hours.[31]

When the company reconvened in Switzerland in 1915, Miassine's prominent position had clearly been solidified. His alliance with Diaghilev and their obvious sexual intimacy were discreetly acknowledged by everyone. The Ballets Russes' structure was strictly hierarchical, and Diaghilev, the supreme seigneur, presided along with his attendant prince, Miassine. Next in line came the council of collaborators, and below them were the various court strata who made up the balance of the company. But Diaghilev and Miassine's public behavior was always restrained, particularly during any interaction with others in the company. Valentina Kachuba, who had come from Moscow to join the troupe, remembers that whenever the two men were in public with other company members, Miassine circumspectly stood behind Diaghilev, remaining at a distance from him and not stepping forward unless he was needed.[32]

Despite the anguish of the war in Europe, the creative ambiance at Bellerive was confident, congenial, and conducive to work. As one visitor, the young composer Maurice Sandoz, described it: "The big Louis XIV house, spread out on its terraces, is dominated by the grassy slopes. Huge clumps of trees, judiciously planted by the English gardeners a hundred years or so ago, did not hide the house or deprive it of its famous view."[33] And: "It was an ideal spot of several acres, abounding in dates and oleanders, pines and maples, lilacs and roses. Following a little path through the miniature woodland, we emerged on a little garden surrounding the smaller villa. 'Here,' [Diaghilev] said, 'is where most members of my colony live,' and then leading me within, we visited half a dozen rooms, in each of which I found a young woman or man busy with pen, pencil, or brush."[34]

Predictably, much of the group's activity centered around Miassine's apprenticeship. Diaghilev had charged Gontcharova and Larionov with furthering Miassine's education in art and choreography. As mentors to pupil, they began working with him on *Liturgie*. As Gontcharova watched over the choreographic sessions, she worked on her designs. Her surviving sketches for this ballet, which show her keen aesthetic grasp of the power of icons, are of finely crafted apostles, gold and silver seraphim, and vermilion-winged angels, all in the Byzantine geometrical style. Gontcharova also worked on the concept of the staging and on the backdrop, in which she depicted Christ, the Madonna, and the apostles in the style of Italian primitives. As the ballet moved toward its final form, Larionov offered further advice on the choreography.

Liturgie was a series of scenes from the life of Christ, centering on the Passion. For the first scene, the Annunciation, Miassine "devised a succession of angular gestures and still, open-hand movements inspired by Cimabue's *Virgin*. For the Ascension I arranged two groups of angels with their arms raised and hands crossed to create the illusion of wings ascending to heaven."[35] These poses were linked to Gontcharova's designs; Miassine later recalled her sketches stressing "such vital details as the Byzantine hand positions and the angular, in-turned arm movements of Christ for the scene of the Resurrection, evoking the effect I was striving for. . . ."[36] He described his rapport with Gontcharova in a letter to Anatoli Petrovich:

I am very enthusiastic about Gontcharova's work, and, perhaps, she is the only one that interests me now. Larionov is a very well-educated artist and much was revealed to me in the course of conversations with him, and I

A rehearsal of the Garden of Gethsemane scene in Liturgie, *Bellerive, 1915*

would like to do much, of course, everything in my sphere, what I feel to be more and more as most congenial to me and at this time I believe the most interesting.

I work on a huge ballet, it seems to me I had written to you already but in few words. The movements will be without music. . . . Music choruses begin only when the curtain comes down and end when the curtain is again risen. It is difficult to say how this came about, one thing followed the other. . . . Costumes and sets are by Gontcharova and she made many interesting things.

Even if it is going to be done in America you have to come to the premiere.[37]

Stimulating friends visited Bellerive. Bakst came from Paris. Stravinsky, who lived at Clarens, frequently made two-hour bicycle trips to Ouchy. There the composer played, for the first time, passages from *Les Noces*, already planned as one of Miassine's future choreographic projects. Of it Leonid wrote to Anatoli Petrovich: "It is extremely interesting and congenial to me and I will be in heaven if I succeed in doing it well. The music is really wonderful and if you like Stravinsky it will be a great joy."[38] Shortly after Diaghilev set up quarters at Bellerive, Mme Khvoshchinsky arrived from Rome to manage the house—whether at the impresario's request isn't entirely clear. But Diaghilev, never altogether comfortable with visits from women, must have been a bit unsettled by the figure cut by this attractive, intelligent young woman, especially since Miassine obviously had taken a fancy to her. (She remained for two months.)[39] Stravinsky introduced another important newcomer, the Swiss musician Ernest Ansermet, into the inner circle. With Pierre Monteux away in the French army, Ansermet eventually became Diaghilev's conductor. Thus, with Diaghilev's collaborators contributing their varied talents, Miassine's apprenticeship was well and truly begun.

Although by now Miassine had choreographed most of *Liturgie*, the work still had to overcome a series of hurdles, not the least of which was

Stravinsky, Mme Khvoshchinsky, Diaghilev, and Bakst at Bellerive, 1915

finding suitable music. Diaghilev had tried to persuade Stravinsky to collaborate, but he refused.[40] Miassine's autobiography tells us that Diaghilev then decided that the ballet would be performed without music, that instead, during the intervals Orthodox chants like those the impresario had heard in Kiev would be heard; but when Diaghilev was unable to obtain the music for them from Russia, the entire project was dropped. In fact, there were production as well as musical problems: In an interview with the Paris-based Russian newspaper *Les Nouvelles Russes* in 1953, Gontcharova discussed the complex, multitiered decor, which was very difficult to execute. She also mentioned that the producers had intended to allow the public to hear the steps of the dancers as a sort of background accompaniment to the choreography;[41] still, Miassine must have been right when he said that the unresolved doubts about the music were one of the reasons that the ballet was abandoned. In any case, *Liturgie* never went beyond the experimental stage.

In the fall preparations got under way for the American tour, which Otto Kahn was to sponsor under the auspices of the Metropolitan Opera. Before leaving Europe, however, Diaghilev arranged two Red Cross benefit performances, one in Geneva, the other in Paris.

Diaghilev needed a new work to introduce before leaving for America and suggested to Miassine that he begin another ballet, one that would not require such a long preparation. *Liturgie* had been an exceedingly personal choice of subject, but this time Miassine opted for one that was straightforwardly, unabashedly Russian: the dances from Rimsky-Korsakov's opera *The Snow Maiden*. When Diaghilev played him the score, Miassine was delighted, for the dances recalled to him the "singing games" of his childhood.[42]

But Diaghilev, as always, was making another, deeper point at the same time. He chose Russian music in order to tap Miassine's cultural roots. And this was in keeping with his own instincts as well, for the impresario shared in the widespread Slavophile stirrings that sought to revive and preserve the venerated Russian virtues and traditions that had been disrupted by the westernizing reforms of Peter the Great.

Diaghilev asked Larionov, who was very knowledgeable about Russian folklore, to design the ballet and assist Miassine in its creation. Gontcharova acted as unofficial collaborator. According to Miassine, Larionov "was intrigued by the idea of a ballet based on Russian folklore, and suggested that it should revolve 'round the person of the sun god Yarila, to whom the peasants pay tribute in ritual ceremonies and dances, fusing with it the legend of the Snow Maiden, the daughter of King

Frost, who is destined to melt in the heat of the sun when she falls in love with a mortal." Miassine also decided to "incorporate into the action the character of Bobyl, the 'innocent' or village half-wit, and to end the ballet with the traditional dance of the Buffoons, for which I devised a succession of interwoven leaps, twists, and turns."[43]

The result of this collective effort was *Le Soleil de nuit*. Larionov and Miassine discussed the structure of the work, and in exploring the anthropological meaning of the old ritual peasant dances Larionov gave the younger man a clearer understanding of their essence. For the choreography Miassine "drew on my childhood memories of the *chorovod* and '*Gori, gori jasno,*' which [Larionov] helped me to embellish with suitably primitive, earthy gestures."[44]

Le Soleil de nuit had no literal story line and, like Fokine's innovative *Les Sylphides,* was conceived strictly in terms of dance; pantomime was unnecessary. Grigoriev saw early on that Miassine possessed originality and skill in the configuration of groups, and had "succeeded in inventing a great many interesting and varied steps and patterns."[45]

During rehearsals Miassine was a bit remote but entirely gracious, treating everyone with the utmost politeness, both in his tactful instructions and in his taking care to use "Mademoiselle" or "Monsieur" when addressing the dancers.[46] Sokolova remembered the dancers' delight not only in performing *Le Soleil de nuit* but in putting the inventions of the young choreographer to the test. His style was eccentric and intensely personal, and they warmly approved.[47] Kachuba admired Miassine's authority and daring in getting his dancers to sit, lie, and roll on the floor.[48]

In addition, in *Le Soleil de nuit* Miassine created a role for himself that set off his charismatic stage presence to greater advantage than ever before:

In my own role as the Midnight Sun I had to match the power of Rimsky-Korsakov's music with a driving energy which permeated my whole body. In my dance, which was based on classical movements, I made use of broad arm movements, and strengthened my performance with rapidly repeated elevations. Larionov had designed for me a sumptuous glittering costume with a fantastic headdress of burning red suns which glowed against the inky-blue of the midnight sky. Attached to my hands by elastic were two more gold suns, the size of dinner plates, decorated with jazzed red borders. As I danced, I flashed them in rapidly alternating rhythms, to the left, to the right, over my head, down below my knees. In order to sus-

tain the illusion of a revolving sun, I was forced to keep every muscle in
my body in constant motion until the end of the dance. But I could feel
power pulsating within me, and by the end I had reached a fever pitch of
excitement.[49]

Miassine's dance was his projection of himself as the star he was to become. As his description suggests, this ballet carried a strong visual impact. Larionov's decor included stage wings painted as huge trees in yellow and green that at first could not be recognized as such; the backdrop depicted a primitive idol against a starred sky.[50] The costumes were variations on traditional Russian costumes with enormous headpieces known as *kitchki* or *kokochniki;* in fact, the headpieces were so large that Miassine asked that his be modified to allow him to jump.[51]

Misia and Sert came from Paris to see the new work. The assurance of Miassine's choreography came as a surprise, since they had blamed him for the failure of *The Legend of Joseph.* Now, in a letter to Cocteau, Misia described "last night, a dress rehearsal for us of what has been done these past months. Something completely new, very beautiful, in which Miassine proves that he really is someone. And how prejudiced we were against him, Sert and I!!!"[52]

The ballet was introduced on December 20 in a single performance at the Grand Théâtre in Geneva, in a program that included *Carnaval, The Firebird,* and *Prince Igor.* On December 22 the *Journal de Genève* reported: "*Le Soleil de nuit* was a delight. It was like a box of Russian toys brought to life and laughter, shining with gold papers and splashed with color. Comic costumes for peasants and clowns, with, among them, Bobyl, a simpleton in a white blouse, and Miassine, the much applauded choreographer, as a puppet with cymbals and a vermillion face."[53]

The enthusiastic reception of *Le Soleil de nuit* gave Miassine a shot of youthful self-confidence. At the age of nineteen he was enjoying his first taste of success and public acclaim. But he soon was brought down to earth by Diaghilev, who after the performance remarked dryly, "I did not hear them cheering."[54] This barb cut deeply enough for Miassine to quote it in his autobiography fifty years later, a sign of how hungry for approval he must have been at the time. The Ouchy period, for all its personal and artistic rewards, was without doubt a time of stress and conflicting demands for Miassine. One can imagine how eager he must have been to prove his artistic worth, not only to himself but, more importantly, to Diaghilev. And he needed the recognition not just to validate his artistic achievement but as compensation for how much he feared he was sacrificing in the process.

Needless to say, Miassine's growing self-confidence was not easy for Diaghilev to accept. He was, after all, a man whose work was a means of self-fulfillment and an extension of himself: Miassine's role was to be an instrument of Diaghilev's own realization, a well-behaved acquisition. Full acknowledgment of his protégé's achievement amounted to granting him an identity and thus an independence that, at least in the early stages of their relationship, he could not bring himself to give. By withholding praise from Miassine's creative efforts at crucial moments—a pattern that would often be repeated—Diaghilev would help to poison some of Miassine's subsequent attitudes toward others.

During his formative years Miassine appropriated much of his identity from Diaghilev's, enough so that assessing the adult Miassine becomes difficult without understanding Diaghilev's aggressive fusion of lightning brilliance with sinister deviousness. For the naive Miassine Diaghilev was a role model, an ideal to which he aspired. Admiring Diaghilev, Miassine also wanted to please him. But at this stage of his life humility and gratitude were the only coinage in which he could do so, and Diaghilev signaled to Miassine the surest way to continue to please him: with *more* humility and gratitude. The unavoidable, if unconscious, anger that this process built up in Miassine in the ensuing years had its seed in these early manipulations of Diaghilev's. The end of their relationship truly was right there in its beginning.

Diaghilev and Miassine spent the holidays in Paris. On Christmas Day a group of friends gathered at Misia's house, where, with Miassine turning the pages of the score, Stravinsky played the first scene of *Les Noces*. The Ballets Russes performed a charity matinée to benefit the British Red Cross on December 29 at the Paris Opéra. The program consisted of *Schéhérazade, The Firebird* (conducted by Stravinsky), *Le Soleil de nuit,* the Bluebird Pas de Deux, and *Prince Igor.* Then, on January 1, 1916, the company sailed from Bordeaux to New York to begin its American tour.

The voyage across the choppy Atlantic was rough, and the smallness of the vessel did nothing to allay the impresario's terror of ocean travel; so Diaghilev distracted himself by poring over the schedules and programs for the tour. Indeed, he became so immersed in the planning that he rarely left his cabin. Miassine, on the other hand, spent a great deal of time on deck, "gazing at the wintry seascape on which the rolling Atlantic breakers formed vast hillocks of foam."[55] Diaghilev never appeared on the open deck without donning a life jacket, and by journey's end his deep dread of the sea had pushed his nerves nearly to the point of collapse. The sudden scream of the onboard sirens sent the skittish traveler scurrying, with Miassine in tow, to the safety of a lifeboat that had been designated for his use in an emergency. To his great relief, he was informed that the siren meant simply that the vessel was passing the Statue of Liberty in New York harbor. As they drew closer and the island lifted its foggy veil, the city and its great skyline stimulated Miassine's imagination; the imposing arrangement suggested to him the geometrical simplicity of "elongated Babylonian temples."[56] Much later he wrote: "What particularly interested me was the fact that each unit of those monumental constructions represented a different aspect of life in New York. I thought it would be amusing to make a choreographic composition based on six individual rooms, superimposed one on another, seen simultaneously, a sort of spiritual and visual counterpoint of various characters and their moods, typical of the daily happenings in this great city."[57]

Since the Metropolitan Opera was still conducting its season, the American debut of the Ballets Russes took place at the Century Theatre. Opening night, January 17, saw the inevitable retirement of "Miassine" and the debut of "Massine." The new spelling was hit upon by Diaghilev, who thought it easier for non-Russians to pronounce. (The Gallicized "Léonide" had been with the dancer from the start of his Ballets Russes career.) The first program consisted of *Firebird, La Princesse enchantée* (as the Bluebird pas de deux was sometimes billed), *Le Soleil de nuit,* and *Schéhérazade;* the repertory for the rest of the engagement included the Polovtsian Dances from *Prince Igor, L'Après-midi d'un faune, Carnaval, Petrouchka, Les Sylphides,* and *Le Pavillon d'Armide.* In addition to his role in *Le Soleil de nuit,* Massine also danced the Faun, Petrouchka, the Golden Slave in *Schéhérazade,* and the Tsarevich in *Firebird.* Later in the tour he danced the role of Amoun in *Cléopâtre.*

Though the Ballets Russes performed well and found favor with American audiences, the press was quick to note the absence of Nijinsky and Karsavina. Generally, the notices were mixed. Of course there were those in the audience for whom classical ballet meant little more than a pretty ballerina floating across the stage in a tutu. Others, like *New Republic* writer Troy Kinney, praised Diaghilev for his synthesis of the old and the new, which engendered what Kinney called "the freedom of richer convention."[58] Diaghilev himself concluded that the barrier was the repertory; New York audiences seemed frankly puzzled by artistic innovations for which perhaps they simply weren't ready.[59] He also confided to Massine that "Americans still seemed to think of ballet as light entertainment, to be enjoyed after a hard day at the office."[60]

Two of the ballets, *Schéhérazade* and *L'Après-midi d'un faune*, were met with shocked protests from the public and the press over their supposed immorality and bad taste. In *Schéhérazade*, the depiction of an interracial orgy in which a white woman takes a black slave as her lover was simply too much for the American public of 1916; the ballet set off an explosive political furor. Grenville Vernon, a writer for the *New York Tribune*, believed that "the remarkable impersonation of the Negro favorite of Zobeide, Princess of Samarcande, by M. [Adolph] Bolm, will render the ballet impossible for production south of Mason and Dixon's line. Even to Northern minds it was repulsive."[61] And of course the simulated act of masturbation in the final moments of *L'Après-midi d'un faune* fared no better, earning from the Catholic Theatre Movement a broadside denouncing certain "objectionable features of the Russian Ballets." The controversy culminated in a hearing in the chambers of Judge McAdoo on January 25. According to the *New York Sun*:

> *M. Serge de Diaghilev and the Russians listened with the grave patience and the puzzled amusement with which intelligent folk from Continental Europe have often watched the workings of the censorship of municipal authorities over the American theater. They were particularly impressed by the abnormal perceptions of some of the protectors of public morals, who discovered "meanings" that had never occurred to those that had many times set the two pieces on the stage. "I believe," said M. de Diaghilev, half amused and half perturbed, "that my mind and the minds of those who planned and executed the ballets are less vicious than the minds of those that made the protest."*
>
> *The spokesmen of sundry "vice" societies were arrogant and vociferous until M. de Diaghilev and the representatives of the Metropolitan Opera House, being quiet men of the world, naturally wearied of noisy bickering and agreed to alter certain items, so that even the agents of the societies in question could not possibly imagine anything into anything.[62]*

In keeping with the agreement, *L'Après-midi d'un faune* was performed that night with the offending finale sanitized; it ended as the Faun (Massine) "placed the drapery gently on the rock and sat gazing at its silken folds."[63] With the performance safely over, huge floral tributes were presented to Massine on stage. A disgusted Diaghilev rose stiffly to take his leave of general manager Giulio Gatti-Casazza, business director John Brown, and the other Metropolitan officials who sat nearby; turning to them all he taunted in French: "America is saved!"[64]

In this charged atmosphere the New York season ended on January 29. Two days later the company opened in Boston, the first leg of a tour that would include sixteen more American cities. Massine soon discovered that the lengthy train rides gave him "the nightmare illusion of being locked in a prison cell while speeding off to an unknown fathomless abyss."[65] Fits of insomnia accompanied his bouts of claustrophobia, causing him to spend many sleepless nights in the cold corridor, staring out windows as the inky landscape sped by. The larger cities allowed the company the luxury of longer presentations and the brief illusion of continuity in their personal lives. In the smaller towns and communities they endured one-night stands. But though Massine found these short, abrupt stopovers exhausting, he enjoyed discovering the various styles of American architecture. He wrote to Anatoli Petrovich: "I take off my hat to these magnificent skyscrapers. They are more beautiful than anything I have ever seen. . . . their simplicity is so much better than all the decorative sculpture which ruins so much European architecture."[66]

The difficult schedule had one advantage: it gave Massine an opportunity to delve into the company's repertory, to take on roles that demanded well-defined and rigorous characterization. In analyzing *Cléopâtre* and *L'Après-midi d'un faune,* ballets in which Fokine and Nijinsky, respectively, had attempted to create a two-dimensional effect reminiscent of bas-relief, Massine concluded that Nijinsky had surpassed Fokine. For him, Nijinsky's choreography achieved the desired effect: by "suppressing the sense of depth, and dispensing with the usual graceful positions, and by twisting sharply in opposite directions the upper part of the body against the lower, Nijinsky evolved a sculptural line which gave an effect of organic beauty such as I had never seen in any ballet."[67] Without ever having seen Nijinsky perform the role, Massine brought to his portrayal of the Faun a similar conception, derived from his own study of Greek statuary and Greek and Roman bas-reliefs. We can assume that Massine discussed the ballet with Diaghilev, and we can be reasonably sure that the impresario was instrumental in Massine's understanding of the work's innovations. But as Massine pointed out in his autobiography, he would receive no praise from Diaghilev for his portrayal of the Faun. The older man's approval of his assuming the role seemed to be enough.

Of the many new roles that Massine undertook, he found Petrouchka the "most rewarding," because in it "my sense of identification with the half-human puppet helped me to project much of my own personality." [68] The most demanding aspect of the role was making explicit "Petrouchka's divided nature, his hopeless love for the ballerina, and his humiliation; all had to be conveyed by constant variations of tiny, grotesque steps woven together to create a pathetic whole." [69] Commentators have often mentioned the parallels between *Petrouchka*'s "triangle" and Nijinsky's emotional and existential conflicts. Some of the triangle's psychological dynamics apply to Massine as well.

Massine's extraordinary good looks and piercing eyes were fit for a Georgian prince, and it is certain that more than one woman in the company fell in love with him. Massine himself was attracted to some of the female dancers, especially those from Moscow. "All the Moscow ladies are kind," he wrote to Anatoli Petrovich, "their manner of speech excites me and causes joy to my ears, as if I hear birds chirping: there is the whole of Moscow in them." [70] Even though flirting with him was "against all the rules," Sokolova recalls that "many of [the women] had a crush on him although no one seemed to be able to penetrate his 'frozen stare.' " [71] As the tour progressed, however, Massine himself—to the amazement of nearly everyone in the company—began to flirt with the company's seductress, the beautiful Lubov Tchernicheva, who was also Grigoriev's wife. This ended abruptly when the company reached Washington, D.C. There, Massine danced Amoun opposite Tchernicheva's impressive Cléopâtre; but later, at an embassy benefit for the Russian Red Cross, the cat came home and sent all the mice scurrying. According to Sokolova:

> We performed several dances in the middle of the ballroom, including that of the nursemaids from Petrouchka, and afterwards we joined in the ballroom dancing. There was a terrific crush, and my partner saw a little room which was empty, so he guided me through the door. Almost immediately we were followed by Massine and his would-be girlfriend. We were all laughing and flirting and having a wonderful time, when to our horror we saw Diaghilev standing in the doorway, a champagne bottle under his arm and glasses in his hand. We froze. He had seen enough; he turned and walked away. The following morning a message came 'round via the bush telegraph—that is, by Vassili, Diaghilev's servant and spy—that anybody who interfered with the peace of the company by disturbing Massine in his work would be expelled immediately. Léonide and the lady did not speak to each other for many a day after that. As for the rest of us, any girl who valued her position in the company was careful to steer clear of Massine. [72]

In Washington Massine watched a group of Sioux Indians perform a series of war dances at the National Theater. From this event he conceived his idea for a ballet based on an American subject. With Ernest Ansermet he visited the Smithsonian Institution, where the conductor studied Native American musical instruments while Massine read up on material dealing with tribal moon dances, nuptial ceremonies, and funeral rites. He had been drawn to the story of the Indian maiden Pocahontas and had decided that she would be the source for his new ballet. Ansermet forwarded to Bakst in Paris colored prints of American Indians and engravings depicting the life of Pocahontas in order to aid the artist in designing a decor. Massine intended to create a *suite de danses* modeled on *Le Soleil de nuit*. In the meantime, the company left Washington for engagements in Philadelphia and Atlantic City before returning to New York to open at the Metropolitan Opera House on April 3.

Ever since negotiations had begun for the United States tour, Diaghilev had hoped to re-engage Nijinsky as the company's premier danseur. However, during the war the Nijinskys were interned twice, first in Budapest and later in Vienna. Finally, through the extraordinary efforts of Diaghilev and Otto Kahn, who called upon the influence and connections of Queen Alexandra of England and her sister the dowager empress Maria Feodorovna, Emperor Franz Joseph of Austria, King Alfonso XIII of Spain, and the Pope (whose intercession was at the request of the Spanish monarch), the dancer and his family were released. They traveled via Switzerland and Paris to Bordeaux and sailed from there for the United States on March 26. They landed in New York on April 4, the day after the Ballets Russes had opened at the Metropolitan.

But no sooner had they arrived than an embarrassing squabble arose between Diaghilev and Nijinsky. In London Nijinsky had won a back-salary judgment against the impresario amounting to half a million gold francs. Now, as he enjoyed his freedom in New York, Nijinsky conveniently overlooked Diaghilev's crucial role in securing his safe passage out of Europe and threatened to boycott the Ballets Russes until he was paid. The press, of course, quickly sniffed out the quarrel and bared the episode in sensational headlines. Nijinsky eventually set aside his argument with his former lover and made his American debut on April 12, but only after Otto Kahn had negotiated a settlement of the dispute.

Nijinsky was once again part of Diaghilev's Ballets Russes, and Massine now alternated with the legendary dancer in some of Nijinsky's own roles. Massine knew that comparisons were inevitable, so he must have been quietly pleased by a favorable review of Nijinsky's Petrouchka that took appreciative measure of both men's abilities: Nijinsky "had to stand a very severe comparison because of the superb work of Massine in the same role. Mr. Nijinsky paid more attention to the puppet's soul and less to his mechanism than Mr. Massine. Those who like this conception will prefer Nijinsky; those who prefer to have the fact that Petrouchka is a puppet emphasized, Massine. Both are as fine as can be in their respective characterizations."[73]

Lydia Lopokova, who had rejoined the company when it arrived in the States and danced the Ballerina opposite both dancers, wrote: "Massine mimed the part with his hands, stiff and hanging—in Massine's mime the hands are very important. Nijinsky moved more with his whole body. Massine's was an intellectual creation, Nijinsky's of inward bodily genius, only half conscious. But both were great creations."[74]

Offstage, Massine found Nijinsky aloof and reserved. But to see him dance! To watch Nijinsky transform himself on stage, to marvel at his effortless control, to be captivated by the fluidity and harmony of his movements, and to witness his profound emotional expressiveness—all this put Massine in ecstasy. He especially respected Nijinsky's Petrouchka, a "poignant representation of a puppet-like but recognizable human figure."[75] He felt that the role came more easily to Nijinsky than to him. He also admired Nijinsky's Bluebird and his Spectre; but what he found even more fascinating was his meticulous coaching of the nymphs in L'Après-midi d'un faune.

In New York, social life for Diaghilev and Massine centered on late-night suppers at the Plaza Hotel, where they enjoyed the company of Grigoriev, Lopokova, Kahn, and Prince Paul Troubetzkoy. They also found time for "delightful parties" coordinated by the well-known society orchestrator Elsa Maxwell. And because the war had driven many Europeans to New York, Diaghilev was able to renew old friendships with, among others, the eccentric photographer Baron Alfred de Meyer and his wife, Olga. For his part, the solitary Massine found time to enjoy the treasures at the Metropolitan Museum and to study and photograph the Morgan Collection of Mayan sculpture.

To follow the Metropolitan engagement, which ended on April 29, Otto Kahn had organized another American tour. He hoped to avoid friction between Diaghilev and Nijinsky by making Diaghilev's presence unnecessary. To that end he proposed renting the company from the impresario. Diaghilev could see that his returning to Europe alone while the war continued would surely disrupt the company, but he also knew that the American tour would secure for the Ballets Russes the continuity it needed. So he accepted Kahn's proposal, but on one condition: the company would first travel to Spain for a string of brief engagements in Madrid, San Sebastián, and Bilbao; Nijinsky would remain in America, awaiting the troupe's return.

Massine outside the Teatro Real,
Madrid, 1916

CHAPTER 4

Spain, May–September 1916

ON MAY 6 the Ballets Russes sailed aboard the *Dante Alighieri* for Spain, where at King Alfonso XIII's invitation the troupe was to perform its first engagement ever at Madrid's Teatro Real. The threat of torpedoes, coupled with Diaghilev's water phobia, made for a nerve-racking Atlantic crossing.[1]

When the *Dante Alighieri* reached Cádiz, the Spanish composer Manuel de Falla was probably at the dock to greet it. He had seen the Ballets Russes perform in Paris and had met Diaghilev there, but it seems to have been Stravinsky who suggested that he travel to Cádiz to welcome the company to Spain. Falla, whose French was impeccable, was a native of Cádiz. He kindly offered his services as cicerone and took everyone sightseeing, exposing the company to its first taste of flamenco.

Despite his rather subdued personality, Falla's intelligence and refinement quickly won over Diaghilev and Massine, both of whom soon befriended him.

Massine was completely charmed by the port town. Its "whitewashed houses [were] smothered in bougainvillea, and the tiny plazas, with their baroque fountains,"[2] were dusted with the scent of lemon blossoms. After the pressures of the American tour and an anxious ocean voyage, Cádiz must have seemed a haven. The young choreographer was very much taken with Andalusia. This first contact with Spain marked the beginning of his lifelong love affair with the country, a passionate attachment that would inspire one of his greatest ballets, *Le Tricorne.* (Cervantes's *Don Quixote,* in Spanish, eventually became one of his favorite books.)

From Cádiz the company set out for Madrid, where the Teatro Real opening was scheduled for May 26.

With Europe at war, Spain had become a refuge for an elegant congregation of citizens without a country, as well as a center of espionage and counterespionage. Despite the deterioration of the local economy, due especially to the catastrophe of the Spanish-American War, for those whom the wartime upheaval had made rich, Madrid was the preferred city for regaining their bearings and recovering their composure. Largely untouched by the hardships of war, the city vibrated with excitement and a sense of anticipation. The grand hotels, notably the Ritz and the recently opened Palace, were crowded with glamorous "survivors." Aristocrats, millionaires, artists, and swindlers all compounded the intrigue. Every newly arrived bejeweled woman sighted at the Ritz or the opera was taken for an American millionairess, a Russian princess traveling incognito, or a cunning spy. Any sleek new male face was thought to be that of an exiled king or a filthy-rich gangster.

Diaghilev and Massine checked into the Ritz, one of the most exclusive quarters in town. Across the street sit the Palacio de Villahermosa and the Palace Hotel; further west stands Parliament. Along the Paseo del Prado is the Canovas del Castillo Square with its fountain of Neptune emerging from the waters. Next to it is the Prado. The entire scene is dominated by the sixteenth-century San Jerónimo Basilica. The Paseo del Prado had long been a fashionable stretch for early-evening promenades. As pedestrians strolled through its park and fountain areas, members of the upper classes, sitting in prominent view in their open carriages, moved alongside them at a stately pace. Massine was enchanted by "how beautiful people are, and the costumes, the shawls."[3] Passing through the famous domed lobby of the Palace, Diaghilev and Massine encountered many of the hotel's celebrated guests; two of the more notorious were the renowned spies Mata Hari and Marthe Richer (who was also one of the first female pilots).

The Teatro Real, opposite the Royal Palace, was the city's most prominent cultural showcase. Opera was enjoying a renaissance. There was fierce competition in the public fancy between long-cherished Italian favorites and the torrential works of Wagner. At the Real it was possible to see the *Ring* cycle performed by some of the best singers and conductors from Bayreuth and Munich. Performances of *Parsifal* extended from the afternoon into the evening, and the audience dined during the intermission, as was the custom in Germany. Two striking divas dominated the scene at the Real. From France there was the red-haired, blue-eyed Geneviève Vix, who had created a sensation there in Richard Strauss's *Salome,* more for her provocative costume than for her vocal abilities. From Russia there was Maria Kuznetsova, who had created the role of Potiphar's Wife opposite Massine's Joseph. She had been romantically linked to Bakst, and Massenet had written his *Roma* for her. In Madrid she created a stir on stage and off. She directed and supervised the premiere of *Parsifal* and sang the role of Kundry as well. Beautiful and enigmatic, she appeared offstage with her arms and head covered with precious stones, the embodiment of Oriental opulence and mystery. She promptly took the Ballets Russes under her wing. An invitation to one of her Russian teas was highly coveted, and Diaghilev, Massine, and other members of the company were often in attendance.

Eager, as usual, to explore new trends in all the arts, Diaghilev and Massine soon were immersed in musical life outside the Teatro Real, attending concerts and recitals at the Ateneo, the Círculo de Bellas Artes, and the Ritz Hotel. These performances featured the most recent compositions of European and Spanish composers performed by prominent musicians and singers, among them Falla, Ricardo Viñes, and Arthur Rubinstein.

The ballet engagement at the Real opened on May 26, with a program consisting of *Les Sylphides, Carnaval, Schéhérazade,* and *Le Soleil de nuit.* It was a glittering social event attended by the royal family, in full regalia, and practically all of Madrid. But the performances immediately following were not supported by the general public. *ABC,* a leading newspaper, reported that although the balcony had been sold out, the tiers and the orchestra seats were only two-thirds filled.[4] Word of mouth must have been good, however, for on May 30 *ABC* reported that the Ballets Russes had become a triumph, playing to consistently full houses.[5]

With the Ballets Russes at the Real, Diaghilev and Massine themselves became an attraction on Madrid's brilliant social scene. Among their most distinguished hosts were the Duchess de Montellanos (at whose home Rubinstein was a frequent guest and performer), the Duchess de Durcal, the Count de Romanones, the Marquise de Ganay, and Mme Eugenia Errazuriz. Yet, true to his custom, Diaghilev soon gathered around him his own entourage, over which he presided with Massine at the Ritz or the Palace. Among the city's luminaries to whom Falla introduced them were the Count de Casa Miranda, the great Swedish diva Christine Nilsson (mother-in-law to the count), the musicians Joaquín Turina, José Cubiles, and Conrado del Campo, and the playwrights Gregorio and María Martínez Sierra. In 1914, after Falla had returned from Paris to Spain, he had traveled with the itinerant theater company of the Martínez Sierras, composing incidental music for them. It was for this group that he created his *El amor brujo* as a vehicle for Pastora Imperio, the greatest flamenco *bailaora* (dancer) of the period. Newcomers to Madrid were entranced by Imperio; Ansermet dubbed her "la Divina."

Stravinsky joined the Ballets Russes for its Madrid engagement. His *Firebird* was performed on May 28, and at his curtain call a thunderous ovation filled the hall.[6] At the first performance of *Petrouchka,* on June 5, the pianist Cubiles played the cymbals as a personal tribute to the composer. While in Madrid, Stravinsky attended bullfights with Falla and visited Toledo and the Escorial with his friends.[7] Both sites made a deep impression on the composer, who thought them a "revelation of the profoundly religious temperament of the people and the mystic power of their Catholicism, so closely akin in its essentials to the religious feelings and spirit of Russia."[8] Massine wrote to Anatoli Petrovich: "The Escorial impressed me more than any other art. I did not find it solemn. In some parts there is the simplicity of Byzantium and everywhere there is powerful spirit and mighty form. I cannot compare it to anything. There are no decorations; only architecture."[9]

At the Martínez Sierras', Stravinsky played passages from *Les Noces* and listened to Falla's work in progress, *El corregidor y la molinera,* a pantomime he was composing for the Martínez Sierras.[10] It was also at one of the playwrights' musical soirées that Diaghilev and Massine heard for the first time Falla's *Noches en los jardines de España* (formerly called *Nocturnos*). They were enamored of the piece; Diaghilev felt that the score offered Massine an ideal opportunity to fashion a ballet on a Spanish theme. But Falla was not keen to hear his music, conceived for the concert hall rather than the theater, accompanying a ballet.[11] To overcome Falla's resistance, Diaghilev enlisted the support of Stravinsky, who cited *Petrouchka* as an example of a work written originally for piano and orchestra and later adapted into a ballet.[12] To entice the wary Falla, Diaghilev proposed a setting: a *fête de nuit* under a starlit sky in the gardens of the Alhambra, with magnificently shawled women and men in evening dress (*"tout à fait vingtième siècle,"* Falla commented).[13] But Falla was even less enthusiastic about this idea, which he felt was more suited to the music hall. He offered another option: he would turn *El corregidor y la molinera* into a ballet.[14]

"El corregidor y la molinera" is a traditional Spanish tale based on the anonymous eighteenth-century romance *El molinero de arcos,* and best remembered as the 1874 novel *El sombrero de tres picos* by Pedro Antonio de Alarcón. (Hugo Wolf based his 1896 opera *Der Corregidor* on the same story.) The Martínez Sierras' two-scene pantomime followed Alarcón closely. Since Falla's compositional draft for the completed first scene is dated August 8, 1916, Diaghilev and Massine could have heard only a partial score for the first scene at the Martínez Sierras'. In any case, the tale interested both men, especially Massine, who hoped to produce his first Spanish ballet in December or January in Rome.[15]

By June 18, Diaghilev submitted a written offer to Falla to produce *El corregidor y la molinera* in ballet form and to do the same with his *Noches.*[16] Falla thought the terms of the offer unfair and made Diaghilev a counteroffer, which the impresario met only halfway.[17] He gave Falla permission to produce *El corregidor* in Spain in the Martínez Sierras' pantomime form.[18] As for the *Noches,* Falla was unable to best Diaghilev, who insisted that he alone would produce it.

In Madrid Diaghilev and Massine delighted in seeing for the first time the works of the great Spanish painters, as well as the impressive collection of Titians in the Prado and the magnificent Goya tapestries at the Royal Palace. In a postcard to Anatoli Petrovich, Massine wrote, "We are all crazy about what we see in the Prado. . . . There is nothing in common with Italy; everything seems new and different to me."[19] Spanish painting would have a lasting influence on Massine, and he now spent most of his free time at the Prado studying the works of Ribera, Murillo, Zurbarán, Goya, Velázquez, and El Greco. Though Goya would inspire the actual choreographic designs of Massine's future works, he was most impressed by Velázquez. This artist, in "the simplicity of his brushwork, the deftness with which he conveyed the forms, and the texture of the surfaces," possessed a style that Massine respected for leaving "much to the imagination, suggesting movement rather than laboring over a minute detail."[20]

On June 4 Massine presented a certificate from Dr. Juan Bergara to the Russian embassy in Madrid and was subsequently exempted from military service on the grounds of pulmonary weakness, which necessitated his remaining in a warm climate.[21]

After the season at the Real ended on June 9, Diaghilev invited Falla to join him and Massine in their travels during the remainder of the month to Seville, Granada, and Córdoba. As they toured these cities Diaghilev and Massine discovered that Falla, a native of Andalusia and a student of Spanish folklore, was a key figure in the revitalization of interest in *cante jondo*—the ancestral southern Iberian form of singing as an expression of pain or joy. With Falla's help they slowly came to appreciate its essence and its finest tradition in the south. The cultural treasures of the region were a revelation. In Seville, Massine was taken to see the most windowed cathedral in the world. He was impressed by its organ as well as by "the altar dances with castanets, and the orchestra in front of the altar." He was amazed, too, by the dancing "accompanied by singing, by little boys, who were also dancing. The singing is really shouting; the dance consists of various steps involving swaying from side to side, and many figures."[22] In Seville he also met the greatest flamenco *cantaora* (singer) of that time, *La Niña de los Peines*. Warm, leisurely evenings were spent at the Café Novedades. Here they met Felix Fernández García, a dancer who would play a major role in the creation of Massine's Spanish ballet.

> One evening, at our favorite café, the Novedades, we noticed a small, dark young dancer whose elegant movements and compelling intensity singled him out from the rest of the group. When he had finished dancing Diaghilev invited him to join us at our table. . . . As we talked to him I sensed that he was a nervous and highly strung creature with a very original talent. He soon made it clear to us that he was not happy in his present life, and although it amused him to dance in the café, he did not find it very rewarding. We made a habit of going every night to see him dance, and were more and more impressed by his exquisite flamenco style, the precision and rhythm of his movements, and by his perfect control.[23]

Massine and Diaghilev found Granada, framed by mountains and olive groves, spellbinding. To Anatoli Petrovich Massine wrote: "I saw a

*Massine with
Manuel de Falla in
Granada, 1916*

miracle, or was it a wonderful, uncommon dream? Such is my impression of what I saw in the Alhambra. There is not a thing equal to that; only St. Mark, however strange it may seem."[24] Here they attended two nocturnal Gypsy feasts, one of them in a garden beneath the Alhambra that looked out onto the adjoining quarter of Albaicin, the old Arabic town. Their host was the famous matador Juan Belmonte. Under a starlit summer sky they revisited the Alhambra.

The evening before they left Granada, they attended a performance by the Madrid orchestra of Falla's *Noches en los jardines de España* at the Palacio de Carlos V.[25] In Córdoba they visited the mosque and came to a fuller appreciation of Andalusia's rich cultural roots in Islam, Judaism, Christianity, and the folkways and beliefs of the Gypsies. It was during this expedition that the gestation of the ballet based on *El corregidor y la molinera* truly began. In a July 7 letter to Stravinsky, Falla reports that by the time he had returned to Madrid from his trip to the south he began revising parts of the score for *El corregidor* and developing the dances.[26]

After returning to Madrid, Diaghilev and Massine proceeded overland to San Sebastián, on the northwest coast. At this time San Sebastián was a fashionable summer resort, along with Santander, where the royal family and the court spent their holidays. Summer in San Sebastián was filled with festive diversions, including sports, the casino, and the theater season. In early July a racetrack was opened to the public for the first time, with the royal family presiding over the inauguration. Diaghilev and Massine's mission in San Sebastián was to arrange for two gala performances of the Ballets Russes at the end of August. Except for a short trip to Paris, they spent the summer between San Sebastián and a small fishing village some forty kilometers south of Barcelona called Sitges, where Misia and Sert were on holiday.

In the early 1890s Sitges was still a quiet fishing village, but by the end of the decade a number of Catalonian painters, most notably Santiago Rusiñol, had made it their home. Rusiñol was the spiritual leader of a group of bohemian artists that included Ramon Casas and Miguel Utrillo. These painters, who had lived in Paris during the 1880s, had enjoyed the admiration and friendship of such Parisian notables as Debussy, Proust, Léon Daudet, and Mallarmé.

At the time that Rusiñol moved to Sitges, it was a simple Mediterranean cove with modest old houses perched along the stone ramparts overlooking it. It was also the site of a church, a medieval hospital, and the chapel of San Juan Bautista. In this quiet, unadorned setting, Rusiñol acquired a pair of old houses next to the hospital and installed in them his vast collection of objets d'art, including two El Grecos, *San Pedro* and *Santa Magdalena*. By the turn of the century, however, Sitges found itself the center of the *modernismo* movement[27] and soon began attracting international personalities. One of these was the Chicago millionaire Charles Deering, who in 1910, with Utrillo's help, acquired the old hospital and several of the old houses around it. Utrillo designed Deering's Mediterranean residence, known as Maricel, by combining elements of the traditional Mediterranean Romanesque, Gothic, and Renaissance styles of architecture. This dwelling became the home of Deering's extensive collection of El Grecos, Zurbaráns, and Goyas as well as works by such contemporary artists as Rusiñol and Casas. Sitges shortly became a gathering place for European artists, many of whom, like Marie Laurencin, were waiting out the war in Spain. Deering invited Misia and

Sert to Maricel in the summer of 1916. So many like-minded people in such a congenial setting proved irresistible to Diaghilev and Massine, who were immediately taken with this charming little village. The intelligent company, plus surroundings that encompassed nature and art at their most magnificent, made Sitges a pleasurable stopover on many of their future visits to Spain.

For the San Sebastián gala Diaghilev planned to offer a ballet on a Spanish theme as a tribute to the Spanish monarchs and an expression of gratitude for their support, with a ballet on a Russian theme as a companion piece. Gontcharova and Larionov, who at Diaghilev's invitation had joined the group in Sitges, once again were delegated to work with Massine. But choosing a subject proved difficult. Diaghilev suggested that they adapt the score of Fauré's *Pavane*. Massine wanted to take Velázquez's *Las meninas,* a portrait of the royal family, as a point of reference and for inspiration.[28] The painting had moved him deeply, and the ballet would be Massine's homage to the Spanish painter.

Diaghilev approved, and the plans proceeded at a steady pace. Sert was to design the elaborate period costumes. Carlo Socrate, the Italian scene painter, was to create the decor, which eventually featured a garden overlooked by a balcony. The story concerns two ladies-in-waiting who secretly, or so they think, meet with two courtiers. The couples perform a pavane as a dwarf—introduced by a cello played pizzicato—makes her presence known and then rushes off, conveying in mime her intention to spread the scandal of illicit love. Massine set a series of pas de deux designed to evoke the ambience of the court of Philip IV. His idea was to communicate "a personal interpretation of the formality and underlying sadness that I had glimpsed in Velázquez . . . counter-balanced by the flowing movements which blended with melancholy strains of Fauré's evocative music."[29]

The ballet was rehearsed in San Sebastián. The dancers were Sokolova, Olga Khokhlova, Leon Woizikowski, Massine, and, as the dwarf, Elena Antonova. At first it had seemed to Diaghilev that a real dwarf was needed in the role. Sokolova describes how things went when a dwarf was brought to Diaghilev's hotel room for the requisite interview with the impresario: "The little man sat for a while, trying to understand what the talk—partly in Russian, partly in French, partly in Spanish—was all about. Then he got bored, slipped off the chair onto his tiny legs, grabbed a lot of cherries from a dish, filled his mouth with as many as it could hold, and began prancing up and down the room, shooting out the stones at everyone in sight. Diaghilev in hysteria kept asking Larionov to 'get rid of the little brute.' "[30] Much to the relief of Sert, who was to design the ballet—and, one suspects, to the relief of just about everyone else—the notion was dropped.

For the Russian novelty Diaghilev suggested one of the fairy-tale settings of Liadov. Massine happily agreed; while a young boy, he had been fascinated by the traditional folk stories he heard in Zvenigorod-Moskovsky. They decided to adapt Liadov's *Kikimora,* the story of a witch who forces her cat to rock her cradle and then, in a fit of rage, decapitates the poor feline. Larionov's decor was inspired by a peasant interior at Abramtsevo, depicting in cubist terms a bright yellow *isba* (a Russian log hut); Gontcharova's two costumes were neoprimitive in style.

San Sebastián that August belonged to the Ballets Russes. Diaghilev and Massine stayed at the Hotel Continental overlooking the Concha. Here they encountered Arthur Rubinstein, and the three men were soon lunching together daily.[31] Rubinstein became closely linked with the ballet company, attending its morning rehearsals and enjoying long afternoons with Gontcharova, Larionov, and Ansermet at the Café Terrace. At night the dancers escorted the young pianist to the empty hall of the casino, where he played for them, and where he became enamored of the beautiful Valentina Kachuba.

In San Sebastián Diaghilev and Massine encountered many familiar faces, among them that of Mme Khvoshchinsky, who planned to spend part of the summer in the old aristocratic enclave. But since she had arrived without her husband,[32] Diaghilev sensed trouble; he feared that her mere presence could awaken Massine's assiduously buried heterosexual leanings. He was right. The agent provocateur, as Diaghilev called her, precipitated the first major crisis between him and Massine.

Exactly how intimate matters became between Massine and Mme Khvoshchinsky is unclear. It's possible they simply promenaded together in plain view or shared amusing conversation over coffee at the hotel, nothing more. They may have gone so far as to flirt openly, perhaps even in Diaghilev's presence. Both Massine and the lady were certainly capable of feigning innocence as they secretly enjoyed skewering Diaghilev's massive ego. In their own eyes the couple may simply have been having a bit of fun, but they were hurting Diaghilev, a man accustomed to exerting monumental control with surgical precision, where he was most vulnerable.

In fact they were playing with fire. For what is known is that they pounded a raw nerve in the tempestuous impresario; he fumed over their flirtation, if that is what it was, for months afterward. Diaghilev had painful memories of women who had threatened his homosexual relationships. First, back in St. Petersburg, the poet Zinaida Hippius (a.k.a. Gippius), in a draining and devastatingly protracted struggle spanning years, had finally claimed for herself Dmitri Filosofov, Diaghilev's longtime lover.[33] The Nijinsky-Romola affair followed, and in that episode the price was not only Diaghilev's loss of his lover but his company's loss of its leading dancer and new, rising choreographer. Now these old wounds to Diaghilev's psyche ached anew. Mme Khvoshchinsky stirred deepseated fears and doubts. Diaghilev was again confronted with the fact that he had taken as a lover a man who was ambivalent about his true sexual orientation, and history suggested to him that he could lose this latest companion to the opposite sex as well.

The first San Sebastián gala took place on August 21; the program included *Les Sylphides, Sadko, Prince Igor,* and *Schéhérazade.* On August 25 *Las meninas* and *Kikimora* were premiered.[34] *Las meninas* was well received; the press was charmed by its "ceremonious and solemn" evocation of ancient Spain, and King Alfonso XIII, who had formally declared himself Diaghilev's protector, came to San Sebastián expressly to attend the performance.[35] Adolfo Salazar, the prominent music critic, wrote: "When we saw that tiny delicate work performed on stage we understood clearly what exquisite and refined art was contained in that production; what fine and subtle talent had been involved in its creation. . . . We are dealing above all with the sketch of an epoch and of a character as conceived by an artistic mind that creates according to sentiments it has been handed down, but that does not attempt to merely copy in a vulgar fashion."[36] When *Las meninas* was shown in Paris, Debussy wrote to Diaghilev, "It has been your pleasure, my dear Diaghilev, that the typical French charm of Fauré's *Pavane* should clad itself in Spanish seriousness. That was a tour de force for which you should be congratulated —you and your prodigious Massine as well."[37] According to Massine, Diaghilev loved *Las meninas* very much, preserving it in the repertory until his very last season in 1929.[38]

Since King Alfonso had become a benefactor of the Ballets Russes, the authorities of Bilbao scheduled series of galas for the end of August to coincide with the monarch's visit to their city to review the fleet. Following the Bilbao galas Diaghilev, Massine, and Ansermet made a short trip to Paris to engage Monteux and Anselm Goetz as conductors to tour with the company. From there they went to Bordeaux, whence on September 8 part of the company sailed for New York. Grigoriev and a nucleus of dancers would remain in Europe to work with Massine.

Diaghilev and Massine returned from Bordeaux to San Sebastián to attend the music festival at the Gran Casino. Misia joined them, probably owing to a request from Diaghilev, who in periods of emotional need or personal crisis counted on her as a confidante (the Mme Khvoshchinsky affair still rankled). The three became inseparable, and together they attended Rubinstein's performance of Rachmaninov's First Piano Concerto on September 20. Falla also came to San Sebastián to help draft the contract for *El corregidor y la molinera,* or *Le Tricorne,* as the ballet was now called, in French, after the title of Alarcón's novel. According to this September 15 draft,[39] Diaghilev would produce the ballet in 1917 in Rome. Falla was to deliver his piano score by November 15, 1916, and the orchestral score would follow on December 15. The draft of the contract does not mention *Noches,* so Falla apparently, with Ansermet's help, succeeded in extricating himself from his original agreement with Diaghilev concerning this work and its future.[40] On September 22 the music festival ended, and Diaghilev, Massine, Misia, and Sert left San Sebastián for Italy.

The Chinese Conjuror in Parade, *1917*

CHAPTER 5

Rome, September 1916–Paris, May 1917

MISIA, SERT, DIAGHILEV, AND MASSINE drove to Italy, making
leisurely stops at Verona, Bologna, Padua, and Venice. At the end of October, in Rome, Diaghilev and Massine rented a furnished apartment,
complete with piano, at the Corso Umberto, via del Parlamento 9. And
since they were soon joined in Rome by Gontcharova, Larionov, Ansermet, and the Cecchettis, this apartment would turn out to be their headquarters until the following May. While the others reviewed plans for
new productions, Maestro Cecchetti gave Massine a daily private class at
the little old Teatro Metastasio.

Stravinsky arrived in November to discuss the ballet *Le Chant du
rossignol,* a reworking of the opera he had begun in 1909, *Le Rossignol.* In
1913 the Free Theater of Moscow had sought to perform the opera, but

before the project materialized the company went bankrupt, in 1914. Diaghilev succeeded in producing the opera that same year. Then in September 1916 at Santander he commissioned Stravinsky to prepare a ballet version by combining the second and third acts of the opera.[1] He visited Stravinsky at Morges later that fall to monitor the work's progress; but now, when Diaghilev once again wanted to discuss *Le Rossignol* in ballet form, Stravinsky had another idea: to turn the second and third acts into a symphonic poem without voices. Diaghilev accepted the new proposition. Feeling confident that he would be able to produce the piece later in Rome, Diaghilev left the composer, who had already begun to revise the music and the scenario for what he now was calling *Le Chant du rossignol.*

Mikhail Semenov, a former music critic from St. Petersburg, joined the Diaghilev circle in Rome, a city he visited frequently from his home in Positano, about twenty miles south of Naples. He, Diaghilev, and Massine would meet at the Caffè Ariana (across the street from the Corso Umberto) for long afternoons of conversation about art and music. Massine in particular drew close to Semenov, a sort of father figure who would eventually provide Massine staunch support during and after his breakup with Diaghilev.

As they had been in other cities, Diaghilev and Massine were soon at the center of Rome's artistic life. Despite the war, the Italian capital provided some of the social and cultural excitement then missing from a beleaguered Paris. They rekindled their association with those futurist painters who were not at the front, particularly Balla and his young follower Fortunato Depero. The futurists stimulated the Russians. In the two years since his first exposure to futurism, Diaghilev had gained a more perceptive understanding of its aesthetic principles, and this visit would mark the first actual collaborations between the Ballets Russes and the futurist artists. (In 1917 Diaghilev would tell Nijinsky: "Futurism [and] Cubism are the last word. . . . I do not wish to lose my place as an artistic guide.")[2]

Massine too felt the pulse of futurism. He later acknowledged that by the time of this stay in Rome futurist painters "had already begun to influence my choreography."[3] Undoubtedly he was beguiled by Marinetti's notion of "total art" (as articulated by Apollinaire), whose aim was to produce a theatrical spectacle with painting, music, and movement equally represented. Marinetti's concept, apart from its emphasis on music hall (variety theater) elements and its affinity for audience participation, coincided in its theory as a theater of synthesis with both the ideal of total theater for which Diaghilev had long prodded Massine to strive and the innovations of the Moscow theater. Futurist theatrical experimentation would infuse *Parade,* the ballet Massine would create in Rome in 1917 with the collaboration of Cocteau, Satie, and Picasso. For the remainder of his life Massine repeatedly singled out *Parade* as an example of a total work of art whose elements were equally represented.[4]

The sojourn in Rome was meant to provide the company with a working period to develop new works, and, above all, to give Massine a chance to sharpen his choreographic skills. During his stay at Bellerive he had worked on *Liturgie* and created *Le Soleil de nuit,* and later, in Spain, he had come up with *Las meninas* and *Kikimora.* With this apprenticeship behind him, at age twenty he was refining the stylistic preferences that would propel his work for the next fifteen years.

Unfortunately, plans for *Le Tricorne* and Stravinsky's *Le Chant du rossignol* had to be postponed because the scores were not ready. Diaghilev began to look for new ideas. Ensconced in Italy, he sensed that an Italian subject would be fitting, as *Las meninas* had been for Spain. Aside from Russia, Italy was the country he loved most, and an homage to her seemed felicitous. He suggested that Massine read Goldoni's comedy *Le donne di buon umore.* Massine quickly seized on Goldoni's musicality and his technique in the manner of commedia dell'arte, a style that blended mime, dance, and acrobatics. This appealed to Massine's own sense of theater and dovetailed with a curiosity about commedia dell'arte that had been apparent on the Russian stage since the turn of the century.

Diaghilev and Massine began to search the libraries of Rome for old Italian music. The composer they lit upon was Domenico Scarlatti (1685–1757), a contemporary of Goldoni. They hired a musician to play some of Scarlatti's more than five hundred harpsichord sonatas on the piano at the Corso Umberto. Of the twenty pieces chosen for the ballet, only two were familiar to concertgoers: a capriccio and a pastorale, both usually performed on the piano in Karl Tausig's arrangements. Vincenzo Tommasini (a young composer whose opera *Uguale fortuna* had won first prize in a 1913 competition organized by the city of Rome) was commissioned to work with Massine on the score and to orchestrate the sonatas. Rehearsals began at the Cantina Taglioni, the dance studio in Piazza Venezia where the company worked throughout its six-and-a-half-month stay in Rome.

Extensive rehearsal time was dedicated to *Les Femmes de bonne humeur,* as the new work came to be known, and the ballet was conceived and created in unhurried fashion. Yet Massine's near-obsessive absorption in his work turned the composition of *Les Femmes* into an intense intellectual and creative exercise. To evoke the style and manner of the period, he began a conscientious study of the seventeenth- and eighteenth-century choreographic treatises Diaghilev recently had acquired for him at auction in Paris. These included first editions of works by Carlo Blasis, Raoul Feuillet and Louis Pecour, Malpied, and Jean-Philippe Rameau.[5] At Diaghilev's suggestion, Massine spent much of his free time studying the paintings of Guardi, Watteau, and Longhi in galleries and art books. He later wrote:

> From Watteau's "Fêtes Galantes" I took the languorous gestures of the women, their delicate hand movements, and the ineffable sadness of their backward glances. Pietro Longhi, with his sharp sense of domestic detail, was an invaluable help when I came to do the choreography for the main scene, the supper-party given by the maid Mariuccia to her admirers, Leonardo, Battista, and the Marchese de Luca, during the absence of her mistress, La Marchesa Silvestra. In this I emphasized the elaborate setting of the table, the placing of knives, forks and plates, the carving of the chicken and the pouring out of the wine.[6]

In transforming the three-act Goldoni play into a one-act ballet, however, Massine was hampered by the stylistic devices and technical trappings of commedia dell'arte, with its masks, disguises, and heightened gestures. To make the complex manageable, he "balanced the action simultaneously on both sides of the stage."[7] In later years he concluded that his solution "worked well in the supper-party scene, but was more difficult in the slower liquid passages."[8]

Massine's steady emergence from apprenticeship to a surer command of his art underlies these passages in his memoirs, which show that he already possessed a keener sense of his identity as an artist than the novice Diaghilev had taken up such a short time before.

Les Femmes was the first Massine ballet notable for both individual and collective characterization, and the first to demonstrate his ability to compose phrases out of idiosyncratic gestures and to intertwine intricate yet cohesive ensembles in which the characters retain their personalities. The contrasts Massine contrived for them served to reinforce their individuality, a result most pronounced in the role of Niccolò, the waiter. Massine confesses that in "pondering over the problem of contrasting him stylistically with the other, more graceful characters, I remembered

Les Femmes de bonne humeur,
Rome, 1917

the puppets I had seen in Viareggio, and decided to give him their floppy, loose-jointed movements."[9]

To intensify this diversity Massine used musical counterpoint to juxtapose the movements of two characters within the same phrase. Moreover, he fixed counterpoint for each dancer by contrasting the torso and the leg movements, devising "broken, angular movements for the upper part of the body while the lower limbs continued to move in the usual harmonic academic style."[10] Sokolova described it as the "jerky, flickering movements of marionettes."[11] Lopokova, who created the role of Mariuccia, believed that "the movements of the dancers' bodies were something quite new in this ballet, different both from classical and from character dancing. . . . The movements were so new that at the rehearsals our bodies began to ache as never before. The knee was always bent and the arms akimbo—the limbs never in a straight line."[12]

This new approach to choreographic movement brought to ballet the aesthetics of angularity as a predominating trend. Lynn Garafola writes:

> *Angularity was perhaps the most dramatic sign of the modernist revolution in ballet. Thanks to Massine, wrote French critic Fernand Divoire in the 1930s, "the invention of the later Ballets Russes in the area of dance was the angular angle, the angle more or less deforming, more or less comic and caricaturing." Under the tutelage of Larionov, Gontcharova, and the futurists, Massine hardened ballet's soft and "beautiful" line. He staunched the flow and cramped the openness of classical movement and substituted contorted gestures for the rounded arms of the traditional port de bras. "All that is plastic, graceful, free from angularity is excluded," wrote Valerian Svetlov. . . . "The times of the 'choreographic tenor,' M. Fokine, in the smart phrase of Massine, are gone for ever. All the movements of the dancers are short, angular, mechanical."[13]*

Characterization in *Les Femmes* was not psychological; it reflected the conventions of commedia dell'arte, in which each character was representative of a type or a personality trait.

Mime—expressive gesture—and dance movement flowed into one another just as, in eighteenth-century opera, recitatives tell the story and the arias that follow let the emotions soar. In most narrative ballets the mime passages remain strictly pantomime (like the *recitativo secco* in opera), but in *Les Femmes* they resembled a *cantinella*, a recitative set to melody (*recitativo stromentato* or *accompagnato*) that was harmoniously blended into the whole work, enhancing its rhythmic cohesion.

Another source of inspiration for Massine was film, with its speeded-up, broken movement and the rapid montage technique for simultaneous action. Nineteen sixteen was also a productive year for futurist cinema, and surely Massine, through his association with this movement, was aware of its developments. The film *Vita futurista*, produced with the participation of Balla, Marinetti, and other futurists, included a dance sequence with transparent figures, achieved by the use of double exposures. (Balla, a close friend of Diaghilev's and Massine's, was one of the signers of the "Manifesto of Futurist Cinema" published in the November 1916 issue of *Italia Futurista*.) And in the same year we find the photographer Bragaglia, who had done experimental work with photodynamism, launching his own company, La Novissima, which produced three full-length films—*Thais, Il perfido incanto,* and *Il mio cadavere*—as well as the comic short film *Dramma in Olimpo*.[14] The futurists' interest in the speed and simultaneity of cinema also touched the theater. In his *Notes on the Theater*, published in the Italian press in installments during 1915–17, Fortunato Depero proposed that "it is necessary to add to the theater everything that is suggested by cinematography."

Another source of Massine's interest in film may have been Gontcharova and Larionov, who had worked with Vladimir Mayakovsky and the Burliuk brothers on the experimental film *Drama at Cabaret 13* before they left Russia.[15] (Gontcharova and Larionov remained committed to Massine throughout his early artistic and intellectual development, not only as mentors but as close friends; Gontcharova served as his confidante, and both were parental figures to him.) Yet another influence came from Massine's fascination with Charlie Chaplin.[16]

Les Femmes was in rehearsal throughout the month of November 1916, and on December 17 Diaghilev wrote to Mme Stravinsky: "Tell Igor that Massine has finished Scarlatti. As an involved colleague it is hard for me to judge, but I think it is a small masterpiece—all merriment and loveliness from beginning to end."[17]

Les Femmes was made on the dancers who had remained in Europe, except for Lopokova, who took over the role of Mariuccia when she returned from the United States tour. The cast Massine chose proved ideal; an indisputable triumph emerged from his meticulous coaching and the dancers' responsiveness to his contrapuntal and angular style.

Diaghilev asked Bakst, who had a great flair for the eighteenth century, to design the production, and in December Bakst left Paris to join his collaborators in Rome. He created a Venetian piazza with buildings that curved inward, as if seen through a concave mirror, giving the work a modernistic semblance. But after the ballet had been performed in Rome and Paris, Diaghilev rejected the concept in favor of the more traditional style of the eighteenth-century Venetian painter Francesco Guardi. Bakst modified his decor,[18] but his costumes were left intact: elaborate gowns richly embroidered in gold and lace for the women, velvet jackets and knee-length breeches for the men, and period wigs for all.

WITH *LES FEMMES DE BONNE HUMEUR* completed, Massine was exhilarated. But as Christmas drew nearer he was stricken with nostalgia for Moscow, which he expressed in letters full of longing to Anatoli Petrovich.

Not everything in Rome had gone as harmoniously as *Les Femmes*. The mere presence in the city of Vasily Khvoshchinsky, in his post at the Russian embassy, revived the fear and jealousy that had racked Diaghilev in San Sebastián, even though Mme Khvoshchinsky was not in Rome. (From San Sebastián she had gone directly to a nearby sanatorium, where she remained throughout most of this period.) Relations between Diaghilev and Khvoshchinsky snapped at a concert on November 19. Arturo Toscanini, conducting Siegfried's Funeral March, was prevented from finishing the piece by shouts from the balcony protesting a performance of Wagner when Italy was at war with Germany. In the theater foyer afterwards, Khvoshchinsky defended the performance and Diaghilev vehemently sided with the protesters, setting off a scandalous row that, according to Diaghilev, ended only "when we called in our seconds, and the affair was settled peacefully, but with great difficulty."[19]

Irrational and out of proportion by itself, the Wagner incident was obviously an excuse for Diaghilev to avenge himself upon Mme Khvoshchinsky, and an outlet for his pent-up anxiety and rage. And, as he would later write to Stravinsky, it afforded him the opportunity he needed to break off his relations, manageably pleasant until then, with the couple.[20] But this was an episode from which Diaghilev would not easily recover, and despite all the exciting work being done in Rome during this period, he confessed to Stravinsky in a letter dated December 3 just how deeply affected by the affair he was. "But my spirit has been depressed. That awful business with Khvoshchinsky is over, but it will be better to talk about it in person." Diaghilev's desperate need for a confidant is made clear in the same letter, in which he declares to Stravinsky, "I will come to Paris when you are there. I am writing all of this to you because of our friendship."[21]

Of course all this turbulence began to erode the bond between Diaghilev and Massine. Diaghilev's uncontrolled fits of temper made life at the Corso Umberto trying. In his fury he was apt to smash the furniture; he once "tore the telephone from the wall and shattered it on the ground."[22] Massine's reaction to such raving was to immerse himself in work. Not only were his spirit and intellect being sorely tested, but his appreciation of Diaghilev as a great man—brilliant, often magnanimous, capable of radical devotion and self-sacrifice in the pursuit of artistic ideals—had to be set against the demanding, sometimes merciless, mistrustful, possessive, and self-centered tyrant he now faced. Nevertheless, since Massine's personal credo dictated the sacrifice of himself to art as to a religion,* any distress his personal situation may have caused him was justified in his mind by the work that grew out of their affiliation. In the creative process he could insist upon an alternative reality, sublimating his private needs to his work and its realization. The dark side of this bargain was that as the years went on art increasingly became for Massine a substitute for and a refuge from real intimacy.

After *Les Femmes*, Massine began a Spanish ballet set to Albéniz's "Triana," from *Iberia*, with decor and costumes by Gontcharova; but this work never advanced beyond the rehearsal stage. Nevertheless, the fascination Spain held for Diaghilev and Massine inspired them to plan more works on Spanish themes. For instance, in notes and sketches surviving from this period, they set out their ideas for *España*, set to Ravel's *Rhapsodie espagnole*, with designs by Gontcharova. (At a certain point this work was probably titled *Rhapsodie espagnole*.) Diaghilev also wanted to produce two additional ballets to accompany the projected *Le Tricorne* on a "Spanish" program, first in Rome, later in Paris. Unfortunately, when Falla was unable to complete his score on time, the other two projects were scrapped.

Diaghilev had hoped that after *Triana* Massine could begin rehearsals for *Le Chant du rossignol*. By November 1916, Fortunato Depero had been contracted to design the new work, for which he envisioned a "fantastic garden scene of huge plastic flowers," and for the costumes,

---

* The sanctity of art was a prevailing belief among the Russian artists of the Silver Age, the Russian cultural renaissance of the turn of the century. As an article of faith it was discussed at length by, for example, Stanislavsky.

"geometrical Chinese masks, cylindrical sleeves, and heads in compart-
ments."[23] Diaghilev found Depero "brilliant," his work on the ballet
"marvelous," and his decorations "splendid." Massine, he reported, "was
dreaming about presenting the work"[24]—his first collaboration with the
composer of *Sacre*. But Stravinsky did not finish the score in time for
Diaghilev to produce the ballet in Rome. It was not staged until 1920,
with scenery and costumes by Henri Matisse.

With both their ambitious projects, *Le Chant du rossignol* and *Le Tricorne* (the latter's score was not completed until 1919), in limbo, Diaghilev
suggested that Massine and Larionov devote some time to the one-act
Kikimora as the starting point of a full-length ballet incorporating other
Russian legends, again to music by Liadov.[25] The ballet eventually consisted of three episodes: the story of Kikimora and the cat; the story of
the swan princess under a spell cast by a three-headed dragon, who is finally set free by a knight; and the story of the ogress Baba Yaga, whose
plot to capture and devour a young girl lost in the forest is thwarted
when the girl saves herself by making the sign of the cross.

Contes russes, as the ballet was titled, grew out of another close creative partnership between Massine and Larionov, just as *Le Soleil de nuit*
had done. Massine later said of Larionov's contribution that his "costumes and decor for the whole ballet were among his most delightful
creations, the elements of Russian folk art being even more cleverly
adapted than in *Le Soleil du nuit*."[26] But the knight's horse in the second
episode, entrusted to Depero, elicited one of Diaghilev's hysterical reactions. Massine describes how he and Diaghilev

> *were summoned to [Depero's] studio on the outskirts of Rome. As we
> walked into the room the artist pointed proudly to his construction—a bul-
> bous outsized elephant! We stood staring at it silently for a few moments
> until Diaghilev, in a sudden outburst of rage, smashed the papier-mâché
> animal with his walking stick. I tried to pacify the shocked and bewildered
> Depero by explaining to him that although his construction no doubt had
> great charm, it was not quite the horse we had envisaged. But poor Depero
> was still puzzled, and explained that he had done his best. This was ex-
> actly how he had imagined the animal. The problem was not finally solved
> until Larionov designed a primitive but graceful animal cut out of thin
> wood and painted white.*[27]

On February 18, 1917, Cocteau and Picasso arrived in Rome to begin
their collaboration with the Russians on a new ballet called *Parade*.

Cocteau had first met Diaghilev at Misia Edwards's Quai Voltaire apartment several days after the sensational opening of the Ballets Russes at the Châtelet on May 9, 1909. It had been through the good offices of Misia and Bakst that Cocteau was able to penetrate the inner circle of the Ballets Russes, and it was following Bakst's suggestion that Diaghilev's impresario in France, Gabriel Astruc, commissioned Cocteau to design the publicity posters for the 1911 ballet season, one of which was the famous rose and mauve poster of Nijinsky in *Le Spectre de la rose*. Cocteau had been engaged by Diaghilev for the first time in 1912, when for the ballet *Le Dieu bleu* he provided the libretto, Reynaldo Hahn the score, Bakst the scenery and costumes, and Fokine the choreography.

But even then Diaghilev had been eager to strike out in new artistic directions, such as Nijinsky's angular, innovative choreography for *L'Après-midi d'un faune* (1912). The formulaic *Le Dieu bleu* did not interest him. He disliked Hahn's score which Prince Peter Lieven, a member of Diaghilev's Parisian entourage, once characterized as "India seen through the eyes of Massenet, sweet and insipid."[28] Diaghilev's decision to employ Cocteau, a poet he did not admire, as librettist on *Le Dieu bleu* in fact had been a scheme to snag Hahn, since, according to Stravinsky, "Diaghilev needed Hahn. . . . He was the salon idol of Paris, and salon support was very useful to Diaghilev at that time."[29] Unfortunately, *Le Dieu bleu* had not been a success, and in a moment of exasperation after its premiere Diaghilev hurled at Cocteau the famous challenge: "Astound me! . . . I will wait for you to astound me . . . !"[30]

These words would come to be the driving force behind *Parade*.

In 1913 the Ballets Russes had premiered Nijinsky's *Le Sacre du printemps*, a succès de scandale. The following year Cocteau, in his indefatigable ambition to be associated with all important artistic events, tried to persuade Stravinsky to collaborate with him on a new ballet libretto he had written called *David*. The project went unrealized; but Cocteau, refusing to abandon it wholly, in 1916 asked Erik Satie to collaborate on a work Cocteau now called *Parade*, an adaptation of his original *David* libretto. Satie, who had gained notoriety in the 1880s and 1890s with his *Gymnopédies* and *Gnossiennes* for piano, was living an obscure and rather bohemian life in Arcueil-Cachan. He accepted Cocteau's offer. Cocteau then asked Picasso, to whom he had been introduced in 1915 by Edgar Varèse, to join the project as designer, and to the utter astonishment of Montparnasse, Picasso accepted the offer from the dubious poet of the Right Bank. Of course, once Satie and Picasso agreed to collaborate,

Cocteau easily secured a commitment from Diaghilev, who admired the composer and the painter immensely.

When Picasso joined Cocteau and Satie in August to begin work on *Parade,* his overbearing personality caused trouble. Two letters to Valentine Gross, who had introduced Cocteau to Satie, tell the tale. In one, dated September 4, 1916, Cocteau implores Gross to

> make Satie understand, if you can cut through the aperitif fog, that I really do count for something in Parade, and that he and Picasso are not the only ones involved. I consider Parade a kind of renovation of the the-ater, and not a simple pretext for music. It hurts me when he dances around Picasso screaming, "It's you I'm following! You are my master!" and seems to be hearing for the first time, from Picasso's mouth, things that I have told him time and time again. Does he hear anything I say? Per-haps it's all an acoustical phenomenon.[31]

The other key letter in the episode, Satie's to Gross, dated Septem-ber 14, is a confession to her of his dilemma:

> Chère et douce amie—if you knew how sad I am! Parade is changing for the better, behind Cocteau's back! Picasso has ideas that I like better than our Jean's! How awful! And I am all for Picasso! Picasso tells me to go ahead, following Jean's text, and he, Picasso, will work on another text, his own—which is dazzling! Prodigious! I'm half crazy, depressed! What am I to do? Now that I know Picasso's wonderful ideas, I am heartbroken to have to set to music the less wonderful ideas of our good Jean—oh! yes! less wonderful. What am I to do? What am I to do? Write and advise me. I am beside myself. . . .[32]

In Cocteau's original libretto for *Parade* three circus performers—a Chinese Conjuror, a Young American Girl, and an Acrobat—emerge from the circus tent to entice passersby in to see the show. Cocteau wanted each character introduced through a megaphone with a sung an-nouncement, in the style of a Greek chorus. "After each music-hall num-ber," he proposed, "an anonymous voice issuing from an amplifying orifice (a theatrical imitation of a circus megaphone, the mask of antiq-uity in modern guise) was to sing a type phrase outlining the performer's activity so as to open up the world of make-believe."[33] Satie and Picasso opposed this idea. According to Picasso scholar Douglas Cooper, the painter shared Satie's belief that the voices would interfere not only with the music but with the choreography and decor as well. Instead, Picasso proposed adding three new characters—who became the French, American, and Negro managers—to introduce the performers. He argued that these additions would exploit "the contrast between three characters [the conjuror, the girl, and the acrobat, played by dancers] . . . and the more solemnly transposed inhuman, or superhuman, characters [the three managers, three-dimensional constructions with dancers inside] who would become in fact the false reality on stage, to the point of reducing the real dancers [the conjuror, the girl, and the acrobat] to the stature of puppets."[34] Disagreement on this point, however, quickly led to arguments, hysterical invective, and threats from Cocteau and Satie to quit the project. But on the eve of their trip to Rome Cocteau finally acceded to Picasso's ideas.

Meanwhile, in Rome, Massine was choreographing Satie's *Gymnopédies* for the Marchesa Casati, one of the very few women admired by the futurists. This gave him an opportunity to experiment with Satie's music and to expose himself further to the composer's style before staging *Parade*. Even though Massine's musical taste, formed at the Bolshoi, was quite traditional, he deeply enjoyed Satie's music, finding it amusing and charmingly original.[35]

Once in Rome, Cocteau and Picasso easily blended into the working dynamic that characterized Diaghilev's ballet productions. They stayed at the Hotel de Russie on the Via Babuino, facing the Piazza del Popolo with its large back garden and its winding paths leading to the slopes of the Pincio. From here Picasso could walk the short distance to his rented studio on Via Margutta, where he continued to work on *Parade*. Activity on the ballet centered around Picasso's studio and the Cantina Taglioni, where the company rehearsed. Despite their hectic schedule, Diaghilev and Massine were delighted to show their beloved Rome to the newcomers; the nights in particular proved ideal for relaxing in the balmy Roman weather. Cocteau, as the group strolled about in the city "made of fountains, shadows and moonlight," was inspired to write his poem "Rome, la nuit."

Meeting Picasso was a momentous occasion for the twenty-one-year-old Massine. Their friendly collaboration would produce four ballets over the next seven years and was critical in refining Massine's aesthetic ideas and orienting his taste. "It seemed to me," he wrote, "that whatever [Picasso] looked at—whether it was a flower, a statue or an architectural composition—went through a process of abstraction in his mind, and emerged as a cubist creation. He was at that time trying to transpose and simplify nature in much the same way primitive African sculptors did in carving their powerful wooden figures and masks. By dissolving surface barriers and clearing away sentimental layers of association, he widened his vision to encompass previously unknown perspectives."[36] Picasso's working methods in fact figured in the evolution of Massine's own approach. Massine was enthralled by the way the painter "would design several dozen of sketches, starting from very realistic ones, before attempting to arrive at a final thought. Then, little by little, this realism would subside like something unnecessary."[37] Massine saw at work beneath Picasso's method the painter's guiding creative principle, a process of trial and error that eventually led to a crystalline idea. "This is something that remained in me," Massine later said, recalling Picasso's admonition "not to take for granted your first step as a final result, but as a point of departure to clear up your thoughts in order to eliminate those elements that could be detrimental to the final conception. An artist arrives at a final result, not as something occasional—because he likes it—but following a principle and a process of thought."[38]

In Rome, Picasso and Cocteau associated not only with other Ballets Russes collaborators, such as Gontcharova and Larionov, but also with the futurists, especially Balla and Depero. Despite their differences, these artists developed a rapport that was founded on mutual respect as much as on the experimental climate of the times.

As *Parade* rehearsals proceeded, Cocteau once again tried to persuade Massine to use voices in the ballet, but Diaghilev and Massine continued to side with Picasso and reject the concept. Massine undoubtedly realized the choreographic potential of the managers, and he saw, too, that the voices would constrain choreography that, if expressive enough, should be able to stand alone. Fortunately, when Cocteau saw Picasso's sketches for the managers, he was won over by the painter's brilliant conception.[39]

During rehearsals some changes were made, the most significant of which was Massine's addition of a female acrobat as part of a parody pas de deux. In adding this character Massine showed a new assertiveness that suggests a view of himself as the creative equal of his collaborators. He also suggested that the Negro Manager, who was to appear on a horse, be omitted altogether, because the "human" figure kept falling off its steed. Picasso discarded the structure of the Negro Manager, but the horse (with two dancers inside) remained.

Another important change resulted from a suggestion by Cocteau. According to a letter from the poet to Misia, Massine was originally slated to dance the male Acrobat, but in rehearsals he imparted such power to the Chinese Conjuror that Cocteau asked him to undertake the latter role in performance.[40]

How rewarding it must have been for Massine that his collaborators made him feel from the very beginning that he was their equal! Indeed, Cocteau sent the young choreographer a letter assuring him of their confidence in him and his work (not a bad tactic, either, for winning Diaghilev's favor):

> My dear Massine:
> Collaborations are full of surprises.
> My theme has surprised Satie and Picasso; their treatment of it in turn has surprised me.
> There remains a blank
> On purpose
> It is yours; it is up to you to fill it, to "surprise" us, so that only the public remains to be surprised. Do not take that blank to stand for something vague, but instead accept it as a manifestation of the excellent construction of Parade, and how much we trust you.[41]

In the midst of their exhilarating and rewarding work, Diaghilev, Massine, Cocteau, and Picasso took time out at the beginning of March to visit Naples.[42] In an exploratory mood the friends visited historical sites (but did not cease thrashing out their vision of Parade). From Naples they made trips to Positano, Pompeii, and Herculaneum. Massine remembered how "Picasso was thrilled by the majestic ruins, and climbed endlessly over broken columns to stand staring at the fragments of Roman statuary."[43] Cocteau captured the occasion with his Kodak. The excursion gave the quartet the opportunity to enjoy both classical art and Neapolitan culture, including good food and fine wine. A special joy accompanied their examination of archaeological sites, historical buildings, and works of art. The introverted Massine, always given to solitude, spent time alone, during the stillness of siesta, "walking through the narrow streets behind the Piazza Garibaldi."[44] An intent observer, he was aware of and admired "the zest and ingenuity of the citizens who, whether they were craftsmen at their work or street sellers displaying their fish and fruit, performed their tasks with such high-spirited style, humor and bravura."[45] Massine was discovering the "richness and diversity of life" in a region to which his future life would be intimately linked.

Picasso, Diaghilev,
Cocteau, and
Massine in Pompeii
and Positano, 1917.
The photos were
taken with
Cocteau's Kodak.

In Rome again, the group resumed work on *Parade* armed with fresh ideas. Diaghilev again presided at long luncheons, usually at the Grand Hotel, where Cocteau's scalding wit amused his friends and sometimes irritated the impresario. On other occasions they would gather in Diaghilev and Massine's domed Corso Umberto salon, where, undoubtedly, one of the topics of discussion was the political upheaval in Russia —for by March 15, the tsar had abdicated the throne and a revolutionary government had been formed by Oleg Kerensky.

The American Ballets Russes contingent was back in Rome by early April,[46] and before the month was out Diaghilev scheduled a short engagement for the company at the Teatro Costanzi. On one of its nights a charity gala was attended by Marchesa Casati and Colette. A second gala, on April 12, saw the premiere of *Les Femmes de bonne humeur*. Eleonora Duse watched the performance from the wings, then came onstage to congratulate the cast. The work scored a great success with the Romans. With *Les Femmes*, Massine had created the first modern comedy-of-manners ballet.

The second part of the evening was a program of Stravinsky's music, conducted by the composer including the fourth tableau of *Petrouchka*, along with the berceuse and final apotheosis of *The Firebird*, which Stravinsky had recently adapted for concert performance. The musical highlight was the 1908 *Fireworks*, which Diaghilev presented as a "ballet without dancers." For this occasion Balla had designed a complex wooden structure covered by paint and canvas, topped by smaller structures covered with a translucent fabric and lit from inside. Against a black background were projected forty-nine combinations of lights (some were repeated), in which scarlet and green predominated. Shadow projectors were also used. The program notes described this experiment as "a purely musical organism that visually evolves at the same pace as fireworks."[47] Balla took a curtain call dressed in a futurist suit and purple straw hat, carrying a square-cut walking stick.

At the time Massine joined the Ballets Russes, Diaghilev had begun to acquire contemporary art works as gifts for him. Shortly, Massine began to buy for himself. Now an impressive selection from his collection was exhibited in the foyer of the theater, including two Baksts, one Braque, six Carràs, one de Chirico, five Deperos, one Derain, two Gleizeses, three Gontcharovas, three Grises, one Larionov, three Legers, three Lhôtes, six Picassos, four Riveras, one Severini, four Survages, and two Zarregas. Taken together, the exhibition and Balla's *Fireworks* made it an evening reminiscent of a *serata futurista*.

When the Costanzi engagement ended, Cocteau returned to Paris. The finale of *Parade* was still being hammered out, and in letters to Massine the poet proposed an ending (which, with some slight modifications by Massine, was close to the actual ending):

> *Here's a good ending which came to me in my sleep. It fits Serge and places emphasis on* Parade: *As the managers collapse in the finale, the acrobats, the young American girl, and the Chinese man could show up timorously, so that they are present and watch terrifiedly as the managers fall, and then they can begin to point with all their strength to the "ingresso," while understanding that the managers have given up on it. That would be a fair way to bring those characters back upon the stage and to help clarify that they are the parade and not the internal spectacle.*[48]

Following their triumph in Rome, the company moved to the Teatro San Carlo in Naples for five performances. This time Stravinsky journeyed south with his friends. En route on the train the others bet Picasso that he could not draw Massine in less than five minutes; he won by doing a pencil portrait of the choreographer in the swiftest academic manner. In Naples they visited the aquarium, which according to Stravinsky was easily the city's greatest attraction for Picasso and himself, a place where they all spent many happy hours together.

After the final performance at the San Carlo, Massine accepted Semenov's invitation to spend several days with him and his wife at their retreat in Positano. The invitation offered him a rare stretch of time away from Diaghilev, who hardly ever let him out of his sight. In Positano Massine was delighted by the "cluster of whitewashed cottages, which looked as if they had been piled up one above the other in a vast cleft in the mountains."[49] In the Semenovs' lovely home, a converted mill discreetly set at the edge of the village, Massine found deep enjoyment in their company.

It was during this visit that he first glimpsed the Isole dei Galli, a group of islands reputed to be part of the legendary sirens' islands braved by Ulysses. The words that follow, written more than half a century later, underscore Massine's yearning for independence at the time:

> *On my first night there I happened to look out my window, and noticed a desolate rocky island several miles off the coast. When I asked Mikhail Nikolaevich about it next morning, he told me that it was the largest of the three islands of Galli, the two smaller ones being hidden from view.*

*The Semenovs'
house in Positano*

*They belong to a local family called Parlato, who used them only for quail
hunting in the spring. During the day we took a boat to the island I had
seen, and discovered that it was composed of rough grey rock with no veg-
etation except for a few sun-scorched bushes. I was overcome by the beauty
of the view across the sea, with the Gulf of Salerno spreading out in the
distance. With Paestum to the south and the three Faralioni of Capri at
the northern tip of the Gulf, it had all the drama and mystery of a painting by Salvator Rosa. The silence was broken only by the murmur of these
and the occasional cry of a gull. I knew that here I would find the solitude
I had been seeking, a refuge from the exhausting pressure of my chosen career. I decided then and there that I would one day buy the island and
make it my home.[50]*

En route from Rome to Paris, the Ballets Russes gave one performance in Florence.

By the end of April 1917 *Parade* was nearing its definitive form. Following Diaghilev's suggestion, Picasso designed a front curtain that was to appear (after the theater's own velvet curtain had been parted) to the accompaniment of Satie's "Prelude to the Red Curtain." The curtain, which drew its inspiration from circus posters, depicted a theater stage framed by red drapes. Seven circus characters sat at a table: two harlequins (one in blue, the other in red), a black man wearing a turban, a toreador with a guitar, a sailor, and two young girls. To the left was a foal beside a winged white mare, and at the top was a ballerina, with small wings, stretching her arms toward a tiny monkey atop a ladder. A dog slept on the floor next to an acrobat's ball and drum. In the background were a garden, an arch in ruins, and, in the distance, Mount Vesuvius. The predominant colors were the greens and reds Picasso had favored in his *saltimbanques*.

The eight characters turned out to be Picasso's friends and collaborators, disguised by him as a private joke.[51] The blue harlequin was Cocteau; the red one, Massine (in a 1917 drawing of Massine by Picasso the dancer appears in the same outfit); the turbaned black was Stravinsky. The toreador was Picasso; the sailor, Diaghilev. The romantic girl next to Cocteau was Maria Chabelska, the dancer who created the role of the American girl; the girl in the hat was Olga Khokhlova, Picasso's future wife; and the ballerina was Lydia Lopokova (who created the role of the female Acrobat). Of course the background, with its view of Vesuvius reminiscent of Naples, had a special meaning for this group.

After the Satie prelude, the front curtain rose to reveal a painted backdrop: a monochromatic urban scene made up of a street, buildings, and trees without perspective and conceived in cubist terms. In the center a crooked rectangular opening, with a balustrade on both sides and covered with a curtain, served as the gateway to the performance tent, through which the four entertainers entered and exited the stage.

The gigantic constructions for the French and American managers were eleven-foot-tall collages of arms, trees, boulevards, skyscrapers, an Uncle Sam hat, megaphones, and signs. Only the legs of the dancers under these structures were visible. The horse (which had been fashioned to carry the figure of the Negro Manager), with a face reminiscent of an African mask, actually had two dancers inside. The Chinese Conjuror wore an Oriental-style outfit in bright yellow, bright red, and black, with a three-cornered hat and a long braid (Massine made up his face with expressionistic features). The American Girl, a bow in her hair, wore a pleated skirt and middy jacket; the Acrobats wore blue and white unitards gaily decorated with spirals and stars.

Massine's choreography fleshed out Cocteau's indications of the personality of each character with a great economy of expressive movement. The Managers marched, turned about, and stomped pompously; the Chinese Conjuror breathed fire, ate an egg that would later be retrieved from his foot, and ran about the stage performing mechanical jumps; the American Girl danced jazzy, Chaplinesque steps. In a parody of the silent serial *The Perils of Pauline*, she swam across a river, drove a car, took pictures with a Kodak, and so on. The horse ingeniously stomped out, and the Acrobats jumped and pretended to walk a tightrope. As the curtain fell, the Managers, frustrated in their efforts to lure the passersby inside, fainted and fell to the floor, the Girl sobbed, and the Conjuror remained frozen in place.

In this unusual ballet, Massine went a step beyond naturalism. The influence of Picasso could be seen in *Parade*'s stylization and deformation of movement, an aesthetic tendency already present in the stylized angular baroquism of *Les Femmes de bonne humeur*. Now, through cubism, Massine undertook a more radical assault on the bodily image, an image that in his hands proved far from a faithful visual sign for actual human gestures.

Sections of the front curtain had been painted in Rome, where Depero helped to construct the large figures of the Managers.[52] When the company arrived in Paris on May 1, Picasso immediately began supervising the reproduction of his designs and also helped to finish painting the curtain. Meanwhile, rehearsals continued. Criticism and comments from the poet Apollinaire helped shape the final form of the ballet.[53] His commentary, published in the *Excelsior* on May 11, was reprinted in the performance program:

The Cubist painter Picasso and that most daring of choreographers, Léonide Massine, have staged Parade, *thus consummating for the first time this union of painting and dance—of plastic and mime—which heralds the advent of a more complete art.*

This new union—for up until now stage sets and costumes on the one hand and choreography on the other were only superficially linked—has given rise in Parade *to a kind of super-realism* [sur-réalisme]. *This I see is the starting point of a succession of manifestations of the "esprit nouveau": now that it has had an opportunity to reveal itself, it will not fail to seduce the elite, and it hopes to change arts and manners from top to bottom. . . .*

. . . Massine . . . has produced a complete novelty, one so marvelously seductive, of a truth so lyrical, so human, so joyous, that it might well be capable of illuminating (if this were worthwhile) the frightful black sun of Durer's Melancholia—*this thing that Jean Cocteau calls a "realistic ballet." Picasso's Cubist sets and costumes bear witness to the realism of his art.*

The sets and costumes of Parade *clearly disclose his concern to extract from an object all the aesthetic emotion it is capable of arousing. Frequent attempts have been made to reduce painting to its own rigorously pictorial elements. There is hardly anything but painting in most of the Dutch school, in Chardin and the Impressionists.*

Picasso goes a good deal further than any of them. Those who see him in Parade *will experience a surprise that will turn into admiration. His main purpose is to render reality. However, the motif is no longer reproduced, but merely represented; or, more accurately, it is suggested by a combination of analysis and synthesis bearing upon all its visible elements —and, if possible, something more, namely, an integral schematization that might be intended to reconcile contradictions, and sometimes deliberately renounces the rendering of the obvious outward appearance of the object. Massine has adapted himself with it, and art has been enriched by adorable inventions like the realistic steps of the horse in* Parade *whose forelegs are supplied by one dancer and the hind legs by another.*[54]

Paris awaited the forthcoming premiere with rapt anticipation. The Châtelet was sold out fifteen days in advance. The season opened on May 11 with a *répétition générale* at four in the afternoon. The evening's program included *Firebird*, the French premieres of *Les Femmes* and *Contes russes*, and the Polovtsian Dances from *Prince Igor*. André Levinson, the prestigious Franco-Russian ballet critic noted for his partiality to the classical tradition, congratulated Massine on his achievement in *Les Femmes de bonne humeur*: "The inspiration of this humorous ballet is so adroit, the execution so homogeneous and free from constraint, the whole so well composed that I freely surrendered myself to the sweetness of living that exquisite hour of forgetfulness."[55] He considered the ballet "a living and original work where the past only appears in the form of a distant suggestion, an echo softened by the passing of centuries."[56] (Levinson once had severely criticized Fokine for relying in his ballets on "ethnography and archaeology" when reconstructing the past.) Levinson admired Mas-

The Chinese Conjuror in
Parade, 1917

sine's choreography for combining "a sense of delicacy with a feeling of fitness in which the laws of the classic dance are rarely abrogated, its normal movements distorted and parodied, heightened and dispersed by the rhythm."[57] He described Massine's style as *"perpetuum mobile,* a movement falling on each note, a gesture on each semiquaver, a continual fidget to which we owe the breathless and spirited animation of *The Good-Humoured Ladies;* now, this restless style, with its insistence on distorted or broken lines, is bound to the imperative of polyrhythmic musical movement or tyrannical syncopation that a Stravinsky imposes on the orchestra."[58]

On the afternoon of May 18, *Parade* received its premiere at a war benefit that had been sold out two weeks in advance. The eclectic audience brought together the Rive Droite and the Rive Gauche: the Ballets Russes circle (the Princess de Polignac, the Count and Countess de Beaumont, the Countess Greffuhle, Misia Sert) and the bohemians of Montmartre and Montparnasse (Juan Gris, Severini, Apollinaire) were joined by Paris' musical elite (Roland Manuel, Ricardo Viñes, Francis Poulenc, Germaine Tailleferre, Louis Durey, and Georges Auric). Picasso's evocative and romantic front curtain was greeted with unanimous applause as it was displayed to the accompaniment of Satie's harmonious prelude—generous welcome from a public that might not have been so warm had it known what was to follow. After the front curtain rose to reveal the cubist decor, the audience was confronted with the huge, sensational constructions of the Managers just as Satie's rhythmic music, composed of integrated noises, began. Of the pandemonium that then seized the auditorium, Poulenc remarked: "For the first time—it has happened often enough since, God knows—the music hall was invading Art with a capital A. A one-step is danced in *Parade!* When that began the audience let loose with boos and applause. All Montparnasse, in the top gallery, shouted, 'Vive Picasso!' Auric, Roland Manuel, Tailleferre, Durey and many other musicians shouted, 'Vive Satie!' It was real bedlam."[59]

By now one segment of the audience was shouting obscenities and loudly demanding that the authors be sent to the front lines. Cocteau described what followed:

> *Women rushed at us armed with hatpins. We were saved by Apollinaire because his head was bandaged, he was in uniform and was therefore respected; he set himself in front of us like a rampart. The piece lasted twenty minutes. After the curtain went down the audience was uproarious for fifteen, and finally fistfights broke out. I was crossing the theater with*

Apollinaire to join Picasso and Satie, who were waiting for us in a box,
when a large lady singer recognized me. "There's one of them!" she
cried—she meant the authors. And she lunged at me, brandishing a hat-
pin, trying to put my eyes out.[60]

The press either massacred the ballet or condescended to it. Pierre
Lalo, son of the composer, virulently attacked it in *Les Temps*. Jean
Poueigh, in *Le Carnet de la semaine,* declared Satie without purpose,
humor, technique, or professionalism. In response Satie sent Poueigh a
postcard bearing the observation that the critic was an ass, and an unmu-
sical ass at that. Unfortunately, since the postcard was not in an envelope
and thus could be read by anyone, Poueigh was able to file a libel suit
against Satie that would go before two tribunals. Eventually, a thoroughly chastened Satie was sentenced to a week in jail and ordered to
pay Poueigh a fine of one thousand francs. Cocteau was a witness at the
second trial. Surrounded by reporters, he not only screamed at them, but
raised his walking stick in a threatening gesture toward Poueigh's lawyer.
For this act Cocteau, too, was fined by the judge.[61]

One vocal segment of the audience at *Parade* considered it a thoroughly lame joke—a joke they resented. The press was especially outraged at Cocteau's audacity in subtitling it "a realist ballet." (To Cocteau,
it was "more true than truth.") The artistic community, on the contrary,
expressed its appreciation and recognition of the ballet's achievement. It
left Stravinsky, for instance, with "the impression of freshness and real
originality."[62] Juan Gris "liked *Parade* because it is unpretentious, gay and
distinctly comic. Picasso's decor has lots of style and is simple, and Satie's
music is elegant. It is not figurative, has no fairy tale element, no lavish
effects, no dramatic subject. It's a sort of musical joke in the best of taste
and without high artistic pretensions. That's why it stands right out and
is better than the other ballets. I even believe that it is an attempt to do
something quite new in the theater."[63] And in a letter to Cocteau, Proust
expressed his pleasure: "I cannot tell you how delighted I am by the considerable stir made by your ballet. It would be almost an insult to you
and your collaborators to call it a 'success.' And yet, inexplicable though
it may seem, the success is real and very great. Even though in this case
the success is no more than a mere foretaste, a propitious aura emanating from the future, it is not to be belittled."[64]

Proust's words were prophetic. As the 1913 *Sacre* is thought to have
been a portent of Europe's forthcoming tragedy, so *Parade* anticipates
the 1920s in its juxtaposition of reality and unreality. With a sort of magi-

cal realism, *Parade* prepared the way for dadaism and for surrealism. (Apollinaire's usage of *"sur-réalisme"* in his commentary anticipates the aesthetic value the term would come to have in the following decade.) Satie's ragtime passages announced the arrival of the Jazz Age and the Roaring Twenties. The Chinese Conjuror's movements were founded in the contraction and relaxation of tension (energy), accurately predicting the dance expressionism of the following decade. *Parade's* mobile decor—Picasso's and Massine's joint achievement was the fusing of the decor with the musical structure—preceded Oskar Schlemmer's *Abstrakter Tanz*, in the Bauhaus style that forged dance from the joining together of painting and sculpture. Already present in *Parade* were seeds of the pictorial visualizations, or frescoes in movement, Massine would create in the 1930s with Joan Miró, André Masson, and Henri Matisse. One can even find in *Parade* premonitions of the pop creations of the 1960s. If the importance of a work of art is measured by its transcending the moment and perpetuating itself in history, then *Parade* is undoubtedly one of the twentieth century's most significant and enduring monuments.

For everyone involved in the creation of *Parade,* the ballet marked a turning point. Satie immediately became a prominent figure in the Parisian musical world. Notwithstanding the influential Apollinaire's dislike for him, Cocteau succeeded in establishing himself as a key personality in the avant-garde; he remained not only a catalyst in the arts but a continuing force for infusing content into the French aesthetic of the twentieth century. His association with Picasso, as Cocteau himself expressed it, meant he gained a better understanding of common reality, the reality that from then on, as he ranged beyond it, became integral to his own creative process. For Picasso, who had not had an individual exhibition in Paris since 1902, the theater clearly offered greater exposure than any gallery could; *Parade* would eventually be seen in Madrid, Barcelona, and London. His work on the ballet reawakened his interest in the human figure, an interest that had waned while he explored the stylistic problems of cubism. He fell in love with and married Olga Khokhlova, and, with Paul Rosenberg as his dealer, left Montparnasse behind and began his rapid rise into high society.

Diaghilev had for some time wanted to attract the artists of the School of Paris; the first of his ultramodern productions, *Parade* was the opening gambit in his campaign to convert his Ballets Russes into an expressive vehicle for the avant-garde. And as for Massine, overnight he ceased to occupy the periphery of Diaghilev's entourage and became a figure of importance in his own right. The young and immature dancer who three years earlier had made his debut in *The Legend of Joseph* now returned to Paris as one of the leading avant-garde artists of the time. Apollinaire wrote to him two days after the premiere of *Parade*:

You have taken up alongside Diaghilev the most prominent position to date as far as scenic art goes.

But what interests us the most is the way in which you embroider with such strangely powerful grace upon those ballets.

It's that force and, I should say, that simplicity of yours, which makes you stand out. . . .

Choreography and music are surreal art forms par excellence, since reality, as expressed by them, always goes beyond nature.

And therein lies the importance of your art and your own artistic importance.

It seemed to me that you are so intent upon penetrating the secrets of the choreographically unforeseeable, that I do not fear in the least for the future of that modern art form.

As for Parade, and even perhaps all ballets in general, I believe that the knees and the elbows have not been paid all the attention they deserve. . . .

There is no doubt that you are the first one to make justifiable the use of the word "art" when speaking of dance.[65]

As a performer and as a groundbreaking choreographer, Massine would dominate ballet for the next thirty years. When the Ballets Russes left Paris in May to return to Spain, the future of modern ballet was his.

Diaghilev and Massine with the company, Seville, 1918

CHAPTER 6

Spain, June 1917–July 1918

AT THE END of May the Ballets Russes was back in Madrid, and so were Picasso, Stravinsky, and Ansermet. Nijinsky, who had remained in Spain with his family since the American Ballets Russes contingent had returned to Europe in April, made his long-awaited official Spanish debut at the company's June 2 opening.[1] That night audiences at the Teatro Real had the rare opportunity of seeing Nijinsky as Harlequin and Massine as Eusebius in *Carnaval*. The first performance was a wild success with public and press alike; and the final curtain came down triumphantly night after night. Once again, the Spanish monarchs attended every performance. In a letter to María Martínez Sierra, who was in Paris at the time, Falla noted that there was not a seat to be had.[2] In addition to the season at the Teatro Real, a number of special performances were given for the royal family and the court at the private Royal Palace Theater.

Diaghilev and Massine quickly joined Madrid's artistic and social life. Arthur Rubinstein was still in town, as were two newcomers to Diaghilev's inner circle, Sonia and Robert Delaunay. These two artists had been much influenced by French chemist Eugène Chevreul's 1839 theory of simultaneous contrasts ("the breaking up of color tone into its component elements").[3] This led them to coin the term *simultanéisme* for the placement of human figures and objects in the same painting. The notion had two main emphases: color, as subject and form, and the rendering of light. The couple were important members of the artistic community of prewar Paris; their studio at rue des Grands-Augustins was a gathering-place for the avant-garde.

The Delaunays had first arrived in Madrid in 1915, then moved on to the Vila do Conde in Portugal, and later to Vigo in northern Spain. By 1917 Sonia's private Russian income had been cut off, so they returned to Madrid looking for financial opportunities. Diaghilev introduced the couple to the capital's elite, and these contacts helped Sonia to open a successful clothing and interior design boutique in the elegant Serrano quarter of the city. In designing clothes for members of the royal court she found herself in competition with the French painter Marie Laurencin, who was also in Madrid. But Sonia's dresses, shawls, purses, umbrellas, and furniture were such hits that she later opened two more shops, in Barcelona and Bilbao.

By day Diaghilev, Massine, Picasso, Stravinsky, Ansermet, the Nijinskys, Falla, and the Delaunays would congregate at the bullfights, and by night they plunged into Madrid's unique after-dark scene, where they relished seeing authentic flamenco and often stayed out until the wee hours of the morning.

Massine and Diaghilev resumed their collaboration with Falla. Soon after they were reunited, Falla played for them his score for the pantomime *El corregidor y la molinera,* which had been successfully premiered in Madrid the previous April. Diaghilev's and Massine's first reactions were relayed to María Martínez Sierra by Falla in a June 8 letter, in which the composer confessed: "As I feared, I will have to make important modifications in the second scene . . . to make it more choreographic. . . . Consequently there will be two versions: the original that will remain as is for the theater companies, and the choreographic one, for the Russians."[4] Although these changes had not yet been discussed in detail, "the only certain thing at the moment is that I have to create a long finale, develop further the scene of the fight and even, perhaps, make it possible for the Miller to return followed by the corregidor's policemen."[5] Diaghilev and Massine agreed that the composer would surely strengthen the piece by "omitting some of the pastiche writing of the music for the corregidor's dance, and expanding the ending into a fuller, more powerful finale."[6] Falla readily concurred. For one thing, *Les Femmes de bonne humeur,* which he had just seen at the Real, had given him a sense of Massine's originality and creative power, and Falla was excited and eager to work with him.[7] Falla continued to revamp his score, and by June 22 María Martínez Sierra had praised some of his changes in the finale.[8] But more hard work lay ahead. According to Massine, the composer felt that in order to expand the score he would have to spend "more time studying native dances and music before I could successfully translate the *jota* or the *farruca* into a modern idiom."[9]

When did Picasso join the project? Douglas Cooper and others believe that when he returned to Paris after his visit to Spain with the Ballets Russes in the summer and autumn of 1917 he was still unaware of Diaghilev's plans to create a Spanish ballet.[10] But it is highly likely that the Russians had already discussed their plans with Picasso in Rome, since *Le Tricorne* was one of the projected ballets for the Roman season. It seems safe to assume that Picasso, a member of Diaghilev's informal artistic council, would not be left out of any discussion of forthcoming productions, especially plans for a Spanish ballet. Another piece of evidence bolsters this assumption. Carlos Bosch, who also frequented Diaghilev's Madrid circle, claims that around this time he introduced the artist Pedro Muguruza to Diaghilev as a possible designer for *Le Tricorne.* Indeed Muguruza prepared preliminary sketches for Diaghilev, but the matter went no further since, according to Bosch, Picasso was already involved in the project.[11]

In Madrid relations between Nijinsky and Massine—past and present lovers of Diaghilev—were cordial but distant. Massine deeply admired Nijinsky as dancer and choreographer and seized every opportunity to observe him at work. He watched transfixed as Nijinsky, rehearsing *L'Après-midi d'un faune,* "demonstrated the most minute details of gesture and movement."[12] And Nijinsky in turn genuinely admired Massine's work; after a performance of *Les Femmes de bonne humeur* the great dancer was unrestrained in his praise. "I was surprised," writes Massine, "to receive a visit from Nijinsky, who came to my dressing room, embraced me, and told me what a beautiful ballet I had created. I was taken by surprise, as I did not feel I knew him very well; but when he said that he would love to dance Battista—one of the principal parts—I felt very honored."[13]

The engagement at the Teatro Real ended with two performances, including *Parade*, which was added at the request of the king. The company then spent June 23 to 30 in Barcelona at the Gran Teatre del Liceu. Picasso accompanied them in order to introduce Olga to his family and friends.

The rapport that had developed between Picasso and Massine during the creation of *Parade* went deeper than an understanding between professional collaborators; the two men thoroughly enjoyed one another's company. In Barcelona, as in Madrid, Paris, Rome, and Naples, they spent many hours together. They would meet at the café-restaurant Lion d'Or, their favorite hangout, or go sightseeing. Of course their talk focused mainly on art. In my conversations with Massine he remembered that on this trip to Barcelona he and Picasso began work on *Le Tricorne*. A sort of personal testament to these fertile Barcelona days is the famous Harlequin that Picasso painted here, for which, back in Rome, Massine had been the model.

The Spanish dancer Felix Fernández García was also in Barcelona. Diaghilev and Massine had become reacquainted with him in June in Madrid, where, during the Teatro Real engagement, they ran across him in a working-class café. Right on the spot Diaghilev had invited Felix to a performance at the Real,[14] and after the dancer had seen *Schéhérazade* and *Thamar* he was eager to join the company. Diaghilev had promptly signed him before leaving for Barcelona. Sokolova saw this as a crucial move:

> The employment of Felix was the first step towards the realization of the great Spanish ballet which Massine intended to create, though at that time neither Diaghilev nor Massine could have known exactly what form it would take. The essential was that Massine and the company should learn to perform Spanish steps in a Spanish way: and Massine in particular had to master the grammar of the Spanish dance before he could work out his choreography. At this stage Diaghilev and Massine probably saw Felix as the eventual star of their Spanish ballet, for if they had only needed a professor, it would surely have been more reasonable to engage an older man with experience of teaching.[15]

In Barcelona, Felix, whom Massine thought "a naturally gifted dancer," began to teach him flamenco.[16] He also introduced Massine to his old Barcelona teacher Señor de Molina, who would give Massine his first lessons in the intricate technique of *zapateado*.

Unfortunately, Barcelona also became the site of renewed antagonism between Diaghilev and Nijinsky. While both men no doubt avoided dwelling on their stormy history, Nijinsky may nonetheless have resented the attention now being paid to Massine, and very likely felt some rejection at being left out of the company's creative process. He realized, too, that Massine had completely replaced him in Diaghilev's life.[17] Perhaps to salve his injured pride—and ill advised by his wife—Nijinsky suddenly balked at going to South America, where he was under contract to appear with the company immediately after the Barcelona run. He rashly tried to flee Barcelona for Madrid, but Diaghilev countered with stern legal measures; according to Spanish law, the dancer was bound both to perform in Barcelona and to tour with the company. Nijinsky was found in a Barcelona train station, arrested, and returned to the company.[18] Thus, after the Teatre Liceu engagement ended, Nijinsky sailed for South America with the Ballets Russes on July 4. (For this tour Grigoriev was in charge and Ansermet was company conductor.)

The Nijinsky incident was quite unsettling to Massine. He wrote to Anatoli Petrovich:

> *I have not written to you for such a long time because everything was not clear in my mind, I could not visualize the future.*
>
> *Today is a special day: the whole company departed for Brazil and with them went Nijinsky, such a difficult and complicated subject. . . .*
>
> *Nijinsky is unacceptable and it seems to me that it is impossible to work with him. In spite of this I have great love for him as a great master who is troubled by thoughts that are similar to mine.*[19]

With the company abroad, Diaghilev and Massine decided to resettle in Barcelona, partly because in hot weather the Mediterranean city was more agreeable than Madrid. Nearby Sitges had become their favorite summer resort on the Iberian peninsula. José María Sert was there during this time, and when not preoccupied with redecorating Charles Deering's home, he would take frequent jaunts into the city. Falla arrived in Barcelona and took Diaghilev and Massine to a performance of *El corregidor y la molinera* at the Teatro Novedades. For the first time Diaghilev and Massine heard the score played by an orchestra, and the music's "pulsating rhythms, played by eleven brass instruments, seemed to us very exciting, and in its blend of violence and passion was similar to much of the music of the local folk-dances."[20]

Few ballets have been as meticulously planned as *Le Tricorne*. In July, Diaghilev organized an excursion to give Falla the opportunity to do still more research on popular tunes, and to allow Massine to immerse himself in Spanish culture studying the personality types and dances that were to find their way into the new ballet. Felix Fernández García came along. The foursome journeyed from Zaragoza, the home of *jota*; to Burgos, the city of the medieval hero El Cid; to the high Renaissance of Salamanca; to El Greco's Toledo, with its blend of Sephardic and Arabic influences; and on through Córdoba, Seville, and Granada, the three southern cities that Diaghilev, Massine, and Falla had visited the year before. The dry, scorching summer heat did not keep them from visiting cathedrals, monasteries, and museums. At night they abandoned themselves to café life and soaked up regional music. Felix outdid himself trying to impress his traveling companions. He was a great asset, for "wherever we went he was automatically accepted as a friend by the local dancers. He was able to arrange several performances for us, and we spent many late nights listening to selected groups of singers, guitarists, and dancers doing the *jota*, the *farruca*, or the *fandango*."[21]

Through Falla and Felix, the Russians were exposed to the best of flamenco. In Seville, where the previous year they had met La Niña de los Peines, they now met the famous flamenco dancers Ramírez and Macarrona. Massine was able to film some of their performances on the 16mm camera he had bought in Rome. These dancers impressed him with their "ferocious power and elegance."[22] In Seville they also watched "a *sevillana* performed by a group of dancers on the roof of an old house in the Triana quarter, lit by warm blue moonlight. In Córdoba Felix organized a performance in a cavern on the outskirts of the city, gathering together the group of cobblers, barbers and pastry cooks who were considered the best dancers in that part of town. After a meal of raw ham and Jerez they danced with such pleasure, spontaneity and native fire that the performances went on until the early hours of the morning."[23]

In Granada they revisited the Alhambra and the Generalife gardens, this time on donkeys. (To the amusement of the others, on the first slope the donkey bearing Diaghilev collapsed under his weight.)

As Massine got to know Falla more intimately, the composer's religious fervor, his ascetic views, and his almost monastic lifestyle, so detached from worldly vanities, all made a deep impression on the younger man. "His natural dignity and humility," Massine wrote, "were expressed in his thin, El Greco shaped face which, with it finely chiselled features and sallow skin, was like an instrument tautly strung."[24] Falla was "an extraordinary, inspiring man . . . unassertive, yet his remarks were often sharp and penetrating. He spoke with compelling intensity, and his conversation—particularly on art and music—was curiously exhilarating."[25] They reached a level of intimacy in which they exchanged anecdotes about their childhoods, about their love for the theater, and about their fascination with puppets. This trip marked the beginning of a friendship that would last until the composer's death in 1946.

Throughout the journey Massine was intrigued by Falla's method of compiling musical sources; he was "continually writing down passages of music in the notebook he habitually carried."[26] Once, in Granada, on their way back to the hotel after "wandering through long Moorish patios and courtyards," they "stopped to listen to a blind man playing a guitar. Falla spoke to the man, asking him to repeat the mournful little tune. . . . While he did so, Falla stood with his eyes closed humming it through and then methodically writing it down in his notebook. He later used that melody for the *sevillana* in the second part of the ballet. . . ."[27]

As the trip continued, *Le Tricorne* began to assume its final shape.[28] First the characters were modified. The miller in the pantomime, as in the novel, was ugly and humpbacked; for the ballet he was metamorphosed into an attractive young man. The names of the two central characters, Lucas and Frasquita, were changed to the Miller and the Miller's Wife, to accentuate their symbolic value in Alarcón's social allegory of the common folk's victory over the aristocracy. The intricate scenario of the pantomime was simplified in order to smooth its transition to dance, and Falla replaced the descriptive musical passages with dance numbers. Yet the action and the score of the first section of the pantomime and those of the corresponding part of the ballet were to remain remarkably similar.

But in the second scene *Le Tricorne* began to assume much larger dimensions. The first scene revolved around the actions of the two main characters, but the second required a full corps de ballet. This was a significant departure for Massine, since in *Les Femmes* and *Parade* he had used only a limited number of dancers. In *Le Tricorne* he would prove his skill in the deployment of large ensembles. And to match Massine's conception for the finale, for the first time in the evolution of the work Falla introduced a full orchestra.

Besides swapping ideas about the new ballet, Massine and Falla talked long and deeply about folklore.[29] For Falla, popular thematic sources served only as a point of departure. He wanted to capture the mood, rhythm, melodic forms, and cadences, but eschewed the perpetuation of the literal popular form, opting instead to try for a personal and original interpretation. According to him, "the essential elements of music, the sources of inspiration, are the nations and their people. I am opposed to music that takes as its base the authentic folkloric documents; on the contrary, I believe that it is necessary to have as a point of reference the live, natural sources and to utilize their sonorities and rhythms in its essence, but not for their exterior appearance."[30] In the first of Massine's ballets rooted in folklore—*Le Soleil de nuit* (1916) and *Contes russes* (1917)—he had unwittingly carried out Falla's dictum. His objective had been to take the essence of the popular dance movement and distort it in order to produce his own personal expressive and suggestive movement. And undoubtedly these conversations on folklore with Falla during the gestation of *Le Tricorne* influenced and altered the course of that ballet as well.

When Diaghilev left Spain in 1916, his intention had been to produce a Spanish ballet in Rome with Spanish dancers, as evidenced by the numerous letters in which he asked Falla to hire Spanish dancers to come to Rome.[31] In the Falla Archives one can read a contract signed in Seville on October 1, 1916, by Falla (acting on Diaghilev's behalf) and the dancer Angela Morillo, who was to join the Ballets Russes in Rome the following November 1.[32] It is possible that in 1917 Diaghilev still felt inclined toward Spanish dancers and that he envisioned Felix Fernández García, as Sokolova suggested, as the leading male dancer of *Le Tricorne*. However, as Massine developed his concept of the work as a stylization of Spanish folklore instead of an authentic interpretation, or re-creation, the choreographer must have realized that Felix was not as suitable for the role of the Miller as he himself was, especially since he was now much more confident in his knowledge of the native dance idiom. By the time their excursion ended and Diaghilev, Felix, and Falla returned to Madrid, Massine was fully imbued with the Spanish temperament, proving again his ability to take what he needed from his cultural surroundings.

Once back in Madrid, Falla set to work on the score, but, deliberate worker that he was, it would take him several more months to complete a satisfactory draft. In the meantime, Diaghilev warded off the stagnation of inactivity by suggesting to Massine that he begin preparing a new ballet. They decided to set it on a series of unpublished pieces by Rossini,

Péchés de vieillesse, which had been brought to their attention in Rome by the composer Ottorino Respighi, and devised a libretto based on the German ballet *Die Puppenfee,* which dealt with toys that come to life. (This work had first been produced in Vienna in 1888, and again in St. Petersburg in 1903 with choreography by the Legat brothers.) Massine liked the music's gaiety and variety, and he easily

> *visualized first two Italian peasant dolls who would dance a tarantella. Then, for Rossini's rousing mazurka, I pictured a quartet of characters from a pack of cards: The Queen of Diamonds and of Clubs, the King of Spades and of Hearts. Another piece of music, an ingenious parody of Offenbach, naturally suggested two vivacious cancan dancers in the spirit of Toulouse-Lautrec's paintings. We all agreed that the ballet should be taken at top speed, the dancers following each other without a break. I much enjoyed making the first rough sketches for the new ballet, which we called La Boutique Fantasque. . . .*[33]

Rehearsals got under way as soon as the company returned from South America in October.

The next Ballets Russes season took place in Barcelona, November 5–18, 1917. *Parade* was presented on November 10. The cubist ballet was not acclaimed by the press. At the end of November the company returned to the Teatro Real in Madrid. But neither autumn season equaled the success of the spring season, for the country was being swept by influenza. In Barcelona the flu had caused the death of many employees at the British consulate, and in Madrid half the populace had fled to the countryside.

For Massine the presence of the Delaunays in Madrid was comforting. His introspective personality made it difficult for him to open up and establish friendships, but he seems to have been able to communicate with certain women, one of whom was Sonia. Happily married, she was no threat to Diaghilev. Like Gontcharova, the other woman close to Massine, Delaunay—also Russian, a painter, and highly intellectual—would come to play a maternal role for the young choreographer.

After the season at the Teatro Real, prospects for the Ballets Russes were more uncertain than ever before. Aside from a forthcoming engagement in Lisbon in December, Diaghilev had not been able to arrange any other bookings. With the rest of Europe at war and with the impresario cut off from his private income as a result of the revolution in Russia, the survival of the troupe was in serious jeopardy.

Upon the company's arrival in Lisbon, revolution broke out, with the aim of overthrowing the government of Bernardino Machado. The upheaval lasted three days and nights, during which Massine and Diaghilev remained barricaded under the main staircase of the Avenida Palace Hotel. While Diaghilev fretted that they were losing valuable rehearsal time, Massine, with his capacity to retreat into the world of his imagination, felt rather stimulated and creative in the presence of so much turbulence:

> *Instead of succumbing to the general panic, I found myself remembering the gaiety and fantasy of Rossini's music. While the fighting raged outside my thoughts went back to the beach at Viareggio, where I had seen two white fox terriers coquettishly chasing and teasing each other. With a vivid picture in my mind of their frisky, flirtatious movements I mentally composed the poodles' dance for the new ballet. Throughout the revolution I remained in a highly creative mood and as a result, once the fighting had stopped, I was able to compose the major part of* La Boutique fantasque *in a few days.*[34]

When the political turmoil came to an end, the company opened its season a day behind schedule at the Coliseu dos Recreios, then moved for two performances to the San Carlos Opera, whose auditorium, at Diaghilev's request, was reopened especially for the Ballets Russes.

During the Lisbon engagements Massine began to rehearse, with Sokolova and Alexander Gavrilov, a Venetian waltz for his Rossini ballet. He also introduced into *Le Soleil de nuit* a solo for Lopokova set to the music of the shepherd's aria from *The Snow Maiden*. (Lopokova first danced it when the company went to London in 1918.)

The performances at the San Carlos ended, and prospects grew dire. Diaghilev and Massine returned to Madrid, leaving an almost starved company behind. Immediately upon their arrival, Diaghilev sent for Falla, who came at once to the Palace Hotel to find him desperate, with tears in his eyes. He confided to Falla the company's circumstances. "I am lost," he said. "What is going to become of me? My only solution is to go into a monastery."[35] Falla offered to help by approaching his friend and solicitor, Leopoldo Matos. Matos had successfully negotiated the rights to adapt Alarcón's *Sombrero de tres picos* to the stage, despite the fact that the writer's will had stipulated that the novel was to remain in its original form. With Matos's assistance the Spanish impresarios Arturo Serrano and Méndez Vigo came to Diaghilev's rescue, offering to organize a forty-seven-performance tour of the Ballets Russes throughout Spain. From Madrid, Diaghilev and Massine returned to Barcelona to spend the rest of the winter at the Hotel Angleterre.

In Barcelona, Massine began to set the tarantella for *La Boutique fantasque.* When the bullfighting season opened he attended the corridas regularly. He especially enjoyed the "poise, control and elegant movement of Juan Belmonte, Gaona, and Joselito."[36] He studied their styles and movements to acquire a better understanding of folk dances like the *farruca,* and befriended Belmonte, who fascinated him in long conversations about bullfighting. In *Le Tricorne,* Massine's inspiration was to give full expression to what he took Spain to be, including the perilous position of the matador and his flirtation with death in the arena. He collected all the illustrated bullfighting periodicals; and when as the Miller he performed his *farruca*—for him more than a dance, "it was a trance"—he envisioned a bull confronting him. Massine poured into his solo "all the highly emotional feelings I had when spending the afternoons at the *corridas.*"[37]

Diaghilev, who had been in touch with Oswald Stoll to arrange an engagement at the London Coliseum, went to Madrid to see about transferring the company to England. By now he felt that he had squeezed Spain of all prospects, and to him the Ballets Russes' future looked grimmer than ever.

By March the tour of Spain had been arranged, to begin at the end of the month in Valladolid. Diaghilev traveled to Lisbon to share the good news with the company. One of his chief hopes was to recruit a superior orchestra. With Falla's assistance, he was able to persuade Joaquín Turina to become the company's musical director and assemble a group of musicians that included members of the orchestras of the Teatro Real, the Madrid Sinfónica, and the Filarmónica.

The tour covered about four thousand kilometers; the company's eighty-six dancers visited Valladolid, Salamanca, San Sebastián, Bilbao, Logroño, Zaragoza, Valencia, Alcoy, Cartagena (where with Serrano's help a threatened musicians' strike was averted), Córdoba, Seville, and Granada. The most successful engagements were the last two. In Seville, Diaghilev invited the company to celebrate at a *venta* (an open-air café) surrounded by orange groves, where Felix danced. In Granada, they performed at the Teatro Isabel la Católica and danced *Schéhérazade* at the Alhambra, for invited guests only, to Diaghilev's immense satisfaction and to high praise from those who later said the company had soared on this special occasion. From Granada they returned to Madrid, where they performed from May 25 through June 2, then moved on to Barcelona.

During this trying period, Massine's privileged position in the company brought on some grumbling among the dancers. During Turina's short association with the Ballets Russes, he clearly perceived its hierarchical structure: "A quite picturesque and rare society of nomadic people. It was classified into three sections: the higher echelon, the bourgeoisie, and the working class, who had the least possible contact among themselves and who kept a most rigorous protocol. The leading dancer, Massine, replaced the famous Nijinsky with very little sympathy from the other dancers who resented his rapid rise to eminence."[38]

The company's ongoing crisis of survival weighed heavily on Diaghilev's shoulders. Three years into the war, he found himself penniless, cut off from most of his friends and supporters, and responsible not only for his company's continuity but for the well-being of a great number of people. This overwhelming burden, added to his other cares, gradually wore him down. The lack of funds, a spreading dread, and repeated sleepless nights drained him, and their effect began to show in the shabbiness of his physical appearance. His dear friend Misia had advised him to drop it all, apparently forgetting that Diaghilev's imperious will would not allow him to surrender.

Diaghilev exhausted every possible connection to help get the company to England. He went to Madrid to make a personal appeal to King Alfonso, and through the intercession of the monarch, the Spanish ambassador in London and the English ambassador in Madrid arranged for the company's entry into England via France. Diaghilev wrote to Massine, who was still in Barcelona with the company:

I am working here from 9:00 a.m. until nighttime. Upon arrival, I found out that the French will not let us through and are falling back on their last refusal. . . . I became like a storm and challenged everybody to their feet. The French did not give in, and again wanted to ask the English to let us go by sea. Again, I howled—new obstacles arose—I did more than I could. There was no one in Madrid who was not somehow involved in helping us! I begged the King three times to let us through and finally obtained the authorization. As soon as I did my nerves cracked and my whole system collapsed.[39]

All of this agitation placed further strains on Diaghilev's intimate relations with Massine. He turned more anxiously than ever to his young companion for emotional fulfillment and love. Massine was unable to respond fully to Diaghilev's needs, adding even more stress to an already unhappy situation. Diaghilev's demands were desperate, histrionic, and permeated with fear. He adopted the role of victim, and the resulting hysteria was calculated to fill Massine with guilt. This classic victim-victimizer scenario was Diaghilev's characteristic modus operandi; its dynamic defined his relationship with Massine. Perhaps unaware that his behavior would inevitably shatter that relationship, by clinging desperately to the younger man Diaghilev drove him away. In the same letter to Massine, Diaghilev dispatched a lover's reproach:

> At times, it's probably necessary to explain oneself, given that you don't want to understand or to feel. . . . I sent you a cable thinking that I was victorious, and received only a cable from the Lopokovs. From you not one word of tenderness, not one word of joy in return for my warmth. I asked frequently whether there was a note from you. . . .
>
> I was very depressed and cried constantly, having to leave the table when I would not hold back my tears. The Delaunays wanted to cheer me up and took me out to a restaurant. . . .
>
> I was ready to leave when I got your note asking me, for the sake of the dancers, to wait and wait and wait. I wanted so badly to go to the sea . . . didn't I deserve a break? If no one is concerned about my tired head then I need to think about it myself.
>
> It is very hard for me to be without my family, my dear ones, without friends, without a drop of tenderness. . . .
>
> Someday you will understand all this and someday a ray of light will illuminate your heart of glass. . . . Can it be that it is not my destiny to infuse you with the warmth of a Russian spring sun?[40]

Before returning to Barcelona, Diaghilev invited the Delaunays to join him and Massine for a short stay in Sitges. With most of Diaghilev's closest friends unavailable to him, the Delaunays had been supportive, and during his frequent visits to Madrid he had spent most of his free time with the couple. In Sitges the four friends settled down in a lovely villa (probably lent to Diaghilev, in view of the catastrophic state of his finances).

This was not the first time that Sonia and Robert had joined Diaghilev and Massine in Sitges, but this sojourn would mark the initial collaboration of the Delaunays with the Ballets Russes. Diaghilev had asked them to redesign *Cléopâtre* for the projected London engagement.

Robert designed a new decor, and Sonia designed some of the costumes, including Cleopatra's. A more creative collaboration, however, took place when Sonia, Robert, and Massine, all of whom had wanted for some time to work together on a ballet, began preparing *Football*, inspired by Robert's 1913 painting *L'Equipe de Cardiff*. Robert wanted to create something with a joyous and mad life, a work that would have repercussions for ballet.[41] Sonia wanted the space around the players (dancers) to remain mobile; as she explained to Massine, art in the past had been characterized by static laws, but the laws of modern art were dynamic. In her view, *Parade* had been a new beginning for a "universal spectacle," with every movement fresh and true and rooted in simplicity; she saw it as a point of departure.[42]

Working with the Delaunays afforded Massine another in a series of insights into art. Gontcharova and Larionov had provided his first important exposure to Russian and modern art; the futurists had given him a taste for experimentation; Picasso had introduced him to the principles of cubism; now the Delaunays would help him explore other artistic movements, including abstraction. They enjoyed his company, and respected his insatiable artistic curiosity and willingness to cross new frontiers. Robert wrote to him: "I find that you are making unbelievable progress and it is work that makes you superior, and in the way you have abandoned certain little prejudices of our friends from yesterday. . . . We see through it that you have also been taken by the liberating and regenerating movement, because a new era begins for the ballet."[43]

Sonia and Léonide spent long afternoons at the beach discussing art, theater, and films. Massine was fascinated by moving pictures and wondered exactly how they would affect the theater arts. Sonia argued that film would not achieve the stature of the other arts until it was delivered into the hands of artists,[44] but Massine, of course, had already proven in *Les Femmes de bonne humeur* the influence of film on his own work.

On July 29, 1918, the French consulate in Barcelona issued a transit visa enabling Massine and Diaghilev to enter France between August 4 and 7 and traverse it on their way to England. Leaving Barcelona on a midnight train, they entered France at Cerbère on the fourth.

The trip was not uneventful. At the French border, two detectives in dark glasses interrogated Diaghilev about his connections in Spain with Mata Hari, who had been executed in France for espionage on October 15, 1917. Fortunately, the letters she had sent to Diaghilev at the Palace Hotel imploring him to take her into the Ballets Russes had been left behind in Madrid.

The Cancan Dancer in La Boutique
fantasque, *1919*

CHAPTER 7

Paris, August 1918–London, August 1919

IN PARIS, Diaghilev and Massine took a taxi from the St-Lazare station
to the Hôtel Meurice. They were shocked at the devastation the City of
Light had suffered during the war, in stark contrast to the untroubled
Spanish landscape they had just left. The façades of the buildings were
covered with grime, the city's "boarded-up shops and kiosks"[1] looked
like barracks, and the few people they encountered showed the weariness of war in their thin, pale faces and stricken appearance. Everyone
seemed "fearful of the shells from 'Big Bertha' which burst over the town
every few minutes."[2]

At the hotel, Diaghilev and Massine were joined by Misia and Sert
and during luncheon the foursome recounted the travails of the past several months. But they clung to their hopes for the upcoming London sea-

son and for Massine's ballets in progress, *Le Tricorne* and *La Boutique fantasque*. Diaghilev was also optimistic about his plans to produce the eighteenth-century Cimarosa opera *Le astuzie femminili*, with, he hoped, a design by Sert.

During their six-day sojourn in Paris, Diaghilev and Massine were overjoyed to embrace old friends. At the Palais Royal apartment of Valentine Gross and her fiancée, the artist Jean Hugo, Stravinsky, just in from Switzerland, played his brand new composition *Ragtime* for, among other guests, Diaghilev, Massine, Picasso, Auric, and Poulenc.[3]

On August 9 Massine and Diaghilev left via Le Havre for England. As they were leaving Paris, a house on rue des Capucines was bombed, and pieces of glass and stone pummeled the roof of their taxi. They soon discovered that London, too, had been dramatically transformed by the war. Victoria Station hummed, and "Oxford Street, Trafalgar Square, the Savoy Hotel, the Coliseum—all were in a perpetual bristle."[4] The two travelers checked into the Savoy and got to work on their Coliseum engagement, which was only four weeks away. Diaghilev soon held auditions to replace those dancers who had defected in Spain when the troupe's survival had seemed most doubtful. Into the Ballets Russes came a group of dancers whose English names were immediately Russianized. The sole exception was petite Vera Clark, who was identified by her real name in company programs for a short while before she changed it to Vera Savina. She would play a decisive role in Massine's future.

The Coliseum engagement was the Ballets Russes' first in a music-hall theater. The company appeared on both afternoon and evening programs; according to Massine, Diaghilev detested seeing his ballets "sandwiched between performing dogs and acrobats, and clowns."[5] Diaghilev also cursed the theater's deficient lighting equipment.

As opening night drew closer, a weighty responsibility fell on Massine. Since Nijinsky and Karsavina were no longer with the company, much of the season's success depended on him. Diaghilev, with good reason, was jittery, particularly about the reception of *Les Femmes de bonne humeur*.[6] London audiences had not seen Massine dance since before the war, and then only in brief appearances as Joseph. Now he returned as both leading dancer and choreographer of the Ballets Russes; the novelties in the repertory would doubly depend on him.

The Ballets Russes opened at the Coliseum on the afternoon of September 5, when Massine was reintroduced to London as Amoun in *Cléopâtre*. The welcome was warm. The dancers were no doubt buoyed to see many of their longstanding society friends and supporters in the audience, including Lady Juliet Duff, Lady Ottoline Morrell, Lady Cunard, the Duchess of Rutland, Catherine d'Erlanger, and the Sitwell brothers. In the evening the company presented its first premiere, *Les Femmes de bonne humeur*, with a new, more realistic decor by Bakst.

To Diaghilev's immense relief and deep satisfaction, *Les Femmes* and its dancers were a sensation. The ballet's cinematic movements and simultaneous action were a revelation to British balletomanes. Wrote *The Observer*: "The merry adventures are unfolded with a rapidity of action that only perfect precision can sustain, and it is this precision with which every gesture is linked to its accompanying musical phrase that is the secret of this remarkable feat of stage production. . . . The result is not only a brilliant work of art, but the most exhilarating entertainment. Wordless wit is not easy of accomplishment, but Massine's choreography has attained to it."[7]

Still, the work's distinctive style and rhythm took the general public by surprise, and even ballet aficionados found it a bit puzzling. The dance historian Cyril Beaumont described his own first impression: "I was not sure whether I liked the ballet or not. The unusual speed of the performance was a little bewildering, and I could not get accustomed to the jerky, puppetlike quality of Massine's choreography, so different from the rounded and flowing movements of Fokine's compositions."[8] Only after repeated viewing did he determine that Massine's "dances did far more than accompany the music and accord with its rhythmical structure; they really translated the spirit of the music in terms of choreography."[9] Beaumont was also much taken by Massine's new, *cantinella*-like mime, which he found "unusual in that it was not separated from the actual dancing but, so to speak, grafted on it. Thus the whole ballet was a continuous flow of expressive movement unbroken until the very end, the sequence being adroitly subjected to variations in mood and speed to afford contrast and variety."[10] If Fokine's dramatic ballets had made their action cohere in terms of pantomime and dance—distinct from one another but of a piece with the narrative—Massine's synthesis of mime and dance, welded to the musical structure, produced a new, quintessentially balletic style of storytelling.

London's artistic and literary lights, unimpressed by Diaghilev's earlier, prewar seasons, now eagerly adopted the company. Osbert Sitwell observed: "Now the leaders of the intellectuals, seven lean years too late, had given the signal OK, and their followers flocked to it, replacing the old kid-glove and tiara audience of Covent Garden and Drury Lane."[11] This new interest was partly motivated by an awareness of Diaghilev's association with Gontcharova and Larionov, and of the controversial creation of *Parade* the year before, tales of which had been circulating ever since. Moreover, the collaboration of Cocteau, Satie, and Picasso had made the Ballets Russes an integrated brigade in the continental avant-garde. England was beginning to feel the sweep of this movement largely thanks to Roger Fry, who was instrumental in bringing foreign art before the tradition-bound British public. (In 1917 Fry had organized an exhibition in Birmingham that included canvases by Constantin Brancusi, Juan Gris, André Marchand, André Derain, and Maurice de Vlaminck, as well as such British painters as Duncan Grant and Vanessa Bell.) Thus Massine—associate of Picasso, Gontcharova, and Larionov, artists whose works marked such a radical stylistic departure from the prewar repertory held in contempt by Bloomsbury—now found himself the focus of that coterie's rapture and respect.

The Sitwell siblings lost no time in capitalizing on their prewar connection with Diaghilev, electing themselves unofficial Ballets Russes hosts for all of Bloomsbury. (It was in their home at Swan Walk that Maynard Keynes met his future wife, Lydia Lopokova.) On a rainy night in November they gave a dinner party for Diaghilev and Massine that coincided with the Armistice, much to Osbert's delight. The official end of the war that had seen the slaughter of more than ten million Europeans left everyone overwhelmed with relief and excitement, so they all left Swan Walk to attend another party at the flat of the collector Montague Shearman. Osbert, Diaghilev, and Massine took a taxi around Trafalgar Square, where it seemed that all of London had gathered to participate in a euphoric celebration. At Shearman's they found the "dark flower of Bloomsbury," as Osbert liked to call the set: Virginia Woolf, Roger Fry, Lytton Strachey, Clive Bell, Maynard Keynes, Duncan Grant, David Garnett, D.H. and Frieda Lawrence, Aldous Huxley, Sacheverell Sitwell, Ottoline Morrell, and Lydia Lopokova. It was an important and jubilant occasion, and with Diaghilev alone abstaining, the revelers danced into the next day.[12]

On November 21, *Le Soleil de nuit*, now titled *Midnight Sun*, was premiered; it now included the solo for Lopokova that Massine had added in Lisbon. Wrote Sydney Carrol in the *Sunday Times*: "Emblematic of Pagan Russia—the savage vitality, the crude color and design, the primitive exuberance of this village dance thrill the senses and arrest the mind."[13] With this neoprimitive Russian ballet, Massine scored another success with both press and public. In a letter to his daughter Pamela, Fry described it as "a sort of peasant festival in honor of the Midnight Sun. Dances of peasant women in wonderful dresses with buffoons and village idiot. Then Lopokova is the Snow Maiden and has a most strange and poetical *pas seul* expressing her longing for the Midnight Sun. Massine, Midnight Sun, dark scarlet red and gold with two great golden discs. He rushes backwards and forwards across the stage, while the peasants keep up a ceaseless dance, very complicated and almost chaotic, but very beautiful. . . ."[14]

On December 23 came the London premiere of *Contes russes*, retitled *Children's Tales,* and Massine enjoyed yet another triumph. Some changes had been made. In order to link the three unrelated episodes Massine had made two additions: a prologue for a street vendor carrying puppets representing the characters in each story; and at the end of the Swan Princess episode, a funeral procession for the dragon slain by the knight Bova Korolevich. The finale, according to Grigoriev, also had been modified and improved.[15] *The Times* declared that Massine had "strung together three old Russian legends in a very ingenious way; the grotesque setting is so quaint and so unlike anything that one usually associates with a children's entertainment, the dancing of the whole team is so exhilarating, that one cannot wonder at the enthusiasm which greeted it."[16] There were also alterations to the decor; because some scenery had been destroyed in a fire in South America, Larionov redesigned the backdrop for the Swan Princess scene. Diaghilev also asked his scene painter, Vladimir Polunin, to change the yellow backdrop of the Baba Yaga episode to green (a decision that displeased Larionov). Even so, Fry was so much taken by Larionov's work in *Le Soleil de nuit* and *Contes russes* that in March 1919 he published, in *Burlington Magazine,* two appreciative articles on these designs.

The successful engagement at the Coliseum closed on March 29 with more than seventeen curtain calls. The six-month season had established Massine as a sublime craftsman and a formidable artistic force, which gave his ego a powerful boost. Massine the "star" began to emerge. In his book *The Diaghilev Ballet in London,* Cyril Beaumont describes an incident that clearly demonstrates how absorbed Massine had become in his newly won status. Entering the theater well before curtain time at a gala performance one evening, he noticed that the name of Lopokova, who also had conquered London and whose popularity was enormous, had been printed in larger type than his own. In a display of temperament, Massine promptly locked himself in his dressing room, fell completely silent, and refused to come out. It was not until much later, after Diaghilev and Grigoriev had pleaded and begged, that the choreographer finally emerged—only moments before curtain time—and went on stage.[17]

Massine's artistic maturation and the recognition it brought accelerated his independence from Diaghilev. He relished running his own life, forming friendships with people like Ottoline Morrell and going off alone to visit Duncan Grant's studio on the top floor of a house in Fitzroy Street, where Grant and his circle of friends held forth. These were Massine's first decisive moves toward becoming his own person.

Their Coliseum engagement over, the Ballets Russes performed in April at the Hippodrome in Manchester, then returned to open a second season in London on April 10 at the Alhambra Theatre, which, like the Coliseum, was under the management of Sir Oswald Stoll. Now in a suitable venue, the company could present its customary three-ballet program. As Massine began rehearsals for *La Boutique fantasque* and *Le Tricorne*, London, like Rome in the spring of 1917, became for Ballets Russes a setting for exhilarating creative collaboration. Ansermet came to conduct the Alhambra season, and in May Picasso and André Derain, the French *fauve* painter, arrived to work on the new ballets. Picasso and Olga took up residence at the Savoy, and Derain stayed at 36 Regent Square in a small flat lent to him by Vanessa Bell.

La Boutique fantasque, the first world premiere scheduled for the Alhambra season, was also the first Diaghilev ballet to be created in England. Planning for it had begun in Italy in 1917. Bakst, who then was working with Massine on *Les Femmes de bonne humeur* and who had designed the Legats' *Puppenfee,* was commissioned to design the new ballet. Throughout 1918, Massine and the painter exchanged letters on various aspects of the production.[18] But when Bakst's preliminary sketches reached Diaghilev in London, he was disappointed: for him, the artist's "pre-war style had lost its appeal."[19]

At the end of the Coliseum engagement, Diaghilev asked Massine to meet with Derain in Paris to discuss his possible collaboration on *Boutique fantasque.* In Derain's rue Bonaparte flat, Massine outlined the plot and explained how he and Diaghilev envisioned the toy shop, "something entirely *fantastique* and imaginary."[20] As he described the characters he hummed the music, and Derain, highly excited by the project, boldly proceeded to sketch the four playing cards, the tarantella dancers, and the cancan dancers.

When the news that he had been replaced reached Bakst, he was, of course, terribly hurt. The breach that opened between him and Diaghilev lasted for two years. But Diaghilev was merely obeying his dictum "In the theater there are no friends."[21] Although Massine believed that "it was certainly a ruthless thing to do," he admitted that "it did not surprise me, for I had long ago realized that Diaghilev was ruthless in anything that affected the work of the company. The artistic perfection of his productions was the most important thing in his life and he would allow nothing, not even a longstanding friendship, to stand in the way of it. When an artist was no longer useful to him, he did not hesitate to drop him. At the time I am afraid I did not consider this a defect in his character, but rather an unavoidable aspect of his professionalism."[22]

When rehearsals began in London, most of the choreography for the characters who had emerged from conversations between Massine and Diaghilev had been laid down. In the first of three scenes, the keeper of the toy shop is displaying his goods to his customers, who include three English ladies, an American family, and a Russian family. The windup toys include an Italian couple, who dance a tarantella, a quartet of playing cards (two kings and two queens), a snob, a melon dealer, a group of Cossacks, a pair of poodles, and two cancan dancers. Unfortunately, each family wants to buy only one cancan dancer, separating the loving couple. As the customers leave the shop, the cancan dancers are placed in separate boxes for future delivery. The second scene takes place at night, when the shop is closed. The toys come out of their boxes and trolleys eager for their lives to continue, but they are saddened by the lovers' tragic separation. An escape is planned for the couple, and the scene ends in a spirited mood as all of the remaining toys dance in celebration of their scheme.

When, in the third scene, the families return the following day to pick up their merchandise, they are dismayed to find the boxes empty. Believing that they have been cheated, they attack the shopkeeper and his assistant. The toys, however, come to the rescue of the owner and his helper and make war on the customers, driving them, terrorized, out of the shop. As the shoppers peer through the window from the street, the toys forgive the shopkeeper; then all unite in a joyous grand finale.

The juxtaposition of human beings and toys that come to life only under the right conditions gave Massine the opportunity to assemble an ironic comedy of manners in which the nonhuman characters win the sympathy of the audience. His people are caricatures—the affected, aristocratic English ladies, the crass, nouveau-riche American family and its merchant-class Russian counterpart—but the toys become ever more human and admirable. The grotesque and satirical elements serve as distancing devices to keep all sentimentality out of the plot.

With *La Boutique fantasque* Massine hoped to give ballet a new kind of realism, what he called "naturalistic realism."[23] The poodles' sexual frolicking and antics (such as the male poodle lifting his leg on the American boy) were examples of this. His burlesque treatment of an old theme was a further departure from the conventions of neoromanticism and was regarded by conservative critics as excessive, cause for extreme uneasiness. According to Clive Bell, "*La Boutique* reminds one oddly of the sculpture of Bernini. It skims the edge of vulgarity: Need I say that there is never the least chance of its falling in? M. Massine has chosen to construct his work of art out of the banalities that have haunted the variety stage these sixty years. There are white frills and pink roses and an apotheosis of *la prima ballerina assoluta*: and Madame Lopokova gives the final touch to an unmitigated can-can with an authentic 'split.' No, Massine is not in the least frightened, but he contrives, like an accomplished funambulist, to give his cultivated audience a twinge of fearful joy."[24]

Massine clearly separated the pantomime from the dance passages. Each expressive mode was reserved for one kind of character: melodic mime for the human beings, dance for the toys. For each toy, dance passages and stylized gestures were so narrowly idiosyncratic that even the toy's nationality was recognizable. It was precisely the absence of any superficially human qualities from the toys' movements and gestures that accentuated the internal human qualities with which Massine endowed them. Each character stood out as an individual, so much so that Sokolova felt that "the interpreters of even the smallest parts could flatter themselves that Massine had taken so much trouble to show them off to advantage as if they had been the stars of the ballet."[25]

For the creation of *Boutique*, Massine owed a debt to two major influences. The general pictorial sources can be traced to the paintings of Seurat and Toulouse-Lautrec, the inspiration for the ballet's period atmosphere and style (the male cancan dancer comes directly from Seurat's *Le Cirque*).[26] The ballet's language, its intricate footwork, derives from Massine's recent immersion in Spanish folk dance, especially flamenco. In *Boutique* he invented a new balletic language of the floor, with constant movement transitions of heel-toe-heel and frequent use of stomping. His choreographic effects tend toward self-containment (for which he was indebted to his classical training under Cecchetti), avoiding open and large movements. In the program notes, Diaghilev noted that Massine's "choreographic mind derives chiefly from the Spanish school

. . . which is what is termed in pictorial art 'miniature.' " [27] Alexandra Danilova, a ballerina who later was to be closely identified with the role of the cancan dancer, remembered: "What made Massine's choreography interesting was its *fantastique* rhythm. The rhythm was all in the feet, the way it is in Spanish dancing, which fascinated him . . . Massine would use heel work . . . His steps came from character dancing: the *farruca*, the *tarantella* . . . always the talking feet." [28]

Rehearsals were in progress, but Massine had yet to devise a finale. He had departed considerably from *Die Puppenfee*, introducing many new characters and imposing upon the work a satiric edge that required a new dénouement. Derain hit upon the solution—the fracas between the toys and the customers. [29] The clash between human and mechanical characters served as a safety valve for the ironic tension, and the image of the ousted customers peering through the shop window provided an object for the work's spirited ridicule and satire.

La Boutique fantasque was Massine's first contribution to a new genre that he himself created: the modern demi-caractère divertissement ballet, in which the dance and mime passages make up an organic whole, and the divertissement is essential in advancing the plot. One of the defining elements of this genre is the "Massine finale," a dramatic expansion of the coda of the traditional classical divertissement. The inner dynamic of Massine's finale is based on escalating tensions, the contrast in mood and tempo as individuals or groups of dancers join the ensemble, one after the other, in ever-increasing numbers, establishing the momentum leading to the climax. But such was Massine's emphasis on characterization that despite their cohesion as a group, the dancers retained their individuality as well as the specific meaning of their movements.

Derain designed a front curtain depicting two figures, a man with a guitar and a dancing woman. The stage decor consisted of a backdrop of arched windows overlooking an exotic bay with foliage and an old, white-wheeled paddle-steamer, and stage wings painted with charts and tables. London audiences lauded the designs and admired Derain's work for its simplicity. Ansermet commended him as "the first painter that I find very much a musician." [30]

The premiere was one of those rare occasions when an audience is completely carried away by its enthusiasm. Indeed, before the curtain had gone up the theater vibrated with the promise of an extraordinary feat. Beaumont had expected a full house but "was not prepared for the enormous audience that had gathered": [31] even the space in the back of the stalls had been taken, and the packed foyer was impossible to navigate. Throughout the performance there was continual applause, which swelled to roars of approval as Lopokova and Massine came on to dance the cancan, whereupon the full house screamed ecstatically: "Massine! Lopokova!" After the finale "the applause was literally deafening. But when the collaborators came forward to call in their turn, Derain was frightened at the warmth of his welcome and had to be dragged on the stage. Massine made repeated graceful bows while Lopokova, half crying, seemed divided between sadness and delight."[32]

London's reception of *La Boutique fantasque* was one of the greatest outpourings of love and acceptance accorded any theatrical event during the years immediately after the war, if not *the* greatest. The ballet won unanimous plaudits from the critics as well as the public and, said *Vogue,* was immediately elevated to the status of a "popular cult."[33] Britain was in need of an antidote to the ravages of war, something to divert its attention, even temporarily, from the depressing social, political, and economic conditions of postwar life. *La Boutique fantasque* fit the bill perfectly, and the public responded with elation. Although "the world was going awry . . . here before our eyes something was enacted which achieved perfection. We could console ourselves that man's powers were not decaying."[34]

As soon as Picasso arrived in London in early May, he vigorously set to work on *Le Tricorne.* Soon the top-floor studio across from the gallery entrance of the opera house (occupied today by offices and the Covent Garden Archives) was his center of operations, with sketches hung at eye level from the ceiling. Meanwhile, Vladimir Polunin and his wife, Elizabeth, busied themselves painting the scenery with their long-handled broom brushes. From the many surviving preliminary sketches one can sense the amount of work Picasso poured into the project. Studying the drawings proved instructive for Massine. He and Picasso held long discussions on the new ballet, and, as before, their talks inevitably came down to crucial aesthetic decisions. One pivotal issue was the recurring question of symmetry versus asymmetry in art. Picasso believed that symmetry was binding and rigid. He directed Massine's attention to his decor for *Le Tricorne,* pointing out that "if I put a house on the right, I do not put a house on the left."[35] From these discussions Massine drew the courage he needed to transform his own choreography; ever afterward he would consciously seek to avoid symmetry in his configurations (though it was not until the 1930s that his work achieved its broadest freedom in movement and spatial formation, when he began to make asymmetry a dominant feature of his symphonic ballets).

Picasso's designs for *Le Tricorne* began with a painted front curtain depicting a bullfighting arena, from which a dead bull is being dragged out by horses. Seated in an arched spectator's box are four women in traditional garb, complete with mantillas, and a man in a scarlet cape. A little boy selling oranges completes the tableau.[36] The arena scene was framed on each side by gray curtains. The front curtain enhanced the theatrical experience in much the same manner as had the curtain Picasso created for *Parade*. Picasso's decor, with very simple lines, in a style that seemed unrelated to cubism, presented a stage landscape in ocher, rose, and salmon. To the right stood the Miller's house, with a porch, a well, and a birdcage. The silhouette of a town could be seen beyond a bridge in the distance. Picasso took Diaghilev's suggestion and enhanced the Miller's home by adding a vine. The costumes were an elaborate collection of traditional regional attire in the spirit of Goya, combining black and gray with a riot of yellows, greens, blues, scarlets, pinks, and mauves.

As in *Parade*, Picasso wanted the front curtain visible during the playing of a prelude. Since Falla's score had none, Diaghilev hastily wrote to him in Madrid, requesting more music and relaying Picasso's idea that Falla use voices in this overture to enhance the emotional impact of the corrida scene.[37] Falla concurred and immediately began working on it.[38]

From Alarcón to Martínez Sierra to Falla—who also made some final additions to the ballet's libretto—the story of *Le Tricorne* had been radically simplified. In Falla's hands the first scene related the story. The second was an allegory that ended with an apotheosis symbolizing the people triumphant over an ineffectual monarchy.

The eighteenth-century tale, which remained the bedrock for Falla's inventions, recounts the intrigues of a miller and his beautiful wife and the attempts of the corregidor (the local governor) to seduce her. And Falla stays with this essential framework. First the Miller and then his Wife are introduced, followed by the Corregidor, who is borne aloft on a sedan chair and is about to make his way, accompanied by his faithful entourage, through the village. The Miller's Wife flirts shamelessly with him, but before the Corregidor can respond, the Miller returns, to the extreme consternation of the Corregidor, who sullenly leaves the scene. With the Governor gone, the Miller and his Wife join their neighbors in a joyous dance.

In the ballet's second part, the Corregidor, determined to seduce the Miller's Wife, arranges to get the Miller out of the way by having him arrested. He then returns to the Wife, who is now alone. They engage in a perilously seductive dance, during which she cleverly manages to send him off the side of the bridge into the mill stream below. She rushes off to find help. The Governor emerges from the stream, removes his wet coat, hangs it out to dry, and lies down to rest upon the bed inside the house.

The Miller returns home, sees his sleeping rival, and dons the Corregidor's coat. As the Miller turns to leave again, he stops and writes upon the wall: "Your wife is no less beautiful than mine."

When the Corregidor wakes to find his coat gone, he puts on the Miller's clothes. As he leaves the house he encounters police officers, who abuse him in the belief that he is the Miller. Villagers congregate, soon becoming an unruly mob. Undeceived by the Corregidor's disguise, the crowd surrounds him and the people take turns beating and berating him. At the finale the villagers, led by the Miller and his Wife, join in a celebration of the Governor's downfall and gleefully dance a mad *jota* as they roll his effigy into a blanket and toss it about.

At the beginning of rehearsals, the role of the Miller's Wife was assigned to Sokolova, with Woizikowski and Massine as the Corregidor and the Miller. Sokolova recalled: "Massine spent hours with me on the stage of the Alhambra in the afternoons, practicing Spanish dancing and working out scenes and numbers we were to do together. We did amazing things with our heads, hands, and arms, and tried out every combination of heel-beats which Massine had taken down from Felix or which he invented. . . . Diaghilev would sit patiently watching us: I think he enjoyed seeing us master the subtle steps."[39] Felix Fernández García, who also attended these rehearsals, "must have thought as he sat there how sadly he had been cheated: for he had taught Massine and the rest of us all we knew about Spanish dancing, and yet he was neither to dance the chief part in the ballet nor to have any credit for his share in the creation. It must have been too much for him to see Léonide, who was not even a Spaniard, dancing what was to all intents and purposes his own *farruca*."[40]

Earlier, in Spain, Massine had been apprehensive about giving the role of the Miller to Felix; now, in London, he had no doubt that Felix was both unsuited to the part and incapable of taking it over. Like most flamenco dancers, Felix was all spontaneity; his dancing was largely improvisational, and it was nearly impossible for him to perform the same step twice in succession. Massine wanted very much to give Felix an opportunity to dance, so he offered him the tarantella in *La Boutique fan-*

tasque.[41] But the result was a disaster. Sokolova recalls: "Massine gave him a metronome to help him learn the dance on time," but instead of being aided by this, Felix would simply "become nervous and hysterical."[42] The tarantella fell to Woizikowski. In another effort to make use of Felix, Massine tried him in the corps de ballet; but the only role in which he did well was the Peddler in *Petrouchka*, which allowed him to improvise as much as he wished.

Soon after the opening night of the Alhambra season, Karsavina joined the company and took over the role of the Miller's Wife in rehearsals of *Le Tricorne*. Although she had not seen Massine since the 1914 London season, when they had danced together in *The Legend of Joseph*, she soon realized that he now was clearly a different person. "I was strongly impressed," she wrote, "by the amazing development of Massine. . . . I found him now no more a timid youth . . . he now possessed accomplished skill as a dancer, and his precocious ripeness and uncommon mastery of the stage singled him out, in my mind, as an exceptional ballet master. It was his complete command of Spanish dancing that amazed me the most. On the Russian stage we had been used to the balletic stylization of Spanish dancing, sugary at its best, but this was the very essence of Spanish folk dancing."[43] Despite her confidence in Massine, though, Karsavina had serious misgivings about undertaking a part that she knew was inappropriate for her: unlike the others, she had not been immersed in Spanish culture. So, to inspire the ballerina, Diaghilev asked Felix to dance for her at the Savoy Hotel. Karsavina recalled the occasion:

> It was fairly late when, after supper, we went downstairs to the ballroom and Felix began. I followed him with open-mouthed admiration, breathless at his outward reserve when I could feel the impetuous, half-savage instincts within him. He needed no begging, and gave us dance after dance. In between, he sang the guttural songs of his country accompanying himself on the guitar. I was completely carried away, forgetful that I was sitting in an ornate hotel ballroom 'til I noticed a whispering group of waiters. It was late, very late. The performance must cease or they would be compelled to put the lights out. They went over to Felix too, but he took not the slightest notice. He was far away. The performance had given me something of the same feeling as listening to the gypsy singers of my own country—savagery and nostalgia. There, no hotel official would come to bring us brusquely back to earth again. To a Russian such a curfew is incomprehensible. A warning flicker and the lights went out. Felix continued

like one possessed. The rhythm of his steps—now staccato, now languorous, now almost a whisper, and then again seeming to fill the large room with thunder—made this unseen performance all the more dramatic. We listened to the dancing enthralled.[44]

The endless frenetic dancing at the Savoy was only the latest sign of Felix's disturbed mental state. His behavior, erratic enough before this episode, had marked him among the members of the company as an eccentric. But this evening and the dramatic events that followed made it clear that whatever gave Felix his tenuous hold on sanity was rapidly deserting him altogether. About his final descent into madness, Sokolova wrote:

It cannot have been more than two or three days after Felix had danced at the Savoy—and it may have been the very next morning—that his behavior at rehearsal became stranger than ever. We were working in the club room in Shaftesbury Avenue, where the men had to dress behind a sort of bar or cloakroom counter. Felix began to pop his head up from behind the counter, wearing different hats and making faces. This was quite funny at first, and we all laughed, but he would not stop. Grigoriev tried to control him without success, and as Felix kept on and on, appearing and disappearing in a variety of hats, one could feel a wave of concern go around the room. At lunch time he went off, with his metronome ticking. Leon Woidzikovsky followed him to the Hotel Dieppe in Old Compton Street, where he was staying, and found him lunching in his room—he was not allowed to have meals in the restaurant, as he behaved strangely and upset people. Felix was eating to the rhythm of the ticking metronome, stopping now and again to adjust it to a different speed. Leon could get no sense out of him and went away.

That night, when Felix should have been on stage he was discovered in the men's dressing room, his face spotted with a mixture of grease paints, grimacing at himself in the mirror. Nothing could be done about this while the performance was in progress, and by the time the ballet was over he was nowhere to be found. He did not return to his hotel, and his disappearance was reported. Later that night he was found doing a demented dance on the altar steps of a South London Church.[45]

Felix was certified insane and taken to a mental asylum at Epsom, where he remained until his death in 1941. Massine wondered if "the seed of his mental illness was not inherent to his genius."[46] Reluctantly, one wonders too if Felix was something of a sacrificial lamb in the creation of Massine's Spanish masterpiece.

As Massine put the finishing touches on his choreography, Picasso was also readying his second work for the stage. The Polunins found it a pleasure to work with him, for not only did he visit the studio daily to supervise the creation of his maquettes, he also took an active interest in the completion of the entire work. Picasso painted directly onto the decor the silhouette of the town in the distance and the seven stars in the sky, and as the Polunins prepared the colors and assisted him in other ways, he painted most of the corrida scene on the front curtain. To Vladimir Polunin, who had reproduced Bakst's elaborate designs, Picasso's decor was amazing in "its total absence of unnecessary detail; the composition and unity of coloring was astounding. It was just as if one had spent a long time in a hot room and then passed into the fresh air." [47]

Diaghilev's lighting design for the mise-en-scène graduated downward from a bright bleached quality for the first part of the ballet to, near the close, almost pitch darkness (with a hopeful dawn at the very end). According to Falla, the progression of the choreographic action and the orchestration was directly inverse to this lighting scheme; that is, in the first part the number of dancers was kept to a minimum in order to keep the focus on the principal characters, and the orchestra was limited by Falla to the size of "a chamber orchestra. Later, on the contrary, from the beginning of the second part the choreographic and orchestral elements gradually increase to culminate in the final dance." [48] Thus in the ballet's first part, which revolved around the personal conflict of the leading characters, the music was intimate, while in the allegorical second part it was more grandiose. According to Polunin, Diaghilev's gradations of lighting, from day to night and night to dawn, were quite effective: "The scene, owing to the presence of some soft reddish tints, acquired the aspect of a Japanese print which, so far from impairing its beauty, endowed it with a certain unexpected charm." [49] For Beaumont, "the disturbing brilliance of the day, and the cool, tender night pervaded the auditorium." [50]

The first performance of *Le Tricorne* was scheduled for July 22. Falla reached London several days in advance, but hours before he was to conduct the premiere he received a cable saying that his mother was critically ill. The company was very supportive, and Ansermet accompanied his friend to the station and saw him off. Sad to say, Falla never saw his mother alive again, for she died that very day. Ansermet conducted the premiere in his stead.

That night at the Alhambra Theater, as the stage was being readied for *Le Tricorne*, Picasso himself applied greasepaint to the faces of the policemen with a "mass of blue, green and yellow dots which under the stage lighting, gave . . . a pockmarked, ruffianly appearance."[51] He gave Woizikowski, the Governor, a most effective makeup, matched-up "dabs of the same blue which was used in the costumes of his bodyguard of policemen."[52] When the stage curtains parted to reveal Picasso's corrida scene, and Falla's vibrating rhythms were heard, shouts of "Olé!," the tapping of heels, and the click of castanets filled the theater. The evening's tone was set, its charged atmosphere established, and the delighted house roared its approval. When the final curtain came down on the *jota,* the entire audience was caught up in a sense of enchantment. The *Sunday Times* summed up the new work's artistic relevance: "In conception and workmanship it rivals all other stories of Russia, Italy, France, and the Orient, told with such splendor, colors and audacity in poetic movement."[53]

However, Picasso's constructionlike dresses and the grotesque colored makeup he employed to dehumanize the minor characters were most disturbing to some critics. For W. A. Propert, the moment the secondary characters entered, "one began to feel less at ease. The beauty began to fade with the insistence of those noisy dresses, dresses that never seemed to move with the wearers or assume the changing curves of their bodies, that looked as if they were cut in cardboard, harshly striped and rayed, with all their contours heavily outlined in black."[54]

In its final form, Alarcón's story line, with its sociopolitical satire and regional localization, was of secondary importance to the creators of *Le Tricorne*. The tale gave the ballet its narrative structure, but it was essentially an excuse for Falla, Picasso, and Massine to present a personal artistic expression of their feelings for Spain, its folklore, temperament, and way of life. Ethnic popular sources were vital to modernist artists, especially those from Spain and Russia, who found in folklore a strong source of inspiration. However, the goal of modernism was not to reproduce folklore but to take it as a point of departure, to stylize it while purging it of banality, and subject it to a process of purification to get closer to its essence. Falla, one of the greatest folklorists of his time, adhered to this principle completely, utilizing popular thematic sources only as a source of inspiration.

For Picasso, *Le Tricorne* occurred during an important transitional moment in his development, bringing about a fusion of predominant elements from his previous creative phase: cubism and his omnipresent concern for the concepts of space and perspective. If the front curtain and the characters of the acrobats in *Parade* already had hinted at a tendency toward a classically oriented aesthetic, then *Le Tricorne* signaled the neoclassical style that came to the fore soon after. As Marilyn McCully has stated, "*Le Tricorne* is a prime example of the synthesis of styles Picasso achieved at this time, and it was, perhaps more than any other, the project that helped him attain this synthesis."[55]

The lengthy period of collaboration and friendship between Falla and Picasso strongly influenced the young Massine. (He was twenty-four when *Le Tricorne* was premiered.) The choreographer already had been exposed to "ethnic modernism" through his association with the neo-primitivist/cubo-futurist Gontcharova and Larionov. Throughout the three-year apprenticeship that culminated in *Le Tricorne* he was able to extend ethnic modernism into its fullest choreographic possibilities.

Massine's work on *Le Tricorne* had been long and arduous, but the result was unquestionably gratifying. He saw in Karsavina's "virtuoso performance" all the "zest and sensuality of a Spaniard," and found that the "languorous, seductive movements of her first entrance quickly established the character of the Miller's bored, dissatisfied wife. . . ."[56] The choreographer also declared Woizikowski as the Corregidor a "wonderful grotesque character, all trembling lust and licentious leers."[57] Yet the personal high point of the ballet for Massine was the *farruca* he danced:

> I began by stamping my feet repeatedly and twirling my hands over my head. As the music quickened I did a series of high jumps, ending with a turn in mid-air and a savage stamp of the foot as I landed. Throughout the dance my movements were slow and contorted, and to the style and rhythm which I had learned from Felix I added many twisted and broken gestures of my own. I felt instinctively that something more than perfect technique was needed here, but it was not until I had worked myself up in a frenzy that I was able to transcend my usual limitations. The mental image of an enraged bull going in to the attack unleashed some inner force which generated power within me. I felt an almost electrical interaction between myself and the spectators. Their mounting excitement had the effect of heightening my physical strength until I was dancing with a sustained force that seemed far beyond my reach at other times. For one moment it seemed as if some other person within me was performing the dance.[58]

Beaumont was convinced that "few of those who saw the first night will have forgotten the color and bravura with which he invested his

The Miller in Le Tricorne, *in the early 1950s*

farruca, the slow snap of the fingers followed by the pulsating thump of his feet, then the flickering movement of his hands held horizontally before him, palms facing and almost touching his breast. All at once this gave place to a new movement in which his feet chopped the ground faster and faster until suddenly he dropped to the ground on his hands, and quickly leapt to his feet and stopped dead, his efforts greeted with thunderous applause."[59] The *farruca* invariably drove audiences into a delirious frenzy. Massine's charismatic stage presence, his ability to enthrall his audience, triumphed. Even motionless, he could marshal a degree of expressiveness that left the audience spellbound.

Le Tricorne is particularly noteworthy for its synthesis of classical movement with the basic styles of Spanish folk dance. Massine skillfully assimilated into his own personal idiom the *farruca,* the fandango, the *sevillana,* and the *jota,* without sacrificing their individual characteristics. Moreover, he used the internal dynamics of Spanish dancing, specifically that tantalizing quality of increasing-decreasing speed, "pursuit of tension, teasing, advancing and retreating,"[60] to establish a mood. He wrote: "*Le Tricorne* had begun as an attempt to synthesize Spanish folk-dancing with classical techniques, but in the process of evolution it emerged as a choreographic interpretation of the Spanish temperament and way of life."[61] Massine had created yet another genre: the modern folk-character ballet.

In homage to Goya, the three *Tricorne* collaborators devised the climactic *jota,* in which the whole ensemble joined to form a magical fresco in movement. Falla's musical inspiration had come from a 1917 visit with the painter Ignacio Zuloaga to Fuendetodos, Goya's native town; Picasso's costume designs sprang from Goya's art and style; and Massine borrowed the tossing of the effigy from his *El pelele.*

Boutique and *Tricorne* had made it apparent to most observers that Massine commanded an impressive range of talent. In a brief career, he had produced ballets on Russian and Spanish themes and had articulated styles that went from commedia dell'arte to the satiric comedy of manners to modernism. He had done wholly narrative ballets and ballets with no story line. And with each work he had enriched and extended his choreographic language. On the personal level, his exploration of new possibilities and his ever-vigilant struggle against repetition had grown out of his ideal of self-perfection. In a short three years, a new page had been turned in ballet history. Writing in *The New Republic* at the end of the Alhambra engagement, Clive Bell compared the "old" and the "new" ballet and concluded that Massine possessed "a creative genius and therefore an authority, which has carried the ballet to a degree of seriousness and artistic importance of which Nijinsky can scarcely have dreamt. It is extraordinary how thin and essentially unimportant the ballets of six years ago seem."[62] In Bell's estimation, only Fokine's *Petrouchka* held its own, yet even that,

> under the Massine influence . . . is something distinctly different from and superior to the Petrouchka of M. Fokine. M. Massine has emptied the puppets of their superfluous humanity, and the protagonists (when Madame Lopokova dances) are more doll-like than dolls, and the ballet, by becoming less theatrical, has become more of a work of art, and infinitely more dramatic . . . [Massine's] greatest achievement has been to rescue the ballet from "the stage"—I use the word in the commonest and most disobliging sense—putting it on the level of literature, music and the graphic arts. His idea of the ballet is an organized whole, detached from circumstance, and significant in itself. . . . The fact is, with his creative imagination and positive intelligence, M. Massine has realized the dream which Mr. Gordon Craig half dreamt, fumbled, dreamt again differently, and never came near realizing. He has given us "an art of the theater."[63]

Of Massine's many innovations, perhaps the most daring was a new kind of characterization. He sought to transfer the center of gravity from the audience to the work itself: the life of each character was to be understood from the interaction of all the characters and their theatrical reality rather than in direct presentation to the audience. Bell compared Karsavina, the embodiment of pre-Massine interpretive technique, with Lopokova, who embodied the new kind of dancer. Karsavina "communicates her gracious and attractive personality directly to the audience . . . ; when not preoccupied with purely technical subtleties, she is apt to express herself, not through the work of art she is interpreting, but immediately, as in conversation. There is complicity between her and the audience."[64] But Lopokova was likened to Mozart or Fra Angelico: "The point is that neither Mozart nor Fra Angelico, nor Lopokova, express themselves directly to the public. They transmute personality into something more precious. The public gets no raw material from them. They pour themselves into works of art from which the public might deduce what it can." Bell continued:

> Since to be a work of art, the ballet must have the detachment of a picture or a symphony, the mimes, it seems, should go through their motions as in

an imaginary screen between themselves and the rest of the world. They have relations with each other, with the music and the scenery, and with nothing else. They may be personal as they please on their own side of the curtain. It is because she sometimes crosses to ours that Madame Karsavina is not perfectly in key with the new ballet: whereas little Lopokova, bouncing in her box, making vivid contacts with every line and color on the stage, impressing her personality on each gesture of her own, and so helping to build up an organic whole, is the choreographer's first violin. In the difference between Madame Karsavina and Madame Lopokova is epitomized the essential differences between the old and the new ballet.[65]

Massine himself proved to be the quintessential actor-dancer, and London's cognoscenti paused to admire. T. S. Eliot wrote: "Massine . . . seems to me the greatest actor whom we have in London. Massine, the most completely unhuman, impersonal, abstract, belongs to the future stage." The poet felt that next to the "conventional gesture of the ordinary stage which is supposed to *express* emotion . . . the abstract gesture of Massine, which *symbolizes* emotion, is enormous." Massine's interpretations bore out Eliot's contention that emotion in art must be transmitted through physical images analogous to the emotion—what he came to call the objective correlative. Such images should derive not precisely from nature but from life experiences. In a similar vein, "the art of every actor is in relation to his own age, and would perhaps be unintelligible to any other. But as the age is not an instant, but an infinite span of time including part of the future, we can still, with our retrospective selves, appreciate such artistry as that of Bernhardt, though we move toward satisfaction in the direction which moves Léonide Massine."[66]

In Ouchy and San Sebastián, where Massine produced *Le Soleil de nuit*, *Kikimora*, and *Las Meninas*, he served his choreographic apprenticeship. Rome, where he fashioned *Les Femmes de bonne humeur*, *Contes russes*, and *Parade*, was the site of his initiation into the ranks of his profession. Then came the Alhambra season in London, where the creation of *La Boutique fantasque* and *Le Tricorne* led to his consecration as a hero in a new balletic age. He was bombarded with rave reviews and flurries of congratulatory letters and cables; he was inundated with invitations, adulation, recognition, and respect. He was sought after by both high society and the intelligentsia. Massine left London in August 1919 haloed in his own light and the light of no other. He was no longer a planet in the solar system of Serge Pavlovich Diaghilev.

London, 1920

CHAPTER 8

London, August 1919–Rome, February 1921

AFTER THE ALHAMBRA SEASON ended on July 30, Diaghilev and Massine left London for Paris, then proceeded on to their beloved Italy. Most of their vacation would be spent at the Lido in Venice and in Naples. In a familiar pattern, they spent their holiday preparing new works. This time a ballet based on the character of Pulcinella began to germinate.

But Italy also put Massine in a reflective mood. "I began," he recalls, "to think seriously about the work I had been doing since 1917, and although I felt I had made great advances in technique, I was far from satisfied with what I had accomplished. Now that I had thoroughly absorbed the theories of Blasis, Feuillet and Rameau, I realized that mere mastery of their notations would not help me to go beyond the so-called 'technical regime' of the classical tradition. In fact, I began to see that their work, if followed too closely, could limit the scope of my choreographic evolution."[1]

His personal life was not all he wanted it to be, either. After six years of a nomadic existence he yearned for the privacy of his own retreat, a home base. The Isole dei Galli beckoned again, and on this Neapolitan excursion Massine moved his dream of ownership a little closer to reality.

In Naples he and Diaghilev renewed ties with their friend Mikhail Semenov, whom they had last seen in 1917. That year, shortly after the exhibition of his art collection at the Teatro Costanzi in Rome, Massine had left the collection in Semenov's care. He also had authorized him to act in his behalf in securing the purchase of the Isole dei Galli. Unfortunately, the "negotiations had been prolonged because the numerous members of the Parlato family could not decide among themselves how much they wanted for [the property]."[2] Those negotiations were still going forward while Massine, on this present excursion to Italy, stopped to see the Semenovs in Positano and to take "another delightful trip to Galli." He became more committed than ever "to buy them, and hoped one day to go and live there."[3]

In September Massine and Diaghilev left Italy and returned to Paris to begin work on *Pulcinella*. Fragments from his past were coming together to make the subject appealing to him now. On his first visit to Italy in 1914 he had become fascinated by the commedia dell'arte. In 1917 he had been charmed by commedia dell'arte street performers in Naples; and that same year, while researching the genre for *Les Femmes de bonne humeur,* he had come across a manuscript, circa 1700, entitled *Les Quatre Polichinelles semblables.* He was beginning to see how a ballet based on Pulcinella might work.[4]

But *Pulcinella* remained in embryonic form in 1917. Preparations for producing it began only after Diaghilev's return to London from Spain in 1918. That year he obtained from the British Museum a sheaf of pieces then attributed to Pergolesi which he hoped to consider for the score. By September, at Diaghilev's direction, the musicologist E. van der Straeten had worked into a score selected movements from several of the sonatas for violin and bass (which are no longer thought to be by Pergolesi). Still more music came from the Bibliothèque Nationale in Paris, and the richest lode of all was found in Professor Ricci's Casa Musicale, a commercial outlet where copies of musical compositions from the Conservatorio di Musica in Naples were sold.[5] Diaghilev probably offered Picasso the commission to design *Pulcinella* in 1919, while the painter was in London working on *Le Tricorne*. In a June 10 letter to Stravinsky written in London, the conductor Ansermet mentions a projected "Pergolesi-Picasso" ballet.[6]

Ideas for *Pulcinella* kept blossoming. In Naples in 1919 Massine continued his research on the commedia dell'arte at the Royal Palace Library. Meanwhile, at the Conservatorio di S. Pietro a Mailla, Diaghilev found yet another collection of compositions by Pergolesi; on the strength of a preliminary selection from these he would later commission Stravinsky to orchestrate the ballet score. In *Expositions and Developments* Robert Craft quotes Stravinsky recalling that "the suggestion that was to lead to *Pulcinella* came from Diaghilev one spring afternoon while we were walking together in the Place de la Concorde: . . . 'I have an idea that I think will amuse you . . . I want you to look at some delightful eighteenth-century music with the idea of orchestrating it for a ballet.' When he said that the composer was Pergolesi, I thought he must be deranged. . . . I wasn't in the least excited by it. I did promise to look, however, and to give him my opinion. I looked, and I fell in love."[7] (Stravinsky errs in placing this conversation in the spring. It was in September, and before the month was out he was conferring with Diaghilev, Massine, and Picasso about the new ballet.)[8]

In truth, in the spring of 1919 relations between the impresario and the composer had been stormy. Between May and July they had quarreled bitterly through intermediaries over the royalties from *Firebird* and *Petrouchka*. And such bickering was not new. Their relationship in and out of the theater had always been plagued by feuds over money and over Stravinsky's loyalty to the Ballets Russes—and to Diaghilev. The staging of any Stravinsky work outside the Ballets Russes inevitably provoked Diaghilev's jealousy and possessiveness, especially when such efforts were successful, as the recent production of *L'Histoire du soldat* in Switzerland had been. Now, however, the complainant was Stravinsky, who accused Diaghilev of robbing him and threatened a lawsuit. Ansermet and Misia were called in to mediate the dispute, and the matter was settled just before Diaghilev and Massine left for their vacation at the end of July. Diaghilev may have still felt sour over the incident, though, since he deliberately avoided seeing the composer that August as he journeyed from Paris to Italy.[9]

Happily, a correspondence between Diaghilev and Stravinsky was resumed that same month, and by September all of the collaborators had arrived in Paris to begin working on *Pulcinella*. By then Stravinsky saw that "the proposal that I should work with Picasso, who was to do the scenery and costumes and whose art was particularly near and dear to me, recollections of our walks together and the impressions of Naples we had shared [in the spring of 1917], the great pleasure I had experienced from Massine's choreography in *The Good Humoured Ladies*—all this combined to overcome my reluctance."[10] He composed the tarantella between September 7 and 10; on the eighth Picasso gave him an inscribed drawing of two figures for the ballet. Diaghilev, Stravinsky, and Massine worked on the libretto and finished it in October.

Pulcinella was not the only ballet that Diaghilev hoped to mount in 1920 with Stravinsky's help. During their reunion in Paris, Diaghilev once again turned his attention to *Le Chant du rossignol,* which he had hoped to stage in Rome back in 1917. At that time, he had commissioned the futurist artist Fortunato Depero to create the scenery and costumes, but now Diaghilev much preferred to work with Henri Matisse.

Ever since his first collaboration, in 1917, with the painters of the school of Paris, Diaghilev repeatedly had tried to enlist Matisse for a Ballets Russes project. In September of 1919 the painter was at his residence in Issy-les-Moulineaux, on the outskirts of Paris, when Diaghilev and Stravinsky arrived unannounced one morning. Stravinsky played the piano score of *Rossignol* for Matisse, who responded with some ideas about decor and costumes.[11] The visitors tried to persuade Matisse to design the ballet, but he refused. As the days went by, however, his ideas continued to ferment; and when Diaghilev approached him again, he easily gave in.

With the collaboration of Stravinsky, Picasso, and Matisse assured, Diaghilev and Massine returned to London. The third ballet season had begun on September 20 at the Empire Theatre. Since the English premiere of *Parade* was the only novelty scheduled during the twelve-week engagement, Massine was able to devote himself to the new ballets. In October Diaghilev invited Matisse to come to London for a day, as an adviser.[12] Matisse's sojourn at the Savoy Hotel had been beautifully—cunningly—prepared for by Diaghilev, who immediately asked Matisse to remain in London not for twenty-four hours but for fifteen days, to supervise the execution of his designs. This opportunity tantalized Matisse, though he was hesitant about neglecting his other work in Paris. Diaghilev prevailed. Matisse would in fact remain in London for more than a month. Toward the end of his stay he was also persuaded by Diaghilev to design the ballet's front curtain.[13]

Matisse and Massine began to sketch out their conception of the ballet, agreeing that the overall look should be achieved through the precise allocation of color as on a canvas. "Those colors were the costumes," said Matisse years later. "The deployment of colors allows the decor's expression to remain the same. It is imperative that a great expression dominates the colors in order to create an ensemble without demolishing the harmony in the rest of the work."[14] In attaining this shared goal, Matisse admitted that he was aided by Massine, who understood what he was trying to achieve.[15] (Five years later, Matisse was terribly disappointed by Balanchine's revised version of the ballet, feeling that the original work had been turned into "a real candy jar.")[16]

During one of their Sunday outings, Matisse, Diaghilev, and Massine paid a visit to Felix Fernández García, whom Massine would continue to visit at the asylum until the outbreak of war in 1939.[17]

Matisse and Massine became fast friends during their collaboration in London. In subsequent years, during engagements in Monte Carlo, Massine made regular Sunday calls on the painter at his home in Nice. Matisse described these visits as the dancer's "Sunday recreation because the rest of the week was very hard on Massine."[18] In his autobiography Massine writes that in Matisse's flat in Nice "one of the best rooms was occupied by a giant bird cage. He had hundreds of exotic birds from all over the world, and was so proud of them that he carried about an official document testifying to the vocal range of his favorite nightingale."[19]* But after *Le Chant,* twenty years would pass before the two would collaborate again.

On December 20, 1919, the Ballets Russes completed its season at the Empire, then moved on to the Paris Opéra, where the season was to be divided into two engagements. The first would begin on December 24 and feature, on January 23, 1920, the French premieres of *Le Tricorne* and *La Boutique fantasque,* followed on February 2 by the world premiere of *Le Chant du rossignol.* The second engagement, slated to begin on May 8, would include the world premieres of *Pulcinella* on May 15 and *Le astuzie femminili* on May 27. During the early days of the run Massine prepared for the premiere of *Le Chant* while, at the atelier of the famous couturier Paul Poiret, Matisse supervised the building of the Emperor's sumptuous cape.[20]

Le Chant du rossignol, which was based on a story by Hans Christian

---

* Massine's recollection of seeing the painter's birds in his flat in Nice may actually come from later visits, for according to Matisse he had not yet acquired them at the time of the creation of *Le Chant du rossignol.*

Andersen, was highly praised by the French press. Louis Laloy wrote in *Comoedia:*

> *The most remarkable aspect of this version is the composition of the en-sembles. M. Massine is not only a ballet master who choreographs steps and formations, he is a painter who executed a series of moving tableaux in space. M. Henri Matisse has furnished decors of elegant simplicity and costumes whose brilliant colors lend themselves to the most divine combi-nations. M. Massine is thus able to exercise his inspiration without di-rectly copying the style of the Orient; instead he can imply the most daring essence of the style.*[21]

Massine's choreography depended on groupings that suggested sculpted images like those seen in Chinese porcelain, paintings, and screens. Sokolova found these groupings "ingenious": "They built them-selves up into flat friezes, rather in the way that acrobats do, but their bodies were packed tight and knitted close together, some men on one leg, some upside down resting on a bent arm, some in a kind of hand stand. These groups suggested to me the grotesque combinations of fig-ures on carved ivory boxes, and I wondered if it was from these that Mas-sine had taken them."[22]

Massine's groupings, in static, pyramid-like configurations, en-hanced the theatrical space. The close collaboration between choreogra-pher and designer was felt throughout the ballet:

> *One of Matisse's concerns in designing* Le Chant du Rossignol *was the manner in which individual costumes could be made to interact and com-bine. The sculptural poses and ensemble movement of the uniformly clad corps de ballet allowed the artist to think in terms of volumetrical model-ing. Matisse designed geometrically cut costumes for the Mourners and Mandarins that deliberately masked the curves of the body, thereby trans-forming the dancers into building blocks of Massine's accumulative archi-tectonic structures. When the costumes were isolated and placed in movement by the figures inside, they became part of an overall fluctuating pattern of stylized shape and color. The Mourners' all-encompassing white felt cloaks and hoods, appliquéd with midnight blue velvet chevrons and triangles, converted the dancer's figure into a planar surface—an ab-stract shape—as did the saffron yellow satin robes of the Mandarins. In scene two, matching his choreography to the spare design, Massine caused these alternately shimmering and absorbent surfaces to move "silently be-*

fore the pale background . . . like spirits passing at dawn . . . [as] the pale hand of Death was outstretched over [all]."[23]

The London critics, who first saw the ballet in July 1920, were not as enthusiastic about these innovations as the French press had been. *The Times* commented that although the dance of the Nightingale was "brilliantly designed and carried out," in it there was "something wrong between the dance and the music. It halts and wavers. . . ."[24] Ernest Newman of the *Sunday Times* declared that since the music was "mostly without rhythm, it has baffled even the genius of Massine to invent a satisfactory"[25] choreography for it. However, the *Daily Herald* admired the production for its theatrical ingenuity. "There are no big dancing opportunities but it is full of quaint devices, of curious and unexpected effects, and consistently remains a fairy tale. It is a fairy tale such as one would never have dared to see in the flesh. Who could have thought they would have lived to see the Emperor really walking on the backs of his courtiers—or, death defeated, see his funeral robes turn magically to an indescribable magnificence?"[26]

As the Paris Opéra engagement continued, Diaghilev and Picasso began an intense struggle over *Pulcinella*. Picasso's first thought was to move the setting to modern times, a notion that Diaghilev immediately rejected. The painter then produced preliminary sketches of a false proscenium framed by tiers of theater boxes, with a nocturnal Neapolitan scene at stage center. These, too, were turned down. According to Douglas Cooper, this particular design was probably inspired by the Teatro San Carlo in Naples. Cooper speculates that "the baroque tradition was probably considered too grand for the occasion, but it shows that from the start Picasso wanted to underline the artificiality of the action, its puppet show element, for the dancers would have to perform in the middle of the false theatre and in front of the inner stage."[27]

Picasso next offered a group of designs transposing the idea of a theater-within-a-theater to the Paris of the Second Empire. Diaghilev exploded in fury. Stravinsky writes that the "designs were Offenbach-period costumes with side-whiskered faces instead of masks. When he [saw] them, Diaghilev was very brusque: 'Oh, this isn't it at all,' and proceeded to tell Picasso how to do it. The evening concluded with Diaghilev actually throwing the drawings on the floor, stamping on them and slamming the door."[28]

Picasso submitted yet another version of the stage-within-a-stage before he produced his final decor, which consisted simply of three panels depicting a Neapolitan night scene. Between two houses a little street stretches away and disappears into a background where a solitary boat sits in the bay and a radiant moon hangs over Mount Vesuvius. Cyril Beaumont described it as a "cubist study in black, blue-grey and white, admirably conveying with a remarkable economy of means a moonlit street overlooking the Bay of Naples."[29] The stage was covered with a floor cloth whose surface was freshly painted white for each performance. As with *Le Tricorne,* Picasso's palette of soft colors for the decor contrasted with the traditional commedia dell'arte costumes of bright red, green, plum, rose, white, and black.

Since his arrival in Paris, Stravinsky had been drawn into the

> *frequent disputes which ended up in pretty stormy scenes. . . . Sometimes my orchestration proved a disappointment. Massine was composing his choreography to the piano reduction, which I was sending to him section by section as I made it from the orchestral score. It often happened that when I was shown certain steps and movements that had already been decided upon I saw to my horror that in their character and importance they in no way corresponded to the very modest volume of my little chamber orchestra. . . . The choreography had, therefore, to be altered and adapted to the volume of my music, and that caused them no little annoyance, though they realized that there was no other solution.*[30]

The completed *Pulcinella* was remarkable in its modernist juxtaposition of traditional and new elements. Stravinsky reinterpreted eighteenth-century melodies in his own musical idiom; Picasso's cubist decor stood in contrast to his traditional commedia dell'arte costumes; and Massine once more expanded his choreographic language by fusing Neapolitan folk dances and commedia dell'arte gesticulation with the academic balletic vocabulary.

Before the second Paris Opéra engagement in May, the Ballets Russes presented seasons in Rome, Milan, and Monte Carlo. During this period Diaghilev and Massine embarked on *Le astuzie femminili.* Diaghilev's avid pursuit of eighteenth-century Italian music had netted him the scores for *Les Femmes* and *Pulcinella,* and now, hoping for a third such success, he was eager to begin work on Domenico Cimarosa's opera. *Astuzie* was composed after Cimarosa's three-year residency in St. Petersburg, where in 1798 he had replaced Paisiello as director of the Italian Theater. The plot concerns a rich heiress who, refusing to wed her

Lubov Tchernicheva, Massine, and Vera Nemtchinova rehearsing Pulcinella, *1920*

guardian or the man her father chose for her before his death, in the end manages secretly to marry the man she loves. Diaghilev commissioned Ottorino Respighi to arrange the music and José María Sert to design the costumes. Massine would direct the movements of the singers in the opera—the first two scenes—and choreograph the ballet which was the work's third and final scene.

In Rome, rehearsals for *Le astuzie* were marked by the first violent creative disagreement between Diaghilev and Massine. "For the last scene," writes Massine, "which was supposed to be a performance of '*Ballo Russo*,' I devised a series of short divertissements. . . . When Diaghilev came to a rehearsal and saw what I was doing, he objected strongly. He said that the divertissements were entirely unnecessary and wanted to dispense with them. I, on the other hand, insisted that a suite of dances was entirely in keeping with the pervading eighteenth-century style of production. This led to a heated argument, but I finally persuaded Diaghilev to let me have my way. . . ."[31] According to Grigoriev, Diaghilev "wanted a connected suite of dances. Their arguments were interminable, but Massine held out. . . . They had, of course, argued before on points of detail. But hitherto Massine had always yielded to Diaghilev's reasoning. So this was a new departure; and whether or not it signified a rebellion on Massine's part, whether or not he had decided to assert himself, it marked in fact the opening of a rift between them, which was to widen as time went on."[32] In other words, Massine, knowing full well that Diaghilev was rigidly uncompromising toward the aesthetic convictions of others, signaled his determination to press new claims both for his own artistic territory and for personal autonomy. His surprising readiness for confrontation must have shaken the impresario. Unaccustomed to having his will thwarted, the man who brooked no disagreement gave in. Why? Was it because he could, or because he could not, see that Massine was after his freedom?

The tremendous success of the postwar London and Paris seasons secured the company's immediate continuity as well as Massine's reputation. To Diaghilev, his protégé's triumph was undoubtedly a source of deep satisfaction. He had sensed Massine's potential, advanced his education, nurtured him, and surrounded him with some of the most prestigious and innovative artists of the era. Indeed, Massine was Diaghilev's greatest creation—a young man made of uncommonly rich clay, which Diaghilev modeled largely for the realization of his own needs. But the mentor-pupil relationship was nearing a crisis, and their remaining months together would be an emotional and professional tug-of-war.

More than fifty years later, Massine regarded the *Astuzie* confrontation with Diaghilev as the "false daring of a young man who is convinced that he is right. The false authority due to age and immaturity."[33] But by then, of course, Diaghilev already had become for Massine an idealized figure, infallible and larger than life.

When the Rome and Milan engagements concluded, the Ballets Russes appeared in Monte Carlo for the first time since the war. From the principality they proceeded to Paris, where they arrived after an unexpected delay:

> On the day we were due to leave Monte Carlo for Paris a railway strike started. Diaghilev was in despair, for our engagement in Paris was scheduled to begin in four days time. Fortunately, at the last minute we heard that there was one train leaving Monte Carlo with four sleepers, enough for Diaghilev, Karsavina, Matisse and myself. Early next morning, as we were speeding toward Paris, I was suddenly aware of a violent jolting, and a heavy ashtray hit me on the nose. The train had been derailed, and turned over on its side. . . . When I climbed out of the carriage I found Diaghilev

and Karsavina a bit shaken, but not injured. Matisse too had emerged safely, and as we all stood there in dazed bewilderment one of the passengers took a photograph of us. We were at a small place called Bar le Duc, about three hours from Paris, and we heard afterwards that a group of strikers had deliberately cut through the railway line. I can still remember standing there in the cold morning air, staring in amazement at the smashed locomotive with the rails jutting up like a broken iron fence.[34]

The four travelers were driven to Paris.

At the Paris Opéra, the premiere of *Pulcinella* on May 15, 1920, marked another triumph for Massine. André Levinson reported:

Just as Stravinsky in the enchanting score has confined the gushing melodies that might be by Pergolesi within a sarcastic harmonic scheme, where the trombone utters insolent persiflage and the bassoon hiccoughs asthmatically, so Massine has used the technique of classic virtuosity in an ironic sense. He treats the great "temps d'école" (like the double turns in the air, the caper or that brilliant ornament the "fouetté") as so many comic themes, expressing the exuberance and mannerisms of cavaliers costumed by Picasso. The "classic" is no longer the grand style, abstract and synthetic. It is used purposely to create character in the same way that the czardas, the bolero and the jig were used in the classic Coppélia. *Only now the roles are reversed. In* Pulcinella *the traditional steps are used to stylize the pantomime.*[35]

When the ballet was premiered in London on June 10, it was warmly received by the British press. Richard Capell wrote in the *Daily Mail:* "It is a comic view of the human puppet show. It looks through the spectacles of the eighteenth century's dry fun and crackling wit.[36] *The Observer* wrote that "the lapses from Italian melodious purity into unadulterated Stravinsky do not jar, as Massine's wonderful choreography follows the changes with such understanding that the dancers—the perfect ensemble—seem to take the lead, and the orchestra merely to follow their spontaneous movements." [37] For Cyril Beaumont:

The whole production was dominated by Massine as Pulcinella, for which character he had invented all manner of grotesque steps, obviously inspired by a careful study of the many pictorial representations of the Mask in question. Massine's dancing was particularly interesting for the way in which he caused certain steps to be expressive in themselves. Remember, too, that his features were almost hidden by his bird-like mask. Yet it was extraordinary to observe how, by the tilt of his head and the angle of his body, and by the varying speed and variety of his movements, he was able to suggest his thoughts and emotions. When I saw his subtle, intensely expressive, and beautifully timed dancing, I was reminded of Garrick's comment on the Italian harlequin Carlin—"Behold how the very back of Carlin has a physiognomy and an expression."[38]

The choreography for each character became a stylistic manifestation of that character, so that while the "two gallants and the girls . . . were cast in a modish vein,"[39] the peasant Pimpinella's dances were rooted in folk style. Edward Dent, writing in *Athenaeum,* called it a "more elaborate *Parade.*"[40] Stravinsky felt that in *Pulcinella* "all elements—subject, music, dancing, and artistic setting—formed a coherent and homogeneous whole."[41]

While Paris was not much taken by *Le astuzie femminili,* the second premiere (May 27) of the Opéra season, the ballet was a tremendous success in London. Ernest Newman wrote in the *Sunday Times:*

There must be a good deal of eighteenth-century light opera that is worth reviving (Mozart by no means exhausted the vein), and apparently it is to M. Diaghilev that we must look for the revivals, for only he, with his thorough methods of preparation, and his equal understanding of all the elements of a production, can deprive us of any excuse for condescension towards these old works. This rippling, sparkling music should be the delight of the town. The new principles of gesture and movement that Massine has gone upon for the opera singers deserve more detailed consideration than I can give them today: briefly, no gesture is made that is not necessary and pertinent. The acting thus wins a curious and paradoxical repose as well as an animation. Massine's ballet (that follows the opera) is one of the most beautiful creations of the extraordinary young genius; it has the quiet harmony that one or two of his later inventions, brilliant as they have been, have lacked.[42]

Edward Dent congratulated Massine as an opera director by remarking that "in the operatic part M. Massine has really succeeded in carrying out convincingly what only a very few producers have even attempted before. . . . What M. Massine has realized is that formal music requires formal movements and groupings. There is no attempt at realistic acting.

Nor are there any of the usual ridiculous movements which we associate with operatic acting. The singers at every moment form a composed group. . . . It is perfectly simple, harmonious and expressive."[43] The choreography for the ballet scene was a variation of the Petipa divertissement which included a pas de trois, a pas de six, a tarantella, a *pas rustique,* a *contredanse* for eight couples, a classical pas de deux, and the finale.[44] Massine juxtaposed numbers based on character dances, such as the tarantella, with numbers strictly based on the *danse d'école,* such as the pas de deux. Diaghilev incorporated the *Astuzie* ballet into the repertory in 1924, and it was thenceforth called *Cimarosiana.*

When the second season at the Opéra ended, the Ballets Russes moved back to England. In June and July at Covent Garden the company performed *Pulcinella, Astuzie,* and *Chant du rossignol.* Diaghilev and Massine then left London for the Lido. On this holiday, however, Massine set aside valuable time for himself. Diaghilev had entrusted him with launching a revival of *Le Sacre du printemps,* and on his own Massine went to Switzerland to discuss the project with Stravinsky.

In autumn the Ballets Russes toured the provinces in Britain. After performances in Liverpool and Birmingham Massine returned to London—surprisingly, without Diaghilev. With him instead were Sokolova, who had been cast as the Chosen Virgin in *Le Sacre,* and Vera Savina, who came along so that Massine could coach her in *Les Sylphides.* On this sojourn in London the delicate balance between Diaghilev and Massine finally collapsed.

Savina, the English Vera Clark, was born in Hempstead on July 12, 1897. The daughter of Jane Helen Kerasly and Ralph Clark, a post office clerk, she received her early training at Stedman's Academy in London, but truly grew as a dancer under the tutelage of Maestro Cecchetti. She had joined the Ballets Russes in 1918. Two years younger than Massine, she was small and technically strong, "with well formed limbs and exceedingly attractive head, blonde, slightly suggestive of [the ballerina Lydia] Kyasht at times."[45] According to Arnold Haskell, she suffered from "stage modesty probably due to her English temperament."[46] She created the role of the female poodle in *La Boutique*; and according to Beaumont, Massine created the *Astuzie* pas de deux for her, although the premiere was given to Karsavina. Savina later danced it brilliantly. Sokolova said that she had "a lovely, long jump with delicate hand and arm movements"[47] and that her dancing of the Mazurka in *Les Sylphides* was done "beautifully and with a wonderful quality of lightness."[48]

Two forces in Savina's life were about to collide, and nothing would be the same for her once they did. First, Diaghilev recently had chosen her to learn the Mazurka, a sure sign of his high hopes for her as a future ballerina. Second, Massine fell in love with her. Sokolova would later write of Savina that "being English and not speaking two words of Russian, [she] was as innocent as a new-born lamb, and she was the only person in the company who had no idea of Massine's situation. But Massine had fallen in love with her. Without realizing any of the implications, she must have been flattered."[49] It must have been liberating for Massine to feel someone utterly unlike Diaghilev responding to him emotionally, guilelessly, passionately. Savina's return of his affections probably emboldened him, too. Here at last, in the flesh, was a personal, obvious challenge to Diaghilev.

From London the Ballets Russes went to Paris for a season at the Théâtre des Champs-Elysées, where Massine's version of *Le Sacre du printemps* received its world premiere. The first choreographic version had been the powerfully erotic handiwork of Nijinsky, and its premiere at the same theater on May 29, 1913, had marked one of the great theatrical scandals of the century. Stravinsky had lauded Nijinsky's controversial choreography at the time, but by 1920 the composer was openly expressing dissatisfaction with it. The essence of his complaint was that Nijinsky had become "subjected to the tyranny of the bar"[50] in trying to achieve a perfect metrical synchronization between the choreography and the music. When Diaghilev offered to produce a new version of the work, Stravinsky, sensing that a whole new estimation of *Le Sacre* lay in prospect, eagerly collaborated with Massine. Before rehearsals began, as the two men discussed the music at length, Massine's own concept of *Le Sacre* began to take shape. His idea was to attempt "a counterpoint in emphasis between it [the music] and the choreography."[51] The solution lay in creating "a bridge over certain passages of music not counting every bar and every note, and to create a counterpoint over it, then, to create another bridge over other passages of so many bars. . . . I did not account each bar as an individual thing to choreograph. From here to there I do a bridge and I do my own rhythm as I felt I should."[52] Stravinsky readily agreed, and the choreographer began to formulate the work.

Neither man hesitated to discard the original libretto. Massine in particular, in a clear departure from his recent work, looked forward to producing a work void of all literal story, one emerging solely out of a synthesis of music and dance. According to the program notes, "*Le Sacre du printemps* is a spectacle of pagan Russia. The work is divided in two parts and has no subject. It is choreography. It is choreography freely created to the music." As the composer himself commented, "[Massine] and I have suppressed all anecdotal detail, symbolism, etc. [that might] obscure this work of purely musical construction. . . . There is no story at all and no point in looking for one."[53]

In fashioning the choreography, Massine "studied numerous archaic Russian icons and wood carvings and found no justification for the bent wrist and ankle movements which Nijinsky had used. I therefore decided to base my production on the simple movements of the Russian peasants' round dances, strengthened when necessary by the use of angular and broken lines which I had evolved from my study of Byzantine mosaic and perhaps unconsciously also from the captivating spirit of cubism."[54] This *Sacre* would depend on the juxtaposition and counterpoint of groups, and on the contrast between tensed, heavy movements and light ones. To set the work consistently in abstract dance terms, Massine used less exaggerated gestures and a cleaner, classical vocabulary. One example was the choreography for the Chosen Virgin. Though Massine gave this dance a barbaric intensity and emotion, he filled it with recognizable *danse d'école* steps such as *grands jetés en tournant* even as, through stylization, he distorted them.

Sokolova, one of five remaining members of the company who had danced in Nijinsky's *Sacre*, described the differences between the two versions.

> *This was a typical Massine production, clear-cut and methodical, with each group counting like mad against the others, but each holding its own. In Massine's choreography nothing was ever left to chance, and if anybody was in doubt about what he had to do or why he had to do it, he had only to ask and everything was explained. I think it was lucky for Massine that he had never seen the Nijinsky production, which had been staged a year before he joined the company: he might have felt obliged to imitate something which had been conceived in a style quite alien to him. The Nijinsky ballet had a sadness about it, with its groups of ancient men with enormous beards, trembling and shuffling. . . . It was a vague work, far less complicated and accurate than Massine's.*[55]

Massine gave Sokolova her greatest triumph as the Chosen Virgin. She describes the choreography:

There were some enormous sideways jumps, which had to be performed very slowly, and every second one had an extra movement in it. . . . The steps Massine had invented for my sacrificial dance bore so little relation to any kind of dancing that had ever been done before and were so violently contrasted one with the other, and followed each other so swiftly with such sudden changes of rhythm, that I think the impression I gave was of a creature galvanized by an electric current. The dance was tragic: it evoked pity and terror.[56]

Grigoriev wrote:

Massine's choreography was highly expert, but to my mind lacked pathos, in which it differed notably from Nijinsky's. It was as if Massine had paid greater heed to the complicated rhythms of the music than to its meaning; and the result was something almost mechanical, without depth, which failed to be moving. Nijinsky's version, comparatively helpless though it was, had better captured the spirit of the music, and whereas it had brought out the general theme and, in particular, the contrast between the two scenes, these somehow became obscured in Massine's composition.[57]

A grateful Stravinsky commended Massine's efforts, explaining to the press, first in Paris and later in London, how Massine had allowed the music and dance to free and not restrict one another:

What enlightened Massine was to hear [Le Sacre] in concert. . . . Thus from the first he perceived that, far from being descriptive, the music was an "objective construction." Massine does not follow the music note by note, or even measure by measure. . . . Take, for example, this measure of four followed by one of five: Massine's dancers stress a rhythm of three times three. . . .

The choreographic construction of Nijinsky was one of great plastic beauty but subjected to the tyranny of the bar: that of Massine is based on phrases, each composed of several bars. This last is the sense in which is conceived the free connection of the choreographic construction with the musical construction. . . . [Le Sacre] exists as a piece of music, first and last.[58]

When Massine's *Sacre* was premiered in Paris on December 15, 1920 (performed in its entirety before the stark backcloth that Nicholas Roerich had designed solely for Part Two of Nijinsky's production), the reception was mixed. In *La Revue Musicale* Emile Vuillermoz, piqued by Stravinsky's pronouncements, counterattacked in a four-page vindication of Nijinsky's choreography, accusing the composer of "ingratitude" toward his previous collaborator, especially when Stravinsky declared that it was "Massine who made him understand the real meaning of his work." Vuillermoz found Massine's version "less novel and less personal" than Nijinsky's.[59] Levinson commented:

> [Massine] denies, with—it would seem—the consent of the composer, the magnificently human motivating basis of the work to conform to a purely abstract conception, which has been consciously emptied of all significance. He simplifies the actions by eliminating all historical reminiscence, all archeological association. To be sure the theatre is not a museum, but Massine filled the void with a succession of illogical movements of niggardly design, without plastic reason for being. Mere plastic exercises, denuded of all expression.[60]

For Jean Bernier, Massine's dancers were men and women rather than anthropological, mythic archetypes, though they belonged to a primitive tribe. "It is not a question of ballet; Léonide Massine dictates a sacred ceremony. Only instinct—no longer science or taste—is his master, his demon. . . . Symbolist with Nijinsky, *Sacre* by Massine is brutal, of implacable realism." For Bernier it was "an explosion of life."[61]

Julie Sasonova felt that "it presented a tremendous contrast to the ethereal classical dance. . . . The male dancers underlined their efforts in lifting the inert bodies of the women. The final dance was a frenzy . . . that seemed to be carved out of stone, so strongly was it permeated with the sensation of weight—one of the rare occasions that Diaghilev's ballet was a precursor of modern dance technique. It was as if Massine wished to show the expressiveness and the constructive possibilities of the contrast between weight and lightness."[62]

In June of the following year the ballet's abstraction was roundly decried in London. Said the reviewer for the *Morning Post*: "Mr. Massine has turned his back on any idea so definite as the ceremonial action which Mr. Nijinsky fitted to the music eight years ago."[63] According to *The Times*:

> There is no drama, no story; only a passionless ritual, in which the men lunge and spar at one another, and lift the women on their shoulders. In the second scene the Chosen Virgin stands in the centre of the stage in a

striking pose, the other participants grouped around her. Sometimes they cluster closely and indulge in a curious spasmodic quiver. At last the chosen one deigns to move in a high-leaping, ungainly dance which is at least a triumph of calisthenic skill. The others leave her to herself; her dance becomes more extravagant, till at last she falls to the ground exhausted. That is all that happens, and through it all Stravinsky's orchestra tears its way in ever-increasing harshness.[64]

Massine's *Sacre* remained in the Ballets Russes repertory off and on until the company's final season in London in 1929. Although by then Diaghilev was in poor health and his visits to the theater were rarer, he did show up at Covent Garden to see *Le Lac de cygnes* and *Le Sacre du printemps*. According to the critic P. W. Manchester, in its 1929 revival at Covent Garden *Le Sacre* achieved a triumph greater than its successes of 1913 and 1920. In the gallery the audiences "were stomping and screaming and yelling and you thought the place would come down that night."[65] *The Times*'s critic declared Massine's version the true landmark: "The revival of Stravinsky's *Le Sacre du Printemps* was devised, no doubt, to form the climax to the season of the Diaghilev Ballet. . . . It is the charter of the modern ballet. . . . After its first presentation, Léonide Massine designed a choreography which not only freed it from the vulgarity of story-telling, but even eschewed any recognisable symbolism or 'programme.' . . . *Le Sacre* is 'absolute' ballet and we are assured that it will come to be regarded as having a significance for the 20th Century equal to that of Beethoven's Choral Symphony in the 19th."[66]

Massine's turn to abstraction in *Sacre* shows him extending his expressive grasp, reaching out to include ballet freed from literal story in favor of the pure integration of music and dance. This not-quite-conscious sense of mission, which intensified during the 1920s, set in motion a developing aesthetic that came to fruition during the next decade with his abstract symphonic ballets. From the 1930s to the end of his life these abstract ballets would continue to appear alongside his dramatic works. He felt especially close to *Le Sacre*, reviving it on four more occasions during his lifetime.

As the season at the Théâtre des Champs-Elysées advanced, so did Massine's pursuit of Savina. Sokolova remembers:

It was about six in the evening, and the place was dark. Vera Savina was standing in the far corner of the stage, when Mme. Sert suddenly came through a door nearby. Misia Sert was a clever, attractive woman of the world, besides being Diaghilev's devoted friend, and there were no secrets between them. Crossing the stage, I overheard Vera say, "Mme. Sert, have you seen Mr. Massine?" "No, Verotchka. Did you want him for anything in particular?" "I have an appointment with him." At this, of course, Mme. Sert pricked up her ears—and so did I. "Oh? Where is your appointment?" "At the Arc de Triomphe, but it's such a big place I don't know exactly where to meet him." "Then," said Mme. Sert, "I should stand right in the middle of the arch if I were you." I was staggered by this, but said nothing. I imagined Misia hurrying off to tell Diaghilev about the appointment, and Vera standing in the centre of the Etoile, waiting in vain.[67]

It was highly probable that Diaghilev was already aware of the latest developments, and Misia's discovery would only have confirmed his misgivings. One day Sokolova

heard Massine calling to me. His room was next to mine, and the door was open. As I walked in, Léonide Feodorovitch congratulated me for the first time in my life. He said, "We could not have achieved this work without each other." I was surprised and touched. I told him I was grateful for all he had done for me. He put his hands on my shoulders and kissed me quite naturally on each cheek. This was done with such sincerity, and I was so overwhelmed to hear these words from the handsome Massine, who never praised anybody, that I returned his embrace with emotion. As he moved away he suddenly froze. Looking round, I saw Diaghilev standing in the doorway. Without a word, he walked past me. I mumbled something and slipped out, leaving an icy atmosphere behind.

Diaghilev must have known at this time that Massine was interested in someone, but I think he may have been uncertain whether it was Savina or [me]. As Mme. Sert had undoubtedly passed on the information about the rendezvous under the Arc de Triomphe I suppose that his suspicions now rested on Vera.[68]

At the dinner after the premiere of *Le Sacre du printemps*, Savina

was seated half-way down the table, and as the evening went on the Diaghilev group began to rag her unmercifully. As she spoke no Russian she was an easy butt. She wore a short pink dress with shoulder-straps, which looked very English among all these sophisticated gowns by Lanvin and Chanel. There was a lot of laughter and they kept saying, "Have a little more champagne, Verotchka." ... Diaghilev must have been anxious about Massine; and Massine must have been longing for some sort of life of his own with Vera. I should have liked to sit quietly listening to Stravinsky, who could be very amusing, and who had, besides, many complimentary things to say about my performance. However, our conversation was interrupted by Massine who jumped to his feet and climbed onto the piano.

"Quiet, everybody!" he shouted. "I have an announcement to make." There were a few encouraging cheers, then everybody was silent. We all realized that he was tight, for he was much too quiet and well-behaved in the normal course of events to make any demonstration.

"The time has come," he said. "I have made up my mind that I am going to run away."

Everyone shouted, "Come on! Tell us who with. Who is it to be?"

"There's no secret about it," cried Massine. "I am going to run away with Sokolova."

The guests all cheered and laughed, taking this for a great joke—pretending to think it funnier than they did—since they were all embarrassed. Diaghilev ... can have found it no more amusing than I did. Massine jumped off the piano, came round the table to where I sat petrified, and kissed my hand. ... I could not imagine what had possessed Léonide Feodorovitch. Was it just a bit of nonsense on the spur of the moment? Was he trying to annoy Diaghilev, in a spirit of frustration? Or was he trying to put him off the scent?[69]

Throughout the Paris season Diaghilev was ill-tempered and irritable. During a lighting rehearsal he asked Grigoriev:

"What would you think if Massine suddenly left us?" This was so unexpected I merely looked surprised; so Diaghilev went on: "Yes," he said, "we are to part." As soon as I could collect my thoughts, I answered that as a dancer Massine could certainly be replaced. But as a choreographer—to replace him at all quickly would be extremely difficult. "You think so?" asked Diaghilev, as if not so sure. Then looking at his watch, he asked me to continue by myself; after which he stood up and went away, leaving me much perturbed.[70]

According to Grigoriev, the "season in Paris ran its customary course; and the only evidence Diaghilev exhibited of the private conflict that was distressing him was that he showed less than his usual interest in the details of our performances. He looked more and more sombre, however; and it was clear that his relations with Massine were rapidly deteriorating."[71]

By New Year's Eve, when the company moved to Rome to open a season at the Costanzi on January 1, Massine's involvement with Savina had become so serious that Diaghilev had hired detectives to follow the pair about and report on their activities. Massine was not intimidated and pursued Vera openly.[72] Diaghilev's next, clearly desperate, tactic was to offer Savina a contract that would assure her of leading roles in the company—if she would leave Massine.[73] Beneath Diaghilev's outlandish bullying and manipulation was the devastating pain he was experiencing in watching his lover go. But Massine had reached the point of no return.

Stories about the remaining emotionally strenuous days abound. One of the most unpleasant has Diaghilev inviting Savina to his room, getting her drunk, stripping her naked, then throwing her into Massine's room next door.[74] Grigoriev writes that one day in Rome he was summoned by Diaghilev and

found him in a state of great agitation. "I am definitely parting with Massine," he declared. "I have come to the conclusion that we can no longer work together. His contract has expired; and I should like you, as régisseur, to inform him before today's rehearsal that I have no more need of his services, and that he may accordingly consider himself at liberty." Diaghilev's face was flushed as he told me this, and he could not keep still, but kept walking up and down the room. I knew, as before over Fokine, that it was useless to argue or make any attempt to overpersuade him. So I remained silent; on which, realizing that I did not agree, he continued even more heatedly. Hadn't he, he cried, done everything for Massine? Hadn't he made him? What had Massine's contribution been? "Nothing but a good-looking face and poor legs!" And now, when, owing to Diaghilev, he had become the dancer and choreographer he was; when, working together, they could have created the most wonderful things—everything had collapsed and they must needs part company!—His voice was full of pain and bitterness. He grew more and more agitated, and continued his pacing to and fro. Then he poured himself out a glass of wine, which he drank off quickly, and, suddenly controlling himself: "So, my dear Serge Leonidovich," he said, "go and deliver my message, please. We'll talk further about this later on."[75]

When Massine arrived at the rehearsal, Grigoriev "immediately took him aside and gave him Diaghilev's message."[76] The choreographer "went deathly pale and turned and walked out of the room."[77] According to Grigoriev, "that night Massine called on me and asked me in detail what Diaghilev had said. I told him as much as I could, adding that I was convinced no power on earth could make Diaghilev revoke his decision. Massine agreed that this was probably so; after which we shook hands and said goodbye."[78] In the theater that evening Sokolova "went to see Vera to find out what was going on, but her dressing-room was empty. I asked the wardrobe mistress where she was and was told she had been put upstairs. I traced her to a room at the top, which she was sharing with three other girls. She had been banished to the corps de ballet . . . I told her she must stand by Massine whatever happened."[79] On February 2 Savina was replaced in a lead role in *Les Sylphides* and Massine's performance as Petrouchka was canceled.

Diaghilev disappeared for several days. Only Walter Nouvel and the impresario's servants were close to him during his collapse. They "feared for his health and even for his reason" and "watched him anxiously day and night."[80] When he finally "emerged, he had such black rings under his eyes that he was barely recognizable."[81]

For Diaghilev, forty-nine years old, the familiar story was repeating itself: a younger man he had skillfully shepherded to international acclaim now fought free of his grasp. Yet he maintained that his attachment to Massine possessed a unique dimension, unlike his liaisons with earlier or future lovers. He eventually called Massine "the most brilliant mind I have ever met in a dancer."[82] Nevertheless, according to Serge Lifar, after their breakup Diaghilev would also blame Massine for all his future misfortunes, including the diabetes that ended his days. No clear resolution of the affair would be possible for him. He once said that of all the friends he had loved, none but Massine had "provided him so many moments of happiness or anguish."[83]

Apparently no civil parting, arrived at in mutual respect, was feasible. In their final months together Massine's need for independence grew stronger, while Diaghilev grew more truculent, turning vicious when faced with his inevitable loss. One can see Massine driving him to the breaking point. First came the artistic disagreement over *Le astuzie*, with the choreographer tenaciously and victoriously holding his ground. Then came a demand by Massine that he be given the title of *maître de ballet* during the final Paris season. Diaghilev at first rejected this out of hand, then complied after the creation of *Le astuzie*—compromising, bitterly, one final time. But Massine, twenty-five years old, forged ahead without regard for the consequences.

PART THREE

The 1920s

*The man who has achieved intellectual
freedom is not so much a traveler towards
a goal as a wanderer on the face of the earth.*

—NIETZSCHE

Massine with Nicolas Efimov in Les Fâcheux, *1927*

CHAPTER 9

Rome, February 1921–Paris, September 1928

NO LONGER UNDER the protection and guidance of Diaghilev, Massine now had to answer life's most persistent question for himself: which way should he go next? Ever since his departure from Russia in 1914, his "life and work had been entirely bound up with the Ballets Russes."[1] In a letter to Anatoli Petrovich written just after the company's departure for South America in 1917, the lonely youth had disclosed that "I have affection for the company as if it was my family."[2] Now, separated from the company once more, he again "felt abandoned and alone."[3] But he proved more resilient than his dejected tone would suggest and before long had taken control of his situation. He had much in his favor: youth, fame, and connections to a network of well-placed, powerful insiders he was soon to exploit brilliantly.

It is difficult to assess Massine's finances at the time of his breakup with Diaghilev. As a member of the Ballets Russes—a company chronically short of cash—he never had been able to save much; so when he was dismissed he was probably not financially secure enough to support Savina and himself indefinitely. But for the moment the happy couple showed no signs of money worries.

One reason may have been Massine's knowledge that he had his valuable art collection to fall back on. Back in December 1917, to keep the collection safe from Diaghilev's maneuvering, he had wired his friend Semenov in Italy to "protect it against all eventuality."[4] Diaghilev had been corresponding with Semenov during this same period, and it is possible that he had proposed the sale of some of the paintings as a stopgap measure to alleviate his own financial problems.[5]

Massine began to enjoy his new life, proudly squiring his future bride to Rome's museums, libraries, and monuments. He also immersed himself in planning future ballets.

By the second week of February, he had his first offer of work. The Italian impresario Walter Mocchi, of Rome's Teatro Costanzi, asked Massine to organize a small ballet company to tour a chain of theaters Mocchi managed in Brazil, Argentina, and Uruguay. The troupe would present ballet programs and also appear with Mocchi's touring opera company. Massine immediately set to work.

He invited Jan Kawetzky, a dancer from the Ballets Russes, to join the venture as régisseur. Kawetzky, unhappy with Diaghilev, seized the moment and quickly recruited other defectors, including Gala Chabelska, Kostecki, Statkiewicz, Grabowska, Edinska, and Norwicka. (Still another group of dancers would join this contingent once the company reached South America.) But Massine's personal attempts to lure Stanislas Idzikowski into leaving Diaghilev proved unsuccessful.[6] With Kawetzky in charge of assembling the dancers, Massine began to prepare the repertory. First he acquired the rights to the music for two of his own ballets, *Les Femmes de bonne humeur* and *Le Tricorne,* and to several pieces that he could use in the future, including Satie's *Gymnopédies,* Liadov's Eight Russian Folk Songs, and the March and Dance from Glinka's *Ruslan and Ludmilla.* A number of sources came through with material: Falla, the music publishers Ricordi, J. and W. Chester, and Durand et Cie, the archives of the Opéra-Comique. Massine then commissioned composer Gian Francesco Malipiero to orchestrate four dances by Cimarosa and a selection of pieces by Johann Strauss the Younger and engaged Respighi to orchestrate a series of Chopin piano pieces.

Massine and Savina were married in London on April 26, 1921, but for the rest of the three-month preparation period they divided their time between Rome and Paris. During this time Mocchi arranged for Massine to meet with Raoul Gunsbourg of Monte Carlo's Casino Theater. On May 24 Gunsbourg offered the newlyweds a tempting contract: following its South American tour their new company would present ballets at the Casino Theater and join the theater's opera season from February through April 1922. Gunsbourg gave Massine until September to accept his offer.[7]

The contract with Mocchi had been signed during the first week of May. It called for Massine to be lead dancer and choreographer, with Savina as ballerina, for four months, during which they would perform in Rio de Janeiro, São Paulo, Buenos Aires, and Montevideo. Among the operas Massine agreed to stage were *Samson et Dalila, Aïda, La Gioconda, Carmen, Marouf,* and *Tannhäuser.* The roster of the opera company was headed by Beniamino Gigli. The new company sailed from Genoa for South America on May 27 aboard the *Principe di Udine.*

While Massine was happy to be directing his own company, the rigorous schedule did not leave him enough time for thorough creative work. When he worked with Diaghilev, he had been given ample time for meticulous planning of his ballets. He now found himself pressed to produce a full repertory and manage a company at the same time. During the first four weeks in Rio de Janeiro he conducted sixty-five rehearsals, choreographed several ballets, and staged eight operas. Of course, not all of that work was grueling; most of the repertory consisted of excerpts or divertissement ballets, though Massine included the full-length *Femmes de bonne humeur.* He considered the tour "physically and mentally more exhausting than any I had ever undertaken. Besides dancing every night, I had to run the company, and felt far from confident in my role as director. Nor did I have any time in which to do my own work."[8] Nevertheless, throughout the hectic months Massine found time to maintain his correspondence with Picasso. From the dancer in São Paulo to the painter in Fontainebleau:

All the blacks here dress themselves like the blackman in Parade's *front curtain. They have such an air of innocence as if America had just been discovered yesterday. All in all, it is a bit curious. Young people wear neck-collars like those from the time of Boutique and one finds in small cafés people wearing wooden hats in the shape of straw hats.*

Nature surpasses all imagination . . . a hundred times more beautiful than what we see in photographs. One eats extraordinary fruits with a taste as strange as their name. . . .

I have had a success as I have never had before, which frightens me, and Vera also. . . . I continue my [choreographic] research although I have very little time for it; however, I feel very comforted by the discoveries I have made.[9]

In another letter he spoke more openly about his work and state of mind: "I think that I am freeing myself of various faults that cluttered my head and my eyes and which were an obstacle toward the realization of my choreographic goals. Here I lack the technical means and the company has such a limited number of dancers that it has affected what I can achieve choreographically. . . . The lines and their harmony have been broken and muddled up, as have all of my ideas. The only thing that sustains itself is *Le Sacre*, which marked the turning point of my present ideas."[10]

Fortunately, the company, billed as Compañia de Bailes Rusos, was enthusiastically received. South America had already seen such famous ballet artists as Olga Preobrajenska, Virginia Zucchi, and Ana Pavlova, as well as the Ballets Russes in 1913 and 1917. A cultivated public awaited Massine's troupe, especially in Buenos Aires and Montevideo. As matters turned out, after his obligations to Mocchi had been satisfied Massine extended the tour on his own. From late October to mid-December the company performed twice a day at the Empire Theater in Buenos Aires; on December 19 it opened a two-shows-a-day, ten-day engagement at Montevideo's Teatro Artigas. But despite success Massine was homesick for Europe and his friends, and his letters to Picasso became more frequent. On November 18 he cabled: "Let me hear about your news. Loneliness unbearable."[11]

Far from Europe, and thriving, Massine was probably better able to grasp the significance of his dramatic break from Diaghilev. As in 1914, when he wrestled with the decision to *remain* with Diaghilev, he wrote to Moscow for his family's blessing and acceptance. His letter was unusually open and heartfelt. He had "left them as a boy" without knowing "that God would send us so many long and painful experiences"; unquestionably his journey "had been very lonely." His recent decision to leave Diaghilev and to marry had been "a turning point in my private and social life." Living with Diaghilev had become unbearable. "I felt as though I was in a gilded cage which suffocated and oppressed my entire spirit. This ended a seven-year period of my life in which I have endured more than others will endure in a lifetime!" He described Savina as "charming" and "humble" and "a great source of support in my life." [12]

On January 12, 1922, the Massines sailed for Europe on the Italian ship *Duca d'Aosta,* which docked in Monte Carlo on February 1. They proceeded to Paris (the contract with Gunsbourg having collapsed after a financial disagreement),[13] where the Hôtel Normandie once again served as their headquarters. While Semenov continued to negotiate the acquisition of the Isole dei Galli, Massine set his professional sights across the Channel.

London was to become Massine's base of operations for most of the 1920s. His extended Ballets Russes engagements there had given him entrée to the city's cultural elite; social and professional relationships with prominent Londoners had followed. Most important, despite Britain's depressed postwar economy, London enjoyed a dynamic theatrical life, and dance was turning from a craze into an obsession. Soon London would (until World War II) replace Paris as the world's ballet capital.

From the Hôtel Normandie, Massine negotiated with Sir Oswald Stoll and with the Hollywood producer Walter Wanger, who had leased the Royal Opera House at Covent Garden, to book performances in London.[14] Covent Garden was undergoing a severe financial crisis during the postwar period; to remain open, it had resorted to scheduling film screenings and revues as part of the Royal Opera House programs. Both Stoll and Wanger offered Massine immediate engagements. The choreographer opted for Covent Garden and soon put together a small company whose nucleus was Savina, himself, and some of Diaghilev's dancers. During the 1921 Ballets Russes season in London, Diaghilev had produced a three-act *Sleeping Beauty* (entitled *The Sleeping Princess*) that had ended in financial disaster, making it easier now for Massine to recruit such dancers as Lopokova, Sokolova, Woizikowski, and Thadée Slavinsky. Ninette de Valois, not yet a member of Diaghilev's company, also signed on with Massine.

Massine settled himself and Savina in a flat at London's Phoenix Hotel and the couple rented a dance studio on New Oxford Street, where classes and rehearsals began immediately. With Lopokova and Massine billed as the "world's greatest Ballet Dancers," his newly formed group opened at Covent Garden on April 3. The repertory introduced London to some of the works created in South America, including *Ragtime,* to Stravinsky's music, as well as *The Fanatics of Pleasure,* a divertissement ballet to music by Johann Strauss the Younger. There were also popular excerpts from *Tricorne, Boutique,* and *Astuzie.* According to *The Times,* "the dancers were given a great welcome by a large audience, especially M. Massine and Mlle. Lopokova in their dance duets." *Ragtime* "seemed to amuse the house very much, in spite of the little invention shown in discovering movements," and the critic "soon tired of the simple, if not childish, idea of the mechanical figure." The Strauss dances, however, "were danced to a happier style."[15] Despite its divertissement quality, Ninette de Valois found the choreography interesting and some numbers full of invention.[16] The performances at Covent Garden were a success with the public, and the company was offered an immediate engagement at the Coliseum. A return to Covent Garden was arranged for July, after a provincial tour.

T. S. Eliot attended the performances at the Coliseum and was further impressed with Massine's artistry and stage presence. "I have been to see him," he wrote Mary Hutchinson, "and thought him more brilliant and beautiful than ever. . . . As I [had never been so close before], I quite fell in love with him. . . . He is a genius."[17] After meeting Massine later in June, Eliot wrote Hutchinson: "Do you think Massine likes me? And would he come to see me, do you think?"[18]

Massine's instinct was to remain aloof, but his career now required him to move in London's social and artistic circles. Renewing former ties, he began to get himself noticed and inquired after.

Lady Ottoline Morrell, the wife of Liberal M.P. Phillip Morrell, was one of England's most prominent hostesses of the day, an aristocrat whose glittering parties and salons at Bedford Square in London and at Garsington Manor, a few miles from Oxford, are part of the British cultural lore of the first three decades of the twentieth century. During the Great War, Garsington Manor became a refuge for pacifists and conscientious objectors, and here she played hostess to many of the era's most brilliant social, political, artistic, and literary personalities, including Raymond Asquith, Bertrand Russell, Maynard Keynes, D. H. Lawrence, Roger Fry, Virginia Woolf, T. S. Eliot, Aldous Huxley, and Lytton Strachey. The ambience at Garsington Manor was decidedly relaxed: sexual freedom was a matter of fact—among Her Ladyship's lovers was Russell—and homosexuality was openly accepted. Lady Ottoline was known for her eccentricities and her oddly striking physical appearance as much as for her kindness toward struggling talent. Massine described her as "dressed in fantastically-coloured satins and brocades," looking like "a majestic bird of prey."[19] She had championed Diaghilev, whom she met before the war, and during the 1918–20 Ballets Russes London seasons she befriended Massine. Their correspondence shows a sincere rapport. Now she aided him in every way that she could, introducing him to the right people, even recruiting wealthy students for his ballet school.[20] They frequently met in London, or the Massines would spend weekends in Garsington. "I come to see you Wednesday next week? . . . Shall we come to Bloomsbury?"[21] writes Lady Ottoline, or, "If you would care to come in on Thursday to tea you would find a *very* interesting man here—James Stephens."[22] Although Massine never had much inclination to entertain—he was also notoriously tightfisted—he would on occasion receive special visitors at his apartment. One of its biggest draws was the modernist paintings on display from his own collection: "I should very much like to come see your pictures, especially your Braque. Also to see you," writes Lady Ottoline from Garsington in April 1922.[23]

Also among Massine's close acquaintances at this time in London were Osbert and Sacheverell Sitwell.

By the beginning of 1923 Massine was actively working in the theater. He created incidental choreography for the play *Arlequin* (produced by Albert de Courville) and choreographed his first revue, *You'd Be Surprised*, starring George Robey, which opened at Covent Garden on January 22. For this, he staged the exotic ballet *Togo*, with music by Darius Milhaud and designs by Bloomsbury artist Duncan Grant, and several dances, including a Chinese dance to music by Johann Strauss the Younger. These may have been stimulating exercises for Massine; but Sokolova, for one, found most of the pieces quite uninspiring.[24]

Many London stage luminaries came to the Massines' studio for coaching: Viola Tree, Gladys Cooper (whom Massine coached in 1923 for *Peter Pan*), Tallulah Bankhead. Bankhead writes:

> *Facing my first London audience in* The Dancers, *on the curtain's rise I was dancing for the supper in a British Columbia saloon, on its fall the toast of Paris, a ballerina! Actor-manager Sir Gerald du Maurier was a perfectionist. Feeling the demands of the part might be beyond my dancing range, he sent me to a ballet teacher. Reluctantly I went to the studio—a bleak, dark and empty room. There I was greeted by a rapt young man.*
>
> *The rapt young man was Léonide Massine, whose jetés and tournées and what-have-yous are discussed in hushed tones, wherever balletomanes engage in their rituals.*[25]

Among his students were the young Frederick Ashton, who would become England's leading choreographer, and Eleonora Marra, who in 1924 would replace Savina in Massine's affections.

Massine surely enjoyed being drawn into London's theatrical whirl, but his professional future must have appeared quite uncertain. He had no guarantee of employment from one engagement to the next. Teaching helped financially but could not nourish him creatively; and in any case, it seems unlikely that Massine was an inspired teacher—he took far more pride in mastering ballet's theoretical problems than in refining the pedagogy of academic dance. (Years later he would develop his own theory of dance notation.) No doubt there were other frustrations as well. He must have sorely missed the Ballets Russes, a company organized and disciplined enough to execute his artistic ideas with poise and authority. But he kept his spirits up by constantly, almost compulsively, exploring possible future collaborations and projects, most of which, unfortunately, never got off the ground. He continued shuttling between England and the Continent, and Paris was soon a second hub of activity.

After the Great War, Paris again became Europe's mecca of illusions and aspirations, with Montparnasse as its artistic and intellectual center. The city was spellbound by the new artistic movements of dadaism and surrealism. Adding to the tumult were the free-spending international set, the "lost generation" of American expatriates, an unruly new dance called the Charleston, and widespread delirium over *le jazz hot*. Coco Chanel transformed the appearance of women, and avant-garde canvases shocked the bourgeoisie. Paris was the major battleground in the war between old and new values. In the forefront were the likes of Man Ray, Jean Cocteau, Tristan Tzara, André Breton, Gertrude Stein, André Gide, Constantin Brancusi, Nancy Cunard, and Cole Porter.

In the midst of this ferment, Massine saw the wisdom of renewing his artistic and social contacts in France. Among them were Ravel, Fauré, Satie, and Milhaud, four composers who in 1924 endorsed Massine's induction into the Société des Auteurs, Compositeurs et Editeurs de Musique to ensure his receipt of royalties for his works currently being performed by the Ballets Russes in France.[26] Picasso, Lucien Daudet, the Delaunays, Gontcharova, Larionov, and Derain were other artist friends Massine contacted. But of paramount importance was the Count Etienne de Beaumont.

Etienne and Edith de Beaumont were leading figures in the Parisian haut monde. The count's lineage could be traced to an aristocratic Touraine family dating from 1191. In 1907 he had married Edith de

Taisne, also of noble birth and a few years his senior. He was tall, flamboyant, possessed of exquisite manners, and homosexual. He had a penchant for lavish entertaining and for sponsoring young artists; he designed jewelry for Chanel and Schiaparelli, arranged charming *soirées musicales,* and had organized an ambulance service during the war. The countess was more reserved, with a serious interest in Greek poetry; her translation of Sappho was later published in an edition with designs by Marie Laurencin. The much-discussed couple's magnificent eighteenth-century *hôtel particulier* in the rue Daruc was a meeting place for Parisian society, artists, and writers. The setting was breathtaking, with salons as sumptuous as those in the Louvre and splendid gardens ornamented with neoclassical statues.

This palatial residence was also the setting for the count's most meticulously rendered social statements: his celebrated masquerade balls. Many of these spectacles were decorated by Picasso, Sert, or Laurencin. The costumes, designed by Picasso, Jean Hugo, or the count himself, blended flights of fancy with bizarre fantasy. Once Princess Soutzo appeared as a Christmas tree and the Maharanee of Kapurthala made a triumphant entrance as caviar, held aloft on a silver tray by four attendants. Every detail of these balls was carefully orchestrated by Beaumont. His guests sometimes had to wait for hours in a drawing room before making their precisely timed entrances, usually as a sort of tableau vivant accompanied by dance and song composed for the occasion. Dress rehearsals were required.

In 1923 Picasso, Satie, and Massine collaborated on a divertissement for a ball dedicated to "L'Antiquité sous Louis XIV." During preparations for this extravaganza Beaumont struck on the idea of organizing a series of performances centered around Massine. (According to Bernard Faÿ, "Beaumont did not hide . . . his cult for the dancer Massine, whom his admirers had renamed *le devin Léonide,* and his [Beaumont's] desire to have the Parisian public recognize the superiority of this artist's genius."[27] Soon Beaumont was gathering some of the most prestigious artists in Paris for the venture. By then he had also developed a sexual infatuation with Massine, but his yearning, the evidence suggests, remained entirely sublimated in their artistic collaboration. The two men established a close friendship that lasted until after World War II.

Preparations for Les Soirées de Paris, as the season was called (after Apollinaire's prewar journal), began early in 1924. It was to take place at the music hall La Cigale from May 17 through June 30 and would mainly consist of a series of ballets, with a few music-hall numbers included.

The count also planned two dramatic pieces: Tristan Tzara's *Mouchoir de nuages* (dedicated to the rebellious and fascinating English heiress Nancy Cunard) and Cocteau's adaptation of Shakespeare's *Romeo and Juliet*. According to Francis Steegmuller, Beaumont enlisted Cocteau to contribute something "in which there would not be a role for Massine, in order that the pro-Massine purpose of the *Soirées* be at least slightly disguised."[28] Steegmuller also notes how "Massine's absence from the cast, strategic though it was, resulted in Beaumont's taking little interest in *Romeo*."[29]

Massine choreographed seven works: *Salade* (book by Albert Flament, music by Milhaud, scenery and costumes by Georges Braque); *Mercure* (music by Satie, scenery and costumes by Picasso); *Les Roses* (a plotless ballet to music by Henri Sauguet); *Gigue* (a baroque piece to music by Bach and Handel, performed at the piano by Marcelle Meyer, with scenery and costumes by Derain); *Premier Amour* (a sketch about a girl who falls in love with a doll in her dreams, set to Satie's *Trois morceaux en forme de poire* as well as his polka from *Petites pièces montées*, interpreted at the piano by Satie and Meyer); *Le Beau Danube* (book by Massine, music by Johann Strauss the Younger, decor after Constantin Guys, and costumes by Beaumont), and *Divertissement* (a plotless *suite de danses*—waltz, variation, pas de deux, rigaudon, and mazurka—to *Chabrier* music, performed against color projections). The American dancer Loie Fuller oversaw the lighting design.

Rue Daruc became Massine's headquarters. He temporarily moved into an annex. Two large rooms in the house served as rehearsal studios, in one of which he taught a morning class to about thirty dancers. The company, recruited in London and Paris, included some Diaghilev defectors, the most important of whom was Idzikowski. Lopokova came to Paris from London to join the venture, but Savina remained in England.

Word of Massine's latest undertaking reached Diaghilev in Monte Carlo. He was furious. For one thing, Les Soirées would coincide with the Ballets Russes' forthcoming Paris season. Though several of the works of Beaumont's enterprise would prove rather amateurish in spite of all the prestigious artists involved, Diaghilev rightly feared that it could draw attention away from his own engagement. Massine and Beaumont's effrontery in competing with him so openly must have been unbearable. Equally galling was the participation of such artists as Satie, Picasso, and Derain, all associated with Diaghilev in the past; others, such as Braque and Milhaud, were collaborating with the Ballets Russes at that very moment. (Perhaps to dispel any hint of disloyalty to Diaghilev, Marie Laurencin, who had just come from designing the scenery and costumes for Diaghilev's *Les Biches*, appears credited as "N." in the program for *Les Roses*.) Diaghilev was both frightened and envious, and the gossip was that "Big Serge" was in "such a rage" that he was willing to engage "everyone possible with a contract forever."[30] Indeed, Diaghilev would not let matters rest, and before long he retaliated. He advised Poulenc and Auric, who had just contributed scores to two new Ballets Russes productions, *Les Biches* and *Les Facheux*, that if they participated in Les Soirées those ballets would not be presented in Paris. He also tried, unsuccessfully, to persuade Milhaud not to collaborate with Beaumont. Milhaud had just composed the score for Diaghilev's production of Cocteau's *Le Train bleu*. Cocteau, afraid of falling out of Diaghilev's favor, wrote the impresario:

> *I was so sorry not to have seen you to say goodbye. I wanted to explain to you about a Cigale project which I should think will please you as it changes the aspect of the whole enterprise.*
>
> *E. de Beaumont wants me to stage* Romeo et Juliette, *to alternate with his music-hall programme. I am working with Jean V. Hugo, and I am having some Scotch bagpipers sent over from England.*
>
> *So I am doing nothing that is in any way like your productions, and am confining myself to theatre theatre.*[31]

With Beaumont, Diaghilev employed a more gracious strategy. In the spirit of requesting a professional courtesy, he asked the count not to engage Idzikowski for the coming extravaganza. According to Lopokova, "The count promised, in the meantime Big Serge tried behind his back to destroy the count's season, so that now the count is furious and engages Stas [Idzikowski] for spite."[32]

The intensive rehearsal period began in February, with two or three sessions a day. The work must have been exhausting, but by April 26 Lopokova wrote to Maynard Keynes that "Massine looks well and seems pleasant to everybody."[33]

As opening night drew near, however, tempers flared. The relationship between Lopokova and Massine became particularly tense, and in her letters to Keynes she complained of not being paid proper attention and protested that her suggestions were not being considered. "I plead [with] Massine to have clear lights in the scene where the psychological moment develops [probably referring to *Le Beau Danube*], but he is difficult."[34] The sometimes open, sometimes buried rivalry between the two dancers was rearing its head: "My friends find as ever that Massine does everything to shadow me and not make me his equal," Lopokova wrote, adding that "we can't change the nature of Massine, it is always twisted in the wrong direction."[35] Contention between the two dated from the Ballets Russes' return to England in 1918, when, just as Karsavina and Nijinsky had done in Diaghilev's prewar seasons, Lopokova and Massine became the sensation and rage of London. After Massine left the Ballets Russes, his ensuing professional instability made him exceedingly wary of anyone he believed might threaten his position; thus the 1922 and 1923 collaborations between the two dancers at Covent Garden and the Coliseum had been marred by Massine's petty squabbling over money and his intrigues to monopolize the limelight. Now as then, Lopokova was fed up with his attempts to upstage her:

> *I went to a rehearsal for that damnation ball tomorrow. Stas came into the dressing room with a newspaper . . . and it said how this charity ball included all the amateurs society and L. Massine. As it is a thing of charity I absolutely want my professional name, and as Count is very busy, I left the dirty theatre. . . . Besides my costume is the same as corps de ballet and they do not take least trouble to make it better. . . . The Count must not overlook these matters, and if he does, there is penalty for him; the announcement certainly comes out of his organisation. Tonight I shall tell him so.*[36]

Lopokova also denounced Massine's rash treatment and incessant overworking of the dancers—a recurrent grievance over the years among his co-workers: "I still work like an elephant. . . . I told Massine that he must give us one free night before Saturday to come into a normal condition."[37] And the following day she wrote: "In the theatre from 2 till 8½ forever waiting, trying on costumes, and [have] not been able to dance with the orchestra except for 7–8 minutes. I told Massine that except [for] himself, he considered the other dancers as mud (in *The Roses* he does not dance), but the ballet with him he rehearsed for hours, so that musiciens [*sic*] when tired were logic[al] to stand up and depart."[38] Massine's obsessiveness could sometimes make him overlook the needs of other dancers, and his impersonal manner often made them feel that they were merely tools for his artistic advancement. His introverted personality did not help. He struck many as cold, insensitive, and untrustworthy. Keeping his distance, he invited suspicions that he harbored ulterior motives. Asked to justify his tyrannical demands, he would simply declare that "I did not ask of dancers what I did not ask of myself."[39] (The young generation of dancers in the 1930s would be devoted to Massine and accept his sometimes unreasonable demands out of respect for his unquestioned genius. Most of his contemporaries' admiration, however, had no cultlike reverence attached to it. They saw his despotism as utterly uncalled for.)

Les Soirées opened with a gala on May 17. Among the works created by Massine, only *Mercure, Salade,* and *Le Beau Danube* received the highest acclaim. *Mercure,* in fact, was mainly disliked by the press, but it was hailed in the artistic community as the high point of the season.

The idea of *Mercure* was credited to Massine in the program, but in a letter to Picasso dated February 21, 1924, Beaumont advanced the concept as his own, passing it on to Picasso to use as a point of reference for a series of designs on which the work was to be based.[40] In a letter to Satie written on the same day, Beaumont informed the composer of his letter to Picasso and proposed a working title for the ballet of *Mercure: Tableaux vivants.*[41] (This later was changed to *Les Aventures de Mercure,* and, finally—more in keeping with the original idea—to *Mercure: Poses plastiques.*)

The ballet consisted of three parts and twelve scenes,* some of which lasted only twenty to thirty seconds. The series of tableaux vivants included dancers and sculptural aids such as wooden silhouettes (made mobile by other, hidden dancers or by strings) and constructs of enmeshed wire. Gertrude Stein commented: "Calligraphy, as I understand it in him [Picasso], had perhaps its most intense moment in the decor of *Mercure.* That was written, so simply written, no painting, pure calligraphy."[42] Such stage sculpture in motion had antecedents in *Parade* and *Le Tricorne* and was an important device in turning these two ballets into what Ornella Volta has described as Picasso's *"Machines de guerre contre le ballet traditionnel."*[43] The male and female costumes were modeled after classic Greek tunics—with the incongruous addition of long white evening gloves for everyone except Mercure himself (Massine). The gloves were not Picasso's idea—it has been credited to Beaumont—but he liked it.[44] Dancers who appeared as stagehands were dressed in black unitards with hoods. One of the most peculiar scenes in *Mercure* featured

---

* The twelve scenes were *La Nuit, Danse de tendresse, Entrée de Mercure, Danse des signes du Zodiaque; Les Trois Grâces, Le Bain de Grâces, Mercure vole les perles des trois Grâces et s'enfuit, Colère de Cerbère; La Fête chez Bacchus, La Polka des lettres, Entrée du Chaos,* and *Enlèvement de Proserpine.*

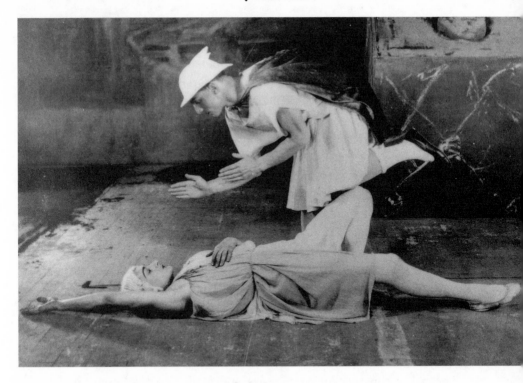

Massine as the title character in the Diaghilev revival of Mercure, *1927*

figures of the three Graces, played by three muscular male dancers *en travesti*, all wearing large papier-mâché breasts and pictured in a vertical bathtub. W. H. Shaw wrote in the *Criterion*:

> Mercure *left one uncertain. The effect produced on the first night audience was indicative. The younger generation led by Louis Aragon became so excited that they leapt from their seats, running through the theatre to the loge of the Comte de Beaumont, screaming in menacing tones, "Vive Picasso! Vive Picasso!," as if uncertain whether to thank or damn him for presenting anything so thrilling. . . . The curtain rose on a tableau representing night in a manner entirely new to Picasso, an abstract composition made of canvas and wire. The three graces were done by three mechanical figures which were many times as large as the dancers who carried them across the stage. The dance of Chaos was executed by a group of dancers entirely covered by different colored tights, reaching even over their faces, crawling across the stage, supporting other dancers on their heads and backs.*[45]

Mercure gave Satie the happy opportunity to work with his admired friend Picasso—and without Cocteau, from whom he had broken off social and artistic relations for good by 1923. In an interview for the *Paris-Journal* on May 30, the composer described the ballet and its music: "I wanted my music to create a body, if you will, to go along with the actions and gestures of the characters. The poses are exactly similar to those that one can see in the fairs. The spectacle resembled the music hall, all together without stylization and not at all in rapport with that which is essentially artistic."[46]

Salade, described in the program as a "choreographic counterpoint in two acts," was a commedia dell'arte imbroglio in which two couples—Polichinelle and Rosetta, Cinzio and Isabelle—pursue all sorts of intrigues, only to end up marrying. But according to Madeleine Milhaud, the composer's wife, Massine did not treat the ballet in a light, commedia dell'arte style. He gave it a "tragic dimension, especially the scene in which the Polichinelle is beaten and which Massine performed heartbreakingly."[47] Although the critic Fernand Gregh described the work as "a rhythmic pantomime, a series of stylized gestures that, for a second, froze the actors in poses that became a tableau,"[48] according to Massine his intention was to show "what was essential to dance uncluttered by any sort of mime, thereby liberating it from anything that is foreign to its nature: dance should appear in its fundamental character. *Le Sacre* was a great monumental symphony; *Salade* would belong to the genre of chamber music. . . ."[49]

Lopokova, who did not dance in *Salade,* found Massine's performance "admirable" and the ballet "one of [his] best."[50] Its structure, she wrote, "develops like a building."[51] She found "the decor by Braque very attractive."[52] Noting the shallowness of the Cigale's stage, the critic Raymond Cogniat described the decor as a "line of arches which spread across the full length of the stage . . . dividing it in two parts or zones which were independently lit from one another and where the actions of the interpreters took place, thus creating at the same time the illusion of a space that would have been impossible to render by the use of perspective if the stage itself had been any deeper. Consequently, the arches did not allow the upstage to look empty."[53] Braque's costumes, with the exception of Massine's pale yellow, employed a color scheme of autumn leaves. As inspiration for the scene Massine gave Milhaud various themes of antique Italian music.[54] The critic Arthur Hoerée found the score one of the composer's best.[55]

Le Beau Danube returned to the demi-caractère divertissement genre

Massine had already explored in *La Boutique fantasque*. Its two scenes depicted a Hussar who, strolling in a Viennese park with his young bourgeois fiancée, encounters his old flame, a Street Dancer. The two women square off and the Hussar temporarily succumbs to the charms of his former lover. However, he is genuinely in love with his young intended, and they are reconciled at the end. The story had been conceived during Massine's difficult days in Rome after his breakup with Diaghilev. According to Massine, *"Le Beau Danube* came as a reaction from the intense seriousness of *Parade* and *Le Sacre du Printemps*. It was an absolute necessity for me to create it. Curiously enough, [it came about] during the very strongest period of jazz, before there was any thought of a return to the Vienna waltz."[56] Massine's selection of danceable tunes by Johann Strauss went against the current trend toward either jazzy or more serious ballet scores. (In the 1920s Strauss's reputation was not high. When Malipiero had arranged his music for *Fanatics of Pleasure*, he asked Massine not to include his own name in the program credits.) *Le Beau Danube* consisted of a series of polkas, mazurkas, waltzes, and marches. The dances—pas de deux, solos, and ensembles, danced by others in the park as well as the three leads—were intertwined with the narrative passages to advance the story line. And Massine employed some of his favorite storytelling techniques, such as simultaneous action and an apotheosis at the finale.

Polunin's decor depicted a tall carriage taking two gentlemen for a ride in the park, a scene inspired by the romantic engravings of Constantin Guys. Beaumont's period costumes relied on a muted color scheme of sepias, russets, dark greens, grays, and burgundies. Although Lopokova found the ballet a little long, she thought that the costumes were the most lavishly produced of the season, and asserted that while the other ballets were for an elite, *Le Beau Danube* was for "the grand public."[57] Indeed, the ballet was Massine's most popular of the season; it was performed seventeen times (*Gigue* was performed fifteen times, *Salade* fourteen).

All of Paris now gravitated toward the two sites where the battle of the impresarios would be played out: La Cigale and the Théâtre des Champs-Elysées. And no matter which side one might be on, with the Ballets Russes performing Massine's *Parade, Sacre, Cimarosiana,* and *Pulcinella* the choreographer was easily the celebrity of the season. The Diaghilev-Beaumont competition fueled tensions and intrigue between their supporting camps. Jean Hugo recalls that during one of Massine's appearances Beaumont shouted "Bravo! and applauded noisily. There was no echo. Misia had entered. She was the Ballets Russes incarnate, which

Massine had betrayed. She did not go unnoticed, and when the curtain fell, many hesitated to applaud."[58]

Diaghilev also came to La Cigale. Pointing to the poster for Les Soirées, he commented, "Only my name is missing."[59] At one performance he was accompanied by Bronislava Nijinska and Serge Lifar, and when Nijinska applauded Diaghilev seemed to become upset.[60] While he felt that Le Beau Danube was "pure trash,"[61] he thought that the lighting and choreography of Salade "had marked a definite step forward."[62] And he admired Mercure, a work he later added to his repertory—the only ballet he ever acquired from another producer.

One can see Massine in his creations for Les Soirées taking two quite distinct aesthetic approaches. The first, in modernist works like Salade and Mercure, is dominated by the collaboration of the painters, Braque and Picasso respectively. These works are almost experimental in their fragmentation of images and stylization of movement. In both, but especially in Mercure, the strictly visual aspects of painting and sculpture overshadow the dancing. In a May 1924 interview in Candide, Beaumont described this approach as one in which the function of the choreographer and leading dancer "takes the place of an instrument within the orchestra of dancers. Composition, optics, movement, lighting are some of the problems that this great artist [Massine] has strived to resolve, giving to himself in the whole ensemble just the importance of a dominating color in a painting."

Le Beau Danube, Divertissement, and Les Roses reveal the opposite tendency; here, dance is the predominant element. (According to critic Paul Ginistry, Les Roses was composed of "harmonious groupings" which served as a background for the virtuosity of Idzikowski.)[63] The fact that Danube was conceived by Massine without the collaboration of any other artist is one clear indication of his new preference for pure dance within a dramatic context. This was a crucial step in his development, but what we can only call an incomplete one. It had been clear for months that in working with Beaumont Massine would be unable to exercise much artistic independence: in a letter dated January 14, 1924, just after Massine had approached Lopokova to dance in Les Soirées, the ballerina told Maynard Keynes that Massine's "friends" and "associates have control over everything, he [Massine] employs his power only as a maître de ballet."[64] Thus one wonders whether had Massine had more freedom during the Soirées season, he would have produced even more dancing ballets instead of following the modernist formula of the 1920s, a course that was very much determined by Beaumont's aesthetics.

Massine's negotiations with theatrical producer Charles B. Cochran to bring Les Soirées to London—a move that incensed Diaghilev—came to nothing. So by the summer of 1924 he had to face his vanished hope to create his own repertory company.

After Les Soirées Massine returned to London, where his marriage ended. (He and Savina would divorce in 1925.) According to Massine's autobiography, Savina felt abandoned during their long separations when he was engaged by Beaumont in Paris. Yet their problems apparently predate Massine's involvement with Beaumont. Mostly, in fact, he writes, their breakup could be traced to her feeling "disillusioned" about the marriage.[65] In a letter to Keynes dated January 20, Lopokova hints that Savina had just returned to Massine after temporarily leaving him. Massine refused to answer Lopokova's inquiries about whether or not he and Vera "were in a state of partition" and declined to discuss his "domestic drama" with her.[66] The fact that Savina did not come to Paris to join Les Soirées was a clear sign that by the beginning of 1924 their relationship had badly deteriorated. Her absence was the beginning of the end.

Into the breach stepped Massine's London student Eleonora Marra, who would be his emotional mainstay for the next few years. She had come to Paris to create leading roles in the repertory. It is impossible to say precisely when their affair began, but it was only the first of many. Extramarital relationships would continue to checker Massine's emotional life. Despite his pleas for solitude, he was incapable of being alone, and one lover was quickly replaced by another. The sheer number of his involvements until the end of his life, coupled with his unending search for new sexual conquests, suggests that sex became a sort of safety valve for accumulated pressure, a mechanism to lower his anxiety. For a man so closed within himself and so detached from others by his inability to communicate on a more intimate level, sex—next to the aesthetic gratification of his creative work—became a primary source of pleasure. While through his art he could ascend to a higher self, it was sex that reconciled him with his human nature.

Since his return from South America in 1922, Massine had made several attempts to renew his artistic relationship with Diaghilev. On separate occasions he had asked Misia and Jacques Rouché, director of the Paris Opéra, to intercede on his behalf, but all such advances had come to nothing.[67] Now, in London, the two men effected something of a reconciliation. Massine writes that Maestro Cecchetti told him that "Diaghilev was in town and wanted to see me. I was surprised at this news, and perhaps a little curious, and readily agreed to Cecchetti's suggestion of a rendezvous at his studio a week later." [68] Diaghilev proposed that Massine return to the Ballets Russes to choreograph two new ballets. As usual, he had more than one motive. Since Massine's departure, Nijinska had been the company's choreographer. By 1924, however, Diaghilev had shown interest in the work of George Balanchine, who had been touring Western Europe with a group of dancers from St. Petersburg. He recruited Balanchine for the Ballets Russes—the reason usually cited for Nijinska's departure in January 1925. (Did she also know that Massine was about to be rehired?) With Nijinska gone and Balanchine not yet established as a choreographer, one can see why Diaghilev needed Massine. One can also see further Diaghilev's ploy to eliminate a competitor.

He was ready to take his onetime protégé back—even under Massine's exorbitant conditions. The art critic Michel Georges-Michel served as intermediary. From Italy, where he had just met with Massine, he wired to Diaghilev the choreographer's astronomical demands: 160,000 francs annually, a rehearsal schedule to be set by Massine himself, plus full casting authority, contingent only upon Diaghilev's approval. [69] Massine was adamant. Diaghilev acceded. (Balanchine, once he was established as a choreographer and principal dancer with Diaghilev, was paid only 2,500 francs a month.) [70]

The negotiations concluded, Massine took Marra to Italy for a long respite on the Isole dei Galli, which he had finally acquired in 1922.

The three tiny islands, lying three nautical miles off Positano in the Gulf of Salerno, are steeped in legend. In antiquity they formed a single island which in profile had the shape of a reclining woman; seamen called it Sirene. Homer immortalized the site as the home of the Sirens whose song had lured Ulysses. In the fourteenth century the islands served as a fortress and lookout for the king of Naples (Robert of Anjou) against Saracen invaders. Later they were used as a prison, and as a hideout for pirates in the seventeenth century.

When Massine bought them, the largest of the three, Isola Lunga (approximately eight hundred meters in length), held a fourteenth-century ruined tower. On the highest island, Brigante, stood the remnants of another tower and a water cistern probably built in the seventeenth century by a nobleman from Sorrento. The third island, Rotunda, slightly larger than Brigante, was empty. From Galli one has a magnificent view across the water to Capri, Amalfi, and, on a clear day, the mountains of Sicily.

During the summer of 1924 Massine ordered the first fleet of workmen and materials from the mainland to Isola Lunga.

Massine

The local people in Positano referred to me as the mad Russian who has bought a rocky island where only rabbits could live. Even my caretaker, Nicola Grassi, was pessimistic, pointing out one tiny fig tree growing among the rocks and telling me that nothing would ever thrive on the island. One day a priest from Capri came to visit me. When I asked him if he thought I should ever succeed in cultivating the land, he bent down, picked up a handful of soil, and said: "This soil is the same as we have on Capri. I see no reason why you should not cultivate your island as we have done." He was right, but it was not as easy as it sounded, and it was many years before I was able to plant the island with vines and trees.[71]

In the course of Massine's life, the mission of building his home on Galli took on pharaonic dimensions. Working against the deteriorating effects of salt, winter weather, and time, he poured unflagging energy and a huge portion of his earnings into creating a refuge from the world. Galli came to stand for his hermeticism; as an almost Nietzschean metaphor, it exalted the individual's isolation in his struggle to live a truly creative life. Over the years his efforts were rewarded. Isola Lunga eventually boasted a private radio station; four beaches built by Massine; an electrical plant generating thirty kilowatts of power; a port with boathouse; four 400-meter terraced gardens planted with fruits, including grapes (the island eventually undertook its own small wine production); a lighthouse (serviced by the Italian government); a two-story central villa—for whose design in the 1930s Massine received suggestions from Le Corbusier—and a terrace with a spectacular view of Capri. A second five-bedroom villa, with a view of Positano, served as the caretaker's quarters. The fourteenth-century tower was eventually restored and became Massine's residence in his last years. Its interior had a sober Florentine aura, with Carrara marble pillars carved after those in the cathedral at Ravenna. On the first floor (above the ground floor) the choreographer erected a large dance studio, floored with Siberian pine and including a mezzanine balcony to seat a string quartet. A kitchen, a dining room, a library, and bedrooms completed the accommodations.*
On Isola Lunga Massine also built an open-air theater, which was destroyed in a mid-1960s storm that sent its columns crashing into the sea.

On Brigante Massine restored a boathouse, built a large dock for fishing and swimming, and at the top of the island dug out two terraces for cultivation. Rotunda, the third island, remained undeveloped. In 1924,

* During my stay in Galli in 1978 I was Massine's guest at the tower.

all three islands were only deserted rocks in the Mediterranean. As time passed they became an indispensable resting place in a vertiginous life.

By 1925 Massine was back at work for the Ballets Russes and "felt again the atmosphere of creative exhilaration."[72] He claimed that after his London meeting with Diaghilev their relationship "was quickly re-established on its old footing" and that in Monte Carlo Diaghilev "welcomed me warmly."[73] Others report that the relationship was polite but distant. Right at the start Diaghilev made it clear to Massine that resumption of any close, friendly contact between them was out of the question.[74] Also, Diaghilev had taken Savina back into the Ballets Russes since her separation from Massine. (Later, after Marra and Massine separated, Diaghilev took her, too, into the company.) Massine's position in the company was undoubtedly difficult. He kept to himself and maintained a calculated distance from his colleagues. According to Sokolova:

> From the first day he appeared embarrassed and uncomfortable with the company. When he said, "How do you do?" he just pressed his lips together and curled up the corners of his mouth: that sufficed for a smile. At rehearsals he spoke to no one, except to give directions: he and Grigoriev exchanged civilities and that was all. . . . Savina was ignored as if she did not exist. She was deeply hurt. Diaghilev and Massine were never seen together, and we gathered there was little love lost on either side. If in the old days it had been impossible to get a glimpse of Massine's inner thoughts and feelings, now he seemed to exist in complete isolation. It would have been interesting to know his opinion of Dolin, Lifar and Balanchine. He was lonely, but refused to be friendly, and although some of our "old gang" were secretly glad to have him back it was clear that an earthquake would be needed to make him show any emotion.[75]

It seems, though, that Massine was more at ease with those who had not been part of the company during his previous tenure. To the young Russian composer Vladimir Dukelsky (who later became famous as a composer of popular songs and musical comedies in the United States under the name Vernon Duke), it was a "delightful surprise" when "this forbidding and admittedly difficult master, certainly the top choreographer of his time, took to me and my music immediately. He smiled repeatedly, nodding his head, and he sat directly opposite me while I played."[76] The composer and the choreographer spent most evenings together, "which annoyed Diaghilev, who insisted that Léonide had no soul, no heart and no taste and was only interested in money."[77] Dukelsky, on the other hand, found "Léonide stimulating company, although he detested crowds, organized gaiety," and "disorganized drinking." [78]

Those who encountered Massine for the first time found him handsome and decidedly aloof, yet with a captivating, effortlessly theatrical air, especially in the rehearsal room, where he wore his habitual costume of black alpaca flamenco pants. They were high-waisted with creases down the sides, and his full-sleeved white crêpe de chine rehearsal shirt had been designed especially for him by Bakst. Dukelsky described him thus: "Although of a small stature, [Massine] was an arresting figure; his head was of extraordinary beauty, the eyes flashing and hypnotic, the smile rare and therefore all the more beguiling. His movements were brusque and oddly, determinedly, virile, with none of the unmasculine grace and softness too often typical of male dancers. . . . His manner was distant, inaccessible and reserved in the extreme." [79]

Massine's two choreographic assignments were both to use libretti by Boris Kochno, who had been Diaghilev's secretary and artistic collaborator since 1921.

The first Massine work rehearsed and premiered in Monte Carlo was *Zéphire et Flore,* a modern adaptation in seven scenes of an eighteenth-century tale in which Boréas, madly in love with Flore, kills Zéphire with an arrow during a game of blindman's bluff and carries Flore off to his cave. As Flore struggles helplessly with her abductor, the Muses arrive with the corpse of Zéphire. The gods intervene and revive Zéphire, the lovers are reunited, and Boréas is punished forever.

This would be another production in the Diaghilev postwar mold of works inspired by the Grand Siècle. The libretto grew out of Kochno's interest in Russian poetry inspired by mythological themes from Greece. When he first brought the idea to Diaghilev, the impresario proposed to do it in the Russian style prevalent at the beginning of the nineteenth century, when princes' private theaters sponsored plays performed by their serfs. [80] The music was commissioned from young Dukelsky; the scenery and costumes from Georges Braque.

According to Kochno, *Zéphire et Flore* marked a return by Massine to lyricism that lent the work an impressionistic quality. He felt that the choreographer was especially successful in realizing a lyrical neoclassicism in the roles of Zéphire and Flore, danced by Anton Dolin and Alice Nikitina. They were juxtaposed with the roles of Boréas (danced by Lifar) and the Muses, rendered in Massine's characteristic angular style. [81] The ballet was not well received in 1925 in Monte Carlo or later that same year in Paris, but it met with greater acceptance in the autumn in London. Writing in the *Morning Post,* Francis Toye described it as "an essay in pseudo-classicism."[82] *The Times* called the choreography "vivid and ingenious. [Massine] does not use concerted movements, like Fokine, but gives to each dancer a separate part, so that the effect may be called, in the musical term, contrapuntal."[83] The ballet also scored a big success in 1926 in Berlin.

Les Matelots was a practically plotless ballet in five scenes. It had a lively score by Georges Auric as well as scenery and costumes by the young Spanish painter Pedro Pruna, an artist who would collaborate with Diaghilev twice more during the 1920s. The action revolves around the adventures of three sailors and two girls and shows what happens when one of the sailors tries to test his girlfriend's fidelity. The scenario was little more than a pretext for the five characters to perform a *suite de danses* consisting of solos, pas de deux, pas de trois, and ensembles. For Massine the highlight of the production was a "carefully synchronized pas de trois in which the sailors, standing on chairs, mime the playing of a game of cards."[84] For Cyril Beaumont, the sailors' "rolling gait, their quick alert movements, their ability to retain their balance in almost every position, their susceptibility to women and their passion for cards, were all admirably expressed in Massine's choreography."[85] Although Valerian Svetlov found its almost nonexistent plot difficult to make out,[86] the ballet was nevertheless a tremendous success in its Paris premiere in 1925. Later that same year in London Raymond Mortimer wrote in the *New Statesman*: "Every movement is unmistakably signed 'Massine.' There is in it wit, satire and good humour, superabundant vitality and continual formal beauty."[87] According to *The Times,* Massine had "shown a great wealth of imaginative invention, which is very welcome after the pale trivialities recently put before us."[88] Diaghilev himself declared in the *Morning Post* that *"Les Matelots* is the most definite success we have had since the war. . . . Massine has achieved nothing so astonishing since the *Boutique.* And the reason why it is so good is that he did it quickly, in one impetus . . . here he has no doubts, no hesitations."[89]

Soon after Massine finished these works, and before the season began in Monte Carlo, he returned to London. Nineteen twenty-five was to be a busy year for him. He collaborated with Cochran on two revues, *On With the Dance* and its sequel, *Still Dancing,* serving as choreographer and dancer for both.

On With the Dance was a revue by Noël Coward, in two parts and twenty-two scenes, with music by Coward and Philip Braham. It featured the beloved star Alice Delysia, all *diamantée* with ostrich feathers, gowned by Paris couturier Jean Patou. Massine contributed three ballets: *The Rake, Crescendo,* and *A Hungarian Wedding.*

The Rake, which had music by Roger Quilter, scenery and costumes by William Nicholson, and masks by Betty Mutz, was inspired by the art of William Hogarth. According to Massine, "to suggest the debauchery of eighteenth-century England I filled the stage with Hogarthian characters—obese women, grotesque musicians and deformed bedlamites. As the Rake, drunk and slouching in his chair, Terry Kendall gave an excellent performance." [90] Cochran considered *The Rake* a "complete success." [91]

Crescendo had scenery and costumes by Gladys Calthrop and a score filled with jazzy tunes. ("Pick Up Your Sins" was its most popular melody.) The program note touted the ballet as epitomizing the 1920s:

> In an age when the romance of Machinery is superseding the lilies and languors of Victorianism, Art must of necessity reflect the angular tendencies of the time. Man becomes a puppet, and Beauty a slave to the new forms of the relentless progress of civilisation. *Crescendo* is an attempt to portray the transition from the ethereal to the material—the gentle tranquility of Les Sylphides is rudely shattered by the insistent clamour of modernity— contemporary types push aside the dim memories of yesterday—Massine as the spirit of the age dominates the scene, and his puppets jib to the tune of cocktails and jazz, until, willy-nilly, they are swept up to a frenzied climax of impressionistic movement.

In an interview with the *Morning Post* Massine described his approach in *Crescendo*:

> Every age has its own way to move and its own dancing modes, and we cannot continue to devise our choreography according to the precepts of the schools of the sixteenth, seventeenth and eighteenth centuries.... What we have to do today to make dancing vital is to learn all we can from the Italo-French School of three hundred years ago, and transpose it into terms of the best in modern jazz. We have to alter the direction of the ancient school, and, by adapting its conventions, its form and its steps, create a new spirit representative of the spirit of the age. [92]

But *Crescendo* had problems from the beginning, and modifications had to be made along the way. Cochran's practical, show-biz assessment in a letter to Massine was that "the opening was splendid, but from that point all dances seem a little on the long side, with the exception perhaps of the three 'Nifty Nats.' The ballet drops badly with the entrance of the three couples after Delysia's and your exit."[93] Cochran suggested that Massine cut two minutes and recommended that the dancers in the closing number, "The Automobile Age," wear motor goggles to convey to the audience the intended parody. Despite weak spots, the ballet had its effective moments, especially Massine's role. Coward wrote: "There is something elegantly vicious in the strange extremities of it; a corruption half base, half spiritual, with the inevitable latent sorrowfulness of conscious, unreluctant sin. The ballet itself is more or less incoherent, and trivial; but it is enough that you have created that strange, half-lunar figure, reaching blindly out to a beauty beyond its own posturing; as though it mocked lightly at things hidden from and sacred to itself."[94]

The evening ended with *A Hungarian Wedding,* led by Delysia singing. Massine and Marra danced in all three ballets.

Collaborating with Cochran in *On With the Dance* taught Massine even more about the dynamics of a musical revue than he had picked up working on *You'd Be Surprised.* Unlike the ballet process, where carefully crafted movements were honed during the rehearsal period into a polished work, in a revue changes were constantly being made on the spot to sharpen the production. Sometimes numbers had to be shortened or additions made, and these changes were always subject to further overhaul based on their success with the audience. The correspondence between Cochran and Massine lays out in detail the working relationship between a theatrical producer and a choreographer. Massine declared it a pleasure to work with Cochran, "for he did everything with vitality and imagination, responding with alacrity to new ideas, and maintaining a wonderful harmony between all his collaborators." Schooled in the ballet, Massine found the challenge of *On With the Dance* an "exciting venture" that brought him "into close contact with a fresh facet of the London theatre." He enjoyed meeting and working with Noël Coward, and was "immediately attracted by his charm and crackling wit."[95]

While *On With the Dance* ran at the London Pavillion, the Ballets Russes presented *Zéphire* and *Les Matelots* in Monte Carlo and Paris, and Massine received congratulatory cables from Diaghilev, Kochno, and Dukelsky. When the company moved to the London Coliseum in the summer, Massine rejoined them as guest dancer. In addition to some of his old roles, his repertory included for the first time the French sailor in *Les Matelots.* His return was not easy for Savina. Diaghilev vindictively paired them in the pas de deux from *Cimarosiana* and again in the Blue-bird pas de deux.

When the London engagement ended, Massine and Marra returned to Galli.

> *From time to time I received letters from Semenoff* [sic] *in Positano, telling me what was happening on Galli. In this way I learned that work on the vineyards was going well, but that more pine trees had been destroyed by the* tramontana—*the bitter north wind that sweeps down from the mountains. I had already realized that the only way to combat the* tramontana, *and the equally destructive* sirocco, *was to continue planting trees every autumn, but not until I had lost hundreds of pines did I discover that the best things to plant on Galli were cypresses, the local Southern pines, and rosemary bushes. Through trial and error I was gradually learning how to cultivate my island. I visited nurseries in Florence and Rome during my holiday in the autumn of 1925, buying hundreds of plants and bushes, and also ordered grape vines to be shipped over from Sicily.*[96]

Upon his return to London from Italy, Massine started work on the revue *Still Dancing,* which opened on November 19, 1925, at the Pavillion. Although this time Coward was not to be involved, Delysia remained the star. Within two parts and twenty scenes, there were four ballets by Massine: revivals of the successful *Rake* and *Hungarian Wedding* from *On With the Dance,* and two new works, *Pompeii à la Massine* and *Pyjama Jazz.*

Pompeii à la Massine had scenery and costumes by Doris Sinkeisen and a potpourri of melodies, mainly by Louis Ganne. The program note read: "The fantasy represents an entertainment presided over by Ariadne. It commences with a dance of flowers and a caterpillar, followed by the repair of Ariadne's heart, broken by the flight of Theseus. After an incident between the Alchemist and his clients, there comes a Chinese visitor. The Pavane, danced by Ariadne, leads up to the finale." *Pyjama Jazz,* the revue's finale, was a 1920s extravaganza led by Delysia, with the whole cast in fashionable pajamas provided for the occasion by Selfridge and Company.

Cochran's association with Massine proved so successful that before 1925 ended he began to negotiate Massine's participation in his next revue, *Cochran's Revue 1926,* scheduled to open on April 29. He wanted Massine and Nicholson, who had collaborated so successfully on *The Rake,* to work together again in a ballet based on an episode from Boccaccio's *Decameron.* Massine in turn suggested that Cochran engage

Massine in costume for the Chinese number in Still Dancing, *1927*

Dukelsky as composer and hire the dancers Nicholas Zverev and Vera Nemtchinova, who were husband and wife, from Diaghilev's company. Diaghilev, his fury held in check, genteelly complained to Cochran:

> *You knew, of course, that Mme. Nemchinova was my pupil and that it was with me that she learned to dance in the past ten years . . . Allow me to add in a friendly spirit that I very much regret . . . the way you exploit the Russian artists whom I have discovered and trained. Dukelsky writing bad fox-trots for musicals is not doing what he is destined to do; Massine dancing in supper clubs and composing choreographies in the style of* Pompeii à la Massine *dangerously compromises himself; likewise, Nemchinova is not made for revues . . . I take the liberty of telling you this in view of our longstanding friendship. One must create works and artists and not exploit those created by others for purposes very different from yours and in an atmosphere having nothing in common with what you do, and what you often do very well.*[97]

For *Cochran's Revue 1926* Massine revived his *Gigue* from Les Soirées and created two new works: a pas de deux, *La Carmagnole,* with decor by Guy Arnox and music by Adolf Stanislas, and the Boccaccio ballet, *The Tub. The Tub,* to music by Haydn, with scenery and costumes by Nicholson, was based on the tale of Giannello Strignario and revolved around the exploits of an unfaithful wife, Peronella (Nemtchinova), her deceived husband, Piero (Zverev), and her lover, Giannello (Massine). While the husband is away, Peronella receives her lover, but to their surprise the husband returns home with a friend who wants to buy a wine barrel. Peronella hides Giannello in the barrel, then, after he emerges, makes her husband believe that he, too, has come to buy it, and all ends well. Less neatly, life was imitating art, or vice versa: the triangle on stage was being paralleled in the performers' lives. Since their collaboration in *Les Matelots,* Massine and Nemtchinova had embarked upon a short-lived love affair.

In January of 1926, Massine had received preliminary offers from Diaghilev to revive *Mercure* and to make two new ballets: *La Pastorale,* to a score by Georges Auric, and *Jack-in-the-Box,* to orchestrated piano music by Satie. For *Jack-in-the-Box,* Massine was to collaborate again with Picasso. But when Massine skipped the Ballets Russes season in order to keep his commitment to Cochran in the spring of 1926, Picasso dropped out of the project and showed little interest in working with Diaghilev on any other. As it happened, Beaumont owned the rights to *Jack-in-the-*

Box and did not hesitate to impose on Diaghilev his choices of Derain as designer and Milhaud as orchestrator. (Beaumont wanted *Jack-in-the-Box* and *Mercure* to coincide with the Satie festival he was organizing as an homage to the recently deceased composer.) Diaghilev then proposed having *Mercure* rechoreographed, since Massine was unavailable; but Picasso objected, and *Mercure* was not to be restaged for Diaghilev until 1927.[98]

For the next two years Massine's life followed a pattern: the summer he would spend in Galli, supervising works in progress; from autumn through spring he would join Diaghilev as guest choreographer and dancer. In 1927 he produced the revival of *Mercure,* a new version of *Les Fâcheux,* and the world premiere of *Le Pas d'acier.* In 1928 he created his last work for Diaghilev, *Ode.*

Les Fâcheux, premiered on May 3, 1927, was another modern adaptation of an earlier work, Molière's 1661 comedy-ballet of the same name. Diaghilev first had produced it in 1924 with music by Auric, choreography by Nijinska and scenery and costumes by Braque. According to Kochno, the 1924 version failed because his libretto concentrated on individual characterizations, a challenge Nijinska was rarely up to, since her abilities were more suited to ensemble work. Massine, on the other hand, was skilled at embellishing the personality of each role. Kochno has called him a "clockmaker" who was able "to translate words into dance movements, contrary to Fokine, who translated words into pantomime." To Kochno, a ballet by Massine was *"une conversation chantée."*[99] Nevertheless, Massine's version of *Les Fâcheux,* following in Nijinska's footsteps, was not very successful.

Without doubt, Massine's boldest venture for the Ballets Russes in 1927 was *Le Pas d'acier,* which was premiered in Paris on July 4. The ballet, in two scenes, depicted two facets of Soviet life: the fields and the factory. It had a score by Prokofiev and scenery and costumes by Georgy Yakulov. *Le Pas d'acier* was Diaghilev's attempt to align himself with the experimental aesthetics of the postrevolutionary art of Russia, the outgrowth of the country's radically transformed political, social, and economic structure. One of the new artistic movements was constructivism, which celebrated the perfection of technology and the era of the machine. *Le Pas d'acier* was to be the Ballets Russes' contribution to constructivism.

Diaghilev's enthusiasm for a Soviet-inspired ballet was born in March of 1923, during the visit to Paris of Alexander Tairov's Kamerny Theater. Initially he planned to engage a team of Soviet artists: Tairov or

Vsevolod Meyerhold as director; Yakulov, Tairov's scenic designer; and Soviet choreographer Kasian Goleizovsky. When only Yakulov accepted his invitation, Diaghilev offered the commission for the stage direction and choreography to Massine, believing him, according to Kochno, the only other appropriate choice.[100]

Prokofiev and Yakulov wanted "to show what was new in the Soviet Union, above all, its achievements in construction." They would propel the "action on stage with big and small hammers, rotating conveyors—belts and fly-wheels and flashing signals. All this encouraged a common creative impulse during which the choreographic groupings both worked at machines and choreographically represented machines in operation."[101] The constructivist elements were to be provided also by Massine's choreography and mise-en-scène.[102] Massine devised a new choreographic lexicon that pictured, through expressive mechanical movements, a world in which human emotion was stifled.[103]

Despite British reservations about a Soviet-inspired ballet, when the new work was presented in London in July *The Times* found the second scene "extraordinarily impressive, and even terrifying."[104] Wrote the *Daily Express*: "Massine has created new postures and steps, strange contortions and movements that give the impression of powerful, complicated machinery, pistons working, wheels turning, and intense labour. The effect is stimulating, exciting, at times comic, and on the whole interesting to the highest degree."[105] For Cyril Beaumont, the second scene "gave a masterly impression of rhythmic power and beauty of machines":

> There were isolated movements which gradually built up into one huge machine, now of this type, now of that. Arms weaved, swung, and revolved; feet pounded the floor; even bodies took part in the movement, swinging from the waist in different arcs and at varying angles. The dancers massed, divided, strung out into line, and, with arms outstretched sideways, sharply turned their hands up and down, flat to the audience, which action ingeniously suggested a flashing lamp; this flashing, arranged in changing patterns, was most effective. So the rhythmic force ceaselessly grew in intensity until there appeared on a central platform two figures bearing giant hammers, which they swung and wielded more and more strongly until, at the height of the tumult, the climax was reached with the constructivist elements adding their quota—signal discs snapping on and off, and wheels spinning faster and faster. At this point the curtain fell to the accompaniment of a frenzied outburst of applause.[106]

Massine with Alexandra Danilova
in Le Pas d'acier, *1927*

This scene renewed Beaumont's "admiration for Massine's rare ability to contrive movements appropriate both to the theme of the piece and to the rhythm of the music, and then to combine the component parts into one vast orchestration of sound and expressive action, ever increasing in intensity until the conclusion was attained."[107]

Yet as the Ballets Russes season ended, Massine began to feel that most of his possibilities for creative work in Europe had been exhausted. He had now produced five more works for Diaghilev, but he remained unhappy. In his autobiography he remembers worrying in 1927 that since by then "Balanchine was doing so much of his [Diaghilev's] choreography . . . there would not be enough work for the two of us."[108] What he does not say is that although Balanchine had created six works in three years (1925–27), two of them—*La Pastorale* and *Jack-in-the-Box*—first had been offered to Massine and turned down by him, or that in 1927 Massine produced three ballets for Diaghilev, Balanchine one. Still, there is reason to believe that Massine chafed at sharing the Ballets Russes with *anyone,* since he had never had to before. And certainly he must have been irritated when Diaghilev commissioned from Balanchine a new version of *Le Chant du rossignol* in 1925, at a point when Massine's own version was only five years old.

But beyond any rivalry with Balanchine, Massine probably felt stunted artistically. His strained personal relationship with Diaghilev rendered him powerless in setting the company's artistic course—that responsibility had been given to Kochno. Massine's chief contribution thus far had been to execute projects that had been conceived by others. He behaved like a competent craftsman: he came, did his job, and left.

So in the summer of 1927 he set his sights across the Atlantic. If the United States was not to offer him the creative outlet he longed for, it might at least provide more generous financial rewards. And there was no denying that money was desperately needed to continue the renovations on Galli.[109] By July he was writing to Otto Kahn in New York to explore the possibility of working at the Metropolitan Opera House. He also contacted three English theatrical agencies, Daniel Meyer Company, Foster's, and Ernest Edelstein, as well as any other London contact who might help him secure a job in the United States—if not at the Met, then perhaps on the Broadway stage, in Hollywood, or with the Chicago Civic Opera. On February 7, 1928, Massine sailed for New York on the *Mauretania,* clutching letters of introduction, including four from Cochran to theatrical tycoons Charles B. Dillingham, Florenz Ziegfeld, Morris Guest, and Max Hart. New York's Plaza Hotel became his center of operations.

By the time his frantic American sojourn ended in mid-March, the agent William Morris had negotiated for Massine a preliminary contract with S. L. Rothafel of the Roxy Theatre in New York. The six-month term of the agreement would begin in December 1928 and included first-class transportation from Europe as well as a weekly starting salary of $350.[110]

Back in Europe, Massine hectically began preparing repertory to bring to the United States. He sought performing rights to some of his works in the Ballets Russes repertory and to the segments he had created for Cochran's revues. He also found creative energy for two new ballets, *Perpetomobile* and *Ode*.

Unsatisfied with doing Ballets Russes work for hire, Massine now began to explore ideas independently. His inclination toward abstraction, which first had shown up in his 1920 *Sacre du printemps*, by 1927 had become nearly all-absorbing. By the end of that year, in search of collaborators for an uncompromising abstract ballet, he approached two old friends, Sonia and Robert Delaunay. In a carefully composed letter, Sonia responded ecstatically, congratulating Massine on his commitment to a new "regenerating and liberating movement" that was to signal the "beginning of a new era for ballet."[111] A sort of budding manifesto, her letter divided ballet into three periods: classicism; the analytical period, which she called the *"époque de nature morte"*; and modern ballet, or the "period of pure dance." Sonia believed that their collaboration could coax modern ballet to "wash off all that junk dealing [*brocante*] of false modernity, of mannerism and idiocy." The aim of their work together was to force ballet to align itself with the new contemporary art and produce "pure dance for the senses and the intellect, without tricks, naked."[112]

Such brave words make it all the more regrettable that even today the history of *Perpetomobile* remains largely unknown. Set to music by Schubert, it was described on a list of productions Massine intended to take to America as "visions of rhythm and colour by L. Massine with scenery and dresses by Sonia and Robert Delaunay."[113] We know that Massine began to rehearse the work in Paris after his return from the United States, and some of Sonia's costume sketches have survived; all other specific information about the work is lost. It is impossible to say whether it was completed and, if so, whether it may have been privately presented or was in fact never seen outside a rehearsal room.

Despite these uncertainties, *Perpetomobile* holds a prominent place in Massine's oeuvre. It marks the high point of his exploration of abstraction during the 1920s, and its conception is a precursor to his purely abstract symphonic ballets of the 1930s. One can see in the description of

Perpetomobile a clear point of departure for his 1933 collaboration with André Masson in *Les Présages,* and its influence is apparent again in his 1939 collaboration with Matisse in *Rouge et noir.*

The argument for *Perpetomobile*'s pivotal role in Massine's growth becomes even more tantalizing when one examines a work completed around the same time, his last for Diaghilev. *Ode: Meditation on the Majesty of God on the Occasion of an Apparition of Aurora Borealis* has long been regarded as one of the Ballets Russes' most elaborate and hypnotic productions. It was a ballet oratorio in three acts to a libretto by Kochno, with music by Nicolas Nabokov, scenery and costumes by Pavel Tchelitchev, and special lighting effects and projections by filmmaker Pierre Charbonnier. It had the barest of story lines: "Nature expands her mysteries to a pupil. She exhibits the stars, and a river, flowers and bacteria, and finally 'the master work, the end of all yet done'—man." [114] The oratorio was based on an ode by the eighteenth-century Russian writer Mikhail Lomonosov. Diaghilev first envisioned it as a period piece recalling imperial coronation festivities, and it is on this idea that Kochno based his libretto. But as work among Kochno, Tchelitchev, and Massine went forward, the original concept underwent drastic revision, and Tchelitchev's notion of building the ballet around "the seven days of creation culminating with the appearance of the Aurora Borealis—the northern lights" prevailed. [115] In the end, *Ode* became for Kochno an evocation of the sumptuousness of the tsarist court translated into modernist terms. [116] For his part, Diaghilev loathed the final conception and doubted that the collaborators could bring it off. [117]

Rehearsals for *Ode* began in Monte Carlo in the spring and continued in Paris. Diaghilev by this time had ceased to take much direct interest in Ballets Russes productions, but in this case he took control of final rehearsals to bring some order to what he considered the chaotic state of *Ode*. Above all, according to Haskell and Nouvel, Diaghilev wanted "to suppress a series of cinematographic projections that horrified him." [118]

Nevertheless, the final result was impressive. *Ode* was a multimedia work whose cosmic/microscopic effects were achieved with the help of slide and film projections on a giant backcloth, making the character of nature itself seem to float on clouds. Phosphorescent costumes and neon light projections heightened the effect. Cecil Beaton was especially taken by Tchelitchev's decor:

> Ode *was remarkable for the fact that Tchelitchev had completely discarded painted scenery. The setting consisted of ropes and two lines, which*

mounted from either wing to meet high above the centre of the back of the stage, on which were hung small dolls. . . . Against a blue void the still, small dolls gave the scene vast size and depth, while the black, white and grey dancers formed triangles of rope, strange mechanical designs.

There was no insistence on the reality of this geometrical immensity. The keynote was suggestion: when Lifar appeared as a cleric, he wore a curé's tabs, but retained the dancer's tights. All the dancers, their faces obliterated with flat masks, were black-gloved symbols in a nocturnal world. Behind gauze screens a man and a tall, thin woman, like a blade, gave an impression of nakedness, without conscious nudity. It seemed as if all humanity had been reduced to embryonic form.[119]

When first approached for *Ode,* Massine had felt that the poem, "a contemplative hymn to nature," was not appropriate for a ballet. But after studying it, he "found a series of images beginning to take shape" in his mind.[120] Together he and Tchelitchev mapped out a cohesive visual spectacle blending stage design and choreography in a totally unified effect. Massine hewed to classical ballet technique, relying for his effects on purity of line and elongated movements. Felia Doubrovska, who danced in the premiere, recalled that with the exception of some of the architectural and geometrical configurations for the corps de ballet and the role danced by Lifar, the choreography was poetic and classical, emphasizing long arabesques, développés, and a formal rhythmic beauty.[121] The classical line was accentuated by the female dancers' costumes: white unitards and headpieces like swimming caps. (Doubrovska's exquisite physical instrument probably served Massine's choreography beautifully.)

Ode was an important advance in the evolution of Massine's "new classicism." Even as early as the *Astuzie* divertissement of 1920, he was beginning to depart from the choreography he had produced under the influence of the neoprimitivist and modernist aesthetics of Gontcharova, Larionov, Picasso, and Falla. In 1926 he had begun to study in London with Nicholas Legat, former director of the Imperial Ballet School in St. Petersburg. Legat helped him to trust his emerging new feeling for flowing movement and openness, and to move beyond Cecchetti's more self-contained classical style and Massine's own deeply imbedded roots in folk dance. The elements of this new classicism stand out in several of Massine's works from the twenties, especially *Le Beau Danube, Divertissement, Les Roses, Zéphire et Flore,* and *Ode,* but it would find its most sublime expression in the symphonic ballets that he began to produce in 1933.

When *Ode* premiered on June 6, 1928, in Paris and on July 9 in London, its reception was mixed. The ballet was visually splendid, yet most critics were perplexed by the multimedia effects or by the work's overpowering surrealism—or both. In London, Edwin Evans reacted coolly to some of the lighting devices and film projections but admired the choreography, calling it "extraordinarily good" and finding in "its soft-hued background and the dancers in pure white before it [a scene] to be remembered long afterwards as a feast of beauty in movement." [122] Cyril Beaumont praised the choreography: "Massine displayed the greatest innovation and originality in the composition of his ever-changing groups, which were never symmetrical and yet harmonious. The actual movements were in the manner of the classical ballet whose linear beauty was here given its full value by reason of the bodies being, for all practical purposes, unclothed. But the lines had an unusually austere and chaste quality, a geometrical rather than an emotional beauty." [123] Beaumont described one of the pas de deux as an "elegy" in which

> the dancers jointly upheld, each with one upraised hand, a slender, horizontal pole, from the first and last third of which was suspended a length of gauze, a little higher than a man and about twice the breadth of his body. This device was like two straight curtains with a gap between them equal to the width of one. A number of beautiful effects were achieved when the dancers danced behind the gauze, which invested them with ectoplastic quality, or else appeared alternately in the open space, so that a solid form danced with a shadow in one; sometimes their arms alone curved and crossed in the intervening space. [124]

For Beaumont, *Ode* had a "strange character," a "celestial beauty," and an "intellectual appeal." A decade later, A. V. Coton called it "the 1928 grand experiment." [125] Lynn Garafola argues that *Ode*, like *Apollon Musagète*, another 1928 Diaghilev production (with choreography by Balanchine), anticipates the 1930s "in the appearance of dreams, romance, and fantasy elements . . . in the new importance assigned to dance in the overall ballet spectacle, and in the renewal of interest in the danse d'ecole." [126]

Before departing for the United States at the end of the year, Massine was engaged by Ida Rubinstein to choreograph two ballets for her newly organized company. They were not to be premiered until the following year.

The Russian-born Rubinstein had made her Paris debut with the Ballets Russes, dancing the leading roles in Fokine's *Cléopâtre* and

Schéhérazade. Her technique rose to amateur level at best, but she excelled in mimed parts where her enigmatic beauty could often be seen to great advantage. After her success with Diaghilev she sponsored seasons in Paris, presenting works created for her by some of the era's most prominent artists. In 1928 she founded her own company, producing ornate works in which she was regarded as the absolute embodiment of fin-de-siècle aesthetics. She held court in her Parisian *hôtel particulier* (decorated by Bakst), surrounded by a number of influential personalities from the worlds of society, the arts, and letters, including Gabriele d'Annunzio, Paul Valéry, Ravel, Gide, and Benois.

Massine's two productions for Rubinstein—conceived, as was customary, by the diva herself—were *David* (libretto by André Doderet, music by Henri Sauguet, and designs by Benois) and *Les Enchantements d'Alcine* (libretto by Louis Laloy after Ariosto, music by Auric, designs by Benois). Both works revolved around a hero's adventures and provided exotic backdrops for Rubinstein's striking presence. They exploited her penchant for playing male parts *en travesti,* a trademark of her productions since her unforgettable creation of the title role in the Debussy-d'Annunzio *Martyre de Saint Sébastien* in 1911. Rubinstein steeped these roles in decadent sexual ambiguity, which delighted her followers.

Massine, however, was not much inspired by her. For one thing, he was being asked merely to prop up, not to elevate, her lurid conceptions. The grande dame herself was yet another problem. "Rubinstein, who was really more of an actress than a dancer, was beautiful and statuesque, but though she had a striking stage presence it was difficult to get her to move gracefully." Since the ballets were "centered on her," Massine "had very little opportunity for original choreography."[127]

Despite this unfulfilling work, the months spent in Paris put Massine in high spirits. Already that spring Nabokov had found the choreographer "at moments even gay and smiling" instead of his usual "stern and taciturn" self.[128] There was good reason: he was in love with a beautiful twenty-year-old Russian dancer, Eugenia Delarova.

Delarova, born in 1907 in St. Petersburg, left the Soviet Union in 1926. She met Massine in Paris in the spring of 1928 in a class given by the Russian ballerina Lubov Egorova. One day after class he asked Delarova about the situation in Russia at the time of her departure. The conversation was brief, but provocative enough to make him go to see her dance at the Folies-Bergère. Later he showed up at a rehearsal of a troupe assembled by Nemtchinova and Dolin, where she was a recent recruit. Finally, he sent her a note at the Folies-Bergère asking her out. After several dates, the love affair grew passionate.[129]

Delarova, extroverted and easygoing, found Massine gloomy and too serious. His lifestyle seemed to her needlessly severe and austere, and she saw no reason for him to dress stuffily in dark clothes. He seemed aloof and guarded all the time. But Delarova had fallen in love, and decided to brighten him up, hoping her ability to enjoy life would prove contagious. And her lack of inhibition gradually rubbed off on him; he allowed for some spontaneity and became much more stylish.

During the summer, on their way to Galli, they motored through some of Massine's favorite Italian towns, lingering in Florence and Naples, where he showed her the paintings and architecture he had learned to love. In Positano they visited the Semenovs, who had become Massine's surrogate family. By then Massine's appearance had begun to show some moderating Delarova touches: sandals, shorts, brightly colored shirts. His inordinate jealousy didn't faze her, and their first few months together were idyllic. Caressed by the southern Italian sun, their days in Galli were filled with romance. By night they would sail in the moonlight, their favorite music pouring lushly from a portable gramophone. As soon as they arrived back in Paris from their holiday, they married, and days later they sailed for America.

PART FOUR

Years of Transition:
The Symphonic Ballets

Only metaphor can provide us with evasion,
and it creates out of real things imaginary
reefs, the blossoming of illusory islands.

—ORTEGA Y GASSET

Massine's dancers in the fourth movement of Choreartium, *1933:*
Tatiana Riabouchinska, Tamara Toumanova, and
David Lichine in the foreground

CHAPTER 10

New York, December 1928–London, June 1936

MASSINE'S ARRIVAL in New York was scarcely publicized. In the *New York Times* John Martin hinted that the Roxy management harbored some misgivings about just how well their new choreographer would adapt to working in the American theater. The Roxy's terse announcement had said only that Massine would assist Miss Ragge and Léon Leonidov in staging the theater's dance offerings. "Assistant" struck Martin as a surprisingly humble job description for one of the world's leading choreographers. But Rothafel was in fact hiring Massine on a trial basis. He had been warned not only that Massine was difficult and demanding but that his productions could be ruinously expensive.[1] In order to dispel just such doubts, Massine had asked Cochran to vouch for him personally with Rothafel.[2] He was fully aware of his predicament: "In Europe I had made something of a reputation, but in America I was just another dancer who had been vaguely associated with the Ballets Russes."[3]

> *The productions at the Roxy, I discovered, were vaudeville-type spectacles performed on a vast raked stage. I was amazed at the way the director, Léon Leonidov, managed to manoeuvre the interminable rows of sequined and high-kicking chorus girls on and off stage. When I was introduced to Leonidov he told me that I would be expected to provide a new ballet every week, with occasional solos and divertissements.*
>
> *It was a staggering responsibility to have to create every week a ballet which would appeal to the enormous Roxy audience, particularly as my productions had to be coordinated with the weekly theme of the rest of the spectacle and in keeping with the seasons of the year. I composed Spring Ballets, Easter Ballets, Christmas Ballets, and ballets for such festivals as St. Valentine's Day, Halloween and Thanksgiving. The music was mostly Victor Herbert, Sigmund Romberg and Franz Lehár. As well as rehearsing the new ballet, which had to be ready by Thursday each week, I also danced four times a day, and five times on Saturday. I did not see much of New York. When I was not at the Roxy I was in my bed, asleep. Eugenia was in the corps de ballet, and she too danced four times a day and five on Saturday. It was a miserable life for her, but she realized we had no choice, and never complained.*[4]

In May 1929 Massine and Delarova made a short trip to Paris to supervise the final rehearsals of *David* and *Alcine* for Rubinstein. Feeling as if they had just been "let out of prison,"[5] they rambled about Paris visiting old hangouts, shopping, strolling through galleries, or enjoying old friends, especially Gontcharova, Larionov, and the Delaunays. At Sonia Delaunay's boutique, Delarova bought new dresses. Then the couple returned to New York and toiling at the Roxy.

In August 1929, the Massines were on a short vacation in Virginia Beach. A member of the local press gave them the awful news: on the nineteenth, in Venice, Diaghilev had died. Massine "sat down on a bench and thought of all the years I had spent with him, all the ballets we had collaborated on, all the times I had danced for him. . . . Although I had twice left his company, I had the deepest affection and admiration for him, and knew too how much I owed him. . . . Having been so closely connected with him for so many years, I think I must have felt his loss more than anyone."[6]

In the years ahead, with the man of flesh and blood actually gone,

Massine's recollections of Diaghilev would gradually shift from memory to myth. Massine, Diaghilev's pupil turned antagonist, eventually became his most fervent apostle. The edge of their stormy relations dulled with time. For the moment, however, his present responsibilities called to Massine and, bewildered as he must have been at this paradoxical loss, he could deal with his sorrow only by quickly returning to New York— and to work.

Immediately after Diaghilev's death Massine wrote to Beaumont:

Etienne! Do you want to take over the direction of the Ballets Russes? I would leave everything here in order to help you—we would create masterpieces—Picasso will help us . . . I am full of enthusiasm—and if you believe that you would like to do it, cable me to come to Europe and I will leave immediately.

We will take another direction—there are so many beautiful things to be done—discuss all of this with Picasso . . . Etienne—you are the only person who could succeed.[7]

Tempting as this offer may have been, Beaumont was not interested in following in Diaghilev's footsteps.

Cole Porter introduced Massine to theatrical producer E. Ray Goetz, who hoped to reconstitute the Ballets Russes in America and present seasons in New York and on tour.[8] (Goetz had wanted to do the same thing in 1928, but no engagements materialized.) Now, with Massine as middleman, Goetz moved to secure the rights to the deceased impresario's properties; but in the United States of 1929 raising cash proved extremely difficult, and he had abandoned the idea by 1931. This was only one of many disappointments for Massine in the years from 1929 to 1931. He drove himself into a frenzy trying to resurrect Diaghilev's company. He talked up the idea continually with the Grigorievs, Woizikowski, Sokolova, Doubrovska, Balanchine, and Lifar, among other Ballets Russes alumni.[9] Looking for financial backing, he found two major prospects: Sir Thomas Beecham at Covent Garden and René Blum at the Casino de Monte Carlo. Negotiations with Beecham lasted until 1932, but nothing came of them. And in Monte Carlo, where at first there was no interest in reviving Diaghilev's company, by 1931 Blum was instead organizing a new permanent ballet company at the Casino in collaboration with Colonel Wassily de Basil of the Paris-based Opéra Russe. The spring of 1932 witnessed the triumphant debut of the Ballets Russes de Monte Carlo.[10]

Yet Massine stood apart from these developments, doggedly trying to keep his career afloat in hectic round trips between the United States and Europe. The artistic highlight of 1930 was a revival of his *Sacre du printemps* for the League of Composers. Nicholas Roerich was to collaborate on the design; Leopold Stokowski would conduct the Philadelphia Orchestra. Cast in the role of the Chosen Maiden was the American modern dancer Martha Graham, who later reminisced:

> It was a great turning point in my life, and it moved me into an area which fed me a very great deal. I had no sense of belonging to the ballet world at that time, and I was struggling to find a language which was, I felt, a little more true than what I had to do in the Follies and in vaudeville, when I was there, and in Denishawn. . . .
>
> The passionate Russian thing—whether it's Russian or whether it's primal doesn't matter, but the rite was a sacrificial one and it had nothing to do with the idiosyncrasies of ballet style or modern dance. You had to accommodate yourself to it, and the music is very, very powerful, as we all know. We go and hear somebody's new composition just this year, and we will say, "Well, that is just straight out of Stravinsky," because he has a lure for people which is very hard to resist. I met him once. I meant absolutely nothing to him. He was in a wrath at the moment—not at me, but just at the world in general.
>
> But Sacre meant spiritually a great deal to me and still does. . . . It's close to me emotionally and it was a turning point in my life.[11]

Stories about the edgy working relationship between Massine and Graham during *Le Sacre du printemps* abound.[12] How true are any of them? Two such volatile personalities would seem to provide ample material for combustion, but in fact there appears to have been only one minor flare-up: Graham refused to rehearse her solo in full force. Such holding back in rehearsal would indeed have been incomprehensible to Massine, who came from a deeply ingrained Russian tradition of zealous commitment to a role from day one. As a result, so the story goes, he threatened to replace her. But *did* he? Anna Sokolow, who danced in *Sacre*, suggested that Graham's decision not to dance full out in rehearsal was due to simple precaution, because she first "wanted to see what we were doing and how we were reacting to the direction of Massine."[13] Bessie Schönberg, another cast member, concluded that Graham "faithfully learned what Massine had to teach her, but then she took it to the studio by herself and made it her own, which I am sure meant that she stressed other things than Massine might have and changed certain things. I am sure she didn't want particularly to exhibit this every time at rehearsal and have Massine say, 'You're not doing it right.' "[14] Also, she cannot have been eager to appear a fool before the eleven members of her own company who were dancing in *Sacre*.

Others recall no temperamental exchanges at all between Graham and Massine. Lily Mehlman, also in the cast, remembered Graham as "very cooperative . . . and there was great respect shown to her by Stokowski and Massine."[15] Said Schönberg: "When she was needed, she was all there."[16] In conversations with the author, Delarova did not recall any particular friction. Massine, also in conversations with the author, described his work with Graham as unqualifiedly productive. In his memoirs he wrote: "Martha Graham's powerful performance as the Chosen Maiden added considerable strength to the production. I found her a most subtle and responsive dancer to work with, and her small stature and delicate movements gave the role an added poignancy."[17] Nor would Graham confirm stories about dissension between herself and Massine:

I'm sorry to disappoint you on that. I had made up my mind that I would follow direction completely, and I did. I never argued with any of them because I felt they were dealing with something which I was not ready to deal with choreographically or musically, and I remember the first time Massine came to my apartment. It was during the Depression, and I had an apartment that looked over Central Park which I got because nobody else wanted it. . . . It had no furniture. I had an army cot, and a chest of drawers, and a kitchen table, a grand piano, and a Victrola. So Massine came and we played the Sacre. He was very nostalgic. He said it was a very different way of hearing it, compared to the last time he had heard it, and it brought back memories which I'm sure didn't encompass a bare living room in the Depression facing Central Park with a small Victrola on the floor and no other furniture except the piano.

But I made up my mind that I would follow his choreography as nearly as I could, and his direction, and I did. There were certain things balletically that I changed a bit. But my style was beginning to develop at that time, and I would do the thing the way I would do it, you see, and usually Massine was very generous and he said, "We'll keep that." For instance a leap or something of that kind. And I remember rehearsing with him at Roseland because there were no studios available—this great big shiny room with all those mirrors. I was very thin in those days and I was in a black dress. And he was very thin and he was in black, kind of Spanish pants that he always had, and he looked at us in the mirror. He was teaching and we were alone. He said, "We look enough alike to be brother and sister." Well, we did in some strange way. . . .[18]

To say the least, stories about strife between Massine and Graham seem to have been much exaggerated.

Massine's *Sacre* was a singular event in the development of American dance. One of the most prestigious ballet choreographers of the day was working in the United States with *modern* dancers; thus it marked an important moment of fusion between two apparently irreconcilable approaches. According to Sokolow, "It was a revelation in the world of modern dance to have a Russian ballet artist come in, introduce us to another world, introduce us to Stravinsky . . . and then watching Massine work, which we did when we stood on the side while he worked on other things. . . . I couldn't help thinking that there was a connection between the approach to dance as Martha Graham had and Léonide Massine had."[19] Bessie Schönberg described Graham's daring solo: "She was in the air practically all the time. They were complete splits in the air with, of course, not her toes pointed, but her heels pointed and her hands at an angle. And they were like little screams in the air, they were like little yells; and it was frenetic, extraordinary; and deeply moving, deeply moving."[20]

The ballet was presented in Philadelphia on April 11 and at the Metropolitan Opera in New York on April 22, sharing the program with the American premiere of Schoenberg's opera *Die glückliche Hand*. The double bill, called the "most important dance event of the entire year"[21] by the New York *Herald Tribune*, was ecstatically received by the press and the intelligentsia. In the *Times* John Martin wrote:

> *There can be little question that it provided a landmark on the road to the theatrical theatre, the theatre of synthesis, or "rhythm," as Mr. Stokowski called it. . . .*
>
> *Of Massine's choreography it is only possible to speak with enthusiasm. Just as the music does not yield its fullness at one hearing, it is doubtful if there is one pair of eyes in a thousand capable of seeing the full richness and beauty of this dance setting. As has been noted already, it was extraordinarily inventive. The movements of the individual dancers were colored with hieratic suggestions and imbued with a tremendous muscular vigor which at the same time seemed to be inhibited by the mental limitations of*

a crude people. Through this combination of opposing ideas the choreographer conveyed without an instant's relief the overpowering influence of something not understood—the mystery, if you will, of nature in its vernal surging. In the mass designs were creations of surpassing beauty, ingenious to the last degree, but none the less stable for that. . . .

In the first part of the ballet there perhaps was the most impressive evidence of Massine's artistry. The dance of the adolescents, in which the men perform tremendous movements before a background of girls seated and moving with their arms; the mock abduction and the spring rounds that follow; the games of the rival tribes, and the intricate and extraordinary mass movement that closes the act, all these are choreography that ranks at the very top of modern dancing. Through its complicated visual counterpoint and its terrific energy, there shines the barbaric passion of elemental human beings. If it were not so near in the physical standards of savagery, akin to that of the animals themselves, it would be sensual and voluptuous beyond what we are accustomed to condone in the theatre. As it is, it is so young, so frank, so strong, that it seems a part of nature itself, a visualization of that rich depth which rolls through the music.

As the maiden chosen for sacrifice, Martha Graham proved once again her right to rank with the foremost of her art. The famous dance which brings the ballet to an end puts a terrific burden upon the dancer. After two acts of mass movement, keyed far higher than any single dancer could be expected to reach, she is called upon to touch the peak of performance. This is a problem for the choreographer as well, and Miss Graham in the movement designed for her by Massine succeeded in doing the seemingly impossible. . . .[22]

But even the complete triumph of *Sacre* could not guarantee Massine further employment. For the next two years the bustling between Europe and the United States continued. Except for commitments to the Roxy in the early spring and guest performances at the Arts Club of Chicago, by 1931 Europe was again the Massines' center of operations.

In April, Walter Nouvel had approached Massine on behalf of Ida Rubinstein to return to Paris the following month.[23] Rubinstein engaged Massine from May 1 through July 15 for her company's Parisian and Covent Garden seasons; he was to supervise revivals of *David* and *Alcine* and to stage a new production, *Amphion*.

The *mélodrame Amphion* revolved around the adventures of the mythical character who received a lyre from Mercury and whose music moved stones. It was based on a poem by Paul Valéry, set to music by

Arthur Honegger of Les Six, with scenery and costumes by Alexandre Benois. Valéry's idea for this pantomime-ballet was to demonstrate expressive parallels among music, mime, and gesture (for him gesture had the triple value of the symbolic, the significative, and the active). He wanted "words, song, orchestra, pantomime, dance, and theatrical design to all merge as a whole."[24]

Valéry's involvement created high anticipation in the Paris press. But *Amphion* opened on June 23 to mixed reviews. Instead of the promised coordination of voice, music, action, and dance, most reviewers found confusion on stage. Louis Schneider lauded Benois's sumptuous decor in the grand opera style as "nothing Greek, nothing classical; conceived, as the costumes, in that modern Russian style that opens the door to all fantasies."[25] André George, on the other hand, deplored its "dark heaviness."[26] Henri Malherbe lamented that the designs, though naturalistic in inspiration, contradicted the symbolic intention of the poet, which was to free himself from the pseudorealistic style.[27]

As always with Rubinstein, the choreography relied more on pantomime than dance. Yet Levinson felt that "Massine's choreography, though relegated to semidarkness since all the light was directed towards the protagonist and surrounded by all sorts of obstacles, manifested originality, although it was compressed by the uncalled-for tyrannical necessities of a paradoxical mise-en-scène."[28] The choreography's "counterpoint of movement" and "monumental gymnastics" were not "exempted of grandeur," and "Massine's Russian constructivism" was justified by the libretto.[29]

Once again, Rubinstein was lambasted for producing works that kept her own persona firmly at center stage. There would always be those who would succumb to her charms, Emile Vuillermoz acknowledged. Nevertheless, he bluntly asked, "Why does she persist in personally engaging in battles in the fields of choreography and diction out of which she would not be able to emerge victoriously?"[30] Levinson complained, "How sad that Mme Rubinstein, who stages so many important productions, persists in spoiling everything by becoming a star."[31]

The Rubinstein engagement ended in July, and the Massines spent the rest of their summer in Galli. The young composer Igor Markevitch—Diaghilev's last lover—was their guest. In the spring Massine had been approached by the British and Dominions Film Corporation to create a new ballet to be included in an English film based on the story of *Le Beau Danube*.[32] He had chosen Markevitch as composer, before having met him, undoubtedly through the good offices of Alexandrine Trousse-vitch. Troussevitch, who had become a sort of secretary to Diaghilev during the impresario's final years, had introduced him to Markevitch; and after Diaghilev's death she backed Massine's efforts to revive the Ballets Russes. (An eccentric chain smoker, Troussevitch spent her last years in a Greek Orthodox convent in Palestine.)

From their first meeting in Paris, relations between Massine and Markevitch were friendly:

Massine and I met in Paris for the first time, and he was so moved by the memory of Diaghilev, which I embodied for him, that he could not hold back his tears. As for me, I remember the atmosphere of exceptional quality which emanated from his personality, which was possessed by the power of his own creativity in a way that was both naive and willful. The more I have become acquainted with Massine at his work, as I saw him implement a choreography or give a course in classical or Spanish dance, and the more I have learned of the first works he created in conjunction with old collaborators such as Picasso or Cocteau, all the more I have reached the conviction that Massine will turn out to have been one of the greatest choreographers and dancers of all times; possibly the most complete of all. . . .

Many artistic affinities brought us close to each other from the start. The Ballets Russes remained for Massine one of those rare subjects on which he would expound, and which seemed to touch him. One felt that they had brought him to himself and that he felt a deep need to keep them in his memory. The rest of the time, as he concentrated upon his work, he did not offer many possibilities for contact and was easily thought of as inhuman.[33]

Their second meeting took place in Naples, where they rented a vertical piano to bring along to Galli. On the island, Markevitch was introduced to Delarova and to Massine's father, Feodor, who had recently arrived from the Soviet Union to visit his son in Italy.

Over the years Massine had maintained a steady correspondence with his family in Russia, although he had not seen them since 1914. His sister, Raissa, and brother Mikhail had both married, and Mikhail had two children. His mother and brother Gregori had died, and Massine now wanted Feodor to spend time with him in Galli. His father helped with domestic chores, and "every evening at sunset he would stand out on the patio, playing his French horn, and I shall always remember him, sunburned, white-haired, but still erect, as he played us the lovely old Russian tunes which were part of my childhood."[34]

On the island Massine and Markevitch immersed themselves in the creation of the ballet score and libretto, and though the work was demanding, their days under the hot August sun were relaxing in all respects but one. Much to Markevitch's astonishment, Delarova—whom he described as "seductive" and "passionate"—began an open flirtation with him. Given Massine's jealous nature, it is easy to see why, according to Markevitch, the "atmosphere became tensed, the island seemed to shrink, Massine's handsome face became impenetrable, and I feared all the time a catastrophe."[35] Getting off the island may have been the only way to ease the strain. Thus, when work on the ballet score was complete, the party, with the exception of Massine's father, returned to the mainland. (Brigitte Helm, the star of the film, so disliked Markevitch's score that the ballet was dropped from the project before it was choreographed.)

Massine and his wife were given to exploring Italy's ruins, architectural sites, and museums. He took special delight in guiding her around a country he had learned to love through Diaghilev's eyes. On this particular excursion, they parted from Markevitch and traveled on their own to Sicily by car.

> From Taormina we drove via Syracuse, Agrigento and Segesta, to Selinus, where I was overwhelmed by the sheer immensity of the ruined Temple of the Giants. Wandering among these fragmentary columns and massive remains of statues of mighty gods, some with severed torsos over forty feet long, I was excited by the challenge which they presented. They immediately suggested to me vast harmonic groupings, and I wondered if it would be possible to create with human bodies a similar feeling of physical grandeur wedded to pure music. I realized that this could only be done by using the symphony of a great composer as the inspiration for my choreography, an idea which was to return to me later.[36]

That autumn and winter Massine pursued various projects that were set to debut the following year. First, he signed with Milan's Teatro alla Scala to choreograph two works to open the following January: a revival of Giuseppe Adami's *Vecchia Milano*, and *Belkis*. The latter, a grandiose pageant in six scenes to music by Respighi, featured the Persian princess-turned-dancer Leila Bederkhan. According to the *Dancing Times*, some of the numbers were successful, especially those performed by the rising Scala star Attilia Radice, but overall Massine's choreography was dull and repetitious.[37]

He was to fare better on the London theatrical stage. In September, Cochran approached him to create the dances for *Helen!*, a new production based on Offenbach's operetta *La Belle Hélène*.[38] It was to be directed by the renowned Max Reinhardt; Oliver Messel was hired as designer; and Evelyn Laye was to sing the lead role. Massine looked forward to collaborating with Reinhardt, whom Diaghilev had considered "a key figure in the development of realism in the theatre."[39] Massine found the Austrian director "a most interesting character, civilized, cultured and easy to talk to." And Reinhardt was astute when it came to stagecraft.

> *Once I had begun working for him I realized also that he was a complete man of the theatre, and one who well understood the value of simplicity in choreography. . . . While doing the choreography for the banqueting scene, the bacchanal, and the battle episodes, I learned some very valuable lessons from him, mainly concerned with the importance of rhythm in large ensemble scenes. He also had a wonderful way of integrating comic situations into large crowd scenes. Although he allowed me complete freedom as far as my own work on the production was concerned, I was always eager for his help and advice, and was flattered when he subtly intimated that he considered my participation in the production . . . almost as important as his own.*[40]

Helen! was rehearsed throughout November in Manchester, where it had its first run before moving to London's Adelphi Theatre on January 30, 1932.

In Manchester, shattering news arrived: Massine's father, who had remained in Galli with the caretakers, had died, like a mythical hero in exile, alone with his French horn and far from his native land. Heartbroken, but unable to leave England, Massine asked his wife to rush to Galli to arrange the funeral and oversee the burial of his father on a hill at the top of Positano.[41]

Flush with the success of *Helen!*, Cochran sought another collaboration with Reinhardt, Massine, and Messel. He wanted to revive a work he had produced in 1911 at the Olympia Theatre, *The Miracle*. Massine described *The Miracle* as "a wordless pageant in seven episodes based on the legend of a nun who breaks her vows for love of a knight, and returning to the convent after many years finds that her place has been taken by the Madonna and no one had missed her."[42]

The Spielmann in Max Reinhardt's The Miracle, *1932*

Cochran's 1911 extravaganza, under the direction of Reinhardt, required two thousand extras and featured a lavish cathedral decor whose rose window was three times larger than the one at Chartres. In 1923 Reinhardt had directed a grandiose production starring the English beauty and social luminary Lady Diana Cooper. It had toured the United States under the management of Morris Gest, who in many ways pushed Reinhardt out of the limelight. Now in 1932, Lady Diana, who had been adored in the U.S. tour, again was to appear as the Madonna; Tilly Losch, the Viennese dancer-actress, was cast as the nun. In addition to creating the dances, Massine was to play the role of the Spielmann, a trickster or minstrel who persuades the nun to abandon her duties. Except for some mild backstage intrigue between Lady Diana and Losch, the production went smoothly.[43]

The Miracle opened at the Lyceum on April 9 and had a considerable success. Lady Diana, as always, received excellent reviews. It was no triumph, however. According to The Times, Massine's choreography was "at its best when its mood has gaiety and light ... before it takes on a tragic colour,"[44] and his performance as the Spielmann had "a genuine power to excite which fails only when, being used in excess, it is dissipated in violence."[45] Lady Diana found him as inventive as her 1923 Spielmann, Werner Krauss, and more reliable.[46] Reinhardt declared it a pleasure to work with Massine, and in a congratulatory letter before the run ended wrote that "the collaboration with you was a wonderful experience for me and I am firmly resolved to repeat it again in the coming future."[47]

Between his stints with Helen! and The Miracle Massine went to Monte Carlo to choreograph a new work for the debut season of the newly organized Ballets Russes de Monte Carlo under the direction of René Blum and Colonel de Basil. From its inception the new company had the potential to make ballet history. Blum and de Basil, with the artistic collaboration of Kochno as conseiller artistique and Balanchine as ballet master, launched the most important enterprise of its kind since Diaghilev's death in 1929. Also signed on were former Diaghilev collaborators Derain, Benois, Miró, and Auric; among the newcomers was the designer Christian Bérard. Serge Grigoriev, Diaghilev's régisseur for twenty years, assumed the same position in the new company, and his wife, Lubov Tchernicheva, was named ballet mistress. A number of Diaghilev dancers, led by Doubrovska and Woizikowski, also joined the effort. But it would be a new generation of young dancers who would define the company's style and personality. Mostly Russian-born, they had been trained in Paris in the strictest Russian tradition by the émigré Imperial Theater stars: Olga Preobrajenska, Mathilde Kchessinska, Lubov Egorova, Volinine. Though they were only in their teens, each possessed dazzling technique and a distinctive stage presence.

Massine had been asked to choreograph two ballets, only one of which materialized: *Jeux d'enfants*, to Bizet's twelve-part, four-handed piano suite, with scenery and costumes by Miró.[48] The ballet portrayed a little girl's dream of toys coming to life. There was no narrative line, only a series of episodes depicting the child's interactions with her toys. The little girl as spectator and participant gave the work its unity.

Massine's choreography blended classical balletic vocabulary with expressive idiosyncratic movement. With their mastery of classical technique as a solid base, the dancers were urged to make the toys recognizably human. A. V. Coton later compared the work to Massine's 1919 *La Boutique fantasque*: "Massine had abandoned all reference to the 'unnatural' toy movement idiom of *Boutique Fantasque* in composing this work. All the toys and games . . . danced perfectly balletic and athletic measures as against the entirely derivative movement idioms of the toys in *Boutique Fantasque*."[49]

Jeux d'enfants was crucial in spelling out the 1930s aesthetic of pure dance as the essential element of ballet. This new dance-music integration differed drastically from Diaghilev's 1920s productions, where dance was generally subordinated to narrative. Of *Jeux d'enfants* Coton wrote that "every phase of the plot's unfolding is continuous within the dancing sequences; neither a bar of music nor a single movement by any of the participants is wasted on action extraneous to the continuity and development of music and dance forms, from curtain to curtain."[50] Classical virtuosity reigned supreme. Here was a company whose ballerinas could perform breathtaking multiple pirouettes and grandes pirouettes on pointe. And thus the prominence of the ballerina was revitalized after her years of subordination to the male dancer in Diaghilev's company.

Although Massine's recent successes in London and New York had been rich learning experiences, collaborating again on a ballet with a major painter proved highly stimulating, helping him to catch up with advances in the plastic arts, most notably surrealism. As he had done with Picasso, Matisse, and the Delaunays, Massine worked closely with Miró to ensure visual coherence in the completed ballet. The design exploded a nursery into a playful jumble of surrealistic geometrical forms in vibrant primary colors. These forms and the still silhouettes of the dancers against the gray-blue backcloth gave an impression of children's paper cutouts. The backcloth set in motion gave the entire scene the magical effect of a moving canvas.

Massine's arrival in Monte Carlo had been eagerly awaited. The young dancers held him in awe but were also wary of his no-nonsense reputation: serious, aloof, and inaccessible. He completely disarmed them. Though he continued to keep to himself, remained earnest about work, and demanded total concentration, he formed a warm working rapport with the company. Tamara Toumanova found him "all kindness from the very beginning,"[51] and Tatiana Riabouchinska did not find him "intimidating at all. He was very reserved but was kind and even gentle; he was soft-spoken and inspiring."[52] Now that he seemed more at ease, his Diaghilev colleagues came to believe that his detachment in the past had likely been aggravated by his personal relationship with the volatile impresario. Also obvious to everyone was the change wrought by his sparkling and sociable wife. Soon Delarova had charmed everyone, and became a welcome member of the company sightseeing parties formed at the Café de Paris and seen strolling through Monte Carlo.

Jeux d'enfants was ideally suited to the young troupe. They had quickly caught on to Massine's style, and their roles suited them perfectly, especially the fifteen-year-old Riabouchinska as the Child and thirteen-year-old Toumanova as the Top. In 1932 the ballet triumphed in Monte Carlo and in Paris. When it was presented in London the following year, Ernest Newman wrote in the *Sunday Times*: "One's first impression is that Bizet's charming music does not lend itself to the action. . . . Yet in a very little while it becomes clear that Mr. Massine has achieved the almost impossible, by a boldness of translation that soon converts our first skepticism into willing belief. *Jeux d'enfants* is a delightful fantasy, in which action, miming, costumes and colors combine subtly to the one end."[53]

After Monte Carlo, the Massines returned to London for *The Miracle*. At the conclusion of its run on July 23 they left to spend their holidays in Galli, stopping over in Salzburg as Reinhardt's guests at his castle in Leopoldoskron.

The summer of 1932 was professionally unsettling. In July Massine had written to Rothafel and Jay Kaufman of the Roxy, inquiring about their plans for a Radio City ballet company. He wondered if he could be hired as ballet master and stage some of the full-length classics from the repertory of the Imperial Theaters. Massine regretted that during his tenure at the Roxy he had not been able to produce a full-length work and insisted that the moment was ripe to revive the classical style. He enclosed a list of twenty-two classics, including *Swan Lake, Sleeping Beauty, Nutcracker, Raymonda, Le Corsaire, Paquita, Coppélia,* and *La Fille mal gardée.*[54] It was a bold proposal, but something even grander was in store for Massine. By December he found himself in Paris as the new ballet master for the Ballets Russes de Monte Carlo.

After the first Monte Carlo season, sharp differences over the artistic direction of the company had arisen between Blum and de Basil on the one hand and Kochno and Balanchine on the other. The latter two departed at the end of the Paris summer season, their contracts having expired. With Balanchine gone, de Basil moved quickly to hire Massine. The director knew a valuable asset when he saw one: Massine was a bigger draw as a choreographer than Balanchine; he was in his prime as a performer; he maintained close ties with the English theatrical establishment (London was de Basil's next objective); and he was indispensable if de Basil was to obtain Diaghilev's scenery, costumes, and props, now owned—through Massine's intercession in the past—by E. Ray Goetz. What's more, hiring Massine eliminated a potential competitor, since up to the summer of 1932 the choreographer had been steadily negotiating with Sir Thomas Beecham about the possibility of founding a permanent ballet company at Covent Garden.

The Massines came to Paris in late autumn to start preparations for the Monte Carlo season, and by January 2, 1933, they had joined the company in the principality of Monaco. Following an exhausting rehearsal period of three and a half months, the landmark engagement at the Théâtre du Casino opened on April 13 with the world premiere of *Les Présages,* set to Tchaikovsky's Fifth Symphony, with scenery and costumes by the painter André Masson. (When Massine in late autumn had outlined for Blum his plans for new works, the director had found the notion of a ballet choreographed to a symphony quite disturbing. Hoping to dissuade Massine, he had enlisted the support of the great conductor Bruno Walter, to no avail.) The first ballet in Western Europe set to a symphony, *Les Présages* signaled a new creative phase for the choreographer and marked a turning point in the history of twentieth-century dance.

Massine's objective in *Les Présages* was to create an abstract ballet without any literal story or narrative line. Tchaikovsky, in his correspondence with his patroness, Nadezhda von Meck, had pondered at length the concept of man's struggle against the forces of destiny. Following their lead, Massine linked each movement of the symphony to a symbolic theme introduced by allegorical characters. The first movement dealt with man's desires, temptations, and diversions, with the main character, a female called Action, symbolizing man's progress. The second movement depicted love in conflict with the baser passions; its main characters were two lovers, who together represented Passion, and Fate. The third movement was an interlude of gaiety symbolized by the character of Frivolity. In the fourth movement man's passion for war is aroused; he struggles mightily against it and vanquishes it at the end. All the leading figures of the previous movements come together in the finale.

The creation of an abstract choreographic counterpart to the structure of the music had a precedent in Massine's *Perpetomobile* of 1928. Indeed, many of his earlier ballets contained the seeds that blossomed into *Les Présages*: choreographic counterpoint, asymmetry, juxtaposition of styles, contrast between the qualities of weight and lightness, mass movement, abstraction. In conversations with critic Arnold Haskell in 1933, Massine asserted that his artistic growth could be measured in the evolutionary process that produced *Les Femmes de bonne humeur* (1917), *Le Tricorne* (1919), and *Les Présages* (1933), a propensity that he described as "the start of a new development which should bring me back to pure choreography."[55]

As usual with Massine, he derived the choreography from his dissection of the score; musical themes found their complement in a solo dancer or group of dancers. Sometimes dancers would represent sections of the orchestra, such as woodwinds or strings. Massine's choreographic counterpoint was so intricate that at times not only the soloists but each dancer in the ensemble became an independent entity.

The masterly juxtaposition of styles began in the first movement, where Action and a male dancer danced to the first and second musical themes, respectively. Here Massine contrasted a freer choreographic idiom to classical ballet technique. The "modern" idiom was appropriate to the role of Action, brilliantly danced by Nina Verchinina. Though classically trained, Verchinina had an affinity for the freedom and expansiveness of Massine's approach; eventually she became its embodiment.[56] The French dance critic Pierre Michaut described Action's choreography as "a play of arms well defined and rich in expression, raised up, extended, soft or rigid, frequently disassociated."[57] Here the emphasis on the torso and arms became as relevant as the leg work.

Verchinina described Massine's method:

"He experimented with movements. First he would create a variation that was more technical and classical in style, sort of a *pas de valse* with piqués and so forth. Then he would start working with me, and the movements began to evolve into something different and much more expressive." (This is reminiscent of Massine's description of Picasso's method.) "We would work until I was able to feel the movements as if the music was passing through my whole body—fingers, hands, head. The objective was to be able to feel Massine's movements inside of me and to understand what he wanted to achieve and to express. He was very responsive, and I was able to see immediately when he was happy, when he was able to transfer into my body his idea of the movement he wanted. He would not explain much, but he would show his basic idea. He mainly strove for me as the interpreter to grasp what he wanted so I could give the movement my own feeling and individual expression. My choreography for Action was a warrior dance, an ode to life, and every movement had a meaning: when I had both palms facing in front of me and I pushed one back, it would mean that I was creating fire; when I would move my rigid straight arms around me—as if I was cutting the air—they were swords; or I would make circular movements as if I was making designs in the space." [58]

The use of space was one of Massine's key principles. Verchinina explained: "Space exists and one must feel it as a presence, and every movement is executed inside (within) the space. Massine would show a circular movement, for example, and after I would perform it he would say, 'Now push through space, feel the pressure of the space around you, feel your body in friction with the space,' and so on until my movement would achieve the corporeal expression that he visualized in it. It was force against the space, my body cutting, piercing through the space, moving through space, whether being pushed by it or pushing it, designing movements within the space. Otherwise there was no dynamics, movement is dead, there is no expression. That is why even when there was no movement one would still project and transmit, because there is a dynamic relationship between the figure and the space." [59]

Massine fixed the dancer in relation to space, symbolizing the individual and the universe. Instead of a vacuum, Massine's space became a medium through which the dancer moved. This dynamics of space imposed on the dancer a dialectic of pressure and void which determined the quality of the movement: tensed, relaxed; flexible, rigid. The dancer's constant friction in space brought along an emotional impulse that gave expressivity to movement.

Massine's regard for the utilization of space and its dynamic relationship to the physical body placed a new emphasis on how a mass was formed and deployed. When he considered "the ancient ruins of Selinus, Agrigento and Paestum, it was the mass and volume of these structures which offered a challenge."[60] In *Les Présages* he "decided to avoid all symmetrical compositions and to render the flow of the music by fluctuating lines and forms both static and mobile. I deliberately chose to follow the movements of the symphony in a logical evolution of choreographic phrases, successively applying the regroupings themselves into new shapes and patterns."[61] Groups emerged and broke up before the audience fully realized that they had been formed. The spontaneity (automatism, according to the surrealist concept) of the fleeting entrances and exits was enhanced by the asymmetry of the corps patterns and the distorted spatial relations.

In the second-scene adagio, Massine created perhaps the first modern romantic pas de deux. Unlike the Petipa classical pas de deux (adagio, variations, coda), or the romantic and neoromantic Fokine pas de deux (a dramatic incitement in the development of the action), the pas de deux in *Les Présages* became its own raison d'être. Massine's creation of a self-contained, self-sufficient pas de deux (which at times became a pas de trois with the appearance of Fate) set a precedent for the many works that were later devised by other choreographers for slower movements of other symphonic or concerto ballets.

Though an all-female corps made brief entrances, the third movement was a solo for Frivolity. Here Massine reached the peak thus far of his new classicism. Riabouchinska explained the ardent connection she felt to the work:

"The rhythm of the choreographic phrase had a great degree of subtlety in the way Massine would join smaller steps as a preparation for bigger, more brilliant ones, to reach some spectacularly difficult ones in a sort of choreographic crescendo. Other times he would invert this order in a sort of decrescendo—always with a great emphasis on the torso and arms. This approach would make certain steps stand out more and enhance their aesthetic value—like when I finish an *enchaînement* in an attitude back in a *cambré* position. It made the technicality of the dance less mechanical, and you were swept away by the phrasing. The choreographic construction was such that you felt part of a grandiose conception. At the time there was nothing as grandiose in contemporary ballet."[62]

This movement employed a strict classical technique, free of any obvious symbolism. For André Levinson, who did not care for the philo-

Les Présages, *1933: fourth movement, the Rockets*

sophical connotations of the work, the audience became euphoric "at the moment of the waltz-scherzo, which defends itself victoriously against all implicit metaphysics."[63]

The finale was an apotheosis in which all the figures from the previous movements reappear—a Massine innovation that subsequent choreographers freely appropriated. The acrobatics of the ballet, especially in the spectacular finale, were novel in the West. By coincidence, they resembled the pyrotechnic style developed in the Soviet Union in the 1930s.

As designer for *Les Présages* Massine had wanted Matisse, with whom he collaborated in 1920 on *Le Chant du rossignol*. The painter declined (though they would work together again six years later). Matisse, who later attended many of the rehearsals in Monte Carlo, recommended Masson.

Preliminary discussions took place in Paris during the winter of 1932. Working together, Massine and Masson eventually conceived the ballet as a painting in motion. *Les Présages,* we can now see, operated on a deep level of symbolism and in a style reminiscent of German expressionism. As Massine explored and developed his symphonic ballet genre, his treatment of the figure / space relationship became a venue for his cosmic interpretation of the world.

Masson's interest in expressionism had begun in 1929 when he broke with André Breton and the surrealist movement. Although his work remained largely surrealistic in character, by 1932 he had begun painting expressionistic scenes of ritual killings. In his work of this period, color, line, figure, and background were united in a dynamic whole, and there are striking similarities between the color scheme of Masson's 1933 *Massacre in the Field* and that of *Les Présages*: bright reds, greens, yellows, purples, blues. All the female costumes were modeled on the classical Greek tunic, probably owing to Masson's recent interest in Greek mythology. The backdrop was a multicolored array of comets, shooting stars, rainbows, tongues of flame, spouting hearts, and other emblems of an apocalyptic vision.

The premiere in Monte Carlo on April 13 was a triumph with the public and the press. But it was the Paris premiere at the Théâtre de Châtelet two months later that launched the "symphonic ballet" controversy that was to rage in full force for years. There, *Les Présages* found vociferous supporters and equally adamant detractors. Some musicians deemed the use of a symphony to bolster a ballet nothing less than a sacrilege (although Isadora Duncan had already had symphonies performed to accompany her dances); and from the artistic community, the design drew outraged objections. Up until then, painters working with choreographers had confined themselves to suggesting an appropriate atmosphere within a realistic ambience. Masson's approach was purely painterly. Even the surrealist *Jeux d'enfants* stayed within the realistic boundaries of the premise, which was, after all, a surrealistic nursery. In *Les Présages* Masson avoided poetry as well as realism, fastening on pure abstraction and symbolism. He had two related aims: to capture the flow of the music in the arrangement of color and, more importantly, to link the movements of the dancers to the design of his backcloth, to suggest color parallels to the music. In the face of the controversy, the ballet was performed without decor and in practice clothes in London in 1935. The critics were nonplussed, and ended up agreeing that Masson's contribution was vital to the work's total effect.

Factions for and against the ballet immediately sprung up. Some people, such as Balanchine and Lifar, argued that a symphony required no choreographic elucidation—though in the 1940s, they themselves would use symphonies and concerti for their ballets.[64] Massine's supporters contended that he was breaking new ground. The two camps couldn't agree on a number of questions: (1) Was it right to superimpose a philosophical allegory on a ballet? (2) Was it fusion or only a mishmash to juxtapose classical ballet technique and an idiom closer to the Central European modern dance movement? (3) Did the innovative, self-sufficient pas de deux in fact stand on its own? (4) What was intended by the use of asymmetrical and almost automatic mass movement? (5) Were the acrobatics justified artistically? (6) Was the abstract choreographic treatment of the music aesthetically satisfying or only a riddle for the audience to puzzle over ad infinitum? It has turned out, of course, that this work was ballet's turning point, ushering in the currently accepted aesthetic of abstraction and nonrepresentational dance.

The controversy was not confined to artistic circles. In the midst of the frightening European economic and political upheavals of 1933 (depression, the burning of the Reichstag, the victory of the Nazi party, the establishment of the "National Revolution," the exodus of German intellectuals and artists), a minority of liberal intellectuals and artists objected to the militaristic tone of Massine's fourth movement with its strong reference to war.

Though opinion was divided, the ballet was an immense success. For Pierre Michaut it "had an imposing sensation as much for its intensity as for its originality. . . . Some passages remain in one's memory: the scintillating, luminous entrance of Frivolity (Mlle Riabouchinska) and the grandiose final movement, a vast composition of ensemble, a true orchestration of masses, where movement, full of force and magnitude, sustains itself by a continuity and dimension truly powerful."[65]

The roles were milestones in the careers of the dancers, who, much like the "symphonic ballet" itself, were seen as representatives of a new generation and style. Nina Verchinina as Action, in her own eclectic way, welded the music to the choreography with unusually angular movements. As Passion, the fourteen-year-old Irina Baronova combined poetry with brilliant attack, suggesting the extraordinary classical-modern ballerina she was to become. As Frivolity, the fifteen-year-old Riabouchinska stamped the role with her speed, lightness, elevation, and ethereal presence. (Along with Toumanova, Baronova and Riabouchinska were the legendary "baby ballerinas.") David Lichine, the male dancer who with Massine was to dominate the international spotlight in the

1930s, was all virility and barbaric exuberance in the roles of Passion and Hero. In his powerfully dramatic appearance as Fate, Leon Woizikowski met the high standards set in his Diaghilev performances.

That July in London, the ballet caused a sensation. Its most ardent advocate, Ernest Newman, dean of British music critics, found that "it is really the music of the symphony that [Massine] has translated into a ballet, and this in such a way that, incredible as it may appear to anyone who has not seen *Les Présages*, the inner life of the work, as an organic piece of musical thinking, is not diminished but actually enhanced. There are points, indeed, at which none of us will henceforth be able to listen to the music in the concert room without seeing it in terms of this ballet. . . ." [66]

The second new work of the Monte Carlo season was a revival of the 1924 *Beau Danube*. Massine eliminated its heavily narrative scenes and modified the choreography to capitalize on the flair and technique of his young cast. The ballet—led by Alexandra Danilova, Riabouchinska, Baronova, and Massine himself—became one of the company's signature pieces. According to Coton: "Of all works in the de Basil repertory this is probably the most popular; certainly no other work except possibly *Boutique Fantasque* has an equal appeal as purely romantic choreography in Massine's own special idiom. . . . It dispenses with formal balletics, and achieves perfection of pattern between dance and musical line." [67] During the company's first London season, Coton noted, *Le Beau Danube* and *Les Présages* "drew people to watch ballet . . . who otherwise might never have been attracted to the ballet theatre." [68]

Beach, the third new work, was an homage to the principality of Monaco. The ballet had an original score by the young composer Jean Françaix (a protégé of Nadia Boulanger), a libretto by René Kerdyk, and scenery and costumes by the French artist Raoul Dufy, who had started as a fauve. *Beach* gently satirized topical characters from the Riviera's smart set. A prologue, two scenes, and an epilogue showed the world of Nereus, with its Nereids and Tritons, being transformed into a collection of fashionable Monte Carlo types, who after an outing at the resort return to their mythological kingdom in the sea.

André Levinson likened the spirit of the piece to a spectacular music hall revue. Massine's choreography, he found, took its inspiration from the Jazz Age and the open-air culture, utilizing tap and the fox-trot as well as stylized sports movements. No doubt Massine was influenced by his years at the Roxy. At the same time, the lyrical pas de deux between Baronova and Lichine was danced in a pure balletic idiom. Dufy's

Massine

designs consisted of beautiful seascapes that gave a fish-tank look to the stage, and the costumes were witty and chic (Dufy designed textiles for Paul Poiret's prestigious *maison de couture*). The evening gowns were by couturière Jeanne Lanvin, who also launched the soon-to-be-fashionable navy-blue dinner jacket.

The final work premiered in Monte Carlo was *Scuola di ballo,* based on a comedy by Goldoni that exposed the intrigues of a teacher, his students, their parents, and an impresario in a dance school. The ballet was set to music by Boccherini as orchestrated by Françaix, with scenery and costumes by Etienne de Beaumont, whose most recent collaboration with Massine had been back in 1924. The choreography took its style from commedia dell'arte, in which the hands, arms, and torso were used to tell the story. However, unlike *Les Femmes de bonne humeur,* which emphasized Massine's *cantinella*-like pantomime, *Scuola di ballo* employed a great degree of technical virtuosity and choreography packed with flowing variations that lacked the flickering quality of the 1917 work.[69]

The ballet required precisely what Massine could call forth from his dancers with ease: idiosyncratic characterizations which gave them an opportunity to excel technically and dramatically. Massine shaped characters to suit his dancers' personalities yet left enough room for them to make the roles their own. Said Baronova: "To penetrate into Massine's roles, dancers had to work on their own and approach the parts as actors do. We had to explore the characters in order to obtain their mannerisms. For Massine, two things were of utmost importance: expressivity in the body and fluency of movement, both subordinated to the music."[70] Riabouchinska added: "After he gave them the basic idea, the dancers had to work on their own. They had to digest and build their interpretations as long as they were consistent with the overall approach."[71] (This was a lingering influence from Massine's early exposure to the Moscow stage.) Every role depended on a strong personality: Massine, Baronova, Riabouchinska, Woizikowski, Yurek Shabelevsky. Delarova made her Ballets Russes debut as Felicita, the inept pupil. Massine described her solo as "a wonderfully droll take-off of an inadequate dancer clumsily caricaturing classical steps blended with grotesque leaps."[72] Her performance was praised as a "real piece of farce."[73]

The ballet was mostly well received in Paris. Emile Vuillermoz wrote: "The lessons, the entrances, the exits are arranged with an astonishing freshness of invention. Never had Massine discovered effects so youthful and so alive, devoid of all that angular trepidation."[74] Only Levinson found it inferior to *Les Femmes* and *Pulcinella.*[75] Haskell, on the

Massine with Tatiana Riabouchinska in Scuola di ballo, *1933*

other hand, declared it in "perfect harmony with the music and the thought of the time."[76] Toumanova, who was not in the cast, called it a gem.[77] Ernest Newman observed:

> *Over all the production there is that sense of "nothing too much" that is always one of the best features of the ballet school that has arisen out of the old Italian comedy: never for a moment does the grotesquerie overshoot the mark. And once more one is astounded at Mr. Massine's genius for translating music into action. Only the musicians in the audience can fully appreciate what he does in this respect; there are a hundred subtleties in the way of capturing the very essence of a rhythm, of an accent, even of a splash of orchestral colour . . . to make them clear to the reader one would*

have to quote this or that bar of the music with a section from a film of the ballet.[78]

"When the de Basil company launched its first big-scale English season," Coton wrote, "the item of news of equal importance with that of the resurrection of ballet was the promised return of Massine to London."[79] That promise was fulfilled in the summer of 1933, in Massine's double triumph as choreographer and lead dancer of a brilliant company. For Haskell it was "a company of extraordinary training and versatility, and, from that point of view at least," it was "the finest and the most complete" the critic had seen.[80] The Ballets Russes de Monte Carlo's historic engagement at the Alhambra Theatre opened on July 4. The three weeks initially scheduled were extended to nineteen. The company took London by storm and throughout a meltingly hot summer performed nightly to sold-out houses. Now, joining the elitist audiences that had supported Diaghilev, a new public was making its way to the ballet. During the 1930s, ballet became the rage in London, and Massine its undisputed star. His new repertory, as well as the older works, earned him even greater critical acclaim than he had received with Diaghilev. Coton tried to put his achievement in perspective: "No other choreographer has experimented in so many forms to produce always interesting, occasionally vivid and beautiful, and never shoddy, work. Out of the living corpus of his work we can construct a document of every phase of experiment of any value since Fokine's heyday; what Massine has done, other choreographers have done—later."[81] He added that in his twenty-eight works Massine had "evolved a richer and wider catalogue of mixed miniatures and grand-scale projections of movement such as neither Fokine, nor any other living choreographer, has achieved."[82]

A Massine ballet created an instant cult. Agnes de Mille recalled how "the furor evoked by the baby ballerinas and the love commanded by Danilova were not in a class with the adulation accorded to the master of all, Léonide Massine. Seeing a Massine ballet had become one of the erotic pleasures of the London season. The expensive spectators in the stalls contented themselves with 'Bravos' and gush. The devotees upstairs gave themselves unrestrainedly to screaming, jumping up and down, beating the railing, hugging one another, slathering at the mouth."[83]

And it was not only Massine the choreographer who was praised; Massine the performer proved irresistible. Haskell summed up the opinion of public and critics alike:

Massine today is at the very height of his powers, both as a creator and as a dancer. There are obviously greater technical performers, but no one who is even nearly his equal as an artist. It is in his case that I have felt the same concrete audience contact as with Pavlova. I once watched Le Beau Danube from the wings. At the moment where Massine stands motionless, centre stage, remembering as he hears the strains of the famous waltz, and then very slowly raises his arm above his head as the crowd of idlers and midinettes passes him by in scorn, I looked into the auditorium by chance. Like some big wave the audience had risen in their seats, craning forward, as if his hand had pulled some unseen string. There is no one else who could achieve such a result by standing almost completely still. It is quite another thing to whip an audience into excitement by a complicated technical feat.[84]

For Haskell, Massine ranked with the masters of movement. "As a mime, Massine could only be compared to Chaplin. His characters were round; they had pathos and humour. The Barman in the otherwise trivial *Union Pacific* [of 1934] was a masterly study, a splendid distillation of the comedy of the silent film. When one adds such varied roles as the Can-Can Dancer in *La Boutique Fantasque* and the Miller in *Le Tricorne*, we have a performer of rare quality, especially in his early days, when the *buffo* dancers were so often stereotypes."[85]

Scheduled to close the Alhambra engagement was the world premiere of *Choreartium*, to Brahms's Fourth Symphony. Tchaikovsky's Fifth had imposed upon the choreographer a dense, specific psychological mood. Brahms's Fourth, not in the strictly academic sonata form, summoned from Massine a resolutely abstract ballet sans theme, symbolic idea, or reference to allegorical characters. He wanted instead a choreographic rendition of the music's structure through continuous sequences of movement. The soloists, couples, trios, and ensembles, interwoven into intricate patterns, mirrored the fluctuations and climaxes of the music. Even more so than in *Les Présages*, the dancers here were tied to musical themes or groups of instruments. Massine particularly wanted to use "women dancers to accentuate the delicate phrases, while the men interpreted the heavier, more robust passages. The music with its rich orchestration and its many contrasts, lent itself admirably to this kind of interplay between masculine and feminine movements."[86]

The opening movement highlights this gender contrast. The principal couple's pas de deux (one critic called it the first allegro pas de deux) becomes a dialogue between the female (Toumanova), dancing to the

Rehearsal of the first movement of Choreartium, *1933*

strings, and the male (Lichine), dancing to the woodwinds. This movement, said Massine, was composed of "airy patterns of moving figures,
continually forming and reforming in evanescent designs" through
which the principal couple "moved like waves, undulating through the
shifting groups."[87]

The first, third, and fourth movements were examples of Massine's
new classicism, where intricate pointe combinations were followed by
large, open, flowing movements for the women, and pirouettes, *tours en
l'air,* jumps, and *batterie* for the men. The second movement was a return
to his modern idiom: a solo for Verchinina before an all-female corps de
ballet in architectural formation.

*I had been told that Brahms had visualized this Second Movement as an
afternoon in Sorrento, but I could not see it that way. To me there was a
spiritual quality in it which suggested medieval Italy, and reminded me of
a fresco I had seen in the Palazzo Campanile in Siena. Most of it had become blurred with the passage of time, but there was a group of women in
deep burgundy red robes which was still visible. I made these women the*

leitmotiv *of the movement, threading the image of them through the ensembles, in which the weaving dancers, with their arms extended, formed a succession of harmonic choreographic progressions and dynamic evolutions.*[88]

Unlike her forceful Action in *Les Présages,* in *Choreartium* Verchinina had to dance introspectively, as it were, differentiating fluid from tensed movements, meticulously contrasting weight and lightness, tension and relaxation.[89] Massine called it "a mystical dance."[90]

Massine's mastery of figure/space relationships let the audience perceive stage movement in three dimensions. His theory of movement at this point was essentially architectural. *Choreartium*'s mass configurations—a dialectic between motion and stasis, arrest and movement—turned the theory into practice.[91]

Coton traced this approach to Massine's final work for Diaghilev.

Choreartium, 1933: first movement

"That Massine had not forgotten his devices of architecturing the choreography of *Ode* when he began to create part of *Les Présages* and, later, most of the fourth movement in *Choreartium*, is obvious."[92] (In fact his interest in architectural formations began as far back as *Le Chant du rossignol* and reappeared later in *Amphion*.)

Choreartium was first presented to a select London audience in a midnight dress rehearsal, the night before its premiere. Osbert Sitwell provided the introduction, to an assembly that included political, social, and artistic luminaries. The ballet immediately became the talk of the town. Massine was accused of blasphemous arrogance in daring to use a symphony (especially one by Brahms) as background music for a ballet, of presumptuousness in trying to interpret a self-sufficient musical work in terms of dance, and of selling out to modern dance in the second movement. London critics divided into two factions. The opposition was headed by composer, conductor, and critic Constant Lambert. The proponents, or Massinists, were led by Ernest Newman. The controversy was played out for a full year in their respective newspapers, the *Sunday Times* (Newman) and the *London Referee* (Lambert). Readers in both camps passionately followed the war of words. Newman wrote:

> *Massine showed the common sense we might have expected of him when he put aside all thought of reading a story into Brahms's symphony and decided to approach it as music pure and simple. . . . If music is to be ruled out from ballet when it is "pure" music, what justification is there for* Les Sylphides, *for example? There is no more programme in Chopin's music than there is in Brahms's; yet the enduring success of* Les Sylphides *proves that choreographic figures can be devised that are felt to be not in the least alien to the spirit and the build of this music. We are bound to grant, I think, that there is nothing a priori incongruous in the mating of "pure" music, whether that of Brahms or of any other composer, with the lines and masses and movements of the ballet. . . . The only question is to what extent the choreographer has succeeded. . . .*
>
> *What has Massine done with the remainder of the symphony? Here I can only wonder at the lack of imagination that prevents some people from seeing the points of genius with which Massine's choreographic score, so to call it, positively bristles. There can, of course, be no question of a translation of the "meaning" of this music as a whole into terms of another art: this kind of music is just itself, the expression of something to which there is no real equivalent in any other art. But if there is no equivalent, surely there can be parallelisms; surely certain elements in the musical design,*

certain gestures of the music, certain softenings and hardenings of the colours, can be suggested quite well in the more objective medium. I found myself profoundly interested in watching these correspondences, many of which gave me a fresh respect for Massine's genius. Unfortunately, as I have remarked before in a similar connection, there is no way of making these correspondences clear to the reader without quoting the musical passages in question side by side with photographs of the particular moments of the ballet with which they are associated. But how any musical listener in the audience who knows the Brahms score and has any imagination at all could fail to perceive these extraordinary parallelisms I confess myself unable to understand.

The opening entry of these two figures for instance, with their curious gliding, undulating motion, seemed to me as perfect a translation into visible motion of the well-known dip and rise of the first phrase in the violins as could possibly be conceived. I could cite similar felicities of parallelism by the hundred; the sense of the musical design conveyed for instance by the entry of the same two figures each time the first subject of the symphony assumed a leading part in the structure, the subtle distinctions invariably made in choreography between the basic elements in the music and the transitional passages—between the bones as it were and the cartilages—the curious correspondence between harshness in the harmonies and musical colors and angularities or violences in the gestures, and so on. In the finale, which, as the reader no doubt knows, is in passacaglia form—a series of variations upon a ground fugue—Massine seems to me to have done wonders. He typifies the commanding main theme by six black figures that persist through the whole movement as the ground bass itself persists in the music; and he intensifies or thins out the action and the groupings in accordance with the changing texture of the variations.[93]

Repeatedly in the years-long debate Newman compared the choreographer to Wagner: "If, it was said, Wagner was allowed to go on as he was doing, it would be the end of true art, just as it is now said that if the nefarious activities of Massine are not checked it will mean the ruin of both the symphony and the ballet. But Wagner quietly went on doing what he had set himself to do, and the public ranged itself on his side, let the critics foam at the mouth as they liked—another parallel with the Massine case."[94]

For Haskell, *Choreartium* was "forty minutes of individual and group movement, always beautiful, logical, and yet surprising, with every member of the huge cast an individual and at the same time part of a fresco." [95] He was certain that "such a feat on this scale has never before been attempted in choreography. It is the birth and triumph of pure dancing and shows that in the hands of a master its possibilities are inexhaustible." [96] Coton argued that in *Choreartium* "Massine had completed the most important experiment in balletic reorientation since the day of Fokine." [97] He traced Massine's accomplishments in *Choreartium* to earlier attempts in *Le Soleil de nuit, Cimarosiana, Ode,* and *Les Présages* (he could have added *Sacre*). [98] Coton felt that "by discarding all scenaric complications and working with no other guide than the musical score he had produced the most complete pattern of 'meaningless' [meaning abstract] movement, absolute and satisfying in itself, in the history of ballet." [99]

Les Présages and, especially, *Choreartium* proclaimed the autonomy of a choreographer freed from the conceptual limitations of scenarist and designer. This was a bold departure not only from the Diaghilev ballet but from the Ballets Russes de Monte Carlo's 1932 productions. The symphonic ballet provided a new, purely reflective pleasure, which found value and aesthetic satisfaction in the choreography alone. Leading world conductors of the time (Beecham, Stokowski, Monteux, Eugene Goossens, Eugene Ormandy) conducted performances of *Choreartium* in England and the United States throughout the decade.

As the season drew to a close, the Ballets Russes de Monte Carlo savored a triumph that was broader and deeper than any under Diaghilev. Their unprecedented success permitted de Basil—aided by Massine's contacts—to set up an impressive sponsoring committee that won the company the Royal Opera House at Covent Garden as its London home base, an arrangement that lasted from 1934 until the outbreak of war in 1939.

The impresario Sol Hurok brought the company to the United States for the first time in December 1933. The first engagement, in New York, had no general support (after the brilliant opening night, the ballet public proved so meager that the houses were practically empty). But by the end of its United States tour the company, led by Massine, the legendary baby ballerinas, Danilova, Verchinina, and Lichine, had achieved financial success and become a vital force on the American artistic scene. Thereafter the troupe toured North America, including Mexico, Cuba, and Canada, for six to seven months a year. The balance of their engagements were in Europe. In grueling one-night stands and in longer engagements in the larger cities, Massine became a household name and built an international following unmatched by any of his predecessors.

Yet, once again, alongside Massine's professional triumph his apparent marital bliss was undergoing a steady erosion. His five-year marriage was being shaken. This time the object of Massine's affection was the beautiful young dancer Vera Zorina. As it happened, the German-Norwegian Zorina, née Eva Brigitta Hartwig, was brought to Massine's attention in 1933 by Delarova herself. Brigitta was appearing in London opposite Anton Dolin in *Ballerina,* a play with ballet interludes. Massine, who rarely attended the theater, was in the habit of sending his wife to new shows to scout young dance talent. After attending a performance of *Ballerina,* she urged Massine to snap up two gifted members of the cast: Brigitta and the Englishman Frederic Franklin.[100] Massine wasted no time (it is uncertain whether or not he attended later performances of *Ballerina*), enlisting the critic Arnold Haskell as middleman in the negotiations with Brigitta. She joined the roster of the Ballets Russes de Monte Carlo during the 1934 Covent Garden summer season under the name Vera Zorina. (Franklin did not join Massine until 1938.)

Massine and Zorina began their affair during the North American tour that followed the London season. Privacy in a touring ballet company is generally hard to come by, but Massine and Zorina were obviously in love. Risks were taken. Delarova, in what seems a last-ditch attempt to save her marriage, accepted Zorina into the life she shared with her husband.

Throughout the American tours, the Massines traveled in a trailer attached to the choreographer's Lincoln. A Lithuanian couple, Alexander and Elizabeth Drevinskas, served them as chauffeur and cook, an arrangement that allowed Massine to bypass the inconvenient schedules of the Pullman trains arranged by Hurok, and thus to live a more regulated life during arduous series of one-night stands. Zorina became a member of Massine's caravan, as it was called, which required a strenuous adjustment.

When the company returned to England in the spring of 1935, the traveling threesome continued. On April 30 in Nice the party of five (including the Drevinskases) obtained a collective Spanish visa to proceed to Barcelona for the company's season at the Gran Teatre del Liceu.[101] After the Barcelona season (the Massines and Zorina stayed at the same hotel), Massine and Zorina made plans to meet secretly in Piešťany, a spa in Czechoslovakia that he frequently visited. According to Zorina, the days spent there "were reassuring, peaceful, and an oasis of peace during those turbulent two years."[102]

Massine was a man with a divided nature. One side was suspicious, aloof, and distant. The other, which predominated only when he was in love, was passionate, romantic, and possessive—as long as the love object yielded to him. He poured out his feelings for Zorina in heartfelt letters after she had left him in Piešťany:

The day you left—Never in my life, I haven't thought that I could love like I love you—Never nobody can tear from me what I acquired with you here. The feeling and the memory of us close heart to heart will be indefinitely vivid in me—Remember suddenly that huge dark cloud with wonderful light ribbon which appeared almost above our heads and sent the dark cloud away as though giving us to understand that the dark stormy cloud of our life might soon be gone too.

The next day—Some force dragged me to the place where we have met the sunset. It is about the same moment now. Coming here I stopped every place we stopped with you. I looked on the ground trying to find the trace of your feet—every place reminds me of you, I feel your breath. Now I am standing there and sun is going almost hidden behind the mountains. "You are like out of gold," you said to me looking in my face—Once you said "I love you—at least you are a true person"—and you sat on the couch, it was almost dark. I looked at you and expression of your face overwhelmed me—you were like some Leonardo da Vinci paintings, so soft and so mysterious lighting was on you.[103]

After the Czechoslovakian interlude, the company reassembled in London for another successful season at Covent Garden. Zorina writes:

After our London season, Léonide invited me to spend my vacation on the Isola dei Galli, the private island he owned off the coast of southern Italy, near Positano. I am unable now to understand how I could have agreed to travel once more in a triangular fashion, but then I am not eighteen any more. I don't believe one can ever again re-experience the ferocious passion, the longing, the hope—ah yes, the hope that things will change. I had no capacity for self-denial—nor could I give up hope—nor was I ready to admit defeat.

We motored through Italy, stopping at Ravenna to admire the pure ivory throne and sarcophagus of the Byzantine Empress Theodora and the wonderful mosaics showing the Empress and her entourage. How mysterious their large-eyed, direct gaze seemed, and how perfect the splendor of their attire, which in spite of the opulence of cascading pearls, emeralds, and rubies, coupled with the utmost regal bearing, nevertheless gave the impression of an austerity. We remained for a few days in Abano, near

Venice, so that Léonide could take mud baths for his ailing knee. From there, we visited Padua and Vicenza.

The Giottos in the chapel in Padua made a deep impression on me. For a dancer, who cannot express anything except through the movement of her body, there was a great deal to be learned. In the physical expression of lamentation, in the hands turned upward like birds in flight, in the raised arms, in the manifestation of sorrow of the spirit expressed silently but powerfully through the body. We stood there and looked and looked, absorbing and trying to remember every detail. The magnificent Palladian villas, and the perfection of the Teatro Olimpico in Vicenza, tiny but with the most miraculously deep perspective of the small stage—what treasures for an eighteen-year-old to see for the first time. [104]

After a visit to Ravello and Positano, the threesome headed for Galli to spend the summer holidays. But though there were delectable moments of swimming, sunbathing, and boating, the atmosphere was thick with tension. Years later, in her autobiography, Zorina wondered "why a man would want to subject two women who loved him to such an unhappy arrangement—both of whom complied in the hope that they would be left alone with him one day." [105]

The next United States tour was more exhausting than the two previous ones had been. It included a more rigorous string of one-night stands; moreover, Massine had openly retained counsel to get him a divorce from Delarova so he could marry Zorina. But this could not be arranged; according to the French courts, the "status and capacity to sue are governed by the law of the nationality of the parties." [106] The marital tensions escalated. Trying another tack, Massine directed New York attorney George Boochever to explore the possibility of obtaining a divorce in the Mexican courts on grounds of incompatibility, hoping that it would be recognized in France. [107] Massine wanted to have everything in order by the time the company arrived in El Paso; from there he would travel to Mexico to initiate the proceedings. [108] But this gambit failed.

De Basil ordered Zorina not to travel in the Massines' caravan. Yet even after she went back to traveling with the other dancers, the anguish did not stop. In Orlando, Florida, Zorina cut her wrists with a razor blade. She later wrote that she "had no intention of committing suicide or any thought of death. It seemed that by inflicting physical pain I might stop the mental pain I was no longer able to endure." [109] Massine, the ardent lover, showed no sympathy. She accused him of simply becoming "annoyed and angry." [110] The resolution of the crisis came during the 1936

Covent Garden season. Massine, writes Zorina, "solved his dilemma by bringing another woman into his life, a woman who was to become his third wife."[111] After the London season ended, Zorina left the Ballets Russes de Monte Carlo and went on to a successful career in musical comedies and films.

Massine and Tamara Toumanova as the Poor Couple in
Jardin public, *1935*

CHAPTER 11

London, June 1936–Paris, June 1939

BY 1936 the professional relationship between de Basil and Massine
had seriously deteriorated. The strain had begun in 1934 during the first
Covent Garden season. The year before, the two men had jointly acquired from E. Ray Goetz most of the scenery, costumes, and props of
the Diaghilev organization—an extraordinarily rich cache. But in May
1934, a Ballets Russes press release asserted that de Basil was sole owner
and proprietor: "Since the appearance of Colonel de Basil's company at
the Alhambra Theatre last year, a group of English admirers have acquired the scenery and costumes belonging to the Diaghilev organization and presented them to Col. de Basil."[1] Massine's solicitors, J. D.
Langton and Passmore, immediately demanded that the managing director of the Royal Opera publicly retract the statement and pledge that

none of the scenery and costumes would be removed from the theater without Massine's consent.[2] After months of litigation, Massine and de Basil agreed that by August 1934 de Basil would purchase Massine's portion of the properties for 143,000 francs, to be paid over a period of one year.[3]

But the quarreling was not over; the prize of the artistic directorship of the company continued to loom between them. Massine had wanted to be named Artistic Director back in 1933, but de Basil had consistently turned him down, deeming his artistic hold on the company already too strong. He had a point. Danilova observed: "With Diaghilev, we had always felt that the success of a new production rested on the collaboration of everyone involved, but with de Basil, we had the sense that the weight of the entire company had fallen on one man's shoulders—our success depended on Massine."[4] To loosen Massine's grip, in 1935 de Basil, always wary of a possible Massine defection, hired Bronislava Nijinska as guest choreographer; she produced a new work, *Les Cent Baisers*, and the following year revived her 1922 Stravinsky ballet, *Les Noces*. De Basil also continued to nurture David Lichine as a choreographer.

Massine's complaints kept piling up. He wanted his name, title (in a compromise de Basil in 1934 had appointed him "maître de ballet and artistic collaborator"), photo, and biographical note included in programs and press releases. He wanted for himself and his wife the same first-class steamship accommodations provided to the de Basils. The régisseur was to notify him of the company's schedules and repertoires at the same time de Basil was informed. He objected to not being consulted about the hiring of Nijinska and several new dancers, or the commissioning of *Le Pavillon* from Lichine in 1936. And he protested that since 1934 he had not been able to win approval for a revival of his *Sacre du printemps* with Verchinina (Nijinska's *Noces* must have been a slap in the face).[5]

By March 1936, while the company was touring the United States, Massine had secretly begun to explore the possibility of leaving de Basil and organizing his own company. He contacted René Blum in Monte Carlo (by 1935 Blum had severed his association with de Basil and gone on to organize the Ballets de Monte Carlo) and Sir Oswald Stoll in London as potential backers.[6] He then approached Lifar, Woizikowski, and Balanchine about joining the venture.[7] These bold moves were like tremors before the quake, which was not to occur for another year.

During the 1936 Covent Garden summer season, de Basil decided to organize a second company to tour Australia while the nucleus performed in Germany and later in America. Massine refused to have his ballets included in the repertory of the Australian company since he could not be there to supervise the performances, and sought a restraining order from Justice Bucknill in London. But when it became apparent that the petition would not be granted before the new company sailed, Massine personally rehearsed his works so that they could be presented to Australian audiences in authentic form.[8]

In the midst of these disputes, Massine created one of his most monumental works, to Berlioz's *Symphonie fantastique*. It would be his last production for de Basil's company.

Since *Choreartium* in 1933, Massine had produced three minor works to fulfill the company's need (and Hurok's demand) for novelties: *Union Pacific* (1934), *Jardin public* (1935), and *Le Bal* (1935). The first was the most successful. Based on the building of America's Union Pacific Railroad, it had a scenario by the poet Archibald MacLeish, music by Nicolas Nabokov, decor by Albert Johnson, and costumes by Irene Sharaff. As the first ballet by an international company based on an American theme and dance idiom, it was designed to bolster the Ballets Russes' publicity campaign in the United States. The general public liked the ballet, but it

The Barman in
Union Pacific, *1934*

stirred artistic controversy, especially in the dance community, where the Russians were resented by those burgeoning elements struggling to create an American ballet school and company. As Grace Robert noted, "It was not greeted with any particular acclaim by the critics, who seemed to think that the Russians were carrying their invasion of the United States too far."[9] *Union Pacific* gave the company's leading dancers some outstanding roles, especially the Barman and Lady Gay, created by Massine and Delarova. Massine's dance always stopped the show, and later the role of Lady Gay became identified with Baronova, who would take it over after the premiere.

Jardin public, based on a passage from André Gide's novel *The Counterfeiters,* had scenery and costumes by Jean Lurçat and a score by Vladimir Dukelsky. It was an attempt at a social ballet where various alienated characters, including a rich and a poor couple, as well as a man who commits suicide, meet in a public park. The ballet was a failure in the United States and England. However, as with *Union Pacific,* there were memorable performances, especially by Toumanova and Massine as the poor couple and Delarova as the woman who rented the chairs. Haskell wrote of her performance: "She has created a character that can be placed beside Massine's barman."[10] In spite of its indifferent reception, Massine remained attached to *Jardin public,* and in 1936 he revised it, with new decor and costumes by the Polish artist Alice Halicka. This new version, however, did not fare any better.

Nineteen thirty-five also saw the premiere of *Le Bal,* a new version by Massine of a ballet originally choreographed by Balanchine for Diaghilev in 1929. Massine chafed at having to rechoreograph an already existing work (this was to become the fashion with de Basil in order to take advantage of the Diaghilev properties he owned). *Le Bal* was a minor addition to the company's repertory and was dropped from it soon after.

These three ballets were created, rehearsed, and produced under strenuous, almost catastrophic conditions during the long and exhausting American tours. In a preunion era, rehearsals were held in any space available, from hotel basements to train station lobbies, and many times would not begin until after an evening performance and go on until three a.m. Only the dancers' dedication and their devotion to Massine enabled them to accept the almost inhuman working conditions. Toumanova recalls: "During our first years with de Basil there was no limitation to our working capacity. There was a collective fervor in the company, and we lived to see those performances come through. Our only concern was to give our very best on stage and to make it happen. It was almost a religious feeling that we had been chosen to keep this art and tradition alive. And of course we worshiped Massine, who was our inspiration. I do not think any of us would have said no to any of his requests. We admired his genius, and each one of his ballets was a revelation—even the ones that were not a great success had something special. Working with him was a constant learning experience and a process of exploring unimaginable possibilities of new movement." [11]

MASSINE HAD FIRST CONSIDERED Berlioz's *Symphonie fantastique* as early as January 1933, probably in lieu of Tchaikovsky's Fifth.[12] However, it was not until 1934 that he began to plan it, and by 1935 he was seriously immersed in the work. In August of that year he wrote to Etienne de Beaumont, who was taking a two-month cure in Germany, soliciting advice about a designer.[13] After a lengthy preparation period, rehearsals began in the late spring of 1936, when the company arrived in Barcelona for its May season at the Gran Teatre del Liceu, and continued in full force at Covent Garden. The rehearsal schedule was demanding, and, as was typical, Massine engaged himself compulsively in the creative process. No other work the Ballets Russes had produced was as rigorously demanding as the Berlioz. The entire company, including soloists and corps, was utilized, and to realize Massine's grandiose conception, extra, day-long rehearsals were scheduled on weekends. After one of these rehearsals Ernest Newman wrote to his wife, Vera:

> They all looked worn out this morning. Riabouchinska looked like a wraith with galloping consumption, and was coughing all the time and Baronova is sick. How they stand this life is a mystery to me. Ballet dancing must be a hard life. They have two more rehearsals and the performance tomorrow. How any girl can take up ballet dancing as a career is beyond my comprehension. And what skinny creatures they mostly are. They remind me of worker bees who work . . . to make money for goodness knows who—for they don't—they get precious little out of it for themselves.[14]

Symphonie fantastique was perhaps Massine's greatest statement of his idea of the dance-drama, and although the work followed the narrative idea set down in the composer's synopsis, the ballet was not dominated by its narrative element. On the contrary, the narrative was minimal, and, with the exception of the fourth scene, dance predominated within the episodic structure of the music. For the five movements Massine devised five independent tableaux, given continuity by the external elements of the main characters, the Musician and the Beloved (who appears only when her musical idée fixe is played). An internal element also provided continuity: the ballet's pervasive mood, which depicted the world as a metaphor for the Musician's tormented soul, the emotional state of mind emanating from the romantic first-person narrator.[15]

In *Symphonie fantastique,* Massine found a point at which to fuse the symbolic as well as the purely abstract approaches of *Les Présages* and *Choreartium.* At the same time, the fourth movement allowed him to

Symphonie fantastique, *1936, third movement: left to right, Paul Platoff, George Zoritch, Tamara Toumanova, Massine; decor by Christian Bérard*

conceive a scene of spectacular realism set to music. As Newman commented: "Nothing so pungently realistic has yet been seen in ballet as the March to the Scaffold and the Witches' Sabbath." [16]

Massine's monumental conception for *Symphonie fantastique* contains the various techniques characteristic of his previous work: an emphasis on mass configurations and pyramid constructions to achieve the illusion of three-dimensional movement through space; counterpoint choreography; contrast between weight and lightness; and the contrast of action and tempo. The fusion of all of these effects and devices enhanced the neoromantic expressionism of the ballet, which was linked to the romantic musical qualities of Berlioz's composition.

Symphonie fantastique marked a turning point in Massine's oeuvre. For the first time there is a glimmer of the self through the exaltation of the romantic ego, a dimension that had been absent from his ballets up to this time. Contrary to his tendency in his comic, *demi-caractère* ballets, in which the hero is integrated into his environment, here Massine moves toward a tragic tradition in which the isolated hero drifts into solitude. This new expression of the self was undoubtedly the result of a subconscious desire for self-expression, and coincided with the two-year period of emotional turmoil over his frustrated relationship with Zorina. In Massine's enactment of the role of the Musician, every movement was imbued with a personal dimension. As with his Joseph two decades earlier, he used parallels with his own character to build his interpretation:

> I was fascinated also by the morbid personality of the chief character, and as I began to interpret the role, which I danced myself, I found it called for a good deal of dramatic action. Here once again my early experiences as an actor at the Maly proved invaluable. In the process of choreographing this ballet I found myself increasingly caught up in the part. This, I think, was inevitable, for if I had not been able to identify myself with the young Musician, my dancing would have been meaningless. [17]

But something else was at work, too. Despite its symbolism and its grandeur, *Symphonie fantastique,* with its connotations of emotional craving and guilt, is one of Massine's most intimate works, and seems to take its cue from the choreographer's personal experience. The choreography also becomes at times the expression of an idea. The second scene is a case in point. As the waltzing grows madder and more frenzied, the Musician is spun about in a confused whirl of dancing couples, the visualization of his inner turmoil. Probably no other ballet has matched the Ball scene in its expression of the romantic sensibility. If the aesthetic creative process was for Massine a means of transcendence, the larger-than-life quality of *Symphonie fantastique* was, almost in a Schopenhauerian manner, the ultimate expression of the artist's will.

At the time of the creation of *Symphonie fantastique,* the symphonic ballet controversy was still very much alive. Just prior to the work's premiere on July 24, Ernest Newman wrote four articles on the subject for the *Sunday Times,* again crossing swords with a colleague, this time J. A. Westrup of the *Daily Telegraph.*[18] Although the new work aroused the ire of some, the ballet was for the most part highly praised, even by those who had not been proponents of Massine's earlier experiments. Nevertheless, one of the staunchest admirers of *Choreartium,* A. V. Coton, complained that with *Symphonie fantastique* "Massine had abandoned further research into the potentialities of absolute movement—pattern-building, divorced from story-telling, character building and commentary. . . ."[19] Newman, on the other hand, gave the choreographer what was for him his highest praise: "One feels, indeed, that had Berlioz had a choreographer like Massine ready to his hand it would have been in some such form as this that he would have planned to have his work presented."[20]

Critics were divided in their appreciation of one or another movement. The reviewer for *The Times* felt that the second, the waltz, was most successful because it was most appropriate for choreographic treatment.[21] Coton described the fifth movement as "a scene which, divorced from the rest of the work, might be Massine's best purely inventive choreography since 1928 [probably referring to *Ode*]: as daring a realignment of choreographic material as the first movement of *Choreartium.*"[22] In general, the third movement was considered the strongest. Constant Lambert, a fervent antagonist of the symphonic ballets, conceded Massine's triumph in this instance: "It was surprising to discover how successfully the pastoral scene 'came off,' for on paper one would have said it was an impossible task. . . . [The designer Christian] Bérard, of course, is more static than dynamic, and Massine more classical than romantic, so when both are treating the most serene and classical music in the symphony we get a closer fusion of three minds than we get elsewhere in this ballet."[23] Newman wrote: "The result has been as convincing a demonstration of [Massine's] genius as he has ever given us, an idyll of the first order, with a new miming and a new translation of music into terms of dance. So skillfully and imaginatively has it all been done that there is soon an end of our first fears of an intrusive realism when we catch sight of the deer in the background; even this animal is woven harmoniously into the general texture of the idyll."[24] The critic W. J. Turner wrote in a congratulatory letter to Massine after the premiere: "I consider the third movement . . . an absolute masterpiece and the finest piece of plastic imagination I have ever seen in choreography."[25] And on the other side of the Atlantic, W. J. Henderson wrote in the *New York Sun*: "The third movement, the pastoral, in which Berlioz essayed to make so much [of] the woodwind dialogue, is the best of Mr. Massine's conceptions. Here the choreography is imaginative, poetic and subtly suggestive, while the series of pictures evolved by the action is not only delightful to the eye, but filled with sentiment and fitness to the study and the music. Mr. Massine found himself quite as much at home here as he did in a similar situation in *Choreartium*."[26]

Edwin Denby, on the other hand, disliked the ballet's "nervousness," its lack of "human feeling," and concluded that "the characters are intellectual references to types; they do not take a mysterious life of their own."[27] No admirer (with rare exceptions) of Massine's work, Denby nevertheless acknowledged that

> *Massine is without doubt the master choreographer of today. He has the most astonishing inventiveness and the most painstaking constructivity. He is an encyclopedia of ballet, character, specialty, period, and even of formulas from modern German dancing. . . . Besides this gift of detail he has a passion for visual discipline, a very good sense of dramatic variety and climax, and one watches the whole* Fantastique—*except perhaps the last finale—with a breathless attention. The prison scene in particular moves as fast as a movie thriller. In the* Fantastique *Massine uses even more successfully than in* Présages *or* Choreartium *the device of a number of simultaneous entrées, giving an effect like a number of voices in music; and his gift for following the details as well as the main line of a score is remarkable.*[28]

Denby found the sets and costumes nothing short of "miraculous." Christian Bérard brilliantly captured the feeling of a romantic mise-en-scène: the mythical landscape in the first scene, the mysterious ballroom, the ruins of the pastoral scene, and the somber, cavernous subworlds of the two final movements. The romantic devices included the illusion of the disappearance of walls and, in the third scene, the flying entrance of the Beloved. The visual impact was enhanced by

Kochno's intricate chiaroscuro lighting design. Each contribution helped to make *Symphonie fantastique* a great theatrical event.

Massine looked for his next challenge. There was much to choose from: a Mozart or Beethoven symphony, a lively Viennese divertissement ballet in collaboration with Etienne de Beaumont, as well as the ever-present possibilities of reviving *Le Sacre* or resurrecting *Liturgie,* his first, unfinished choreographic essay. For the new *Liturgie* he was planning to draw inspiration from a series of Mantegna friezes in the National Gallery and set them to music from the fifteenth and sixteenth centuries, to create a series of rhythmic tableaux on religious themes.[29] He hoped to persuade Nadia Boulanger to consult with him on the score. He also considered staging Zoltán Kodály's *Háry János.*[30]

At the end of the Covent Garden season, the Massines first visited Piešťany, then, en route to Galli, stopped in Salzburg to visit their friends Alice and Hugo von Hofmannsthal. In September Le Corbusier visited the Massines in Galli.

Nineteen thirty-seven would mark Massine's definitive break with de Basil. The 1936 petition for a restraining order was followed by a famous 1937 copyright suit. Massine's patience was wearing thin. He was already irritated that he had been forced to go to court to stop de Basil from using his ballets in the Australian repertory. Now, more inclined than ever to break away, form his own company, and establish sole ownership of his ballets, he filed suit against the Colonel when the company returned to London in the summer of 1937. The case stirred a great deal of talk in artistic circles and was thoroughly raked over by the international press, especially in England and the United States.

The ballets to which Massine laid claim fell into three categories: eight works that he had choreographed before he and de Basil signed a contract on June 1, 1932; the six he created under that contract; and the three works executed after they made a new agreement in August 1934. On February 23, 1938, Lord Justice Greer ruled that four ballets in the first group would go to Massine and four to de Basil. To Massine's dismay, the other nine ballets, including the three symphonic ballets, would go to de Basil, who had paid for them. By the time of this ruling, however, Massine had already defected, having performed for the last time with de Basil's company in San Francisco on January 30.

As it happened, during the American tour in the spring of 1937, Massine had found in Julius Fleischmann, a Cincinnati industrialist (of a yeast, liquor, and coffee fortune), the financial support needed to create his own company. When the loss of Massine became imminent in 1937, de Basil hired Michel Fokine as guest choreographer. Fokine's departure from Blum's Ballets de Monte Carlo opened the way for Massine to re-contact Blum and to propose reorganizing his company with American capital. The troupe would be sponsored by World Art, Inc. (a name taken from Diaghilev's journal *The World of Art*), with Hurok as its American manager, Fleischmann as president of the board, and Serge Denham, a Russian-born banker, as vice-president. Since Massine was ballet's most prestigious international figure, he of course became the operation's driving force. On January 2, 1937, he promised Denham that he would leave de Basil in order to become the new company's artistic director, choreographer, and premier danseur. Massine also guaranteed the participation of famous artists such as Hindemith and Matisse, both of whom wrote letters of intent to Denham—all of this in order to secure the backing for the enterprise.[31] To Hurok, Massine agreed to extend his expiring contract with de Basil until the 1937–38 American tour, with the crucial proviso that Hurok would sign a "proper" contract with Denham before May 15, 1937.[32] Blum's company, renamed the Ballet Russe de Monte Carlo, was to have headquarters in both Monte Carlo and the United States. On November 19, 1937, Blum sold the Ballets de Monte Carlo to World Art, Inc. (later to be called Universal Art), with the purchase to take effect on February 1, 1938.[33]

Massine's Ballet Russe de Monte Carlo would gather an impressive roster of dancers: Toumanova, Danilova, Delarova, Alicia Markova, Mia Slavenska, Lubov Rostova, Nini Theilade, Nina Tarakanova, Nathalie Krassovska, Lifar, George Zoritch, Michel Panaiev, Igor Youskevitch, Frederic Franklin, and Roland Guérard. Efrem Kurtz left de Basil's company to become its leading conductor. The rival companies attracted the attention of the international press early in 1938, and the Battle of the Ballets, as it was known, became an artistic and social war that involved some of the most important personalities of the time in Europe and the United States. But in the long run, the outcome of this crisis would prove detrimental to Massine. After five years of work, he possessed an out-standing and versatile company trained, coached, and molded to give body to his choreographic ideas. As Haskell had observed the previous year: "Massine's departure will not only damage the company as a whole, but Massine himself perhaps even more. It has taken all of five years, hard work and sacrifice to build up this magnificent ensemble. . . . It would take more than five . . . to create another such."[34]

In January 1938 Massine returned to Europe to organize the new enterprise. He approached old collaborators and friends such as Count

Etienne de Beaumont, who once again took an active part in his projects. After Massine settled in Monte Carlo, preparations could begin for the company's spring debut in Monaco. With complete control of his own company, he tried to establish a creative atmosphere reminiscent of his early days with Diaghilev. The whole company was overtaken by an almost frenzied mood of artistic collaboration. Monte Carlo became a feeding ground for dancers, composers, painters, and prominent supporters; there were Dalí, Chanel, Kochno, Bérard, Beaumont, Hindemith, Tchelitchev, all enraptured by the creative process. Even Massine's relationship with the dancers grew closer; during the day-long rehearsals, the leading members of the company would gather at his villa outside Monte Carlo for sandwiches and relaxation.

Massine's return to France put him back in touch with the artistic trends prevailing in Paris. He recontacted friends, especially painters, some of whom (Masson, Miró, Dalí, Duchamp, Ernst, Man Ray) had enjoyed a rousing success during January and February with the famous surrealist exhibition at the Galerie Beaux-Arts. His return to the Continent also exposed the choreographer to the darkening political, social, and economic reality of Europe. His previous five years had been spent mostly within the sheltered milieu of the Ballets Russes, in England and America. England throughout the 1930s had tried to remain insulated from the ominous events unfolding in continental Europe; and in America the approaching cataclysm was dulled by distance. Massine was never acutely political, but in Paris he could not avoid reality. Days were somber. The "May crisis" that followed the Anschluss, Hitler's annexation of Austria, made it evident that he also had designs on Czechoslovakia, and signaled Germany's plans for territorial expansion.

The spring engagement at Monte Carlo's Théâtre du Casino was to include only one premiere by the company's choreographer: *Gaîté parisienne*. (Massine was not appointed artistic director until March 23, 1939.)

Gaîté parisienne probably had as its point of departure the divertissement ballet on a Viennese theme that Massine was discussing with Beaumont in 1936. But, undoubtedly in reaction to the frightening events in Austria, Beaumont changed the setting to Tortoni's, a fashionable Parisian café of the Second Empire, to which came various characters in pursuit of love and pleasure: a Glove Seller, a Flower Girl, a Peruvian, a Baron, an Officer, a Duke, and other topical characters mingled with dandies, cancan dancers, and brilliantly uniformed soldiers. The score consisted of excerpts chosen by Boulanger from a number of Offenbach works,[35] orchestrated by Manuel Rosenthal in collaboration with Jacques

Monte Carlo, 1938. Standing: Eugenia Delarova, Igor Youskevitch, Christian Bérard, Massine. Seated: Barbara Karinska, Alicia Markova, Boris Kochno, Etienne de Beaumont, and the Countess de Beaumont

Brindejonc-Offenbach, the composer's nephew. The scenery and costumes were designed by Beaumont. *Gaîté parisienne* followed in the tradition of *La Boutique fantasque* and *Le Beau Danube*. Here the slight plot of flirtations, amorous intrigues, and conquests unfolded as a series of solos, pas de deux, and ensembles, including a climactic cancan. (According to Frederic Franklin, Massine intended to end the ballet with the cancan, and it was Kochno's suggestion to add the final scene.[36]) Less balletic than *Boutique* and *Beau Danube*, the Offenbach piece was fashioned more in a glorified music-hall style.

A sensational hit with the public, this piece of sheer escapism met with a mixed reception from the European press. In London, Newman found it "lovable,"[37] and Fernau Hall, writing for the *Dancing Times*, compared it favorably to *Boutique*, *Beau Danube*, and *Union Pacific*:

> *The dance of the soldiers, for example, is much more clean-cut and vital than the corresponding dance of the Cossack toys in* Boutique, *and it has a gloriously impudent quality which sets the atmosphere of the whole bal-*

let. As for the fight, it is incomparably better than the fight in Union Pacific, and one of the finest scenes Massine has ever arranged. No actual
fighting takes place, but the effect given by the complex dancing movements
is far more real than the real thing could ever be. All the experience Massine has gained in handling large groups in his symphonic ballets is brilliantly applied in this scene, so that although the whole stage is filled with
dancers, all of whom constantly remain "in character," the general effect is
always clear and definite. As for the Peruvian himself, he is a pure joy, and
quite unlike any other Massine role.

The Can-Can dances are built up to a fine climax, with some very effective virtuoso effects on the way.[38]

Haskell and Cyril Beaumont, however, did not fall under its spell. Beaumont found it inferior to *Le Beau Danube* and lacking the latter's "homo-
geneity" and "charm."[39] In the United States, the ballet won praise from
public and press alike. John Martin in the *New York Times* found it superior to *Le Beau Danube* and "fresh as a daisy, extraordinarily skillful and inventive."[40]

In America, the ballet became the company's signature piece, as *Le
Beau Danube* had been de Basil's. It was an ideal piece to end a performance, and much of its success depended on the brilliant, unforgettable,
and (even in their own day) legendary performances of Danilova as the
Glove Seller, Massine as the Peruvian, and Franklin as the Baron.

In March there was an unexpected development: a scheme to
merge the warring Ballets Russes factions.[41] The idea was Hurok's. He
envisioned managing what he called "the finest ballet company that . . .
ever existed."[42] His ploy had a double aim: to merge the companies and
to oust de Basil in the process. Agreements were signed and repudiated.
Lawsuits and counterclaims were filed. The merger failed to materialize.

For the upcoming summer season at the Drury Lane Theatre in
London, Massine's company would face direct competition from de
Basil's under the artistic guidance of Fokine. Counterprogramming, Massine premiered two new ballets: *Seventh Symphony* (Beethoven's) on July 12
and *Nobilissima Visione*, set to an original score by Hindemith, on July 21.

Massine had first considered the symphony as early as 1936, after
Symphonie fantastique. (He no doubt had been encouraged to do so by
some words of Newman's published that year in the *Sunday Times*: "Les
Présages and Choreartium . . . draw full houses at Covent Garden; and we
unregenerates now hope that Massine, having at last got the Berlioz ballet off his hands, will turn his genius to the Beethoven No. 7.")[43] Without

The Peruvian in Gaîté parisienne,
1938

the abstraction that had characterized *Choreartium,* and closer in mood to *Les Présages, Seventh Symphony* was Massine's depiction of the creation and destruction of the world, utilizing universal archetypes derived from the Bible and classical mythology. He wrote:

> *I had for some time been intrigued by the problem of interpreting this monumental work, whose powerful chords in the First Movement suggested the formation of the earth, with moving masses of soil and water creating rivers, hills and valleys. The clarinet theme which follows seemed to me to represent the evolution of plant life, while the chords of the next passage conjured up in my mind the flight of birds and the running of small animals through the forest. Standing on Galli one summer afternoon, watching the waves, whipped up by a sudden storm, pounding the unyielding rocks, I found the theme of the ballet clarifying itself in my imagination. I saw in the first scene the basic forces of nature, Earth, Air, and Water, assembled by the Spirit of Creation. Plants, birds and animals appear. Finally, Man, Woman, and the Serpent emerge from the living rock. The second scene I conceived as the story of man's guilt and despair, symbolized by Cain and Abel and the introduction of death with man's first murder. The third scene introduced the gods of Olympus. Beginning in a mood of gaiety, I created a choreographic movement which led on to the debauched bacchanal of the Fourth Movement, concluding with the destruction of the world by fire.*[44]

Although relying less on counterpoint than in his first three symphonic ballets, Massine drew on all his characteristic techniques for *Seventh Symphony.* However, whereas in *Choreartium* and, especially, *Symphonie fantastique* he had achieved an architectural quality by emphasizing the construction of moving masses on stage, *Seventh Symphony* produced a sculptural effect. Here, apparently amorphous groups would begin to fall into formations representing air, water, earth, and fire. These visual images were essential to the mise-en-scène and stood in contrast to the actual formal dancing of the other characters. Forty years later Massine observed: "The richness and beauty of the human body lays in its manifold possibilities of movement, whether it is classical technique, folk dance, or simply visual images that can be created through corporeal rhythmic movement. In the *Seventh Symphony* I wanted to expand the possibility of body movement to the utmost, not just through dancing, but exploring the potentialities of rhythmic corporeal movement as well."[45]

Seventh Symphony, *1938: Fourth movement, final moment of the bacchanale*

However, the corporeal movement in *Seventh Symphony* could be called plastic only insofar as it caught and expressed a visual image inspired by painting or sculpture. Even as it captured such an image, the movement quickened. Massine avoided the trap awaiting any choreographer who tries to re-create visual images in movement: his plasticity kept the work from feeling static. On the contrary, the film of the ballet shows, as Jack Anderson noted, that the dancing is characterized by a kinetic dynamism. Albertina Vitak, writing in 1940, said that the ballet had "more straight dancing with less theatricalities than Massine's previous symphonic works."[46]

Like those predecessors, *Seventh Symphony* provoked a great deal of controversy. Some critics admired the result; others were skeptical about the use of a Beethoven symphony; and still others felt that Massine simply hadn't succeeded, whether a viewer thought his goal worthy or not. Some looked back to *Les Présages* and *Choreartium* as models and regretted that he had departed from them. Francis Toye wrote in the *Daily Telegraph*: "We have had enough of the symphony ballets. Not because of their lack of reverence for Beethoven . . . but because they are a bore." [47] But Newman, though he felt that the scherzo movement did "not lend itself well to choreographical parallelism," [48] again championed Massine, comparing him favorably to Fokine:

> What I cannot understand is why Massine should be censured for doing well what other choreographers aim at doing but do not succeed in. Examine certain of Fokine's ballets from L'Oiseau de Feu onwards, and you will see that he too has constantly aimed at finding choreographic equivalents for features of the music that in themselves have no connection to external reality. . . .
>
> Now Fokine is constantly "pointing" to this or that feature of the music in his choreography; the trouble, so far as I am concerned, is that too often the pointing is almost unbelievably naive. I do not mind so much when, in L'Epreuve d'Amour, he adopts the very obvious device of making his dancers stamp when Mozart's cellos and basses seem to stamp: it is not very brilliant invention, but it may pass. But when, in those long woodwind chords in the Midsummer Night's Dream overture, he makes his elves do a jerk of now head, now body, on each chord in turn, I feel that the limit has been reached of my tolerance of naiveté. When Massine points a phrase in this fashion—take, as an example, the movements of the Spirit of Creation at the commencement of the Beethoven—the dancer's movements and gestures not only mean something in themselves but form an organic part of a large design. [49]

In New York the second scene, with its possible reference to Christ's Descent from the Cross, created a bit of an uproar and was even found sacrilegious by some. As Jack Anderson expressed it in 1981, "In this day of rock musicals based upon the Bible, it is hard to imagine such a scene causing any hullabaloo." [50] Denby was scornful of the entire enterprise:

> Like a cigarette company, he is using famous names to advertise his wares. But I cannot help resenting it, because they are names of living things I have loved. It is hardest to bear in the case of his Seventh, where the orchestra is constantly reminding me of the Beethoven original.
>
> Trying, however, to put aside this private resentment, I still am disappointed. . . . I could see a kaleidoscopic succession of clever arrangements, but there was no thrill in the order in which they came. There was no sequence in the movement that awakened some kind of special feeling, some

kind of urgency. It all occupied the eye as long as it lasted, and left no real-
ity, no secret emotion behind. I missed the sense of growth and interplay,
of shifting kinds of tensions, the feeling of drama, almost, that makes the
best choreography mean much more than a string of effects. As a pictorial
arranger Massine is inexhaustible. But dancing is less pictorial than plas-
tic, and pictures in dancing leave a void in the imagination. . . .

Because Massine's tension is static he can never make us feel the curious
unfolding that is like tenderness. Like a Hollywood director, he gives us no
sense of human growth (there isn't time), he keeps everything at a con-
stant level of finish; everything is over as soon as it starts. He has no equiv-
alent for mystery except to bring down the lights.[51]

The ballet received some of its most eloquent reviews when it
reached Paris in 1939. Vuillermoz was a firm admirer:

It is fashionable to be dynamic, and in this regard we must grant that Mas-
sine is a full embodiment of that restless ideal of his time. Once the cur-
tain falls at the end of each of his creations, the interpreters are all out of
breath, but so too are the spectators. . . . Massine excels in architectural
combinations, in which he utilizes the different parts of his dancers' bodies
simply as construction materials, obtaining thereby arabesques of new
and unforeseen interest. This all happens, of course, in the midst of vio-
lent, carried-away motions which infuse his rhythms with the power of a
hurricane. . . .

There are some purists . . . who have deemed it proper to cover their
faces and to cry out against the sacrilege of someone daring to translate
into choreographic terms the rhythmical indications of a Beethoven sym-
phony! Allow me to smile at such prudish qualms!

. . . There is never any sacrilege in attempting to uphold in the
synesthetic creation of a plastic medium, the grandeur of a rhythmic
creation. . . .

The fact is, the beautiful images which accompanied the four move-
ments of the Seventh Symphony—the Creation, the Earth, the Heavens,
and Destruction—are a most respectful, noble, and, I dare say, Beethoven-
like embodiment of the clear and legible tempo indications appearing in a
score that is not at all esoteric.[52]

Of special interest were the reactions of leading French composers.
Florent Schmitt, among those who had called the adaptation of a symphony into dance a "sacrilege," succumbed once he saw the work itself,

describing it as "a spectacle full of great pathos that owed its birthright to music itself."⁵³ And Henri Sauguet in *Le Jour* noted that the ballet "does not shock the musician who sees come to life with intelligence the different voices of the symphony." He felt that the ballet was full of "boldness, fire, invention, and real grandeur."⁵⁴

The second premiere of the Drury Lane season, *Nobilissima Visione,* was inspired by the *Little Flowers of Saint Francis.* Massine had considered collaborating with Hindemith as early as 1935, and in the summer of 1936 the Hindemiths and the Massines went sightseeing together in Italy. From Poverello they proceeded to Florence. Massine wrote: "The idea for this work came to me from Paul Hindemith. . . . He had just come from the great church of Santa Croce [in Florence], which contains the frescoes by Giotto depicting the life of St. Francis of Assisi. He had been deeply impressed by them; taking me by the arm he hurried me back to the church to see them. I too was struck by their spiritual beauty and could well understand why they had so profoundly moved Hindemith."⁵⁵

After much thought, Massine was still hesitant about the idea, and he approached the writer François Mauriac for advice. Although Mauriac was also unconvinced, by then the idea had so intensely fired Massine's imagination that there was no turning back. (Later Mauriac commented: "I must admit that when Léonide Massine spoke to me for the first time of his project for St. Francis, the idea seemed to me worse than bold—it was even sacrilegious. This is because I had not realized that the dance, as this great artist has conceived of it, can express what is most beautiful and sacred in this world: the love of God taking possession of the soul of a young man.")⁵⁶ At the end of the summer of 1937 Massine invited the Hindemiths to Galli to work on the new ballet. In fact, however, most of the preliminary planning had already taken place earlier in the summer in correspondence between the two. In its embryonic stage the scenario was to concentrate on Saint Francis's miracles. But in a letter dated August 12, 1937, Massine suggested to Hindemith that they focus instead on the character of Saint Francis himself, structuring the action on "three distinct periods, that is to say, his life before the conversion, the period of the conversion and the miracles." Massine continued: "It seems to me that this idea is superior to the first one. It allows for a greater episodic variety, a strong contrast between the first and the third parts and a very beautiful moment, that of the conversion. It also brings to the fore the character of Saint Francis, an aspect that seems interesting to me due to his profound and rich spirituality and his reactions to all the events of his life." Massine proceeded to list the eight episodes that he found most remarkable in the saint's life and which, in fact, were incorporated into the final scenario.[57]

The rehearsals for *Nobilissima Visione,* as well as those for *Seventh Symphony,* took place during the spring of 1938 in Monte Carlo. During the rehearsal period Hindemith played the score at the piano and advised Massine on "the structure of some of his musical phrases, which were extremely complex and difficult."[58] Pavel Tchelitchev, with whom Massine had worked previously on *Ode,* was commissioned to design scenery and costumes in medieval style.

Nobilissima visione, later better known as *Saint Francis,* had five scenes:

First Scene: The Shop of Pietro Bernadone. Francis and his companions are spending time at his father's shop. Motivated by the arrival of a knight, Francis departs for war, dreaming of military honor and glory.

Second Scene: A Country Road. Francis is disappointed by the knights' greed and abusive behavior when they attack an unarmed group, carrying off the women and whatever loot they find. Francis prays for guidance, whereupon Poverty, Obedience, and Chastity appear as allegorical figures. The latter two vanish and Francis follows Poverty.

Third Scene: The House of Pietro Bernadone. At a banquet celebrating Francis's return, a group of beggars show up, and Francis gives them the gold vessels from the table. His father is furious and strikes his son. Francis takes off his rich clothes and, laying them at his father's feet, leaves the house.

Fourth Scene: Francis Finds Happiness as a Hermit. He meets a wolf. His three companions join him. As Francis sleeps, Poverty appears to him in a dream. As he awakens, he welcomes her as a bride. They exchange sashes and the companions celebrate their marriage with bread and water.

Fifth Scene: A Landscape with a Great Rock in the Distance. Surrounded by nuns and monks, Poverty leads Francis to the summit of the rock against a blazing sky.

Choreographically, the ballet was rooted in the *terre à terre,* nonvirtuosic modern idiom that had characterized the second movement of *Choreartium.* The steps were stylized, with an Oriental Byzantine touch derived from Italian primitive painting, especially from the works of Giotto. Some of the phrases were reminiscent of martial art. For Massine, *Nobilissima Visione* "was not a ballet at all. It was a dramatic and

*Massine as
Saint Francis, with the
three Companions and
with Nini Theilade
as Poverty, in*
Nobilissima
Visione, *1938*

choreographic interpretation of the life of St. Francis in which Hindemith, Tchelitchev and I tried to create and sustain throughout a mood of mystic exaltation."[59] The ballet, possessing great sobriety of style, had very effective and ingenious movements. For example, in their pas de deux Saint Francis (Massine) and Poverty (Nini Theilade) "danced an adagio which was more like a slow allegro. There was not one lift. They danced a lot of the same movements together, facing each other."[60] And in the final scene the alleluia was sung silently by the hands of the Franciscan monks and nuns.

Opening night had all the excitement of a traditional Massine premiere. In attendance were Lady Cunard, Lady Juliet Duff, Sir Kenneth Clark, Lord Berners, Baron Gunzbourg, Alice von Hofmannstal, Edward James, and the Sitwells. In a letter to Massine after the premiere Hindemith wrote: "We have admired your devoted art and the sublime passion with which you capture the spirit and the heart at the same time." The composer acknowledged that "the birth of this work has marked a period full of happy and productive discoveries."[61] Although the ballet was greeted with twenty-one curtain calls, its critical reception was mixed. Haskell felt that the music sounded "like so much unpleasant noise, signifying nothing," and that the choreography was "dull."[62] Francis Toye strongly disagreed with the suitability of the subject and added, "I have no desire to see Massine impersonate St. Francis, who after all is one of the major saints in the calendar. It would be a pity if he were now encouraged to try his hand at St. Paul or one of the apostles."[63] When the ballet was presented in the United States, it found admirers in press and audience alike. According to Grace Robert, this was in part because the public had grown accustomed to the seriousness of modern dance works, especially those by artists such as Martha Graham, and "welcomed an appeal to more adult emotions."[64] Denby, predictably, disliked it: "*St. Francis* seems a slinky posturing, a Sakharoff-Kreutzberg parody of illuminated Books of Hours and Minnelieder, with a grand finale of anthroposophic chorus girls.

"No one but Massine could have got any theatrical effect out of this hodgepodge of minor pictorial devices, no one but he could have held the stage with a solo only half executed—but everyone acknowledges his stupendous gift of showmanship, and eminence, for that matter."[65] By 1940, however, he admitted that *St. Francis* had been the "last time Massine took a chance with novel choreography."[66]

John Martin, on the other hand, praised the ballet in the *New York*

Times as "one of the most memorable and beautiful dance works of our day." He added:

> *Unorthodox in subject matter, elevated in tone, and revolutionary in its choreographic procedure, it is one of those creations which, like Bronislava Nijinska's* Les Noces, *grew out of boldness of conception without regard for precedent or consequences.*
>
> *Massine has caught not alone the particular development of Francis "so little and simple and rude of speech," but has evoked a masterly picture of the Middle Ages in which he moved. It is perhaps not so much thirteenth century Italy in detail as the entire medieval period he has sketched in little, with its sumptuousness and its misery, its cruelty and its vision . . .*
>
> *The movement, though it does not deny its ballet premises, is touched in an extravagant style definitely influenced by medieval illuminations and those painters we have come to call "primitive" and richly evocative. If it is designedly naive, it is never merely quaint or whimsical, but eminently dignified and honest. For all its distortions and inhibitions, it has great pace and flow, and proves itself in every way fitted to convey feeling in eloquent terms. Like St. Francis himself, it is both ascetic and joyful; sparing and full of color.* [67]

Hurok called it "one of Massine's greatest triumphs and one of his very finest works. The ballet, unfortunately, was not popular with mass audiences; but it was a work of deep and moving beauty." [68] Similarly, George Amberg wrote: "The work was a rejection of the prevailing realistic tendency in the ballet and an affirmation of true spirituality. . . . In no other ballet did Massine seem so totally absorbed in the world of his creation. In no other ballet did the limited realms of stage space and stage time seem to expand into such unlimited poetic dimensions. . . . As the story unfolded, the actual events appeared as symbolic stations of human inspiration progressing toward ultimate transfiguration." [69]

In Paris the following year the work aroused special interest in the musical world (Hindemith's music was forbidden in Germany during the Third Reich). While Schmitt found the score monotonous, except for the scene of the wolf, [70] and Sauguet felt that it lacked definition and color, [71] Milhaud praised it warmly. For him it had "great loftiness of thought and it was all imbued with an extremely mystical feeling." [72] In general, the choreography was praised, and Sauguet singled out the last scene when "the hands of the dancers seem to leave their bodies, mute, like birds taking flight toward the heavens with St. Francis's soul."[73] Even dancers who were not in the cast found the ballet moving, plastically beautiful, and extremely spiritual. Danilova today considers it her favorite work by Massine.[74]

BEFORE THE COMPANY left Europe in the fall of 1938 to tour the United States for the first time, Massine finally divorced Eugenia Delarova. The last months of the marital breakup were stressful and dramatic, as was the postdivorce period, since Delarova remained on the roster of the Ballet Russe for the next two years. There was no divorce settlement. Most dancers were saddened by the separation, since for them Massine and Delarova had become an institution, and she in particular was highly esteemed not only for her charm and friendliness but for her kindness to everyone, and her undisputed devotion to Massine and his career. "She was behind it all," declared Franklin. "She watched rehearsals; she brought to Massine's attention those dancers who had talent and special qualities and could be made into soloists. Delarova was always part of the creative process, and she was there as a sort of diplomat trying to orchestrate everything for Massine, and when anyone had a problem she was always there to take care of it."[75]

During the United States tour Massine produced one new ballet, based on Slavic mythology. The idea for a Russian ballet had been proposed to Massine by Hurok, who wanted to emulate the tremendous success the de Basil company had enjoyed the previous year with Fokine's *Le Coq d'or*. The impresario demanded that the American tour include a world premiere, so *Bogatyri* was rehearsed during the hectic London season, and premiered in October 1938 at the New York Metropolitan Opera House. It revolved around the adventures of the half-historic, half-legendary hero who had defended Prince Vladimir, the first Christian ruler of Russia. In the ballet, the handsome Bogatyri Dobryna Nikitich (Panaiev) sets out to rescue Princess Anastachiuska (Mia Slavenska), the daughter of Prince Vladimir, from the clutches of the twelve-headed snake dragon. In the course of the Bogatyri's search, a battle takes place with a Tartan tribe after which the tribeswomen seduce the Bogatyri, causing them to forget their mission. In the meantime Alyosha (Frederic Franklin) discovers the dragon's garden and saves the princess. When they return safely home, a huge wedding celebration takes place. The ballet was set to Borodin's Second Symphony, the two movements of his unfinished Third Symphony as orchestrated by Alexander

Glazounov, and the Nocturne from his String Quartet No. 2 as orchestrated by Nicolas Tcherepnine. Perhaps the most noteworthy aspect of the production was Nathalie Gontcharova's magnificent scenery and costumes.

At the end of the United States tour, the company returned to Europe. On March 14, 1939, Massine married his third wife, the statuesque and strong-willed Tatiana Orlova, née Milishnikova. They had met a few years before when she took some Spanish character-dance classes he was teaching at Egorova's studio in Paris. In the interim, Orlova was in and out of Massine's sight until the relationship suddenly blossomed.

In the spring of 1939, the deterioration of the political situation was immediately evident. In September 1938, England, France, and Italy had surrendered Czechoslovakia to Hitler in Munich, allowing his armies to march into that country on October 1, and now Europe slid inexorably towards war. On March 15, 1939, German troops marched into Bohemia and Monrovia; that evening Hitler himself made his entry into Prague. Clearly Poland was his next objective.

The Monte Carlo spring season introduced two new works by Massine: *Capriccio espagnol* (May 4) and *L'Etrange farandole* (May 11), later better known as *Rouge et noir.*

Massine had invited to Monte Carlo the renowned Spanish dancer Argentinita as guest artist to take over the role of the Miller's Wife in *Le Tricorne.* The choreographer came up with the idea of co-creating with her another ballet based on Spanish folklore. The choice of music was Rimsky-Korsakov's *Capriccio espagnol,* a dance suite that "portrayed a country fair, with gypsies dancing in a rousing *bulería* until the dancing becomes general and the watching couples swing into a frenzied *jota.*"[76] *Capriccio espagnol* became a flashy vehicle for Massine and Argentinita. Later Denby wrote:

Capriccio Espagnol *has the benefit of Argentinita's exhaustless repertoire of regional steps, and of Massine's equally exhaustless repertoire of effective theater. Most of it is pleasant to watch and the end is one of those bang-up finales that are indispensable to ring the curtain down if you have a lethargic audience. Massine has a solo, and in it he makes the other men look like little boys. The showmanship, the bite of his stage presence is superlative; look at the slow curling of his hands as his dance begins. It is inaccurate to call such a dance as his Spanish in the specific sense . . . and foolish to compare him with a real gypsy, who would probably have no gift*

*for dominating a crowded stage and would hardly be visible at that mo-
ment to an ordinary audience.*[77]

Rouge et noir was the second and final collaboration between Massine and Matisse. The idea had arisen when Massine visited the painter's
studio while the painter was at work on a huge panel decoration commissioned for the Barnes Foundation in Pennsylvania. Massine was so
taken by the sense of movement and rhythm in Matisse's work that he
asked his old friend to collaborate with him again on a ballet.[78] But it was
not until 1939 that this joint creative effort materialized.

For the music Massine selected Dmitri Shostakovich's First Symphony, which Matisse then visualized in five basic colors, taking the great
arches of his decoration for the Barnes Foundation as a point of departure for the decor. Matisse recalled that he "divided the background in
four colors, blue, red, black and yellow, with white arches. I dressed the
dancers in the same colors of the decor in blue, red, black, yellow and
white unitights. . . . I was satisfied with the idea because I managed to
free myself from all those insignificant accessories that had no direct relation with the plastic element and the dynamism of ballet."[79] In a letter to
Massine dated May 18, 1938, he wrote:

> *I should tell you I believe that in order to facilitate your choreographic
> composition of the First Symphony it seems to me to be indispensable to
> dress your male and female dancers in colored tights or work costumes for
> the torso and the legs—and even the arms since the volumes of color which
> you will have to move around should not be hacked down and cut up into
> small pieces by having the arms and the legs dressed in any old colors. The
> extra cost will be really insignificant if you compare it with the benefits
> you will obtain.*[80]

Massine was not completely satisfied with Matisse's initial idea for the
front curtain, however, and suggested that the painter change it. Matisse
replied: "You have made a just observation regarding the curtain and it
has set my brain in motion, so that since your arrival I have worked on it
and have come up finally with a new curtain which I hope will please you
entirely."[81]

Massine gave allegorical meaning to the colors: white (man and
woman), yellow (wickedness), blue (nature), red (materialism), and black
(violence). (Massine told Danilova that white stood for Russia, black for

fascism, and red for communism.)[82] Though more abstract than *Les Présages*, *Rouge et noir* was a sequel to the Tchaikovsky ballet, and as in *Les Présages* each movement was given a symbolic theme.

First Movement (Aggression). Man, symbolizing the poetic spirit, is pursued and overtaken by brutal forces.

Second Movement (Field and City). The men of the city encounter the men of the field and drive them off.

Third Movement (Solitude). Woman parted from Man is tormented in her solitude by an evil spirit.

Fourth Movement (Destiny). Man eludes the brutal forces and finds Woman again. But their joy is short-lived, for in freeing himself from his worldly enemies he is conquered by destiny.

While in *Les Présages* the hero triumphed over fate and the adverse forces of war, paralleling the European reality of 1933, *Rouge et noir* presented a pessimistic finale of wretchedness and disillusionment. In his treatment of it Massine summoned the anguish of the age, its overwhelming feelings of alienation, despair, failure, and the angst of loneliness, stressing a cosmic level of identification outside the self. In this ballet he proved his ability to conceive emotional ideas in terms of forms. *Rouge et noir* was a personal metaphoric expression of the philosophical and political ideas that permeated the historical moment. The political connotations of the ballet did not escape audiences or critics. Pierre Michaut commented that for some the ballet's "abstraction hid an esoteric meaning . . . a political allegory: the dramatic crushing of helpless nations, victims of the violence and brutality of victimizing nations—Abyssinia, Austria, Czechoslovakia. . . . Woman . . . who survives, symbolizes the spirit that prevails and cannot be defeated."[83] However, Michaut felt that although the symbolic theme did not impose any action or narrative development and the work was purely an abstract ballet, it nonetheless produced in the spectator "a dramatic impression quite oppressive, a clear sign that its agitation is not pointless."[84] Jack Anderson later pointed out that "one of its most effective moments, a solo lamentation for Markova, symbolized to some audiences the grief of Czechoslovakia overcome by Germany."[85] Danilova described Markova's solo as "a cry—she *bourréed* all around the stage, changing the positions of her arms, of her body. She was weeping without tears, with her soul."[86]

Rouge et noir was a visualization of music in absolute dance terms, but Massine resorted less than in his four previous symphonic ballets to architectural constructions and to counterpoint. Here his objectives were abstraction of content (despite the symbolic theme) and abstrac-

Rouge et noir, *1938*

tion of line (linear development). While in *Les Présages* and *Choreartium* the choreographic line is clearly defined as geometrical, with each image contoured and modeled, the line in *Rouge et noir* fuses abstract formations, achieving, in part through its fluctuating velocity, a galvanic power. Abstraction not only serves the thematic structure but is at the heart of the choreographic impulse, showing a greater degree of introspection than ever before from Massine. In its handling of mass formations that were constantly shifting and regrouping, the choreography became a device to manipulate the audience's visual field. As Grace Robert commented: "It was extraordinarily effective scenically, though best seen from a distance. . . . The groups formed and came apart, making wonderful blocks of color like an abstract painting set in motion."[87]

The opinions of the Paris critics were mixed, the majority preferring *Seventh Symphony* and *Nobilissima Visione* to the pessimistic *Rouge et noir*. But Pierre Michaut nevertheless admired the result, describing the choreography as "various groups that form, scatter, and re-form. It is a simple handling of lines and formations in movement. The handling of forms is accompanied by a play of colors; the various leading characters detach themselves from the large background figures, by which they are reabsorbed. A visual symphony of forms and colors in movement is superimposed on the musical symphony." [88]

In the United States, too, notices were mixed. Denby disliked it:

> *The set and underwear costumes, effective for a while, become rather professorially meager long before the piece is over (and rather unpleasantly indecent). . . . The choreography I am at a loss to describe because it does not seem to relate itself to anything I feel. I will gladly accept it as my fault that it all seems to me to happen in a vacuum. I can see ingenious arrangements and good technique, a touching opening in the third scene, and an odd feeling of a conventional anecdote at the very end. When I like something I am sure I am right; when I don't, I'm not. I should like to read a sympathetic criticism of this ballet to help me get interested.* [89]

John Martin's reservations centered on the fact that the ballet was "partly abstract, partly programmatic, partly dominated by a color symbolism that is far from clear. Another is the ground of the willful mysticism of the theme." [90] Grace Robert admired the group formations: "Massine had taken a lot of criticism of previous symphonic ballets on the subject of the unballetic scurrying of dancers on their way to form one of his famous architectural tableaux. To a certain extent this criticism was justified, and he answered it superbly in *Rouge et noir*, where the groups (many and fascinating) click into position as though placed there by a gigantic hand working a jigsaw puzzle." [91] Robert Lawrence thought it was one of Massine's finest efforts: "Although [he] provided a philosophic program, *Rouge et noir* is—as its title implies—an abstract play of color and line which may be enjoyed without any recourse to a deeper meaning. Massine's patterns are self-sufficient; and in few other ballets by any master is emotional content so compellingly wedded to formal design." [92] For George Beiswanger it was Massine's "best constructed and most poetic ballet." [93]

Massine's symphonic ballets of 1938 and 1939 reflect in their themes the historical context as well as the aesthetics of the time that produced them. *Seventh Symphony* and *Rouge et noir* were very much concerned with cosmic events, with conflict, violence, loss of love, sacrifice, destruction, and death—a corollary to the anxiety of a continent facing depression, civil war, fascism, Nazism, and the portent of holocaust. The themes of these ballets were recurrent in the works of other European artists of the immediate prewar years, especially those associated with surrealism. For Michaut, *Seventh Symphony*, with its "apocalyptic destruction of humanity," and *Rouge et noir*, a "symbolic drama of the condition of man," hinted that "Massine was probably suffering a mystical crisis as he had in the past." He compared the choreographer's crisis with Stravinsky's and added that "when we think of the situation of these great spirits, living in exile, separated from the land of their ancestors and their first masters . . . Massine has imprinted on his ballets a pessimistic and desperate accent. More and more he distances himself from futility. And his worry about these immeasurable questions reveals an anxiety of the soul."[94] Nonetheless, to counterbalance the devastating *Seventh Symphony* and *Rouge et noir*, there were *Gaîté parisienne* and *Capriccio espagnol*, two pieces of theatrical escapism, and *Nobilissima Visione*, a work that reiterates spiritual values and wherein man finds salvation. The Saint Francis ballet was Massine's return to the mysticism and religious fervor that from childhood had given him a vision of transcendence. On the edge of a world catastrophe, *Nobilissima Visione* was a reiteration of the Dostoyevskian perception that man must not become alienated from his spiritual world, otherwise human existence can only tilt toward tragedy.

PART FIVE

The War Years

*Being essentially the instrument of his work, he [the artist]
is subordinate to it. . . . He has done the best that there is in
him by giving it form. . . .* —JUNG

*It is not others' hopes that you have to fulfill. You're going
nowhere, they say? Whatever you offer of yourself, it will
be your all and not what others would expect from you.
. . . Let them study you or let them leave you. You ought not
to lower your soul to their lack of understanding.*

—UNAMUNO

CHAPTER 12

Paris, June 1939–New York, August 1946

AFTER THE 1939 Paris season ended in late June, the members of the Ballet Russe de Monte Carlo scattered on holiday, planning to reassemble for a Covent Garden engagement on September 4. The opening never took place. On September 1 Nazi troops invaded Poland. As Hitler's armies marched into Warsaw, German war planes bombarded the Polish capital in the first of hundreds of air strikes that would devastate Europe over the next six years. On September 3 England and France declared war on Germany.

Paris grew frantic. Massine's and de Basil's dancers found themselves stranded there, unable to leave Europe. Life was immediately conditioned by war. Restaurants and shops were boarded up or closed. Some Parisians quickly joined an exodus toward the south. Those who remained behind sometimes had to carry gas masks or make their way to bomb shelters during air raid drills.

The first transatlantic passage that Massine was able to book he turned over to Delarova. She was now, since their divorce, quite alone and a source of great anxiety to Massine, who wanted her safely out of Europe as soon as possible.[1] Fortunately, Massine and Orlova were also able to leave soon afterward, on the *Rotterdam*. They arrived in the United States on September 14. The difficulties of transporting a ballet company across the Atlantic during wartime (especially given the variety of the dancers' nationalities) caused the scheduled Metropolitan Opera engagement to be moved back from October 10 to October 26. To be certain of making the new date, Massine trained a second ensemble in case members of his company were unable to leave Europe.

On October 26, the Ballet Russe opened its revised schedule at the Met (most of the dancers having arrived only that morning). On November 9 Massine's *Bacchanale* received its world premiere. A surrealistic outing with scenario, decor, and costumes by Dalí, it was set to excerpts from Wagner's *Tannhäuser* (including the Venusberg music and, as the finale, the Pilgrims' chorus).

The first planned collaboration between Dalí and Massine went back at least as far as 1937, when the two artists discussed a ballet called *Tristan fou*, with a scenario by Dalí based on Wagner's *Tristan und Isolde*.[2] Besides excerpts from *Tristan*, the music was to include jazz and traditional Spanish *pasos dobles*. Elsa Schiaparelli was to contribute the costumes.[3] Dalí signed a contract with Denham on November 11, 1937,[4] but *Tristan fou* did not materialize until 1944. By the spring of 1939, Dalí and Massine had instead begun work on *Bacchanale*, first in Paris and later in Monte Carlo.

Massine's friendship with Dalí (they met in the mid-1930s) and genuine admiration for his painting cemented the collaboration. And Massine's choice of the flamboyant designer was firmly endorsed by the Ballet Russe management. A master of self-promotion, Dalí by the end of the 1930s had a high profile in the United States as well as Europe. His work had been exhibited in America since 1932, and he had first visited in 1934. By 1939 he was notorious in New York, especially after the uproar that year over his designs for Bonwit Teller's windows. When the store's management altered them, the painter, in a fury, destroyed his own work. The fracas ended with him smashing the windows themselves.

The scenario for *Bacchanale* traced the mounting delirium and eventual suicide of King Ludwig II of Bavaria, Wagner's patron. It was Dalí's attempt at a psychoanalytic ballet, a tribute to Freud, who, he claimed, had allowed him to understand Wagner.[5] He painted a harrowing picture of a man in the grip of despair: "The subject represents the Bacchanalia of Tannhäuser as it develops in the imaginative and delirious confusion of Ludwig II of Bavaria's brain. He will remain until the end of the performance the *sole and unique* protagonist, the action being executed only by a Bacchanalia of mythological hallucinations, of images and sentiments to which he is prey."[6] Among the characters that appeared were Venus (stepping out of a Botticelli-like seashell), Lola Montez, Sacher-Masoch (accompanied by his wife), two satyrs who observed the performance while knitting red socks, and an assortment of other mythological creatures. Massine's description of the action further catalogued some of its bizarre details:

> In this mingling of symbolism, psychology, fantasy, and reality, we showed Ludwig, imagining himself to be Tannhäuser, approaching Venus (danced by Nini Theilade), and being almost blinded by the effulgent vision. She becomes a dragon, and as Lohengrin Ludwig kills it. But his sight grows worse, and his last vision, as he dies wearing Lohengrin's helmet with Tannhäuser's pilgrim robe, is of Leda embracing the swan—"the symbol," to quote Dalí, "of heterosexual love." The final symbols of Ludwig's death were the parasol and Lola Montez emerging from the belly of the swan.[7]

Bacchanale's theme reflected the surrealist preoccupation with the dark, irrational motives buried in the unconscious. Ever since the movement's 1929 manifesto, a credo strongly influenced by the psychoanalytic study of dreams, a generation of artists had searched the hidden corners of the psyche for images too ghastly to embrace yet too powerful to disown. Dalí's designs had utilized the same illusionist dream imagery that tantalized other surrealists of the 1930s, such as Magritte and Tanguy. (The designs Miró had produced in 1932 for Massine's Jeux d'enfants were closer to the ideas of the first surrealist wave of 1924, whose manifesto emphasized automatism and improvisation.) Working in the style of his oil-painted dream photographs, Dalí centered the decor on an enormous swan, wings spread, with a large hole in its breast through which the dancers made their entrances. The background depicted Spain's Emporda Valley (Dalí's birthplace); and center stage, above the swan, the temple from Raphael's Betrothal of the Virgin was visible. The costumes, with highly charged sexual overtones, were a riot of imagination: one fe-

Backdrop by Salvador Dalí for Bacchanale, *1939*

male dancer had a large rose-colored fish head; Lola Montez wore a hoop skirt over harem trousers; some male dancers' tights were festooned with large red lobsters symbolizing their sexual organs; Venus wore a long blond wig as well as full-body pink tights to give the illusion of total nudity; and the three Graces wore absurdly large breasts. (Many of these "obscene" motifs were modified in later performances, sanitizing the production.) Chanel had built the costumes in Paris, but during the war they couldn't be transported across the Atlantic, so when the production opened in the United States they were reproduced there by Karinska.

Bacchanale was such an elaborate visual spectacle that its dance elements were overshadowed by Dalí's paraphernalia. Massine himself acknowledged that his work was circumscribed by the painter's conception: "As I had to sustain in my choreography Dalí's bizarre atmosphere, without intruding on his scenic creations, I did not have in this ballet the scope for choreographic invention which I had had in *Symphonie Fantastique*; this was a more demented dream world. Also I found myself somewhat inhibited by the surrealist setting and costumes."[8] In league with Dalí's allusive imagery, Massine's choreography and mise-en-scène aimed at creating a dreamlike aura. He put classical vocabulary at the service of unusually distorted and grotesque steps. Sensational plastic and visual images, such as the striking entrance of Venus, became ends in themselves. According to Danilova, the goddess's appearance "was erotic and quite beautiful—a Botticelli-like scene with Nini Theilade, as Venus, dressed in pink leotard, with white [sic] long hair, posed like a pearl on a shell at the rear of the stage."[9] Another eye-popping moment came in Ludwig's death scene, in which a series of umbrellas sprung open on stage. Jack Anderson, writing about the film of the ballet (preserved in the New York Public Library's Dance Collection), was spellbound by the scene with Sacher-Masoch and his wife, "she forcing him to the floor and kicking him while he cringes with delight and degradation," and the portrayal of death as a dancing umbrella: "His mincing, fidgety steps are ludicrous, yet unsettling." Anderson called this character a descendant of the grotesque managers in *Parade*.[10]

The ballet, as expected, was a *succès de snobbisme*. John Martin in the *New York Times* found that Dalí's "fantasies benefit greatly by the addition of the time element, for they can develop to climaxes with a degree of shock and surprise that static presentation . . . cannot hope to approximate."[11] Robert Lawrence, chiding Massine, concluded that *Bacchanale* marked "a lamentable point in the evolution of Léonide Massine. . . . Massine abdicated as a generative force, contributing instead a danced framework for a pictorial background."[12] Not everyone was quite so disappointed. Alfred Frankenstein declared that:

> *For all the grandeur of its architecture [the music] belongs in the same bracket with the nymphs of Bouguereau and other Victorian purveyors of sweetness and light. It also extols that hefty, Germanic, cymbal-and-drum vulgarity of which Wagner was sometimes guilty. . . .*
>
> *Dalí, it seems to me, thoroughly appreciates this, and embodies it in his figure of the mad King Ludwig, whose attitudinizing is almost the ultimate satire on inflated, rhetorical grandiosity. At the opposite pole to Ludwig are the two imps soberly tending to their knitting. These are the imperturbable answer of common sense to Ludwig's soaring, Olympian ambitions. . . . They are a kind of choreographic Bronx cheer.*[13]

Massine

For George Amberg,

> *its significance . . . was much broader than its insistent and ostentatious Freudian symbolism, for it was revealing evidence of our artists' ceaseless endeavor to articulate the processes of the subconscious. Massine's method was debatable, but not his intentions. The cryptic symbols and mystification he used are as irritating in the theatre as in any other medium and they ultimately condemn Bacchanale as a repertory piece. The essential motivation, however, is perfectly valid. If we find Tudor's sensitive probing into the subconscious more convincing and powerful, we still cannot deny the theatrical magnificence of Dalí's terrifying images and grandeur of vision.*[14]

During 1940 and 1941 four new Massine works were produced: *The New Yorker, Vienna 1814, Labyrinth,* and *Saratoga.* None of them proved successful.

The New Yorker (October 18, 1940) and *Saratoga* (October 19, 1941) were, of course, based on American themes. By 1940 the emergence and establishment of American ballet was a fact, further exacerbating the hostility that the dance community had felt since the 1930s toward the various manifestations of the Franco-Russian ballet. With Europe at war and the Ballet Russe forced to operate solely and indefinitely in the western hemisphere, the company decided to align its programming with local taste, so Massine was coaxed into producing ballets on American subjects and at the same time all but ordered by Denham to discontinue his work on symphonic ballets. (In November 1940 he expressed to the press his "patient regret that he had not been permitted to continue his work on creating large dance works to the great symphonies."[15] By then he had "advanced very far in a Mozart work" and had been planning to choreograph a Schubert symphony in collaboration with Bérard, who as Massine spoke was in occupied France.[16])

The idea for *The New Yorker* was suggested to Massine by one of the magazine's writers, Rea Irwin, and was inspired by cartoons from its pages by Peter Arno, Helen Hokinson, William Steig, and Otto Soglow. The score was selections from George Gershwin made with the assistance of his brother, Ira. They included a collection of hit songs, the *Cuban Overture,* a small segment of *An American in Paris,* and excerpts from the Concerto in F.

The New Yorker did not have a propitious beginning. Massine, utterly uninspired, suggested to Denham that he hire an American choreographer for the project, perhaps Eugene Loring. But Denham declined to follow the advice,[17] and the work was prepared in correspondence between Denham in New York and Massine as he toured with the company in South America. Through July and August of 1940 Massine struggled, in sometimes bitter exchanges, to come to an agreement with Denham about scenario, designer, music, and orchestration. He thought the libretto "not a brilliant one"[18] and "far from . . . satisfactory."[19] He had suggested either Peter Arno or James Thurber as the designer, feeling that Irwin, "who in two years had designed only one page in *The New Yorker*,"[20] did not qualify. This correspondence was filled with Massine's complaints that his artistic advice "did not get any attention and contrary action has been taken."[21] Denham's thoughtless insistence on the dismissal of dancers from the corps had, Massine charged, forced "the principal artists" to take part "in the ensemble, which never happened since Diaghilev's time."[22] What irked him most was the "lack of someone capable to organize our work on the new productions normally, so that they should be decided upon and completed during nine months instead of rushing them through three months, which is a real tour de force."[23]

Massine's comments on *The New Yorker* after its creation reveal his obvious reservations and lack of enthusiasm. "It was not easy finding a style for this comic ballet. . . . The Gershwin music which has real melodic quality is really either too close to some of us or too outdated for present swing enthusiasts. In a hundred years such a ballet would be very easy to formulate." About the characters he added: "It may not provide stock characters as profound as the traditional *commedia dell'arte* of the Italians, but everyone recognizes the Hokinson lady, the Peter Arno clubman, the petty flappers, Soglow's Little King. Unfortunately, for a ballet, these characters are perhaps too familiar. Everyone has his own idea. . . ."[24]

The New Yorker followed the divertissement structure of *Gaîté parisienne*, and the choreography integrated various American dance idioms, including tap. The ballet was pleasant entertainment but not a success. Denby acknowledged that the work was "entertaining, with many excellent caricatures,"[25] and John Martin found Massine's own interpretation of the Timid Man "funny, inventive and completely off the beaten track."[26] On the road it was generally well liked. But Irving Kolodin wrote that "all of Massine's good intentions and wit did not compensate for the orientation that might have been supplied by an American choreographer."[27]

The gestation of *Vienna 1814* (October 28, 1940) goes back to Massine and Count Etienne de Beaumont's 1936 plan to create a ballet on a Viennese theme.[28] *Concert d'Europe,* as the ballet originally had been titled,[29] was to be set to piano music by Carl Maria von Weber as orchestrated by Hindemith, with scenery and costumes by Bérard. By 1940 Denham had resurrected the idea, insisting on "a lively ballet."[30] Massine devised a divertissement that attempted to "recreate the splendour and gaiety of a ball given to the diplomatic corps in Vienna by Prince Metternich to celebrate the defeat of Napoleon."[31] The ballet ends with the news of the emperor's escape from Elba. Some of Weber's piano pieces, his Siciliana, and his *Turandot* Overture were arranged by Broadway's Robert Russell Bennett, and the scenery and costumes were by Stewart Chaney. The ballet offered some good dancing opportunities for the cast but passed without praise.

Before Massine began work on his second ballet on an American theme, he collaborated with Dalí on *Labyrinth,* another surrealist extravaganza. This time they agreed on Schubert's Seventh, which Massine once had hoped to adapt in collaboration with Bérard. But Bérard was in Europe, so Massine decided to work instead with Masson, who had arrived in the United States in the summer of 1941.[32] However, this arrangement, which Denham opposed, did not materialize. This seems a pity when one considers Masson's important creative American phase from 1941 to 1945 and his influence on the younger generation of artists, especially Jackson Pollock.

Dalí's scenario for *Labyrinth* was based on the myth of Theseus and Ariadne in the labyrinth. The labyrinth and the minotaur were recurring images among the surrealists of the 1930s. According to Massine, Dalí "envisaged the uninterrupted continuity of Schubert's melody as a musical parallel to the ball of thread which Ariadne gave to Theseus to guide him out of the Labyrinth. His idea was to employ a blend of choreographic and surrealist images to suggest the turmoil aroused in Theseus's mind by his encounter with the Minotaur."[33] At first, the choreographer was not much moved by the idea, but:

> Dalí was a persuasive talker, and I found myself carried away by his bizarre symbolism. As we discussed the individual scenes, I was both amused and revolted by the images he invented. For the episode in which Theseus kills the Minotaur, he wanted to use a real calf's head to be followed by a scene in which the dancers would ceremoniously cut chunks from the head and eat them. One evening, after we had begun rehearsals, Dalí and I took a taxi to Sixth Avenue, where we visited one restaurant

after another in search of a calf's head. The waiters were stunned, but po-
lite; the best they could offer us was a veal sandwich!

There were times when Dalí's imagination got completely out of hand.
When he suggested that, as a symbol of destruction, we should drop a
Steinway onto the stage, I drew the line.[34]

Massine found certain scenes effective, however, singling out one that showed "a girl in a transparent tunic lying motionless on the stage. Several dancers were suspended above her, hidden by the backcloth, except for their feet, to which we attached live white pigeons. In this way we created the illusion of a nude girl with doves fluttering above her."[35]

As he had done with *Bacchanale,* Dalí again stole the show. According to Robert Lawrence, "isolated moments of Massine's genius managed to filter through this mass of philosophic double talk and scenic weightiness. Certain passages of the scene within the labyrinth, the jovial cockfight of the scherzo, the excellent pas de deux for Castor and Pollux in the finale, indicated that the choreographer could rise above his scenario."[36] Denby was put off by Dalí's grandstanding: "Dalí hogs the show so completely he won't let you see Massine's part of it, or hear Schubert. . . . He focuses your eye at a spot so high on the drop that every time you pull it down to look at the dancers below you feel acutely uncomfortable. Besides dwarfing the dancers he dresses them in incredibly bad taste."[37] Walter Terry, on the other hand, found the painter's work "more significant than any that ballet has disclosed before. Strangely enough, they are not silly, and although the opening scene reveals a tremendous cracked skull and a chest with a doorway in it, the effect is one of archaic grandeur."[38]

Massine's final ballet of 1941, *Saratoga,* had from its beginning little possibility of success. The project had been imposed on Massine as a fait accompli, part of the company's new policy. Massine writes: "I was disappointed to be told that the directors had decided in the future to produce only ballets directly sponsored by individual backers. . . . It was therefore no surprise to me to be asked to produce *Saratoga.*"[39] The action of the ballet took place at the fashionable racing resort at the turn of the century. The scenario and the music were by Jaromír Weinberger, the decor and costumes by Oliver Smith. In 1949 George Amberg wrote: "It was an ambitious, not to say pretentious, production with a pleasant theme, attractive decor and costumes and some lovely dancing. Potentially, *Saratoga* may have had some of the ingredients of an American

Gaîté Parisienne, but it turned out to be an uninspired piece of no particular description or spirit. The score was especially poor."[40]

Massine's final productions for the Ballet Russe de Monte Carlo were not successful, but the choreographer took consolation from the rapturous reception his other works in the repertory were enjoying, especially *Le Beau Danube, La Boutique fantasque, Gaîté parisienne, Capriccio espagnol,* and *Le Tricorne.* Also, when de Basil's company, now renamed the Original Ballet Russe, returned to the United States in September 1940, its Massine ballets were a resounding success. Anatole Chujoy, writing in *Dance,* voiced the consensus about the first symphonic ballets. *Les Présages,* he maintained, "holds the interest of the audience as much as it did before. The pas de deux . . . in the second movement . . . is the finest example of a modern adagio found anywhere." Reassessing *Les Présages* in retrospect, he concluded that "only now, having seen all of Massine's other symphonic ballets, can one appreciate how much the choreographer put into *Destiny (Les Présages).* It served as a source of material for a number of sequences in his later work." Chujoy found *Choreartium* "still one of the finest Massine ever did," and claimed that *Symphonie fantastique* "remains as exciting a composition as it was when it was first presented here."[41] These ballets were given outstanding performances by an impressive roster that included most of the original dancers: Baronova, Riabouchinska, Toumanova, Verchinina, Lichine. *Scuola di ballo* was presented with Delarova as Felicita, the role she created.

The four unsuccessful productions for the Monte Carlo company—*The New Yorker, Vienna 1814, Labyrinth,* and *Saratoga*—made Massine an easy target for critics. "The current weakness of the Ballet Russe de Monte Carlo," wrote Walter Terry about the 1942 season, "is not a sudden occurrence. The process of enervation commenced months, perhaps years ago, and a good share of the blame must be laid to its artistic director Léonide Massine. . . . Every creator needs a rest, and Massine has needed one for the last two years."[42] But Massine was being asked to shoulder the blame for all of the company's ills, whether he had been responsible or not. For instance, the choice of the season's opening-night program—*Saratoga, Labyrinth,* and *Gaîté parisienne*—was lambasted by Terry. In fact, the selections had been made not by Massine but by Hurok, who, according to his rival Denham, was making a "deliberate attempt to undermine" the Ballet Russe.[43] (It is interesting to note that during Massine's tenure as artistic director he expanded the repertory of the company to include works by Ivanov and Petipa [*The Nutcracker* and Acts II and III of *Swan Lake*], Fokine, Nijinsky, Ashton, Lifar, and Nini

Theilade, as well as the full-length *Coppélia* and *Giselle*.) For some time it had been evident that the working relationship between Denham and Massine had turned edgy and tense; these harsh criticisms of Massine further disturbed the delicate balance between them.

During the 1938–39 season, the Ballet Russe de Monte Carlo had been in every way a choreographer's company: Massine's. He was ballet's superstar, and his reputation had been indispensable in attracting sponsors to back the creation of a new company. His international prestige was such that by 1938 his name alone could draw money from investors on both sides of the Atlantic. This, of course, gave him a great deal of power over the company's artistic policies. Still, from the beginning Denham had been inclined to insert himself into the decision-making process. In a letter dated August 26, 1937, he advised Massine to ignore the opinions of his "pederastic friends" concerning *Gaîté parisienne*, declared that there was no need for an orchestrator for Offenbach's music, and suggested that the choreographer completely rework the libretto of *Seventh Symphony*.[44] A year later, in a letter dated August 13, 1938, Massine was finding it necessary to curb Denham's meddling:

> I would urge you to refrain from interfering in my department, as we are already paying heavy punishment for your interference with the artists. . . .
>
> I would therefore again ask you not to have anything to do with the artists individually or in group, not to interfere in the artistic advice of it or make any remarks which may result in financial and moral losses to the company. If you have any complaint or defects to register you could ask me or tell me.
>
> I hope it will not be necessary for me again to call your attention to these matters as I have so much to do—preparing new productions, watching the old productions and rehearsing the company—[and] should not have to give my valuable time on unnecessary evils.[45]

When the Ballet Russe returned to the United States in 1939, the relationship between the two men was showing pronounced cracks. With the company stranded indefinitely, far from its home base in Monte Carlo, Denham tried to restrict Massine's artistic control. (It is possible that Denham had already realized that in the United States Massine was becoming ballet's bête noire; the local critical and financial establishments were increasingly shifting their support to American ballet and to Balanchine.) In 1940—before Massine had made any of his unsuccessful ballets—Denham commissioned Balanchine to mount on the Ballet Russe two works he had created for Lincoln Kirstein's American Ballet: *Le Baiser de la fée* for Denham's spring season and *Poker Game* for the fall. By 1941 rumors, obviously unsettling to Massine, abounded that Balanchine was set to replace him at the Monte Carlo company.[46] (Denham's invitation to Balanchine must have given Massine a chilling sense of déjà vu; he had only to recall the invitation de Basil extended to Nijinska back in 1935–36.)

By 1940 Massine was astonished that he was being prevented from choreographing any new symphonies, which, he told an interviewer for *Dance* magazine, was what "most of all interests me."[47] (It is clear that at least as early as 1939 Denham had lost interest in Massine's symphonic genre. When Massine had proposed that year to create a second ballet with libretto and designs by Matisse, Denham bluntly informed him that such an artistic decision rested solely with the company's directors. In a letter to Fleischmann Denham worried: "I am somewhat afraid that by force of gravity, but perhaps against his own wish, Léonide will fall into his usual 'symphonical choreography.' ")[48]

If all of this artistic haggling weren't demoralizing enough, Massine's years in exile were also taking their toll. He felt "separated from Europe" and from his "most trusted collaborators."[49] By 1942 his grievances were multiplying. He quarreled heatedly with Denham over rehearsal time for *Mysteria,* another Dalí-Massine ballet (set to music by Bach), which never materialized. He angrily pointed out that his title of artistic director was omitted from posters, that his salary was slow in arriving, and that he was receiving neither royalties nor traveling expenses.[50] Sensing that his authority was ebbing, he specifically "spoke against further attempts to acquire repertoire or personnel from the . . . American Ballet," writes Jack Anderson. "Yet he did not oppose guest choreographers in principle. He suggested that forthcoming seasons offer two new productions by himself and two by someone else: Fokine, Balanchine, or any other appropriate choreographer."[51]

At the same time, despite all the turmoil, Massine in 1942 was eagerly trying to salvage his association with "his" company. In January, perhaps in an attempt to boost his own confidence, he sent Denham a list of twenty ballets he was prepared to undertake over the next few years.[52] In 1941 Massine had contacted Manuel de Falla, who was living in Argentina, having fled his beloved Spain after Franco's takeover and the assassination of his dear friend Federico García Lorca. Massine had proposed four Spanish literary works to Falla as possibilities for collaboration; they eventually settled on Cervantes's *Don Quixote,* but Falla died in Argentina in 1946, still at work on the score.[53]

Yet it is clear that by 1942 Denham was ready to sharply curtail Massine's influence within the company. Early that year Denham had begun negotiating with Lincoln Kirstein for performance rights to twelve ballets from the American Ballet repertory. In his correspondence with Fleischmann on this subject, Denham revealed a complete lack of interest in Massine as company choreographer, having concluded that "as a matter of policy, we will have to curb him [Massine] and let him do something where he can display his ability and his wit."[54] By April of that year Massine, quite aware of Denham's intentions, had bowed to the inevitable, openly talking about a "friendly discontinuation" with the Ballet Russe, a proposition that Denham saw as a "great relief of our finances."[55] Massine's services had never come cheap.

The wild card in the Massine-Denham crisis was the rivalry between Denham and Hurok. In the 1930s and 1940s Hurok was synonymous with the ballet establishment in the United States. He had begun his career as a dance impresario in the 1920s; in December 1933 he took a major risk by bringing de Basil's Ballets Russes to America for the first time. At first the company was mainly a success with "café society" opening-night audiences, but by the end of its 1934–35 tour it had become a coast-to-coast artistic and financial success. Throughout the rest of the thirties the company performed six to seven months a year throughout the United States, bringing ballet not only to large cities but to small and mid-sized communities in a series of one-night stands. By 1936 *Time* magazine was reporting that "ballet has suddenly become a rage not only in Manhattan but in 100 other U.S. cities visited by the Monte Carlo dancers since last October. The fever began in earnest last season when the company toured 20,000 miles. . . . It played to capacity audiences . . . [in] houses in Little Rock, Ark.; El Paso, Tex.; Portland, Me. In Brockton, Mass., a leading citizen was impressed because the ballet's appearance there was one of the rare occasions when he had known his townsfolk to turn out in formal evening clothes."[56] In the heyday of the Ballet Russe, its Russian dancers were household names. Massine, Danilova, Baronova, Riabouchinska, Toumanova, and Lichine became as popular as movie stars and in the process transformed ballet into a full-fledged commercial enterprise. Hurok the impresario dominated the scene, for in addition to his far-reaching booking apparatus, until 1946 he held the exclusive lease for ballet at the Met. He exerted wide influence over the internal affairs of the companies he sponsored.

From 1940 on, Hurok launched a series of outright attacks on Denham, claiming that he had become "infected with Diaghileffitis" and that "with the 1940–41 season, deterioration had set in in the vitals of the Monte Carlo Ballet Russe."[57] (Indeed, by then Denham had grown completely intractable in his artistic directives.) Hurok observed:

> *I could not be other than sad, for Massine had given of his best to create and maintain a fine organization. He had been a shining example to the others. The company had started on a high plane of accomplishments; but it was impossible for Massine to continue under the conditions that daily became less and less bearable. Heaven knows, the "Colonel" had been difficult. But he had an instinct for the theatre, a serious love for ballet, a broad experience, was a first-class organizer, and an untiring, never ceasing, dynamic worker.*
>
> *Sergei Denham, by comparison, was a mere tyro at ballet direction, but, amateur or not, he was convinced he had inherited the talent, the knowledge, the taste of the late Serge Diaghileff.*[58]

Wanting "to be free to experiment"[59]—actually, hoping to mastermind the entire ballet explosion singlehandedly—Hurok in 1941 dropped his exclusive contract with Denham's company and signed on with Lucia Chase's fledgling Ballet Theatre as manager.

The struggle between Denham and Hurok necessarily involved Massine. With no further interest in Denham's company, Hurok naturally wanted to secure Massine's services; he was fully aware that to the general American ballet-going public, ballet was *Russian* ballet, which meant Massine. The three men were soon craftily double crossing one another. In the spring of 1942 Massine was given permission to create two ballets as guest choreographer for Ballet Theatre later that year, a temporary break that Denham took as a welcome financial boost, "so that we may be able to save his two and one-half months' salary."[60] By November Massine's permanent departure from the Monte Carlo company was imminent; on the sixth he signed a new agreement with Universal Art that annulled his old contract (due to expire in 1948) as the organization's artistic director. Massine writes:

> *I was informed that my ten-year contract with Universal Art Inc. had not been ratified by the Board of Directors. After working for them for three years, I was summarily dismissed. It was a bitter blow, which left me feeling bereft and disillusioned. Although I protested vehemently, there was*

nothing I could do. Ever since I had been appointed Artistic Director to the Company, I had devoted all my time to it, thinking I was building on a sure foundation. I had gathered together and trained a superlative group of dancers, and through my own efforts, and my artistic contacts, I had brought distinguished artists to work for it, among them Bérard, Dalí, Derain, de Beaumont, and Matisse. I felt that I had more than fulfilled the original aims of the Board by reviving traditional ballets and creating new ones with both American and European participation.[61]

In a recurrent nightmare, Massine once again initiated litigation over the ownership of his ballets. But unlike the outcome with de Basil back in 1938, the decision was now rendered in the choreographer's favor. The case was heard by the American Arbitration Association, and arbitrator James Gifford ruled that "the scenic properties and costumes for most of my own ballets, including *Le Tricorne, La Boutique fantasque,* and *Capriccio Espagnol,* should be assigned to me without fail. He also established my legal right to perform all or any of my own works anywhere I chose, and to make copies of the costumes and scenic material which had been used in the productions which I had done for the Ballet Russe de Monte Carlo." When the ordeal ended, Massine was "moved" by the decision, and "after everything had been settled I went to thank him [Gifford]. As we shook hands at farewell he smiled and said 'Just remember that bankers must not have the right to dismiss artists so easily.' "[62]

On November 10 Massine joined Ballet Theatre. His departure from the Ballet Russe de Monte Carlo marked the last time that he would be affiliated with a ballet company in the role of resident choreographer. From his breakup with Diaghilev in 1921 he had tried to establish his own company. When he finally succeeded, it was to last only four years, of which the final two were marked by his diminished authority and gnawing uncertainty. Beginning in 1942 he embarked on a long international career as guest choreographer and performer—though in 1960 he would make one last attempt to realize his dream: a company of his own.

DURING MASSINE'S GUEST ENGAGEMENT with Ballet Theatre in the summer of 1942, he created two new works, *Aleko* (September 8) and *Don Domingo* (September 16); both ballets were premiered in Mexico City.

Aleko was based on Pushkin's dramatic poem *Gypsies* and was set to

Tchaikovsky's Trio in A minor (orchestrated by Erno Rapee). The idea for the ballet had been in Massine's mind since 1941 (it had been called *Gypsies* on the list of potential productions he had sent to Denham in January 1942). The work had spectacular decor and costumes by Marc Chagall, who was also waiting out the war in New York. Massine and Chagall had met briefly in Paris, but upon Chagall's arrival in New York German Sevastianov, Ballet Theatre's general manager, reintroduced the two men. (Sevastianov, husband of ballerina Irina Baronova, previously had been associated with de Basil during Massine's tenure.) While working on *Aleko*, Massine and Chagall, two Russians in exile, forged a bond that would rise to a special level of intimacy. In his memoirs, Massine reminisced that Chagall "never forgot that he was a disappointment to his family. His mother, who had intended him to become a photographer, had had ambitions for her son, wanting him to settle down in a suburban house with a wife, a family, and a lot of good solid furniture." [63]

Aleko was Massine's first Russian ballet since *Bogatyri* (1938) and his most important since *Le Pas d'acier* (1927). It came at a time of professional uncertainty and personal anxiety for both artists, who, "meeting in the world of Tchaikovsky and Pushkin," according to the Chagall biographer Franz Meyer, "looked upon it as a fragment of their homeland brought to life by their joint efforts out of a common 'memory.'" [64] Working with Chagall must have provided a respite for Massine after the pressures he had recently endured with Denham. For the painter, too, the experience was consoling: "For Chagall and his wife the months spent working with Massine were among the happiest of their stay in America and years later a few bars of the Tchaikovsky Trio sufficed to evoke the wonderful unison of the period." [65]

Aleko took shape in a spirit of teamwork. In their adaptation of the poem, each artist tried in his own medium to bring the richness of Pushkin's imagery to life. The preparation took several months, during which Massine and Chagall met regularly at the painter's Manhattan apartment. Massine would bring his record player so that they could talk out the conception of the ballet as they listened to the score. One sign of their close collaboration can be found in Chagall's sketches, which include detailed notations on the choreography and the action. [66]

The ballet was divided into four scenes, the first and second of which were set to the first movement of the trio. In the first scene Aleko abandons city life and arrives with the Gypsy Zemphira at her camp. Other main characters are introduced: Zemphira's father (the Chieftain), the Young Gypsy, who also falls in love with her, and the Fortuneteller.

The second scene presents a carnival with a picturesque assortment of acrobats, street dancers, and clowns. As Zemphira dances, she is swept up in the collective euphoria. In the third scene a group of youths go bathing on a bright summer afternoon. A love interlude between Zemphira and the Young Gypsy is interrupted by the arrival of Aleko, who pleads with Zemphira to return to him. She rejects him in favor of her new lover. In the finale Aleko in his delirium confronts visions from his past. The line between reality and fantasy disappears, and in a moment of despair he murders the lovers. Zemphira's father banishes him from the camp and he is condemned to wandering.

The planning and groundwork were accomplished in New York, and in Mexico City, where the company had been invited for a five-month period as guests of the government, the choreography was worked out and the scenery and costumes took shape. Over Massine's objections, Chagall had not been allowed on the stage of the Metropolitan Opera House because he was not a member of the American Trade Union, so Massine invited him to Mexico City, where he would have no interference in executing the backdrops.[67] The Chagalls and the Massines settled in the San Angel district, an artistic colony on the outskirts of the city; but as the work on *Aleko* grew more intensive, they took lodgings at a hotel close to the Palacio de Bellas Artes, where Ballet Theatre's season was to take place. Although free time was hard to come by, Massine managed to lead the Chagalls on brief excursions and to introduce them to several Mexican luminaries as well as some of the other European artists and intellectuals who had found refuge in Mexico City. Massine remembered the capital well from his first tour there with de Basil's company in 1934. On that occasion the company had inaugurated the newly built Palacio de Bellas Artes with its dazzling Tiffany proscenium.

While Chagall and his wife, Valentine, who was in charge of costume construction, worked at the theater, Massine rehearsed the company in the Hotel Reforma. Fokine, who was also in town as guest choreographer for Ballet Theatre, shared a dressing room with Massine. It was to be their last encounter:

He was as withdrawn and uncommunicative as ever, as aloof as when I had gone to his room in St. Petersburg for my first audition in 1914. He was always polite, but formal, and I could never relax in his presence. I had always had the greatest admiration for him as a choreographer, and I found it puzzling that a man who had created such rich, flowing movements should be, as an individual, so cold and inflexible. I remember noticing in Mexico City that he wore a shirt and tie and a tightly buttoned-up suit for rehearsals, and when he had finished I could see the sweat rolling down his face. I wanted to suggest that he would be more comfortable in a rehearsal costume, but of course I never dared to do so.[68]

Staging *Aleko* with the new company meant that Massine had to introduce his unorthodox working habits, which took some getting used to. Dancers such as Markova and George Skibine, who had worked with him before, easily adapted to his rehearsal style. Others had difficulty. Two aspects of Massine's method were especially disconcerting. One was his penchant for devising different choreography for the same musical phrase, then asking the dancers to perform all the versions, from which he would choose the one that he felt was most appropriate. The other was his routine lack of verbal communication with the dancers. As Skibine explained: "He would show the steps to you and then just sit and look. He wanted you to improvise; he showed you the steps so fast that you never really caught exactly what he did. You worked on it yourself— he let you create the parts."[69] Dolin, who had been cast as Aleko, dropped out of the ballet during rehearsals; he explained in his autobiography that he could not endure Massine's way of proceeding. (Massine was not happy with the choice of Dolin for the male lead and thought that Skibine could more convincingly portray the young and temperamental Aleko. This probably contributed to the wary working relationship between Dolin and Massine which led to Dolin's walkout.)

Chagall's contribution to *Aleko* consisted of four backdrops and more than seventy costumes. Leland Windreich described the backdrops:

For the opening scene Chagall created a troubled cobalt sky at nightfall, dominated by Pushkin's pearly-white, uncanny moon and its reflection in a lake, with a brilliant red cock flying to reach it. Sidney Alexander, a Chagall biographer, notes the phallic symbolism in this image, which is repeated in a motif painted on Zemphira's costumes for this scene. Two lovers embrace in a cluster of clouds. The second scene shows a fiddle-playing bear floating over a tilted village, a couple drifting in space, and a monkey dangling from a branch of lilacs. A golden wheat field dominates the third painting, with two huge blood-red suns: one has jagged rays, and the other is a bull's eye encompassed in rings. A fish head and a peasant's sickle emerge from the tall grass, and an inverted birch branch floats earthward. In the finale a doe-eyed white pony with hind quarters which melt into the wheels of a carriage streaks across a black sky lit by a gold chandelier.[70]

According to Meyer, there was a close relationship between the backcloths and the artist's earlier works—"Act I with the lovers in the sky, a fantastic scene of 1938; that for Act III with the scythe in the tall grass, one of the *Fables*"—but the stage provided Chagall with a new ambience that was "more spacious and flowing."[71]

The costumes were built by Mme Chagall under the close supervision of the painter, who personally decorated them. For Chagall, said one art critic, "a stage costume is not a garment but the means by which the character who is represented physically and morally can participate in the life of a whole."[72] The lighting design, directed by Chagall, was an important element in creating the visual poetic imagery: "The 'poem' is born of the blue night, grows in the cool light of morning, becomes radiant color in the bright noontide and finally dwindles away in the lonely distance of a starry night."[73] According to Windreich, "spotlights behind the first and last backdrops effectively accentuated the figures depicted as charging into the sky and gave the moons the effect of having been painted on stained glass."[74]

It was typical of Massine's eclecticism that the choreography was composed of the various techniques that had characterized his *demi-caractère* and symphonic ballets. For instance, in the fortune-telling episode in the first tableau and in the ballet's fourth scene, he juxtaposed different kinds of action, with many activities occurring simultaneously on stage. Action montage was the means by which Massine expanded the physical space into a series of subspaces—an appropriate treatment of a story in which the external reality and the hero's inner world cohabited. Another choreographic technique was the juxtaposition of styles, about which Grace Robert noted: "It joins classical with free plastic dancing in a manner that does violence to neither style. The wild dances of the gypsies in the first scene, the stylized Russian dances in the third, are exhilarating. The pas de trois is a strictly classical exposition of line . . . the spirited mazurka performed in the third scene by Zemphira and the Young Gypsy is an interesting elaboration of a folk-dance form for balletic purposes."[75]

Massine's most recent symphonic ballet had been *Rouge et noir* (*Labyrinth* had been completely dominated by Dalí's conception); *Aleko* pointed to the new direction he was taking in the genre. In it he focused less on massive vertical formations, such as pyramids, and more on elaborate horizontal configurations, and an incredible wealth of choreo-graphic detail that signaled a new "baroquism," to some extent a return to that of his early Diaghilev years.

In mood, *Aleko* represented the neoromantic expressionism of the 1930s and was related more to *Symphonie fantastique* than to any other work. Both depicted the romantic introspection of the hero, manifested in his delirium. Choreographically, both emphasized sweeping ensem-bles and the employment of dancers as part of the mise-en-scène. A case in point was the fourth scene in *Aleko,* which Grace Robert described as "rich in plastic groupings." Robert declared a moment in the work where "girls wearing black gloves, with arms extended in the form of a Latin cross, are held high in the air to make a background for the drama . . . es-pecially memorable."[76] This image was reminiscent of the crosses cre-ated by the walking monks in *Symphonie fantastique.*

Alicia Alonso, whose performance as Zemphira (the role created by Markova) was highly acclaimed when the ballet was presented in Lon-don and Paris in 1953, still had vivid recollections of the choreography in 1988: "[It] was imbued with a dramatic style which was very characteris-tic of Massine. There was a great richness of movement: a classical step or position would be stylized in a sort of demi-caractère sense. There was a great deal of contrast between the leg work, torso and head move-ments, all subject to the musical rhythm. The whole choreography was a question of style; even the development of a character was a question of style, all marked by Massine's own personality. There was a multiplicity and variety of movements, angles, positions. This style is very much in contrast to the choreography that prevails today: dynamic, dry, in a straight line, the dancing taking place with the dancer facing or with his back to the audience. Today's choreography is like modern construc-tions—cutting, geometrical. On the contrary, Massine's choreography had innumerable nuances of body movement." About the group config-urations she added: "Sometimes a specific block or group of dancers did not mean much by itself until it would be seen within the context of the whole picture effect as each group was integrated to another. The aes-thetic balance depended on the composition of the various groups in their collective formation. It was a fascinating clockwork mechanism."[77]

The choreography was extremely difficult, and the lifts were mur-derous. Skibine withdrew with a back injury after the Mexico City pre-miere. Markova later was reported to have fainted twice during performances of the ballet, and "panicked at the thought of doing it"; in 1943 she underwent surgery for a hernia which, she said, was "aggravated" by the choreography in *Aleko*.[78] The ballet ended with one of those grand Massine finales, the stage swirling with movement, the work exerting its seductive power over audiences. Marcia Siegel described Massine's ballets as "busy, explosive, full of great rushes and changes of energy. They must have been enormously appealing to the audiences' emotions—you can sense a kind of Broadway programming of the sensibilities, the great sweeps of emotion and the long pregnant pauses, the melodramatic multiple pirouettes. Massine was fond of large choral groups, which he designed in harmonizing or contrapuntal masses, in the manner of the modern dancers."[79]

With nineteen curtain calls, the premiere on September 8 was a thunderous success with the cosmopolitan Bellas Artes audience (which included Diego Rivera). The Mexican press reported that Massine had brought to *Aleko* "a humanity, an emotional and poetic depth which he has never before achieved."[80] The work was introduced at the Metropolitan in New York with Skibine as Aleko, Markova as Zemphira, Hugh Laing as the Young Gypsy, and Antony Tudor as the father, and proved to be Massine's greatest success since the outbreak of the war. Robert Lawrence wrote in the *Herald Tribune* that "the double murder of the gypsy girl and her lover by Aleko is one of the most shattering experiences not only in the dance, but in the whole world of theatre."[81] For Denby the work was "Massine's finest since *Fantastic Symphony*. It has lots of his expert stylization of local color (in this case, Russian gypsies and peasants), lots of his stylized dance-pantomime, lots of his ballet counterpoint. . . . It has as prize plum a long last scene with the breathless melodramatic thriller rush that Massine does better than anyone else."[82] Of course Denby, an admirer of very little of Massine's work, also pointed out the qualities of *Aleko* that he disliked: "an agitation that seems senseless, a piling up of scraps of movement and bits of character like so much junk from Woolworth's, patterns but no room for them, accent and meter but no rhythm and flower of phrase. The duets are bizarre without intimacy; the man has to jerk from one position to another by turning his back awkwardly on his partner."[83]

But when Massine took over the role of Aleko several months later, Denby felt that the whole ballet became more intelligible and delineated:

The title part of Aleko *is difficult because the character, who stands in opposition to the entire company, is at the center of the action only at the beginning and at the very end. At other times when he appears, he seems to express a sort of self-pity that is not especially communicative, and his ges-*

ture is "inward." Other stars do not hold the attention in these portions. Massine, however, dominated the stage with ease. He also gave the story a lively beginning by showing convincingly how pleased a city youth would be to be accepted by gypsies as one of their alien world.

Though Massine avoided a few technical feats Dolin adds to the role, his superior understanding of the story, and of its specifically Russian aspects, made the ballet itself clear.[84]

Alfred Frankenstein wrote in the *San Francisco Chronicle*: "*Aleko* is a hyper-romantic, rhetorical subject, and if you accept that as its premise, it follows that the dance Massine has created for it is perfectly in keeping. It is rich in pattern and pace, inventive within the framework of Massine's well established style, fervent and vivid both as dance and as dramatic expression."[85] And four years after it was first seen in New York, Grace Robert wrote: "*Aleko* is a brilliant montage of a gypsy life that never existed out of the realm of poetry. When a realistic touch appears, it is only for the purpose of pointing up the fantasy. One must see this ballet many times before the wealth of detail may be absorbed."[86]

Massine's second Mexico City premiere was *Don Domingo de Don Blas*, created in collaboration with the Mexican composer Silvestre Revueltas and the Mexican artist Julio Castellanos. Based on a seventeenth-century drama by the Spanish playwright Juan Ruiz de Alarcón y Mendoza, the ballet revolved around the rivalry between Don Domingo and Don Juan, the rich and poor suitors of Doña Leonor, Don Ramiro's daughter. The action was transferred to Mexico; according to Charles Payne, "The ballet was designed as a flattering tribute to Mexico, which Sevastianov hoped would persuade its government officials to make the Palacio de Bellas Artes available to the Ballet Theatre as its summer residence; it at least accomplished this purpose."[87] Although Massine employed a team of teachers from the Mexican Ministry of Education to coach the cast in Mexican dances, the ballet was an uninspired work whose tepid reception, especially in the United States, made its stay in the repertory a brief one.

ONCE MASSINE JOINED Ballet Theatre in the summer of 1942, his family life became more normal. From the moment of their arrival in the United States in 1939, the Massines had constantly been on the go, in part because the Ballet Russe de Monte Carlo was primarily a touring company. To make life easier during these peripatetic years, Massine had bought

a large Lincoln, with a trailer fitted with a modern kitchen and a comfortable bed-sitting room. This was driven by a Russian chauffeur, Georgi Lanbourinsky, who came of an old Cossack family. Since Tatiana and I both disliked hotel cooking, we also engaged an Italian cook, who travelled with us, hundreds of miles, from one engagement to another, usually by night. It was not a very satisfactory way of living, but at least it spared us the monotony of long train journeys and the anonymity of a different hotel each night too.[88]

In 1941, while Massine was in Los Angeles filming *Gaîté parisienne* and *Capriccio espagnol* (now retitled *The Gay Parisian* and *Spanish Fiesta*) for Warner Bros. under the direction of Jean Negulesco, the couple's first child was born. They named her Tatiana, after her mother. As a father Massine found that "day to day life seemed to have a deeper meaning, and I even found myself dancing with renewed energy." However, it did not take long before they had to "face the problem of trying to fit Tatiana into our hectic and nomadic life. It became too much of a strain to travel with both of us, a small baby, a nurse, a cook and a chauffeur crammed into the Lincoln, even with the space provided by the trailer. We decided that as soon as possible we must find a permanent home."[89] In the spring of 1943, with a reduced touring schedule to fulfill with Ballet Theatre, they decided that they "could not endure another oppressive summer in the city, and so we bought a house at Long Beach, on Long Island. Built in the 1930's, it had a pseudo-Gothic tower and a large garden, which I enlarged by buying several adjoining lots to safeguard our privacy. . . . Tatiana swore [it] was the ugliest house in Long Island, though she admitted that it was a pleasant and comfortable one to live in and bring up our family . . ."[90]

Now that he "seemed to be permanently settled on Long Island, Massine had a large dance studio built onto the house, and was able to practice there every morning before going into New York for rehearsals."[91] He "began work on another production for Ballet Theatre, a companion piece, in a way, to *Gaîté parisienne*, a light-hearted evocation of Paris during the 1790s. I discussed the project with Efrem Kurtz, and we agreed that Le Cocq's [sic] *opéra-bouffe*, *La Fille de Madame Angot*, which was based on a vaudeville of 1796, would provide suitable material for it. He helped me to select extracts from that and operettas by Le Cocq, which were orchestrated for us by Richard Mohaupt."[92]

To make the plot of the Lecocq work more amenable to dance, Massine modified the identity of the characters. The ballet was divided into three scenes. As the program synopsis described it:

> *Soubrette, betrothed to a barber, falls in love with an artist. He caricatures an old official and his aristocratic mistress, whose beauty so entrances the artist that he loses all thought of Soubrette.*
>
> *The artist, fleeing the Hussars sent to arrest him for his damaging cartoons, crashes a party given by the aristocratic lady. She conceals him and diverts his pursuers. During the ball the artist is discovered and ordered to prison by the minister, a scene witnessed by the lovelorn Soubrette, who arrives with her equally unhappy barber. The artist, however, snatches this of all moments to declare his love to the titled lady.*
>
> *Soubrette retaliates by arranging a masque to which she invites her friends, the lady, the official and the released artist. The love affair between the lady and the artist is exposed to the duped old official, and Soubrette, healthily disillusioned, returns to her barber.*[93]

The four leading roles were taken by Nora Kaye, Rosella Hightower, Massine, and André Eglevsky.

Mademoiselle Angot, which premiered at the Met on October 10, 1943, marked Massine's return to his comic-narrative *demi-caractère* ballets. As always with his works in this genre, the commedia dell'arte interpretive style kept the piece light and the dancing nimble. The characters were stock theatrical types, which meant that there was virtually no development. Each character was relevant to the others only within the boundaries of their shared theatrical truth. Making a connection with the audience wasn't the main goal; making a blatantly theatrical impression was. T. S. Eliot had honored Massine's characters by calling them "impersonal," since according to Eliot a work of art was relevant only within its own terms; not even its relationship to its creator should mediate in order to explain or illuminate it. It could remain impersonal insofar as its objectivity (Eliot's theory of the objective-correlative) served to keep the work's emotional content at a distance. As Eliot would express it: "The progress of an artist is a continual self-sacrifice, a continual extinction of personality."[94] But while Massine's characters indeed remained impersonal with respect to any relations outside their theatrical selves, they throbbed with personal vitality within the terms of their aesthetic truth.

It's not surprising that Massine's personages were criticized as stereotypical and shallow at a time when psychological characterizations were becoming more usual in ballet. But this subjective mode didn't fit with Massine's objective theatrical realism. Massine's characters were given coherence by plot development, not by internal conflict. His character types, in other words, did not leave room for speculation.

Of course, in his symbolic symphonic ballets Massine did permit himself a more subjective emotionalism. These works expressed (albeit metaphorically) an inner turmoil, an inner vision. He sometimes could be at his most personal only when his posture was loftiest—indeed, cosmic. This is the gem to be found at the core of his symphonic ballets. Working at this high-minded level, where he could resort to symbol and myth, Massine was free to let his feelings of alienation, anguish, rejection, fear, and despair, as well as his experience of the angst of loneliness, pour out. *Rouge et noir* is a good example: through abstraction and symbolism he transcends the personal and particular in favor of the poetic and universal.

As produced by Ballet Theatre (there was a subsequent, revised version in Europe), *Mademoiselle Angot,* according to the critics, had two major handicaps. While it offered some excellent dancing opportunities for the cast, it lacked a cohesive narrative structure. The critics discerned no clear plot development, and they were not prepared to let the choreographer off the hook by labeling the work a dance suite. Furthermore, Massine's stylistic and choreographic "baroquism" (a quality very much rooted in his earlier immersion in the rhythms and counterrhythms of flamenco, maintained by the feet, waist, arms, *épaulement,* and head) departed from the openness of movement, simplification of detail, and clear definition of line that he had embraced from *Le Beau Danube* onward.

Some found "baroquism" oppressive in its lack of expansion and pointless in its excess. Denby was disturbed by so much "superactivity," complaining that "as dancing it is a constant jumping about, fluttering of dresses and arms and legs that has no cumulative effect. . . . The plot of Massine's ballet disappears in fact under a load of separate dance numbers that have neither logical connection nor dramatic destination. . . ."[95] In a later review he added: "The trouble with *Mademoiselle Angot* is simply that for all its constant commotion it seems endless and pointless; the

Massine

successive dances seem to flounder around without either a steady subject or any consecutive form."⁹⁶

But perhaps it is more reasonable to see *Mademoiselle Angot's* busy and intricate choreography and stylistic embellishment—well-known characteristics of Massine's early ballets—as a return to a more familiar way of working. This was, after all, a time when his personal and artistic fortunes were highly uncertain, in fact quite unknowable. The dislocation of the war, the loss of his company, hostile criticism, professional instability, artistic isolation—these forces would contribute to his introversion, and were reflected artistically in his choreography and personally in his Long Beach refuge with its Gothic tower.

Over the next three years Massine produced only two new works. November 27, 1944, saw the premiere of Beethoven's *Moonlight Sonata,* a rather sentimental pas de deux for Toumanova and himself, both appearing as guest artists with Ballet Theatre. On December 15 *Mad Tristan* was presented by the newly organized Ballet International under the sponsorship of the Marquis George de Cuevas.

Originally planned in 1937 as *Tristan fou, Mad Tristan* was a two-scene piece set to excerpts from Wagner's *Tristan und Isolde* arranged by Ivan Boutnikoff. The libretto was hallucinogenic:

> *The first [scene] opens with Isolde waving the fatal scarf and proceeds to a horridly confused acrobatic love duet with Spirits of Death like shivering maniacs and Spirits of Love like enormous dandelions in seed milling about. It ends with the revelation of two Isoldes, both equally fascinating and differently horrid; King Mark with two soldiers wondrously armed enters.*
>
> *The second scene shows Tristan on a version of Böcklin's Isle of the Dead, plagued by a sardonic Shepherd, plagued by a beautiful bouncing ship, plagued by the Isoldes and the Spirits and other faceless figures. It ends with Tristan dying for love as upstage his own repulsive mummy is lowered into a vault caressed by white wormlike dismembered living arms.*⁹⁷

As expected, *Mad Tristan* was Dalí's show. Denby called it

> *a masquerade that only a genius could invent. Dalí takes Wagner's music and Massine's choreography and uses them as props for a spectacle, and what a show he puts on. . . .*
>
> Mad Tristan *is nothing like a classic ballet, it is not something to be*

seen over and over. It is fascinating as a contradiction of classicism. It is fascinating too for its imaginative abundance, for the largeness of its pictorial presence. And it is wonderful how Dalí turns whatever pictorial reference he offers into an immediate insignia of the unconscious world within us. To put it more simply, as a show and the first time you see Mad Tristan *there isn't a dull moment in it.*[98]

Grace Robert commented:

The symbolism employed in Mad Tristan *has become obscure, and is less related to the textbooks of abnormal psychology than in the two former [Dalí/Massine] ballets. Dalí seemed to have become obsessed with wheelbarrows, which were pushed about the scene by a group of dancers realistically pantomiming the tics of spastic paralysis. There were several female dancers dressed in what looked like white tulle evening dresses, their heads concealed by globe-shaped arrangements of flowers or dandelion seeds.*[99]

For George Amberg the "controversial" *Mad Tristan* was Ballet International's artistic event of the season. "This 'paranoiac ballet,' " he wrote,

was a surrealist masterpiece. It was a thoroughly serious and valid piece of operating visualization which proceeded with the haunting and compelling irrational consistency of a dream. As ballet it was disastrous, and it must have been the despair of choreographer and dancers. But it was frank and legitimate theatre and, incidentally, the first notable attempt in many seasons at an imaginative use of the stage illusion as a creative medium. . . . Mad Tristan *has probably not furthered the cause of ballet, but it has revived faith in "theatrical" theatre. Eventually the ballet may benefit.*[100]

With *Mad Tristan*, Dalí and Massine completed their surrealistic triptych. "All three productions were cerebral works," observed Amberg, "the freezing point of emotion, and their shock effects were carefully planned."[101]

BY 1944 MASSINE'S professional life had become more unstable. The relationship between Hurok and Ballet Theatre had deteriorated considerably; the company resented his employment of a roster of Russian guest stars that justified the promotion tag: "The greatest in Russian

Ballet by Ballet Theatre." In 1945, with the appointment of Lucia Chase and Oliver Smith as administrative directors, Ballet Theatre embarked on a campaign of de-Russianization. With Denham's company no longer a viable option, the future for Massine in the United States grew increasingly uncertain. Moreover, the arrival of his second child, Léonide Jr. (later known as Lorca), rendered his financial responsibilities more pressing. In 1945, capitalizing on the Ballet Russe's reputation and his own popularity, he organized a performing group called the Ballet Russe Highlights, with the participation of leading dancers including Baronova, Eglevsky, Yurek Lazowsky, and Anna Istomina. Under the management of Fortune Gallo, the group toured from coast to coast with a divertissement program. A second tour took place the following year, without Baronova but with Igor Youskevitch, Rosella Hightower, and Komarova added to the roster. But as Massine explains:

> *While we were on tour Tatiana and I and the children again travelled in the Lincoln and the trailer. We visited about twenty cities, including Chicago, Boston and Philadelphia. But although the performances were well received by audiences and press alike, I soon found that expenses were eating up all the profits. It was a hectic life, too, for every evening we performed about twenty dances from our repertoire, with only one interval. This meant quick changes and perfect coordination between cast, stagehands and orchestra, for each dance lasted only a few minutes. It was impossible to use any scenery, and our costumes and makeup had to be kept very simple. In the end Ballet Russe Highlights, though highly gratifying artistically, proved to be a very strenuous and unprofitable affair.*[102]

In the spring of 1946 Massine received an offer from England to appear in a murder mystery play, *A Bullet in the Ballet*. Deferring to his wife's judgment that the tours were "impractical" and "a strain on the whole family,"[103] he accepted. In August, after an absence of seven years, the Massines and their two children sailed for Europe.

Massine's years in the United States during the war marked the lowest ebb of his artistic reputation. The combination of two factors—the conditions that prevented him from further exploring his interest in symphonic ballets, and the emergence of a new American art whose triumph was consolidated by the end of World War II—contributed immeasurably to this decline.

In the early 1940s, Massine was highly admired by the general public, and his name was undoubtedly one of the biggest box-office draws.

Each production of his ballets was an event. As a performer he was a star; although he was nearly fifty, even those critics most antagonistic toward him as a choreographer continued to find him a titanic stage presence. About his performance in *Le Tricorne* Denby wrote: "He still dances all of it, and especially the farruca, to great effect, though he dominates the stage more by his matchless stage presence than by technical virtuosity. He almost alone of ballet dancers seemed formerly to have something of the edge of the great Spanish dancers, something of their brilliant attack and unpredictable rhythm." [104] And about his *Petrouchka* the critic said: "Massine . . . is by far the most intelligible Petrouchka we have. He throws himself in despair through the paper wall. When he reappears on the roof he is eerily derisive; and his final collapse is scary." [105] In 1941 Massine and the Ballet Russe brought twenty-five thousand people to the Hollywood Bowl. That same year, thirty-six thousand New Yorkers made their way to Lewisohn Stadium to see him, despite temperatures in the mid-nineties "on two of the most humid evenings of the summer." [106] In 1945 his Ballet Russe Highlights brought twenty-five thousand people to Lewisohn Stadium and fifteen thousand to Philadelphia's Robin Hood Dell.

But despite his popularity, the war years were a period of creative stagnation for Massine. He remained insulated from the germinating and fermenting American artistic scene; his spiritual headquarters were always in Europe. His aesthetic and personal maturity had been channeled into his symphonic ballets, a genre he longed to extend and amplify. When he was not allowed to do so—and was actually obliged by the Ballet Russe management to produce works that were of little interest to him—much of his creative momentum was dissipated. This meant heavy reliance on collaborators like Dalí to provide him with scenarios, a situation unlike that during his highly fruitful period of 1933–39, when he did the job singlehandedly. So it was not surprising that, in a 1940 interview, he voiced a rather unusual public complaint that he was forbidden by his employers to choreograph symphonies. [107] Also detrimental to his unstable personal and professional circumstances was the strong anti-Massine bias of the cognoscenti. Unfortunately, his presence in the United States led neither to a new phase of artistic re-evaluation within the dance community nor to any significant redefinition or reorientation. Yet he himself was chastised for not moving on to a new style. Possibly his greatest fault, at the age of fifty, was his loyalty to his own aesthetic vision—and to little else. Amberg wondered why "none of Massine's contacts with American life and art show in his work, since his art had so thoroughly and easily assimilated the indigenous qualities of other peoples and he had so keenly reflected the temper of his time and environment and so sharply caught the essence of human types and characters. But nothing in his creation or performance indicates that he was touched at all by the folk or society, the countryside or the climate, the thought or the feeling of America." [108]

The 1930s had seen the awakening of a consciousness that fostered an indigenous expression that once and for all would end European domination of America's artistic life. In ballet the aesthetic principles of Lincoln Kirstein—the driving force behind the creation of the School of American Ballet—were an adaptation of the Diaghilev formula, with the crucial accent on Americanism. "With the Depression," writes Marcia Siegel, "came a period of introspection and patriotism in all the arts and by the mid-1930s the idea of finding an American dance had become institutionalized." [109]

Resentment against Europe gave birth to a new nationalism and the writing of belligerent letters of protest, pamphlets, and manifestos which turned the cause of an American Art into an intellectual battle cry. These writings were mainly aimed at overturning the aesthetic judgment of the establishment, represented in the art world by museums (especially the Museum of Modern Art) that supported the European modernist tradition and served a highly functional purpose within the dealer-critic system, and in the ballet world by Sol Hurok. The general feeling of the American dance community was expressed by Agnes de Mille: "[In 1933] Hurok imported de Basil's Ballet Russe de Monte Carlo and the craze that was to endure seventeen years and sweep everything else to corners." [110] And according to George Amberg: "The Ballets Russes became synonymous with ballet for the uninitiated American public, a misunderstanding which hindered the development of a native ballet." [111]

Kirstein, the champion of George Balanchine and of American ballet, directed his censure—though it also touched Martha Graham and the American modern dance movement—against the Franco-Russian ballet and Massine. A glance at his titles reveals his journalistic militancy: *Blast at Ballet,* "Let's Go Native," "Stardom: Slave and Native," "Lincoln Kirstein Smacks at the Ballet Russe," "Ballet Blitz"—all were crafted to attract attention and alert the audience to his mission. His attacks on the Franco-Russian ballet were incessant: "Ballet is in a bad time in America today because the blackmail of the Russian organization primed by publicity and patronage still works." He described the Franco-Russian reper-

tory as "vitiated" and a "dying formula."[112] Massine did not fare any better. As noted by Jack Anderson: "Massine may also have been used as a
pawn in an ideological battle. He found himself domiciled because of
the war in America during a period when it was necessary to demonstrate the viability of American ballet. Because he failed to produce the
kind of American ballet certain advocates demanded, Massine, the personification of Ballet Russe, was open to attack, and some critics attacked ferociously."[113] Kirstein dismissed his symphonic ballets as "silly"[114]
and, in a frontal assault, noted that "Massine has a right to embellish the
old music-masters, but it is scarcely a creative act when he does so. It is,
pure and simple, an inferior art; the art of illustration."[115]

The disruption caused by the war and the lack of encouragement
must have been debilitating indeed. Massine must have nearly suffocated
from demands that he align himself with a cause that had nothing to do
with his own artistic values. The prevailing judgment of the time coincided with Amberg's: "Massine's American career contributed immensely to the ballet education of this country but, for all its brilliance
and fecundity, did little to further the growth of a native tradition."[116] But
it was precisely the new American ballet that had produced the change in
aesthetic taste, to which taste Massine's work was now anathema. Balanchine, Tudor, and de Mille were the new pacesetters. Interestingly, Eugene Loring, more than forty years after his seminal ballet *Billy the Kid,*
suggested that the time had come for a reassessment of Massine's influence, and described Massine's ballets as models against which American
choreographers of the 1930s and 1940s reacted in search of their own
style, or from which they assimilated new ideas. Specifically, Loring drew
attention to the influence of the cinematographic technique of *Union Pacific* and *Symphonie fantastique.*[117]

Edwin Denby was the apologist for the new aesthetics, especially
the dogma of neoclassicism. Although he approved of Massine's Diaghilev pieces, he took exception to the symphonic ballets, and his criticism, when not generally negative, appeared to question Massine's artistic integrity. "If one took him seriously," Denby wrote, "he would be
guilty of murdering the Beethoven Seventh, the Scarlatti, and even tender little Offenbach. . . . There is of course no reason for taking Massine
seriously; he doesn't mean to be, he doesn't mean to murder."[118] If art, as
some would have it, is the illusion that provides an aesthetic truth,
Denby's incompatibility with Massine's art never allowed him to gain a
closer glimpse of that truth. Even when it came to his best work of the
time, the most that Denby could muster was a nod toward the achieve-

ment of a master craftsman who, like a prestidigitator, always had a good, effective trick up his sleeve.

As Amberg wrote, "Massine's serious substantial compositions did not touch the general American public in a profound, emotional sense."[119] And the negative attitude of tastemakers Kirstein and Denby further debased Massine's artistic reputation, especially in subsequent decades when his symphonic ballets were not in the active repertory and thus could not speak for themselves.

With the coming of war, patriotism swelled. Walter Terry wrote in "Recipe for American Ballet" that "the days of our national inferiority complexes are over, and the United States is feeling proud of its governmental system, its industries and its culture. Relegated to the dimming past are the beliefs that only exotic names can produce art and the 'Dubinskayas' are discovering that the Patsy Bowmans and the Eugene Lorings are of no mean ability."[120] After the war, the triumph of the economy and the liberal ideology of the United States also marked the apogee of American ballet, modern dance, and painting (the New York school).

Massine was profoundly affected by these events—artistically and physically uprooted, denied the chance to explore his full creative potential through his symphonic ballets, and made the target of savage criticism. Throughout his long career and despite its ups and downs, he had been accorded respect by critics and artists who were themselves, in their respective fields, luminaries—Apollinaire, Clive Bell, Roger Fry, T. S. Eliot, Ernest Newman. By 1939 and the outbreak of World War II the choreographer seemed at his zenith, permanently fixed in the firmament like a glorious star. Only a decade later, after sixteen years (including his Roxy period) of advancing and contributing to the cause of dance in America, he now found himself the ballet establishment's persona non grata.

PART SIX

Europe and the Postwar Years

The poet begins where man ends. The
destiny of the latter is to live his human
itinerary, the mission of the former is to
invent what does not exist.

—ORTEGA Y GASSET

CHAPTER 13

London, September 1946–Edinburgh, September 1960

A BULLET IN THE BALLET was a dramatization of a mystery novel by
Caryl Brahms[1] and S. J. Simon, revolving around the backstage intrigue
in a ballet company where every dancer cast as Petrouchka is murdered.
The play included Fokine's *Petrouchka*, revived by Massine with the assistance of Idzikowski, *Gaîté parisienne*, and a new *ballet blanc*, *Reverie clas-
sique*, choreographed by Massine to the music of Chopin and led by
Massine and Irina Baronova. The musical was rehearsed in London,
opened in Edinburgh on October 1, 1946, then proceeded to engagements in Glasgow, Manchester, Leeds, Blackpool, and Liverpool. It had
considerable success during its provincial tour; but backing for a London
engagement was never found, and the show closed after its final performance in Liverpool.

Massine's presence in England for the first time since the onset of war was in itself an event in the ballet community and fed speculation about his future. Discussions were held about his joining the Ballet Rambert,[2] but nothing came of them. During the tour of *A Bullet in the Ballet,* Ninette de Valois, founder-director of the Sadler's Wells Ballet (later to become the Royal Ballet), invited Massine to revive *Le Tricorne* and *La Boutique fantasque* and to act as guest choreographer and dancer early in 1947.[3]

De Valois, a *demi-caractère* dancer and choreographer much influenced by Massine, profoundly admired him. By 1946 her company was a well-organized institution that had achieved artistic excellence during the war years by relying on the choreographers Frederick Ashton, Robert Helpmann, and de Valois herself. Now de Valois wanted Massine as the company's first guest choreographer. She believed that his introduction to ballet of "the character and demi-caractère technique, always supported by classicism," was already vitally important to her troupe's artistic development. She saw no "other master choreographer who could really bring to classical ballet the techniques of character and demi-caractère. His knowledge in this field was tremendous, and he alone had the capacity to make it belong to the classical school—character ballets of the classical school, not character ballets on their own."[4] De Valois realized how important it was for her dancers to get to know his work, for "he had a definite style of his own. It was a character style underneath it all, imposed on classicism. Also he was a long-term pupil of Cecchetti, and a lot of the Cecchetti background work and the Italian style was strongly felt in his work, and this was indispensable if the dancers were to grasp a better understanding of the demi-caractère style."[5] De Valois valued Massine's *demi-caractère* ballets not only for their dancing opportunities but also for their sharp, universally recognizable characterizations. His ballets such as *Mam'zelle Angot,* remarked Alexander Bland, "abounded in character roles of the type which de Valois, following in Massine's footsteps, liked to create and which deployed the dramatic abilities that she encouraged in her artists."[6] De Valois also felt that exposure to Massine's sense of musicality and rhythm would benefit the company. One of her chief concerns was the development of the male dancers, for whom Massine was especially important.

But hiring Massine was also a political ploy, for despite the hiatus of the war years the choreographer and the Ballets Russes still had a strong following. As Bland noted: "It was a shrewd move, for it brought back those members of the Russian ballet audience who had been reluctant to transfer their allegiance to the home-grown Company."[7] And in revival the two Diaghilev works "with their imaginative Ecole de Paris designs and their nostalgic echoes of pre-war triumphs amply fulfilled their function—to set the mantle of the Ballets Russes firmly on the shoulders of the Sadler's Wells troupe."[8]

By the beginning of 1947 the Massines were settled in a four-room flat in Kensington High Street near Kensington Gardens, where the children played in the afternoons accompanied by their nanny. The flat was decorated in the austere English manner with Chippendale furniture from shops in Chelsea and Kensington. Other pieces were acquired at Sotheby's and Christie's.

Massine's first contact with de Valois's troupe took place one Sunday morning when she assembled the company for a special class on the old Sadler's Wells stage. It was Massine's chance to decide whether he wanted to work with her company. Only days afterwards rehearsals began for the spring season revivals of *Le Tricorne* and *La Boutique fantasque*.

Working again at Covent Garden, the site of so many triumphs, Massine felt "as happy there as in my early years with the Diaghilev company."[9] As usual, the schedule was exhausting, but as the dancer Alexander Grant recalled, working with him was "a learning experience, because we took a lot by watching him demonstrate during rehearsals and especially watching him perform his roles on stage."[10]

For most of the dancers, Massine still had the aura of his prewar eminence. Margot Fonteyn, who danced the role of the Miller's Wife, described him this way: "The great Massine was already a legend; a strange, quiet man, with those marvelous eyes that fascinated yet also had the effect of a closed door. Occasionally a quick smile lit up the impassive face, and the door opened briefly. But even then I felt at a great distance from him."[11] Although she felt that she was not "particularly good in the role . . . the exhilaration of swirling about in the fandango opposite the intense face of Massine, and then watching him stand absolutely motionless at the end of the Miller's dance while the audience cheered wildly for five minutes, was so overwhelming. . . ."[12] But despite the success of the revivals, especially *Le Tricorne* (the ballerina Moira Shearer, in a secondary role, found it fresh and inspiring to dance),[13] the company had trouble grasping the proper style, phrasing, and sweep of movement of these ballets. The leading female roles in particular failed to come to life. Fonteyn was beautiful to look at in *Le Tricorne*, but her movements were not convincing. As for *La Boutique fantasque*, "the inability of the Wells to produce a Danilova robbed the can-can of a climax."[14]

Massine with Margot Fonteyn in Le Tricorne, *1947*

Although de Valois considered the works to be masterpieces of twentieth-century ballet, she also felt that with the war an era dating back to Diaghilev had come to a close. However, it was still too soon to fashion a proper method of reinterpretation. She cited Lopokova, who observed that "it is easier to revive a work whose style [is] a hundred years old than one that is twenty."[15] Grant believed that the difficulty in Massine's ballets was that they required a unique type of actor-dancer. "In the 1930s the Ballets Russes artists were able to convey character through movement. The choreography was the movement that gave them the key to characterization, and they were able to convey what they were, and who they were, through their dancing because they were actor-dancers. They were incredible artists to be able to do that, and they were an inspiration at the time for all of us who saw them. These Massine ballets require artists who are such dynamic and charismatic people that they can hold the attention of a whole audience with a single movement."[16] In the postwar generation, said Grant, such actor-dancers were almost nonexistent.

Massine returned to the London stage as a performer when he was already past fifty. He was still slim and agile and possessed a commanding theatrical presence, but some younger members of the audience had not seen him before. While they found him charismatic, some of the impact of his dancing, about which so much had been written, was missing from his performances. P. W. Manchester commented: "It's very difficult to watch a dancer in his middle forties if you never saw him when he was thirty-five . . . because . . . when we watch dancers over a period of twenty or thirty years, we don't really notice the erosion. It is very gradual. But if they are great artists they will still, for us, have something. But to be presented with somebody whom you never saw before, to suddenly see Massine in 1947 . . . how could you possibly have really seen him? You know he never taught anybody that great slide at the end of his dance [in *Le Tricorne*], where he had a slide across the stage and then leaped to his feet and stood absolutely still. By [1947] . . . he wasn't able to do that."[17]

As the successful Sadler's Wells ballet season drew to a close, Massine was approached by the British film director Michael Powell to participate in his next picture, *The Red Shoes*, which was to include a ballet based on the Hans Christian Andersen story of the same name.[18]

The team of director Powell and writer Emeric Pressburger had by 1947 achieved international recognition for a series of outstanding films, especially *A Matter of Life and Death* (*Stairway to Heaven* in the United States; 1946) and *Black Narcissus* (1947). Pressburger had written *The Red Shoes* back in 1937 at the request of producer Alexander Korda as a vehicle for Merle Oberon, soon to become Mrs. Korda. The film did not materialize, and almost a decade later Powell and Pressburger bought the script back from Korda and persuaded Arthur Rank to produce it. Powell had agreed to participate with Pressburger on two conditions: (1) the leading role of the ballerina Victoria Page must be taken by a dancer, and (2) the film would include a twenty-minute ballet. This was a risky proposition, one that even Pressburger feared; he suggested cutting the ballet to ten minutes. "In the end," Powell recalled in his memoirs, "and mainly through Emeric's pressure, the ballet ran seventeen minutes."[19]

Powell felt that his exposure to ballet and his knowledge of the form were indispensable to the making of the film. During the 1920s he had lived on the French Riviera, where he attended Ballets Russes seasons in Monte Carlo, met some of the dancers and even, once, Diaghilev himself. He had thrilling memories of Massine's performances. During the 1930s he had followed the Ballets Russes de Monte Carlo seasons in London and was very much impressed by the symphonic ballets.[20]

The story of *The Red Shoes* revolved around a ballet company and its impresario, Lermontov, a character patterned after Diaghilev (and played in the film by Anton Walbrook). The impresario demands from his artists complete dedication and devotion to art. When his prima ballerina, Victoria Page, falls in love with the company's musical director, Julian Craster, Lermontov turns vengeful and implacable. Linked to the story of Victoria Page, who is faced with the dilemma of choosing between art and life, is the actual creative process and performance of *The Red Shoes,* a ballet about a girl who cannot stop dancing until she is driven by her red shoes to her own death. The ballet itself, as a dramatic device, is inextricable from the context of the film story and becomes a symbol for the main plot. To quote Pressburger: "The gem of the whole thing, in one sense, does lie in Andersen's story, for the ballet grew out of that story, and the main plot out of the ballet. One stage followed another. Above all, I wanted to have a film in which a work of art would not merely be discussed, but in which it would appear. That was my aim."[21]

Powell's choice of choreographer and leading dancer for the film was Robert Helpmann of the Sadler's Wells company, a personal friend of Powell's who had worked on his 1942 film *One of Our Aircraft Is Missing.* The leading female role was given to the marvelously young, striking-looking Moira Shearer, also from Sadler's Wells, whom Powell had recently seen in Helpmann's ballet *Miracle in the Gorbals.* The role of the prima ballerina was taken by the French dancer Ludmilla Tcherina, and the dual role of the choreographer Ljubov in the film and the Shoemaker in the ballet *The Red Shoes* was given to Massine. Powell admired Massine tremendously and was convinced that he was the right choice for the part. When the director "heard that he had arrived in London just when I was casting for *The Red Shoes* I felt that fate had brought us together just when I needed for the film all the genius of the world."[22]

Powell had briefly met Massine during the Diaghilev years, but it was not until their collaboration in *The Red Shoes* that a very special friendship evolved that united the two men for the rest of their lives. Powell "worshipped him as an artist for twenty-five years of his brilliant career, and loved him as a friend for the next thirty years. We loved to work together and together we created magic."[23] He described Massine as "intensely musical, a superb mime and a good actor. He could pass from dignity to buffoonery in a flash, one moment a monk, the next a monkey."[24]

However, asking Massine to dance another choreographer's work made Powell hesitant. He writes about their first meeting:

He had taken an apartment in one of those tall stone and red brick Kensington houses, just around the corner from Barker's department store, and we met there. He was preternaturally solemn and stared at me with a look that was centuries old. I explained what we were up to and that Grischa Ljubov was based, perhaps, partly upon himself. He bowed. Then I mentioned the ballet, spoke of Brian Easdale [who was composing the film's score] and Sir Thomas Beecham [who would conduct the Red Shoes ballet], and explained Bobby Helpmann's part in the proceedings. The temperature of the room went down perceptibly. Massine picked his words carefully. He had nothing against the Sadler's Wells Ballet and its leading male dancer, and of course it was my privilege to appoint whom I wished as choreographer. But if he were to dance the Shoemaker in the Hans Andersen story, he would obviously create the part himself, and would want credit for doing so. I was so mad about him by now—he brought half a dozen qualities to the film which had been sadly lacking—that I strode over this minor obstacle, merely saying that I was sure Robert Helpmann would agree to this.[25]

Shooting began in June 1947 on location in France. The ballet itself was filmed later at Pinewood Studios outside of London. From the beginning Powell was fascinated with Massine's interpretation and his intuitive understanding of the camera. Powell described him as a "genius" who developed his own relationship with the lens and its power.[26] That is probably why, according to the essayist Monk Gibbon,

Again and again through the ballet, Massine furnishes the film with some of its most striking visual effects. Powell has given not only some wonderful close-ups of the great Russian, which for colour and animation have never, I believe, been equaled on the screen, but he has used him to reconcile us to the whole macabre and magical aspect of the story. Massine contemplating his victim, Massine leaping forward to pour ink over a little bit of rag and so turn day into night, Massine crouching forward upon the church steps quite indifferent to the threat of the knife upheld in the girl's hands, all these moments are unforgettable. They are unforgettable because the personality of the dancer is as colourful as his costume or the setting.[27]

Robert Helpmann, Moira Shearer, and Massine in The Red Shoes, *1947*

Gibbon goes on to praise Massine's openness to the camera, especially when

> *at one point in the ballet, when a close-up of Massine, the cobbler, shows*
> *him either as renewing the spell which he has cast over the dancing girl or*
> *perhaps merely contemplating her with cynical detachment, his whole ex-*
> *pression seemed to me such a masterpiece of inspired facial control that I*
> *almost cried out with pleasure. Powell has seized on a particular gesture,*
> *a sudden twist upwards of the palm, with the hand extended, accompa-*
> *nied by a facial expression full of such subtle implications as to be almost*
> *indescribable.*[28]

The working relationship between Powell and Massine was one of tacit understanding and complicity. Shearer remembers that Powell never gave him any direction.[29] Powell found him such a "formidable actor" that he gave him complete freedom to interpret his role. "I simply used to tell him, 'This is the shot, Léonide, you only have one and a half seconds to do it, and we are shooting from here. Let's run it.' "[30] The rapport between director and actor was so strong that Massine did not hesitate to make his own suggestions. Gibbon writes:

> He [Powell] takes the occasion when the cobbler shuts up his shop and proceeds to turn day into night. "In the original sketch the Shoemaker in his role as Magician appeared with his hat on and stood in the foreground with his arms wildly extended and the girl dancing away in the background." I said to [Hein] Heckroth [the designer of the film], "This is static and obvious. How about bringing his hands together, and having a close-up of the hands and letting the audience see the girl beyond them?" ... But when it came to taking the shot the musical score had been refined down to leave only twelve seconds for Moira to leave her home and come right across the square dashing into the crowd, as well as for the business of the Shoemaker and his hands. I said to Helpmann, "You can have eight seconds for Moira. I want four seconds for Massine." Helpmann speeded Moira up still more, so that she spun across the set like a whirlwind. She became a teetotum. Massine was standing with his back to the audience and with upraised arms watching her. The camera had been following Moira. Massine said, "Why don't I turn and come up to the camera and blot the girl out?" Later he [Massine] added the touch of coming up and looking through his suddenly vibrating hands.[31]

According to Powell, it was also Massine's idea to leave Shearer alone on stage while she took her curtain-call bows.[32]

The Shoemaker should be added to the impressive gallery of portraits that Massine created throughout his career. He himself called the Shoemaker a rather "shady character, a mixture of magician and charlatan."[33] But the shadiness had broader dimensions. For Gibbon, the Shoemaker was "the apotheosis as it were of all human puppetry."[34] To allow Massine greater opportunity for characterization, Brian Easdale studied Massine's dancing in order to bring to the Shoemaker's music a compatible style and mood.[35]

That he created the role of the Shoemaker within the terms of Helpmann's choreography testifies to Massine's theatrical craftsmanship.

Shearer herself was unaware at the time that he was doing his own choreography.[36] While his solo scenes may not have presented much of a problem, Massine's perceptive understanding must have been tested in the scenes where his character interacts with others. There, his immersion in the collective dynamics is brilliant; but in addition these scenes become a fully realized study-in-movement of the protagonists' relationships. Together with Shearer's solos, any scene in which Massine appears lights up *The Red Shoes*. His impact is doubled, in fact, by the ballet's circular structure: it opens and closes with the Shoemaker performing "macabre antics outside his cobbler's shop."[37]

In the Shoemaker Gibbon saw reminders of other famous Massine characters, such as those in *Pulcinella* and *Les Femmes de bonne humeur*. In *The Red Shoes*, says Gibbon, Massine gives the spectator

> the very quintessence of his specific talent. . . . Massine's intense vitality shows itself at every stage. Though the whole of the Fun Fare is a vortex of hectic activity, the Shoemaker moving with "a cat-like elegance and sinuousness" stands out nevertheless as far more highly energized than anyone at the fair. He is a dynamic force behind all, not demonic, not even suggesting evil very strongly, but so highly magnetized and magnetizing, so charged with an electric force which is evident in every gesture, that he seems to control everything. It is the force of his character which makes the fairy tale side of the ballet so realistic for us. He "steals the show," but it is not a deliberate theft, nor does he take from anyone else. He steals it simply because the part he plays is the axis on which everything else turns, and because without the whimsical, capricious, sinister cobbler there would be no ballet at all. . . . His energy is revealed not merely in that terrific leap seen in one of the "stills," but it is implicit in every movement and every gesture, implicit most of all perhaps when he is not stirring at all.[38]

According to Powell, Massine had a "dramatic and human tension that became an integral part of his acting or dancing."[39] The director found a combination of these qualities in all of his scenes. He pointed out the facial expressions in his scene with Lermontov while they are backstage watching the excerpt from the second act of *Giselle*, when Massine delivers the line, "That is all very fine, very pure and fine, but you cannot alter human nature." Powell also commended the scene on stage, also with Lermontov, before the *Red Shoes* ballet begins, when Massine cries out, "Chaos, chaos, chaos!" while he clings to Lermontov, and then suddenly goes limp in Lermontov's arms for a fraction of a second, like a lifeless puppet, only to spring back to life with overwhelming vitality. (It is impossible to watch this scene without Petrouchka coming to mind.) For Powell, the final sequence of the ballet, just before the girl dies, illustrates Massine's impressive acting ability and his intuitive understanding of the theater. Powell was particularly impressed because a lot of the ballet, particularly Massine's scene here, "was simply made up on the spot, improvised to bring the whole thing down to storytelling. In this scene Massine had twenty to thirty seconds which I broke down into ten shots."[40]

Massine found filmmaking absorbing (he felt quite comfortable working with Powell) and

> *infinitely more complex than working in the theatre. The day-to-day work was repetitive, for if a single detail in a scene was not quite right, we had to take it over and over again. This was very exhausting, and I found it a great strain to repeat my scenes with the same conviction and intensity each time. Meticulous preparation was essential, and I had to sketch out the choreography in detail before each day's filming. While I was dancing I was always acutely aware of the camera, picking up and magnifying the most minute detail. I had to be careful to avoid excessively fast rhythms, which would have come out merely as a succession of jerky movements.*[41]

Despite Massine's reserve and distance throughout the making of the film—he never mixed with other members of the cast or the crew, appeared on the set only when he was needed, and always lunched alone in his dressing room—he developed a friendly rapport with Moira Shearer. At Covent Garden, the stunning redhead had appeared in *Le Tricorne* and had danced the *Boutique* cancan opposite Massine. From the beginning of the shooting they spent a good deal of time together. (Location scenes on the Continent were shot first, and on the morning of their flight there Shearer's eyes widened as she watched Massine consume three substantial breakfasts: one before boarding, one on the plane, and yet another on arrival.) She found him courteous, friendly, and charming, but he never struck up a conversation without prodding. She was fascinated by his personality and tantalized by the air of mystery about him, the hints of a deeper, more cryptic, and quite unreachable level. At the same time, she wondered how a man so enigmatic and withdrawn could seem to be the force behind almost everything happening in the course of the filming. She detected a great "sense of humor just with his eyes, and felt that if he had let himself be, he would have said a lot of wicked and funny things every five minutes about everyone and every-thing."[42]

When they began to shoot the ballet segments at Pinewood Studios, she got to know him even better. They often shared a cab to the studio and, later, to the rehearsals for the Sadler's Wells *Mam'zelle Angot*. By then he had relaxed a bit and did not seem to mind when she asked questions, especially about the Diaghilev days. But he never talked about current work or any aspects of the film, and never offered his opinion about their work together. "His attitude at work was practical. He wasn't troubled about anything and he stood back very dispassionately. He never showed emotion at any time of any variety."[43]

When the film was completed, it was £200,000 over budget and dismayed the producers. According to Powell:

> When the Rank organization saw it they thought they were sunk. I didn't show it to Rank and John Davis, but Emeric did ... When the film finished, they got up and left the theatre without a word because they thought they had lost their shirts. They couldn't understand one word of it. Universal were their partners and as soon as they could get a print they showed it to some executives ... An executive stood up and said, "This film will not make a penny."[44]

In addition, "most of them shared the opinion of [co-producer] Arthur Krim that it was an art film, and would require tough selling."[45] The film, however, became an immediate hit; in New York it ran for two years and seven weeks at the Bijou Cinema on Fifty-fifth Street and Broadway. Powell wrote: "I think that the real reason why *The Red Shoes* was such a success was that we had been told for years to go out and die for freedom and democracy, for this and for that, and now that the war was over, *The Red Shoes* told us to go and die for art."[46]

TOWARDS THE END of the summer Massine began to rehearse (atop the Stoll Theatre) his new production for the Sadler's Wells company, *Mam'zelle Angot*, a revised version of *Mademoiselle Angot*, his 1943 ballet for Ballet Theatre. This was his first "new" ballet work for Sadler's Wells and the first Massine premiere in London since 1939. The ballet remained close to the 1943 original, and although there were no major changes in structure, the story was clarified and the choreography varied to capitalize on the technique and personality of his new cast. The English cast featured four of the company's most brilliant dancers: Fonteyn in the title role, Shearer as the Aristocrat, Michael Somes as the Caricaturist, and Grant as the Barber. (Of these dancers, Fonteyn in her soubrette role was the least suitable.)

Working with Massine on a third ballet, the company by now better understood his idiosyncratic style. His emphasis on characterization was "all through dancing," recalled de Valois. "There was no mime, but the characters came through the movements he had choreographed. Everything was in the choreography and in the attitude of the character. In the case of the aristocratic lady the movements were elegant, in legato, regal, as a character sort of detached in contrast to the others. But all these characters were achieved through the painting of broad strokes, to show certain types of behavior through movement."[47] The ballet resorted to Massine's customary *demi-caractère* techniques: juxtaposition of action (one example is the pas de deux of Mam'zelle Angot and the Caricaturist against a pas de quatre for four male dancers), and quick, staccato steps with a great deal of rhythmic movement of the torso and arms.

True to himself, Massine exhausted and dismayed everyone during the rehearsal period. De Valois remembers that "some of the dancers could not take the strain in his work,"[48] and Grant felt that "he took for granted that no one got tired."[49] But, amazingly, he himself was able to keep pace and continue his practice of demonstrating each role. As usual there was very little verbal communication. Shearer discovered that "he expected the dancers to understand their characters through the movements. He was able to show and demonstrate when he wanted—especially specific visual images. He gave the straight choreography, no trial-and-error approach; there was very little experimentation. He never praised nor criticized, and when he pressed on to something else, dancers guessed that he was happy."[50] According to Grant, "He would work you until you would get it right to his satisfaction and so in the process you understood your character. A very important aspect of working with him was that he demonstrated each role and that he was extremely musical. But this was not a disconcerting approach for the company because Ashton was the same way—the more you did a movement, the more you understood what it was. There was very little explanation."[51]

Mam'zelle Angot marked the reunion of Massine with his friend André Derain, who designed new scenery and costumes. Derain came to London to supervise the execution of his designs and himself painted the flowers and vegetables on the backcloth.

Mam'zelle Angot premiered on November 26, 1947, and was an unqualified success. Mary Clarke called the press's reception of the work "ecstatic."[52] The reviewer for *Dancing Times* wrote: "The choreography bears all the hallmarks of Massine's genius and his demands are great. . . . Once the market is open they must be ready for all kinds of intricate *enchaînements* and lifts for unusual hand and arm movements which are a vital part of the roles he has created, . . . The thing that strikes one most is the contrast he draws between the dances."

While regretting the work's overreliance on atmosphere—especially in Mam'zelle Angot's waltz, where the "charm" and "purpose" of various actions were lost—the reviewer saw the "many deft touches of humour" as "evidence of Massine's close study of human nature and its foibles, proving that everyday life still plays a large part in artistic designs of all kinds. Perhaps the greatest compliment one can pay to Massine is to say that one must see this work many times before discovering all these delightful human touches, and their correct place in the setting to be fully valued."[53]

In a *Dance Magazine* article titled "Massine in England and America," Mary Clarke suggested some of the possible reasons Massine's ballets, notably *Mam'zelle Angot,* worked better for the English dancers than the Americans. Admitting that "neither English nor Americans approach Massine's choreography in the same manner as the Russians used to, [because] they lack the complete unselfconsciousness and personality that seems to be the birthright of every Russian dancer," Clarke argued that

> [*the reason*] *Sadler's Wells has taken happily to Massine's style is doubtless due to their having been previously trained in Ninette de Valois's ballets, which are often period evocations . . . and which are based on movement which at its worst is fidgety but at its best sets the whole stage alive with vigorous character dancing. . . . De Valois has emphasized the importance of acting in ballet and has demanded neat characterization from her dancers rather than strong dance ability, leaving the creation of pure dancing to her leading choreographer, Frederick Ashton. . . . The division, however, has tended to become rather too marked and Massine's first complaint in England was that there were no true character dancers here: they either acted or they danced but not both.*[54]

Mam'zelle Angot remained in the repertory of the Royal Ballet until 1968; it was revived in the spring of 1980 as a tribute to Massine.

BY 1948 MASSINE was operating on an extensive international circuit, for his works were in great demand. During the next few years he staged his ballets for La Scala, the Royal Danish Ballet, the Teatro Colón, the Opéra-Comique, the London Festival Ballet, the International Ballet, the Rome Opera Ballet, the Teatro Municipal in Rio de Janeiro, the Royal Swedish Ballet, the Paris Opéra, and many more. The revivals were mainly his classics from the Diaghilev repertory and de Basil's *Le Beau Danube*. Perhaps the ones that were best able to recapture the stylistic mood and the nuances of the period were those by the de Cuevas Company, where Massine's guest appearances found him performing opposite his Ballets Russes stars Riabouchinska, Toumanova, and Lichine.[55] He also staged several opera ballets, mostly in Italy. Until well into the 1950s Massine's wife acted as his assistant, bustling all over the world to supervise the preliminary rehearsals of his ballets for various companies while he worked on others. Massine would then arrive for the final rehearsals.

Nineteen forty-eight saw two new works. *Capriccio* was presented at La Scala on a gala Stravinsky program that also included a revival of Massine's *Sacre du printemps*. A more ambitious production than *Capriccio* was *Clock Symphony* (to Haydn) for the Sadler's Wells company, with scenery and costumes by Christian Bérard, his first collaboration with Massine since *Seventh Symphony* in 1939. Massine found that "the persistent rhythm of the *Clock Symphony* had reminded me of the revolving figures in delicate porcelain often found on baroque clocks, and I conceived the new ballet as an animation of these figures, modeling them on the delicate Meissen figurines I had seen in Dresden in 1927."[56] He

> devised a fairy-tale plot about a young Clockmaker and a Princess living in the Kingdom of Insects. When the king announced that he was taking a suitor for his daughter the poor young Clockmaker brought him an elaborate and intricate clock which he had designed and made himself. The other suitors, seeing that the Princess was attracted to the Clockmaker, secretly hid one of their pages inside the clockcase to dislocate its mechanism. In the final scene the hands of the clock go in reverse, but when the page has been extracted and the suitors banished from the kingdom, the Clockmaker is able to repair it and so wins the Princess in marriage.[57]

The complicated production, with a huge cast, featured a giant clock that opened up to allow the many dancing figures to emerge from it. The opening was dazzling: the curtain rose on Shearer, in a black and night-blue tutu, seated commandingly on a throne under a white canopy. The role of the Clockmaker was danced with gusto by Alexander Grant.

Even though this was Massine's fourth staging for Sadler's Wells, and the company had grown familiar with his style, the choreography for *Clock Symphony* presented them with a new degree of difficulty, a return to Massine's overemphatic baroquism of the earlier 1940s. The staccato leg work, with arm, torso, and head movements, was, according to Grant, "exhausting and very Massinesque . . . a type of technique that demands an extensive quick allegro footwork that is not used today in the same manner."[58] Shearer was afraid that "he was beginning to overchoreograph—to put too many steps per musical bar that gave the impression that the choreography was too full."[59] In his earlier works, Shearer thought, his choreography had a longer line, with more flowing movements; *Clock Symphony* was so packed with choreography that it became frenetic. The allegro technique demanded by the role of the Princess presented a painful test for Shearer. Throughout the first and second movements she remained sitting without moving, but when the third movement began she had to "leap into action, by this time stiff, stiff, but straight into the most tremendous quick jumping, leaping movements."[60]

Premiered on June 26, *Clock Symphony* was not a success. The story was difficult to follow without reference to the program notes; moreover, the reviewer of *Dancing Times* felt as Shearer did, that the piece was handicapped in that "Massine appears to have so overloaded his choreography with exceedingly intricate dances that in many instances there is no clear pattern."[61]

BY 1949 THE MASSINES had settled in Paris. Work commitments on the Continent, particularly in France and Italy, motivated the move. In Paris, the family bought a large four-story house at Neuilly-sur-Seine, where a great many of their belongings from London and Long Island found a new home. The decoration of the house was left to Tatiana, always the organizer, who created an elegant but sober environment, taking into consideration Massine's dislike of furniture that was not essential.

Although many of the works in Massine's impressive art collection had been kept in storage in New York since before the war, the walls at Neuilly were soon hung with Derains, Légers, Mirós, and Picassos, including the latter's series of zodiac signs. A photograph of Diaghilev radiated a strongly felt spiritual presence. The library contained an important collection of art and dance books, musical scores, and books by Russian authors. On the top floor Massine built a dance studio, so that he could avoid the crowded and badly heated Parisian ateliers. This studio also made it possible for his children to take ballet instruction at home from Maria Gourileva, a Cecchetti-trained teacher whom Massine thought outstanding.

From his early morning class, which he held alone in the studio, until night, life at Neuilly revolved around the master's work and needs. A butler, a governess for the children, a cook, a chauffeur, and maids were on hand, all subject to Massine's strict discipline and meticulously planned daily schedule. He was most relaxed during his leisurely luncheons with his family. Even here, however, talk of present and future work dominated the conversation. Massine apparently had little else to talk about. Surely the children were bored; as Lorca remembered, "He did not leave much room for anyone. We listened while he talked about his work, laughed when he laughed, and stopped when he stopped."[62]

Still, life in Paris was less nomadic for the family and a bit more sociable. Some of Massine's artist friends were frequent visitors. Also, Tatiana tried to arrange dinners and parties for guests from the worlds of art and dance. Her efforts sometimes aggravated her husband, who disliked social life and entertaining (with exceptions made for those few friends he enjoyed unreservedly, such as Derain, who always managed to arrive accompanied by a beautiful woman) and hated to waste time away from his work.

The family's summer residence was the Isole dei Galli. They returned for the first time after the war to find that the caretakers had kept everything in the best possible condition given the circumstances. It was a pleasant surprise to discover that the vineyards had produced six hundred liters of wine. Work resumed to refurbish and improve the islands, and the crucial construction of the main villa got under way.

For holidays the family would leave Paris in their Buick, suitcases tacked on the roof, and travel caravanlike through Italy. Frequently their destination was Positano, where they would board the boat to Galli. Each journey of this kind was designed as a learning experience; Massine organized visits to museums, cathedrals, churches, and historical monuments, in the course of which he would lecture his family about painting, sculpture, architecture, and music. The islands of Galli were a refuge for rest and work, from which strangers were banned. Only a few friends visited, including the Stravinskys, the Hindemiths, Powell, and Marke-vitch, and it was common for them to spend most of their time sightsee-ing on the mainland, in particular Naples and environs, which Massine loved. (Once when the Stravinskys and the Massines were visiting Pres-tum, Vera Stravinsky heard that there was a case of cholera in the vicin-ity and the group had to leave immediately for Galli.)[63] Guests' stays on Galli were always kept brief.

In 1949, in a burst of activity, Massine returned to La Scala. In Feb-ruary he choreographed the ballets for *Carmen* and *Khovanshchina* and produced a minor new work, *Quattro stagione.* Set to Vivaldi's score, with scenery and costumes by Pierre Roy, the ballet was a series of vignettes that captured the mood of each of the four seasons. Winter was in the style of a *ballet blanc,* ending in a pas de deux by a poor couple in the rain. Spring depicted a shepherd's dream of unrequited love and his awaken-ing to reality. Summer was in the style of a *ballet de cour.* Autumn pre-sented a series of episodes related to harvest rituals, ending in a bacchanale. One Italian critic reported, "In the choreography, imagina-tive, noble and comic scenes alternate with one another."[64]

For most of the year, however, Massine was busy reviving works for various companies and performing as a guest with the Marquis de Cuevas Ballet. While with de Cuevas he choreographed a pas de deux for Toumanova and Skibine set to Debussy's "Clair de lune." (It was never performed due to Toumanova's departure from the company.)[65]

At the end of 1949 Boris Kochno commissioned a pas de deux from Massine for his Ballets des Champs-Elysées. The work was based on an idea by Kochno about the allegorical relationship between an artist and his model, which disintegrates into a victim/victimizer relationship. A struggle ensues in which the artist attempts to possess his model but is destroyed by her in the end. The creation of *Le Peintre et son modèle* was an experiment. Massine worked without a score, devising movements to rhythms and tempi that he provided to the rehearsal pianist. Only after the pas de deux was completed did Georges Auric compose a score based on the movements.

The choreography departed from Massine's staccato style; it was long of line and acrobatic. Irene Skorik, who danced the model opposite Youly Algeroff's artist, found it remarkable, with an aspect of violence, cruelty, and dramatic power that made a welcome change from the lyri-cal roles with which she was identified.[66] The scenery and costumes were by Balthus.

In April 1950 Massine created two new works for Les Fêtes d'Avènement in Monaco, which were performed in the palace courtyard in the presence of Prince Rainier III. These were *Concertino,* an abstract ballet set to Françaix's 1932 work for piano and orchestra, and *Platée,* set to music from Rameau's *ballet bouffon,* a suite of dances—*musette, tambourin, passepied, rigaudon, contredanse*—in the style of Feuillet and Blasis.

In 1950 and 1951 Massine supervised various revivals for the Opéra-Comique and created two new works, *La Valse* and *Le Bal du Pont du Nord.* Set to Ravel's score and with scenery and costumes by Derain, *La Valse* was adapted from Mikhail Lermontov's play *Maskerad,* a story of jealousy, passion, and murder involving an officer, his best friend, and the officer's wife, with all of the action taking place during a ball. But aside from some "effective moments" Massine considered it "a failure, partly because the music was too repetitive. I had hoped to overcome this problem through the dramatic elements in the libretto, but the choreography was defeated by the monotony of the music."[67]

Le Bal du Pont du Nord had a libretto by Hubert Deviellez based on a dramatic Flemish tale, music by Jacques Dupont, and scenery and costumes by André Masson. In the ballet Adèle, daughter of the town's bell-ringer, steals away from her father's appointed watch to meet her lover at the fair, where she finds the swain flirting with her friend Marion. Adèle commits suicide by throwing herself from the Pont du Nord. To re-create the feeling of the story, the ballet was designed in the style of a Flemish painting. At its premiere in Lille it was titled *Meure flamande.*

Before returning to London to work again with Michael Powell on his film *The Tales of Hoffmann,* Massine was approached by Henri Sauguet to choreograph *Les Saisons (Symphonie allégorique)* for the de Cuevas company for the Bordeaux International Music Festival of 1951. Sauguet collaborated with Jacques Dupont on the music and libretto; Dupont designed the scenery and costumes. The choreography consisted of a suite of *tableaux vivants* illustrating man's relationship with nature as the four seasons follow one another.

Sir Thomas Beecham was the force behind *The Tales of Hoffmann.* After conducting the score to the *Red Shoes* ballet, he had offered to participate in any opera film Powell wanted to make. When Powell eventually took up the offer, Beecham suggested Offenbach's opera, a work dear to the conductor ever since he first brought it to Covent Garden in 1911.[68]

The new film reconvened most of the creative team that had produced *The Red Shoes:* Powell, Pressburger, Beecham, designer Hein Heckroth, Shearer, Tcherina, Helpmann, Massine. A major addition was

Frederick Ashton, who was to choreograph the balletic passages and appear in the film as well. Massine, as in the previous film, created his own roles.[69]

Hoffmann was shot in nine weeks at Shepperton Studios in London. The filming went smoothly, much more so, according to Shearer, than that of *The Red Shoes,* because the dancing passages were designed to run longer and the dancers could become even more engrossed in their performances.[70] Powell combined actors and dancers who lip-synched, singers who sang off-camera, and other singers who appeared on camera, singing and acting their roles. The various casts meshed flawlessly, giving brilliant performances in a visually striking film.

Massine played three roles: Spalanzani in the balletic first act, Schlemil in the dramatic second, and Franz in the operatic third. He brought an original interpretation to all of them, and played each with such conviction that Powell felt fully vindicated in his belief that Massine was a truly gifted actor.[71] Monk Gibbon, in his book on the film, discusses each Massine characterization, beginning with Spalanzani:

> *a light, plausible, perfumed creature, taking an immense pride in his mere showmanship. Though the costume and makeup for the part are a shade bizarre, the face of Massine as Spalanzani, when he is not acting but sitting in his chair near the set, has a strange, graven beauty which might also be Egyptian. . . . He is light as a feather, he might be blown thistledown.*[72]

The role of Schlemil—"the man without a shadow—is in itself the mere shadow of a part," for Gibbon.

> *His face expresses a profound sadness; he is the battered old soldier, the indomitable failure, the man who has had his heart broken in the cruellest fashion. . . . [His face] is a deathly white, and, but for the two huge and immensely wistful and melancholy eyes, it might almost be a skull and not a face. It suggests sorrow and disillusion and despair but it is the stoicism of despair rather than its desperation.*[73]

And in Schlemil's death scene Massine's "body turns slowly on its own axis, the black train winds itself round his legs, the mouth gapes open, the deep-set eyes seem for a moment to attain an unnatural brightness, and the body, run through by his opponent's sword, tilts tragically in an excessively difficult and uncomfortable pose, which he is able to hold

Massine as Spalanzani with Moira Shearer as Olympia in
The Tales of Hoffmann, *1951*

rigidly for a matter of seconds. Finally, just before he drops, the eyes widen into a grim stare and almost make us believe that they are about to slowly glaze."[74]

Powell agreed with Gibbon that Massine's performance of Franz is the film's masterpiece.[75] Gibbon writes:

> *Massine brings a lovely innocence into his characterization of Franz. He makes it unforgettable. It is built up by innumerable small touches. He nibbles his fingertips, he cocks his head on one side, he screws up his mouth and makes his eyes as round as O's; he rubs his hands in his apron to clean them or merely to occupy them. . . . Every expression of Franz's face is inimitable. . . . He is normal with the normality of peasant earth and of a lifetime of normal labour; he is immutable; he is the soil; he is, as Powell put it one day, "something that has been in that spot for 3,000 years, something that might almost have the pointed tips of the horns of a faun. . . ."*[76]

Gibbon regarded Massine's dance segment as Franz as

> *an improvisation in which the dancer seems conscious of the stiffness of his joints but indifferent to it. In it the old man liberates all his repressed aspirations and ambitions. Little by little he reveals an agility surprising in view of his years but which is in entire accord with his temperament. Massine has taken the rather obvious burlesque which Offenbach probably had in mind and turned it into something much more subtle, human and universal.*[77]

The Tales of Hoffmann instantly joined that special group of films that have become unclassifiable, and many historians consider it a masterpiece. Yet it was not a big success. Although it was awarded the Special Jury Prize at the 1951 Cannes Film Festival, Powell believed it could have won the Grand Prix if the final sequence had been deleted (a suggestion, probably made by the producers, that he had rejected).[78]

The ballet press found the film somewhat disconcerting. Though Shearer's dancing was widely praised, the choreography was judged formal, unimaginative, and predictable. According to Fernau Hall: "At no point in the film did Ashton create dance images expressive of the characters and moods of the personages involved, and this made the film as a whole into a bewildering succession of shots with little or no relation to the singing or each other. . . . Massine's superb acting in one of the cen-

Franz in The Tales of Hoffmann, *1951*

tral roles, with his professional assurance and complete grasp of the film medium, showed very clearly what was wrong with Ashton's choreography."[79]

Today Michael Powell is considered among the most important auteurs of English cinema, and *Tales of Hoffmann* is regarded by some as a film that was in many respects ahead of its time. In 1968 Thomas Elsaesser wrote:

Tales of Hoffmann *is no doubt seriously flawed, over-ambitious and uneven. It creates a confusing complexity, in which images of startling force are side by side with a rather too obtrusive, mechanical symbolism. But it is a film which is genuinely disturbing, not least by its uncompromising pessimism. Its importance derives from its partial failure; made in 1951, it foreshadows the decline of the great American cinema, and very accurately feels its way towards the modern "continental" cinema, haunted as the latter is by an often paralyzing self-consciousness about the limits of the cinematic medium. Powell's unresolved formal problems stem directly from his themes, which seem to belong more to the 1960's. The almost prophetic urgency of his themes has, as it were, wrecked the traditional narrative form and, today, one is inclined to view the fragments with singular affection and admiration.*[80]

WHEN FILMING CONCLUDED on the *Tales of Hoffmann,* Massine joined the Sadler's Wells Ballet to start work on *Donald of the Burthens,* which had been in its planning stages for more than two years and was to be his last new work for the English company.

Donald of the Burthens was based on a Scottish legend about a wood-cutter who makes a pact with Death. In return for the gift of healing, he agrees never to pray and to make his fortune only under Death's banner. If Death is seen at the foot of a patient's bed, the patient will live, but if Death appears at the head of the bed, the patient must die. When Donald is asked to heal a dying king, he arrives to find Death already positioned at the head of the bed. To fool Death, Donald instructs the servants to turn the bed around; thus he heals the king and sends Death into a rage. But in celebrating the king's recovery, Donald forgets his vow and teaches a group of children a prayer; the pact is broken, and he is compelled to dance to his death.

The ballet was set to an original score by the Scottish composer Ian Whyte, with scenery and costumes by the Scottish artists Robert MacBryde and Robert Colquhoun. Rehearsals began at Covent Garden in September and lasted until December. The elaborate production required special coaching for the company in Scottish folk dances, such as the sword dance and the reel, which already had been integrated into Massine's choreography. According to Alexander Grant, who danced the role of Donald, the rehearsals, during which certain passages had to be drilled over and over, were taxing; but the company took heart from Massine's creativity and his unflagging energy, especially when he demonstrated movements himself—everyone agreed that no one else danced his choreography with quite his panache.[81] For the ballerina Beryl Grey, who danced the demanding role of Death, working with Massine was "exhilarating" and a revelation. Her biographer Pigeon Crowle wrote:

No detail was too small to be worked on again and again until [Massine] had achieved the desired effect, from corps de ballet upwards, and he was able to dance each movement himself—and so much better than anyone else. [Grey] learned much from watching him dance—he was so swift and light, able to draw with immediate ease a complete and clear picture, with every movement full of meaning and character. He was quiet and of few words, but had a fine sense of humor which was often reflected in his penetrating brown eyes. His rare praise meant a great deal.[82]

Donald of the Burthens marked Massine's return to character ballet aesthetics, as exemplified in *Le Tricorne*. Only Grey's allegorical role of Death remained within the bounds of strict classical technique, and she alone danced on point. Her difficult and intricate choreography was "full of short, sharp, crisp movement,"[83] in contrast to the Scottish folk idiom. The second scene featured a divertissement performed for the monarch, and after Donald's death, the ballet culminated in a characteristic, grandiose Massine finale with the whole cast (minus Donald), led by Death, performing a stylized reel.

At its premiere on December 12, 1951, *Donald of the Burthens* received seventeen curtain calls and, according to *Dance and Dancers*, "the loudest reception accorded to any new ballet since the war."[84] But its success was not lasting; like *Clock Symphony*, it was handicapped by a plot too intricate to unfold with clarity. While the Scottish press heralded *Donald* as a landmark, the more specialized London press was considerably less receptive. *Dancing Times* praised the cast and the folk-inspired dances, especially the opening, a sword dance superbly led

by Brian Shaw and eight men, whose performance is an object lesson in precision. Then comes a delightful Country Dance in which the manipulation of the four Danseuses' skirts stress their lilting movements and patterning. Alexander Grant then has a brilliant solo in which Massine exploits to the full the niceties of capers, high-cuts, turns and shakes, until Grant as Donald the woodcutter seems to be possessed of the very Devil. The finale is tremendously exciting, for Death compels everyone to dance her bidding after she has taken Donald's life, and here Beryl Grey dominates the stage and although this role is confined to eccentric movements, her tremendously forceful personality makes her dance stand out above all.

But the reviewer also had reservations:

Despite Massine's flair for revealing the subtleties and qualities of every kind of folk dance, the real essence of Scottish dance, with its rugged characterization of the Scottish people, has eluded him. He has caught its wonderful patterning, lilting quality, impetuous and neatly complicated footwork, but he has failed to express the strange mystical belief of the Scottish people in the supernatural, their pawky humor, lyricism, and above all their romanticism and love of clear-cut statement.[85]

Clive Barnes in *Dance and Dancers* agreed that "any ballet by Massine could never be less than competent" but nevertheless complained that the two-scene ballet was "poorly constructed," since the first scene, consisting of two episodes, was "hardly more than half the length of the final scene." He also noted that the narrative was obscure and that "by the time the ballet had got going, in the divertissement danced before the resuscitated King leading to the excellent and exciting Highland-fling finale, it is nearly finished." Still, he praised "the floor-patterns, with their ingenious use of obliquely-placed blocks of dancers and the circular finale." He also thought that the best choreography in the ballet had been given to "a group of children. Their 'prayer scene' had a pathos that the rest of the ballet conspicuously lacked, and their 'follow the leader' jumping entry into the finale was a fine piece of choreographic craftsmanship."[86] The critic in *Ballet Annual*, too, singled out the "superb ground patterns." In addition, "the dancers are brought on and off in a way one rarely sees today, and the finale is a masterpiece."[87]

Fernau Hall suggested that the work's fundamental flaw was Massine's inability to realize the incompatibility of the folktale with his expressionistic treatment, which ended with a puzzling "cheerful climax." (But Hall seems not to take into consideration the fact that throughout history subjects have been reinterpreted in the particular style of a period or according to the personal stylistic preferences of an artist. It is not so much a question of the incompatibility of subject and treatment as, rather, of whether or not the work of art is fully realized.) According to Hall, Massine's myopia could be explained by "the fact that to a choreographer of his generation expressionism is not a style of art: it is art itself." He concluded:

In 1919, in the heyday of expressionism, Massine had gaily satirized the moribund Petipa-style of ballets of the nineteenth century in La Boutique Fantasque. *He was now faced with a situation in which his natural style offered no further possibilities of development and had lost its appeal to the public, whereas the Petipa-style ballets popularized by Diaghilev and Pavlova had become more reliable box office attractions than most types of modern ballet. It is therefore easily understandable that he should attempt to ensure the success of* Donald of the Burthens *(his most ambitious production for over a decade) by giving it the shape of a Petipa ballet—even though this shape was completely unsuitable to the theme and represented the most violent possible departure from the aesthetic ideals of his youth.*[88]

Alexander Grant agreed with the *Dancing Times* reviewer, who found the music unsuitable and thought it suffered from a "lack of drama and emotional content."[89] Grant remembered being fascinated by the choreography but also recalled the story as unduly complicated. Ninette de Valois, too, found the choreography "very interesting. . . . There were some lovely passages and Massine, a very thorough person, did tremendous research on Scottish dance."[90] Grant concluded that *Donald of the Burthens* had happened at the wrong time, when dance was moving towards abstraction and neoclassicism, and a folk ballet with "a complicated story seemed to be no longer part of the balletic scene, when all the new contemporary abstract ballets were becoming the rage."[91] Though Massine had made a profound impression with his abstract ballets in the 1930s, Grant noted, he now fiercely championed his character and *demi-caractère* ballets, sensing perhaps that these genres were in danger of extinction.

Alexander Bland wrote in 1981: "There were, in fact, some moving passages, but . . . uncertain translations of folk-dance into ballet bogged the piece down."[92]

IN 1952, during Massine's association with the Maggio Musicale Fiorentino, for which he staged the dances in Cavalli's *Didone* and Rossini's *William Tell* and *Armida* (with Maria Callas in the title role), the festival's director, Francesco Siciliani, introduced the choreographer to *Laudes dramaticae Umbriae,* "a thirteenth-century Italian version of a Latin liturgical play dealing with the life of Christ. I was much moved by the simplicity and sincerity of the dialogue, and began to wonder whether in using it as the basis for a ballet I might not at last accomplish what I had set out to do so many years before in *Liturgie.* Here, surely, was a genuinely primitive treatment of the subject which lent itself admirably to the kind of simplified choreography I had been trying to evolve then with Larionov."[93]

Massine found the adaptation of the *Laudes* the most inspiring project he had undertaken in years. Siciliani offered to have the new ballet produced in the autumn for the Sacra Musicale Umbria, of which he was the artistic director. *Laudes evangelii,* as the work was titled, was to be produced in the fourteenth-century church of Santo Domenico in Perugia. The scenario, based on the life and Passion of Christ, was by Giorgio Signorini; the music, based on *laudes* by Jacopone da Todi and other thirteenth-century composers, was orchestrated and adapted by Valentino Bucchi. The scenery and costumes were by Ezio Rossi.

Working on a "sacred drama" reminded Massine of his first unfinished ballet. "It seemed strange, after so long, to be working on something so similar to *Liturgie*. Everything—text, music, the possibility of production—had fallen into place so easily that it seemed almost as if Diaghilev himself were giving me back my lost opportunity."[94] (Actually, in the summer of 1952, in Galli, Massine made copious notes on the choreography of *Liturgie*.)

Laudes had seven scenes: the Annunciation and the Visitation; the Nativity and the Flight into Egypt; the Entrance into Jerusalem; the Garden of Olives (Gethsemane); the Flagellation and the Via Crucis; the Crucifixion and Deposition; and the Resurrection and the Ascension. The spirit of the work derived from the ancient Umbrian *laudatori*. Massine recounts that in order "to evoke the atmosphere of the pre-Giotto *Laudi* I had based my choreography on the attitudes depicted in Byzantine mosaics, and on the paintings of the primitive Lucca and Pisa school."[95] A painting by Giotto, an artist whom Massine had always found fascinating, was the inspiration for the scene of the kiss of Judas. However, Massine's purpose was not archaeological reconstruction but the creation of a style of dramatic choreography that would require a personal vocabulary of symbolic gesture. The burden of the production in Massine's mind was to transform the spirit of the *laudatori* into a new theatrical language. Giorgio Signorini commented:

> The Laudes, *in fact, is not a miracle play or a sequence of dramatized hymns of praise; nor does it imitate the original Umbrian and Tuscan theatrical productions of the fourteenth century. But while it is no "imitation" as far as faithfulness to those dramatic forms is concerned, it nevertheless aims at a close correspondence with their narrative content, in which "narration" is indeed both chronicle and drama, a vein of pure, profoundly popular, poetry. The intention behind* Laudes Evangelii *was*

to translate a story reconstructed from old manuscripts into a new form of theater; to create a contemporary vision of that language.[96]

Valentino Bucchi added: "Regarding the musical text of this work, we followed, with very few exceptions, the old *Laudi,* remaining faithful, as far as language went, to the original harmonized melody according to the canons of the *ars antiqua.* Having made this musical language our base, however, we felt we could use the utmost freedom in the arrangement of the individual components, the instrumentation and the tonality."[97]

For the performance of *Laudes evangelii* Massine assembled a fifty-member company, with dancers from La Scala and from other troupes he had already employed for the Maggio Musicale. Rehearsals began in the summer in the Villa Romana at the top of a hill above Positano—a special arrangement made to allow Massine to commute daily from Galli. The rehearsal period was strenuous; dancers working with Massine for the first time came face to face with his compulsive work ethic. All needs save those of work had to be set aside. The final rehearsal ran twenty-four hours. Massine himself recalled that by then his "nervous system was so overstrained that in the middle of the night I woke up and found myself on the floor."[98]

A drama-ballet about the life and Passion of Christ did not go unnoticed by Perugian church officials, who doubted the religious integrity of the project. When a photograph of the French ballerina Geneviève Lespagnol (cast as the Virgin Mary) in rehearsal tights and leotard appeared in Roman newspapers, a delegation of priests was dispatched to oversee rehearsals and to certify that appropriate precautions were being taken with sacred matters.

The two-hour *Laudes evangelii* premiered on September 20, 1952, at the church of Santo Domenico. It was a spectacular production. The music employed four soloists, a chorus of ninety-two, and a fifty-five-piece orchestra. The stage was set at the head of the central nave, and a steel-supported ramp running the length of the church accommodated twenty-five hundred spectators. The tri-level stage was built in two sections, one of which floated to allow for the changes of scene. The first three scenes took place at stage level. The next two, the Garden of Olives and the Via Crucis, took place on a double ramp with all of the action going uphill. The final two, the Crucifixion/Deposition and the Resurrection/Ascension, unfolded on the highest level. A gold mosaic backdrop created an arch beneath the seventy-five-foot stained glass rose window, which was lit from the outside. As for the scenery, there was a chapel in the first scene, a grotto in the second, and a palm tree and fountain at the entrance to Jerusalem in the third.

The success of *Laudes evangelii* was tremendous. The Italian press raved, calling Massine a magician. (Despite the ballet's success, a Vatican spokesman would only go so far as to say that church authorities had taken no position on the matter. He did, however, permit himself to wonder aloud whether a church should be turned into a theater.) The work was also hailed by the international press. Arnold Haskell considered it a "masterwork: it is religious in feeling and scholarly in its understanding of liturgy and of the spirit and movement of the period from which it derives. Massine alone could have created it."[99] The work was such a success that for the next decade it toured cathedrals and festivals in Europe, including Nantes and Edinburgh. In 1959 it was presented at La Scala, where a scene called "Massacre of the Innocents" was added. In 1961 it was filmed by Associated Television with the Glyndebourne Festival Chorus; the production featured the younger Tatiana Massine as Mary, the elder Tatiana as Elizabeth, and Lorca Massine as Saint John. It was shown on television throughout England, Holland, Denmark, Canada, and Italy; and on April 8, 1962, it was aired in the United States. Jack Iams of the *New York Herald Tribune* thought it "splendid": "I know of no single word to describe the combination of ballet, mime, background music and voices through which the story was told. Perhaps it could be called a pageant—certainly the production was rich in pageantry, with its splendidly garbed figures moving against equally splendid, and effectively stylized, settings. The choreography by Léonide Massine was breathtaking, and the music, based on old canticles, was solemnly majestic."[100] Jack Gould of the *Times* hailed it as "stunning":

> Through his exquisite design of movement, Massine achieved an uncanny blend of forms; at times the presentation almost seemed to be a succession of religious tableaux coming to life out of a stained window. The delicacy and inventiveness of the choreography, complemented by the soloists and chorus, imparted a mood of sustained awe mixed with the excitement of unfolding creativity.
>
> In the Ascension scene there was a grandeur of pictorial composition and a majesty of dimension rarely seen [on television]. Similarly, the scene of the Crucifixion was unforgettable, a visual tour de force of Christ towering in agony above the boisterous soldiers fighting over his garments.[101]

Until the end of his life Massine would regard *Laudes evangelii* as one of his most important postwar achievements.

IN 1953 MASSINE created no new ballets. During the summer, however, Ballet Theatre included *Aleko* in its repertory for a European tour. The eleven-year-old Chagall-Massine ballet was brilliantly led by Alicia Alonso and Igor Youskevitch and enjoyed a triumphant reception. London and Paris were warm in their praise:

> *The choreography is a masterpiece. The four tableaux are held together by one single emotion that does not pause while drawing the spectator inside. There are no holes; no weaknesses. The action never falters. Although the piece takes place over a long period of time, we are never made to feel it. That is only made possible by the richness of Massine's perpetual choreographic invention, backed up by his enormous experience, which enable him to draw upon a repertory of forms and motions accounting for his constant renewal. . . .*
>
> *His expertise shows in the fast pas de deux full of dramatic élan and never falling into meaningless "expressiveness," which can be of such dire consequences to dance as an art form. As everyone knows, Massine's specialty lies in the arrangement of ensembles seemingly disconnected and free-flowing, as if they had arisen spontaneously yet following a rigorous pattern that obeys the strict logic of the composition. That is . . . a sign of the great masters. The entire choreography provides constant fulfillment.*[102]

The year's creative work was confined to choreographing the Dance of the Hours in *La Gioconda* for La Scala and staging and choreographing *The Snow Maiden* for the Rome Opera. But the year also brought Massine back to films, this time for *Carosello napolitano,* directed by Ettore Giannini.

Carosello napolitano was Giannini's only commercial film as a director. He had enjoyed a distinguished theater career as a writer and director and had produced some of the best Pirandello, Shaw, and O'Neill in Italy. He was also one of the first theater directors to work for the Italian operatic stage. His production of *The Abduction from the Seraglio* with Maria Callas for La Scala was an artistic highpoint of 1952.

Carosello napolitano—a history of Naples through song, dance, and pantomime—had been in Giannini's mind since the late 1940s, but backing for the project had proven difficult to obtain. Giannini explained:

"After the war there was a vogue in Italy for American cinema and neo-realism. Any subject dealing with folk was associated with fascism, and Neapolitan folk especially was at a very low ebb." [103] So in order to raise money for the film, Giannini first produced *Carosello napolitano* as a musical show. It had its premiere in Florence in April 1950, then successfully went on the road in Italy and later in South America.

When preparations at last got under way, Giannini wanted Massine for both his international prestige—essential for the financial backing—and his experience in film. The two men had met the year before at La Scala, where Massine was reviving *Le Tricorne* with the renowned Spanish dancers Antonio and Mariemma. When discussions about the film began, a close rapport developed between them. From the beginning Giannini felt as if they had worked and known each other for many years. He particularly appreciated Massine's economy with words, and they both seemed to have an aptitude for sustained concentration. [104]

The film depicted the history of Naples from medieval invasions through World War II. It was an allegory of the spirit of the Neapolitan people and their capacity for survival as seen through the experiences of a poor family of carnival players. Giannini's intention was to create a portrait of the city through various episodes that cohesively combined dance, song, pantomime, and acting. The spoken drama would fluidly link one passage to the next, allowing story, dance, fantasy, and reality to flow into one another. The episode of Margherita, for example, begins as a straight dramatic scene with spoken words, then develops into dance. Giannini called his approach "*realismo magico*: the method was realist, the reality was magical." [105] He aimed to diversify a cinema that he felt was completely dominated in content and practice by a realism tied to a strong social and political message.

Carosello departed from the traditional musical or ballet film in that it gave the dancers no opportunity to show off at center stage. With few exceptions, dancers in each scene were part of a collective whole, and many of them complained that they were not being given a place commensurate with their star status. According to Giannini, their protest eventually waned thanks to the example set by Massine, whose only concern was for the work and the realization of his artistic vision. [106]

Massine was to stage several pantomime scenes and choreograph four of the five dance episodes: the Pulcinella ballet, danced by himself and Rosella Hightower (the role of Pulcinella was originally conceived for an actor, but Giannini wanted Massine to appear in the film); the music hall cancan; the tale of Margherita (danced by Yvette Chauviré);

and the final tarantella, led by Antonio and Rosiata Segovia. (A stat-uesque, pre-Hollywood Sophia Loren was featured in a nondancing role.)

Giannini began by describing to Massine the action of a scene, which the latter then choreographed or staged. If Giannini approved, the scene was shot. The collaboration was so close-knit that the result was seamless; it was hard to determine where the work of the choreographer ended and that of the director began.

The fifteen weeks of shooting on *Carosello napolitano* took place in Theater 5 (Fellini's favorite) at Cinecittà. However, the ballet's climactic scene, the tarantella, was shot on location in Naples, as Giannini wanted to break the monotony of studio shooting and, above all, to end the film showing the real face of the city.[107]

Appearing in the heyday of neorealist cinema, *Carosello* sparked controversy among Italian critics, who found it difficult to categorize. Yet its international success was absolute. *Le Figaro* called it "something com-pletely new that does not belong to any known genre, a sort of *suite chan-tée et dansée* . . . that never bores, though it is not aided by a story or characters to follow and has as its only theme the streets of Naples."[108] Ernest Borneman in *Ballet Today* felt that it was

> in many ways the most remarkable musical film to be made anywhere the world over. . . . Here is a fascinating, ingenious, provocative film—but a film which is bound to remain almost wholly unintelligible to the vast ma-jority of filmgoers. . . . The idea is simple. . . . But the execution is fantas-tically complex. Since there is no continuity of plot, all continuity is either optical or acoustical. Visual metaphors, sound similes, musical allusions abound. Choreographed movements are used to carry one action through time and space. . . . This is Massine at his best. . . . This isn't dancing, this is an allegory. And it is beautifully done, . . . taking bits from the damnedest places and blending them all with an astounding degree of style.[109]

In 1954 *Carosello,* having been applauded continually throughout the screening, was awarded the Grand Prix at the Cannes Film Festival by a jury presided over by Jean Cocteau. Film historian Gian Piero Brunetta re-evaluated it in 1980: "Of all the Italian musical films made in the 1950's it is the only one that deserves to be compared with the great American musicals, because of its stage inventiveness, its close connection with the national tradition, the richness of its costume designs, and its awareness of the complete possibilities of spectacle. . . ." Yet Giannini's *realismo magico* did not fail to dig beneath the surface of postwar Italy. As Brunetta noted: "Beyond the colors, the dances, and the songs, one perceives throughout the whole film the feeling of a painful path, the telling of a story of hunger and misery never overcome and never vanquished by a journey destined to continue."[110]

While working on *Carosello napolitano* Massine was asked by the Rome Opera Ballet to create a *pièce d'occasion* for guest artist Yvette Chauviré. Very much an *hommage* to Fokine's *Les Sylphides*, *Les Dryades* was an abstract ballet in the neoromantic classical style, with symmetrical ensembles and soloists in the foreground. The score was made up of thirteen Chopin pieces, including preludes, waltzes, one mazurka, one étude, and a fantasie, all orchestrated by Vieri Tosatti. The scenery and costumes were by Dimitri Bonchiere.

The tremendous success of *Laudes evangelii*, which was still being performed around Europe, led the philanthropist Count Vittorio Cini in 1953 to invite Massine to produce another "sacred drama," this one to inaugurate the Teatro Verde on the Venetian island of San Giorgio Maggiore. Until the end of the 1940s the island had belonged to the Italian army; then, under Cini's supervision, it was converted into an impressive international cultural and artistic center that housed schools of navigation and the arts and crafts, as well as the open-air theater. These institutions were named the Giorgio Cini Foundation after the count's son, who had died in a plane crash a few years earlier.

The inaugural program of the Teatro Verde in July 1953 consisted of a revival of Benedetto Marcello's opera *Arianna*, with baroque dances choreographed by Massine, and the "sacred drama" *Resurrezione e vita*, with a scenario by Orazio Costa from Christ's words "Ego sum resurrectio et vita." The score employed music by the sixteenth- and seventeenth-century Venetian composers Monteverdi and Gabrieli, orchestrated and arranged by Virgilio Mortari. The scenery and costumes were by Virgilio Marchi, Valeria Costa, and Veniero Colasanti.

Rehearsals took place throughout the summer at the Teatro Verde. The Massine family stayed at the Villa Korompay on the Lido.

Massine's approach to *Resurrezione e vita* differed from his method on his previous "sacred drama":

> *I soon realized that this spectacle would have to be presented in an entirely different style from that of* Laudes Evangelii, *where the influence of the Umbrian text and music had inspired a portrayal of Christ's Passion in a*

primitive Italian pre-Giotto style. For Resurrezione e Vita . . . *we decided on a broader, more animated approach. It was to be in two parts, with a prologue portraying the Nativity, the Massacre of the Holy Innocents and the Presentation in the Temple. The first part embraced the episodes of the Christ-Child in the Temple, the parable of the Wise and Foolish Virgins, the Woman Taken in Adultery, the Prodigal Son, the Raising of Lazarus and the Temptation in the Wilderness. Part Two included the Entry into Jerusalem, the scene of the Mount of Olives, the Trial of Jesus, the Crucifixion and the Resurrection. The movements and groupings in my choreography were based on the paintings of Titian and Veronese.*[111]

At this time Massine's wife and children began to play an important role in his work—an arrangement that not only would expand with time but would eventually disrupt a family that had always been dominated by one personality. In *Resurrezione e vita,* the elder Tatiana played Mary Magdalene, the younger Tatiana an angel, and Lorca the child Jesus in the temple.

Anticipation ran high in Venice, but the day of the premiere, July 11, did not pass without complications. A fleet of vedettes and gondolas carrying the elegantly attired opening-night audience, which included Greta Garbo, made its way to the island that evening—but so did a tornado. Everyone was forced to take cover in the Palladio cloister, whence they later were rescued by the *vaporetti,* Venice's motorboat buses. The next night the same ritual took place, but this time among the passengers' minks and ermines one could also see raincoats and umbrellas with mother-of-pearl inlaid handles. Garbo arrived under a wide-brimmed, rainproof sailor's hat. As Count Cini addressed the audience with his message of welcome, a storm broke, again driving the guests to the cloister. They waited out the deluge until midnight, soothing their nerves with champagne. On Wednesday the thirteenth, in a third procession of gondolas and vedettes, Garbo and company made their way yet again to San Giorgio Maggiore, where the premiere finally took place.

Resurrezione e vita was an impressive artistic spectacle. The stage was composed of three revolving levels that allowed the life of Christ to emerge into view as if seen through frescoes, the scenes brought to life by Massine's expressive dance vocabulary. The press hailed the work. *Le Monde* wrote: "Let us repeat it again: the success was complete. . . . [Massine] did not try to be intellectual or even mystical. What he wanted was to give a new look, or, better, a new youth, to a centuries-old glory. He bowed low before the Italian Renaissance and in this way he resurrected it in all its luxurious effervescence." The reviewer added: "Among the most successful scenes I shall mention is the majestic arrival of Gasparus, king of the Magi, in front of the crèche, on which the swinging incense lamps converge, and the flagellation, in which Massine had mustered for the seasoned soldiers of Pilate a *variation grotesque* to poignant effect."[112]

Resurrezione e vita completed the sacred triptych Massine began with *Saint Francis* and *Laudes evangelii*.

AFTER FULFILLING HIS COMMITMENT to Count Cini, Massine returned to Galli to rest and prepare himself for his return to the United States. He and Denham had buried the hatchet to the extent of negotiating for a new work for the Ballet Russe de Monte Carlo.[113] Massine suggested a revival of *Laudes evangelii* with new scenery and costumes by Georges Rouault,[114] but although Denham was very interested in the idea (he pursued it until 1955), he came to realize that the demands of the production made it impractical. Instead, he proposed the creation of a new ballet set to Berlioz's *Harold in Italy*.[115] Denham's invitation was not unwelcome; not only was the idea attractive financially, it came at a most opportune time, when the Massines, naturalized American citizens, had to fulfill their obligation to return to the United States every five years to comply with immigration law. At the same time Massine was also interested in organizing a series of talks for Columbia Concerts at which he would lecture and demonstrate his theory of choreography, which he had been working on for some time.[116]

Harold in Italy was set to the four movements of the Berlioz work, which the composer called "Harold in the Mountains," "March of the Pilgrims," "Serenade," and "Orgy of the Brigands." The action revolved around the Italian sojourns of the poet Childe Harold, from Byron's poem. Like the Musician in *Symphonie fantastique*, Harold was a rather static first-person narrator.

When rehearsals started in autumn, Massine must have been delighted to find that Frederic Franklin, one of his favorite dancers during his tenure with the Ballet Russe, was now the company's ballet master. But despite this piece of luck, the rehearsal period was difficult and frustrating, and the work advanced slowly. The scrupulous choreographer would pursue a problem to its limits, then find it difficult to admit that what was clear to him might not be clear to others. Franklin remembers the whole process as "a struggle. . . . After so many years of absence, his choreography had become alien, especially considering that since 1944 the Balanchine era of the Ballet Russe had begun. [Massine] demanded artists who could express, who could act, who could feel stuff to come out of them, but by then dancers were getting away and away from this sort of ballet."[117] Some members of the company found Massine "very manic" and "out of another age."[118]

When *Harold in Italy* was premiered, certain critics dismissed it; Doris Hering in *Dance Magazine*, for example, called it outmoded.[119] But P. W. Manchester felt that despite some weak spots (a "poetic" blowing of leaves and yet another lyrical impression of deer, both stale holdovers from earlier Massine ballets), the "choreography for the ensembles is masterly, with its strongly marked masculine and feminine characteristics. How beautifully, too, he uses the upper part of the dancers' bodies, with a fluid grace that ripples to the fingertips." She especially praised the pas de deux of the happy couple and a country dance for the moutaineers led by shepherds who "discover their love for each other with an awestruck, simple wonderment which Massine transcribes beautifully into a folk dance idiom."[120] And Ann Barzel wrote: "Massine's reaction to the music is entirely emotional and his choreography is concerned with evoking emotion rather than with making formal design."[121] She agreed with Manchester that the final movement was the weakest: "The first three movements are epic in poetry and grandeur and epitomize the Symphonic Ballet at its best. The fourth movement, The Brigands, is a letdown. The episode is confusing and choreographically underdone. If Massine could be recalled to give *Harold in Italy* a worthy concluding movement it might be the summation of his credo on symphonic ballet, a truly monumental work."[122]

Seeing a rehearsal film of *Harold in Italy* thirty years after its creation, Jack Anderson commented on the "impressive ensemble movement. But," he added, "on first viewing, the principal trouble seems to be Harold himself"—a role to which perhaps only Massine himself could have done justice. "Not only does he appear to be the stock Romantic poet, and a rather droopy, soggy one at that; choreographically speaking, he has little to do except make overblown gestures. However, if one adjusts to such attitudinizing, then the presence of Harold becomes not only dramatically, but kinetically interesting. For with his slow, steady, meditative gestures and his periods of immobility, he becomes the ballet's focal point, the weight of his presence serving as a contrast to the ensemble's restlessness."[123]

Denham regarded his renewed collaboration with Massine as a success, and offered to make him the company's permanent artistic consultant, which would require that he "make one or more trips abroad for the purpose of collecting artistic materials for new productions, rehearsing our company, creating new productions for us, etc."[124] But Massine longed to remain in Italy, his spiritual home.

In 1955, however, Massine again crossed the sea, this time to South America as guest choreographer for the ballets of the Teatro Colón in Buenos Aires and the Teatro Municipal in Rio de Janeiro. His affiliation with the Teatro Colón had a tremendous impact on the Argentine ballet world, which considered him the greatest living dance personality. As the prestigious critic Fernando Emery wrote in 1955: "It is true that Europe and America have other creators. Balanchine, Lifar, Robbins, Lander, Christensen. . . . But for those who know and remember, Léonide Massine, through the years . . . still represents the unreachable zenith of classical dance."[125]

Between 1948 and 1955 Massine had revived eight works for the Colón: *Le Tricorne, Capriccio espagnol, Symphonie fantastique, Rouge et noir, Seventh Symphony, Gaîté parisienne, Jeux d'enfants,* and *Choreartium.* Now he was to create his first original production for the company, *Usher,* based on Edgar Allan Poe's *The Fall of the House of Usher.* Its score, by the Argentinean Roberto García Morillo, had been composed for the Colón but never had been used.

Usher was a return to a highly expressionistic neoromanticism reminiscent of *Symphonie fantastique.* However, despite several phantasmagoric scenes, *Usher* centered on three human protagonists: Roderick; his sister, Madeleine; and the Poet, who served as narrator. The group scenes appear and recede as brief visions in the protagonists' hallucinatory drama. Consequently the memorable choreographic qualities of *Usher* were to be found not in the ensemble groups (which in *Symphonie fantastique* were organically linked to the allegorical main characters) but in the long solos and pas de deux of the three principals, who most of the time were alone on stage. The highlights were the lengthy and acrobatic pas de deux: one with Roderick and the Poet (in which Massine anticipated the male pas de deux of the 1960s and 1970s), and two featuring Roderick and Madeleine, which disturbed both audience and critics by their implied incestuous eroticism. According to the critic Dora Kriner:

> *The combination of two techniques, classical and modern, provokes unexpected tension. Technically the use of elongation, that is to say beginning a choreographic combination with the torso excessively bent instead of*

straight and then developing the body into a classical figure . . . demands a calculated effort different from the customary. This play of imbalance that must be performed in an abrupt way creates in the space an angular and severe design that surprises us and which can produce various states of anguish.[126]

The technical as well as the expressive and interpretive demands of the roles were tremendous and were brilliantly met by José Neglia (as Roderick), Jorge Tomin, and Maria Ruanova. (When the Teatro Colón Ballet presented the work in Paris in 1960, Neglia was awarded a special prize from the city for his interpretation.) After the premiere, Fernando Emery wrote:

In his untiring search for new possibilities, Massine gives us moments of great pathetic intensity: Roderick's first three poses as he lies on his bed, his body tensed up like a bow that is being violently stretched; the convulsive, epilepticlike gait of the servant who opens the doors of the castle to him; the flowing duet of the two friends, in which the two premiers danseurs perform real acrobatic feats with a show of outlandish gestures; Roderick's and Madeleine's pas de deux; . . . the great frightening epileptic scene, so reminiscent of the sacred trembling of the Chosen Maiden in The Rite of Spring; *and the last grand scene in* Usher—*all of these combine to make out of Massine's new choreography a very vivid, tremendously dramatic and suggestive ballet. . . .*

Among the possible objections which one could bring up are the excessive complexity of the choreography and that the pantomime gestures do not always seem accessible to the public's understanding.[127]

For most dancers who performed the ballet, the pas de deux and the solos were bona fide choreographic challenges.[128]

FROM BUENOS AIRES MASSINE went to Rio de Janeiro, where he revived six old works (*Boutique, Tricorne, Gaîté, Présages, Capriccio espagnol,* and *Beau Danube*) with an impressive roster of guest stars (Franklin, Chauviré, Eglevsky, Maria Tallchief, Lupe Serrano, Michael Lland) and created a rather uninspiring *Hymn à la Beauté,* "based on a poem by Baudelaire, with a score by the Brazilian composer Francisco Mignone, and scenery by Georges Wakhevitch. The spirit of Baudelaire's beautiful poem evoked a stream of dramatic images, which took the form of scenes portraying Faith, Murder, and First Love. Each episode was chore-ographed within the context of the poem."[129]

ALTHOUGH IN THE SECOND HALF of the 1950s Massine contin-ued to revive earlier ballets, requests for original works declined signifi-cantly. More and more companies were launching, or associating themselves with, their own choreographers, and the generation of new talent that had begun to emerge in the 1950s was impressive. Other trends were also becoming apparent. The taste of the public was moving away from Massine's stylized, overly detailed, and distinctly personal story ballets and toward neoclassicism. Moreover, an elaborate Massine production could be mounted only by major opera houses, many of which were experiencing fiscal difficulties. And not only was Massine himself an expensive acquisition, so were his chosen collaborators—a matter in which he expected carte blanche. Most insidiously of all, Massine's unsuccessful works had begun to create for him a dubious rep-utation. In his advancing years he was looked upon as an artist who stood for an outdated aesthetic. His name might still bring prestige to a ballet company, but the demand was more and more fulfilled by revivals; in undertaking these, a troupe could offer its audience not only the great Massine—a legend who was still performing—but also the mas-terly accomplishments of such artists as Picasso, Derain, Stravinsky, and Falla.

The last four years of the 1950s saw only two new Massine produc-tions, *Mario e il mago* and *Don Juan. Mario,* which was premiered at La Scala on February 25, 1956, brought Massine together with the Italian the-ater and film director Luchino Visconti. The gestation of the ballet dates back to 1951, when Visconti met Thomas Mann, one of his idols, at the home of the writer Alba de Céspedes. Visconti already had the idea of adapting Mann's novella *Mario and the Magician*—whose theme was the psychology of fascism and the failure of willpower—into a two-act opera-ballet. He discussed his concept with Mann, who welcomed the idea; and upon Mann's agreement that the project was properly de-scribed as a "choreographical action," a contract was signed on August 27, 1951.[130]

The music for the new work was commissioned from Franco Man-nino, Visconti's brother-in-law, the scenery and costumes from Lila de Nobili, and the choreography from Massine.

Mario e il mago had first been scheduled to premiere at La Scala in

1954 but was canceled due to Visconti's wish to crowd the stage with bicycles in one scene. In a recent production of the opera *La città in campagna,* the La Scala audience had booed the appearance of a car on stage,[131] and the management felt it prudent to postpone the production until Visconti agreed to reduce the number of bicycles.

Mario e il mago was a hybrid of dance, mime, song, and pure dramatic speech, a grandiose spectacle that from the moment it began took the audience's breath away. As the curtain went up on the first scene, a railroad gate came down; soon a train passed through, emerging from the right wing, and Mario, played by the French dancer Jean Babilée, rushed to the gate looking for a girl. Placing one leg over the gate, he suddenly flew off on it and disappeared through the sky, only to reappear moments later, flying on a bicycle, which eventually landed on stage.

Babilée, one of the most fascinating male dancers of the postwar era, had met Massine briefly in London in 1949 when both artists participated in a gala in honor of Nijinsky. Babilée had been surprised back then to learn that Massine, who he thought had retired long before, was still dancing. Watching him perform the Miller's dance from *Le Tricorne,* Babilée was overwhelmed; Massine was "magical, especially his sense and control of the stage whether he was moving or still."[132] When he was asked in 1954 to create the role of Mario, Babilée eagerly accepted the invitation to collaborate with "this legendary master,"[133] and when work began at La Scala he was constantly astonished: "Massine was prodigious," he recalled. "Very intelligent, and every movement he created was not only interesting but new, unusual. Gestures were at times stylized, unnatural, and there was always this quality of surprise in what he did, because nothing was evident or obvious. This of course made the choreography very difficult, because one had to really understand the movement process."[134]

Babilée found Massine's originality and richness of gesture and movement a wonder: "In *Mario e il mago* there was a sort of world tour— India, China, etc.—and the movements that Massine created for these pastiche dances were fascinating, as if he had been able to extract the essence to produce his own personal evocation that was poetic, magical, and at times mysterious. It was like a modern *Thousand and One Nights.* He was extremely clever with gesture. Even the choreography that utilized simple daily gestures had a very strong theatrical value, and could, when needed, sustain an emotional and symbolic content."[135] Discussing the choreography of *Mario e il mago* more than thirty years after its creation, Babilée still remembered it as something "extremely personal, beautiful, and unique—something that today would be striking and contemporary. Beauty and true art are never dated." [136]

Babilée found working with Massine deeply inspiring, and even, at moments, charmingly impromptu. At age sixty-one Massine "showed everything himself, and that had an incredible force. Although he always seemed very distant, and he valued the quality of silence while working, he also developed a special working rapport. Once he showed this variation which was extremely difficult technically and interpretation-wise, for it depicted all the essence of Mario's character. I was astounded. I worked very hard to master it, and when I finally did assimilate and understand it, I could see that it gave him as great a pleasure as it did me. Once during a rehearsal of his *Pulcinella,* which was staged for La Scala after Mario, I was dancing Massine's original role, and he made me repeat various times the same difficult variation. When I ended I was so exhausted and pale that I thought I was going to faint. He looked at me and like a robot gave me a shot of whiskey from a flask which he had in his pocket." [137]

Babilée, enthralled, felt that he and Massine had developed a solid working relationship. But their communication stopped there. "He was a solitary character. He was always in complete control, did not show emotions, and never wasted a minute on anything superfluous to work.

"Once, after we had already worked in *Mario,* I was on the La Scala stage rehearsing one of my ballets when I saw Massine enter with his black suitcase. I stepped out of the rehearsal to greet him and he explained that he was on his way to Paris from Rome, but had a few hours in Milan before catching the train. He wanted to work! I gave him the keys to my dressing room. He changed into his practice clothes and came to a corner of the stage to do his barre. While he was doing his demi-pliés and battements he was completely immersed in reading a book. When he finished, everyone on stage applauded. He simply left." [138]

Lila de Nobili, the designer of *Mario,* admired Massine's "exceptional capacity for work, his incredible concentration on his choreography, his complete control of the company—something that gave me the impression that I was having a chance to experience to a small degree the working spirit of Diaghilev's Ballets Russes." [139]

The working relationship between Visconti and Massine seemed to be based on mutual artistic respect. The *Mario* concept was in many ways similar to that of *Carosello napolitano* in its eclectic mixture of pure theater, rhythmic pantomime, song, cinematic technique, and choreography, all set to music except for the spoken dialogue of Cipolla, the Magician, played by the renowned actor Salvo Randone. (Babilée, as Mario, spoke only one word: "Sylvia.") The scenes without spoken dialogue or dance, set at the café or the beach, were completely cinematographic, filled with Visconti's beautiful, evocative, and languid images as well as the eloquent rhythm characteristic of his later films, particularly *Death in Venice.*

The collaboration between Visconti and Massine went very smoothly. According to Babilée, they discussed the concept of the scenes that Massine was to arrange, but Visconti never became involved with the dances in any way. Visconti's aesthetic, a sort of supra-realism, blended well with Massine's idiosyncratic movements to produce a stylized, multilevel story in which symbolism played a major role. For Lila de Nobili, achieving harmony in Visconti's realist mise-en-scène was not easy, but observing Massine and Visconti work together was "the privilege of witnessing the encounter of two heavenly stars."[140] The charismatic Babilée gave a performance that "was remarkable for its psychological penetration, telling mime and outstanding vigorous dancing."[141] The production won La Scala's coveted Diaghilev Prize.

Before Massine rejoined La Scala in 1959, he was approached by Michael Powell to collaborate with him on an English-Spanish co-production, *Luna de miel (Honeymoon).* The film, which was shot entirely in Spain, revolved around a ballerina's honeymoon journey through the Iberian Peninsula, with the leading roles taken by Ludmilla Tcherina and Antonio. Besides various vignettes featuring Spanish folk dancing, the film included two main dance numbers: Falla's *El amor brujo,* with choreography by Antonio, in which Massine appeared in his own creation of the role of the Spectre, and *Los amantes de Teruel,* led by Tcherina and Antonio as the tragic lovers, with choreography by Massine to the music of Mikis Theodorakis. (In this ballet most of the crowd scenes were staged by Powell; Massine was responsible mainly for the solos and pas de deux.) At the 1959 Cannes Film Festival the film was awarded the Special Prize of the Commission Supérieure Technique. Yet despite excellent performances (which aficionados still enjoy), the film has never been regarded by dance or film critics as more than a colorful travelogue.

In early 1959 Massine was once more associated with La Scala, where he staged *Laudes evangelii* and the dances for Glinka's *A Life for the Tsar* and also produced a new ballet, *Don Juan.*

Gluck's original score of *Don Juan* was first choreographed by Gasparo Angiolini, a master of eighteenth-century *ballet d'action,* in Vienna in 1761. While Angiolini's scenario derived from both Molière and a version of the story by Tirso de Molina, Massine's adaptation had primarily Molière as its literary source. Massine writes:

> *I wanted to present Don Juan not simply as a romantic adventurer, but as a man in conflict with himself. In the ballroom scene I had the advantage of working to some of Gluck's finest music. After the guests had left I made Don Juan and Doña Elvira linger together in the deserted ballroom. The ghost of Doña Elvira's father had already appeared to Don Juan, and the lovers were intensely aware of the hopelessness of their situation. At this point I created a pas de deux which expressed both Doña Elvira's sadness and the insoluble conflicts within Don Juan's character. In the final scene, where Don Juan is driven to desperation by the tormenting furies and demons, the ghost of Doña Elvira appeared, holding a skull, and danced round him as he lay distraught on the ground. For this dance I used the haunting strains of the Siciliana, played on the oboe, with which Don Juan had serenaded her in the opening scene. This heightened the pathos of Don Juan's final condemnation and made a dramatic and ironic conclusion to the ballet. It was a complex work to choreograph.*[142]

The favorable reception of *Don Juan* by the press testifies that though Massine's work of the 1950s was at times inconclusive and uneven, he could still produce ballets of arresting quality. Although Robert Laurence, writing in the *Saturday Review* of May 16, 1959, found the final scene relatively weak,* he thought the ballet in general

> *a triumph of theatrical invention, extraordinarily vivid, dramatically, and cohesive architecturally. . . . [Massine's] wonderful treatment of the central character, both in motion and repose, is quite the equal—in another sphere—of da Ponte's, or perhaps even superior. This Don Juan of Massine is no mere philanderer, gripped by a last-minute terror, but a poetic spirit constantly at war with himself. . . . The pathos of [Doña Elvira], the tragic conflict in the soul of Don Juan, have been here projected incandescently by Massine in a pas de deux which is the legitimate, tragic heir of the brilliant grand duo in Gaîté. I had thought this kind of enkindling*

---

* By now the last scenes in Massine's ballets had become generally the weakest. During his later years he became so extremely meticulous and detailed in his choreography that by the time rehearsals for a ballet reached its last scene, the dancers were exhausted, the time schedule was very limited, and the rehearsals became a literal tour de force.

emotion lost forever to theatrical dance; but there it is, burning up the stage and the audience unashamed, elemental, imaginative in the highest. . . . Massine the creator, like the Phoenix, has risen from his own ashes.[143]

Don Juan was Massine's first ballet with La Scala's rising star Carla Fracci, the Doña Elvira. They would work together in three more productions the following year, the first of which, the one-act *Fantasmi al Grand Hotel,* premiered at La Scala on February 11, 1960, with Fracci and Mario Pistoni in the leading roles. The scenario, by Dino Buzzati (who also designed the costumes and scenery), was the story of a country girl who arrives in the big city in search of fortune and is trapped instead by a group of gangsters headquartered in the hotel. She is accused of the murder of a gang leader but is saved from death by a mysterious man. At the end they both escape as the hotel collapses.

Although *Fantasmi al Grand Hotel* was an important production, Massine's time and energy were by then being taken up by the planning and organization of his most ambitious undertaking in many years. In 1959 he had been approached by the industrialist Ariodante Borelli to act as artistic director of the Fifth International Festival of Ballet at Nervi in Genoa the following year. Previously, the festival had been composed of international guest companies, but this year Massine was asked to put together a ballet company from scratch, with a guarantee of complete artistic control over roster and repertory. With substantial financial backing from the festival, the municipality of Genoa, and various industrialists, including Borelli himself, Massine was to embark on his last truly spectacular project.

At a press conference held at Maxim's in Paris, Massine declared that the Nervi Festival was nothing less than a "resurrection of the Diaghilev era."[144] Certainly it represented his own attempt to return to the Diaghilev aesthetic of total theater—of ballet as a fusion of all the arts, of literature, music, and painting—and to reproduce the creative momentum of the artistic teamwork that the impresario had fostered. Massine believed himself to be the last bastion of a form of theater he feared was on the brink of extinction, and Nervi was to be a reiteration of his own aesthetic.

The festival repertory included a revival of Fokine's *Schéhérazade*; two ballets by young choreographers (Maurice Béjart's *Alta tensione* and Jack Carter's *Señor de Manara*); and five Massine works: three new productions—*La commedia umana, Bal des voleurs,* and *Il barbiere di Siviglia*—and revivals of *Choreartium* and *Le Beau Danube.* The variety of the

Massine repertory testifies to his eclecticism, a survey of the broad range of genres he had explored throughout his career. Of primary importance was *Choreartium,* his earliest example of purely abstract choreography. However, it would be a mistake to regard Nervi as an act of nostalgia, for at its heart nostalgia is an attempt to recapture a fantasy, a feeling or event that never took place. Massine acknowledged the past but never ceased to keep the future firmly in his sights.

Rehearsals began in April. The fifty-five-member company assembled in Nervi was the cream of a new generation of talented dancers from all over Europe: Carla Fracci, Ethery Pagava, Duska Sifnios, Yvonne Meyer, Tessa Beaumont, Milorad Miskovitch, Paolo Bortoluzzi, Vasili Sulich. The roster also included Lorca and Tatiana Massine and five ballet masters: Leon Woizikowski, Tatiana Leskova, René Bon, Harry Haythorne, and Massine's wife. *Ballet Annual* in London dubbed the new company the "Italian Renaissance."[145]

Nervi instantly became an international art center reminiscent of Monte Carlo in the days of the Ballets Russes. The list of personalities arriving in Genoa was impressive: Georges and Nora Auric, Alfred Manessier, Jean Anouilh, the theatrical designer Jean-Denis Malclès, the *costumière* Barbara Karinska, and the French critic Irène Lidova were among them. The designer André Beaurepaire, who previously had collaborated with Bérard, Kochno, Cocteau, Petit, and Ashton, had never experienced "such a collaboration of artists, enthusiasm, collective energy and extravagance in spending in such elaborate productions and lavish designs."[146]

Massine's work reached new levels of compulsion. According to Vladimir Augenblick, his personal assistant, the choreographer worked obsessively and kept everyone else going at his pace. He drove himself to an almost frenetic degree and expected the same level of commitment from the others. He would arise at 5:00 a.m. to prepare his work; company classes began at 8:45, and rehearsals went on until midnight. When exhaustion overcame him during the long sessions, he would take a short nap in the studio, on a cot behind a screen. Augenblick saw him imposing his "iron willpower" on everyone. "Once, with a 40-degree [centigrade] fever he did his customary barre and then called his technical assistant, Carlo Faraboni, to give him instructions about the ballets."[147]

If the dancers could hardly believe how hard they were being driven, they were even more astonished by Massine's own Promethean determination. Sulich felt that for any choreographer the creation of one major work such as *La commedia umana* was sufficient for a season; but

Massine was not only producing *three* new works, he was responsible for the entire enterprise. He displayed incredible physical energy for a man in his mid-sixties. Sulich remembers that Massine once performed the Hussar's waltz in *Le Beau Danube* with full force to show Miskovitch how it should be danced. The dancers looking on were duly impressed but a little anxious, fearing that he might not make it through the demonstration.[148]

Although he was extremely patient with the dancers, Massine remained aloof. He was becoming even more distant, disconnected from those around him, more impenetrable and isolated. Lorca summed up his experience working with his father as "sweat and steps—little human contact."[149] Lidova, too, observed how detached and hermetic he was, and his almost inhuman disregard for the needs and limits of others. She was astounded by his habit of working eighteen hours a day.[150]

Nevertheless, the Massine mystique was unquestionably in full force. Beaurepaire saw him as almost mythical, an artist whose "attitude about work, his complete immersion in himself, and his aura of inaccessibility enhanced the dimension of a legendary personality." Moreover, he sensed that Massine was conscious of the effect that he had on others. Obsessive and distant as he found Massine, collaborating with him was a fascinating lesson in theater art. "Especially one was in awe of his culture," said Beaurepaire, "of his knowledge about painting and art and history."[151]

The first ballet premiered at Nervi was *La commedia umana,* the idea for which dated back to 1954, when Massine had planned to collaborate with the writer Curcio Malaporte on a new ballet for the Maggio Musicale Fiorentino. That project did not materialize; but when preparations for Nervi began in 1959, Massine, through the good offices of Francesco Siciliani, asked the Italian scholar and Boccaccio specialist Vittore Branca to assist him in adapting eight episodes from the *Decameron* for a ballet scenario.

La commedia umana was intended to be the festival's magnum opus and the most monumental undertaking of Massine's career. It would run more than two hours and boast forty-seven solo roles plus corps de ballet. Inspired by Massine's beloved Quattrocento, it was to be a study/dance fresco depicting the universal human condition and celebrating the choreographer's bond with Italy's humanist tradition.

Massine's interpretation of the *Decameron* followed Boccaccio's idea that, as Branca explains in the program notes, the lives of men are governed by forces of Fortune, Love, and Ingenuity, and that the power of

Virtue—the force that will guide man towards self-realization—is greater than all three together. The ballet incorporated eight episodes in three acts, with a prologue and an epilogue. Act One, "The Triumph of Fortune," included the tales of Andreuccio and Ginevra. Act Two, "The Triumph of Love," featured the tales of Guardistagno and Nastagio. Act Three, "The Triumph of Ingenuity," told the stories of Peronella, Elena, and Calandrino. In the epilogue, "The Triumph of Virtue," the tale of Griselda preceded the ballet's finale.

To adapt such detailed narratives for dance was a daunting task. Massine made use of many of his choreographic techniques and styles—angularity, a contrast between flowing and staccato movements, ensemble counterpoint. He described the range of his choreography: from "varied and vigorous ensemble movements like those in the prologue to the tragic and comic dances of the second and third parts and the light, gay ensembles of the third and fourth."[152] *La commedia umana* was a study in form, language, and style. It was an indulgence in choreographic detail, a reaffirmation of his choreographic "baroquism." At a time in dance history when the choreographic line had been simplified and ballets had a more melodic physical allure and an easy sensuality, appreciating Massine's overwhelmingly rich choreography required a vigilant and attentive eye as well as the sustained collaboration of the viewer.

Owing in part to its longueurs and to its uneven quality, the work had a perplexing and disconcerting impact. According to Lidova, it possessed novel and brilliant moments but was too long, too scholarly an adaptation, and needed to be cut.[153] Sulich felt that the story was too detailed and complicated and the choreography too intricate, despite the fact that it was the work of an experienced craftsman; with the exception of some beautiful passages, such as Fracci and Adolfo Andrade's pas de deux, it lacked inspiration.[154] The reviewer for *Le Figaro* said of *Commedia*:

> *A grandiose medieval fresco takes place in a frame of greenery, a spectacle composed of dancing, sound, and lighting, of a vastness never before equaled. . . .*
>
> *The principal fault of the choreography is, without doubt, a relative disproportion among the various episodes; but Massine, besides possessing an innate theatrical sense, a very sure taste, knows how to direct the ensembles, how to juxtapose the feminine qualities to the virile dances, and to evoke, without the slightest trace of vulgarity, the farce or the cruel games of love set to fourteenth-century music.*[155]

A more negative review came from Clive Barnes (who saw the company later on, in Edinburgh, where, he felt that, in addition to the work's inherent problems, the dancers were underrehearsed):

> *In his vintage years Massine, in such a work as* The Three-Cornered Hat, *based on an Alarcón fable, showed an almost unbelievable ability to make a complicated story clear in ballet terms. But what he could do once, it appears he can now do no more, and certainly his* Commedia Umana *was quite incomprehensible without constant reference to the printed scenario. . . .*
>
> *The choreography . . . had a sort of competence in that it at least never quite petered out, yet it was so full of padding, so loaded down with triviality, so lacking in any real inspiration or originality that the total effect was crushingly dispiriting. In fairness there were a few patches of quality among some of the solos and pas de deux. . . .*
>
> *The one real quality of the ballet was in its suggestion of a genuinely medieval atmosphere, and this Massine sustained moderately well throughout the evening. In this he was helped by the music, which while in itself monotonous and unsuitable for choreographic purposes, had been based on authentic medieval airs. He was also assisted by the curiously stylized settings and costumes of Alfred Manessier. These designs—and there were dozens of sets and well over two hundred costumes—succeeded in conveying an appropriate sense of period while being in themselves quite modern.*[156]

In a later evaluation of *La commedia umana,* Alfio Agostini wrote: "Massine's choreography was now as far removed from the brilliant historical and folk characterizations of his youthful works as from the severe classicism of his symphonic ballets or the dense gestural symbolism of his mystical creations. In this late work it achieved a perfect balance between dance and mime, classical style and modern influences, choreographic substance and narrative clarity."[157]

Massine's second new production for the Nervi Festival was a one-act ballet based on Jean Anouilh's *Bal des voleurs,* a comedy with musical interludes that had first been produced in 1938, with decor and mise-en-scène by André Barsacq and incidental music by Darius Milhaud. The new production had music by Massine's old friend Georges Auric, and the scenery and costumes were by Jean-Denis Malclès, who had been proposed for the assignment by Anouilh. In his autobiography, Massine described the gestation of the ballet:

I was also anxious to include in my programme something French, original and contemporary, so I asked my daughter, who was well read in modern French literature, to find something suitable for me. When she suggested Anouilh's Bal des Voleurs *I read it at once, and was delighted by the iridescent wit of the dialogue and the delightfully satiric and amusing characters, immediately feeling that the play would offer me the right ingredients for a lighthearted but highly polished ballet. I wrote to Anouilh, who invited me to visit him in his charming apartment situated in one of the old squares of Paris. He was not at all what I expected. A slight, bespectacled man, his manner was precise and businesslike, quite unlike his light, witty plays. He was pleased to hear that I wanted to make* Bal des Voleurs *into a ballet; in fact, he told me, he had originally conceived it as a comédie-ballet. But he wanted to be sure that his characterizations would not be lost in adaptation, so we went carefully through the text together, discussing each character scene by scene. Many months later, when most of the programme for Nervi was already taking shape, there were still a number of questions in my mind about* Bal des Voleurs, *so I went to see Anouilh at Lausanne, where he was staying at the time, and we had another long talk. He made it clear that the choreography must emphasize the basic situation of the rich Englishwoman so bored by her idle life that she invites into her home three obvious thieves.*[158]

Although an elaborate production, *Bal des voleurs* was an ephemeral ballet, although it was revived by the Royal Ballet in 1963 when Carla Fracci (who created the role of the Englishwoman) made her company debut as a guest artist.

The third new Massine work presented at the festival was *Il barbiere di Siviglia*, the choreographer's homage to Rossini. Following the concept of Diaghilev's 1914 staging of Rimsky-Korsakov's *Le Coq d'or*, *Il barbiere* was danced on stage while the singers sang in the orchestra pit. Besides admiring Rossini's music and especially *Il barbiere*, Massine also wanted to produce this work because he

always felt that in the operatic version much of Beaumarchais's wit and humor evaporated because of the physical demands of the singing. In many scenes where the text obviously demanded movement, the singers had to stand perfectly still while rendering their arias. In our production the opera was sung from the orchestra pit, which meant that I was free to create movements and gestures which fully exploited the comic situations inherent in the dialogue. It was, however, an unusually heavy task for me

. . . since the method chosen for the production called for continual dancing and no pantomime.[159]

According to Beaurepaire, the opera's designer, Massine's concept was "that of a *fête du théâtre* as a sort of apotheosis of the opera buffa."[160] *Il barbiere* was a sumptuous production styled after the eighteenth century; one costume was more elaborate than the next. (All of them were executed by Lydia Douboujinsky, who, as she had done for *La commedia umana*, supervised most of the shopping for fabrics in France, England, Switzerland, and Italy.) The production was a luxurious theatrical pageant.

Once the festival ended, the Ballets Européens de Nervi, as the company was called, appeared at the Edinburgh Festival, where they presented *Schéhérazade*, *Le Beau Danube*, *La commedia umana*, and *Choreartium*. Even though there were other attempts to book the company, it soon disbanded.

According to Lidova, the whole enterprise was "an extravaganza that was proof that Massine had lost touch with reality and had lost his ability to organize and manage a company's finances. The working schedules were exhausting and draining, and he showed no regard for the expenditures. Besides a large company, there was a full orchestra and chorus from the Genoa opera; some of the leading singers came from La Scala, and there were three conductors. He brought designers and composers to Nervi, and even Madame Karinska had settled there for three months, where she opened an atelier especially to execute the costumes for some of the works. The productions were outrageously lavish and cost a fortune. After the festival ended it went into bankruptcy, and the following year there was no festival. Massine's ideas were so impractical that he hoped to keep it as a company without realizing that most dancers were under contract to other companies, such as La Scala, and had been on leave just for the summer. The scale of the productions and the expenses of the enterprise made it prohibitive for any producer to undertake the project."[161]

Nervi was Massine's last adventure as a choreographer and artistic director of any company. The mixed critical reception of the works presented at Nervi dealt the final blow to his already faded reputation. Clive Barnes wrote:

Unquestionably the slump in Massine's reputation from its pre-war pinnacle has been among the truly remarkable aspects of post-war ballet. Once, and only a few years ago at that, regarded as the world's leading choreographer, Massine has now slid so far down the slippery pole of fashion that to the young generation of balletgoers he is rapidly becoming little more than a name. A few of his ballets are still regularly performed in the repertoires of the world, yet I cannot help feeling that his fame is slowly diminishing into that of an historically important, but nevertheless comparatively minor figure. Such an assessment I feel does Massine a grave injustice. Although he occasionally was overestimated in his heyday, fashionable ballet opinion today tends to neglect him.

Looking at Commedia Umana *and also recalling Massine's other creations over the past twenty years or so, I cannot but regretfully record my opinion that creatively his powers have now dwindled away to little more than competence.*[162]

Thus, the grandiosity of Nervi inspired a chorus of fatal whispers that Massine had become hopelessly extravagant and self-indulgent, out of touch and perhaps permanently off his stride. After the festival he began to withdraw from the ballet world into self-imposed seclusion.

PART SEVEN

The Late Years

I want to make things as hard *for myself
as they have been for anybody: only under
this pressure do I have a* clear enough
conscience *to possess something few
men have ever had—wings, so to speak.*

—NIETZSCHE

Massine in rehearsal during the 1960s

CHAPTER 14

Moscow, June 1961–Borken, West Germany, March 1979

FOR MASSINE the following year, 1961, was one of homecoming and touching roots. Asked by the Soviet Export Film Company to produce a number of his ballets in the Soviet Union for distribution to American television, he returned to Russia, in June, after an absence of forty-seven years. Massine traveled by train with Lorca—he avoided planes whenever possible—while his wife flew ahead to Moscow. (Tatiana remained in France.)[1]

The sight of Moscow filled Massine with long-buried passions, sensations, and memories. The Massines stayed at the Metropole Hotel, the very place the eighteen-year-old dancer had first met Diaghilev in 1913. But its splendor was no more. "Its nineteenth-century grandeur had faded; the carpets were threadbare, the walls flaking, the porters had discarded their gold braid, the lobby was no longer thronged with princes and grand dukes but with American businessmen carrying briefcases, European diplomats, young Russian technocrats, and other workers obviously content with the present conditions of life."[2] Yet at first it seemed that the city of his youth had not changed as much as he had expected:

> As I looked at the towers and walls of the Kremlin, the vast Red Square, and the gay onion domes of St. Basil's Cathedral, it was as if my childhood and youth were unrolling before my eyes like a film. When we passed the Theatre School I recognized the massive door through which I had been taken, nearly half a century before, for my first physical examination by Dr. Kazansky. A flood of memories came back to me: my first appearances in ballet, the Gogol and Ostrovsky plays, my painting classes with Anatoli Petrovich Bolchakov. . . .
>
> I remembered that afternoon in 1914, and my uncertainty and confusion before making the great decision to leave Russia. I felt it was indeed written in my stars that I should meet Diaghilev. Destiny had played a big part in the pattern of my life. I thought of some of the curious circumstances that had affected the course of my career. If Nijinsky had not broken away from Diaghilev's company, if he had danced the role intended for him in La Légende de Joseph, then Diaghilev would not have come in search of a new young dancer to create this part. If I had remained in Moscow I would perhaps have become a competent actor at the Maly instead of a choreographer. I might even have been killed in the Revolution. Then, for no reason, I found myself thinking of Galli, of my first view of it in 1917, of my decision to buy it. It seemed to me that it had always been more than just a place of refuge; it represented something in my life which I had yet to discover.[3]

The first obligatory visit was to the Theater School, where arrangements had been made for Massine to practice each day in a rehearsal room that once had served as the school's dining room. Massine found it "strange to walk through my old school and find it so unchanged. I went from room to room, remembering the games we played and my classmates calling me 'the gypsy,' my first teacher, Domachov, in his crumpled dinner jacket, instructing us in the first five positions, and our visits to the Bolshoi for rehearsals."[4]

Of course the most emotional event of his Russian sojourn was the family reunion at Zvenigorod-Moskovsky. His brother Mikhail, now retired, had moved with his wife, Sophie, back into the old family dacha about forty miles from Moscow. Massine's sister, Raissa, now a widow living in southern Russia, had returned to the dacha to embrace her celebrated brother once again, and Mikhail and Sophie's two grown daughters, Helena and Eugenia, were there with their husbands and children. Massine's childhood took hold of him again and offered him a welcome solace.

> From the garden I could still see the lovely monastery of St. Saavo across the river, its lime-washed walls and cupola looking just as I remembered them; I was sad to hear that the bell tower had long been silent, the silver and brass bells having been melted down for ammunition in the last war. Also a row of suburban houses had been built in the village, ruining the atmosphere of our wooded hilltop. But our house remained unchanged, and everything was as I had left it: the dark red walls, the green roof, the little square sitting room with its comfortable chairs and its birchwood cupboard. I was thrilled to see the brass samovar on the table and the old-fashioned sink with its pump handle where as a child I had so often washed my hands and face. . . .
>
> After a quiet hour in the garden, I walked in the cool of the evening to put flowers on the graves of my parents* and of my brother Konstantin. I could hardly find their tombstones, the graveyard was so overgrown with long grass and weeds.[5]

Reunited for the first time in nearly half a century, the family indulged in unrestrained Slavic expansiveness. Over the years, and despite the distances, Massine had preserved his emotional ties to his kin. He had confided in them when he was in distress, especially in his youth, and during his years in the West he had helped them materially whenever possible. So the bonds were solid. But forty-seven years of separation had inevitably planted doubts in their minds as well, and Mrs. Massine noted with tenderness how very eager he was to be accepted by them again.[6]

Upon his return to Moscow, Massine was invited to sit in on classes at the Theater School. He also visited the Stanislavsky Museum as well as the Theater Museum, escorted by its founder's son, Yuri Bakhrushin.

> The framed pictures of actors at the Maly in Ostrovsky's and Gogol's plays brought back memories of playing juvenile roles with Rybakov, Sadovsky and Padarin, and I realized what a great influence these men had had on my career. From them I had learned the fundamentals of expressive gesture

---

* Of course Massine means his mother's grave; his father had been buried in Positano.

and mimicry and a strong technique which later applied to my dancing and choreography. I was very interested to see Petipa's original notebook. Although his sketches were somewhat primitive, I had no difficulty in interpreting them, and could easily follow the patterns he had set down for the pas seuls and pas de deux and for the intricate ensemble movements with which he had so deftly filled the stage.[7]

From Moscow the Massines went to Leningrad (the once and future St. Petersburg), a city Massine had visited only twice before, with Diaghilev. He was delighted to find on the walls of the Hermitage Museum works by his friends Derain, Picasso, and Matisse which previously had belonged to the private collections of the country's prerevolutionary merchants.

Professionally, the trip home was not successful; contracts to make the ballet films failed to materialize. Massine returned again in 1963, accompanied by his daughter. This second trip was not a business success, either; and it was marred by the sudden death of Mikhail. Massine and Tatiana attended the funeral in Zvenigorod-Moskovsky, which was like a vignette of old Russia. Mikhail was buried with full military honors, and as the cortege slowly made its way to the cemetery, family and friends followed the open black casket with its red velvet interior. Snow fell on Mikhail's corpse and the procession of uniformed men and women wrapped in black fur.[8]

Undaunted, Massine next tried Western Europe, where he plunged into an exhaustive work schedule. But aside from a 1966 *Nutcracker* for French television and various opera ballets for La Scala (where he also staged his own version of *Les Noces* at the Piccola Scala),[9] new Massine productions were rare throughout the remainder of the 1960s. (Among the La Scala productions, however, was a joint choreographic effort with Lorca of Rousseau's opera-ballet *Le Devin du village*.) Mostly, Massine mounted Diaghilev revivals—for the Royal Ballet, La Scala, the Cologne State Opera Ballet, the Vienna Opera Ballet, and the Ballet du XXE Siècle. These revivals sometimes provoked decidedly mixed reactions, partly because contemporary dancers had trouble understanding and immersing themselves in Massine's style, in mastering the dramatic and interpretive demands of a Massine role. But even more troublesome was the conflict that had arisen among dance writers, as historical sensibility clashed head-on with critical response. Some critics, such as Mary Clarke and Richard Buckle in England, appreciated these works within their historical context; others dismissed them as hopelessly dated. Massine's early aesthetics and idiosyncratic choreography differed so drastically from the predominant trends of the day that a generation of dance critics had sprung up who were indifferent or hostile to works that only a few years earlier had been hailed as groundbreaking. Some critics charged that even in his prime he had been "overestimated" by his contemporaries—a judgment often voiced by Clive Barnes, among others.

Although offers for Massine's services had fallen off considerably, he was a compulsive worker who could not remain idle. Two new projects absorbed his time: he began to work more systematically on his theory of choreography, a project he had been mulling over for decades, and he began to dream of converting Galli into an international art center.

Massine's fascination with dance notation, which he believed was essential to preserve choreography, had been born at the Moscow Theater School, where he was the best pupil in the notation class of Maria Gorshkova. Back in 1917, though he was excited by the idea of filming his ballets for posterity, Massine had confided to Anatoli Petrovich his hope that "cinema will not replace choreographic notation."[10] Now, in the deep autumn of his career, he returned to the search for a scientific method. Relying on Stepanov's notation, fully aware of the rules that govern the motion of the body, he concentrated on developing a theory that would serve not only as a method to record dance but as an aid in composition. As he painstakingly reviewed all of his choreographic notes since 1920, one question drove him:

What is choreography? And I had no answer to it. I was like a child designing pages and pages, volumes and volumes, lines and lines, but nothing, you see. Until I met Paul Hindemith. It is from Hindemith that I first put my foot on the ground. I saw that what is in music must also exist in dance. So I tried that, and from there on I had no difficulty. Just work, work, work until I get sort of a possibility to make it concrete. What it represents, how it moves, what is the result of postures. From there on I felt much better. No more hesitation. I can write and continue my research work. No more discouragement to find out what it is all about.

And then I discovered Stepanov. It was [Nicholas] Sergeyev who gave me that book. He said look at it and maybe you will be interested. I knew the book and had even had it in school, but I had never really studied it.*

---

* It is conceivable that Massine's notation textbook at Theater School was Gorsky's fairly simplified version of Stepanov's work. This might explain why he could get by brilliantly in school without having studied it closely.

Now I grab at the book and read it. This is a brilliant work. Where Stepanov stops, I now continue. But it is he who invented it. The good of it is not just that it is a recording system—it is a system that permits you vertically to compose and see what we have in every bar. It has a magic effect. By that, you see at once what the time signature is, you see at once whether it fits contrapuntally or not, and you see if in your body you get something to look at, whether it be dynamics, melody, dance or harmonic posture. And you get your posture in the right place, like in music, where the melody often needs heavy support and where the chords appear. The same process in composing the choreography. It is immense what Stepanov invented, you see.[11]

In the course of expanding his own thinking, Massine reabsorbed the theories of Pecour, Rameau, and Blasis, theoreticians he had encountered earlier in his career. He now had to see them afresh as he delved deeper "into the realm of harmonic and dynamic progression in choreography."[12]

Most of the actual writing of his theory of choreography was accomplished on Galli. Life on the islands was austere, with an almost spartan, ascetic quality. By the 1960s Massine was living in the renovated fourteenth-century tower. He believed in physical discipline, rising early in the morning, taking his customary daily barre, swimming twice a day, walking, hiking, working most of the day, then retiring early. Vladimir Augenblick recalls an episode that attests to the physical fitness of the seventy-one-year-old Massine. One day, as the boat to Galli sailed toward the islands, a storm rose up that was so violent the two men feared for their lives, but it subsided, and they arrived safely on the main island. As soon as they docked, Massine took off his clothes and swam to one of the smaller islands and back—a total distance of two hundred meters. The feat was clearly a sudden burst of rejoicing in his own capacity for survival as well as a reaffirmation of life when the end had seemed so near. This event also illustrates Massine's visceral rapport with the most basic aspects of nature. Though inclined to contemplation and analysis, he never relinquished a strong physical connection to his environment— a leitmotif from his childhood days at Zvenigorod-Moskovsky to his ageless form astride the landscape of Galli.[13]

During this period Massine wrote his memoirs, *My Life in Ballet*, published in 1968. *Massine on Choreography* followed in 1976. (When he died in 1979 he was working on a second volume of theory and practice, *Elaborations and Variants*.)

Massine with his students on the Isole dei Galli during the 1960s. The isles of
Rotonda and Gigante are in the background.

Massine had begun seriously considering the idea of converting
Galli into an international art center as early as 1963. He wanted musicians, choreographers, painters, and writers to be able to meet in the
spirit of the Diaghilev tradition and create new works "away from the en-
croaching materialism of modern life."[14] He had two goals: to safeguard
Diaghilev's ballet aesthetic, which he feared was being obliterated, and to
reaffirm his own. For Massine, the survival of ballet as total theater became an engrossing crusade. A cultural center on Galli would be his final
tribute to Diaghilev, the greatest any disciple could offer.

Surely this goal was in part a humble attempt to honor his artistic forebear. But was it also an acolyte's subtle reworking, and rewriting, of the past? It was true that Diaghilev's aesthetic sprang from a view of art and ballet that Massine himself continued to elaborate until the end of his life.[15] But now Massine's memories were filtering out all negative aspects of Diaghilev's character in favor of his finer qualities, which Massine idealized to almost cultlike dimensions. It was the tribute of the apostle through whom the master achieves his surest immortality. Anyone who knew Massine could also, if he simply looked deeply enough, know a piece of Diaghilev as well. Such veneration exalted Diaghilev at the same time it showed the world a shining path to him, and that path was Massine. Reverence and ultimate control of the revered one were deftly combined; the master was at last mastered.

Massine revived *Parade* in 1964 for Béjart's Ballet du XXE Siècle. It was the first time that he had revived the work since its final performance with Diaghilev's company. As he did so, he stressed over and over in the press the ballet's importance as a visual manifesto of Diaghilev's idea of the total theatrical work of art, of the balanced, equally important roles that decor, choreography, music, and literature play. In his memoirs Massine paid a posthumous homage to Diaghilev, and in later conversations and interviews he constantly relived their aesthetic relationship. At one point he told *Dance Magazine*: "I certainly regret having argued with him. A great genius he was. Now, the more distant he is the more I realize his principles and the way he conducted his artistic life are not to be deviated from." He added that Diaghilev "was intransigent. Uncompromising . . . he was like a comet—a star. Nothing like him will ever appear again. Meeting him changed my life and also changed the course of art in the West. Diaghilev was a perfectionist. Live life as it ought to be—not as it is, he would say."[16] It was Massine's concern for this legacy that prompted him to spend the last two decades of his life championing Diaghilev productions by Fokine and Nijinsky; he was personally responsible for revivals of *Petrouchka* and *L'Après-midi d'un faune.*[17]

THE MASSINE FAMILY'S solidarity was beginning to deteriorate. Tatiana and Lorca ventured out to organize their own company, Les Ballets Europeéns—a natural step towards independence, but in this case accelerated by the choreographer's excessive demands. Massine's often tyrannical relationship with his family was due in part to the exigencies of his creative work. But even in the personal sphere he imposed upon himself and his environment, just as Diaghilev had, rigorous intellectual formulae by which he measured everything, from aesthetic issues to human relations. The resulting tensions were at times unbearable.

In 1963 Massine went to revive *Le Tricorne* in Cologne, where, in a café, he met Hannelore Holtwick, a Bayer Aspirin employee who offered to be his German interpreter and soon became his assistant and lover. Their child Peter was born in Switzerland in 1964, followed a year later by a second son, Theodor, who was born in Germany. Massine bought a house in Weseke, Germany, where he would stay with Holtwick and the children when he was not traveling to fulfill artistic commitments. In 1968 he and his wife were granted a divorce by a French court, yet he would not marry Holtwick until just before his death.

In addition to reviving his old ballets, Massine gave a great deal of his time to teaching. In 1968 he was invited to teach his theory of choreography at the Royal Ballet School in London, and in 1969 at Pittsburgh's Point Park College. By the 1970s his assignments would include several summer programs and workshops in Europe and the United States, where he also gave lecture-demonstrations and improvised choreography in front of an audience.

An important period of revivals began in 1969, when Massine staged *Le Tricorne* for the City Center Joffrey Ballet, the first time he had worked with an American company since 1954. The Massine association gave a serious boost to Robert Joffrey's prestige as a ballet director with a keen sense of historical consciousness. The company's thorough and faithful revivals of twentieth-century classics won acclaim in the 1970s and 1980s from a new generation of ballet critics who believed in letting the past speak for itself without making it accountable to the values and aesthetic principles of the present. Within the next few years Massine revived three more works for the Joffrey: *Le Beau Danube* (1972), *Parade* (1973), and *Pulcinella* (1974). *Parade* became a staple in the Joffrey repertory; indeed, today it remains the only American company where Massine has been consistently represented. In the 1970s he would also stage major revivals for American Ballet Theatre, the Australian Ballet, the London Festival Ballet, the Royal Ballet, the Sadler's Wells, La Scala, and the Vienna State Opera Ballet.

The last major chapter in Massine's creative life opened in 1975, when he choreographed *Till Eulenspiegel* for his students at Point Park College. No offers to create new works from ballet companies were forthcoming, so he produced them in workshops, in which he could put into practice his concepts and theory of choreography. Unfortunately,

Till Eulenspiegel, with its slow rhythmic movements and choreographic asymmetry, was never performed outside of the rehearsal studio.

After reviving Nijinsky's *L'Après-midi d'un faune* with Romola Nijinsky for the Paris Opéra in 1976, Massine traveled to northern California to give a series of seminars at the invitation of Mary Otis Clark of the Rossmoor Ballet Guild. These seminars caused a stir in the Bay Area dance community, and Massine was invited back to the guild the following year.

In December 1976 he went to Palm Beach for the premiere of the newly organized ballet company Dancers, whose director, Dennis Wayne, hoped to commission a ballet from him. In Florida Massine met Ariane Csonka, an attractive young opera singer who managed two ballet studios in the area. Csonka fell under "the spell of his magical and mystical presence"[18] and soon became a supporter and collaborator who would accompany him in some of his travels. It is fascinating to note how the eighty-one-year-old Massine still exerted a seductive power over women, especially younger women. His enigmatic personality, larger-than-life allure, and almost Machiavellian sense of control never failed him until the very end of his life. Women gravitated to him until his death, and throughout his final years he continued to form intense relationships with them that provided him with emotional support, vitality, and renewed inspiration.

In the spring of 1977 Massine returned to the Bay Area to conduct a series of successful seminars and workshops in choreography. Again he was a hit, and a revival of *Le Beau Danube* for the San Francisco Conservatory of Ballet (now the Marin Civic Ballet) soon followed. Massine was beginning to find himself a force in the Bay Area ballet community, and to this end Fred and Elena Maroth became a constant source of support and friendship. Fred was a National Public Radio music producer, and Elena a onetime dancer from Cuba who now taught ballet. The Maroths became a sort of surrogate family for Massine during his sojourns in northern California, helping him to meet his professional commitments and serving as his assistants. He was also more than once a guest in their Oakland Hills home.

The summer of 1977 spent in Galli was productive. Massine invited Ariane Csonka and Susan Gieliotti-Ford, a dancer from the Palm Beach area, to join him on the island in June. Lorca and his wife joined them two weeks later. (Massine's personal guests stayed in the tower along with their host, while Lorca and his family were lodged in the main villa.)

As usual, life on Galli was disciplined, revolving around work and

Massine rehearsing in California during the 1970s

rest. After breakfast Ariane, Susan, and later Lorca (whom Massine, standing in a window, always summoned from the main villa with a megaphone) would join the choreographer in the tower's second-floor dance studio, where film and sound equipment stood ready to record each new choreographic session.[19] The first piece that Massine worked on, *The Inconstant Lover* (inspired by Shakespeare's poetry), was choreographed without music, although Massine later asked Csonka to improvise music to it in performance. *The Inconstant Lover* was a pas de deux staged on Ariane and Susan, and Csonka describes its creation as both a phenomenon and a revelation. "It was fascinating to see how he worked with both of us, even though we are both so different. To begin with, I am not a professional dancer and Susan is. . . . The movements he created for Susan and the mood that he gave to them absolutely depicted Susan's personality, while those he devised for me felt absolutely right. . . . The spirit of the characters reminded me of Ariadne and Zerbinetta in *Ariadne auf Naxos*.

"The choreography itself was slow, consisting of bodily interweaving. It was a pas de deux for two women who could have been lovers, friends, or any other kind of human relationship. We came together and parted, and yet Massine somehow showed through our gestures that upon parting we took along something of the other. She took with her some of my movements and I some of hers. It was so to the heart of life. Everything he did, even if it was abstract, was emotional, to the heart.

"Throughout the choreographic process he applied his theory of choreography to give us directions, since he could not actually show the movements. Yet he explained very little. The movements themselves would give the emotions, and he would only make a remark like, 'Surrender to it,' and in so doing he brought out my personality through his movements. He would give a movement that was so right for me that it was like finding my own center."[20]

Working with Lorca, Massine began to experiment with Bach's *Art of the Fugue*; Fred Maroth had recently given Massine a recording of it with a new orchestration by William Mallock. Massine also choreographed the Italian song "Se tu m'ami" on Lorca and Csonka, and Lorca found the wealth of movement that his father conceived astonishingly innovative.[21]

Csonka was touched by Lorca's compliance and patience with his father, who was never easy to work with or to please. In fact Lorca was spending most of his vacation time in the tower instead of with his family. Even his wife, a Béjart dancer who was pregnant at the time, joined some of the choreographic sessions.

But most rehearsal time was allocated to *Parisina,* a ballet based on Lord Byron's poem of the same name and set to Villa-Lobos's *Bachianas Brasileiras.* The piece had been commissioned in San Francisco by ballerina Natalia Makarova. The scenario revolved around Parisina's infidelity to her husband, Prince Ago of the house of Brunswick, with her son-in-law, Hugo. It was conceived by Massine and Csonka in three scenes: in the palace Ago discovers that Parisina has been unfaithful to him; in the garden the lovers meet and dance an ardent pas de deux; in the closing scene Parisina is executed. The sections of *Parisina* created in Galli were staged on Susan, and according to Csonka the choreography was beautiful and intensely emotional. "What was prominent in Massine's choreography was the image of this girl being caught in the agony of her guilt and remorse. . . . She danced out her passions as well as her memories of her love affair with her son-in-law and how he had loved her. At the end the guards came for her . . . Susan was standing in the middle of the studio and suddenly Massine had her listening to the guards coming and depicting her reaction when they finally came. He put all those feelings into physical motion. And then at the end, she went off with her arms behind her and head down as if they were dragging her off. Each minute detail was imbued with that emotion. It was very strong."[22]

In the autumn Massine began working with Makarova in San Francisco, but unfortunately their efforts came to nothing. It was unlikely that two such mercurial personalities could ever mesh. And Makarova simply could not accept the fact that *Parisina* had already been partially staged on someone else.

But being back in the Bay Area gave Massine the opportunity to resume work with the Marin Civic Ballet. He choreographed two new works for the company, *Venus and Adonis* and Mozart's *Bastien und Bastienne.*

During his final years Massine became an avid reader of poetry; *Venus and Adonis* was a pas de deux inspired by Shakespeare's poem of that name. Young Adonis, roving through the woods, comes upon Venus, who helplessly succumbs to his beauty. She bares herself to him in hopes of enticing him, but he turns from her, horrified. The choreography was in the simple and economical style of Massine's later oeuvre, stressing slow, sculptural movements rather than the staccato passages that had characterized his earlier work. He wanted very much to make a powerful connection with young, talented artists in the community, so he set the pas de deux to an electronic score commissioned from a young local composer. But Massine was still Massine, and he asserted his control by giving strict directives about length and measures for each section of the piece.[23] Unfortunately, as in the case of *Till Eulenspiegel, Venus and Adonis* was never performed outside the rehearsal room.

Late in life Massine took up yet another challenge: choreographing vocal compositions. Although Mozart's Mass in C Minor was one of the projects he longed to see realized, he knew that its scale was too vast for the resources of the Marin Civic Ballet. From Palm Beach, Csonka proposed the one-act opera *Bastien und Bastienne* instead and promptly brought its score to Massine in the Bay Area. They immediately began collaborating on the scenario.

Mozart's chamber opera centers on the shepherdess Bastienne and her lover Bastien; the only other character is the wise man/magician Colas, who ill advises the young lovers. (The three-character ballet also featured children playing a flock of sheep.) The ballet closely followed the opera's action, though it did manage to trim ten minutes from its forty-five-minute length.

Choreographing *Bastien und Bastienne* was made difficult by the working conditions. Massine had been invited by the Marin Civic Ballet to choreograph a full-length version of the Hans Christian Andersen story "The Red Shoes" (a work that, though he busied himself preparing for it, in the end never materialized). He was also peremptorily asked to donate to the company a second ballet, for which he was not to be paid. If this siphoning off of his energies weren't enough, when work on the Mozart piece got under way, the company's administrators had so poor an understanding of his requirements that they neglected to provide him with a rehearsal pianist. On top of that, it was *Nutcracker* season, so practically no rehearsal time was allocated to him.[24] It sometimes seemed that the company, rather than truly respecting Massine, only wanted the luster of his name. Massine, however, endured the annoyances with great dignity and was delighted with the artistic result. He hoped to recruit André Beaurepaire, with whom he had worked in Nervi, to design the ballet. Unfortunately, *Bastien und Bastienne* was never performed outside the studio. Yet according to eyewitnesses, especially the Maroths, the ballet was a first-rate addition to Massine's oeuvre.

Massine spent the Christmas holidays of 1977 with Hannelore and their children. In January 1978 he returned to the Bay Area, which he considered his working base. His life became more settled, due in great part to his devoted new personal assistant, twenty-five-year-old Mary Ann de

Vlieg. A native of Detroit, de Vlieg was studying linguistics at the University of California at Berkeley when she met Massine. She also held down a job as day supervisor of the Holiday Inn that Massine always stayed in when he visited the area.

One day, while he was staging *Le Beau Danube*, he approached de Vlieg with his easy, old-world grace. He kissed her hand, addressed her as "Madame," then extolled her diligence, efficiency, and discretion (he had taken particular notice of the fact that she rarely spoke with anyone). He promptly offered her a job. De Vlieg was knocked off her feet. Of course she had noticed this eccentric stranger, dressed in black and gray, of whom it was whispered around the hotel that he was Russian and a great man of ballet. His air of self-esteem and poised eminence suggested to her a recently fallen grand duke.

She began handling Massine's correspondence, accounts, and urgent business matters in the evenings.[25] Shortly she dropped out of college, quit her job, and, working as Massine's assistant from eight a.m. to midnight (with an afternoon break), became his most devoted and constant companion. In Diaghilev's manner, Massine provided for her room and board as well as all her personal travel expenses. But the salary he had promised her at the beginning of their association was never forthcoming (though when she needed money to buy her father a birthday gift, Massine delightedly handed it over at once). By now most of Massine's precious art collection had been sold, and de Vlieg soon realized that he was plagued with financial obligations that were quite beyond his means, including the caretakers' salaries on Galli, tuition for the children in Germany, taxes on the Swiss apartment, and heating bills for the house in Paris. Nevertheless, de Vlieg recalls, at difficult moments a royalty check for performances of his ballets in Vienna would miraculously arrive, or Massine would discover a forgotten Picasso drawing—stuck between the pages of an old book in his library—that could be sold. Thus was more than one financial crisis averted.[26]

The octogenarian Massine had conceded nothing to the coming of age, and de Vlieg quickly grew to appreciate his methodical, almost ritualistic physical regimen. He would rise early to do his Cecchetti barre, followed by a steam bath (a habit he had acquired at the Piešťany spa, which he still visited every three years), then rest in bed for forty-five minutes. Breakfast, the main meal of the day, varied according to the country he was in, though it always included freshly squeezed orange juice. As they rode in de Vlieg's car, he did not permit any conversation— he often wore a black eye mask—or radio playing, an act he considered disrespectful to the music as well as a distraction to the driver. In the afternoon he always took in healthy amounts of fresh air. De Vlieg would drive him into the hills, where to her amazement he would climb to the highest accessible spot. There he would sit with his eyes closed, in silence. (It seemed to her that he meditated.) He allowed conversation only if the matter was urgent or related directly to his work—a stricture, he claimed, that had also been insisted upon by Diaghilev. His days were usually occupied by near-compulsive work or study, along with the continual mapping out of new projects. He believed that as an artist he followed a path not chosen of his own free will but divinely ordained.

In 1978 Massine's schedule in the Bay Area was extremely hectic. He worked intensely with Fred Maroth to complete a television documentary on Diaghilev, and continued to conduct lecture-demonstrations. Igor Youskevitch and Walter Ducloux from the dance and music departments, respectively, of the University of Texas at Austin invited him to create a new work to inaugurate a new campus theater scheduled to open in December 1979. Massine chose to choreograph a version of Handel's *Messiah,* on which he began work with dancers from the Contra Mesa Ballet. De Vlieg later arranged for a group of modern dancers to work with him. These rehearsals were a great success, Massine felt, because the dancers seemed to grasp his style more readily than did ballet dancers, who he maintained were too stiff. Also that year, through the intercession of Fred Maroth, the Oakland Ballet commissioned from Massine a revival of *La Boutique fantasque* as well as a new work, which the choreographer decided would be a new version of *Le Soleil de nuit,* now titled *Snow Maiden.*

In the spring Tatiana Riabouchinska invited Massine to Los Angeles for the opening performances of the Southern California Ballet at UCLA, a company of which Riabouchinska is founder-director. The purpose of this invitation was to allow Massine to assess the young company and decide whether he wished to create a new work or revive an old one for it. The Massine-Riabouchinska reunion was poignant, and at the close of the master class he taught in her studio the pair performed the initial section of their mazurka from *Le Beau Danube* before the spellbound company and guests. The outcome of this trip to Los Angeles was to have been a 1979 revival of *Jeux d'enfants.* Miró was immediately contacted, declared himself thrilled by the prospect, and agreed to design a souvenir program for the occasion.[27]

After his usual summer in Galli, this time accompanied by Hannelore and the children, Massine revived *La Boutique fantasque* for the

Sadler's Wells touring company, then returned to the Bay Area to complete his work on *Snow Maiden,* which was scheduled for the following year.

Before leaving northern California in December 1978 Massine worked with a local pianist-composer, Bruce Nalezny, on an album for Terpsichore Records in Berkeley. Nalezny's original concept was to produce a ballet class record as a teaching aid, a proposal to which Massine objected, because he never had been interested in teaching basic ballet classes, only choreography.[28] Instead he selected five pieces to choreograph, which were notated according to Massine's own theory by a local dancer, Janet Karkowski, in the record's instruction booklet. Massine choreographed two additional pieces, a Tchaikovsky work for eight dancers and a solo dedicated to Nijinsky, which were not included in this album but were intended to appear on a second recording (which never came to pass).[29] These seven pieces were Massine's last choreographic works.

During the summer Massine had been taken seriously ill on Galli for a few days. Fearing the worst, he prepared a handwritten will. The episode took place during a storm, so it was difficult to get medical assistance to the island. After the crisis had passed, he never complained to de Vlieg about any pain or discomfort. He had a general physical examination and was declared in good health.

Massine returned to Germany to spend the Christmas holidays with Hannelore and the children. He planned to meet de Vlieg in New York afterwards. But de Vlieg remembers that at the airport, as he was departing for Germany, he somberly told her, "You'll never see me again."

In Germany Massine's condition—prostate cancer—worsened. In March de Vlieg received a telephone call in New York informing her that he was gravely ill. She immediately flew to Germany and went directly to the hospital in Borken. "You must hurry," the staff told her as she strode down the hallway. She found Massine alone in his room. He recognized her, tried to speak, but could not. She stayed with him awhile, but once she realized how critically ill he was she went into the hallway to telephone his daughter, Tatiana, in New York.

By the time she returned to the room Massine had died. It was March 15, 1979.[30]

EPILOGUE

AFTER DECADES OF NEGLECT of Massine's serious works (his *demi-caractère* and character ballets have always found a place in the international repertory), the last few years have seen a renewed interest in the symphonic ballets. This revival has stimulated both critics and balletomanes. Rudolf Nureyev took the first valiant step by commissioning a revival of *Les Présages* (1933) for the Paris Opéra. The work, though representative of the expressionistic aesthetics of its time, received high critical acclaim. Anna Kisselgoff wrote in the *New York Times* (March 9, 1989):

> *In fact, the production is a complete triumph not only because it is exceedingly well danced by the Paris Opera Ballet, but also because the choreography has a dynamic invention that stands up on its own. . . .*
>
> *A revelation of the production is how strongly classical and formal the choreography looks. Massine's influence over Sir Frederick Ashton (his pupil) and even George Balanchine is evident. . . .*
>
> *The original criticism about the heaviness of the allegory—man battling his destiny—still holds true. In this production, however, the message falls by the wayside. One is left with the complexity of Massine's contrapuntal groups of dancers . . . and the sheer and striking classicism of most of the choreography. . . . The pas de deux in the second movement is actually a neoclassic duet of superb invention and fluidity. . . .*
>
> *We see the Ashton of the future in fleeting passages. His walking-on-air*

trademark is visible in the duet, and the arm movements he used in Sym-phonic Variations are also present. To see the martial gestures in Les Présages *is to recall similar arm work in the Balanchine-Stravinsky Sym-phony in Three Movements. One can note a passing resemblance to cer-tain lifts and images in other Balanchine ballets. . . . It is time to see* Les Présages *in a new light.*

And later, on May 7, 1989, Kisselgoff added:

Les Présages *suggests that a revisionist view of Massine is in order. In this revival, he emerges as a major neo-classical choreographer. For all the so-called Expressionist influences in the torso and gestures, the footwork is in the classical idiom, fluent and inventive. . . .*

Les Présages *shows us something else: a choreographer in firm command of the classical idiom and a complex interplay of dance structures. . . .*

Les Présages *also clarifies the relationship of Massine's work to Bal-anchine and Frederick Ashton, 20th century ballet's greatest neo-classi-cists. Ashton, Massine's pupil, acknowledged the older choreographer's influence. . . .*

The Joffrey Ballet subsequently revived *Les Présages,* in 1991.

Of paramount importance was the revival of *Choreartium* (1933)—Massine's first absolutely abstract ballet, a forerunner of abstraction, mu-sical visualization, and neoclassicism. The staging by the Birmingham Royal Ballet in 1991 received rapturous reviews. Clement Crisp wrote in the *Financial Times* (October 28, 1991): "What Massine proposes in *Chore-artium* is certainly a response to Brahmsian device in the immediate terms of thematic and formal structure, but it is one overlaid with an emotional—a Russian emotional—interpretation of mood. . . . The restoration of Choreartium to the repertory brings back to life a work that should retain an honoured place in any assessment of this century's ballet." The *Sunday Times* (November 3, 1991) declared that "it is time to reinstate Léonide Massine's full worth as a choreographer. . . . What first hits you about Choreartium is its epic scale." *The Times* (October 28, 1991) noted that "Massine created a complexity of detailed, distinct choreography, not just for the ten soloists, but for the entire ensemble. His patterns extend across the whole stage in contrast and variety, but are always possible for the eye to take in at once (this is surely something learned from his study of paintings)." And Jack Anderson wrote in the

New York Times (December 1, 1991): "*Choreartium* is a vast mural in motion that makes much recent choreography seem puny by comparison."

Ninette de Valois called Massine a "genius" and predicted that "[his] works will come back and [he] will be again a very prominent figure in our history." Now at last the reconsideration and re-evaluation of Massine's oeuvre are irreversibly on the ascent. He has been re-established as one of the century's most influential and innovative choreographers.

Notes

1. Moscow, July 1895–November 1913

1. Massine's school records, Central State Archives of Literature and the Arts, Moscow, fond. 659. Letter from Elizabeth Souritz to the author, April 21, 1991.
2. Mr. Miassine retired on September 1, 1911, and Mrs. Miassine retired on September 1, 1904.
3. Léonide Massine, *My Life in Ballet* (London: Macmillan, 1968), p. 13.
4. Ibid., p. 15.
5. Ibid., p. 13.
6. Ibid., pp. 12–13.
7. Ibid., p. 13.
8. Ibid., p. 20.
9. Ibid.
10. Ibid., p. 14.
11. Ibid., p. 17.
12. *Dance Magazine*, 51, no. 12 (December 1977), p. 68.
13. Ibid., pp. 20–21.
14. Miassine's school records, Central State Archives of Literature and the Arts, Moscow, fond. 682.
15. Undoubtedly a driving force in early-twentieth-century Russian ballet was Vladimir Telyakovsky, who was appointed director of the Moscow Imperial Theaters in 1897, and later was promoted to general director of the Imperial Theaters. Telyakovsky's greatest concern was to elevate the standards of artistic excellence at the Imperial Theaters. It is he who should be credited with hiring the bass Feodor Chaliapin for the Bolshoi in 1899, transferring Gorsky to the Bolshoi Ballet in 1900, appointing Vsevolod Meyerhold the Imperial Theaters' principal producer in 1907, helping to launch the career of Michel

Fokine, and supporting Stanislavsky's reforms to the extent of persuading him in 1915 to teach acting to the singers at the Bolshoi. See Natalia Roslavleva, *Era of the Russian Ballet* (London: Victor Gollancz, 1966).

16. A Russian cultural renaissance had blossomed during the nineteenth century, perhaps as an artistic revolt against the Europeanization of the Russias under Peter the Great in the late 1700s and early 1800s. This Russian renewal was responsible for the development of a strong Russian identity in the arts. The subsequent artistic fermentation reached its apogee in the early part of this century and continued until the 1930s, when art became a voice for ideological propaganda.

Moscow had been Russia's capital from the end of the Mongol occupation in the fourteenth century until the beginning of the eighteenth, when Peter the Great designated St. Petersburg as his capital. Nevertheless, Moscow remained the economic center of the country, and with the help of industrialization the city in 1900 reached its peak rate of economic growth. Prosperity detonated a population explosion, from 1,038,000 in 1897 to 1,762,700 by 1914.

The cultural renaissance in Moscow was shaped by two vital forces. First, there was the affluence provided by the eco-social phenomenon of the wealthy merchant class, which reached its heyday by the close of the nineteenth century. This group—bankers, manufacturers, industrialists, and railroad tycoons, most of whom came from peasant stock—spent their fortunes on art patronage as well as on industrial and scientific development, thus enriching Russia's cultural and intellectual life. They founded art and literary journals, libraries, and drama and opera companies. Their extensive private art collections, some of which were open to the public, provided sponsorship for Russian and European modernist artists, thus helping to create a market for modern art. Among the most notable members of this class were the Shchukins, the Morozovs, the Mamontovs, the Riabouchinskys, and the Tretyakovs, all of whom were champions of the Slavophile movement, whose philosophy was rooted in a revitalization of the national heritage.

Another factor in the cultural renaissance was Moscow's nationalistic tradition, which so differed from the sophisticated cosmopolitanism of St. Petersburg, which was defined by European criteria. Moscow's search for artistic identity was opposed to St. Petersburg's occidentalism and sought to revitalize and reassert the Russian traditions venerated by the Slavophile movement. This search gave Moscow its pre-eminence as a center for experimentation and modernism.

The Wanderers were a group of Slavophile artists formed in 1863 that rebelled against St. Petersburg's Academy of the Arts (founded in 1757), after which they settled in Moscow and enjoyed the support of the wealthy merchants. In 1870, with the assistance of Pavel Tretyakov, this group founded the Traveling Exhibition Society, whose primary objective was to bring in art from outside the country's two leading cities, and whose artistic credo was to free itself from Western influences so that a national art could be created that depicted Russian themes and the true realities of the Russian social landscape. Understandably, the Wanderers' hero was Leo Tolstoy.

Four years after the creation of the Traveling Exhibition Society, Savva and Elizaveta Mamontov, leading members of the Muscovite merchant class, gathered together a colony of artists at their estate at Abramtsevo, near Zagorsk. Abramtsevo became a center of Russian arts and crafts and came to include among its members Konstantin Korovin, Mikhail Vrubel, the Vasnetsov brothers, and Valentin Serov. It provided the site for the genesis of one of the most important theatrical manifestations of the time: out of the colony of artists gathered by Mamontov emerged his Private Opera Company, which opened in 1885 with the artistic objective of staging works by Russian composers and achieving a theater of synthesis. The productions, mounted in collaboration with the Abramtsevo artists, signaled the future importance of theatrical design.

The creation of the Private Opera Company heralded the development of Moscow as a theatrical center. In 1896, Mamontov invited the bass Feodor Chaliapin to join his company. Unhappy with the conditions at the Maryinsky Theater, Chaliapin gladly joined Mamontov's enterprise, where in three seasons he sang twenty roles. The singer's association with the Private Opera Company was vital for his artistic growth, and the mood of experimentation in the company encouraged him to focus on developing his approach to interpretation. According to historian Varvara Strakhova-Ermans, "The years Chaliapin spent at Mamontov's theater must be regarded as a period of extreme intellectual exertion and great fecundity. . . . This was the moment when his genius burst forth. . . . when Fedor Ivanovich became *Chaliapin*" (Quoted in Victor Borovsky, *Chaliapin: A Critical Biography* [New York: Alfred A. Knopf, 1988], p. 252). Stanislavsky, the great theatrical innovator, who had considered opening an acting workshop for opera singers, stated that "the only correct approach to opera is Chaliapin's approach, which proceeds not from the external reality of the character being portrayed, but from its inner reality, its psychological depth" (Borovsky, p. 9). See Beverly Whitney Kean, *All the Empty Palaces: The Merchant Patrons of Modern Art in Pre-Revolutionary Russia* (New York: Universal Books, 1983), and Serge Faucherau, *Moscow, 1900–1930* (New York: Rizzoli, 1988).

17. The theater had always occupied a revered place in the hearts of the Russian intelligentsia; and even though since the early eighteenth century the Russian theater had been couched in Western European traditions, by the last two decades of the nineteenth century it had begun to find its own identity. Theater would eventually become one of the most artistically fertile areas of the Russian cultural renaissance, with Moscow emerging as the country's theatrical capital.

One of the most influential theatrical movements at the turn of the century was the Moscow Art Theater, founded in 1898 by Konstantin Stanislavsky (born Alexeyev to a merchant family) and Vladimir Nemirovich-Danchenko. The Art Theater introduced new concepts in acting and production that enlisted decor, costumes, props, lighting, music, and sound to create a cohesive dramatic whole that gave birth to a new realism and artistic truth on the stage. From its inception up until 1904, the Art Theater concentrated on realism and naturalism. Yet the emphasis on the outer truth of the theatrical experience led, paradoxically, to its discovery of the inner dimension; and thus from 1905 on the theater's creative direction moved toward psychological realism and the theater of mood. See Nicolai A. Gorchakov, *The Theater in Soviet Russia* (New York: Columbia University Press, 1957), and Marc Slonim, *Russian Theatre from the Empire to the Soviets* (Cleveland: World Publishing, 1961).

18. Elizabeth Souritz, *Soviet Choreographers in the 1920s* (Durham, N.C.: Duke University Press, 1990), p. 86.
19. Among Miassine's classmates, only Margarita Kandourova, a leading ballerina in the 1920s, became famous. Vera Svetinskaya, although only a coryphée, became known as the object of Gorsky's love letters and poetry.
20. Massine, *My Life*, p. 23.
21. Ibid., p. 24.
22. Ibid., p. 26.
23. Ibid., p. 27.
24. Souritz, *Soviet Choreographers*, p. 104.
25. Massine files, Central State Archives of Literature and the Arts, Moscow, fond. 682. On May 4, 1909, Leonid was moved to third class. On April 20, 1911—a year before his graduation—he was moved to fifth class with a special certificate of merit.
26. Letter from Elizabeth Souritz to the author, March 8, 1991.
27. Natalia Roslavleva, *Era of the Russian Ballet* (London: Victor Gollancz, 1966), p. 160.
28. Massine, *My Life*, p. 29.
29. Ibid. pp. 29–30.
30. Ibid., p. 30.
31. Ibid., p. 41.
32. Ibid., p. 32.
33. Ibid., p. 33.
34. Ibid., p. 34.
35. Ibid., p. 30–31.
36. In the certificate of christening in Massine's school records she appears as Alexandra Alexandrovna Minina—probably her maiden name.
37. Massine, *My Life*, pp. 38–39.
38. *Theatre*, no. 976, December 13, 1911.
39. *Theatre*, no. 979, December 16, 1911.
40. *Season News*, no. 2306, December 14, 1911.
41. Massine, *My Life*, p. 32.
42. Ibid., p. 37.

Anatoli Petrovich Bolchakov was born on November 5, 1870, in the village of Novaya Andronovka, near Moscow, and came from a family of peasants. In 1883 he applied for admission at the School of Painting, Sculpture, and Architecture in Moscow, and during his studies there he was so poor that he had to repeatedly petition for his tuition to be waived. (Central State Archives of Literature and the Arts, Moscow, fond. 680). Upon his graduation, probably in 1895, he taught drawing at several ordinary Moscow schools and opened his own art school in his private apartment. (Letters from Elizabeth Souritz to the author, April 21 and May 12, 1991.)

43. Massine, *My Life*, p. 38.
44. Letter from Massine to Anatoli Petrovich Bolchakov, October 9, 1914, State Central Theatrical Museum, Moscow, no. 181575.
45. Massine, *My Life*, p. 71.
46. Ibid., p. 38.
47. Ibid.
48. Letters from Massine to Bolchakov sending his regards to these friends, State Central Theatrical Museum, Moscow.
49. School records, Central State Archives of Literature and the Arts, Moscow, fond. 682.
50. Personal file of L. F. Massine, Central State Archives of Literature and the Arts, Moscow, fond. 659, reg. 3, unit 2532, p. 20.
51. Ibid., p. 21.
52. Massine, *My Life*, p. 35.
53. Souritz, *Soviet Choreographers*, p. 30.
54. Ibid., quoting the critic B. Asafiev, p. 93.
55. Ibid., p. 116.
56. Ibid., pp. 116–17.
57. Massine, *My Life*, p. 39.
58. Ibid., p. 40.
59. Gorchakov, *Theater in Soviet Russia*, p. 12.
60. Massine in conversations with the author, Rennes, France, 1978.

2. Moscow, December 1913–Paris, August 1914

1. Richard Buckle, *Diaghilev* (New York: Atheneum, 1979), p. 41. For a closer analysis of Diaghilev's relationship with Filosofov, see Vladimir Zlobin, *A Difficult Soul: Zinaida Gippius* (Berkeley: University of California Press, 1980).
2. Quoted in William Richardson, *Zolotoe Runo and Russian Modernism: 1905–1910* (Ann Arbor, Mich.: Ardis Publishers, 1986), p. 17.
3. Buckle, *Diaghilev*, p. 61.
4. Ibid., p. 91.
5. Alexandre Benois, *Reminiscences of the Russian Ballet* (London: Putnam, 1941), p. 238.
6. Buckle, *Diaghilev*, p. 102.
7. Ibid., pp. 158–280. See also Arnold Haskell, *Diaghileff* (New York: Simon and Schuster, 1935), pp. 184–255.
8. While in Moscow, Diaghilev also approached Gorsky about producing Nicolas Tcherepnine's *The Masque of the Red Death* for his Ballets Russes. Elizabeth Souritz, *Soviet Choreographers in the 1920s* (Durham, N.C.: Duke University Press, 1990), p. 163.

9. Buckle, *Diaghilev*, p. 269.

10. Ibid., p. 270.

11. Léonide Massine, *My Life in Ballet* (London: Macmillan, 1986), p. 42.

12. Ibid., p. 270.

13. Massine in conversations with the author, Rennes, France, 1978.

14. Massine, *My Life*, p. 43.

15. The date on which this trip took place cannot be determined. In Massine's records from the Imperial Theater School there are several one-day petitions to visit his family.

16. Massine, *My Life*, p. 45.

17. Ibid., p. 46.

18. Petition in Massine's personal school records at the Imperial Theater School, Central State Archives of Literature and the Arts, Moscow, fond. 659, reg. 3, unit 2532.

19. Hugo von Hofmannsthal and Richard Strauss, *Correspondence Between Richard Strauss and Hugo von Hofmannsthal* (London: Collins, 1961), p. 222.

20. Personal school records from the Imperial Theater School, Central State Archives of Literature and the Arts, Moscow, fond. 659, reg. 3, unit 2532.

21. Letter from Diaghilev to Massine, January 22, 1914, Massine's private collection. The contract was extended an additional year, to August 1, 1916.

22. Massine, *My Life*, p. 51.

23. Ibid., p. 48.

24. Lydia Sokolova, *Dancing for Diaghilev* (London: John Murray, 1960), pp. 60–61.

25. Massine, *My Life*, p. 51.

26. Ibid., p. 52.

27. Ibid.

28. Ibid., pp. 53–54.

29. Telegram from Bakst to Misia Edwards, Massine's private collection.

30. Massine, *My Life*, p. 54.

31. Ibid., p. 57.

32. Ibid.

33. Massine in conversations with the author, Galli, 1978.

34. The 1917 cubist ballet *Parade* (music by Satie; libretto by Cocteau; scenery, costumes, and curtain by Picasso; and choreography by Massine) was to be the result of this meeting.

35. Massine, *My Life*, p. 60.

36. *The Lady*, March 7, 1914.

37. *Sunday Times* (London), June 28, 1914.

38. Tamara Karsavina, *Theatre Street* (London: Dance Books, 1981), pp. 298–300.

39. The letters from Massine to Anatoli Petrovich Bolchakov were deposited at the State Central Theatrical Museum, Moscow, by Bolchakov's widow.

40. Letter from Massine to Bolchakov, June 13/1, 1914, State Central Theatrical Museum, Moscow, no. 181566.

3. *Italy, August 1914–United States, April 1916*

1. In his autobiography Massine sometimes tries to play down his relationship with Diaghilev by implying that on certain occasions he traveled or lived independently. This trip to Milan, which he says he made alone, is an example. In fact, up to the time their relationship began to crumble, it is unlikely that Massine was ever far from Diaghilev's sight for long; and when he was, Diaghilev almost certainly knew his precise whereabouts.
2. Léonide Massine, *My Life in Ballet* (London: Macmillan, 1968), p. 66.
3. Ibid.
4. Richard Buckle, *Diaghilev* (New York: Atheneum, 1979), p. 284.
5. Letter from Massine to Anatoli Petrovich Bolchakov, October 9, 1914, State Central Theatrical Museum, Moscow, no. 181575.
6. Massine, *My Life*, p. 66.
7. Ibid., pp. 67–69.
8. Ibid., p. 69.
9. Ibid.
10. Ibid., p. 70.
11. Ibid., p. 71.
12. Ibid., p. 69.
13. Ibid.
14. Massine in conversations with the author, Galli, 1978.
15. Massine interview with Fred Maroth, Oakland, California, 1978.
16. Massine, *My Life*, p. 70.
17. Buckle, *Diaghilev*, p. 286.
18. Massine, *My Life*, pp. 71–72. Original letter in State Central Theatrical Museum, Moscow.
19. Letter from Massine to Bolchakov, December 20, 1914, State Central Theatrical Museum, Moscow, no. 181574.
20. Letter from Massine to Bolchakov, December 22, 1914, State Central Theatrical Museum, Moscow, no. 181573.
21. Massine in conversations with the author, Galli, 1978.
22. Caroline Tisdall and Angelo Bozzolla, *Futurism* (New York: Oxford University Press, 1978), p. 103.
23. Lynn Garafola, *Diaghilev's Ballets Russes* (New York: Oxford University Press, 1989), p. 77.
24. *Stravinsky: Selected Correspondence,* ed. Robert Craft, vol. 2, letter dated November 25, 1914 (New York: Knopf, 1984), p. 16.
25. Letter from Massine to Bolchakov, January 19, 1915, State Central Theatrical Museum, Moscow, no. 181571.
26. Buckle, *Diaghilev*, p. 288.
27. *Stravinsky: Selected Correspondence,* vol. 2, p. 138.

28. Tisdall and Bozzola, *Futurism*, p. 117.

29. Tatiana Loguine, *Gontcharova et Larionov* (Paris: Klincksieck, 1971), p. 197.

30. Aline Isdebsky-Pritchard, *The Art of Mikhail Vrubel* (Ann Arbor, Mich.: UMI Research Press, 1982), passim.

31. Valentina Kachuba in conversations with the author, Madrid, 1987.

32. Ibid.

33. Buckle, *Diaghilev*, p. 291.

34. Ibid., p. 295.

35. Massine, *My Life*, p. 288.

36. Ibid.

37. Letter from Massine to Bolchakov, January 1916, State Central Theatrical Museum, Moscow, no. 181570.

38. Ibid.

39. Buckle, *Diaghilev*, p. 288.

40. *Stravinsky: Selected Correspondence*, ed. Robert Craft, vol. 1 (New York: Knopf, 1982), p. 138.

41. Gontcharova's remarks read:

> *Dès le début, Diaghilev ébaucha une chorégraphie en cinq épisodes de la vie du Christ: la Nativité et l'Adoration des Mages, l'entrée dans Jérusalem, la prière dans le Jardin de Gethsémané, le Portement de la Croix, Golgotha. Plus tard fut ajouté le Sermon sur la montagne et une version de l'Annonciation: le dernier épisode fut, symboliquement et chronologiquement, une introduction à tous les Mystères. Les projets de Diaghilev étaient très vastes.*
>
> *Le Sermon sur la montagne était figuré exclusivement par le mouvement, la plastique et le développement des situations dramatiques. Parfois l'action était précédée par la musique et le choeur. D'autres fois, l'action était accompagnée par la musique et le chant à l'unisson, comme cela faisait dan l'ancienne Russie. La transportation du vieux motif musical fut en partie réalisée par le maître de chapelle de la Cathédrale orthodoxe de Genève, Kibaltchitch, qui était le fils du célèbre révolutionnaire russe. Suivant les exigences de l'action, soit le choeur se déployait au milieu de la scène, soit il en partait, soit encore il se tenait "en escalier" sur les côtés des premières coulisses. Sur scène apparaissaient les personnages principaux. . . .*
>
> *L'entrée dans Jérusalem se déroulait sur l'avant-scène avec pour fond le rideau baissé, réalisé sur le modèle des châssis qui entourent les icônes. Les quatre évangélistes portaient une reproduction d'âne stylisé, aux pattes projetées en avant et en arrière. Sur le dos de l'animal était placée une sculpture qui représentait l'entrée du Christ dans Jérusalem. Les apôtres marchaient sur les toits de la ville, figurés au niveau de la scène. Le sol devait avoir une certaine résonance, le rythme de la danse et le bruit des pas devaient être perçus distinctement par les spectateurs dans la salle. C'est pourquoi on installa, à vint-cinq centimètres du sol, un faux-plancher fabriqué dans un bois "sonore," une espèce de chêne à la texture sèche. Après le passage de la procession, le rideau se levait et l'épisode suivant se déroulait sur la scène.*
>
> *Les Nouvelles Russes*, 1953, no. 427, p. 6.

42. Massine, *My Life*, p. 74.

43. Ibid.

44. Ibid.

45. Serge Grigoriev, *The Diaghilev Ballet, 1909–1929*, trans. and ed. by Vera Bowen (London: Constable, 1953; rpnt. Penguin Books, 1960), p. 117.
46. Kachuba in conversations with the author.
47. Lydia Sokolova, *Dancing with Diaghilev* (London: John Murray, 1960), p. 71.
48. Kachuba in conversations with the author.
49. Massine, *My Life*, p. 76.
50. Massine in conversations with the author, Galli, 1978.
51. Kachuba in conversations with the author.
52. Arthur Gold and Robert Fizdale, *Misia* (New York: Knopf, 1980), p. 173.
53. *Journal de Genève*, December 22, 1915.
54. Massine, *My Life*, p. 77.
55. Ibid.
56. Ibid.
57. Ibid.
58. *The New Republic*, January 15, 1916.
59. Massine, *My Life*, p. 80.
60. Ibid.
61. *New York Tribune*, January 18, 1916.
62. *New York Sun*, January 26, 1916.
63. *New York Times*, January 26, 1916.
64. Ibid.
65. Massine, *My Life*, p. 82.
66. Ibid., p. 81.
67. Ibid., p. 84.
68. Ibid.
69. Ibid.
70. Letter from Massine to Bolchakov, January 1916, State Central Theatrical Museum, Moscow, no. 181570.
71. Sokolova, *Dancing*, p. 75.
72. Ibid.
73. *Musical Courier*, April 1916.
74. Milo Keynes, *Lydia Lopokova* (New York: St. Martin's Press, 1982), p. 211.
75. Massine, *My Life*, p. 97.

4. Spain, May–September 1916

1. Richard Buckle, *Diaghilev* (New York: Atheneum, 1979), p. 311.
2. Léonide Massine, *My Life in Ballet* (London: Macmillan, 1968), p. 88.
3. Letter from Massine to Anatoli Petrovich Bolchakov, June 5, 1916, State Central Theatrical Museum, Moscow, no. 181580.
4. *ABC* (Madrid), May 28, 1916.
5. *ABC* (Madrid), May 31, 1916.
6. *ABC* (Madrid), May 29, 1916.

7. Letter from Manuel de Falla to María Martínez Sierra, June 18, 1916, Archivo Manuel de Falla, Granada.

8. Igor Stravinsky, *Chronicle of My Life* (London: Victor Gollancz, 1936), p. 47.

9. Letter from Massine to Bolchakov, June 13, 1916, State Central Theatrical Museum, Moscow, no. 181519.

10. María Martínez Sierra, *Gregorio y yo* (Mexico, D.F.: Biografías Gandesa, 1953), p. 144.

11. Falla, in a letter to the dancer Nirva del Río dated June 20, 1929, states: "It has always been a definite criterion of mine not to change the character or destiny of my works. The *Noches* were composed as a symphonic piece. . . . I had already received several propositions (especially from Diaghilev's Ballets Russes, even before the premiere of *Tricorne*)." Archivo Manuel de Falla.

12. Jaime Pahissa, *Cuando el maestro Falla fue al pueblo de Goya*, Archivo Manuel de Falla.

13. Letter from Falla to María Martínez Sierra, June 18, 1916, Archivo Manuel de Falla.

14. Pahissa, *Cuando el maestro Falla*.

15. Letter from de Falla to María Martínez Sierra, June 18, 1916, Archivo Manuel de Falla.

16. Ibid.

17. Diaghilev offered Falla 5,000 francs for a five-year exclusivity for each work and a 100-franc royalty per performance for a minimum of ten performances a year. Falla proposed instead 6,000 francs for a three-year exclusivity for each work, a 125-franc royalty per performance and a minimum of fifteen performances a year, and his right to retain the exclusivity of these works for Spain. Diaghilev's counteroffer was of 5,000 francs for a three-year exclusivity and a 100-franc royalty per performance for a minimum of ten performances a year. Falla was to retain the exclusivity for concert performances in Spain. Archivo Manuel de Falla.

18. Ibid.

19. Letter from Massine to Bolchakov, June 5, 1916, State Central Theatrical Museum, Moscow, no. 181580.

20. Massine, *My Life*, p. 89.

21. Doctor's certificate, dated June 4/17, 1916, presented at the Russian embassy in Madrid, private collection.

22. Letter from Massine to Stravinsky, undated, quoted in *Stravinsky: Selected Correspondence*, ed. Robert Craft, vol. 2 (New York: Knopf, 1984), p. 160.

23. Massine, *My Life*, p. 144.

24. Letter from Massine to Bolchakov, June 25, 1916, State Central Theatrical Museum, Moscow, no. 181578.

25. Letter from Falla to Stravinsky, July 7, 1916, quoted in *Stravinsky*, vol. 2, p. 160.

26. Ibid.

27. The *modernismo* movement was the Catalonian expression of European modernism.

28. Massine, *My Life*, p. 89.

29. Ibid.

30. Lydia Sokolova, *Dancing for Diaghilev* (London: John Murray, 1960), p. 83.

31. Arthur Rubinstein, *My Young Years* (New York: Knopf, 1973), p. 469.

32. Letter from Gerald Tyrwhitt to Stravinsky, August 16, 1916, quoted in *Stravinsky*, vol. 2, p. 136. Tyrwhitt informs Stravinsky that Mme Khvoshchinsky has fallen ill in San Sebastián, where she has been for a month.

33. Zinaida Hippius and her husband, Dmitri Merezhkovsky, were pioneers of symbolism in Russia at the turn of the century. They were key figures in the St. Petersburg literary life and collaborated with the *World of Art* circle. One of the most influential poets of the Russian Silver Age, Hippius was instrumental in the Russian religious revival within the turn-of-the-century intelligentsia.

34. Both Massine and Sokolova give August 22 as the date of the premiere of *Las meninas*. But the first gala took place on August 21, and no new works were presented that evening. Ansermet in a letter to Falla dated August 22 mentions that the first gala had taken place the night before and that the program consisted of *Les Sylphides*, *Sadko*, *Prince Igor*, and *Schéhérazade*. He adds that *Las meninas* is being rehearsed and that Diaghilev wants to hear nothing except about *Las meninas* and *Kikimora*, which obviously were to be premiered at the second gala on August 25.

35. Cited in Fernando García-Pérez, "A la busqueda de Mrs. Keynes," *Papeles de Economía Española* (Madrid, 1983), pp. 341–71.

36. Alfredo Salazar, "Algo más sobre los Bailes Rusos," *Revista Musical Hispano-Americana*, August 1916.

37. Massine, *My Life*, p. iii.

38. Massine in conversations with Fred Maroth, 1978.

39. Draft of *Tricorne* contract, Archivo Manuel de Falla.

40. During the Ballets Russes' stay in San Sebastián, Falla wrote several times to Ansermet asking him to persuade Diaghilev to drop his initial idea to use the *Noches* for a ballet. Letters from Ansermet to Falla, August 22, September 2, and undated, Archivo Manuel de Falla.

5. Rome, September 1916–Paris, May 1917

1. *Stravinsky: Selected Correspondence*, ed. Robert Craft, vol. 2 (New York: Knopf, 1984), p. 489.

2. Romola Nijinsky, *Nijinsky* (New York: Simon and Schuster, 1980), p. 374.

3. Léonide Massine, *My Life in Ballet* (London: Macmillan, 1968), p. 107.

4. Massine in conversations with the author, Galli, 1978.

5. In his memoirs Massine claims that he bought the books, but I share Richard Buckle's opinion, in his biography *Diaghilev* (New York: Atheneum, 1979), that it was the impresario who did (p. 319).

6. Massine, *My Life*, pp. 96–97.

7. Ibid., p. 97.

8. Ibid.

9. Ibid., p. 98.

10. Ibid., p. 95.

11. Lydia Sokolova, *Dancing for Diaghilev* (London: John Murray, 1960), p. 98.

12. Milo Keynes, *Lydia Lopokova* (New York: St. Martin's Press, 1982), p. 210.

13. Lynn Garafola, *Diaghilev's Ballets Russes* (New York: Oxford University Press, 1989), p. 86.

14. Caroline Tisdall and Angelo Bozzolla, *Futurism* (New York: Oxford University Press, 1978), pp. 143–45.

15. Ibid., p. 145.

16. By 1916 Massine already had the visionary idea of documenting ballet on film, for it was about this time in Rome that he bought his first camera, to shoot rehearsals and performances of his ballets. However, in a letter to Anatoli Petrovich Bolchakov the choreographer wrote: "I take great interest in cinematography. I tried to shoot movies, but so far did not succeed. I hope the cinema will not replace choreographic notation." (July 4, 1917, State Central Theatrical Museum, Moscow, no. 181569.) The surviving films are now part of the Dance Collection of the New York Public Library.

17. *Stravinsky,* vol. 2, p. 34.

18. Buckle, *Diaghilev,* p. 346.

19. *Stravinsky,* vol. 2, pp. 29–30.

20. Ibid.

21. Ibid., p. 23.

22. Serge Lifar, *Serge Diaghilev* (New York: G. P. Putnam's Sons, 1940), p. 208.

23. *Stravinsky,* vol. 2, p. 30.

24. Ibid.

25. Massine, *My Life,* p. 98.

26. Ibid., p. 100.

27. Ibid., pp. 99–100.

28. Prince Peter Lieven, *The Birth of the Ballets-Russes* (Boston: Houghton Mifflin, 1936), p. 170.

29. Quoted in Francis Steegmuller, *Cocteau* (Boston: Little, Brown, 1970), pp. 75–76.

30. Ibid., p. 82.

31. Ibid., p. 167.

32. Ibid.

33. Steegmuller, *Cocteau,* p. 165.

34. Douglas Cooper, *Picasso Theatre* (London: Weidenfeld, 1968), p. 21.

35. Massine in conversations with the author, Galli, 1978.

36. Massine, *My Life,* pp. 106–107.

37. Massine in conversations with Fred Maroth, Oakland, Calif., 1977.

38. Ibid.

39. Massine in conversations with the author.

40. Letter from Cocteau to Misia Sert, undated, cited in Vicente García-Márquez's *España y los Ballets Rusos,* catalogue to exhibition in Granada, 1989, p. 25.

41. The original letter read:

    Mon cher Massine:

    Une collaboration est faite de surprises.

J'ai surpris Satie et Picasso avec mon thème, ils me surprennent avec la manière dont ils le traitent.

Reste un vide

Exprès

C'est le votre—c'est à vous de la remplir, de nous "surprendre" et ils ne restera plus à surprendre que le public.

Ne prenez pas ce vide pour du vague, mais pour un preuve de la bonne architecture de Parade *et de notre confiance en vous.*

Letter from Cocteau to Massine, undated, private collection.

42. In his memoirs Massine mistakenly dates the trip to Naples with Cocteau after the Ballets Russes' performance at the Teatro Costanzi in Rome, which took place in April. Cocteau was by then in Paris.

43. Massine, *My Life*, p. 108.

44. Ibid.

45. Ibid.

46. Buckle, *Diaghilev*, p. 325.

47. ". . . *un'organismo puramente musicale che si svolge con lo stesso andare di un fuoco d'artificio anche nell'ordine visuale.*" From the original program for the April 12 gala, private collection.

48. The original French reads:

Voici une Bonne fin que J'ai trouvée en sleeping. Elle arrange Serge et elle souligne Parade: *Pendant la final où les managers se detraquent les acrobates, la petite fille américaine et le chinois peuvent apparaître craintivement, assister avec épouvant à la chute des managers et se mettre à leur tour à indiquer de toutes leurs forces l'"ingresso" ils comprennent que les managers y renoncent. C'est une manière honnête de les ramener en scène et d'aider à faire comprendre qu'ils sont la Parade et non le spectacle intérieur.*

49. Massine, *My Life*, pp. 108–9.

50. Ibid., p. 109.

51. Nesta Macdonald, *Diaghilev Observed* (New York: Dance Horizons, 1975), p. 239. Also Marianne Martin, *Futurist Art and Theory, 1909–1915* (New York: Oxford University Press, 1968), p. 103.

52. Massine in conversations with the author, Galli, 1978.

53. Ibid.

54. Steegmuller, *Cocteau*, pp. 513–14.

55. Quoted in Lifar, *Serge Diaghilev*, pp. 217–18.

56. Ibid.

57. Ibid.

58. Cited in Garafola, *Diaghilev's Ballets Russes*, p. 87.

59. Francis Poulenc, *Moi et mes amis* (Paris: La Palatine, 1963), p. 88.

60. Steegmuller, *Cocteau*, p. 186.

61. Ibid., pp. 187–88.

62. Ibid., p. 190.

63. Ibid.

64. Ibid., p. 188.

65. The original French reads:

Vous avez assumé auprès de Diaghilev le rôle le plus important vis à vis de l'art scenique d'aujourd'hui en générale.

Mais ce qui nous interesse le plus c'est cette danse sur laquelle vous dessinez ave une grâce étrangement forte.

Cette force, cette simplicité dirai-je même sont les qualités qui vous distinguent. . . .

La chorégraphie et la musique sont par excellence des arts sur-réalistes puisque la réalité qu'ils expriment dépasse toujours la nature.

Voilà la raison même de l'importance de votre art et de votre propre importance artistique.

Vous m'avez apparu si appliqué à pénétrer les arcanes de l'imprévu chorégraphique que je n'ai aucune crainte sur l'avenir de cet art moderne.

Pour ce qui touche Parade et peut-être les ballets en générale je crois que les genoux et les coudes n'ont pas obtenu tous les égards qu'ils méritent. . . .

Vous été sans doute le premier qui ayez donné occasion d'employer ce mot à propos de danse.

Letter from Apollinaire to Massine, Paris, May 21, 1917, Archives de la Fondation Erik Satie, Paris.

6. *Spain, June 1917–July 1918*

1. Nijinsky previously had danced in Spain in 1914 in Madrid, at the wedding reception of Kermit Roosevelt.
2. Letter from Falla to María Martínez Sierra, June 4 and June 8, 1917, Archivo Manuel de Falla, Granada.
3. See C. E. Gauss, *The Aesthetic Theory of French Artists* (Baltimore, 1966), pp. 24–25. Chevreul concentrated on experiments in the physics of light and color.
4. Letter from Falla to María Martínez Sierra, June 8, 1917, Archivo Manuel de Falla.
5. Ibid.
6. Léonide Massine, *My Life in Ballet* (London: Macmillan, 1968), p. 115.
7. Letter from Falla to María Martínez Sierra, June 12, 1917, Archivo Manuel de Falla.
8. Letter from María Martínez Sierra to Falla, June 22, 1917, Archivo Manuel de Falla.
9. Massine, *My Life*, p. 115.
10. Douglas Cooper, *Picasso Theatre* (London: Weidenfeld, 1968), p. 37.
11. Carlos Bosch, *Mneme* (Madrid: Espasa-Calpe, 1942), p. 155.
12. Massine, *My Life*, p. 113.
13. Ibid.
14. Massine's autobiography is not accurate in its chronology of events. It was during the 1916 trip that he met Felix in Seville; he re-encountered him in Madrid in 1917, the year Felix joined the company.

15. Lydia Sokolova, *Dancing for Diaghilev* (London: John Murray, 1960), p. 113.
16. Massine, *My Life*, p. 114.
17. In his diary for 1918, Nijinsky expresses his feelings of resentment towards Diaghilev, as a betrayed lover.
18. Richard Buckle, *Nijinsky* (New York: Avon, 1971), p. 115.
19. Letter from Massine to Anatoli Petrovich Bolchakov, July 4 1917, State Central Theatrical Museum, Moscow, no. 181569.
20. Massine, *My Life*, p. 115.
21. Ibid., p. 117.
22. Ibid., p. 118.
23. Ibid., p. 119.
24. Ibid., p. 116.
25. Ibid., p. 117.
26. Ibid., p. 118.
27. Ibid.
28. For a more detailed study of the differences between the pantomime and the ballet, see Andrew Budwig, "The Evolution of Manuel de Falla's 'The Three-Cornered Hat,' 1916–1920," *Musicological Research* 5 (1984), pp. 191–212.
29. Massine in conversations with the author, Galli, 1978.
30. Manuel de Falla, *Escritos* (Madrid, 1947), p. 77.
31. Diaghilev-Falla correspondence from July 1916 to February 1917, Archivo Manuel de Falla.
32. Archivo Manuel de Falla.
33. Massine, *My Life*, p. 119.
34. Ibid., p. 121.
35. Jaime Pahissa, *Cuando el maestro Falla fue al pueblo de Goya*, Archivo Manuel de Falla.
36. Massine, *My Life*, p. 122.
37. Massine in conversations with Fred Maroth, Oakland, Calif., 1978.
38. Alfredo Morán, *Joaquín Turina: A través de sus escritos*, vol. 1 (Madrid, 1981), pp. 227–28.
39. Letter from Diaghilev to Massine, undated (Wednesday), Madrid, Palace Hotel, private collection.
40. Ibid.
41. Bernard Dorival, *Robert Delaunay* (Paris: Jacques Dermase Editions, 1975).
42. Letter from Sonia Delaunay to Massine, January 18, 1928, private collection.
43. Letter from Robert Delaunay to Massine, 1918, quoted in Dorival, *Robert Delaunay*.
44. Letter from Sonia Delaunay to Massine, January 18, 1928, private collection.

7. Paris, August 1918–London, August 1919

1. Léonide Massine, *My Life in Ballet* (London: Macmillan, 1968), p. 127.
2. Ibid.

3. Jean Hugo, *Le Regard de la mémoire* (Paris: Actes Sud, 1983), p. 137.

4. Massine, *My Life*, p. 128.

5. Ibid., p. 129.

6. Serge Grigoriev, *The Diaghilev Ballet, 1909–1929*, trans. and ed. by Vera Bowen (London: Constable, 1953; rpnt. Penguin Books, 1960), p. 150.

7. *The Observer*, September 11, 1918.

8. Cyril Beaumont, *The Diaghilev Ballet in London* (London: Adam and Charles Black, 1951), p. 107.

9. Ibid., p. 108.

10. Ibid.

11. Cited in John Pearson, *The Sitwells: A Family Biography* (New York: Harcourt Brace Jovanovich, 1978), p. 123.

12. Richard Buckle, *Diaghilev* (New York: Atheneum, 1979), pp. 349–50.

13. *Sunday Times* (London), November 24, 1918.

14. Roger Fry, *Letters of Roger Fry*, ed. by Denys Sutton (London: Chatto & Windus, 1972), p. 440.

15. Grigoriev, *Diaghilev Ballet*, p. 150.

16. *The Times* (London), December 24, 1918.

17. Beaumont, *Diaghilev Ballet*, pp. 117–18.

18. Letters in private collection.

19. Massine, *My Life*, p. 132.

20. Ibid.

21. Ibid., p. 133.

22. Ibid.

23. Massine in conversations with the author, Galli, 1978.

24. Clive Bell, "The New Ballet," *The New Republic*, July 30, 1919, pp. 414–16.

25. Lydia Sokolova, *Dancing for Diaghilev* (London: John Murray, 1960), p. 138.

26. Massine, *My Life*, p. 137.

27. Ballets Russes souvenir program, London, 1918.

28. Alexandra Danilova, *Choura* (New York: Knopf, 1986), p. 141.

29. Massine in conversations with the author.

30. Cited in *Diaghilev, Les Ballets Russes*, exhibition catalog (Paris: Bibliothèque Nationale, 1979).

31. Beaumont, *Diaghilev Ballet*, p. 134.

32. Ibid.

33. *Vogue* (London), August 1, 1919.

34. Roy Harrod, *The Life of John Maynard Keynes* (London: Macmillan, 1951), p. 334.

35. Massine in conversations with Fred Maroth, Oakland, Calif., 1977.

36. According to Nesta Macdonald, some of the characters in the front of the curtain can be identified, from left to right, as: Picasso (the man in the cape), Olga Khokhlova (the woman with the mantilla next to him), Stanislas Idzikowski (the little boy), Massine (the young man in the bull ring), and Diaghilev (disguised as a woman in blue sitting down). *The Observer*, November 2, 1986.

37. Letter from Diaghilev to Falla, London, May 24, 1919, Archivo Manuel de Falla, Granada.

38. Letter from Falla to Diaghilev, May 24, 1919, Archivo Manuel de Falla.
39. Sokolova, *Dancing,* p. 135.
40. Ibid.
41. This is probably why the tarantella employed a variety of Spanish folk steps.
42. Sokolova, *Dancing,* p. 134.
43. Tamara Karsavina, *Theatre Street* (London: Dance Books, 1981), p. 298.
44. Ibid., p. 300.
45. Sokolova, *Dancing,* pp. 136–37.
46. Massine, *My Life,* p. 143.
47. Quoted in Nesta Macdonald, *Diaghilev Observed* (New York: Dance Horizons, 1975), p. 230.
48. Copy of a letter from Falla to the director of the Teatro Colón, Buenos Aires, in regard to a revival of *Le Tricorne,* Manuel de Falla Archives, Granada.
49. Macdonald, *Diaghilev,* p. 231.
50. Beaumont, *Diaghilev Ballet,* p. 144.
51. Sokolova, *Dancing,* p. 142.
52. Ibid.
53. *Sunday Times* (London), July 27, 1919.
54. W. A. Propert, *The Russian Ballet in Western Europe, 1909–1920* (London: John Lane, 1921), p. 52.

The French reception of *Le Tricorne* was more controversial. Nevertheless, following its French premiere at the Paris Opéra on January 23, 1920, it was well received by the daily press; *Le Figaro* (January 24, 1920) reported long ovations after each entrée. But those French intellectual critics who had championed the prewar Ballets Russes (Henri Ghéon, Jacques Rivière, André Suarez, Fernand Gregh) did not subscribe so quickly to Diaghilev's abandonment of his earlier Russian aesthetic in favor of modernism. Massine the performer was much admired; for Rivière, his *farruca* was almost a "hallucination" ("Les Ballets Russes à l'Opéra," *La Nouvelle Revue Française* 78 [1920]: 463). Unfortunately, no other dancer has been able, as Massine was, to give this character its dramatic and essentially archetypal symbolic quality.

When the ballet was presented in Spain the following year, the issue became modernism versus traditionalism, internationalism versus nationalism. While intellectuals like Adolfo Salazar (*El Imparcial,* April 6, 1921), the dean of Spanish critics, championed *Le Tricorne,* the conservative Spanish press charged the ballet with modernist snobbery and with inaccuracy in its combination of styles of various regions, as well as contending that it departed from Alarcón's original and that even Falla's and Picasso's own work lacked authenticity. Here again, some of the critical objections to modernism were brought to bear.

55. Marilyn McCully, paper given at the symposium "España y Los Ballets Russes," Granada, 1989.
56. Massine, *My Life,* p. 141.
57. Ibid.
58. Ibid., pp. 141–42.
59. Beaumont, *Diaghilev Ballet,* p. 145.
60. Massine in conversations with the author.

61. Massine, *My Life*, p. 142.
62. Bell, "The New Ballet," loc. cit.
63. Ibid.
64. Ibid.
65. Ibid.
66. T. S. Eliot, "Dramatis Personae," *Criterion*, April 1923, pp. 303–06.

8. *London, August 1919–Rome, February 1921*

1. Léonide Massine, *My Life in Ballet* (London: Macmillan, 1968), p. 144.
2. Ibid.
3. Ibid.
4. Massine in conversations with the author, Galli, 1978.
5. Vera Stravinsky and Robert Craft, *Stravinsky in Pictures and Documents* (London: Hutchinson, 1979), pp. 183–84.
6. Ibid.
7. Igor Stravinsky and Robert Craft, *Expositions and Developments* (New York: Doubleday, 1962), pp. 126–27.
8. *Stravinsky: Selected Correspondence*, ed. Robert Craft, vol. 1 (New York: Knopf, 1982), p. 134. However, according to Massine the three met in Paris in 1918.
9. V. Stravinsky and Craft, *Stravinsky*, pp. 177–81.
10. Igor Stravinsky, *Chronicle of My Life* (London: Victor Gollancz, 1936), p. 37.
11. "Conversations with Henri Matisse," unpublished manuscript of interviews conducted by Pierre Courthion, 1941 (trans. by V. G.-M.), Special Collections, Getty Center for the History of Art and the Humanities, Los Angeles.
12. Ibid.
13. Ibid.
14. Ibid.
15. Ibid.
16. Ibid.
17. Ibid.
18. Ibid.
19. Massine, *My Life*, p. 147.
20. "Conversations with Matisse."
21. *Comoedia*, February 4, 1920.
22. Lydia Sokolova, *Dancing for Diaghilev* (London: John Murray, 1960), p. 147.
23. Nancy van Norman Baer, *The Art of Enchantment: Diaghilev's Ballets Russes, 1909–1929*, exhibition catalog, Fine Arts Museum of San Francisco, 1989, p. 75. Quote within extract is from Walter A. Propert, *Russian Ballet in Western Europe, 1909–1920* (London, 1921), p. 60.
24. *The Times* (London), July 17, 1920.
25. *Sunday Times* (London), July 18, 1920.

26. *Daily Herald* (London), July 17, 1920.
27. Douglas Cooper, *Picasso Theatre* (New York: H. N. Abrams, 1968), p. 46.
28. Igor Stravinsky, *Conversations with Igor Stravinsky* (New York: Doubleday, 1959).
29. Cyril W. Beaumont, *The Diaghilev Ballet in London* (London: Adams and Charles Black, 1951), p. 159.
30. Stravinsky, *Chronicle* (London: Victor Gollancz, 1936), p. 42.
31. Massine, *My Life*, pp. 148–49.
32. Serge Grigoriev, *The Diaghilev Ballet, 1909–1929* (London: Penguin Books, 1960), pp. 161–62.
33. Massine interview with Maroth, Maroth Collection.
34. Massine, *My Life*, p. 149.
35. André Levinson, "Stravinsky and the Dance," *Theatre Arts Monthly* 8 (November 1924), pp. 741–54.
36. *Daily Mail* (London), June 11, 1920.
37. *The Observer* (London), June 13, 1920.
38. Beaumont, *Diaghilev Ballet*, p. 160.
39. Ibid.
40. *Athenaeum*, June 18, 1920.
41. Stravinsky, *Chronicle*, p. 39.
42. *Sunday Times* (London), June 27, 1920.
43. *Athenaeum*, July 2, 1920.
44. Later a pas de quatre was added with choreography by Bronislava Nijinska.
45. Arnold Haskell, "The Younger Russian Dancers," *Dancing Times*, London, May 1928, pp. 135–37.
46. Ibid.
47. Sokolova, *Dancing*, p. 159.
48. Ibid., p. 160.
49. Ibid., p. 161.
50. *The Observer*, July 3, 1921.
51. Massine interview with Fred Maroth, Maroth Collection.
52. Ibid.
53. *Comoedia*, December 11, 1920.
54. Massine, *My Life*, p. 152.
55. Sokolova, *Dancing*, p. 162.
56. Ibid., pp. 160, 166.
57. Grigoriev, *Diaghilev Ballet*, p. 167.
58. *Comoedia*, December 11, 1920; *The Observer*, July 3, 1921.
59. Emile Vuillermoz, "La nouvelle version chorégraphique du Sacre du printemps, au Théâtre des Champs-Elysées," *La Revue Musicale*, February 1, 1921.
60. Levinson, "Stravinsky and the Dance," pp. 741–54.
61. Jean Bernier, "La Chorégraphie du Sacre du printemps," *Comoedia Illustré*, January 1921, p. 171.
62. Quoted in Arnold Haskell, *Balletomania Then and Now* (New York: Knopf, 1977), p. 104.

63. *Morning Post* (London), June 28, 1921.
64. *The Times* (London), June 28, 1921.
65. *Ballet Review* 6, no. 3 (1977–78), p. 59.
66. *The Times* (London), July 23, 1929.
67. Sokolova, *Dancing,* p. 163.
68. Ibid., pp. 163–64, 167.
69. Ibid., pp. 167–68.
70. Grigoriev, *Diaghilev Ballet,* p. 168.
71. Ibid.
72. Richard Buckle, *Diaghilev* (New York: Atheneum, 1979), p. 370.
73. Ibid., p. 371.
74. Ibid.
75. Grigoriev, *Diaghilev Ballet,* p. 169.
76. Ibid., p. 170.
77. Ibid.
78. Ibid.
79. Sokolova, *Dancing,* p. 171.
80. Arnold Haskell, *Diaghileff: His Artistic and Private Life* (New York: Simon and Schuster, 1935), p. 289.
81. Buckle, *Diaghilev,* p. 371.
82. Haskell, *Diaghileff,* p. 272.
83. Serge Lifar, *Serge Diaghilev: His Life, His Work, His Legend* (New York: G. P. Putnam's Sons, 1940), p. 208.

9. *Rome, February 1921–Paris, September 1928*

1. Léonide Massine, *My Life in Ballet* (London: Macmillan, 1968), p. 154.
2. Letter from Massine to Anatoli Petrovich Bolchakov, Barcelona, July 4, 1917, State Central Theatrical Museum, Moscow, no. 181569.
3. Massine, *My Life,* p. 154.
4. Copy of telegram from Massine to Mikhail Semenov, Avenida Palace Hotel, Lisbon, December 24, 1917, private collection.
5. Serge Lifar, *Serge Diaghilev: His Life, His Work, His Legend* (New York: G. P. Putnam's Sons, 1940), p. 208.
6. Correspondence between Massine and Jan Kawetzky, February and March 1921, private collection.
7. Contract between Massine and Raoul Gunsbourg, May 24, 1921, private collection.
8. Massine, *My Life,* p. 156.
9. Letter from Massine to Picasso, São Paulo, August 19, 1921, Musée Picasso, Paris.
10. Handwritten draft of a letter from Massine to Picasso, undated, private collection.

11. Cable from Massine to Picasso, Buenos Aires, November 18, 1921, Musée Picasso, Paris.
12. Draft of letter on the Parque Hotel letterhead, Montevideo, undated, private collection.
13. Copies of cables from Massine to Gunsbourg, undated, private collection.
14. Contract with Walter Wanger dated March 25, 1922, private collection.
15. *The Times* (London), April 4, 1922.
16. Ninette de Valois in conversations with the author, London, 1987.
17. T. S. Eliot, *The Letters of T. S. Eliot*, ed. Valerie Eliot, vol. 1 (London: Faber and Faber, 1988), p. 253.
18. Ibid., p. 530.
19. Massine, *My Life*, p. 134.
20. Correspondence between Ottoline Morrell and Massine, private collection.
21. Postcard from Morrell to Massine, October 16, 1922, private collection.
22. Postcard from Morrell to Massine, private collection.
23. Letter from Morrell to Massine, April 23, 1922, private collection.
24. Lydia Sokolova, *Dancing for Diaghilev* (London: John Murray, 1960), p. 198.
25. Tallulah Bankhead, *Tallulah: My Autobiography* (New York: Harper and Brothers, 1952), p. 13.
26. Entrance forms dated October 1, 1924, private collection.
27. Bernard Faÿ, *Les Précieux* (Paris: Librairie Académique, 1966), p. 69.
28. Francis Steegmuller, *Cocteau* (Boston: Little, Brown, 1970), p. 327.
29. Ibid., p. 328.
30. Milo Keynes, *Lydia Lopokova* (New York: St. Martin's Press, 1982), p. 98.
31. Richard Buckle, *Diaghilev* (New York: Atheneum, 1979), p. 426.
32. Polly Hill and Richard Keynes, *Lydia and Maynard: The Letters of L.L. and J.M.K.* (New York: Charles Scribner's Sons, 1989), p. 169.
33. Ibid., p. 174.
34. Ibid., p. 194.
35. Ibid., p. 197.
36. Ibid., p. 207.
37. Ibid., p. 219.
38. Ibid.
39. Massine in conversations with the author, Galli, 1978.
40. Ornella Volta, "Parade et Mercure," unpublished paper given at the conference "España y los Ballets Rusos," Granada, 1989. (According to Douglas Cooper, the whole conception of the ballet's mise-en-scène was essentially Picasso's. This probably explains why Massine in his autobiography does not discuss *Mercure*. It is evident that by 1924 the choreographer was moving away from this modernist trend.)
41. Volta, ibid.
42. Gertrude Stein, *Picasso* (London: Scribner's Sons, 1939), p. 54.
43. Volta, "Parade et Mercure."
44. Volta in conversations with the author, Paris, 1989. Jean Hugo, in his memoirs, *Avant d'oublier* (Paris: Fayard, 1976), p. 177, recalls a conversation in which Picasso claimed that the gloves were not his idea but that he liked it.

45. Cited in Lincoln Kirstein, *Ballet: Bias and Belief* (New York: Dance Horizons, 1983), p. 16.
46. *Paris-Journal*, May 30, 1924.
47. Madeleine Milhaud in conversations with the author, Paris, 1987.
48. "Chronique dramatique: Les Soirées de Paris," *Les Nouvelles Littéraires*, May 24, 1924.
49. Quoted by Anne Bertrand in *Les Soirées de Paris du Comte Etienne de Beaumont*, unpublished dissertation, Université de Paris X, Nanterre, p. 212.
50. Hill and Keynes, *Lydia and Maynard*, p. 196.
51. Ibid., p. 194.
52. Ibid.
53. Quoted in Bertrand, *Les Soirées*, p. 210.
54. Darius Milhaud, *Ma Vie heureuse* (Paris: Belfond, 1973), p. 131.
55. Bertrand, *Les Soirées*, p. 212.
56. Arnold Haskell, *Balletomania Then and Now* (New York: Knopf, 1977), p. 94.
57. Hill and Keynes, *Lydia and Maynard*, p. 180.
58. Jean Hugo, *Le Regard de la mémoire* (Paris: Actes Sud, 1983), p. 232.
59. Boris Kochno in conversations with the author, Paris, 1983–89.
60. Hill and Keynes, *Lydia and Maynard*, p. 200.
61. Massine in conversations with the author. Massine could not conceal his satisfaction that *Le Beau Danube*, which Diaghilev had called "pure trash" in 1924, became in the 1930s and well into the 1950s one of the most popular works in the international ballet repertory.
62. Massine, *My Life*, p. 142.
63. Quoted in Bertrand, *Les Soirées*, p. 229.
64. Hill and Keynes, *Lydia and Maynard*, p. 140.
65. Massine, *My Life*, p. 162.
66. Hill and Keynes, *Lydia and Maynard*, p. 145.
67. Massine in conversations with the author and with Fred Maroth.
68. Massine, *My Life*, p. 162.
69. Handwritten copy of telegram, undated, private collection.
70. Lynn Garafola, *Diaghilev's Ballets Russes* (New York: Oxford University Press, 1989), p. 266.
71. Massine, *My Life*, p. 161.
72. Ibid., p. 163.
73. Ibid., pp. 162, 163.
74. Kochno in conversations with the author, Paris, 1989.
75. Sokolova, *Dancing*, pp. 229–30.
76. Vernon Duke, *Passport to Paris* (Boston: Little, Brown, 1955), p. 135.
77. Ibid., p. 137.
78. Ibid.
79. Ibid., p. 135.
80. Kochno in conversations with the author, Paris, 1989.
81. Ibid.
82. *Morning Post*, November 13, 1925.
83. *The Times*, November 13, 1925.

84. Massine, *My Life*, p. 166.
85. Cyril W. Beaumont, *Diaghilev's Ballet in London* (London: Adam and Charles Black, 1951), p. 248.
86. Quoted in Garafola, *Diaghilev's Ballets Russes*, p. 136.
87. Nesta Macdonald, *Diaghilev Observed* (New York: Dance Horizons, 1975), p. 312.
88. *The Times* (London), June 30, 1925.
89. *Morning Post*, May 20, 1925.
90. Massine, *My Life*, p. 166.
91. Letter from Charles B. Cochran to Massine, May 19, 1925, private collection.
92. Quoted in *Dancing Times*, August 1925, p. 1139.
93. Letter from Cochran to Massine, May 19, 1925.
94. Note to Massine attributed to Coward, private collection.
95. Massine, *My Life*, p. 168.
96. Ibid.
97. Garafola, *Diaghilev's Ballets Russes*, p. 235.
98. Letter from Massine to Edith de Beaumont, January 23, 1926, Archives de la Fondation Erik Satie; correspondence between E. de Beaumont and Diaghilev from January 28, 1926, through April 29, 1926, Fonds Kochno, Bibliothèque de l'Opéra, Paris.
99. Kochno in conversations with the author, Paris, 1989.
100. Ibid.
101. Elizabeth Souritz, "Soviet Ballet of the 1920's and the Influence of Constructivism," *Soviet Union* 7, pts. 1–2 (1980), p. 122.
102. Letter from Marcel Ballot of the Société des Auteurs et Compositeurs Dramatiques, stating that Massine was to receive a percentage as co-author with Prokofiev and Yakoulov, private collection.
103. Kochno in conversations with the author, Paris, 1989.
104. *The Times* (London), July 5, 1927.
105. *Daily Express*, July 7, 1927.
106. Beaumont, *Diaghilev Ballet*, p. 279.
107. Ibid.
108. Massine, *My Life*, p. 174.
109. Eugenia Delarova in conversations with the author, New York, 1981–90.
110. Massine papers, private collection.
111. Letter from Sonia Delaunay to Massine, January 18, 1928, private collection.
112. Ibid.
113. Private collection.
114. Parker Tyler, *The Divine Comedy of Pavel Tchelitchew* (New York: Fleet Publishing Corporation, 1967), p. 328.
115. Ibid.
116. Kochno in conversations with the author, Paris, 1983–89.
117. Nicholas Nabokov, *Bagazh* (New York: Atheneum, 1975), p. 152.
118. Arnold Haskell, *Diaghileff* (New York: Simon and Schuster, 1935), p. 135.
119. Cecil Beaton, *Dance Index* 5, no. 8, August 1946, pp. 194–95.
120. Massine, *My Life*, p. 173.
121. Felia Doubrovska in conversations with the author, New York City, 1981.

122. *Dancing Times*, no. 215, August 1928, p. 491.
123. Beaumont, *Diaghilev Ballet*, p. 287.
124. Ibid., pp. 287–88.
125. A. V. Coton, *A Prejudice for Ballet* (London: Methuen and Co., 1938), p. 90.
126. Garafola, *Diaghilev's Ballets Russes*, p. 142.
127. Massine, *My Life*, pp. 176–77.
128. Nabokov, *Bagazh*, p. 153.
129. Delarova in conversations with the author.

10. New York, December 1928–London, June 1936

1. Letter from Massine to Charles B. Cochran, April 25, 1928, private collection.
2. Ibid.
3. Léonide Massine, *My Life in Ballet* (London: Macmillan, 1968), p. 174.
4. Ibid., p. 175.
5. Ibid., p. 176.
6. Ibid., p. 177.
7. Anne Bertrand, *Les Soirées de Paris du Comte Etienne de Beaumont,* unpublished dissertation, Université de Paris X, Nanterre, p. 358.
8. Vicente García-Márquez, *The Ballets Russes* (New York: Knopf, 1990), pp. 3–4.
9. Copies of cables, private collection.
10. García-Márquez, *Ballets Russes*, p. 4.
11. Oliver Daniel, *"Rite of Spring,* First Staging in America: Stokowski-Massine-Graham." *Ballet Review* 10, no. 2 (Summer 1982), pp. 67–71.
12. These stories have been handed down mainly by Claire Reis and Dick Hammond, who were closely involved in the production.
13. Transcript of the Dance Critics Association panel on Léonide Massine's *Le Sacre du printemps,* New York City, November 7, 1987.
14. Ibid.
15. Ibid.
16. Ibid.
17. Massine, *My Life*, pp. 178–79.
18. Daniel, *"Rite of Spring,"* p. 70.
19. Transcript of Dance Critics Association panel.
20. Ibid.
21. *New York Herald Tribune,* April 20, 1930.
22. *New York Times,* April 27, 1930.
23. Cable from Walter Nouvel to Massine, April 1, 1931, private collection.
24. Huguette Laurenti, *Paul Valéry et le théâtre* (Paris: Gallimard, 1973), p. 430.
25. *Revue de France,* August 1931.
26. *Les Nouvelles Littéraires,* July 18, 1931.
27. *Temps,* July 1, 1931.

28. André Levinson, *Les Visages de la danse* (Paris: Editions Bernard Grasset, 1933), p. 111.
29. Ibid., pp. 111–12.
30. *L'Excelsior,* June 29, 1931.
31. *Candide,* July 2, 1931.
32. Confirmation of Massine's engagement with British and Dominions Film Corporation, July 28, 1931, private collection.
33. Igor Markevitch, *Être et avoir été* (Paris: Gallimard, 1980), pp. 210–11.
34. Massine, *My Life,* pp. 180–81.
35. Markevitch, *Être et avoir été,* p. 212.
36. Massine, *My Life,* p. 181.
37. *Dancing Times* 258 (March 1932).
38. Letter from Cochran to Massine, September 19, 1931, private collection.
39. Massine, *My Life,* p. 182.
40. Ibid.
41. Delarova in conversations with the author, New York City, 1981–90.
42. Massine, *My Life,* p. 185.
43. Philip Ziegler, *Diana Cooper* (London: Hamish Hamilton, 1981), pp. 147–49.
44. *The Times* (London), April 11, 1932.
45. Ibid.
46. Diana Cooper, *The Light of Common Day* (London: Rupert Hart-Davis, 1959), p. 112.
47. Cable from Max Reinhardt to Massine, May 15, 1932, private collection.
48. Cf. my discussion of *Jeux d'enfants* in *Ballets Russes,* pp. 28–37.
49. Ibid., p. 31.
50. A. V. Coton, *A Prejudice for Ballet* (London: Methuen & Co., 1938), p. 213.
51. Toumanova in conversations with the author.
52. Riabouchinska in conversations with the author.
53. *Sunday Times* (London), July 11, 1933.
54. Copy of letter to Rothafel and Jay Kaufman, July 11, 1932, private collection.
55. Arnold Haskell, *Balletomania Then and Now* (New York: Knopf, 1977), p. 94.
56. Verchinina in conversations with the author, Rio de Janeiro, March 18, 1990.
57. Pierre Michaut, *Le Ballet contemporain* (Paris: Pion, 1950), p. 93.
58. Verchinina in conversations with the author.
59. Ibid.
60. Massine, *My Life,* p. 187.
61. Ibid.
62. Riabouchinska in conversations with the author, July 1980, May 1983, and August 1985.
63. Levinson, *Visages de la danse,* p. 83.
64. Lifar was quite outspoken against Massine's symphonic ballets. In 1936 he wrote: "One could discuss his method of transposing an orchestral score onto a dance-canvas. At the present, Massine never idealizes material images; he submits entirely to the power of the sentiments aroused in him by those musical symphonies whose choreographic translator he wants to be." Undated clipping, Bibliothèque de l'Opéra, Paris.

65. Michaut, *Ballet contemporain*, p. 94.

66. *Sunday Times* (London), July 9, 1933.

67. Coton, *Prejudice for Ballet*, p. 65.

68. Ibid., p. 68.

69. Riabouchinska in conversations with the author.

70. Baronova in conversations with the author.

71. Ibid.

72. Massine, *My Life*, pp. 190–91.

73. *New York Times*, January 3, 1934.

74. *L'Excelsior*, June 16, 1933.

75. Levinson, *Visages de la danse*, p. 89.

76. Haskell, *Balletomania*, p. 172.

77. Toumanova in conversations with the author.

78. *Sunday Times* (London), July 16, 1933.

79. Coton, *Prejudice for Ballet*, p. 207.

80. Haskell, *Balletomania*, p. 167.

81. Coton, *Prejudice for Ballet*, p. 212.

82. Ibid., p. 214.

83. Agnes de Mille, *Dance to the Piper* (Boston: Little, Brown, 1952), p. 152.

84. Haskell, *Balletomania*, p. 92.

85. Ibid., p. 101.

86. Massine, *My Life*, p. 191.

87. Ibid.

88. Ibid., pp. 191–92.

89. Verchinina in conversations with the author.

90. Ibid.

91. Cf. my discussion of *Choreartium* in García-Márquez, *The Ballets Russes*, p. 92.

92. Coton, *Prejudice for Ballet*, p. 88.

93. *Sunday Times* (London), October 29, 1933.

94. Ibid., July 5, 1936.

95. Haskell, *Balletomania*, p. 174.

96. Ibid.

97. Coton, *Prejudice for Ballet*, p. 89.

98. Ibid., p. 5.

99. Ibid., p. 126.

100. Delarova in conversations with the author.

101. Official visa granted by the Spanish consulate in Nice, April 30, 1935, private collection.

102. Vera Zorina, *Zorina* (New York: Farrar, Straus & Giroux, 1986), p. 106.

103. Ibid., pp. 106–07.

104. Ibid., p. 110.

105. Ibid., pp. 111–12.

106. Letter from Voltaire A. Gicca (Mexican and Brazilian attorney) to George Boochever, January 17, 1936, private collection.

107. Letter from George Boochever to Massine, January 17, 1936, private collection.

108. Ibid.

109. Zorina, *Zorina,* pp. 111–12.
110. Ibid.
111. Ibid., p. 118.

11. *London, June 1936–Paris, June 1939*

1. Letter from J. D. Langton and Passmore to Colonel de Basil, July 12, 1934, private collection.
2. Letter from J. D. Langton and Passmore to the managing director, Covent Garden Opera House, July 17, 1934, private collection.
3. Agreement between Colonel de Basil and Massine, August 10, 1934, Mme de Basil Collection, Paris.
4. Alexandra Danilova, *Choura* (New York: Knopf, 1986), p. 118.
5. Draft of letter from Massine to de Basil and letter from de Basil to Massine, March 27, 1936, private collection.
6. Correspondence between Massine and Blum and Stoll throughout March 1936, private collection.
7. Copies of cables to Lifar, Woizikowski, and Balanchine, May 3, 1936, private collection.
8. Tamara Tchinarova in conversations with the author, 1982.
9. Grace Robert, *The Borzoi Book of Ballets* (New York: Knopf, 1946), p. 346.
10. *Daily Telegraph,* July 24, 1935.
11. Toumanova in conversations with the author, Beverly Hills, 1985.
12. Letter from Ernest Ansermet to Massine, January 15, 1933, Mme de Basil Collection, Paris.
13. Letter from Etienne de Beaumont to Massine, August 9, 1935, private collection.
14. Vera Newman, *Ernest Newman: A Memoir by His Wife* (New York: Knopf, 1964), p. 155.
15. Cf. my discussion of *Symphonie fantastique* in *Ballets Russes,* pp. 158–68.
16. *Sunday Times* (London), August 2, 1936.
17. Léonide Massine, *My Life in Ballet* (London: Macmillan, 1968), pp. 201–02.
18. *Sunday Times* (London), July 5, 1936; July 12, 1936; July 19, 1936; July 26, 1936.
19. A. V. Coton, *A Prejudice for Ballet* (London: Methuen and Co., 1938), p. 127.
20. *Sunday Times* (London), August 2, 1936.
21. *The Times* (London), July 25, 1936.
22. Coton, *Prejudice for Ballet,* p. 140.
23. *Sunday Referee,* August 2, 1936.
24. *Sunday Times* (London), August 2, 1936.
25. Letter from W. J. Turner to Massine, July 25, 1936, private collection.
26. *New York Sun,* October 30, 1936.
27. Edwin Denby, *Dance Writings* (New York: Knopf, 1986), pp. 39–40.
28. Ibid.

29. Letter from Etienne de Beaumont to Massine, June 26, 1936, private collection.
30. Copy of a letter from Massine to Zoltán Kodály, December 14, 1926, enclosed with a draft of a contract, private collection.
31. Letter from Massine to Serge Denham, January 2, 1937; letter from Denham to Massine, October 1, 1937; Denham Papers, Dance Collection, New York Public Library.
32. Letter from Massine to Sol Hurok, April 13, 1937, Denham Papers.
33. *New York Times,* November 20, 1937.
34. *Dancing Times* 322 (July 1937), p. 413.
35. Copy of a letter from Massine to Beaumont, March 3, 1937, private collection.
36. Frederic Franklin in conversations with the author, New York, 1986.
37. *Sunday Times* (London), July 17, 1938.
38. *Dancing Times,* August 1938.
39. Cyril Beaumont, *Supplement to Complete Book of Ballets* (London: Putnam, 1952), pp. 47–48.
40. *New York Times,* October 13, 1938.
41. *New York Times,* April 24, 1938.
42. Sol Hurok, *Impresario* (New York: Random House, 1946), p. 204.
43. *Sunday Times* (London), July 26, 1936.
44. Massine, *My Life,* p. 206.
45. Massine in conversation with the author, Galli, 1978.
46. Jack Anderson, *The One and Only: The Ballet Russe de Monte Carlo* (New York: Dance Horizons, 1981), p. 69.
47. *Daily Telegraph,* July 13, 1938.
48. *Sunday Times* (London), July 24, 1938.
49. Ibid.
50. Anderson, *The One and Only,* p. 19.
51. Denby, *Dance Writings,* pp. 52–53.
52. *Excelsior,* June 3, 1939.
53. *Le Temps,* June 17, 1939.
54. *Le Jour,* June 3, 1939.
55. Massine, *My Life,* p. 207.
56. François Mauriac, foreword, Ballet Russe de Monte Carlo souvenir program, n.d.
57. Letters from Massine to Paul Hindemith, August 8 and August 29, 1937, Dunham Papers, Dance Collection, New York Public Library.
58. Massine, *My Life,* p. 209.
59. Ibid.
60. Danilova, *Choura,* p. 140.
61. Letter from Hindemith to Massine, August 1938, private collection.
62. *Bystander,* August 10, 1938.
63. *Daily Telegraph,* July 22, 1938.
64. Robert, *Borzoi Book of Ballets,* p. 266.
65. Denby, *Dance Writings,* pp. 53–54.
66. Ibid., p. 66.
67. *New York Times,* October 23, 1938.

68. Solomon Hurok, *S. Hurok Presents ... The World of Ballet* (London: Robert Hale, 1955), p. 129.

69. George Amberg, *Ballet in America* (New York: Mentor, 1955), p. 53.

70. *Le Temps*, June 24, 1939.

71. *Le Jour*, June 4, 1939.

72. *Ce Soir*, June 6, 1939.

73. *Le Jour*, June 4, 1939.

74. Danilova in conversations with the author, New York, 1986.

75. Frederic Franklin in conversations with the author.

76. Massine, *My Life*, p. 211.

77. Denby, *Dance Writings*, pp. 59–60.

78. Massine, *My Life*, p. 211, and in conversations with the author, Rennes, 1978.

79. "Conversations with Henri Matisse," unpublished manuscript of interviews conducted by Pierre Courthion, 1941 (trans. by V. G-M), Special Collections, The Getty Center for the History of Art and the Humanities, Los Angeles.

80. Letter from Matisse to Massine, May 18, 1938, private collection.

81. Letter from Matisse to Massine, undated, private collection.

82. Danilova in conversations with the author.

83. *L'Opinion*, July 1, 1939.

84. Ibid.

85. Anderson, *The One and Only*, p. 34.

86. Danilova, *Choura*, p. 140.

87. Robert, *Borzoi Book of Ballets*, pp. 257–58.

88. *L'Opinion*, July 1, 1939.

89. Denby, *Dance Writings*, p. 60.

90. *New York Times*, November 5, 1939.

91. Robert, *Borzoi Book of Ballets*, p. 258.

92. Robert Lawrence, *The Victor Book of Ballets and Ballet Music* (New York: Simon and Schuster, 1950), p. 374.

93. *Theatre Arts*, July 1940, p. 26.

94. *L'Opinion*, July 1, 1939.

12. *Paris, June 1939–New York, August 1946*

1. Delarova in conversations with the author, New York, 1981–1990.

2. Ballet libretto handwritten by Salvador Dalí, signed and dated Monte Carlo, April 20, 1938, private collection. (According to a letter from Stravinsky to Massine, the composer was eager to collaborate with the choreographer on a Dalí ballet. Obviously, the collaboration did not materialize. Letter from Stravinsky to Massine, March 27, 1938, private collection.)

3. Ibid., specifications in ballet libretto by Dalí.

4. This contract was rectified on July 6, 1938. Letter from Dalí to Massine, October 23, 1938, private collection.

5. Robert Descharnes, *Salvador Dalí* (New York: H. N. Abrams, 1985).

6. Gerald Goode, *The Book of Ballets* (New York: Crown, 1939), p. 19.

7. Léonide Massine, *My Life in Ballet* (London: Macmillan, 1968), p. 215.

8. Ibid.

9. Alexandra Danilova, *Choura* (New York: Knopf, 1986), p. 142.

10. Jack Anderson, *The One and Only: The Ballet Russe de Monte Carlo* (New York: Dance Horizons, 1981), p. 37.

11. *New York Times,* November 19, 1939.

12. Robert Lawrence, *The Victor Book of Ballets and Ballet Music* (New York: Simon & Schuster, 1950), p. 46.

13. *San Francisco Chronicle,* February 3, 1940.

14. George Amberg, *Ballet in America* (New York: Mentor, 1949), p. 53.

15. *Dance,* November 1940, p. 9.

16. Ibid.

17. Letter from Massine to Denham, June 7, 1940, Denham Papers, Dance Collection, New York Public Library.

18. Letter from Massine to Denham, June 16, 1940, Denham Papers.

19. Letter from Massine to Denham, August 24, 1940, Denham Papers.

20. Ibid.

21. Letter from Massine to Denham, September 7, 1940, Denham Papers.

22. Letter from Massine to Denham, August 16, 1940, Denham Papers.

23. Ibid.

24. *Dance,* November 1940.

25. Edwin Denby, *Dance Writings* (New York: Knopf, 1986), p. 66.

26. *New York Times,* October 30, 1940.

27. *New York Sun,* October 19, 1940.

28. Letter from Massine to Etienne de Beaumont, June 4, 1936, private collection.

29. *Dance,* November 1940, p. 9.

30. Letter from Denham to Jacques Rubinstein, December 19, 1939, cited in Anderson, *The One and Only.*

31. Massine, *My Life,* p. 216.

32. Massine in conversations with the author, Galli, 1978.

33. Massine, *My Life,* p. 218.

34. Ibid., pp. 218–19.

35. Ibid., p. 219.

36. Lawrence, *Victor Book of Ballets,* p. 255.

37. Denby, *Dance Writings,* p. 80.

38. *New York Herald Tribune,* October 19, 1941.

39. Massine, *My Life,* p. 220.

40. Amberg, *Ballet in America,* p. 50.

41. *Dance,* January 1941.

42. *New York Herald Tribune,* April 19, 1942.

43. Letter from Serge Denham to Julius Fleischmann, April 15, 1942, Denham Papers.

44. Letter from Denham to Massine, August 26, 1937, Denham Papers.

45. Letter from Massine to Denham, August 13, 1938, Denham Papers.

46. Anderson, *The One and Only,* p. 46.
47. *Dance,* November 1940, p. 9.
48. Letter from Denham to Fleischmann, July 5, 1939, Denham Papers.
49. *Dance,* November 1940, p. 9.
50. Anderson, *The One and Only,* p. 50.
51. Ibid.
52. The list reads as follows:
    1. *Dulle Griet* ("Mad Meg") (based upon paintings by Pieter Brueghel the Elder, scenery and costumes by Dalí);
    2. *Audubon* (character ballet by Glenway Wescott, music by David Diamond, scenery and costumes by [?] Platt);
    3. *Don Pasquale* (classical ballet, music by Donizetti, scenery and costumes by Giorgio de Chirico);
    4. *Brazilian Ballet* (music by Heitor Villa-Lobos, scenery and costumes by Cándido Portinari);
    5. *Lieutenant Kije* (music by Serge Prokofiev, scenery and costumes by Sergei Soudeikine);
    6. *Johnny Goes to Town* (American ballet, music to be composed by Roy Harris, libretto by Archibald MacLeish, scenery and costumes by [?] Saalburg or Aron Borhod);
    7. *Mayan Ballet* (music to be composed by Carlos Chávez, scenery and costumes by Diego Rivera);
    8. *Sacrifice* (Spanish ballet by Dalí, music by Bach or Handel to be arranged, scenery and costumes by Dalí);
    9. *English Ballet* (based on work of Gilbert and Sullivan, scenery and costumes by Oliver Smith and Alvin Colt);
    10. *The Gypsies* (by Pushkin, music by Tchaikovsky, scenery and costumes by [?] Anisfeld);
    11. *The Golden Age* (suite of dances by Dmitri Shostakovich, scenery and costumes by Alexander Calder);
    12. *Golden Wife* (based upon Finnish legend, music by Sibelius (En Saga), scenery and costumes by Pavel Tchelitchev);
    13. *Le Mariage Forcé* (by Molière, music by Mozart to be arranged, scenery and costumes by [?] De Molas);
    14. *Elegie* (classical ballet, music by Chopin to be arranged, scenery and costumes by Lydia Doboujinsky);
    15. *Hungarian Rhapsody* (music by Liszt);
    16. *Astuzie Femminili* (revival);
    17. *Soleil de nuit* (revival);
    18. *Pulcinella* (revival);
    19. *Le Sacre du printemps* (revival); and
    20. *Le Roi valet* (story by Derain, music to be composed by Jean Françaix, scenery by Tchelitchev (if André Derain was not available).
53. Letter from Massine to Manuel de Falla, November 27, 1941, Archivo Manuel de Falla, Granada.

54. Letter from Denham to Fleischmann, January 23, 1942, Denham Papers.
55. Letter from Denham to Fleischmann, April 15, 1942, Denham Papers.
56. *Time,* April 20, 1936.
57. Hurok, *The World of Ballet,* p. 130.
58. Ibid.
59. Ibid., p. 132.
60. Letter from Denham to Fleischmann, May 5, 1942, Denham Papers.
61. Massine, *My Life,* p. 221.
62. Ibid., p. 222.
63. Ibid., p. 223.
64. Franz Meyer, *Marc Chagall: Life and Work* (London: Thomas Hudson, 1964), p. 438.
65. Ibid.
66. Ibid.
67. Jean-Paul Crespell, *The Love, the Dreams, the Life of Marc Chagall* (New York: Coward-McCann, 1970), p. 231.
68. Massine, *My Life,* p. 225.
69. Peter Anastos, "A Conversation with George Skibine," *Ballet Review* 10, no. 1 (Spring 1982), p. 75.
70. Leland Windreich, "Massine's *Aleko,*" *Dance Chronicle* 8 (1985), p. 160.
71. Meyer, *Chagall,* p. 438.
72. Jacques Lassaigne, *Marc Chagall: Drawings and Watercolors for the Ballet* (New York: Tudor, 1959), pp. 14–15.
73. Meyer, *Chagall,* p. 438.
74. Windreich, "Massine's *Aleko,*" p. 170.
75. Grace Robert, *The Borzoi Book of Ballets* (New York: Knopf, 1946), p. 26.
76. Ibid.
77. Alonso in conversations with the author, Rome, 1988.
78. Charles Payne, *American Ballet Theatre* (New York: Knopf, 1979), p. 335.
79. Marcia Siegel, *The Shape of Change* (Boston: Houghton Mifflin, 1979), p. 100.
80. *Novedades,* September 9, 1942.
81. *New York Herald Tribune,* October 25, 1942.
82. Denby, *Dance Writings,* p. 98.
83. Ibid., p. 99.
84. Ibid., p. 118.
85. *San Francisco Chronicle,* July 3, 1943.
86. Robert, *Borzoi Book,* p. 25.
87. Payne, *American Ballet Theatre,* p. 77.
88. Massine, *My Life,* pp. 215–16.
89. Ibid., p. 220.
90. Ibid., p. 226.
91. Ibid., p. 227.
92. Ibid., p. 226.
93. Souvenir program, Ballet Theatre, October 10, 1943.
94. T. S. Eliot, "Tradition and the Individual Talent," in *Selected Essays* (New York: Harcourt, Brace & World, 1964), p. 7.

95. Denby, *Dance Writings*, pp. 148–49.
96. Ibid., p. 154.
97. Ibid., p. 275.
98. Ibid., pp. 275–76.
99. Robert, *Borzoi Book of Ballet*, p. 37.
100. Amberg, *Ballet in America*, p. 167.
101. Ibid., p. 53.
102. Massine, *My Life*, pp. 227–28.
103. Ibid.
104. Denby, *Dance Writings*, p. 113.
105. Ibid., pp. 118–19.
106. *Dance*, July 1941, p. 7.
107. *Dance*, November 1940, p. 9.
108. Amberg, *Ballet in America*, p. 47.
109. Marcia Siegel, *At the Vanishing Point* (New York: Saturday Review Press, 1972), p. 109.
110. Agnes de Mille, *Dance to the Piper* (Boston: Little, Brown, 1952), p. 220.
111. Amberg, *Ballet in America*, p. 42.
112. Lincoln Kirstein, *Ballet: Bias and Belief* (New York: Dance Horizons, 1983), p. 168.
113. Anderson, *The One and Only*, p. 71.
114. Lincoln Kirstein, *P.M.*, December 1, 1940.
115. Kirstein, *Ballet: Bias and Belief*, p. 245.
116. Amberg, *Ballet in America*, p. 45.
117. Eugene Loring in conversations with the author, Irvine, California, 1980.
118. Denby, *Dance Writings*, p. 52.
119. Amberg, *Ballet in America*, p. 54.
120. *Dance*, February 1940, p. 31.

13. London, September 1946–Edinburgh, September 1960

1. Brahms was the editor of *Footnotes to Ballet* (London, 1936) and the author of *Robert Helpmann, Choreographer*.
2. Richard Buckle, *The Adventures of a Ballet Critic* (London: Cresset Press, 1953), p. 90.
3. Ninette de Valois in conversations with the author, London, 1987.
4. Ibid.
5. Ibid.
6. Alexander Bland, *The Royal Ballet* (New York: Doubleday, 1981), p. 90.
7. Ibid.
8. Ibid.
9. Léonide Massine, *My Life in Ballet* (London: Macmillan, 1968), p. 230.
10. Alexander Grant in conversations with the author, London, 1987.

11. Margot Fonteyn, *Autobiography* (New York: Warner Books, 1967), p. 97.
12. Ibid.
13. Moira Shearer in conversations with the author, Wiltshire, England, 1987.
14. *Dance Magazine* 22, no. 4 (April 1948), p. 29.
15. De Valois in conversations with the author.
16. Grant in conversations with the author.
17. *Ballet Review* 6, no. 3 (1977–78), p. 72.
18. Michael Powell in conversations with the author, Avening, England, 1987.
19. Michael Powell, *A Life in Movies* (New York: Knopf, 1987), p. 627.
20. Powell in conversations with the author.
21. Cited in Monk Gibbon, *The Red Shoes Ballet* (London: Saturn Press, 1948), p. 51.
22. Powell, *A Life*, p. 642.
23. Ibid.
24. Ibid.
25. Ibid.
26. Powell in conversations with the author.
27. Gibbon, *Red Shoes*, p. 68.
28. Ibid., p. 30.
29. Shearer in conversations with the author.
30. Powell in conversations with the author.
31. Gibbon, *Red Shoes*, pp. 77–78.
32. Powell in conversations with the author.
33. Massine, *My Life*, p. 233.
34. Gibbon, *Red Shoes*, p. 17.
35. Ibid., p. 58.
36. Shearer in conversations with the author.
37. Gibbon, *Red Shoes*, p. 14.
38. Ibid., pp. 67–68.
39. Powell in conversations with the author.
40. Ibid.
41. Massine, *My Life*, p. 237.
42. Shearer in conversations with the author.
43. Ibid.
44. Ian Christie, *Powell, Pressburger and Others* (London: British Film Institute, 1978), p. 37.
45. Powell, *A Life*, p. 654.
46. Ibid., p. 653.
47. Shearer in conversations with the author.
48. De Valois in conversations with the author.
49. Grant in conversations with the author.
50. Shearer in conversations with the author.
51. Grant in conversations with the author.
52. *Dance Magazine* 22, no. 4 (April 1948), p. 28.
53. *Dancing Times* 448 (January 1948), pp. 180–81.
54. *Dance Magazine* 22, no. 4 (April 1948), pp. 28–29.
55. For de Cuevas, Massine danced in *Le Tricorne* with Toumanova and Lichine

and in *Le Beau Danube* and *Les Femmes de bonne humeur* with Riabouchinska and Lichine.

56. Massine, *My Life*, p. 231.
57. Ibid., p. 232.
58. Grant in conversations with the author.
59. Shearer in conversations with the author.
60. Ibid.
61. *Dancing Times* 455 (August 1948), p. 578.
62. Lorca Massine in conversations with the author, Rome, 1987.
63. Tatiana Massine in conversations with the author, New York, 1990.
64. *The Simon and Schuster Book of Ballet* (New York: Simon and Schuster, 1979), p. 254.
65. Tamara Toumanova in conversations with the author, Beverly Hills, 1990.
66. Irene Skorik in conversations with the author, Paris, 1989.
67. Massine, *My Life*, p. 237.
68. Powell in conversations with the author.
69. Ibid.
70. Shearer in conversations with the author.
71. Powell in conversations with the author.
72. Monk Gibbon, *The Tales of Hoffmann: A Study of the Film* (London: Saturn Press, 1951), p. 58.
73. Ibid., p. 57.
74. Ibid., pp. 57–58.
75. Powell in conversations with the author.
76. Gibbon, *Tales of Hoffmann*, pp. 58–59.
77. Ibid., p. 60.
78. Christie, *Powell, Pressburger*, p. 41.
79. Fernau Hall, *Anatomy of Ballet* (London: Andrew Melrose, 1953), p. 197.
80. Christie, *Powell, Pressburger*, p. 62.
81. Grant in conversations with the author.
82. Pigeon Crowle, *Beryl Grey* (London: Faber and Faber, 1952), pp. 69–70.
83. David Gillard, *Beryl Grey: A Biography* (London: W. H. Allen, 1977), p. 81.
84. *Dance and Dancers* 3, no. 2 (February 1952), p. 14.
85. *Dancing Times* 496 (January 1952), p. 202.
86. *Dance and Dancers* 3, no. 2 (February 1952), pp. 13–14.
87. *Ballet Annual*, no. 7 (1953), p. 17.
88. Hall, *Anatomy of Ballet*, pp. 134–35.
89. *Dancing Times* 496 (January 1952), p. 204.
90. De Valois in conversations with the author.
91. Grant in conversations with the author.
92. Bland, *Royal Ballet*, p. 104.
93. Massine, *My Life*, p. 239.
94. Ibid.
95. Ibid., p. 241.
96. *Simon and Schuster Book of Ballet*, p. 260.
97. Ibid.

98. Massine, *My Life*, p. 241.
99. Arnold Haskell, *Balletomania Then and Now* (New York: Knopf, 1977), p. 105.
100. *New York Herald Tribune*, April 9, 1962.
101. *New York Times*, April 9, 1962.
102. *Arts*, June 5, 1953.
103. Ettore Giannini in conversations with the author, Rome, 1987.
104. Ibid.
105. Ibid.
106. Ibid.
107. Ibid.
108. *Le Figaro*, Paris, April 6, 1954.
109. *Ballet Today*, November 1954, p. 9.
110. Gian Piero Brunetta, *Storia del cinema italiano* (Rome: Editori Riuniti, 1980), p. 246.
111. Massine, *My Life*, p. 245.
112. *Le Monde*, July 16, 1954.
113. Correspondence between Serge Denham and Massine, Denham Papers, Dance Collection, New York Public Library.
114. Letter from Massine to Denham, October 1, 1953, Denham Papers.
115. Letter from Denham to Massine, June 23, 1954, Denham Papers.
116. Letter from Massine to Columbia Concerts, February 5, 1954, Denham Papers.
117. Frederic Franklin in conversations with the author, New York, 1986.
118. Jack Anderson, *The One and Only: The Ballet Russe de Monte Carlo* (New York: Dance Horizons, 1981), p. 59.
119. *Dance Magazine* 28, no. 12 (December 1954), p. 57.
120. *Dance News* 25, no. 3 (November 1954), p. 7.
121. *Ballet Annual*, no. 10, p. 118.
122. Ibid.
123. Anderson, *The One and Only*, p. 71.
124. Letter from Denham to Massine, November 23, 1954, Denham Papers.
125. *Lyra* (Buenos Aires), August 1955.
126. Dora Kriner, *Ensayos sobre ballet* (Buenos Aires: Ricordi Americana, 1964), p. 106.
127. *Lyra*, August 1955.
128. Ricardo Naymanovich in conversations with the author, Buenos Aires, 1990.
129. Massine, *My Life*, p. 248.
130. Gaia Servadio, *Luchino Visconti* (New York: Franklin Watts, 1983), p. 127.
131. Ibid., p. 141.
132. Jean Babilée in conversations with the author, Paris, 1987.
133. Ibid.
134. Ibid.
135. Ibid.
136. Ibid.
137. Ibid.
138. Ibid.

139. Letter from Lila de Nobili to the author, November 1987.

140. Ibid.

141. *Simon and Schuster Book of Ballet*, p. 264.

142. Massine, *My Life*, p. 256.

143. *Saturday Review* 42, no. 20 (May 16, 1959), p. 83.

144. Vasili Sulich in conversations with the author, Los Angeles, 1990.

145. *Ballet Annual*, no. 15 (1961), p. 698.

146. André Beaurepaire in conversations with the author, Paris, 1987.

147. Vladimir Augenblick in conversations with the author, Paris, 1987.

148. Sulich in conversations with the author.

149. Lorca Massine in conversations with the author.

150. Irène Lidova in conversations with the author, Paris, 1987, 1989.

151. Beaurepaire in conversations with the author.

152. Massine, *My Life*, p. 266.

153. Lidova in conversations with the author.

154. Sulich in conversations with the author.

155. *Le Figaro*, July 16, 1960.

156. *Dance and Dancers* 11, no. 11 (November 1960), p. 23.

157. *Simon and Schuster Book of Ballet*, pp. 269–70.

158. Massine, *My Life*, pp. 261–62.

159. Ibid., p. 260.

160. Beaurepaire in conversations with the author.

161. Lidova in conversations with the author.

162. *Dance and Dancers* 11, no. 11 (November 1960), p. 23.

14. *Moscow, June 1961–Borken, West Germany, March 1979*

1. Tatiana Massine in conversations with the author, New York, 1987.

2. Massine, *My Life in Ballet* (London: Macmillan, 1968), p. 268.

3. Ibid., pp. 267–68.

4. Ibid., p. 269.

5. Ibid., p. 270.

6. Tatiana Massine in conversations with the author.

7. Massine, *My Life*, p. 271.

8. Tatiana Massine Weinbaum in conversations with the author, New York, 1987.

9. Massine had first suggested to La Scala that the organization would do well to invite Nijinska to stage *Les Noces*. When Nijinska declined, however, Massine sought her permission to choreograph his own version. Draft of telegram from Massine to Nijinska at the Hotel Rembrandt, London, undated, private collection.

10. Letter from Massine to Anatoli Petrovich Bolchakov, Barcelona, July 4, 1917, State Central Theatrical Museum, Moscow, no. 181569.

11. *Dance Magazine* 51, no. 12 (December 1977), p. 70.

12. Massine, *My Life*, p. 276.
13. Vlademir Augenblick in conversations with the author, Paris, 1987.
14. Massine, *My Life*, p. 277.
15. Massine in conversations with the author, Galli, 1978.
16. *Dance Magazine*, December 1977.
17. Even during his years with de Basil's and Denham's companies Massine had supervised revivals of *L'Après-midi d'un faune*. In 1958 he revived *Petrouchka* for the first time, for the Vienna State Opera Ballet. In the ensuing years he became a vocal champion of both of these works. The enshrinement of his past continued to the end of his life. He included *Schéhérazade* in the repertory of the 1960 Nervi Festival, and just before his death he offered to revive *Petrouchka* for the Oakland Ballet.
18. Ariane Csonka in conversations with the author, Palm Beach, Fla., 1988.
19. Lorca Massine in conversations with the author, Rome, 1987.
20. Csonka in conversations with the author.
21. Lorca Massine in conversations with the author.
22. Csonka in conversations with the author.
23. Fred Maroth in conversations with the author, Oakland, Calif., 1987.
24. Ibid.
25. Mary Ann de Vlieg in conversations with the author, London, 1987.
26. Ibid.
27. Letter from Joan Miró to Tatiana Riabouchinska, Los Angeles, March 24, 1978, Riabouchinska collection.
28. Bruce Nalezny in conversations with the author, Oakland, Calif., 1987.
29. Ibid.
30. Mary Ann de Vlieg in telephone conversation with the author, September 1992.

Bibliography

Acton, Harold. *Memoirs of an Aesthete*. London: Methuen, 1948.

Amberg, George. *Ballet in America*. New York: Mentor, 1955.

Anderson, Jack. *The One and Only: The Ballet Russe de Monte Carlo*. New York: Dance Horizons, 1981.

Apollinaire, Guillaume. *Apollinaire on Art: Essays and Reviews, 1902–1918*. Edited by LeRoy C. Breunig. New York: Da Capo Press, 1988.

Auric, Georges. *Quand j'étais là . . .* Paris: Bernard Grasset, 1979.

Axson, Richard H. *"Parade": Cubism as Theatre*. New York: Garland, 1979.

Baer, Nancy van Norman. *The Art of Enchantment: Diaghilev's Ballets Russes, 1909–1929*. San Francisco: Fine Arts Museum, 1989.

Bankhead, Tallulah. *Tallulah: My Autobiography*. New York: Harper and Brothers, 1952.

Barnes, Albert C., and Violette de Mazia. *The Art of Henri Matisse*. Merion, Pa.: Barnes Foundation Press, 1963.

Beaton, Cecil. *Diaries, 1922–1929: The Wandering Years*. London: Weidenfeld and Nicolson, 1961.

———. *Ballet*. Garden City, N.Y.: Doubleday, 1951.

Beaumont, Cyril. *The Diaghilev Ballet in London*. London: Adams and Charles Black, 1951.

———. *Supplement to Complete Book of Ballets*. London: Putnam, 1952.

Benois, Alexandre. *Reminiscences of the Russian Ballet*. London: Putnam, 1941.

Berg, Shelley C. *"Le Sacre du printemps": Seven Productions from Nijinsky to Martha Graham*. Ann Arbor, Mich.: UMI Research Press, 1988.

Bland, Alexander. *The Royal Ballet*. New York: Doubleday, 1981.

Borovsky, Victor. *Chaliapin: A Critical Biography*. New York: Knopf, 1988.

Bosch, Carlos. *Mneme*. Madrid: Espasa-Calpe, 1942.

Bowlt, John E. *The Silver Age: Russian Art of the Early Twentieth Century and the "World of Art" Group*. Newtonville, Mass.: Oriental Research Partners, 1979.

Braunsweg, Julian. *Ballets Scandals*. London: George Allen and Unwin, 1977.

Brodovitch, Alexey. *Ballet*. Text by Edwin Denby. New York: J. J. Augustin, 1945.

Brunetta, Gian Piero. *Storia del cinema italiano*. Rome: Editori Riuniti, 1980.

Buckle, Richard. *The Adventures of a Ballet Critic*. London: Cresset Press, 1953.

———. *Diaghilev*. New York: Atheneum, 1979.

———. *Nijinsky*. New York: Avon Books, 1971.

Cabanne, Pierre. *Le Siècle de Picasso: 1887–1937*. Paris: Editions Denoël, 1975.

Carrieri, Raffaele. *Futurismo*. Milan: Edizione del Milione, 1963.

Castillo, Alberto del. *José María Sert: Su vida y su obra*. Barcelona: Librería Editorial Argos, 1947.

Chase, Gilbert, and Andrew Budwig. *Manuel de Falla: A Bibliography and Research Guide*. New York: Garland, 1986.

Christie, Ian. *Powell, Pressburger and Others*. London: British Film Institute, 1978.

Chujoy, Anatole. *Ballet*. New York: Robert Speller, 1936.

Clarke, Mary. *The Sadler's Wells Ballet*. London: Adam and Charles Black, 1955.

Cochran, Charles B. *I Had Almost Forgotten*. London: Hutchinson, 1932.

Cooper, Diana. *The Light of Common Day*. London: Rupert Hart-Davis, 1959.

Cooper, Douglas. *Picasso Theatre*. London: Weidenfeld, 1968.

Coton, A. V. *A Prejudice for Ballet*. London: Methuen, 1938.

Crespell, Jean-Paul. *The Dove, the Dreams: The Life of Marc Chagall*. New York: Coward-McCann, 1970.

Crowle, Pigeon. *Beryl Grey*. London: Faber and Faber, 1952.

Danilova, Alexandra. *Choura*. New York: Knopf, 1986.

Deaken, Irving. *Ballet Profile*. New York: Dodge, 1936.

Delaunay, Sonia. *Nous irons jusqu'au soleil*. Paris: R. Lafont, 1978.

Demarques, Suzanne. *Manuel de Falla*. Paris: Flammarion, 1963.

Denby, Edwin. *Dance Writings*. New York: Knopf, 1986.

Desanti, Dominique. *Sonia Delaunay: Magique magicienne*. Paris: Editions Ramsay, 1988.

Descharnes, Robert. *Salvador Dalí*. New York: Harry N. Abrams, 1985.

de Valois, Ninette. *Come Dance with Me: A Memoir*. London: Dance Books, 1973.

———. *Invitation to the Ballet*. London: John Lane, 1937.

Dorati, Antal. *Notes of Seven Decades*. London: Hodder and Stoughton, 1979.

Dorival, Bernard. *Robert Delaunay*. Paris: Jacques Darmasse Editions, 1975.

Duke, Vernon. *Passport to Paris*. Boston: Little, Brown, 1955.

Eliot, T. S. *The Letters of T. S. Eliot*. Edited by Valerie Eliot. Vol. 1. London: Faber and Faber, 1988.

———. *Selected Essays*. New York: Harcourt, Brace & World, 1964.

Falla, Manuel de. *Escritos*. Madrid, 1947.

Fauchereau, Serge, ed. *Moscow, 1900–1930*. New York: Rizzoli, 1988.

Faÿ, Bernard. *Les Précieux*. Paris: Librairie Académique, 1966.

Ferreira, Paulo. *Correspondance de quatre artistes portugais avec Robert et Sonia Delaunay*. Paris: Presses Universitaires de France, 1972.

Fokine, Michel. *Memoirs of a Ballet Master*. Boston: Little, Brown, 1961.

Fonteyn, Margot. *Autobiography*. New York: Warner Books, 1976.

Fry, Roger. *Letters of Roger Fry*. Edited by Denis Sutton. London: Chatto and Windus, 1972.

Gambillo, Maria Drudi, and Teresa Fiori, eds. *Archivi del futurismo*. 2 vols. Rome: Lucia Editore, 1958.

Garafola, Lynn. *Diaghilev's Ballets Russes*. New York: Oxford University Press, 1989.

García-Márquez, Vicente. *The Ballets Russes*. New York: Knopf, 1990.

Gauss, C. E. *The Aesthetic Theory of French Artists*. Baltimore, 1966.

Gibbon, Monk. *The Red Shoes Ballet*. London: Saturn Press, 1948.

Gillard, David. *Beryl Grey: A Biography*. London: W. H. Allen, 1977.

Gold, Arthur, and Robert Fizdale. *Misia: The Life of Misia Sert*. New York: Knopf, 1980.

Goode, Gerald. *The Book of Ballets*. New York: Crown, 1939.

Gorchakov, Nikolai A. *The Theater in Soviet Russia*. New York: Columbia University Press, 1957.

Grigoriev, Serge. *The Diaghilev Ballet*. London: Penguin Books, 1960.

Hall, Fernau. *An Anatomy of Ballet*. London: Andrew Welrose, 1953.

Harrod, Roy. *The Life of John Maynard Keynes*. London: Macmillan, 1951.

Haskell, Arnold. *Balletomania Then and Now*. New York: Knopf, 1977.

———. *Diaghilev*. New York: Simon and Schuster, 1935.

Hill, Polly, and Richard Keynes, eds. *Lydia and Maynard: The Letters of Lydia Lopokova and John Maynard Keynes*. New York: Charles Scribner's Sons, 1989.

Hippius, Zinaida. *Selected Works*. Edited and translated by Temira Pachmuss. Urbana: University of Illinois Press, 1972.

Hugo, Jean. *Le Regard de la mémoire*. Paris: Actes Sud, 1983.

Hurard-Viltard, Eveline. *Le Groupe des Six*. Paris: Méridiens Klincksieck, 1987.

Hurok, Solomon. *S. Hurok Presents . . . The World of Ballet.* London: Robert Hale, 1955.

Isdebsky-Pritchard, Aline. *The Art of Mikhail Vrubel.* Ann Arbor, Mich.: UMI Research Press, 1982.

Karsavina, Tamara. *Theatre Street.* London: Dance Books, 1981.

Kean, Beverly Whitney. *All the Empty Palaces.* New York: Universe Books, 1983.

Keynes, Milo. *Lydia Lopokova.* New York: St. Martin's Press, 1982.

Kirstein, Lincoln. *Ballet: Bias and Belief.* New York: Dance Horizons, 1983.

Kochno, Boris. *Diaghilev and the Ballets Russes.* New York: Harper & Row, 1970.

Kriner, Dora. *Ensayos sobre ballet.* Buenos Aires: Ricordi Americana, 1964.

Kupferman, Fred. *Mata Hari.* Brussels: Editions Complexe, 1982.

Lassaigne, Jacques. *Marc Chagall: Drawings and Watercolors for the Ballet.* New York: Tudor, 1959.

Laurenti, Huguette. *Paul Valéry et le théâtre.* Paris: Gallimard, 1973.

Lawrence, Robert. *The Victor Book of Ballets and Ballet Music.* New York: Simon and Schuster, 1950.

Levinson, André. *Ballet Old and New.* New York: Dance Horizons, 1982.

———. *Les Visages de la danse.* Paris: Editions Bernard Grasset, 1933.

Lifar, Serge. *Serge Diaghilev: His Life, His Work, His Legend.* New York: G. P. Putnam's Sons, 1940.

Litvinoff, Valentina. *The Use of Stanislavsky Within Modern Dance.* New York: American Dance Guild, 1972.

Loguine, Tatiana, ed. *Gontcharova et Larionov.* Paris: Klincksieck, 1971.

Macdonald, Nesta. *Diaghilev Observed.* New York: Dance Horizons, 1975.

Magarshack, David. *Stanislavsky: A Life.* London: Macgibbon & Kee, 1950.

Marcadé, Valentine. *Le Renouveau de l'art pictural russe.* Lausanne, 1971.

Markevitch, Igor. *Etre et avoir été.* Paris: Gallimard, 1980.

Martin, Marianne W. *Futurist Art and Theory.* Oxford: Clarendon Press, 1968.

Martínez Sierra, María. *Gregorio y yo.* Mexico City: Biografías Gandesa, 1953.

Massine, Léonide. *My Life in Ballet.* London: Macmillan, 1968.

Masson, André. *Peindre et une gaguere, le plaisir de peindre.* Paris, undated.

Meyer, Franz. *Marc Chagall: Life and Work.* London: Thomas Hudson, 1964.

Michaut, Pierre. *Le Ballet contemporain.* Paris: Librairie Plon, 1950.

Milhaud, Darius. *Ma Vie heureuse.* Paris: Belfond, 1973.

Morán, Alfredo. *Joaquín Turina a través de sus escritos.* Vols. 1 and 2. Madrid, 1981.

Morrell, Lady Ottoline. *Ottoline.* Edited by Robert Gathorne-Hardy. London: Faber, 1963.

Muñoz, Matilde. *Historia del Teatro Real.* Madrid: Editorial Tesoro, 1946.

Nabokov, Nicholas. *Bagazh*. New York: Atheneum, 1975.

Naifeh, Steven, and Gregory White Smith. *Jackson Pollock: An American Saga*. New York: Clarkson N. Potter, 1989.

Newman, Vera. *Ernest Newman: A Memoir by His Wife*. New York: Knopf, 1964.

Nijinsky, Romola. *Nijinsky*. New York: Simon and Schuster, 1980.

Obolensky, Serge. *One Man of His Time*. New York: McDowell, Obolensky, 1958.

Orozco, Manuel. *Manuel de Falla*. Barcelona: Ediciones Destino, 1985.

Payne, Charles. *American Ballet Theatre*. New York: Knopf, 1979.

Pearson, John. *The Sitwells: A Family Biography*. New York: Harcourt Brace Jovanovich, 1978.

Penrose, Roland. *Picasso: His Life and Work*. London: Victor Gollancz, 1958.

Powell, Michael. *A Life in Movies*. New York: Knopf, 1987.

Propert, W. A. *The Russian Ballet, 1921–1929*. London: Bodley Head, 1931.

———. *The Russian Ballet in Western Europe, 1909–1920*. London: Bodley Head, 1921.

Richardson, William. *Zolotoe Runo and Russian Modernism: 1905–1910*. Ann Arbor, Mich.: Ardis Publishers, 1986.

Robert, Grace. *The Borzoi Book of Ballets*. New York: Knopf, 1946.

Roslavleva, Natalia. *Era of the Russian Ballet*. London: Victor Gollancz, 1966.

———. "Stanislavsky and the Ballet." *Dance Perspectives*, no. 23 (1965).

Rubin, William, and Carolyn Lancher. *André Masson*. New York: Museum of Modern Art. 1976.

Rubinstein, Arthur. *My Young Years*. New York: Knopf, 1973.

Rusiñol, Santiago. *Obres completes*. Barcelona: Editorial Selecta, 1956.

Servadio, Gaia. *Luchino Visconti*. New York: Franklin Watts, 1983.

Siegel, Marcia B. *At the Vanishing Point*. New York: Saturday Review Press, 1972.

———. *The Shapes of Change*. Berkeley: University of California Press, 1985.

The Simon and Schuster Book of Ballet. New York: Simon and Schuster, 1979.

Sitwell, Osbert. *Laughter in the Next Room*. London: Macmillan, 1949.

———. *Great Morning*. London: Macmillan, 1948.

Slonim, Marc. *Russian Theater, from the Empire to the Soviets*. Cleveland: World, 1961.

Smakov, Gennady. *The Great Russian Dancers*. New York: Knopf, 1984.

Soby, James Thrall. *Joan Miró*. New York: Museum of Modern Art, 1959.

Sokolova, Lydia. *Dancing for Diaghilev*. London: John Murray, 1960.

Sopeña, Federico. *Vida y obra de Falla*. Madrid: Turner Música, 1988.

Souritz, Elizabeth. *Soviet Choreographers in the 1920's*. Durham, N.C.: Duke University Press, 1990.

Stanislavsky, Constantin. *My Life in Art*. Boston: Little, Brown, 1924.

Steegmuller, Francis. *Cocteau*. Boston: Little, Brown, 1970.

Stein, Gertrude. *Picasso*. London: Charles Scribner's Sons, 1939.

Stokes, Adrian. *Russian Ballets*. London: Faber and Faber, 1946.

———. *To-night the Ballet*. London, 1935.

Strauss, Richard, and Hugo von Hofmannsthal. *Correspondence Between Richard Strauss and Hugo von Hofmannsthal*. London: Collins, 1961.

Stravinsky, Igor. *Conversations with Igor Stravinsky*. New York: Doubleday, 1959.

———. *Chronicle of My Life*. London: Victor Gollancz, 1936.

———. *Stravinsky: Selected Correspondence*. 3 vols. Edited by Robert Craft. New York: Knopf, 1984.

——— and Robert Craft. *Expositions and Developments*. London: Hutchinson, 1979.

Thomson, Virgil. *Virgil Thomson*. New York: Knopf, 1966.

Tisdall, Caroline, and Angelo Bozzolla. *Futurism*. New York: Oxford University Press, 1989.

Tyler, Parker. *The Divine Comedy of Pavel Tchelitchew*. New York: Fleet, 1967.

Vaughan, David. *Frederick Ashton and His Ballets*. New York: Knopf, 1977.

White, Eric Walter. *Stravinsky: The Composer and His Works*. Berkeley: University of California Press, 1984.

Ziegler, Philip. *Diana Cooper*. London: Hamish Hamilton, 1981.

Zlobin, Vladimir. *A Difficult Soul: Zinaida Gippius*. Berkeley: University of California Press, 1980.

Zorina, Vera. *Zorina*. New York: Farrar, Straus & Giroux, 1986.

Index

Permissions Acknowledgments

Grateful acknowledgment is made to the following for permission to reprint previously published material:

A & C Black (Publishers) Limited: Excerpts from *The Diaghilev Ballet* by Cyril Beaumont (Huntingdon, England: A & C Black [Publishers] Limited, 1951). Reprinted by permission of A & C Black (Publishers) Limited.

Richard Buckle: Excerpts from *Dancing for Diaghilev* by Lydia Sokolova, edited by Richard Buckle (San Francisco: Mercury House, 1989), copyright © 1960 by Richard Buckle. Reprinted by permission of Richard Buckle.

Robert Craft: Excerpts from *Stravinsky: Selected Correspondence,* vol. 2, edited by Robert Craft (New York: Alfred A. Knopf, Inc., 1984). Reprinted by permission of Robert Craft.

Dance Horizons: Excerpts from *The One and Only: The Ballet Russe de Monte Carlo* by Jack Anderson, copyright © 1981 by Jack Anderson. Reprinted by permission of Dance Horizons.

Farrar, Straus & Giroux, Inc.: Excerpt from *Zorina* by Vera Zorina, copyright © 1986 by Brigitta Lieberson. Reprinted by permission of Farrar, Straus & Giroux, Inc.

David R. Godine, Publisher, Inc., and Constable & Co. Ltd.: Excerpts from *Cocteau* by Francis Steegmuller, copyright © 1970 by Francis Steegmuller. Rights in the United Kingdom administered by Constable & Co. Ltd., London. Reprinted by permission of David R. Godine, Publisher, Inc.

William Heinemann Ltd.: Excerpts from *A Life in Movies* by Michael Powell (London: William Heinemann Ltd., 1987). Reprinted by permission of William Heinemann Ltd.

Photographic Sources

Central State Archives of Literature and the Arts, Moscow: 3, 11, 14 (both), 15, 19 (both), 22

The Hulton-Deutsch Collection: ii, 137, 167, 193, 197 (both), 257 (all), 311, 331

40: Photographs by Durnkoof, Berlin, 1914, private collection
106: Fundación Archivo Manuel de Falla, Granada
141: Photograph by Foulsham & Banfield Ltd, private collection
207: Photograph by Maurice Seymour, private collection
218: Photograph by Pearl Freeman, private collection
231: Photograph by Hoyningen-Huene, private collection
243: Photograph by Anthony, private collection
245: Photograph by Iris, private collection
264: Photographs by Maurice Seymour, private collection
277: Photograph by Max Erlanger de Rosen, private collection
314: Photograph by Baron, private collection
333: Photograph by Robert Cann, private collection

All other photographs are from private collections.

A NOTE ABOUT THE AUTHOR

Vicente García-Márquez, the author of The Ballets Russes:
Colonel de Basil's Ballets Russes de Monte Carlo,
*1932–1952, was director of the 1992 Tribute to Diaghilev in
Granada. He consulted with the Paris Opéra Ballet and other
companies when they mounted Massine revivals.
Mr. García-Márquez died in 1993.*

A NOTE ON THE TYPE

*This book was set in a PostScript version of Dante,
a typeface designed by Giovanni Mardersteig. Conceived
as a private type for the Officina Bodoni at Verona, Italy,
Dante was originally cut only for hand composition by Charles
Malin, the famous Parisian punchcutter, between 1946 and 1952.
Its first use was in an edition of Boccaccio's* Trattatello in laude di
Dante *that appeared in 1954. The Monotype Corporation's version of
Dante followed in 1957. Although modeled on the Aldine type used
for Pietro Cardinal Bembo's* De Aetna *in 1945, Dante is a
thoroughly modern interpretation of that venerable face.*

Composed by Dix!, Syracuse, New York

*Printed and bound by Quebecor Printing Martinsburg,
Martinsburg, West Virginia*

Designed by Iris Weinstein

DATE DUE FOR RETURN

This book may be recalled before the above date.

This book may be recalled before the above date.

A. COLIN WRIGHT is a member of the Department of Russian Language and Literature at Queen's University, Kingston.

After a career during which his work was persistently attacked by orthodox communist critics, a number of his plays banned, and, after 1927, publication of his writings suppressed, Mikhail Bulgakov has received posthumous recognition since the publication of *The Master and Margarita* in 1966-67. Although interest in Bulgakov has increased steadily during the past decade and numerous articles have been published, this is the first comprehensive study of the Russian writer's life and works, from his early years in Kiev until his death in Moscow in 1940.

Bulgakov was a prolific and highly versatile writer. He wrote plays, opera libretti, film scenarios, novels, and short stories best known for their realism and their penetrating satire. His place in Russian and world literature has been difficult to assess, however, because much of his work has been virtually inaccessible until recently; even specialists in the field tend to be unfamiliar with much of his writing. This book examines all Bulgakov's major writings, outlines their background and history, and provides information about their critical reception that will enable the reader to place his works in perspective.

In addition to the published sources, Professor Wright has been able to consult archives in Moscow and to interview Bulgakov's surviving relatives, and the result is a work of unusual and impeccable authority.

A. COLIN WRIGHT

Mikhail Bulgakov:
Life and Interpretations

UNIVERSITY OF TORONTO PRESS
Toronto Buffalo London

© University of Toronto Press 1978
Toronto Buffalo London
Printed in Canada

Library of Congress Cataloging in Publication Data

Wright, Anthony Colin, 1938–
  Mikhail Bulgakov : life and interpretations.

  Bibliography: p.
  Includes indexes.
  1. Bulgakov, Mikhail Afanas'evich, 1891-1940.
  2. Authors, Russian – 20th century – Biography.
  PG3476.B78z95   891.7′8′4209   78-3872
  ISBN 0-8020-5402-1

This book has been published with the help of a
grant from the Humanities Research Council of Canada,
using funds provided by the Canada Council,
and a grant from the University of Toronto Press.

Contents

Preface

Since the publication of *The Master and Margarita* in 1966-67, Mikhail Afana-sievich Bulgakov (1891-1940) has suddenly become popular both in the Soviet Union and abroad, after being virtually ignored for a quarter of a century by all but a handful of writers, scholars, and friends. After a career during which he was constantly attacked by orthodox communist critics, with his works (after 1927) not published, and a number of his plays banned, he has at last achieved posthumous recognition. Numerous articles have appeared on him and continue to appear, and there is a wealth of material for research (although his major ar-chive, in the Manuscript Division of the Lenin Library in Moscow, has as yet not been catalogued and remains inaccessible to scholars). To date, however, there has been no overall study, although one other work is announced for publication.

In this book, then, I have attempted first of all to give as complete as pos-sible an account of his life and career - in the hope that this will both provide basic information (some of it little known) for future researchers and also be of interest to those trying to form a picture of Bulgakov the man. At the same time I have tried to give a comprehensive critical account of his works, in order that his place in Russian and world literature may be more easily assessed. Even the specialist in the field will be unfamiliar with much of Bulgakov, although more of his work is gradually becoming available - while the general reader is likely to know of only a small part of his quite considerable output. I have therefore pro-vided here at least some discussion of every major work or group of works - excepting, of course, possible 'new discoveries' (although my frank opinion is that there now remain no major works to be discovered). I should add that in my discussions, although I have not neglected questions of form, I have taken an unashamedly ideological approach, hence the 'Interpretations' of the title. It seems to me that a reader is initially concerned with the outlook an author has on the world and society, and that a detailed examination of his techniques, however important, can safely be left to individual articles or later monographs. While, then, I have indicated what I would consider to be important in this regard, the reader wanting a detailed analysis of, say, Bulgakov's humour will need to look elsewhere.

For their assistance to me in compiling this book, I am indebted to a large number of people, and notably to Lyubov Yevgenievna Belozerskaya-Bulgakova, Konstantin Petrovich Bulgakov (C.P. Bulak), Irina Ivanovna Bulgakova-Koeppen, Lyudmila L. Chernichenko, Marietta O. Chudakova, Mr Peter Doyle, Mr Michael Glenny, Monsieur Yves Hamant, Professor Elizabeth Hill, Vl. Lakshin, Yu.V. Larionov, Vl.A. Lyovshin, Miss Lesley Milne, Carl and Ellendea Proffer, Miss Avril Pyman, K.L. Rudnitsky, L.A. Shilov, M.M. Yanshin, Yelena Andreevna Zemskaya. Particular thanks are due to Dr N.E. Andreyev, reader in Russian Studies at Cambridge University, for reading and commenting on the manuscript; Monsieur Michel Vassilieff of the Sorbonne for willingly supplying copies of almost inaccessible texts; Mrs Wendy Chambers, Mrs Sheila Slots, Mrs Margaret Boesch, and Mrs Eloise Davis for their typing of the manuscript. I of course take responsibility for any errors in the text, and for any inadvertent omissions from the above list. I am also grateful to the Canada Council, the Arts Research Committee of Queen's University at Kingston, Ontario, the Department of Slavonic Studies at the University of Cambridge, the Academy of Sciences of the USSR, and the staff of the Institute of Russian Literature (Pushkinsky Dom) in Leningrad, for their assistance, financial and otherwise, towards the necessary research. Finally, I am deeply grateful to my wife, Mary Anne, for the understanding she has shown during the long and difficult period while this book was being prepared.

For transliterations from Russian I have relied on J. Thomas Shaw, *The Transliteration of Modern Russian for English Language Publications* (Madison: University of Wisconsin Press, 1967): system one for personal and place names within the English text, and system two for isolated Russian words and the bibliography, where a more exact rendition is necessary.

A.C. WRIGHT
Kingston, Ontario

MIKHAIL BULGAKOV: LIFE AND INTERPRETATIONS

1

Development of a writer, 1891-1921

Mikhail Afanasievich Bulgakov was born in Kiev on 3 May (or 15 May by the new style) 1891, the eldest of seven children. His father, Afanasy Ivanovich – cousin of the well-known writer and philosopher, Sergey (later Father Sergy) Bulgakov – was a professor of divinity at the Kiev Theological Academy, and a specialist on the Anglican church: not surprisingly, perhaps, he was a traditionalist, believing firmly in discipline and order. Mikhail's mother, Varvara Mikhaylovna Pokrovskaya, was ten years younger than her husband, a well-educated woman of outstanding personality, and equally convinced of the importance of family life. As the eldest, Mikhail had a certain responsibility for the other children; his 'feeling for the family' was an important influence on him in his early years: it was here that he learnt the value of politeness and respect towards others, something that would remain with him throughout his life.

The children's education was of the best. Besides Russian, they knew at least some German (the girls all went to the German High School in Kiev). They had some knowledge of French too, although as a linguist Mikhail was not particularly talented. The whole atmosphere in the house was one of scholarship and intellect, conservatism of the best kind. An unhesitating belief in God and in Russian tradition was part of the family's life. On occasions, colleagues of Afanasy Ivanovich would come to the house and discuss matters of theology. Later Mikhail himself would have long conversations with his brothers about spiritual matters, and in the course of his life would read many books on esoteric subjects. Brought up as a believer, he would never lose his interest in religion and his conviction of the importance of the spiritual life.

In many ways it was a typical intellectual family, and well known in Kiev. Some idea of the strength of its ties may be had from Bulgakov's novel, *The White Guard*, whose characters reflect the life of the author's own family in their apartment in Kiev at No 13, Andreevsky Spusk (St Andrew's Hill) – called

Alexeevsky Spusk (St Alexey's Hill) in the novel. From the author's descriptions we can easily imagine the comfort and feeling of ease that life in this house provided: a sense of security from the outside world. The writer Viktor Nekrasov has described how he discovered the house itself, some twenty-five years after Bulgakov's death.[1] It is in one of the older parts of Kiev; on a long, winding hill leading down from the town centre to the more commercial district known as the Podol. At that time, according to Konstantin Paustovsky, another writer from Kiev, 'from the windows of their apartment there could be constantly heard the sounds of a piano and even of a penetrating French horn, voices of young people, running and laughter, arguments and singing.'[2] The whole family was fond of music: Mikhail himself played the piano reasonably well, and at one time even had the ambition to become a singer.

In the holidays, from 1902 on, the whole family would go regularly to their wooden dacha at Bucha, in the country outside Kiev. There they would be joined by other relations: Mikhail's grandfather, his cousins Nikolay and Konstantin, his uncles Mikhail and Nikolay Mikhaylovich Pokrovsky. Varvara Mikhaylovna, even on holiday, would ensure that her children were always kept busy in some way: Mikhail's favourite sister Nadya has recalled how this became the subject of an 'anonymous' poem, which was suddenly circulated one morning. The author, of course, was none other than young Misha, and later he would refer to this in a letter to his friend P.S. Popov, saying that he hated poetry and himself wrote only satirical poems, 'causing indignation in my aunt and grief in my mother, who dreamt of one thing, that her sons should become transportation engineers.'[3] Playing tricks on the family, making jokes, pulling people's legs, was something he loved as a boy, and, indeed, this trait stayed with him, so that we can find constant references in his later life to his love of *mistifikatsiia*, as it is expressed in Russian. (This occurs in his writings too, so that his readers have sometimes to be careful about taking everything he says at face value.)

Yet, despite this, he was somewhat reserved, did not communicate his feelings easily. In many ways he was an idealist who was destined to endure constant disappointments. There was often a certain distance between himself and others. 'In my youth,' he would later tell his friend Sergey Yermolinsky, 'I was very shy ... Perhaps until the end of my life I never succeeded in getting rid of this weakness, but only pretended.'[4] This shyness would at times cause him to be sharp with people, or to appear haughty, whereas in fact, like all his family, he had a basic kindness. Sometimes his shyness would take the form of aggressiveness, which was not understood.

1 **391, 168**
2 **419**, p. 61
3 Quoted in **379**, p. 165
4 **266**, p. 79

In 1900 he had entered the First Kiev High School, which was known for its excellent teachers. It was here that Paustovsky first became acquainted with him. In his *The Story of a Life*[5] Paustovsky describes the regular fights between the more 'aristocratic' elements and the 'democrats.' Bulgakov fought alongside the second group: he 'thundered over the whole school,' Paustovsky later told him. His brother and cousins were there as well – in fact the two Nikolays were in the same class – so that at one time there was talk of the 'Bulgakov terror.' Bulgakov's own account, as related by Yermolinsky, gives a somewhat different view: 'It seems to me I didn't thunder, all I did was defend my independence. But that the school authorities didn't like me – that's quite true. For some reason they always suspected me, suspected that such a quiet person as myself would suddenly take it into my head to play some trick or other. In general, all my life I have been unfortunate with authorities ... and I so much wanted to live as an exemplary boy.'[6] He must surely be speaking with tongue in cheek, for he had too much spirit to be an exemplary pupil. Paustovsky talks of his 'extraordinary vitality, the ruthless tongue which made people afraid of him, and the sense he gave us of determination and strength – we felt it in everything he said, however trifling' – traits that would later stand him in good stead when he would be attacked by critics on all sides. He too refers to Bulgakov's love of playing tricks and particularly to his ability for inventing nicknames for the teachers and making up improbable stories about them – often in the course of forbidden excursions on the River Dnieper with his friends.

Bulgakov's great joy during his school days was to go – with or without the school inspector's permission – to the theatre: the Kiev opera, or more particularly the Russian Solovtsov Theatre where a variety of plays were performed. Here he would see such actors as Kuznetsov, Polevitskaya, Radin, Yureniev. The whole atmosphere was one that he loved, the sights and smells – even the dust of the theatre was evidently some special kind of magic for him. And in the holidays at Bucha, like his predecessor Chekhov, he would organize amateur theatrical performances in which the whole family would take part. He even found a name for their company: the Pickwick Club. (Later he would both direct and act in a play of that name, an adaptation from Dickens, for the Moscow Art Theatre.)

It is, of course, during his early years that many of Bulgakov's literary tastes were formed. At the age of nine he started to read Gogol: *Dead Souls*, he thought, was an adventure story. The great Russian writer was destined to be a lasting influence on him; it was Gogol whom 'he invariably set up as a model for himself and together with Saltykov-Shchedrin loved most of all the classics of

5 **420**. Subsequent references are to pp. 179, 187. What follows is also based on **372**, pp. 378-88. These passages appear in other editions too.
6 **266**, p. 80

Russian literature.'[7] It was Gogol's wealth of imagination and fantasy that chiefly appealed to him, although he must have enjoyed Gogol's satire as well, as his liking for Saltykov-Shchedrin and another favourite, Sukhovo-Kobylin, would testify. During the latter days of his school life he was himself writing satirical verses. Imagination, fantasy, satire: all these are essential elements in both Bulgakov and Gogol, but, as one critic has written, 'Bulgakov does not imitate Gogol. For him Gogol is his homeland as much as is Kiev, the same living earth in which his gifts will grow.'[8] In his school days he also read Fennimore Cooper, Leskov, and most of the Russian classics. Dostoevsky and Chekhov, apparently, he was not fond of, nor did he like poetry, with the exception of that of Pushkin, whom he did not consider a poet at all. Interestingly, he is reported as having once written an analysis of the image of the cat in Pushkin's 'Ruslan and Lyudmila':[9] in later years a cat would become a major figure of his novel *The Master and Margarita*.

It is difficult to say with any certainty when Bulgakov's own literary efforts began. He apparently wrote a short story entitled 'The Adventures of Svetlana' at the age of seven,[10] but such juvenilia are hardly significant. At the university he would certainly make some literary attempts, but again we should not take these very seriously. Altogether the wisest course is to take his own word that his first short story dates from 1919, a considerably later period.

In 1907, when he was sixteen, his father died of nephrosclerosis in his forty-eighth year – an indication perhaps of kidney problems in the family, for Bulgakov himself would die of the same disease at almost the same age. But now he had even greater family responsibilities. In 1909 he completed his high school education and entered the Medical Faculty of Kiev University, where he remained until graduation in 1916. It is puzzling to know why, with his love of literature and the theatre, at least some indications of talent in writing and in music, and a further interest – according to Popov – in law, he should have chosen to become a doctor. He himself explained that a doctor's work appeared 'splendid' and that he was fascinated by the secrets of the microscope.[11] More likely he was influenced by his family. His two uncles, Mikhail and Nikolay Mikhaylovich Pokrovsky, whom he respected greatly, were both doctors; so was a good friend of the family whom his mother was later to marry: it may well have been that, to a young man with no clear idea of what he was going to do, the profession he had frequently heard discussed at home seemed the logical choice. (His younger brother, Nikolay, was later to become eminent as a bacteriologist.)

7 Quoted in **491**, p. 87; see also Popov's unpublished memoirs in **187**, folio 556
8 **217**, p. 264
9 **233**
10 **258**; based on Popov's memoirs
11 Reported in **2**, p. 5

Bulgakov was not the only writer who started out as a doctor, and it is remarkable that both Veresaev and the far better-known Chekhov had also turned first to medicine, which they later abandoned for literature. In some ways Bulgakov's career would be similar to that of Chekhov: writing humorous pieces for newspapers, then plays, and working closely with the Moscow Art Theatre. But the similarities, however striking, are superficial, for if in a sense Bulgakov grows out of the Chekhov tradition, he is basically a very different writer, who goes far beyond it.

Of Bulgakov's life as a medical student very little is known, except that he worked hard and continued to enjoy the theatre, opera, and concerts. While at the university, on 25 April 1913, he married Tatyana Nikolaevna Lappa, and for the occasion Bulgakov wrote an amateur play. In it, the members of the two families are portrayed as 'well-wishers' – one of them says: 'Why shouldn't they get married? They'll live in the bathroom: Misha will sleep in the bath and Tatyana in the wash-basin – she's small and thin.'[12] Considering the length of time Bulgakov was with Tatyana, or Tasya, as she was usually called – eleven years, longer than with either of his two subsequent wives – she remains a somewhat elusive figure. It appears that she was the daughter of the president of the tax-office in Saratov and that her aunt was a good friend of Bulgakov's mother.

As a young man Bulgakov must have been aware that the time he was living through represented the end of an era in Russia, and that the kind of life he knew in his family was likely soon to disappear. He had been born into an age of transition. When he was fourteen there had taken place the first revolution, of 1905: successfully repressed, but sufficient to force the tsar at last to allow an elected constituent assembly, or duma. Monarchy was now ailing, if still absolute. On the international scene, too, there was unrest, conflicts and alliances between the various European powers – which in 1914 finally erupted in the First World War, with Russia's disastrous defeats in East Prussia.

NIKOLSKOE AND VYAZMA

Bulgakov, in 1916, graduated as a doctor with distinction. In April he was enlisted into the army: as a soldier of the reserve of the second category, so that he might be put to use as a military doctor. For the remainder of the spring and summer of 1916 he served in front-line military hospitals in Kamenets-Podolsk

---

12 **243**, p. 233. Further information on Tatyana Nikolaevna may be found in **10**, pp. 18-20. This collection of materials appeared too late to be of assistance in the preparation of the present book, but it does contain a number of useful documents which I have quoted or referred to from earlier sources.

and Chernovsty, in the southwest Ukraine; in the autumn he was transferred to the rear for service in zemstvo (district) hospitals. Thus on 29 September Bulgakov arrived with his wife in the remote village of Nikolskoe, in the Sychyovka district of Smolensk province, where he was to spend the next year.

This period in his life was important for the stories that it ultimately produced, most of which were later collected to form his *Notes of a Young Doctor*. These are virtually the only evidence we have for his life at this time apart from three textbooks marked in his hand and his certificate of service at the hospital (which confirms that he indeed performed many operations as he describes – including one tracheotomy, the subject of his story 'Steel Throat').[13] But the stories are obviously based on personal experience and can be relied upon for a general description of his life at the time. Names and dates are changed, but only in one respect are they frankly misleading: his narrator, in 'Murievo,' is a bachelor and alone; Bulgakov, in Nikolskoe, was with his wife.

His isolation seems to have been what weighed upon him most. He longed for the life of the city, but could not even go to the provincial town – forty kilometres away – for at least a month. Blizzards, he thought, 'howled only in novels. But it turned out that they really did howl. The evenings here are unusually long ... I dreamt of the provincial town' (p. 59).[14] At first he had few patients and there was little to do in the evenings. He was the only doctor for miles around, and worried about his inexperience. He was concerned, he tells us, at the ignorance of the people and at the prevalence of syphilis – which explains, perhaps, how he later came to specialize in venereology. Yet we know that as a doctor he was successful. Indeed, he appears to have made a most favourable impression in the area – there is even an unconfirmed report that the inhabitants later wanted to have the hospital named after him.

But he apparently made efforts to get away from Nikolskoe, seeking release from his military service for health reasons. After almost a year there, on 18 September 1917, he was transferred to the town hospital in Vyazma, some seventy kilometres to the south of Sychyovka, and somewhat larger. 'In a word this was civilization, Babylon, the Nevsky Prospect,'[15] he writes ecstatically in his story 'Morphine.' The hospital was luxurious, and there were other doctors to share the responsibility: Bulgakov was put in charge of the infectious and venereological department.[16]

While he had been in Nikolskoe there had come the news of the overthrow of the tsar; now, in Vyazma, he learnt that the liberal provisional government had

13 **243**, pp. 233-4, and **187**, folios 520, 521, 523
14 Page references to **2** are given in the text.
15 This and the following quotation is from **139**, no 45, pp. 11, 12.
16 This and the following is based on **243**, p. 234.

been overthrown in the October Revolution. There was a Bolshevik government in Russia, although its future was as yet uncertain. In the countryside he was far removed from the main course of events. 'If the revolution catches me up on its wing,' he writes, 'then perhaps I'll have to travel a little again ...' Alas, Bulgakov's future, like that of many others, would indeed be determined by the outcome of revolution. In December he travelled to Moscow to try to obtain his release from military service, and also made a most difficult journey to see his wife's parents. Back in Vyazma again he wrote to his sister Nadya of his boredom there and his desire to return to Kiev, or to Moscow. 'In two hours it will be New Year. What will it bring me?' Bulgakov finally received his discharge on 6 (19) February 1918, in Moscow, where he stayed with his sister Varvara. Shortly afterwards he and Tasya left Vyazma for good and returned home to Kiev.

NOTES OF A YOUNG DOCTOR

The publication of Bulgakov's medical stories dates from a later period, but he probably made notes for some of them while he was still in Nikolskoe, and certainly he made drafts before he left Kiev again in 1919. There are nine of them altogether, all except one published in a medical journal, *Meditsinskii rabotnik*, between 1925 and 1927. In order of publication these are: 'First Breech,' 'Snowstorm,' 'Egyptian Darkness,' 'Starry Rash,' 'Towel with a Rooster,' 'The Missing Eye,' 'I Killed,' and 'Morphine.'[17] It seems that Bulgakov intended to publish at least some of these as one book, in imitation perhaps of Vikenty Veresaev's very successful *Notes of a Doctor* of 1901. But it was not until 1963 that five of the above were published together, in a small paper edition put out by the 'Ogonek' library, under the title *Notes of a Young Doctor*. Included too was one story, 'Silver Throat,' not previously published in *Meditsinskii rabotnik*, somewhat revised by the editors to make its details consistent with other stories.[18] The same five stories were reprinted in the authoritative *Selected Prose* edition of 1966, and now Bulgakov's 'Steel Throat' was substituted, unamended, for the 'Ogonek' editors' 'Silver Throat,' and placed second instead of third.

   It is convenient to treat the six stories of *Notes of a Young Doctor* as one work, leaving aside for the present 'Starry Rash,' 'I Killed,' and 'Morphine,' which were not included. Apart from the inconsistencies of 'Steel Throat' (chro-

17 **136-48**. See also the references in **532**, p. 456. There are also two other stories about doctors but not really about medicine: 'On the Night of the Third' and 'The Extraordinary Adventures of a Doctor.' Popov, in his unfinished biography **187**, folio 556, also mentions one written in the early days of the Revolution, 'A Day in the Life of a Chief Doctor,' but this has not been found.
18 **146**. Three of the stories appeared the same year in **143**.

nological detail, the narrator's age, the number of his patients) and a few other minor discrepancies, the stories are relatively consistent with each other, linked by setting and characters, principally the narrator, and follow in a definite time sequence. They involve a doctor's first year of practice: his fears because of his inexperience, the operations he performs successfully (an amputation, a tracheotomy, a breech delivery), his own secluded life, the growth of his practice.

Made up of individual incidents over the course of a year, these stories have a charm and simplicity which is extraordinarily appealing, and indeed this collection belongs to the best of Bulgakov. It has received praise, justifiably, from critics and doctors alike.[19] In some ways the stories are almost written to a formula, involving three stages: the narrator's thoughts and fears, or memories of other cases; some sudden happening involving the need for decision and action; and the successful conclusion, bringing about a greater understanding on the part of the narrator. In the six collected stories there is little variation from this set pattern. Underlying them too is an outlook on life which reflects Bulgakov's own, for many of the themes which occur in his later works can be found here in some form or other.

The centre of interest in these stories is the personality of the narrator: a narrator who is all too human, even if he is a qualified doctor. The reader can identify with him precisely because his attitudes are those of all of us in unfamiliar situations. Afraid of his youth and the impression he makes, he deliberately tries to make himself look older, without success. He stands in awe of things he does not understand, instruments in the hospital he is unfamiliar with, the well-stocked pharmacy. While even the assistants and midwives seem to be more experienced than he is, above all he is tormented by the memory of his predecessor, who of course knew everything and compared to whom he is a 'False Dmitry,' an impostor. Objectively, his fears are exaggerated, for we as readers well know that he will come through; but it is for this reason that we can smile upon the narrator's sense of inadequacy, at his feeling cold with fear when faced with a difficult case, at his constant sweat when operating. Bulgakov frequently makes use of an interior monologue or a dialogue with some inner voice to express the narrator's thoughts, which are amusing in that they dwell always on the possibilities of disaster:

'... and what will you do about a hernia? fear stubbornly insisted in the form of a voice.

'I'll sit him in the bath,' I defended myself in a rage. 'In the bath. And I'll try to reduce it.'

19 See, for example, **283**

'A strangulated one, my dear fellow! What earthly use are baths then! A strangulated one,' fear sang in a demonic voice. 'You'll have to cut him open ...' (p. 52)

Yet contrasting with this fear there is an equally exaggerated pride, in which the narrator delights: he performs operations without spilling a drop of blood; when his assistants compliment him, as is frequently the case, he pretends to be more experienced or assured than in fact. But he is honest enough to admit to this boasting and to be ashamed of such pretensions. Underneath everything, he knows that potentially he is a good doctor, but still only at the beginning, that he must constantly be learning. It is this that is emphasized in the last story, 'The Missing Eye,' where after thinking over all that he has been through and learnt he becomes boastful – 'I positively cannot imagine their bringing me a case which could stump me ...' (p. 106) – then makes a mistake which could have cost a boy his eye, and is duly humbled.

These feelings that Bulgakov is describing are common to anyone placed in a position of responsibility: the clinical details are not important so much as the choices the narrator is called upon to make and his own attitude towards them. There is here a certain fundamental honesty. Bulgakov shows an extraordinary ability to make fun of himself through his narrator: to look humorously at his actions and analyse his inner feelings, his fears, his depressions, his pride in the job he is doing.

In Bulgakov's later work one of the principal themes is that of the writer and his struggle in life. Here his doctor is just as much of an artist, struggling against inner and outer forces, and taking pride in his hard-won professionalism. On a more general level, this applies to any conscientious person. The first struggle is with oneself, one's own treacherous thoughts and the temptation to take the easy way out – '"Die. Die quickly," I thought, "please die. Otherwise what shall I do with you?"' (p. 55). But man finds surprising reserve powers for, despite the cowardice of his thoughts, his inner self takes over and accomplishes things he would not have thought possible. This is no mere accident but, in medicine at least, the result of training and the acquisition of certain attitudes – and the same surely is true of other professions. It leads one to act seemingly against one's own interests, even against common sense – as when, in 'Steel Throat,' the narrator persuades a mother and grandmother to allow an operation he does not know if he can do. Here, the contrast between the narrator's desires and the words he speaks provides an obvious source of comedy: 'Within myself I thought "What am I doing? I'll just butcher the girl." But I spoke differently: "Hurry up, hurry up, agree! Agree! Look, her nails are already turning blue"' (p. 62). Even in a different situation, when the narrator is almost attacked by wolves when returning from a patient, this inner man takes over, avoiding agonizing decisions in the face of the need for action. It is the same with Bulgakov's later heroes. As men of integrity, all do what they know they must despite the real dangers they face.

In *Notes of a Young Doctor* man's interior struggles are often expressed in physical form, on the down-to-earth level of comfort as opposed to necessity: the narrator is constantly being interrupted – from sleep, from having a bath, from shaving. This is the whole point of the story 'Snowstorm,' where he is called out from a day of rest to a girl who then dies before the doctor can do anything. What is important is the bath he can at last enjoy, contrasted with the discomforts of the drive and then the cold misery of the return when he and the coachman get lost in the snow. The story is reminiscent of Tolstoy's 'Master and Man' but with the difference that in Tolstoy the main character is a merchant travelling to make a profit, whereas here we have a doctor who is travelling only because of his sense of duty. And he, in contrast to the merchant, lives, swearing that he will never go out again like this – but knowing quite well that he will not refuse when the time comes. This is the first time that Bulgakov uses the image of the snowstorm – emphasized by an epigraph from Pushkin – but we shall find it again in other of his works. It has been suggested that the storm is the aesthetic equivalent of the Revolution, that the way through it is shown by the lamp of the hospital symbolizing science and light.[20] But it is hardly necessary to find such a specific reference. Man is simply alone in an apparently hostile world: he cannot tame it or change it, but he can find his own area where there is light and civilization, try to cling on to this and extend it.

A related theme, which we shall find again later, is the struggle against ignorance, the 'Egyptian darkness' which impedes the growth of civilization and, like the storm, is a force of its own. It finds its expression most often in the ignorance of the peasants, those 'benighted people' who lack understanding and actively prevent enlightenment: the grandmother in 'Steel Throat,' superstitiously afraid of the surgeon's knife and sure all the child needs is some medicine when she is already on the point of suffocation; a father-in-law who makes a pregnant woman walk five kilometres to the hospital to give birth because he does not want to give her horses for nothing. The story 'Egyptian Darkness' opens appropriately with a description of physical darkness – in the village where the nearest kerosene lamps are nine kilometres away. There follows a whole series of stories of peasants' stupidity: the woman who gets enough medicine to share it out with all the village, or the man who applies mustard plasters on top of his sheepskin coat. And the narrator, determined to struggle with this darkness, gets caught out himself with a patient of seeming intelligence who takes all his pills at the same time because he thinks that this will be more effective.

Such themes we can find in many of Bulgakov's feuilletons, and in some of his later works as well. Darkness is not only a matter of ignorance: it is often one of self-interest, narrow-mindedness, dogmatism, or, on a more philosphical level, of evil. And to achieve light in one's own life is a struggle, too, involving both learning and experience: '"One can obtain great experience in the country," I thought as I went to sleep, "but one must just read, read, as much as possible ... read"' (p. 75).

Of course, there is a more fundamental struggle too, between life and death: the basic *raison d'être* of the doctor. As a medical student Bulgakov had on his wall a sign which read *quod medicamenta non sanat, mors sanat* (Hippocrates): what medicine does not cure, death cures. This might almost have been an epigraph to these stories, when it would sound not as a piece of cynicism but as a grim warning. As a doctor, Bulgakov is aware that death is his one real enemy. 'Death' plays an important role in his other works, too; later he will explore its meaning, the whole problem of immortality and of the life which has gone before, particularly in *The Master and Margarita*. Here it is expressed in simple physical terms. It is always ugly, as opposed to those it threatens who, significantly, are young and beautiful. Theirs is the beauty of life itself, and sometimes, inevitably, it is extinguished.

Such are the human problems which are presented even in these early stories. Yet for all their seriousness, they are humorous, even light-hearted, for the reader knows that in the end all will turn out well, even after the death in 'Snowstorm.' There is here an optimism that difficulties will be overcome. 'Bulgakov writes lightly and gayly. Only his is the gaiety not of heedlessness but of conquered timidity and inexperience – which makes it the most lasting and intelligent gaiety there can be.'[21] Bulgakov's light-heartedness stems partly from his condescending treatment of his own narrator and partly from his use of dialogue. He never allows a description to continue too long without inserting dialogue in some form: either another person's words, or the narrator's own thoughts, or the narrator's 'second voice.' In this is reflected at different times the comical speech of the peasant, the seriousness of the medical staff, and of course all the different tones of the narrator himself: fear, pride, boastfulness, urgency. Because we see through the narrator in all his assumed roles, the total effect is a humorous one.[22]

If we turn to the three medical stories not included in *Notes of a Young Doctor*, we find that thematically there is a certain similarity, but the light-hearted

21 **336**, p. 190
22 For a detailed discussion of Bulgakov's humour, see **418**.

tone is absent. 'Starry Rash,' about the horrors of syphilis, is another story emphasizing the 'darkness,' the ignorance of the peasants. But it is too didactic, and the concern too specific: we are no longer interested in the narrator but in a medical and social problem. So too with 'Morphine,' a wearisome account of a doctor's addiction (when it was republished in *Russkaia mysl'* in March and April 1970, a whole page of the original was omitted accidentally without its being noticeable). 'I Killed' is more interesting, showing a doctor taking life in order to escape from the brutal soldiers of the Ukrainian nationalist Petlyura in 1919; but again, it is lacking in humour and hardly belongs in the cycle of the other stories.

Quite apart from the opposition of Bulgakov's widow to publishing 'Morphine,' it would seem unlikely that he himself intended these three stories to be collected with the others. (He made no attempts even to bring names in 'Morphine' in line with the rest.) The main reason for setting them aside was undoubtedly an artistic one. The inclusion of any one of them would destroy the collection's present artistic unity, for they take us outside the world of a young doctor in his first year of practice; nor do they have the same uniformity of style.

Notes of a Young Doctor, as it is, makes a consistent, satisfactory whole. Its tone is humorous throughout - and Bulgakov is often at his best when serious issues are combined with comedy. He is, of course, writing in a minor form. A work such as Veresaev's *Notes of a Doctor*, which treats broadly the same subject, is far more weighty and gives a deeper insight into the kind of moral dilemmas a doctor may face. Bulgakov has none of Veresaev's long theoretical discussions.[23] But artistically his work is more satisfying, its strength lying in its careful selection of incidents, which give an *impression* of a young man's problems in his chosen profession. The reader relates to the narrator as a person rather than as a doctor, for in this collection (if not in 'Starry Rash' and 'Morphine') literature comes before medicine. Bulgakov in his stories aimed basically at simplicity as the hallmark of good writing. In *Notes of a Young Doctor* he achieves this admirably, while raising issues to which he was to devote a lifetime of thought.

KIEV AND THE CAUCASUS

At about one o'clock in the afternoon, after an hour or two's delay, the River Dnieper appears from behind the Darnitsa woods, the train goes on to the railway bridge patched up after the explosions ... and on the other shore there unfolds in the green of the hills the most beautiful town in Russia - Kiev.

23 For a detailed comparison, see **282**.

Now there is a tremendous tiredness in the town after the terrible reverberating years. Peace.[24]

Bulgakov wrote the above words in 1923, but when he returned to Kiev at the beginning of March 1918 he was just about to live through the most dramatic of the 'terrible reverberating years.' After the February Revolution in Petrograd, 1917 in Kiev had been marked by the rise of a Ukrainian government known as the central rada, whose principal concern was to establish and maintain Ukrainian autonomy. But the Bolsheviks, who came to power in Russia in the October Revolution, also had ambitions in the Ukraine: in February 1918 the Red Army occupied Kiev. The rada, forced to flee to Zhitomir, appealed for assistance to the Germans, with whom a separate peace had already been concluded. The Germans entered Kiev on 1 March, re-establishing the rada (the same month the Treaty of Brest-Litovsk was signed with Russia, ending the war on Germany's eastern front). It was about this time that Bulgakov returned to the city. The Ukrainian rada, however, was now dismissed in favour of the German nominee Skoropadsky, 'elected' at the end of April as 'hetman' (an old Ukrainian title specially revived). The Germans remained the real masters in the Ukraine, but only as long as they could still win the war in the west; in the meantime opposition to them was growing in the countryside under the Ukrainian nationalist Semyon Petlyura. After the armistice in November, the Germans withdrew, the hetman fled, and Petlyura's troops entered Kiev. Less than two months later, Petlyura himself was driven out by the returning Bolsheviks, but he continued the struggle and reattacked at the end of August 1919, entering Kiev at almost the same time as the now victorious White forces under Denikin – who lost little time in forcing Petlyura out again. The Whites were still in control of the city when Bulgakov departed once more in the autumn of 1919. In December Kiev once again fell to the Bolsheviks, who held it until May 1920, when it was taken by Petlyura's Polish allies. This final occupation, however, was short-lived: the Bolsheviks re-entered the city on 11 June and remained. 'By the reckoning of the Kievans,' Bulgakov wrote, 'they had 18 violent changes of government. Some of the hot-house writers of memoirs have counted 12; I can state accurately that there were 14, and moreover I personally experienced 10 of them.'[25]

After his return to Kiev, Bulgakov had, at this difficult time, opened up a private practice as a venereologist and dermatologist, with his office in the same house he had lived in as a child. The family was still there, except for Varya, who

24 **121** and **110**, p. 4
25 **110**, p. 2. For a detailed account of this period, see **459**.

was in Moscow (where, according to a letter from her to her sister Nadya in May 1918, things were infinitely worse), but she returned home shortly afterwards. Living below was the landlord (immortalized as Vasilisa in *The White Guard*), whose daughter has recalled Bulgakov at this period, tall, fair, and with bright blue eyes, with the habit of constantly tossing back his hair: 'And he walked very fast ... And his character – sarcastic, ironic, caustic. Not an easy person to get on with, on the whole ... Yes, and for some reason the faucets in his consulting room were always running. And his basin was always overflowing. And seeping through the floor, so that the water dripped onto our heads ...'[26] In the summer of 1918 Mikhail, his wife Tasya, sisters Vera and Varya, and their cousin Kostya, all remained in the city, while their mother and the younger children went to the dacha in Bucha. Varvara Mikhaylovna was by this time remarried, to the family friend Doctor Ivan Pavlovich Voskresensky, and after the summer she moved into his house at No 38, Andreevsky Spusk, further up the street.

Bulgakov's novel *The White Guard* tells us something of what Kiev was like at this time. Refugees poured in from Moscow: businessmen, merchants, politicians, army officers, actresses, prostitutes. To cater for them restaurants, clubs, and gambling dens were opened up; the merchants did a tremendous business, while new arrivals rushed about transferring money and trying to get abroad. 'They dreamed of France, of Paris, in anguish at the thought that it was extremely difficult, if not nearly impossible, to get there.'[27] The refugees were united by one passion: hatred for the Bolsheviks who had caused them to flee their homeland. Under the hetmanate they could take comfort in the German army, majestically parading through Kiev. Life seemed to go on much as usual, and there was even an atmosphere of gaiety, abandon – but it was a false existence, unlikely to last. Above all, in the city with its large Russian population there was little understanding of life in the countryside nearby, or of the feelings of the Ukrainians. Until suddenly there was news of the abdication of the German kaiser Wilhelm, an armistice was signed, and there came the realization that the German armies would leave the Russians in Kiev to their fate.

It is difficult to know how Bulgakov was affected personally by the entry of the Ukrainian nationalist Petlyura into the city on 14 December 1918. *The White Guard* is fiction; its author may have actually experienced some of the events he describes, he may not. But the atmosphere is authentic: the rumours surrounding Petlyura, the atrocities committed, the fear. The Bulgakovs were Russian intellectuals, as were most of the upper classes in Kiev, a Ukrainian town. Petlyura represented the forces of anarchy, of ignorance, the 'benighted

26 **168**, pp. 311-12
27 **168**, p. 58. The following quotation is from p. 60.

people' who were about to triumph over what, for Russians, was civilization. Towards Petlyura they could feel only contempt. They feared and hated the Bolsheviks too, ultimately a more significant force. But abandoned by the hetman (who, although a puppet in the hands of the Germans, had provided some hope for the kind of life they valued), they were powerless to do more than tolerate Petlyura and wait for his overthrow – then throw in their lot with the Reds or the Whites as the case might be.

It was undoubtedly a difficult time for Bulgakov, as for everyone else. Like his hero, Alexey Turbin, he had 'returned home ... to rest, recuperate, and start again by building a new life, not a soldier's life but an ordinary human existence'; like Alexey Turbin he could not avoid being caught up in events, and even, it seemed, served for two weeks himself as a doctor in the hetman's army – if not in Petlyura's too. In the story entitled 'The Extraordinary Adventures of a Doctor' Bulgakov describes one doctor who is constantly being mobilized by each new army to enter Kiev; two other stories, 'On the Night of the Third' and 'I Killed,' have as their subject a doctor who is forcibly evacuated by Petlyura's men at the time of their withdrawal, and later escapes. Certainly there were cases like this, and one is tempted to wonder if it could have happened to Bulgakov himself: regrettably there is no direct evidence. At all events, he must have felt great relief at the defeat of Petlyura by the Reds in February 1919: after their atrocities, he writes, 'I too started to wait for the Bolsheviks.'[28] Bulgakov lived under the Bolsheviks for seven months, spending the rest of the winter and spring of 1919 in the city, and the summer in Bucha with his wife and two brothers.

The year and a half in Kiev marked a turning point in Bulgakov's career. In 'I Killed' he describes a doctor obviously based on himself: fastidious in his dress, fond of the theatre, reserved but a good story-teller. 'You're a very fine doctor,' he states significantly, 'but nevertheless you haven't taken the right road and you should only be a writer.'[29] We know that he himself was writing at this time: drafts of some of the *Notes of a Young Doctor* stories, a drama called 'The First Flower,' and the outline of a work entitled 'Illness' which, as the Soviet scholar M. Chudakova suggests, may possibly have been the genesis of *The White Guard*.[30] At the end of August Kiev was captured by the Whites, and in November Bulgakov and his wife suddenly left for the south. (His brothers were later to follow the Whites' subsequent withdrawal and eventually emigrate to Paris.)

28 **136**, no 44, p. 14
29 **136**, no 44, p. 13
30 **243**, pp. 236, 242-5, and **532**, p. 456. 'The First Flower' is also mentioned in **306**, p. 327. For the rest of this chapter I have made extensive use of these sources.

What exactly prompted this flight from Kiev, with Tasya, first to Grozny then to Vladikavkaz (now Ordzhonikidze), is impossible to say with certainty. If he had wanted to emigrate, as has been suggested, he would surely have gone to Odessa rather than the Caucasus. He himself had probably no very clear idea of what he wanted to do. It may be that he was simply fleeing before the advancing Bolsheviks, who took Kiev again the following month. The future of the south – which would be occupied by Denikin's White troops a little longer – was politically uncertain: here he might find a certain respite from the constant upheavals in his home town and be free to decide more calmly about his own future.

It is from the time of this flight that his serious literary activity begins, reputedly on 19 November 1919: 'One night in 1919, in the dead of autumn, travelling in a rickety train, by the light of a candle stuck in an empty kerosene bottle, I wrote my first little story. In the town the train had been taking me to, I took the story to the editor of a newspaper. There it was printed. Then they printed several feuilletons. At the beginning of 1920 I abandoned my degree with distinction and wrote.'[31] The story, published in February 1920, was entitled 'Tribute of Admiration' and also described Kiev during the civil war. It was only one of a number written that year for local papers. The decision to abandon medicine dates, apparently, from 15 February. After that time Bulgakov would sometimes go to sick friends of his, at least for the period he was in Vladikavkaz, but he was never to return to the actual practice of medicine. Later he would rarely give the impression of having been a doctor – except perhaps in his love for chemists' shops and his habit of constantly washing his hands. He appears not to have regretted his decision.

In Vladikavkaz, Bulgakov was overtaken by events. Once again, evidence of his intentions comes mainly from what he himself wrote, in his autobiographical sketches, 'Notes on the Cuffs.' Bulgakov's editor suddenly left in face of the impending 'catastrophe': the capture of the town by the Bolsheviks in March 1920. But Bulgakov himself was confined to bed with typhus. The 'Notes' tell us that in his delirium he was constantly disturbed by thoughts of what he had to do, of a journey he had to make but could not. The thought of going abroad at this time was clearly in his mind: 'I'm tired of this idiotic war! I'll flee to Paris, I'll write a novel there, and then I'll go into a monastery ... Doctor! I demand to be sent to Paris immediately! I don't want to stay in Russia any longer ...' (*Vozrozhdenie*, p. 7).[32] There were many victims of typhus in the town at that time,

---

31 **491**, p. 85

32 The Caucasian episodes of 'Notes on the Cuffs' are **131** and **154**. As neither version is complete in itself, it is necessary to combine the two for a full picture. For quotations the relevant version with page reference is indicated in the text.

and Bulgakov nearly died from it. It lasted over a month, and he had at least two relapses, despite the constant care and attention of his wife Tasya. When he recovered the town was already in the hands of the Bolsheviks. He remained, and for the time being seemed to accept the situation.

After his illness his immediate problem was to earn enough money to support himself and his wife. A constant theme through the early chapters of 'Notes on the Cuffs' is 'what will become of us?' 'what are we to do?' The answer appears to have been provided by Bulgakov's writer colleague, Yury Slyozkin: they would open up a 'sub-department of the arts.' This was by no means a far-fetched idea. In the years following the Revolution the organization of the arts in the new Soviet state was a matter for constant discussion, and many such departments grew up under A.V. Lunacharsky's People's Commissariat of Enlightenment (*Narkompros*). In most cases – and here too – ambitions were considerably greater than finances. Nevertheless, the Vladikavkaz sub-department of the arts became a reality, with Bulgakov and Slyozkin doing what they could to encourage the local writers (most of them in search of what the sub-department had least to offer, money) and provide the populace with a cultural education.

Bulgakov, as 'literary manager,' worked hard, organizing literary concerts, writing, and delivering lectures. Two such occasions, a 'Chekhov evening' and a 'Pushkin evening' are described in one of the most amusing sections of the 'Notes.' He was reported in the press as introducing symphony concerts, taking part in literary discussions. Tasya too was in a number of theatrical productions. More important, Bulgakov himself started to write plays for the local theatres, the first of which, a one-act vaudeville called *Self-Defence*, was performed in June 1920. Into the office of the sub-department there came a constant stream of poets and writers: Yevreynov, Ivnev, Mandelshtam, Pilnyak, Serafimovich. There was a local union of poets too, and its young administrator, D.A. Odollamsky, has recalled seeing Bulgakov at a literary evening in the Summer Theatre, sitting beside Slyozkin on the stage in a carefully pressed grey suit and reading short witty stories.[33]

It was at one of the meetings of the poets' group that Bulgakov aroused the wrath of the local critics by defending Pushkin – for at this time there were many fervent communists who wanted to reject the past completely. The public, according to Bulgakov, was receptive: 'But it was different afterwards!! But afterwards ... I was a "wolf in sheep's clothing." I was a "mister." I was a "mouthpiece for the bourgeoisie."' He seems even to have feared for his safety:

---

33 Apart from his own 'Notes on the Cuffs,' 243, and 532, the most useful information on his activities and plays in Vladikavkaz is provided by 236 and 237, both of which I have used extensively in the rest of the chapter. See also 174

'I am no longer literary manager. No longer theatrical manager. I am a stray dog in the attic. I sit squirming. They'll telephone me at night – I shudder' (*Naka-nune*, p. 6). Bulgakov here is referring to an article in the local paper *Kommunist* of 10 July 1920, where one M. Skromny had written that Bulgakov and his colleague Boris Beme were using language as a weapon in the bourgeois cause – by finding something in common between Pushkin and the Revolution.

This was not the first time that Bulgakov had been attacked in the press. On 1 May he had spoken at a concert 'where he managed to avoid ticklish discussions of "politics"'; in *Kommunist* of 4 June 1920 the reviewer of a symphonic concert, M. Voks (himself 'against Tchaikovsky's lyrical slush'), had taken exception to Bulgakov's laudatory introduction. In a town which was literally on the frontiers of Soviet power – for Transcaucasia was still in the hands of the Mensheviks – a primitive conception of literature and art and their role in the struggle against the not-too-distant bourgeoisie was to be expected. Bulgakov, as a man of culture, was incapable of adopting a crude class viewpoint. Yet such attacks were mild compared with those that were to follow in future years.

But anything that was likely to affect Bulgakov's scant income was of concern, for his immediate worry, Slyozkin's too, was still how to get enough money to eat. Feuilletons written for the local papers were one means of support. And another play, *The Brothers Turbin*, opened in October 1920. But a serious blow was the prohibition of the sub-department's literary evenings. The problem became acute. Bulgakov moved to a poorer apartment, which he described to his cousin Konstantin in a letter dated 1 February 1921: 'I live in a nasty room at Sleptsovskaya Street, no 9, apartment 2. I lived in a good one, I had a writing desk, now I don't have one and write by a kerosene lamp.' His only interest at this time seems to have been his projected novel. 'I am working persistently,' he says in the same letter. 'I am writing a novel, the only thought-out thing in all this time.' Two weeks later, on 16 February, he asked for the notes for 'Illness,' left behind in Kiev, and eventually Nadya managed to send them to him. (Later, in Moscow, his friend Slyozkin, using him for a character in one of his own novels, would further indicate how important this work was for him: 'The only thing he would like to write is a novel ... The novel will not leave him ...'[34])

In the winter of 1920-21 Bulgakov also wrote three plays: *The Perfidious Pope* or *The Clay Suitors, The Paris Communards*, and *The Sons of Mullah*. The third of these, a joint effort with a local lawyer, and performed in May, turned out to be profitable, bringing him a hundred thousand roubles. And with the money there came again the thought of escaping to Paris. Once again, Bulgakov

34 From *Stolovaia gora*. Quoted in **236**, p. 76

does not seem to have been particularly resolute in his intentions. On 26 May he left Vladikavkaz, crossing the Caucasus to the south, and went first to Tbilisi. (The civil war had ended six months previously with the complete victory of the Bolsheviks: by this time Georgia too was a Soviet socialist republic.) Tasya followed on 11 June and they stayed in Tbilisi until mid-August. While there, Bulgakov met the poet Osip Mandelshtam again: years later they would be neighbours in Moscow. Then he and Tasya went on to Batumi, on the coast, by which time Bulgakov's money appears to have run out. His account shows him beset by doubts, with no clear idea of what he intended to do, and no really strong desire to leave his native land. There is no mention of his wife here, and we know only that on about 24 August she returned to Kiev, and from there, on 4 September, made her way with considerable difficulty to Moscow, apparently to find out about living conditions. Two weeks later she sent Bulgakov a telegram saying she wanted to come back – by which time he himself had left.

In Batumi, too, Bulgakov wrote feuilletons for the local papers. He was hungry, and tired. According to 'Notes on the Cuffs' he sold his overcoat and tried to embark on a ship about to sail for Constantinople, only to be refused at the gangplank. Worn out, tired of struggling, he decided to return home. First he went to Kiev, arriving on 17 September and spending several days there. (To his mother he later wrote: 'My pleasantest memory recently is – guess what? When I slept on your sofa and drank tea with French rolls. I'd give a great deal to live like that again even for two days, drinking tea, and not to think of anything.') Between 23 and 26 September he went to Moscow, stayed for a while in a student hostel, and then went to live with his brother-in-law, A.M. Zemsky.

THE VLADIKAVKAZ PLAYS

From the point of view of Bulgakov the writer, the most significant thing about this period of his life is his sudden plunge into literary activity. For the first time he was forced to write in order to live: first feuilletons (which have not yet been researched) and then, in an amazingly short time, five plays. It may well be that they were poor plays, as Bulgakov himself judged. They must still have required considerable energy – and confidence – to write.

The one-act vaudeville *Self-Defence* was performed on 6 June 1920: of its precise contents we know nothing, but it has been suggested on the basis of its title and characters that it concerned the preparations of the townspeople against attacks from bandits. It was followed in October and November by 'a hastily written – the devil knows how – four-act drama,' *The Brothers Turbin*. In his letter to his cousin Konstantin, Bulgakov described the tumultuous applause this received and his own confusion at his dream coming true so grotesquely: 'Instead of the Moscow stage the provincial stage, instead of the drama about Alyosha Turbin I cherished, there is this immature thing, done in haste ...'[35] From M. Voks' review in *Kommunist* of 4 December 1920 we know that *The Brothers Turbin* concerned 'everyday episodes from the revolutionary spring of 1905,' and that its heroes, the Turbins, were from the petite bourgeoisie. It seems that Bulgakov for a number of years was toying with the idea of writing about a family similar to his own, and that this play was an early attempt to do so – an unsuccessful one, as his reference to Alyosha Turbin would indicate. In June of that year he wrote to Nadya that he was turning the *Turbins* into a large drama. At this stage his ideas were forming only gradually: Alexey Turbin would finally be the name of his hero in the novel he was working on.

'Then,' the letter to his cousin continues, 'besides stories which there is nowhere to publish, I wrote a vaudeville *The Clay Suitors*. Of course it wasn't taken into the repertory, but they suggest they'll put it on one fine day.' The play, also referred to as *The Perfidious Pope*, and which must have been written at the end of 1920 or the very beginning of 1921, was a farce about the Uniates, a religious sect. 'My work is sharply divided into two parts,' Bulgakov wrote to his sister Vera that April, 'genuine and forced. My best play of the genuine type I consider the three-act farce of the drawing-room type *The Perfidious Pope (The Clay Suitors)*. And just this one is not being performed, and will not be performed, despite the fact that the commission listening to it guffawed throughout all three acts.'

In ten days, in January 1921, Bulgakov also wrote the three-act play, *The Paris Communards*, which he intended for a competition organized by the theatrical section of *Narkompros* on the occasion of the fiftieth anniversary of the Paris Commune. Initially he was not overly optimistic about its success, although he was sure it would be accepted by the local theatre. 'It's all junk, *The Turbins*, *The Suitors*, and this play. I do everything in a hurry.' From a letter to Nadya in April, it seems that the play was at least accepted and rehearsed in Vladikavkaz (whether it was actually performed or not is not clear), and later he expressed concern about its fate in the competition in Moscow. But in June, when he had already left Vladikavkaz for Tbilisi, he was relatively indifferent to it, saying, if it were accepted for performance, 'fine, let it be put on as a triumphant show for some festival. As a play it's no good. If it hasn't been accepted – so much the better. Burn it in the stove of course.' He adds, however, that he would not like any major changes to be made in it.

His fifth play in Vladikavkaz was by far the most successful. The previous autumn, in September 1920, Bulgakov and Slyozkin had started teaching in

---

35 In **532**, pp. 454-5; also quoted in **491**, p. 90

drama studios, where they had met a local lawyer of Scottish origin, Boris Richardovich Beme. It was at his suggestion that Bulgakov had decided to co-operate with him in writing another play, *The Sons of Mullah*. Beme was deeply interested in literature and had himself written a novel. (It was he, too, who had been attacked with Bulgakov for their views on Pushkin.) Furthermore, he had a good knowledge of the native peoples and customs on which the play was to be based, and about which Bulgakov knew little – although he did take some interest in the local Osetin population. The play was written – in seven days, Bulgakov says – in February or March 1921. In 'Notes on the Cuffs' he gives a humorous account of how the work proceeded, with Beme saying how he loved to create, and both him and his wife giving advice – while Bulgakov gloomily decided it would be his last play. 'From the point of view of lack of talent, it was something completely extraordinary, stupendous. Something crass and impudent stood out from every line of this collective creativity. I didn't believe my eyes! What can I hope for, I must be crazy, if I write like this?' (*Vozrozhdenie*, p. 17).

The theme was a love-story in a native village, set against the background of the struggle between old and new: the hatred of two Ingush brothers, a white-guardist and a revolutionary.[36] *The Sons of Mullah* was first performed in May 1921 by amateur groups both in Vladikavkaz and in Grozny, with great success, and translated into the Ingush and Osetin languages. T.T. Malsagova, who acted in it in Grozny, has given her impression of its reception: 'There were masses of people, the public reacted violently, even at one pathetic moment a gun went off in the audience, the curtains had to be closed.' Bulgakov's memories are similar: 'In the mist of a thousand breaths there shone daggers, cartridge cases, eyes. In the third act, after the heroic riders burst in and seized the police inspector and his men, the Chechens, Kabardins, and Ingush shouted out: "That's the way! Scoundrel! Serve him right!"' (*Vozrozhdenie*, p. 18).

We have no texts available on which to judge these plays. It is probably just as well. According to Sergey Yermolinsky, Bulgakov's later friend, whenever Bulgakov spoke of them it was with a sour expression as of something distasteful. 'I placed three plays on the local stage,' he himself wrote in his autobiography. 'Subsequently in Moscow in 1923, after rereading them, I hastily destroyed them. I hope that not a single copy has remained of them anywhere.'[37] A typewritten text of *The Sons of Mullah* in Ingush translation was discovered, however, in 1960, in the archives of A. Goigov, an Ingush writer. So far it has not been retranslated into Russian.

36 See also **314**, II, p. 427
37 **491**, p. 85

2

Moscow and journalism, 1921-24

Bulgakov's arrival in Moscow in September 1921 and the difficulties of finding work and accommodation are described in the second part of 'Notes on the Cuffs': the immediate continuation of his autobiography.[1] Six months earlier the New Economic Policy (NEP) had been introduced by Lenin in order to re-establish the country's economy: but after the upheaval of the civil war Moscow remained a difficult place to live in, and for the next few years Bulgakov's struggle for survival was to continue. According to his story 'Forty Times Forty' he nearly died of starvation before learning how to cope with this new way of life. Elsewhere he writes of how he went all over the city, to offices which were invariably on the sixth floor, looking for work, and of his envy of those who, unlike himself, had no difficulty finding an apartment.[2] 'For a long time in Moscow I lived in anxiety,' Bulgakov would later write. 'To support my existence I worked as a reporter and writer of feuilletons in newspapers and hated these callings without distinction. At the same time I hated editors. I hate them now and will hate them until the end of my life.'[3]

His first job lasted two months, from 1 October to 1 December. The Literary Department (LITO) of the People's Commissariat of Enlightenment (*Narkompros*) had been established in December 1919 as the official and powerful liaison body between the government and the literary world. Now, after the reorganization of *Narkompros* at the end of 1920, it was subordinated to another organization under *Narkompros*, the Chief Administration for Political Education (*Glavpolitprosvet*), along with a number of other organizations involving the arts. By

1 The Moscow scenes of 'Notes on the Cuffs' are **153**.
2 **115**, 27 May, p. 2; 12 June, p. 3. The first of these references can also be found in **127**, p. 3.
3 **491**, p. 85

autumn 1921 LITO had lost the influence it once had had – and its funds, like those of *Narkompros* itself, were severely limited.[4] Bulgakov's expectations of a Moscow literary organization were immediately disappointed: LITO, he tells us in 'Notes on the Cuffs,' occupied but one room and its employees instead of being famous writers were one old man (the manager) and a younger one, both unknown. The young man, A.I. Erlikh, himself had only just arrived there and later left a description very similar to Bulgakov's. Both were looking for work, and they decided between them who was to occupy which position: 'A quarter of an hour later it was determined that Bulgakov would be the secretary of the department' (p. 164).[5]

Bulgakov claims that it was he himself who managed to 'turn LITO on': 'To my future biographer,' he writes, 'it was I who did this.' For a while, at least, the work continued, and young writers would bring their manuscripts for advice – which by now was all LITO was in a position to give them. Bulgakov is of course writing satirically and probably exaggerating the apparently amateur nature of the department's operations. None the less, the problems were real. 'Every day it became clearer that LITO was an accidental and unnecessary establishment,' Erlikh writes. 'The department had neither definite functions nor a material basis' (p. 165). Employees were paid irregularly, partly because of bureaucratic mismanagement and partly because of the general financial situation: *Narkompros* was struggling to find the money even to pay its teachers, to whom it was seriously in debt.

Bulgakov became sick, again he was hungry. The New Economic Policy was not without its hardships. Speculators were everywhere. There was unemployment. 'Briefly I can say there is a mad struggle to exist and adapt to new conditions of life,' he wrote to his mother on 17 November 1921.[6] In his letter he described something of his life in Moscow. He and Tasya were living at the apartment of Nadya's husband, Andrey Zemsky (who, however, had returned to Kiev): Bolshaya Sadovaya Street, no 10, apartment 50. He was working morning to night, with no free days at all; if his office were closed down, he had possible plans for working in a flax trust or in a trade newspaper, the *Torgovo-promyshlennyi vestnik* (Trade and Industrial Messenger). 'Moscow,' he writes, 'is changing over to a new type of life not seen here for a long time – fierce competition, running about, showing initiative, etc. You can't live outside such a life or you'll go under.' Prices were constantly rising, people counted only in hundred thous-

---

4 See **276** for a detailed account of the organizations under *Narkompros*; pp. 136-9 and 236-42 refer more specifically to LITO.

5 **262.** Page references to this are given in the text. A similar account can be found in **261.**

6 **448**, pp. 447-50, and **532**, pp. 459-62; see also **243**, pp. 251-2. I have made extensive use of these publications in this and the following section.

ands and millions. 'Black bread is 4600 roubles a pound, white 14,000 roubles.' Tasya, who found such a life very difficult, helped him a great deal and was trying to get a job as a shop assistant. 'With the huge distances I (literally) have to run across Moscow every day, she saves me a great deal of energy and strength by feeding me and leaving for me only what she cannot do herself: chopping firewood in the evenings and dragging in potatoes in the mornings.' Of necessity he had become very thrifty; their only thought was how to get through the winter, and then, in three years, to re-establish normal life: an apartment, clothing, and books.

Despite difficulties caused by lack of time, Bulgakov was still managing to write: in the letter he mentioned *Notes of a Young Doctor* and 'Illness.' And in a long postscript to his sister Nadya, he asked her to try to find material on Nicolas II and Rasputin in 1916-17, particularly on the murder of Rasputin and the overthrow of Nicolas: papers, memoirs, descriptions of costumes, portraits, and above all else he needed the diary of Vladimir Purishkevich. 'I cherish the thought of creating a grandiose drama in five acts by the end of 1922 ... The idea utterly fascinates me.' Nothing was to come of this. In a later letter to Nadya he also mentioned two feuilletons he had written, 'Eugene Onegin' for the journal *Ekran* (not accepted) and 'The Muse of Vengeance,' for which he had received 100 roubles from *Glavpolitprosvet*, for publication – perhaps – in *Vestnik iskusstv*.

LITO was not to last long. 'The government,' Erlikh writes,

gave up many excesses of a short time previously and it became clear that such establishments as MUZO, IZO, TEO, and LITO would be eliminated first of all.

When instead of our regular pay they gave us in LITO a box of matches each, there no longer remained any doubt that our establishment was living out its last days. (p. 166)

Fortunately, before LITO closed Bulgakov had had the offer of another job – temporary, as it turned out – to go to: the *Torgovo-promyshlennyi vestnik*, which was about to open as a weekly chronicle publishing largely various pieces of information on trade and industry, collected from all over Moscow. Bulgakov became its manager – and found himself having to get advertisements for it.[7] The first issue of the paper appeared on 29 November 1921: a copy exists in Bulgakov's archive with the items for which he was responsible marked in blue pencil.[8] For six weeks (seven issues) he was overburdened with work, but at least earning

7 **115**, 27 May, p. 2; **127**, p. 3
8 **187**, folio 271

sufficient to live on. Then this paper too closed down. 'You will understand what I must feel today,' he wrote to Nadya on 13 January, 'going up the chimney together with the *Messenger*.'

It was impossible to find work. He and his wife had barely enough to eat, and he even tried joining a troupe of strolling players, which took up so much time that he could not write and which still brought in very little money. On 1 February came another tremendous blow for him: his mother suddenly died of typhus – causing him increased concern lest the family should drift apart. Then, at last, about 16 February there was new hope, and he went to work in the daily *Rabochii* (Worker), which started publication on 1 March. On the 24th he wrote to his sister Vera that he was also managing the publishing division of a scientific-technical committee, under the direction of Andrey Zemsky's brother Boris, who became a good friend of his. (Of Bulgakov he would write: 'He understands his fate – it won't escape him.') Later he added work as a lecturer in a small theatre.

In 1921 and 1922 Bulgakov worked for a number of newspapers and wrote for still more, so that it is difficult to know the exact sequence of events. Indeed it is not known when he left *Rabochii* or exactly when he joined the staff of *Gudok* (Whistle), at the suggestion of Erlikh (who had joined *Gudok* after leaving LITO and met Bulgakov again that winter when he was in difficult circumstances). Bulgakov, in his unfinished manuscript 'To a Secret Friend,' relates how the other took him to apply for work as a literary adapter: 'this was what they called people who transformed barely literate material into something literate and fit to print.'[9]

Gudok was the organ of the railwaymen's union, and its office was situated in the enormous Palace of Labour on the Solyanka, overlooking the Moscow River. Here were the central offices of all the trade unions; that of the water-transport workers with its journal *Na vakhte* (which Konstantin Paustovsky joined in 1922) was next door, and there were many others. The atmosphere of the Palace of Labour with its editorial offices, and the writers making the rounds from one office to another trying to get published, emerges most clearly in caricature form, in the novel *Twelve Chairs* by the well-known satirists Ilya Ilf and Yevgeny Petrov, who themselves worked in *Gudok* (here the paper is named *Stanok* [Lathe] and the building the House of the Peoples). There was a constant bustle, constant disorder. 'The corridors of the House of the Peoples were so long and narrow that people walking down them inevitably quickened their pace.'[10] The canteen, where writers could meet, was almost the focal point of the building.

9 **491**, p. 93. A similar but more detailed account is found in **177**.
10 **310**, p. 214

Bulgakov hated his work correcting other people's material. 'One thing I can say, in all my life I never did more disgusting work. Even now I dream of it. It was a flow of hopeless grey boredom, unbroken and inexorable.'[11] None the less, *Gudok* provided a good training ground for many writers and the atmosphere must have been interesting, despite Bulgakov's feelings, if only for the literary contacts it provided. Basically a daily trade paper, carrying standard political items and articles of interest to railway workers, *Gudok* grew rapidly in popularity and consequently in size as well. Once a week it ran a regular edition in Ukrainian. The most popular part of the paper was the 'Fourth Page' (*Chetvertaia polosa*), which contained all kinds of humorous and often satirical stories, based on real situations. Where these were the result of bureaucracy, stupidity, bad management, or even dishonesty, the publicity given to them in *Gudok* frequently led to improvements. The system was simple. All over the country were 'working correspondents' (*rabkory*), railway employees who would send in information. Of the hundreds of letters received a number were selected and either were published, after grammatical corrections, essentially as they were, or became the basis for very short, humorous stories or poems.

If one looks through the issues of *Gudok* for 1922 and 1923 it is impossible to tell which items on the 'Fourth Page' were corrected or written by Bulgakov. It is a delightful jumble of stories, poems, jokes – some with authors' initials, but the majority inserted under pseudonyms or simply signed '*rabkor* No ...' if they are signed at all. Nothing on this page bore Bulgakov's signature or initials: his later signed feuilletons in the paper were elsewhere.

Yevgeny Petrov has recalled his first impression of the office where the 'Fourth Page' was prepared, with its two tables under the window where four of the writers worked. Above all he was struck by the pleasant atmosphere and sharp wit of those present. 'Anyone going into this atmosphere would start to crack jokes himself, but mostly he would be the victim of their raillery.'[12] One feature of the office was a huge board on the wall, bearing the heading '*Sopli i vopli*': 'Sobs and Sighs.' Here were posted up all kinds of printed howlers: newspaper errors, ungrammatical or ambiguous sentences, unsuccessful photographs and drawings. Everyone took part in collecting these, and many of them went into the newspaper under the same heading.

Others too have commented on the constant banter and gaiety in the office, and on the many stories invented on the basis of letters received – stories which were purely for office consumption and never written down. Bulgakov excelled

11 **491**, p. 94
12 **515**, p. 15. See also on *Gudok*, in the same volume, 'Chetvertaia polosa' and 'V starom *Gudke*'; elsewhere, **409**, pp. 140-2.

at this and appears to have fitted into the company very well. Of his colleagues, one, Valentin Kataev, had already achieved some measure of distinction as a writer. Others would do the same. Ilya Ilf and Yevgeny Petrov were later to become famous for their humorous novels *Twelve Chairs* and *The Golden Calf*: it was here that the two met after Valentin Kataev had introduced his brother Yevgeny (Petrov was a pseudonym) to the office. Others were Semyon Gekht, Mikhail Shtikh, Boris Perelman, and the poet Yury Olesha – later to become well known for his novel *Envy* but at this time publishing light poems in *Gudok* under the name of 'Chisel' (*Zubilo*).

Bulgakov was particularly close to Kataev and Olesha, both of whom would visit him in his flat on the Bolshaya Sadovaya Street. He and Kataev would sometimes drink champagne, have long discussions, and give advice to a neighbouring young writer. Although Bulgakov could be witty and sarcastic, he was serious and penetrating in his criticisms, trying to give encouragement even when he thought the writing poor, while Kataev was more outspoken. Both thought very highly of Olesha, whom Kataev considered the most talented writer in Russia.[13] Olesha and Bulgakov shared a mutual respect and had a similar approach to writing: both described what they saw, both started out with material they knew well and understood. When Olesha published his first collection of feuilletons, he wrote a dedication to Bulgakov (30 July 1924): 'Mishenka, I shall never write abstract, lyrical verses. No one needs them. A poet must write feuilletons, so that there should be a practical use for people who receive a salary of seven roubles. Don't be angry, Mishunchik, you are a good humorist (Mark Twain is a humorist too).'[14]

It is doubtful whether Bulgakov would have agreed about writing feuilletons – although he certainly never wrote abstractly. When later his own signed feuilletons appeared in *Gudok* (between 1923 and 1926, but mostly in 1924 and 1925), it was a matter of producing eight of them a month, for a higher salary than for his correcting work. These were sometimes signed with his own name, but often with mere initials or pseudonyms: M. Ol-rayt (a transcription of the English 'I'm all right'), G.P. Ukhov (from the GPU, the secret police), Emma B. (the pronunciation of his own initials), F. S-ov, Neznakomets, Ivan Bezdomny, M. Bull, Tuskarora.[15] This kind of writing came easily to him and his one desire was to do it as quickly as possible so as to get home to work on his novel. To compose a feuilleton of seventy-five to a hundred lines took him from eighteen

---

13 **349**, p. 115
14 Quoted in **244**, p. 7. 'Mishenka' and 'Mishunchik' are affectionate forms for Mikhail.
15 The two final ones are reported by Vl. Lakshin in **2**, p. 8. I cannot vouch for them personally.

to twenty-two minutes, plus eight minutes for it to be typed. It then went to the editor, whose main concern was to find any 'criminal thought with regards to the Soviet system,' after which he would make corrections while Bulgakov waited, nervously smoking cigarettes. Then, when the feuilleton was accepted, Bulgakov's work was finished – but he usually could not go home, for writers had to stay in the afternoons in case they were needed for corrections, even though there was nothing to do. Bulgakov hated to waste valuable time, and according to Erlikh even took to doing his own writing at the office, working calmly without making any corrections or blots, and filling up an entire oilskin-covered notebook.

Bulgakov did not write only for *Gudok*: Paustovsky recounts how he would sometimes come into the office of *Na vakhte* next door, look over one of the letters received, dictate in five to ten minutes 'such a story that the editor would just clutch at his head and the staff would fall off their chairs with laughter.' Then he would collect five roubles on the spot and go off with plans on how to spend it.[16] Even the prestigious *Trud* (Labour) invited him to write feuilletons for it, in January 1923.

By far the most important of the newspapers Bulgakov worked for, however, was the daily Berlin émigré newspaper *Nakanune* (On the Eve), with its editorial office in Moscow. After the publication in it of the first part of 'Notes on the Cuffs,' Bulgakov wrote for *Nakanune* a number of feuilletons, which appeared between 1922 and 1924, and it was these that really began to make his reputation. It all started when in January 1922 he sent his sister a feuilleton he had written entitled 'Moscow Trades' or 'A Commercial Renaissance,' for her to take to a newspaper editor in Kiev with the suggestion to employ him as Moscow correspondent for the paper. Nothing came of this, but Bulgakov continued with the idea of writing about Moscow and, as it turned out, for a Berlin audience instead. *Nakanune* has been described in detail by E. Mindlin, the secretary of its Moscow office, in his memoirs.[17] In many ways the office must have been very similar to that of *Gudok*. It was situated on Bolshoy Gnezdnikovsky Lane on the first floor of the highest building in Moscow, still known as Nirenzee House from the name of its former owner (its later name was House of the Soviets). Here too were a large number of different editorial offices and on the tenth floor was a popular restaurant next to the Moscow Association of Writers. Journalists and

16 **372**, pp. 384-5. The list of journals and newspapers Bulgakov collaborated on in some
measure between 1922 and 1924 includes, besides *Rabochii, Gudok,* and *Na vakhte*:
*Golos rabotnika prosveshcheniia, Krasnaia gazeta, Krasnaia panorama, Krasnyi perets,
Krasnyi zhurnal, Krasnyi zhurnal dlia vsekh, Nakanune, Petrogradskaia pravda, Rabochaia gazeta, Rupor, Smekhach*.
17 **382**. A subsequent reference is to p. 146. Part of the same material also appears in **381**.

writers were constantly in and out of the *Nakanune* office, which shortly after its opening in 1922 became almost a literary club, while others would gather to find out what news there was from Berlin. Although published in Berlin, *Nakanune* was sold in major cities in Russia too, and enjoyed considerable popularity. Originally, it had been founded by a group of émigré writers who saw the New Economic Policy in Russia as indicating a return to the ideas of capitalism and who therefore called on Russians abroad to support the new Soviet state by returning home. They had published these ideas in a collection of articles entitled 'Changing Landmarks' (*Smena vekh*) and the same label was then applied to describe the newspaper too. Later the term became one of abuse in Russia – Bulgakov was frequently called a 'changing landmarks' writer (*smenovekhovskii pisatel'*), corresponding roughly to 'counter-revolutionary' – but at this time it embraced a large variety of people who for one reason or other thought of returning to the Soviet Union, including the well-known writer and editor of *Nakanune*'s literary supplement, Alexey Tolstoy. (He returned in 1923: it was a big event for all the staff of the paper.) None the less, *Nakanune* itself, although generally more pro-Soviet than otherwise, was regarded with considerable suspicion, along with the whole 'changing landmarks' movement.

Bulgakov was only one of many well-known writers who contributed. Amongst others were Yury Slyozkin (his old acquaintance from Vladikavkaz), Alexey Tolstoy himself, Vsevolod Ivanov, Lev Lunts, Konstantin Fedin, Alexandr Grin, Mikhail Zoshchenko, the poets Sergey Yesenin and Osip Mandelshtam, the philologist Roman Yakobson. Nor was Bulgakov the only writer to contribute from amongst those working for *Gudok*: Valentin Kataev became a regular contributor and later introduced several other young writers, including his brother Yevgeny Petrov and Semyon Gekht. Bulgakov and Kataev soon became the most popular writers in the paper. Mindlin recounts how Tolstoy was constantly asking him to send him more Bulgakov, but that although he sent material once or even twice a week it was often appropriated for the main paper and never reached Tolstoy for his literary supplement.

On his first appearance in the office Bulgakov charmed everyone with his well-bred, aristocratic manners which contrasted so sharply with those of the younger writers. Everything about him, his stiff, shining white collar, his carefully knotted tie, his not fashionable but well-tailored suit, pressed trousers, his fur coat, set him apart – as did his over-polite, old-fashioned style of speech, his kissing of ladies' hands, and almost ceremonial bows. A certain sense of style remained with him, although he was far from wealthy at this time. In many ways he must have appeared an anachronism, comical even, but amongst young people not used to this he commanded a certain respect. (He himself was very conscious of being already over thirty.) Mindlin describes how, for his feuilleton on the

First All-Russian Agricultural Exhibition,[18] Bulgakov presented an enormous bill for expenses, which included costs for two in sampling the various dishes in the restaurant. Even the economically minded office manager Kalmens had to give way to his logic: 'First, I never go to a restaurant without a lady. Second, I have indicated in my feuilleton which dishes are most to the taste of a lady. As you please, but I would most respectfully ask you to recompense me for the working expenses incurred by me.'

He had other eccentricities. When a colleague published what he considered to be a particularly good article in *Nakanune*, he would come specially to the office and wait to formally congratulate the author. When he was invited to become the secretary of a new journal, he started by serving his visiting authors with tea, real sugar, and a French loaf each on every occasion – something unheard of in those days, so that the news spread and authors rushed to the office. The journal folded up after three weeks.

In his evenings he was of course writing more important things: his novel, and a number of stories too. He was invited to contribute to other journals. The second part of his 'Notes on the Cuffs' appeared in *Rossiia*, a journal considered to belong to intellectuals of 'changing landmarks' persuasion, although their views differed from their counterparts abroad. (Here too Bulgakov was in good company, with many of the other writers from *Nakanune*.) *Nakanune* itself folded up in 1925, when interest in it subsided.

'NOTES ON THE CUFFS'

'Notes on the Cuffs' is, as Bulgakov's widow has pointed out, written 'in the first person and is to a certain degree autobiographical, like many literary works. But, as the author has testified, it is a literary work and in no way an autobiography.'[19] This may generally be true, but it is still fair to say that it is the most autobiographical of Bulgakov's writings, being a fairly straightforward, if episodic, account of his life in Vladikavkaz and Batumi (Part I) and his work for LITO in Moscow (Part II).

He seems to have written the first part between 1920 and 1921, possibly on the basis of his own diary, while still in Vladikavkaz; finishing it in Moscow (where it was dictated to a typist who agreed to wait for its publication before being paid).[20] It first appeared in the literary supplement of *Nakanune* on 18 June

18 **132**
19 Letter to A.A. Zvorykin (deputy chief editor of the *Bolshaia Sovetskaia entsiklopediia*), 19 Jan. 1951, in **187**, folio 556
20 See for this, and for a discussion of dates of writing and publication, **243**, pp. 248-51.

1922, with a number of omissions indicated by dotted lines in the text. The second part – which cannot have been completed before mid-1922, after the closure of LITO – appeared in *Rossiia* in January 1923. The following month, the 'Nakanune' publishers suggested publishing 'Notes on the Cuffs' in book form, by the coming May – but only what had appeared in the newspaper, with a few additions, and Bulgakov's suggestion to include the second part as well was turned down. The whole undertaking seems to have collapsed when on 20 April he refused to accept a clause in the contract allowing the publishers to shorten the work without his permission.[21] In the meantime, the first part was republished, more fully but with some extra deletions, in the second edition of an almanac, *Vozrozhdenie*, which appeared in May 1923. (At some time, Bulgakov seems also to have written a third part, which he offered with the two others to the 'Nedra' publishing house on 26 May 1924, but nothing came of this.)

It is interesting to compare the varying texts of the first part of the work. *Nakanune* had as its aim to persuade Russians to return to their homeland, and therefore cut out those passages which were unlikely to be encouraging: Bulgakov's wanting to get out of the Soviet Union when he had typhus, the fiasco of the literary evenings and their ultimate suppression, his writing a play and thinking of going to Paris on the proceeds, and references indicating that he himself may have tried to leave for Constantinople. The Moscow publishing house 'Vremia' (which published *Vozrozhdenie*) did not have quite the same scruples when it republished the work. It retained some of the omissions, but restored the above-mentioned passages as there was not the same reason to keep them out – although there must have been some doubt about their political appropriateness. The further cuts made in *Vozrozhdenie* were comparatively minor. Some were for purely stylistic reasons, while at least two more would seem to be the result of a change in audience: Bulgakov's emphasis on returning home *to Moscow*, and the epigraph obviously directed to Russians in Berlin: 'To the voyaging, travelling, and suffering Russian writers.' Others must have seemed simply inadvisable for a Soviet audience: Bulgakov's fearing for his safety after his defence of Pushkin, Slyozkin's being thrown out of the sub-department, an exhortation to Russian writers not to be malicious, and a reference to himself, after his illness, as being 'taken down from the cross.'

Taking the two versions together, we find that there are still at least two sections missing, and parts of others.[22] But quite apart from this the work is frag-

---

21 According to **531**, p. 333, the book was actually printed but destroyed before publication. This is not too reliable in other aspects, however.

22 There is, so far, no trace of the missing sections and we may wish to consider the possibility that Bulgakov never wrote them, using his rows of dots as a mere literary device, as was favoured by some of the romantics.

mentary, a collection of isolated episodes rather than a book – the author himself refers to it as 'something like memoirs.' The writing is impressionistic, the
form that of a diary. At its best this has its advantages; there is an immediacy in
his descriptions which avoids the need for long narrative links. The deliberately
casual style has a certain freshness, and there is tension too: one senses a lack of
stability, reflecting Bulgakov's own life at the time, his disorientation and uncertainties. But the trouble is that it is difficult to sustain this style over two parts.
The second, where the writing is more of a narrative, is anti-climactic. What
starts with a certain originality of technique becomes a straightforward story.

Nor is the first part entirely successful, because of certain mannerisms of the
author. As can be the case in immature works, the author sometimes seems more
interested in the process of writing than in creating an artistic whole. Thus we
get constant repetition of words for their own sake, and description of his own
thought processes. All this slows down the action and appears to be an invitation
for the reader to look at the writer and admire him for his tricks – which do not
always come off. This is particularly true of the early sections describing the
author's illness and recovery: 'My god! My god! My go-o-od!' 'Mama! Mama!
What will we do! – True enough. Wha-at wi-ill we do-o?' Such bleating sounds
like mere self-pity. The narrator may, of course, be laughing at himself but we
are not sure: there is none of the delightful self-satire we find in *Notes of a
Young Doctor*, on which he was working at roughly the same time. (One wonders whether he may have conceived the two as companion volumes, this one being a kind of 'Notes of a Young Writer' and treating his inexperience in this field
in a similar way to his inexperience in medicine.) Despite certain similarities –
the conversational style, frequent use of interior monologue – this work lacks
the charm and the artistic unity of the other.

Its strength undoubtedly lies in its humour. There are a number of scenes that
are memorable indeed: Bulgakov's defence of Pushkin, the Chekhov evenings,
the Pushkin evening with a portrait that Bulgakov mistakes for Gogol's Nozdryov, the writing of *The Sons of Mullah* and its performance, Bulgakov's arrival
in LITO, a slogan-writing competition, his hunting desperately for his office
after it has been unexpectedly moved. The personal tone can be appealing, for
all its rather sententious statements of opinion: 'Only through suffering does
truth come ... That's true, rest assured. But for knowledge of the truth they
don't pay any money or give any rations. It's sad, but a fact.' At times it reads as
though the author were sitting recounting a tale to an audience of friends (something Bulgakov was very good at), indulging in pleasant conversation with them
at the same time. It needs, perhaps, to be read aloud by a good actor – when the
author's fascination with individual words, particularly Soviet acronyms such as

LITO, TEO, DYUVLYAM, would be appreciated. But the rhetorical, exclamatory style ('O dusty days! O stifling nights!') does not always go down well on the printed page, for all its undoubted ironical intent, and again suggests immaturity.

The question arises as to why Bulgakov, at the age of thirty, should have chosen to write an autobiography at all. One wonders if he were not showing more than a little arrogance in considering his life that interesting: after all, at the time he was no more than a struggling writer, and as a book the work could hardly be expected to have much general appeal. But ultimately it is not as a book that it is best considered. Part I was the first piece of Bulgakov's to appear in *Nakanune*, where it would be followed by a whole series of his feuilletons: largely descriptions and tales of life in Moscow. And, in fact, 'Notes on the Cuffs' is closer to a collection of short feuilletons than to a usual narrative, with its interest in short, often amusing, descriptions; its immediacy and lack of explanatory material; its dialogue and colloquial, chatty language; its exclamatory style. Artistic unity then becomes a secondary consideration, and Part II can be read as a description for its own sake rather than as an unsuccessful conclusion to the first part. As reportage it is interesting, entertaining. If we consider the work in this way, there is no problem as to why it was written: Bulgakov merely takes as his subject matter scenes from everyday life – his own – as with his other feuilletons.

This is not to say that he had no further aim. It was an age of experimentation in literature and in art – communism had not yet established its dictatorship entirely – and he may well have conceived this as an experiment, to create a new art form from typical feuilleton material arranged in sequence. For all the work's fragmentary nature one can see at least a certain thematic unity between the two parts, linked by Bulgakov's own career and the repeating themes of literary organizations, the necessity of earning a living, hunger. But unfortunately there is no real development in the second part, where events echo those in the first but do not go beyond them. 'Notes on the Cuffs,' as a separate work, is unstructured, without a beginning or an end (it just stops when LITO is closed), a description of a certain period of a man's life chosen accidentally by history.

It is, of course, a work written by an author during his apprenticeship – and it is worth noting that many early attempts at books are heavily autobiographical. In it there is much of merit, in Bulgakov's ability to find humour in the everyday events; in his enjoyment of satire, which we may trace from this through the feuilletons to the *Diavoliada* stories and ultimately to the later works; in his dialogue and felicitous choice of scene. 'Notes on the Cuffs' is representative of journalistic writing on the highest level, but it is not quite a literary work in its own right.

THE *GUDOK* FEUILLETONS

Of all the feuilletons Bulgakov wrote at the beginning of the twenties, those published in *Gudok* are the least ambitious from a literary viewpoint. Therein lies
their charm. Totally unpretentious, written hastily for monetary reward, they
are amusing, simple, and direct: revealing Bulgakov's mastery in just telling a
funny story. There are over a hundred readily identifiable stories of this type in
Gudok for the years between 1923 and 1926, and it is probable that there are
other similar ones either overlooked or hiding under unidentified pseudonyms,
both in *Gudok* and elsewhere. We may add to these Bulgakov's published volume
of *Stories* of 1926, containing a number of reprints from *Gudok*, a number from
Nakanune, and five more not published earlier but also of the *Gudok* type. (This
volume was published by *Smekhach*, a humorous magazine which the 'Gudok'
press printed. Another collection of stories, advertised for publication by *Nedra*,
never appeared, having apparently been banned.[23])

The feuilletons are essentially based on true events, on information sent in by
the 'working correspondents.' Taken as a whole, they provide a surprisingly vivid
picture of life among the ordinary workers in the years following the Revolution
and civil war. They are characterized by brevity, by their concentration on one single humorous incident or situation, and by their satirical purpose. They are almost
entirely situational comedy, with considerable reliance on dialogue. The style is
conversational: Bulgakov, for example, will often add 'serve him right!' to a story
where a wrong-doer is caught and punished. Some have a strong plot (as the story
about a locksmith who simulates various illnesses to make money on medical pay-
ments, until he is caught: 'A Nasty Type'); some are purely descriptive with
scarcely a plot at all. Frequently the emphasis is on abuses brought about by people's ignorance and stupidity, and there is a constant, sometimes expressed, hope
that things will improve after those responsible have been made to look foolish.[24]

The feuilletons are described most easily in terms of a few of their recurrent
themes. Bureaucracy of one kind or another is perhaps the most prominent target of Bulgakov: workers not getting what they are entitled to ('The R.K.K.,'
'The Libertine'); the need to get official stamps and signatures on documents
('The Trouble with Stamps'); officiousness or overzealousness making life difficult ('Skull-Hunters'); or officialdom being a hiding-place for fraud and deceit
('False-Dimitry Lunacharsky,' 'A Bewitched Place,' 'How the Local Committee
Bought a Present with an Old Woman's Money'). On the one hand, workers –
such as telephone operators – use their job to their own advantage ('On the Tele-

23 5. 'Chas zhizni. Rasskazy' (Moscow: Nedra, 1925) was advertised in *Rossiia* in 1925: see
   446, p. 443; also **379**, pp. 152, 170.
24 For the *Gudok* feuilletons, see **46-86**. A few are also in **5**.

phone,' 'The Undismayed Operators,'); on the other, getting paid is a constant problem ('The Effective Remedy,' 'The Desired Payment,' 'Three Kopecks'). Party meetings are another theme: speakers do not turn up ('The Station-Master's Cradle') or come with an agenda three years out of date, which is still discussed ('The Wrong Trousers'); a drunk gives a lecture on syphilis for women's day ('Festival with Syphilis'); another is thrown out of a theatrical performance (*'Inspector General* with an Ejection'). Drunkenness itself is a frequent theme ('A Story of Beer,' 'On the Usefulness of Alcoholism,' 'A Drunken Steam-Engine'). There are stories about the problems of getting rations ('How Buton Got Married') or about inefficiencies in the commercial trusts ('A New Method of Book Distribution'). As we might expect, there are a number of medical stories too ('Man with a Thermometer,' 'The Flying Dutchman'). And there are more grotesque ones with corpses continuing, by habit, to do what they did when alive ('Adventures of a Dead Man,' 'When the Dead Rise from Their Graves,' 'The Dead Walk'). Or there are the simple oddities: the shunning of a man with the same name as the White general Wrangel ('Trick of Nature') or a dream about the former tsar travelling by tram ('The Conductor and a Member of the Imperial Family'). Typical of Bulgakov at his most amusing is 'Political Director of Divine Worship,' in which a school and a church are in adjoining buildings and everything can be heard from the other – with the result that there is a hilarious dialogue of political and religious slogans, while the deacon gets drunk and is almost converted to communism. Ludicrous and yet all too probable in this new society, exaggerated perhaps and always containing a strong element of social satire – with the author's sympathy on the side of the individual – stories like this had an immediate appeal to *Gudok*'s readers.

One of the earliest feuilletons published there is rather different from the others: 'The Raid,'[25] concerning a sentry, Abram, who is captured and beaten up by the enemy, only just escaping with his life. Years later, someone in a workers' club is telling of his war adventures and the others turn to Abram, now deaf, never expecting that he will have anything to tell: when he does, they can hardly believe it is true. It is simple and unpretentious, as are the other feuilletons, and very moving. Without humour or satire, describing instead the simple feelings of an ordinary man and his one moment of involuntary heroism, it is a step away from journalism into the realm of literature.

ARTICLES IN *GOLOS RABOTNIKA PROSVESHCHENIIA*

More serious than the *Gudok* feuilletons are four pieces written for the pedagogical journal *Golos rabotnika prosveshcheniia* (which had been initiated by

25 63. In 8, pp. 208-16

I. Lezhnev, the editor of the journal *Rossiia*): 'CNA and CA' (Candidate Not
Acceptable and Candidate Acceptable), 'In the School of the Village of the
Third International,' 'The First Children's Commune,' 'Birds in the Attic.'[26] Although good examples of Bulgakov's ability to make basically descriptive material lively (largely by a heavy reliance on direct speech), these are hardly literary
works at all, but more in the nature of short articles on educational themes: the
hiring of teachers, conditions in a school, an experiment with a children's commune, and the terrible conditions in a students' hostel. Bulgakov shows himself
as a serious reporter – particularly in the last story, where he hopes to bring
about improvements – but there is comparatively little in them of literary interest. The same might be said of a later series of feuilletons on the Crimea in 1925,
published in the evening edition of the *Krasnaia gazeta*.

THE *NAKANUNE* FEUILLETONS

The *Nakanune* feuilletons are altogether more ambitious, longer, and more
varied in scope.[27] Leaving aside the first part of 'Notes on the Cuffs,' already discussed, and two others which were part of an early version of Bulgakov's novel
The White Guard ('On the Night of the Third' and 'Evening at Vasilisa's'), we
may divide them into those that are largely literary description and those that
tell a definite story. In all of them, Bulgakov is very much the writer of the town,
and indeed he has been described as the 'singer' of Moscow in the same way that
Pushkin, Gogol, Dostoevsky, and Blok were the singers of St Petersburg.[28]

His descriptions relate entirely to the Moscow he was living in, and specifically to the time of the New Economic Policy, which allowed, temporarily, for
the re-establishment of private enterprise and ownership. Bulgakov describes the
'nepmen' – those who took advantage of the policy – and the new 'red specialists,' also the black market ('Under a Glass Sky'). He talks too of the ordinary
people in the shops, and the outward show and glitter of the goods there as opposed to the real hunger that still existed ('Red-stoned Moscow'). The most successful of such descriptions is 'Forty Times Forty,' which contrasts the 'heroic'
Moscow of 1921 with the new Moscow of the NEP. Starting as a gradual humming
of which everyone soon becomes aware, the NEP develops into all the noise of a
busy, thriving city, with its bright lights, businesses, fashionable restaurants.
Although Bulgakov clearly takes pride in the growth of 'mother Moscow' he has
no particular love for the nepmen, whom he fears 'at the thought that they were
filling all Moscow, that they had gold ten-rouble coins in their pockets, that they

26 41-5
27 For the *Nakanune* feuilletons, see **105-33**.
28 **339**, p. 58

would throw me out of my room, that they were strong, had large teeth, were wicked, with hearts of stone.' Yet he is impressed by the vigour of the new society around him, by such achievements as the impressive Agricultural Exhibition ('The Golden Town'), by the new orderliness, which he praises in 'Chanson d'été' and 'The Capital in My Notebook.' The second of these particular feuilletons serves as a vehicle for Bulgakov to describe all kinds of things going on in Moscow: reconstruction, nepmen flourishing, the opera, a well-behaved schoolchild, a man so wealthy he is a trillionaire. (These last two scenes appeared in English translation the same year, in *The Living Age*.) He expresses his opinion of the theatre, and in particular his dislike of Meyerhold's 'biomechanics.' He is concerned, too, with what will become of the intelligentsia, but shows optimism, despite everything, that it will survive.

Bulgakov is remarkably fair towards the society he is describing: he does not condemn or praise as a whole, although he does not hesitate to describe his individual likes and dislikes. His own experiences clearly play a large part in what he writes (see, in particular, 'A Day of Our Life,' with its conversations and with its frustrations), but despite this he never forces his views on the reader or implies that things were better in former times. Indeed, he seems to have accepted the new order, and writes with a simple love of his country, with all its faults. Each piece reads like a 'letter from Moscow' – which, of course, to his readers in Berlin it undoubtedly was. The appeal is mainly to those who know and love Moscow: the interest was in 'what it's like now,' and Bulgakov provides details both of the familiar and the new. Thus in 'Red-stoned Moscow' he tells what the NEP is like, but finishes with an image of eternal Moscow, with the chimes from the Kremlin bell and the 'Kitay-gorod' lying close by. It is similar in 'Travel Notes,' which describes a train journey: there is a new Bryansk station, but the same old queues; boys are still selling preserves at stations en route, but illegally, since passengers are now supposed to use the special shops. Even the descriptions of demonstrations against Lord Curzon ('Lord Curzon's Benefit Day' – also translated in *The Living Age*) are interesting largely in that they take place against the familiar background of Moscow, for which Bulgakov shows a love that the reader can be expected to share. So, too, in 'Kiev – a Town,' in all Bulgakov's survey of the recent history, in all his discussions on Kievans as compared with Muscovites, on churches, on the NEP, there lies a basic appeal to the reader's familiarity with Moscow itself, to his love for it – which Bulgakov still shares deeply: 'In a word, a beautiful town, a happy town. The mother of Russian towns.'

Bulgakov shows a remarkable sense of his audience. Today we can still feel something of this appeal – the Russian certainly can – but now for most of us these feuilletons must seem more like period pieces, essays representing journalism of high quality rather than strictly literary writing.

The same may be said of some of those that tell a story. Two such feuilletons, 'Golden Documents' and 'Sparkling Life' (both subtitled 'From My Collection'), consist of a number of tales of the same type that are in *Gudok*: four of these even appear alongside them in the 1926 *Stories*. 'Sparkling Life' has some particularly weak items, hardly more than funny jokes. A few other feuilletons too are typical newspaper stories: a friend who has a final fling before being arrested ('Cup of Life'), a horse-dealer who makes money by murder ('The Komarov Case'), a bank director ruined by his speculator brother ('The Belobrysov Story').

A number, however, demand greater attention. One, 'The Crimson Island,' a low burlesque on the Revolution, was the basis for a play, and will be dealt with later. More important is 'The Adventures of Chichikov,' which would be included in the *Diavoliada* collection – and was also at one time forbidden for public reading.[29] It is linked with the other feuilletons in *Nakanune* in that primarily it is a satire on life in Moscow and on the NEP. It differs from them in that it is a comic imitation of Gogol, using not only his situations and characters – mainly but not exclusively from *Dead Souls* – but many of his actual sentences as well. In a 'dream,' Chichikov, the hero of *Dead Souls* (which had 'The Adventures of Chichikov' as an alternative title) reappears in Moscow in Soviet times, and finds there all his old acquaintances. Very little has changed, except for the names. Chichikov first wangles extra rations for himself, following Sobakevich's example, then, inspired by Nozdryov, goes into the export business and builds up a completely non-existent enterprise (in Gogol's original he has, of course, built up an estate of non-existent serfs).

The elements of satire need little elaboration: the little change since Gogol's day, the same people still occupying important positions, the petty crooks such as Chichikov and Nozdryov managing to survive in Soviet times very nicely. There are some clever instances of parody too, with sufficient of Gogol's thought kept intact and combined with the modern situation to create incongruities almost of the type that we find in his own prose. Thus Gogol's famous description of the troika and the Russians' love of speed is applied to the motor car and a rather different picture from the uninterrupted drive through the Russian countryside results:

What Russian does not love a swift ride?

Selifan loved it, too, and therefore at the entrance to Lubyanka he was forced to choose between a trolley car and a plate-glass store window. In a brief instant of time Selifan chose the latter, swerved away from the trolley, and like a whirlwind, screaming 'Help!' drove through the store window.[30]

29 See **379**, p. 152
30 **8**, p. 169

'The Adventures of Chichikov' is an amusing and witty story, but not perhaps a work of major importance. Its merit lies in its basic idea – the application of Gogol to modern times. The imitation is well sustained, the parallels are ingenious, but beyond this there is not a great deal of depth.

One of the earliest feuilletons deserves to be better known: 'Red Crown (*Historia morbi*)' of 1922. (The Soviet scholar M. Chudakova suggests that this may be identified with the 'Illness' Bulgakov mentions in his letters – and that it may also be a stage in the composition of *The White Guard*.[31]) It is about a narrator haunted by the image of his dead brother Kolya, and by that of a man hanged by the White general whom Kolya served. It is a powerful story of the horror and senselessness of the civil war, and the bestiality of the hangings that took place. The responsibility for this, however, lies not with the general alone but also with the narrator, and a bond is formed between the two in their common guilt: 'Who knows, perhaps that dirty begrimed man from the lamppost in Berdyansk comes to you. If so, we suffer justly. I sent Kolya to help you hang others, and you did the hanging.' The burden of accepting such guilt is intolerable: the narrator goes mad. The story is a brilliant precursor to Bulgakov's play *Flight*, where the theme of responsibility and illness brought on by repeated hangings is central.

Four of the *Nakanune* stories were republished in 1926 in a paper book entitled *A Treatise on Housing* – the name of the first of them.[32] This story was originally the first part of a feuilleton entitled 'Moscow of the Twenties' (the second – about the ruses people employ to obtain or keep an apartment – was not republished). From a literary point of view 'A Treatise on Housing' is the least satisfactory of the four. The housing shortage in Moscow and the pressures caused by overcrowding are illustrated by a story of three people living in a telephone receiver [*sic*] and their inevitably muddled conversations, and by the arguments that go on in the author's own apartment block. Although Bulgakov's usual witty style can be appealing ('This winter Natalya Egorovna threw a mop rag on the floor and couldn't unstick it because it was nine degrees above the table and on the floor there were no degrees at all – and it even lacked one'[33]) there is a certain facetiousness, particularly in the hyperbole of the telephone receiver, that is annoying; it is neither fantasy nor realism.

31 **243**, p. 243
32 The collected edition is **127**. Original publications in *Nakanune*: **113, 114, 115, 120, 122.** All of *Traktat o zhilishche* (that is, without the second part of 'Moskva 20-kh godov') has been translated in **8**.
33 **8**, p. 184. This version has the inhabitants living in a telephone *booth*, which would certainly seem more logical. However, the Russian word in both printed versions is undoubtedly *trubka*: receiver.

The same theme is treated more effectively in 'Four Portraits.' In the Moscow of that time a person was allowed only a certain amount of 'living space': anyone with more had to accept other lodgers, often total strangers, who could nevertheless not be ejected. The process was known as *uplotnenie* – which is most easily translated as 'doubling up.' The story concerns a man's efforts to prevent this, and our sympathies are entirely with him rather than with the commissions who come to inspect his apartment. He is, in fact, an early example of the 'sympathetic crook' who is to feature in many of Bulgakov's later writings. The third story, 'A Lake of Home-brew,' describing a drunken brawl which goes on for nearly twenty-four hours in the narrator's own apartment block, is interesting largely for what it tells us about Bulgakov's own life.

Most outstanding, however, is 'A Psalm,' one of the best stories of this period: about a neighbour's four-year-old boy, his father, who has gone away, and his mother who returns to kiss with the narrator after the boy has gone to bed. It is a most moving story of loneliness yet affection as a result of grief – emphasized by the boy with his ordinary child's concerns and lack of understanding. It is remarkable, too, for its use of leitmotifs: cones of light from the kerosene lamp; door hinges, which sing pleasantly and unpleasantly; buttons, which are a constant problem for the narrator; and above all the refrain of the poem 'I'll buy shoes to match my coat, and at night I'll sing a psalm, I'll get a dog, and somehow we'll get by.' More than this there is little to hope for.

OTHER EARLY STORIES

Two stories in *Rupor* in 1922, 'The Extraordinary Adventures of a Doctor' and 'Spiritual Séance,' need not particularly detain us.[34] But two others published in the newspaper *Krasnyi zhurnal dlia vsekh* are far more important: 'No 13 – the Elpit House – Workers' Commune' of 1922 (well known since it was republished in the *Diavoliada* collection) and 'Fire of the Khans' of 1924.[35] Both have clearly been strongly influenced by Konstantin Fedin's 'The Orchard,' which has an almost identical theme – destruction of the old by fire – and had been published in *Nakanune* (in the same issue as 'Notes on the Cuffs') some six months earlier than 'No 13.' In 'No 13' the once-elegant five-storey Elpit House becomes, after the Revolution, a workers' commune, but its manager, Khristi, is retained. He tries to keep up the building for its former owner but, when there is an oil shortage, a woman lights a stove she has illegally installed in her apartment, causing a fire. Khristi watches, weeping, as the building burns.

34 **178, 181**
35 **25** and **35, 36.** The former was republished in **22, 23, 29, 30** and translated in **8.**

It is arguably Bulgakov's earliest masterpiece – the imitation of Fedin not-withstanding. The main theme is more than nostalgia, it is the difference of two worlds, one of which is characterized by the ignorance and stupidity of the new class. 'We are ignorant people. Benighted people. We fools must be taught,' thinks Annushka, the woman who caused the fire. What was splendid about the past has been destroyed, needlessly, and we cannot help but weep with Khristi at this destruction. We may also see the Elpit House as symbolical of the old régime, with all its luxury and decadence, until taken over by communism, personified in the new name of the building and its inhabitants. Despite hopes for survival, the old is totally destroyed – and indeed, when this story was later published in the *Diavoliada* collection, Soviet critics were not slow to point out Bulgakov's apparent feeling that the change had been for the worse.[36] But Bulgakov's sympathies were not necessarily entirely with the old order. In this story he merely points to certain glories of the past and the neglect that follows from making over their use to those who are unappreciative, or have no sense of history.

A similar theme is the basis of 'Fire of the Khans.' A group of tourists is shown round the former mansion of the princes Tugay-Beg Ordynsky by the old servant Iona, who clashes ideologically with a most objectionable man dressed only in shorts and a cap. The reader's sympathy is all with Iona, particularly when he gets the better of his opponent. When the others have left, one man returns: the present, disinherited, prince, whom Iona had not recognized. Angry at the treatment of his family and at the new régime, Tugay-Beg sets fire to the house and makes his escape. The theme of the glories of the past and the vulgarity of the new – epitomized in the odious half-naked party member – is still very much present. Iona fulfils a similar role to that of Khristi, by looking after the house for the hoped-for return of the legitimate owner – or indeed to that of the gardener in Fedin's story, who himself burns down the dacha attached to the orchard in disgust. But of the three former owners of house, estate, and orchard, Tugay-Beg, consumed with hatred for the new régime, is the least sympathetic. He is shown as unable to reconcile himself with the new, questioning his own existence in this world, and becoming bitter, malicious as a result.

Bulgakov's own attitude remains ambiguous, although it would appear to be more pessimistic than Fedin's since, although he is not uncritical of the past, he shows greater love for it. In both his stories he struggles to maintain a certain objectivity, describing sadly what he recognizes to be inevitable and showing the futility of struggling against it.

Bulgakov's works before 1924 – and some for the following two years – are largely journalistic. In them we can find many stylistic features which would be-

36 See **401**, p. 46

come part of his mature writing: his use of dialogue, his love for a simple direct story, his witty narrator who enjoys making his own comments. It is successful journalism, but would hardly be of great literary interest were it not for Bulgakov's subsequent achievement. In a few stories, however, he shows deeper insights and more universal concerns than is possible in mere reportage. The human emotion portrayed in 'No 13,' 'Fire of the Khans,' 'Red Crown,' and 'A Psalm' gives them a more than local interest and makes of them literary works in their own right.

3

The turning point, 1924-25

The house described in 'No 13 - the Elpit House - Workers' Commune' (and referred to in several of the feuilletons as well) was that where Bulgakov and his wife actually lived from 1921 to 1924: No 10, Bolshaya Sadovaya Street. Their apartment, number 50, is indeed mentioned in several works, and it seems that many of the persons Bulgakov describes in his stories at this time - Elpit, Khristi, a 'sanitary inspector,' and probably others too - were based on real people. In real life the five-storey building was known as the Pigit House, from the name of its former owner. Built in the early years of the century, it is today just one of many on the Sadovoe circle, but formerly it was more impressive: the only multi-storey building on that side of the road, with imposing balconies and a neat garden separated by a cast-iron fence from the pavement. The list of its one-time residents and their visitors is impressive, including wealthy bankers and merchants, intellectuals, artists (such as Konchalovsky and Yakulov), theatrical celebrities (Moskvin, Kachalov, Meyerhold), and writers.[1] The poet Sergey Yesenin is said to have met Isidora Duncan there. The house had had its moments of drama: in August 1918 Fanny Kaplan, the would-be assassin of Lenin, had hidden there briefly before her arrest and execution. After the Revolution the 'class-hostile elements' had been removed, workers moved in, and it became the first workers' commune in Moscow. A few intellectuals, such as the Bulgakovs, remained - although the new society's attitude towards such people was at best suspicious.

Bulgakov's time there was not a happy one. It coincided with his financial troubles after returning to Moscow, with several years of working at something he hated, and with his growing literary ambitions which were constantly being frustrated. Many of his complaints are clearly set out in his feuilletons. Interfer-

1 See **349**. The subsequent quotation is from p. 115.

ing troublesome neighbours and dreary work day after day are the themes of 'A Day of Our Life,' while the tragic squalor of such an existence is recreated in 'A Psalm.' In 'A Treatise on Housing' Bulgakov talks of his impossible apartment owner (whom he calls Vasily Ivanovich and who will become almost a stock character for him): 'In a word, he is not thinkable in human society ...'[2] In 'A Lake of Home-brew' he describes how the whole apartment block gets drunk, talks of 'our accursed corridor,' mentions again Vasily Ivanovich and another recurring character, the troublesome and stupid Annushka. He tells us, too, how he cannot afford to get on the wrong side of the block's supplier of home-brew, because that person is powerful enough to 'poison my existence' and if he does this 'I can't write feuilletons, and if I can't write feuilletons, there'll be a financial crash.' In the story his own wife pleads with him: 'I can't take it any more. Do whatever you must, we have to get out of here ... You will never finish the novel. Never. Life is hopeless. I'm going to take morphine.'

It was probably because of this situation that in the winter of 1922-23 the Bulgakov family moved to flat 34, in a different wing of the building – although, remarkably, he himself managed to retain flat 50 for his own use. Living with his parents in the new apartment at that time was one V.A. Lyovshin, then a young man of literary ambitions, who remembers Bulgakov and Tasya in the apartment until it was finally given up in 1925. His descriptions of Bulgakov's elegant appearance and accurate dress, and of their conversations on literature (with Bulgakov always holding up Gogol as his 'number one' writer), make fascinating reading. Lyovshin never saw him actually writing, probably because most of this was done at night. 'I waited for the night with all the impatience of a young man waiting for his beloved,' Bulgakov would write in his autobiographical work *Theatrical Romance*. 'Only then was it quiet enough in my accursed room.'[3] Sometimes in the evening he would go for a walk with Lyovshin to the nearby Patriarchs' Ponds, aware of his surroundings but usually thoughtful, preoccupied with his work.

Apart from housing, things were not all bad in Moscow. There was at least the theatre, and the society of other writers. 'After a cartoon province without papers, with wild rumours – here is Moscow, a huge town, the only town, the state: it's the only place to live,' Bulgakov wrote in 1923.[4] Particularly in the theatre, it was an exciting time, with the constructivist experiments of Meyerhold and Mayakovsky – although Bulgakov himself hated such 'formalism.'

2 8, p. 182. The following quotations are from pp. 205-7.
3 160, p. 20
4 107

(Mayakovsky, the Soviet Union's one great revolutionary poet, was in addition rapidly coming to see Bulgakov as his ideological enemy.)[5]

But other things were happening that were to have a more lasting effect on artistic life. In literature, a successful struggle had been carried out against the excesses of the *Proletcult* (Proletarian Cultural and Educational Organizations). Amongst the many groups that sprang up in these years was the Russian Association of Proletarian Writers (RAPP), concerned solely with the social purpose of literature, and which would play an enormous role for almost the rest of the decade. The secret police, the OGPU, were also becoming increasingly active in ensuring political uniformity. And then Lenin died at the beginning of 1924: his successor, Stalin, would soon begin imposing his will on the whole country. Yet that very year was a good one for Bulgakov personally, for it was now that he started to give readings from *The White Guard*: excerpts from the final version appeared in *Nakanune* and *Krasnyi zhurnal dlia vsekh.*[6]

Lyovshin recalls accompanying Bulgakov to one such reading and the mastery of his performance. Afterwards they returned with a lady Lyovshin did not know, and accompanying her home Bulgakov asked him to tell his wife he had stayed at the meeting. In these years he had his personal problems too: Lyovshin comments that Bulgakov's wife seemed more of a casual companion than someone who shared his life. In the autobiographical feuilletons she is at best a shadowy figure, while it is perhaps significant that in other works which reflect his life – *Theatrical Romance, Notes of a Young Doctor*, 'A Psalm' – the writer appears as a bachelor. 'If in the eleventh year of life together you don't separate,' Lyovshin reports Bulgakov as saying, 'then you'll stay together for a long time.' 1924 was his eleventh year of a marriage that was almost over, although he evidently continued to see Tasya, who remained in apartment 34 until the following year, for some time after the divorce.

In January, at a 'writers' evening,' he had met Lyubov Yevgenievna Belozerskaya, the wife of the feuilletonist I.M. Vasilevsky, who wrote in *Nakanune* under the pseudonym Ne-Bukva. They had just returned to the Soviet Union from abroad in the footsteps of Alexey Tolstoy. Lyubov Yevgenievna had lived in Constantinople, Paris, and Berlin, where she had read Bulgakov's feuilletons in *Nakanune* and become an admirer of his work. Generally she found him interesting, and that evening, in a Tolstoyan blouse, he was charming, witty, and amusing as usual. Within half a year they were married (at the beginning of the sum-

---

5 Kataev tells of how Bulgakov once made fun of Mayakovsky, pretending enthusiasm for a name the other had invented for his hero in 'The Fatal Eggs.' See **323**, pp. 108-9

6 **130, 180**

mer of 1924), and they lived for a while in apartment 50 before moving in 1925 to No 9, Obukhov Lane.

The year 1924 is the turning point of Bulgakov's whole career. Not only was he remarried but at last success and popularity came to him as a writer. The immediate cause of it was the publication that year, in the fourth issue of the almanac *Nedra*, of a longish satirical tale entitled 'Diavoliada.' *Nedra* was reviewed regularly, and 'Diavoliada' was singled out as interesting, even if its content was dubious. People at least were beginning to sit up and take notice. This story was then followed by another satirical piece, 'The Fatal Eggs.' Before its publication Bulgakov gave a reading of it at the home of one of the *Gudok* writers, Leonid Sayansky. According to A.I. Erlikh (who may be exaggerating), as it progressed the bewilderment amongst Bulgakov's colleagues – not in any case used to the idea that he was now a celebrity – increased and they were dismayed that the satire seemed to be directed against the new Soviet society.[7] Later they tackled him in the office. In a brand-new suit and a spotted bow-tie, Bulgakov twirled his stick with its silver knob and tried to turn everything into a joke, but he seemed upset nevertheless. It was Ilya Ilf who finally came to his defence: 'Misha has only just, with great reluctance, become reconciled to the liberation of the peasants from serfdom, and you want him immediately to become a soldier of the socialist revolution! ... You'll have to wait a little!'

'The Fatal Eggs' was published in *Nedra* in 1925; the same year it was reprinted in Bulgakov's first collection of stories in book form, *Diavoliada*. His reputation seemed secure, particularly when the critics howled their protests at the contents of tales which immediately appeared to be critical of post-revolutionary society.

But Bulgakov's most significant achievement in 1925 was, at long last, the publication in *Rossiia* of two parts of his novel *The White Guard*, which he dedicated to his new wife, Lyubov Yevgenievna. Its success, it is true, was only partial, for the journal was closed down before the third part could appear. But it was this novel and its rewriting as a play that marks the change of direction in Bulgakov's career. As a result of his successes, Bulgakov would at last be able to leave the newspaper work he detested so much: only a few odd feuilletons of his appeared in *Gudok* after 1925. And, if his novel and then the *Diavoliada* collection again were even more vigorously condemned by the critics – hardly surprising, perhaps – this did not diminish his popularity.

And now his admirers included the great hero of Soviet literature, Maxim Gorky, living at the time in Sorrento. On 8 May 1925 Gorky had written to M.L. Slonimsky that he liked 'The Fatal Eggs' very much, except for the ending; he

7 For the following, see **262**, p. 173.

also mentioned it to D. Lutokhin, M.F. Andreeva, A. Demidov, and Romain Rolland,[8] and others wrote to him about it. By December 1925 Gorky was writing to Vsevolod Ivanov: 'I would very much like to get you and Fedin here. And Zoshchenko too. And Bulgakov. We would sit here by the sea on the warm stones and would talk of all kinds of things.' On 7 February following, he wrote to the Belgian writer Franz Hellens, mentioning Bulgakov and two others as artists who were to be taken seriously: 'I follow them with ever increasing interest and become more and more concerned about them.'

A further admirer of Bulgakov's was V. Veresaev, whose book *Notes of a Doctor* had in a sense provided a model for Bulgakov's medical stories. Bulgakov had actually become acquainted with Veresaev some time earlier: his diary entry of 14 February 1922 records a public discussion of the book and the favourable impression its author had made upon him. In the autumn of 1923 Bulgakov had gone to see Veresaev, 'just to shake the hand of the man who had written *Notes of a Doctor.*'[9] Now, on 30 June 1925, Veresaev too wrote to Gorky: 'Have you paid attention to Bulgakov in *Nedra*? I expect a great deal of him.' In November he wrote to Bulgakov himself, offering to help him because he wanted 'to save at least the small artistic force of which you are the bearer. In view of that harassment which is carried on against you, you will be pleased to know that Gorky (I had a letter from him in the summer) has very much noticed you and appreciates you.'

Their friendship became stronger, and later Veresaev would indeed lend Bulgakov money. But in 1925 this was hardly necessary. Bulgakov, 'harassed' by the critics, was now popular, even lionized. That year there was only one failure: the story 'Heart of a Dog,' submitted to *Nedra*, did not pass the censor.

DIAVOLIADA

The publication in May-June 1925 of the *Diavoliada* collection is significant in Bulgakov's life in two respects. First of all, it confirmed him as an established writer, and a successful one, despite the vigorous attacks that followed from the doctrinaire critics. More important, from the point of view of his writing the *Diavoliada* stories mark the end of a particular period and it is for this reason that we shall consider them before *The White Guard*, which was published the same year. Afterwards, Bulgakov was never again to write prose of the same type:

8 **293** has Gorky's letters to Slonimsky and Demidov, and a letter from A.P. Chapygin to Gorky, pp. 389, 152, 645. The letter to Hellens is in **295**, pp. 98-9; the one to Ivanov in **315**, pp. 34-5. Others mentioned are quoted in **195**, pp. 158-64.
9 **243**, pp. 254-5, and **346**, pp. 252-3. Information for the story the latter tells was supplied by Bulgakov's widow.

the short, satirical story based on a particular circumstance and with little development of character.

Of the five stories in the collection, two date from three years earlier, and have already been discussed: 'The Adventures of Chichikov' and 'No 13 – the Elpit House – Workers' Commune.' Four of the stories were republished in a collection entitled *The Fatal Eggs* in Riga in 1928, but a second edition of *Diavoliada* in the Soviet Union was apparently not allowed.[10] Nor was publication of the story 'Heart of a Dog,' which is similar to the others in its style and mood.

'Diavoliada: The Story of How Twins Ruined a Clerk'

I'll write about a certain establishment in a huge building ... about the departments continually moving from one floor to another, about old-timers driven crazy by their own muddles. In a word, about an active turmoil of idlers ... Well, of course, about receiving matches instead of money and so on. You'll recognize a lot there ... Deviltry, a diavoliada![11]

The initial impetus for this story had come from Bulgakov's employment in LITO and his getting paid in matches when it closed down. Over the next few years, however, the idea of 'diavoliada' developed, so that ultimately the confusion and bureaucracy would be exaggerated to fantastic proportions. A story which begins as fairly realistic satire turns into a nightmare of absurd events and characters. The incident with the matches remains, difficult office conditions are described by an editor satirized as a living statue of the Polish king Jan Sobieski, but otherwise there is nothing recognizably autobiographical in the story. In the Soviet Union it has been published twice, in *Nedra* in 1924, and in the collection to which it gave its name the following year. It also appeared in the Riga collection, *The Fatal Eggs*.

The hero is a small clerk, Korotkov, who works for 'Spimat' (Main Central Base of Match Materials) and is paid in matches when there is no money. Fired by his new boss, Kalsoner, because of a misunderstanding, he desperately tries to catch him to explain, discovering during the course of the chase that both he and Kalsoner have doubles. After a number of fantastic events, he goes berserk, and is pursued by an enraged crowd to the top of an eleven-storey building, from where he jumps to his death in the street below.

Critical reaction to the story when it first appeared was comparatively mild. It was considered 'talented but confused.' 'The story – again a psychological one!

10 See **379**, p. 152
11 **262**, p. 167

- produces the impression of some realistically confused delirium. It partly irritates, partly wearies one.' Yevgeny Zamyatin, who had himself written but not yet been able to publish his anti-utopian, anti-socialist novel *We*, considered it the only 'modern' work in that edition of *Nedra*.[12] The critic V. Pereverzev pointed out what should have been obvious, that the story was based on Gogol's 'The Overcoat' and Dostoevsky's *The Double*, of which he considered it a fairly successful imitation.[13]

The parallels with both are readily apparent. Like Dostoevsky's Golyadkin, Korotkov is undermined and outshone by his own double, a mere mirror image of himself (Korotkov, unlike Golyadkin, actually meets him only in mirrors). This double - a man opposite in every way, successful at work, successful with women - is clearly the man Korotkov would like to be, yet he is incapable of changing his personality and of coping with the different image his double has provided for him. For Korotkov's double is not actively hostile towards him: there is nothing except his own timidity and short-sightedness to prevent his stepping into the other role and enjoying success. Kalsoner has his twin, too, his mild and gentle counterpart, but Korotkov, although finally understanding that they are doubles, does not realize they are at the same time opposites, and treats both as enemies. The subtleties of life in a dire situation - for Korotkov *has* been fired - are too much for him to understand. We might draw the conclusion that a change in man's fortunes (here the replacement of one boss by another) has its two faces, providing opportunity as well as a threat. Korotkov cannot take advantage of this because of his own inadequacy - which is pointed out to him ironically when Kalsoner, believing him to be his double, tells him to write a report criticizing himself.

The similarities to the world of Gogol are stronger, however, and indeed one criticism of the story might be that the imitation of him is just a little too close. As in Gogol, initial realism and social satire turn into fantasy and mingle with many irrelevant and absurd details: a cashier coming into work with a chicken he has just bought, a car driver who almost runs Korotkov over. As in Gogol, names often have a meaning: Korotkov (short), Chekushin (from the Cheka), Skvorets (starling), Sotsvossky (socialist resurrection), Dyrkin (hole). Korotkov in many ways, even in his speech, is at times reminiscent of Akaky Akakievich of 'The Overcoat.' Basically, he is the Gogolian 'little man,' refusing to believe that 'the so-called vicissitudes of fate do exist in the world.'[14] He, like most of us, expects security, a place in the world by divine right, with no upsets. Convinced he will

12 **443**, p. 309; **389**; **530**, p. 217
13 **423**
14 **8**, p. 3

spend the rest of his life in the match-material office, like Akaky Akakievich he has few outside interests, few desires except a vaguely lascivious one of seeing the secretary Lidochka de Runi in underpants, and no ambition except to ensure his daily existence. Like Akaky Akakievich, too, he appears alone in the world, separated even from those in the office, and this loneliness is emphasized by the author's insistence on applying to him a string of depersonalizing adjectives – 'the cunning Korotkov,' 'the excessively cautious Korotkov,' 'the comic Korotkov' – which cause us constantly to observe him from without and regard him merely as an object of interest rather than as a human being.

But security is not granted to man by divine right. In the tradition not only of 'The Overcoat' but of 'The Nose' too, disaster strikes in an absurd and unexpected way – emphasized here not so much by a totally extraordinary event (to lose a job is after all easier than to lose one's nose) but by the physical grotesqueness of the new boss Kalsoner, who causes it. Loss of his position is for Korotkov the equivalent of loss of his entire personality. In this situation he is incapable of any logical course of action. Initially, to explain to Kalsoner the mistake for which he was fired would seem reasonable, but it soon becomes apparent that it is the activity of the pursuit itself which engages Korotkov's mind rather than its aim. His actions remain futile until the end, involving mainly chases up and down stairs, where each individual becomes an enemy or at least a problem: an old man, women who have been seduced by his double, and a multitude of minor characters who are terrifying only because they get in his way. But when he hits out at them in a blind rage they react accordingly.

The reader can hardly find Korotkov sympathetic, in that he appears just too insignificant. He is like an insect scurrying about in all directions at once, 'for stopping meant destruction,' or like one of Kafka's heroes struggling vainly to prove his innocence and clutching hold of every non-essential detail for his case in a bureaucratic labyrinth. Indeed, the similarities with Kafka's *The Trial* are remarkable, the more so since Bulgakov could not have read it: completed by 1920, it was not published until 1925. But the age they lived in was the same, and so basically was its bureaucracy.

Korotkov may be seen, of course, simply as a victim of this, and, in a sense, literally 'driven crazy' by its muddles. In the story there is obviously a great deal which is satirical: the payment in matches that starts the trouble, the constant replacement of personnel, the reliance on impersonal slogans in an impersonal system. A whole office staff is replaced by workers who are all alike; Kalsoner, transferred from an editorial office to 'Spimat,' manages to take all the furniture with him. A secretary is taken out of a drawer, ready for work; others speak in ready-made phrases. Documents are more important than people – which has its advantages, as when Korotkov realizes he cannot be arrested without them. Yet in this work there is more than satire. We are here in a fantastic world of logical nonsense which no one questions. Even the physical surroundings are ludicrous – the office is in a former restaurant, the 'Alpine Rose,' complete with a working organ and desks which are kitchen tables. Kalsoner's activities are just as futile as Korotkov's, for he too runs around to no purpose. Korotkov ends his life trying to combat the machine-guns of his pursuers with billiard balls which are just lying on a table, in a final burst of violence which surprises no one (and indeed is enthusiastically encouraged by a boy who takes him up in the lift). Faced by the absurdity of the world, he lives his life as in a dream, ending almost as the type of modern gangster who kills in order to take his revenge on society.

It is also possible to reduce the whole story to a simple nightmare, introduced when, at the end of the second chapter, Korotkov falls asleep. He dreams of a billiard ball on legs in a green meadow: an image which is repeated both in the appearance of the Kalsoners with their egg-like heads (on one occasion bending over a green cloth) and in the balls he takes from the billiard table at the end for ammunition. He then wakes to a smell of sulphur, then once more goes to sleep 'and did not wake up again.' From then on, as in a nightmare – a terrifyingly realistic one – Korotkov has no control of events, and the situation of the moment becomes all important, the past forgotten. Boundaries between present and past disappear, so the organ of the former 'Alpine Rose' can happily play again, and the office porter, Pantaleymon, can again become a waiter. Other fantastic events are quite compatible with this dream world. A more sinister, if related, possibility is that we are experiencing Korotkov's death, his descent into hell with its sulphurous fumes – in which case the title 'Diavoliada' takes on a further significance. An important secondary character is a little 'lustrine' old man, who informs Korotkov he has 'crossed him off the lists.' Immediately afterwards, Korotkov discovers his documents are missing, before again noticing a smell of sulphur (which is later repeated elsewhere). Later it is the old man who carries Korotkov off to another superior, the 'terrible' Dyrkin, under the folds of a black cloak. Finally, he is prominent in the chase that drives Korotkov over the parapet onto the street below. All this is suggestive of the approach of death in a symbolical form.

Yet none of it is entirely satisfactory; there is just too much confusion, too many loose ends. We stand outside Korotkov, and watch his antics as we might watch a somewhat brutal cartoon film, with the uneasy suspicion that, despite our lack of sympathy, his dilemma might be applicable to us, but not quite sure how. The story perhaps tries to do too much. But for all its eclecticism, for all its mixture of different elements, it is still a remarkable achievement. Its strength lies in its pace. Korotkov, hardly stopping his mad pursuit, moves from security to destruction in exactly one week. The story tends to repel by the stark brutality of the ending, totally lacking in pathos: but man lives in a brutal world. This, perhaps, is Bulgakov's message.

'The Fatal Eggs'

'The Fatal Eggs' belongs more to the category of early science fiction than to fantasy as such, and is set in the future: 1928, four years after it was written. A Professor Persikov discovers a 'red ray' which stimulates and accelerates the growth of living organisms. Despite his opposition, this is taken over by the communist Rokk (whose name means 'fate') to build up the country's chicken population, decimated by plague. But there is a mix-up over the eggs to be hatched, and Rokk produces a crop of reptiles which threaten to overrun the country, until fortunately they are destroyed by an abnormally severe frost.

The story appeared first of all in 1925 in the journal *Nedra*, and in abbreviated form with the title 'The Ray of Life' in the journal *Krasnaia panorama*.[15] Until the last minute, it seems, Bulgakov had doubts about the ending, for Lyovshin tells of his phoning the editor of *Nedra* for an advance before the story was completed, making up a totally different ending from that finally printed: in this version the residents of Moscow were evacuated.[16] (Gorky's one criticism of the story, we might note, was that Bulgakov missed a great opportunity in not showing the reptiles' advance on Moscow.) Reprinted the same year in the *Diavoliada* collection, 'The Fatal Eggs' was never again published in the Soviet Union, although in the West after an initial publication in Riga in 1928 it has appeared on several occasions. (Interestingly, when it was serialized in the Paris *Russkaia mysl'* there was some confusion over Bulgakov's pun and it was mistakenly entitled 'Rokk's Eggs': *Rokkovy iaitsa* instead of *Rokovye iaitsa*. The mistake was only corrected with the tenth installment.[17])

Critical reaction to the story on its first appearance in *Nedra* was mixed, admitting of a certain talent but generally deploring the inappropriateness of the subject to post-revolutionary society. Bulgakov's work was described as a foreign body in Soviet literature; he was said to be completely uneducated politically.[18] Most critics seemed to feel, with some justification, that there was more to this story than satire on certain aspects of Soviet reality, and that it was the whole system which was being attacked. Indeed, according to Mayakovsky one American newspaper had seized on the events described and reported them as though they were the truth, with the aim of discrediting the Soviet Union.[19]

15 **27, 24**
16 **349**, p. 114
17 **26**
18 **286**, p. 147
19 **362**, p. 230

The basic idea of 'The Fatal Eggs' comes from H.G. Wells' *The Food of the Gods*, which Persikov's assistant Ivanov refers to at the end of the third chapter. There, two scientists produce a food which, used against their wishes, brings forth a whole race of giants, who become a menace to the population of England – although in many ways they are superior to ordinary mortals, whose terror of them is more a result of their size than because they are malicious.[20] In Bulgakov's tale there is no idealization of the creatures produced; they are simply vicious animals created, and eventually destroyed, by accident: in fact, the whole accidental nature of the events was one of the principal features noted by critics as an undoubted weakness of the story. It could almost be a simple horror story, were it not for the comparative lack of emphasis on the terror the animals provide, described in only two of the twelve chapters. It is rather the whole story and its everyday events that are 'nightmarish' (so at least the newspaper vendors think): whether it is the post-war conditions of hunger and shortage before 1928 (described at the beginning), the creation of the ray itself, the distortion of news by the press to astounding proportions, or the ravages of the chicken plague. The characters themselves are hardly significant, stereotypes in a Soviet setting: the absent-minded professor, the hard-nosed reporters, the well-meaning but decidedly limited Rokk, the professor's long-suffering servant Pankrat, a debonair spy, taciturn figures from the GPU. As in 'Diavoliada' we can hardly identify with anyone, least of all with Persikov who, although brilliant and devoted to science, is unfeeling, prefers animals to men, constantly shouts to Pankrat for his slightest needs, and terrorizes his students. Openly hostile towards Soviet society, he shows nothing but contempt for Marxism and its servants.

Yet it is hardly on account of Persikov's attitudes that the critics found the story unacceptable, for Bulgakov in no way holds him up as a hero. Indeed, from a communist standpoint, the trouble is that there are no heroes at all, and Rokk, the activist manager of the 'Red Ray' collective farm, is merely ridiculed. Rokk is carried away by an idea and it matters little to him whether it has been properly tested or not: he is concerned with results rather than principles. In him, indeed, Bulgakov satirizes some of the people whom the Revolution has brought to positions of power. Both Rokk and Persikov have been equated by various critics with Lenin, although more often Persikov has been accorded that honour.[21] There are certainly a few physical resemblances: Persikov's baldness, his protruding lower jaw, his manner of speech, and his age – the same as Lenin would have been in 1928. But there is little tangible evidence for such an assumption, nor is it necessary to make such identifications. For it is easy enough sim-

20 For a more detailed comparison, see **418**, pp. 139-42.
21 See **432**, p. 135, favouring Rokk, and **415**, favouring Persikov

ply to see the 'red' ray as allegorical of the Revolution itself: and in view of its disastrous consequences in the story it is no wonder that party critics were aghast.

The central idea of the story is, in fact, not in the hatching of the eggs, but in the discovery of this ray; the terror lies not in the monsters advancing on Moscow but in the unleashing by man of elemental forces beyond his control. We need not necessarily interpret this allegorically: it could refer to any serious tampering by man with the natural environment. The ray itself, created significantly not by natural light but by the electric bulb, interferes with natural law in one respect only: speeding up the processes of growth and reproduction. Then natural law itself takes over, it is a question of the survival of the fittest, with only the fiercest and most malicious creatures able to thrive and benefit from the ray's effects. In essence, civilization brings about its own destruction, and a complete return to nature, in a very un-Rousseauesque form, is accomplished. Throughout we are reminded that civilization itself, even in this brave new society, is only a veneer, in the same way as Moscow with its seemingly secure Prechistenka, Herzen Street, Zoological Institute, Cathedral of Christ is only a backdrop for fantastic and ugly events. Newspaper men hound the professor as though he were their prey; a reporter, Bronsky, with his 'speaking newspaper' has all the power of a demagogue over the crowd. It is the crowd itself that panics at the approach of danger, and finally murders Persikov and his assistants. People are described in terms of animals, animals are personified: a frog being dissected thinks what bastards his murderers are. Like 'Diavoliada' the story is brutal, with a total acceptance of violence. The most terrible chapter in the story begins with an idyllic description of the beauties of an evening in the country (set, actually, in Bulgakov's old region of Nikolskoe, near the provincial town 'Grachevka'), but ends with Rokk going swimming on a hot afternoon and meeting a giant snake, which snatches up his wife, crushes her bones, and swallows her in a few instants. Similar, brutally matter-of-fact descriptions are given of the deaths of two police officers and later of Persikov, Pankrat, and the housekeeper Marya Stepanovna.

Standing against this inhumane view of life there is only a kind of mock heroism: the country that aspired to create a new type of society is shown valiantly struggling not against foreign invaders but against chicken plague, or making all the preparations, amid a hardly admirable panic, to combat an army of snakes more terrible than the French invasion of 1812 (and advancing from the same direction, with Smolensk again left in flames).

Along with this is a great deal of satire, on Persikov himself, on Soviet institutions, on communist attitudes, on Soviet goods as compared with foreign ones, on newspapers that write nonsense. Cockroaches show a malicious attitude towards 'war communism.' The country's leader is just a mysterious voice in the Kremlin who telephones his instructions (as, in fact, was to happen to Bulgakov himself some years later). The secret police, the GPU, is shown as inspiring terror, ruthlessly efficient, and so well informed that it can identify a spy by his galoshes. The old régime, on the other hand, is referred to as 'eternally dear, enchanting to the point of tears.'

Generally Bulgakov's attitude is one of cynicism. He, as it were, stands on the side, writing of a society of which he is part but which he still finds uncongenial. Thus he mocks at its pretensions, and his satire becomes sarcastic or facetious. In his humour, names are again used to convey a meaning: Persikov – 'peach,' Rokk – 'fate,' Ptachka-Porosyuk (chief of the animal breeding department) – 'bird-piglet.' There is even – unusual for Bulgakov – a certain facile vulgarity, due to the common use of the word 'eggs' for 'testicles': 'All citizens who own eggs must immediately surrender them at their local police precincts,' 'Oh, Mamma, what will I do without eggs?' 'Don't whet your teeth on our eggs, Mr. Hughes – you have your own!'[22]

The story has its merits, but ultimately it is disappointing. Twice the length of 'Diavoliada,' it is too long for the central idea taken from Wells. Thus much of the early part seems like mere preparation for the time when the ray is used with disastrous results: the pace is altogether too slow and consequently the story appears wearisome and contrived. It is the emphasis that is wrong, if we accept that the main theme concerns the terrible potential of the ray. For by showing that it is the wrong *eggs* that cause the dire events, Bulgakov confuses the issue: he could equally well have allowed Rokk to produce his chickens, with similar results. Thus the story tends to lack focus, and what one is left with is simply an impression of Bulgakov's cynicism about his society.

'A Chinese Story'

Shorter and less pretentious than either 'Diavoliada' or 'The Fatal Eggs,' 'A Chinese Story' is at the same time more effective. First published, as far as is known, in the *Diavoliada* collection, it has never been included in the other collections of Bulgakov's stories. A destitute Chinese coolie turns up in Moscow and, although he knows no Russian, gets into the Red Army, where it is discovered that he is a 'virtuoso' with a machine-gun. But the first time he sees action he is killed, understanding nothing except that he still has not received his just reward.

Contemporary critics tended to see the figure of the coolie, called Sen-Zin-Po, as a malicious parody of Vsevolod Ivanov's Sin-Bin-U, the heroic Chinaman of

22 8, pp. 85, 89

his *Armoured Train 14-69*.[23] Compared with the conscious heroism of the latter for the sake of the cause, Sen-Zin-Po's futile death, for no reason that is clear to him except to receive a bonus, is indeed a mockery of Soviet-style heroism.

Yet the story, if brutal like the others, is far more moving and has none of their somewhat facetious humour. Satire there may be, but it is comparatively slight: we are here more interested in the hero and his problem. Not that we know a great deal about him or that we can readily identify with him – indeed we are set apart from him by our being told that he speaks in an incomprehensible language. We know little of his feelings or of his past; there is doubt about his age. But we understand the circumstances in which he finds himself: our interest results largely from his very lack of comprehension of these, so that we too are forced to look at the circumstances – Moscow during the civil war years – with the eyes of a stranger. The story is remarkable for this deliberate technique of alienation, in which there is not a little humour. The coolie is like a child, understanding nothing, feeling that the very city is hostile, with its cold river that flows stupidly through the centre, and its terrible grey sky. He gets into the Red Army without understanding why, he just knows that a certain combination of three words (a common oath) produces unexpected results. He does not understand what he is doing with a machine-gun, but merely that he can do it well and that people are pleased by this. In battle he hardly realizes he is firing at people to kill them; they are not men but 'chains' and he is 'playing a rhapsody' like the Kremlin bells he has heard on his arrival in Moscow. In the few moments before his death he shouts 'bonus' despairingly: he has done his job, why then should he not be paid?

Sen-Zin-Po is typical of any drifter, wanting only security and some kind of purpose, however futile this may be. For if we can read the story as a bitter commentary on man in the civil war, we can also understand it on a less specific level as representative of the little man in any war or disturbance, wandering through circumstances with no understanding of them, let alone any control over them. Or we can similarly understand it as man's existential position in life itself: not understanding an absurd and alien world, governed by circumstance and the will of others, and finally resentful that life has not lived up to its vague promises. Thus the coolie, initially a man without purpose in Moscow, finds like many of us that his purpose is allotted to him by other people: namely that he was born to fire machine-guns. On this a legend is built up, and the readiness with which others accept this enables him to believe in it too. He is partially influenced, it is true, by his opium dreams of becoming a hero, acquiring a beautiful girl (Nastya), and of winning the approval of a Chinese Lenin, but these have no basis in real-

23 See, in particular, **204**

ity, as subsequent events prove to his cost. And even in his dreams the rewards he desires are nothing but peals of bells: symbolizing a pleasant experience, something recognizable in an alien land. ('Bonus' as such is hardly more than a word for him, which probably means the same thing.) Why he has come to Russia in the first place we never learn: it is accidental, like everything else in his life.

There are a number of leitmotifs (such as the bells) which occur throughout the story with special significance: his 'saffron' smile and angelic appearance which help him with others, the buckets of water once carried by the coolie's mother to quench his thirst, the shoots of golden kaoliang, the shadow of an oak tree and the hot sun which remind him of home. To go home to his mother, in fact, seems to be his one deep desire beyond the immediate ones of finding food, shelter, and opium. But this is the one thing that is impossible, travel permits cannot be had, and the Red Army seems to provide the best alternative. Ironically, the oath which gets him into the Red Army, which will carry him away from home and mother for good and only give him death in exchange, is the one blaspheming against motherhood.

We have here a story about a perfectly ordinary man, and a charmingly naïve one, whose view of life is as simple as the statement of another Chinaman in the story of what there is (cold, stabbing, home-brew, bandits, Lenin, the Red Army, music) and what there is not (bread, opium, the bourgeoisie, travel permit). The coolie indeed remains uncorrupted and innocent in the midst of slaughter. If anything, the other soldiers are to blame for using him not as a man with his own desires but as a tool for a purpose he does not appreciate. His only fault, and it is a major one, lies in not trying to understand more himself.

'HEART OF A DOG'

'Heart of a Dog' (originally entitled 'A Dog's Happiness'[24]) was written in 1925 and also dedicated to Bulgakov's wife, Lyubov Yevgenievna. Intended for publication in *Nedra*, whose editor was favourable to Bulgakov, it was none the less rejected, presumably by the censor. The following March Bulgakov also signed a contract with the Moscow Art Theatre for a stage version of it, but this too was abandoned. 'Heart of a Dog' has never appeared in the Soviet Union. It was first published in 1968 in the Frankfurt journal *Grani* and (an inaccurate version) in the London Russian-language magazine *Student*; an authoritative version corrected by Bulgakov's widow was published in Paris the following year. In 1973 it was also announced that the Italian film director, Alberto Lattuada, was making a film of it in Poland.

24 See **446**, pp. 60-1; also, for the contract, **187**, folio 143

A Professor Preobrazhensky operates on a mongrel dog, Sharik, and turns him into a man: however, he turns out to be a drunkard and loafer, although he constantly spouts political phrases supplied to him by the obnoxious house committee chairman, Shvonder. When the situation becomes intolerable the professor performs another operation reversing the process, and Sharikov (as the man has been called) reverts to a dog. It is a far more satisfactory story than either 'Diavoliada' or 'The Fatal Eggs.' The themes are clearer, there is nothing accidental (except for a minor miscalculation in the effect the operation would produce), and no *deus ex machina* situations. It is more, too, than entertaining fantasy or science fiction – although it has a place in this tradition, as have a number of Bulgakov's works. For one has only to accept the one incredible circumstance, the actual transformation, and thereafter the story becomes entirely realistic. Dogs have been treated as though human elsewhere, of course, notably in Gogol's 'Diary of a Madman' and, more seriously, in Kuprin's 'Dog's Happiness' (the title Bulgakov had originally used) and Chekhov's 'Kashtanka'; there have been transformations too: one might think of that from an extremely high-minded ape to man in Kafka's 'Report for an Academy.' What sets Bulgakov's story apart from these is the complete lack of sentimentality or idealization, his portrayal of the dog's limitations once he becomes a man, and the credibility of events that follow. This is the way a dog-become-man would behave, one feels. Clearly, he would have more in common with the lowest elements of society than with the civilized Preobrazhensky. Thus the story becomes a study in conflicting human attitudes which may be described as those of the intellectual as opposed to the uneducated masses.

Raised cultural culture of

In many ways the story would seem to be a second, and more successful, attempt at 'The Fatal Eggs' which preceded it. Preobrazhensky is a somewhat more cultured resurrection of Persikov, his assistant Dr Bormental of Persikov's Ivanov, whereas the other servants are equally shadowy figures in both stories (in 'Heart of a Dog' we have one extra character: the beautiful and elegant, but otherwise characterless, assistant Zina). The professors in the two stories live in the same area: in 'The Fatal Eggs' it is on the Prechistenka, in 'Heart of a Dog' on a street leading to it, Obukhov Lane (where Bulgakov himself was now living). And the central theme is the same: the interference in natural processes that are insufficiently understood, with results that are potentially disastrous. In 'Heart of a Dog' these turn out to be reversible, so the end is a happy one, but the implications remain. Preobrazhensky, unlike Persikov, actually questions the value of what he has undertaken. 'But what in heaven's name for? That's the point. Will you kindly tell me why one has to manufacture artificial Spinozas when some peasant woman may produce a real one any day of the week?' (p. 108).[25]

25 89. Page references are given in the text.

From the Soviet viewpoint there is a great deal that is unacceptable about the story. It raises, first of all, the whole issue of how possible change in man is. Preobrazhensky's 'mistake' was that he thought the pituitary the key to mankind, rather than being, as we are told, the individual brain in miniature. The pituitary he implants in the dog's brain is that of a criminal, uncultured man: the suggestion is that those of this type will never change, despite the benefits – here a good home and economic advantages – to which they have access. This runs counter to all of communist theory. It is true, of course, that the character of Sharikov in the story is determined more by his canine origin than by the deceased owner of the implanted pituitary and testicles: he is more dog-made-man than man resurrected in a dog's body. But he is, none the less, quite conceivable as a man, as a poorly developed type with criminal instincts which, despite the theory, communism has not succeeded in eliminating.

As a dog, Sharik is intelligent. He has taught himself to read. He is content, once his material needs are satisfied, and loyal to his provider. Although governed by his instincts (hence his hatred for cats and suspicions of a stuffed owl owned by the professor), in a dog this is hardly out of place. He even shows a remarkable amount of common sense in some of his opinions of man, whom he observes with shrewdness. But these qualities are quite insufficient when he is forcibly lifted higher up the evolutionary scale. His instinctual behaviour – concern only for himself, lack of courage and conscience, uncontrolled anger at what he dislikes (cats), and lack of sexual restraint – is contrary to everything held important by civilized man, whose standards he regards (correctly) as unnatural. The 'rules' Preobrazhensky makes for him are but a futile attempt at exerting control when it is already too late: Preobrazhensky has already, like Persikov, unleashed the forces of natural law.

Sharikov immediately identifies himself with the proletariat, and a natural assumption is that in the author's view the proletariat is not very much different. 'You belong,' Preobrazhensky says to Sharikov, 'to the lowest possible stage of development ... You are still in the formative stage. You are intellectually weak, all your actions are purely bestial. Yet you allow yourself in the presence of two university-educated men to offer advice, with quite intolerable familiarity, on a cosmic scale and of quite cosmic stupidity, on the redistribution of wealth ...' (p. 95). Here the implied comparison with the proletariat is obvious, and such remarks are equally true of Preobrazhensky's attitude towards Shvonder and his house committee, with their lack of education, insistence on the importance of rules and papers, and real, although recently acquired, power. Sharikov's 'insolence' to the professor is no different from theirs, and the whole thing boils down to a battle between the intellectual and the proletariat, where there is no common basis for discussion. Sharikov merely adopts the slogans and the arguments of others in this struggle, whether he understands them or not, and is hostile towards everything the professor represents, his civilized manners included. In this particular struggle, it is the intellectual who wins, the process is reversed and Sharikov put back in his place: a good example of wish-fulfilment, no doubt. But the same cannot happen in the case of the ignorant masses who would seem to threaten the light of culture: their 'liberation,' unlike Sharikov's, cannot be reversed. As a dog, Sharik was not free, but contented, even lovable. Greater possibilities coming for him unexpectedly, which he did not seek but which were created by a well-meaning intellectual, brought greater demands and greater discontent: he was better off *before* his revolution. Again, a direct comparison with the fate of the proletarian masses is difficult to escape.

Such may not have been the interpretation intended by Bulgakov, but the possible implications are clear enough, and explain why the book was not published in the Soviet Union. Preobrazhensky himself, far more than Persikov, shows an undisguised hatred of the revolutionary society, and at no point is he ever shown to be wrong. He has unfortunate 'social origins,' and he says quite bluntly that he does not like the proletariat. A large part of the story consists of the expression of his ideas, with only the unsympathetic Sharikov or the house committee in opposition. He talks of former, better times, when galoshes could be left in hallways without being stolen and when the central heating always worked. He believes in how things *should* be: vodka of a certain percentage, hors-d'œuvres hot, rooms used for the purposes for which they were intended regardless of limits on living space. From any point of view, Preobrazhensky is very much a counter-revolutionary in attitude – even if he rejects the word as being almost meaningless – and although Bulgakov does not idealize him he has the reader's sympathies throughout. The story implies a definite political viewpoint, intentional or not, and goes far beyond simple satire.

Technically, it is interesting from the point of view of the nice balance between dog and man and for its unusual narrative technique, with the dog taking over the narration for much, but not all, of the story. This, in fact, provides a useful device for alienation, for seeing human actions interpreted, naïvely but not incorrectly, by a creature of less sophistication: Sharik's descriptions of what a typist has to do to stay in the favours of her lover are an example. This may remind us to some extent of Gogol's dogs in 'Diary of a Madman,' although at times the dog's remarks are used almost like a Chekhovian 'chorus element,' as commentary on the action: witness his admiration (as a dog) for the way the professor deals with the house committee. Both as a dog and as a man Sharik is a useful vehicle for satire: on the food stores, on the proletariat itself, on the patients that come to the professor (for rejuvenation – his specialty).

The main fault of the story is in the lack of characterization, something it shares with those of the *Diavoliada* collection. Bulgakov tends at this time to give us stereotypes, with little development. Indeed, in the case of Preobrazhen-sky, he seems to use leitmotifs rather than character as a means of identification: constant snatches of song the professor hums throughout. But this is of relatively minor importance; it is rather the forceful exposition of its theme that makes this work so successful.

The five stories of the *Diavoliada* collection, with 'Heart of a Dog,' share a common basis of satire and humour, and a critical if not hostile attitude to the new Soviet society. A common theme is the ignorance and lack of culture of the new class, whether in simple peasants, workers, or bureaucrats. Bulgakov may have considered he was only pointing to inadequacies in his society, yet one cannot fail to detect certain doubts as to its viability as a whole. Many of these stories, too, contain an element of violence, with the emphasis on action rather than on character. This is perhaps not surprising. The country had recently gone through a revolution and civil war, brutality was a fact of life, and Bulgakov was doubtless influenced by this. That he could write with depth of understanding of his characters was evident from his novel *The White Guard*. In these stories it is more the dehumanizing influences in everyday life which concern him.

Criticism of the collection as a whole, caught up in the increasing momentum of protest following the publication of his novel and production of his plays, became increasingly more violent – it could hardly have been more so if 'Heart of a Dog' had been published. It was as though it suddenly became fashionable to criticize Bulgakov – which, for any self-righteous socially minded critic, was not difficult to do: 'To the question *how*? one can answer: not badly. But *what* he writes ... We need satire, but this satire must be filled with passion for our cause ...'[26] It was suggested that the five stories gave the impression of being émigré anecdotes, and that Bulgakov only saw the anecdotal in Soviet life while remaining basically a nihilist.[27] Such criticism became standard fare for many years to come. As late as 1960 we can still read that 'The Fatal Eggs' 'is a malicious pamphlet against the Revolution,' that in 'Diavoliada' 'M. Bulgakov makes an attempt to ridicule and discredit contemporaneity, in which he can see only disorder, general confusion, and senseless bustle.'[28] Such attacks were hardly surprising, for at no time could Bulgakov be described as more than a fellow-traveller, unable to repress in himself significant doubts about the new society – even, if he was prepared to give it his intellectual support.

26 **204**
27 **388**, pp. 86-7
28 **267**, pp. 214, 215

4

The novelist, 1925

The 1920s was a period of tremendous literary diversity in the Soviet Union, and despite the attempts of the Communist party – from about 1925 on – to gradually assert its control over literary production, there still remained a hope that writers might continue to exert a certain freedom. The critics of the RAPP, however vociferous, were not the only ones, and there were indeed those who were more sensitive to aesthetic as well as social considerations – one might think, in particular, of Alexandr Voronsky. Nor did the writers submit easily to demands from without, but continued along quite independent paths as far as they were able.

Since the turn of the century there had been a general turning away from nineteenth-century realism: in the works of symbolists such as Blok, Bryusov, Bely, and Remizov; in the futurists with their one great poet and playwright Mayakovsky, and then in his Left Front of Art, established in 1923; also in the *Proletcult*, founded in 1917 by A.A. Bogdanov, and its off-shoots, the Smithy and October groups – which in their attempts to produce a 'proletarian art' often showed a tendency towards 'formalism' rather than realism. The one writer in the twenties who had an enormous influence – and who himself, in the thirties, would 'disappear' – was Boris Pilnyak, whose extraordinary and original novel, *The Naked Year*, was published in 1922. Bulgakov himself did not like Pilnyak, but his *Diavoliada* stories clearly show the preoccupation of many writers of the age with experimentation.

As opposed to this non-realistic tendency there stood the writers with a greater social commitment, whose style, intended to be 'understood by the masses,' was more or less realistic: Furmanov, with his *Chapaev* of 1923; Serafimovich, with his *The Iron Flood* of 1924; Gladkov, with *Cement* of 1925. These would be followed by Fadeev with *The Nineteen* in 1927, and Sholokhov, whose *Quiet Don* would begin to appear in 1928.

In a sense, the bridge between the two groups was to be found in the so-called 'fellow-travellers,' those who accepted the new society but whose principal concern was none the less literary rather than social. Most important were those connected with the Serapion Brothers, who created in a variety of styles but were united by the one desire to maintain the independence of art: Zamyatin with his novel *We* (not published in the Soviet Union); Fedin with his 'The Orchard' and novel *Cities and Years* (1924); Zoshchenko, with his satirical stories – to mention only three of the better-known ones. Others whose outlook on art was similar were Isaak Babel with his stories of the First Cavalry Army and Leonid Leonov, whose *The Badgers* appeared in 1924. It was against this background that Bulgakov entered upon the scene of Soviet literature – and in the next few years his friends and acquaintances would also produce works of significance: notably Olesha with his *Envy* of 1927, Kataev with his *Embezzlers* of the same year, and Ilf and Petrov with their *Twelve Chairs* of 1928. Bulgakov himself was not a Serapion, but his views of literature as being above governmental control coincided with theirs – and indeed it was a struggle he would wage all his life. In style he approached the realists more than the experimentalists, although he would inherit a healthy dose of fantasy from his literary master, Gogol. Unlike many of the writers of this time, he would manage to maintain a relative independence from the Party politicians – although not without facing constant problems in his own life as a result – and ultimately he would come to outshine most of them, with the exception, perhaps, of Babel, Zamyatin, and Mayakovsky. It is to his first novel that we must now turn.

THE WHITE GUARD

'For a year I wrote a novel, *The White Guard*. This novel I love more than all my other things.'[1] Bulgakov wrote this in 1924, but in fact the book had taken far more than a year to complete. It would seem that the beginning had been as early as 1919 in Kiev, when he had made a draft for 'Illness.' In 1920 he used the name of Alyosha Turbin, his later hero in *The White Guard*, for the protagonist of one of his propaganda plays: from then on, it seems, to write a novel became his one dream. In his *Theatrical Romance* he recalls, in very general terms, how his novel originated:

It began one night when I woke up after a nightmare. I had been dreaming of my home town; snow, winter, the Civil War ... In my dream a snowstorm whirled soundlessly before my eyes and then came a grand piano and people standing around it.

1 491, p. 86

...

That was how I started writing my novel. I described the snowstorm from my dream. I tried to describe how the side of the grand piano shone in the light of a shaded lamp. It did not work out, but I persevered (pp. 19-20).[2]

To his friend, Popov, Bulgakov wrote that he composed *The White Guard* in 1922, after his mother's death, which had provided the impetus for it[3] - and which indeed is referred to in the opening chapter.

Two further related stories appeared in 1922: 'The Extraordinary Adventures of a Doctor' in *Rupor* and, more important, a feuilleton in *Nakanune* entitled 'On the Night of the Third (from the novel "The Scarlet Stroke"),' referring to events of 1919 and Petlyura's departure from Kiev.[4] In this there are obvious, thinly disguised, autobiographical references: the hero is a doctor, Mikhail Bakaleynikov, he has a brother Kolka (Nikolay), his wife bears the name of Bulgakov's sister, Varvara Afanasievna, and the family live at No 17, St Andrew's Street (as opposed to the real No 13, St Andrew's Hill). Here characters which were later to appear in *The White Guard* are already clearly recognizable, so too are certain scenes and motifs.

Many changes had still to be made, however, for the novel itself was to be set largely at the time of Petlyura's entry into Kiev in December 1918 rather than the time of his departure. (Another story concerning his departure, 'I Killed,' was only published in 1926.) The name Alexey Turbin (whose surname had probably been taken from Bulgakov's grandmother's maiden name - although there was also a general with this name in the civil war) was now restored in place of Mikhail Bakaleynikov. Varvara became Alexey's sister Yelena and another character from 'On the Night of the Third,' Yury Leonidovich, became their friend Leonid Yurievich Shervinsky. Nikolay remained the same. So too did Vasilisa, 'bourgeois, engineer, and coward,' the owner of the house, which finally settled at No 13, St Alexey's Hill. By 1924 the novel, now with the title *The White Guard*, appears to have been ready: two extracts published in May and June that year as 'Evening at Vasilisa's' and 'Petlyura Goes on Parade' are essentially parts of chapters fifteen and sixteen of the final version.[5]

Historically, the book is a fairly accurate description of events in Kiev in 1918 and 1919 although, as at least one historian has pointed out, the treatment is not fully objective.[6] Nor indeed should it be: Bulgakov shows events as seen

2 **160**. Page references to this will appear in the text.
3 **379**, p. 174
4 **129**
5 **130, 180**
6 **459**, p. 204n; compare also **303**

through the eyes of his own class, the Russian intellectuals in Kiev. His central characters, based on members of his own family, cling to their own particular values and to the atmosphere of well-bred manners and comfort in their household. We see this family – the Turbins – as the period of German rule through the hetman Skoropadsky is coming to a close. The elder brother, Alexey, a doctor, enlists with the troops preparing to defend the city against the Ukrainian nationalist Petlyura, but in the meantime the hetman leaves the city together with the Germans. So too does Talberg, the Baltic-German husband of Alexey's sister, Yelena. Consequently, the loyalist troops, inexperienced cadets, are disbanded by their colonel, Malyshev, but there is some fighting. Alexey and his younger brother Nikolka, also a cadet, only just escape: Alexey later nearly dies of typhus. Petlyura enters the city, but forty-seven days later is driven out by the Bolsheviks, when life virtually returns to normal for the family. Around this outline is built a complicated structure of characters and sub-plots which make of *The White Guard* a rich and fascinating novel.

Its first public reading is described in *Theatrical Romance* and, although in all Bulgakov's autobiographical works one must beware of taking everything he says as fact, the passage has a certain ring of truth about it. 'They all said as one man,' Bulgakov writes, 'that my novel was unprintable because it would never be passed by the censorship. Only then did I realize that while I had been writing the novel it had never occurred to me whether it might pass the censorship or not' (p. 22). This indeed seems likely: on other occasions, too, Bulgakov would show a naïve unconcern about such matters.

The White Guard did appear at least in part, in 1925, in the journal *Rossiia*, whose editor, I. Lezhnev, had published the works of many of the writers Bulgakov had known while working for *Nakanune*. But after the first two instalments had been printed, the journal was closed down because of its 'changing landmarks,' neo-bourgeois persuasions – *The White Guard*, it seems, was the last straw – and Lezhnev, its editor, was forced to go abroad to Germany.[7] (Later he would admit his 'mistaken' views and return to Russia.) 'Never in all my life,' Bulgakov would write in *Theatrical Romance*, 'has there been anything quite so mysterious as the incident of Rudolfi [that is, Lezhnev] and my novel' (p. 50). In the Soviet Union *The White Guard* would appear in its entirety only with its publication (with a few minor textual changes) in the *Selected Prose* edition of 1966 and then in the collection of *Novels* in 1973. Indeed many people who knew the play based on it, *Days of the Turbins*, were ignorant of the fact that the novel existed.[8] Abroad, it appeared in Paris in 1927-29 under the title *Days*

7 See **478**, p. 21, **446**, p. 81, and, for what follows, **379**, p. 170; **350**, p. 4; **351**, pp. 8, 315
8 **165**, p. 18

of the Turbins (The White Guard); also in Riga, where public demand for the complete work was so great that it was published in a fraudulent version, with the part missing from *Rossiia* simply invented (apparently by Boris Svobodin) on the basis of the later play. It was translated into English in 1971.[9]

Critical reaction to the novel on its appearance was mild, and initially it seems to have gone almost unnoticed except for a few minor reviews. In *Pravda* one critic said that Bulgakov wrote well, but that *The White Guard* lacked a social viewpoint; in *Novyi mir* it was suggested that a cadet stopped by Nikolka in the book represented Bulgakov himself 'armed with a gun to shoot, but exactly where he hardly knew himself.'[10] But after the publication of the *Diavoliada* collection and the production of *Days of the Turbins* attention returned to the novel. Inevitably, it was now compared with the play, and usually came off worse: it too was included in the general plethora of attacks upon Bulgakov. *The White Guard* was called a 'counter-revolutionary, Philistine chuckle,' deeply anti-social; 'an attempt to represent great tragic events in terms of a farce.' There were complaints of Bulgakov sympathizing with the Whites and trying to 'rehabilitate' them. 'The best representatives of Bulgakov's class are cowards and scoundrels. The best representatives of his class hate the native people.'[11] There was also some fear that the novel reopened the whole complex problem of nationalities, after in theory it had been solved.

Such criticisms, from a communist viewpoint, are partly justified: certainly Bulgakov shows sympathy for his class and its predicament. It could hardly have been otherwise. But to state that he turns tragic events into a farce, or that his heroes are cowards and scoundrels, is clearly nonsense. Since the work's complete publication in Russia, criticism has been less simplistic. More attention has been paid to the positive virtues of the Turbins, their courage and deep sense of honour. Bulgakov is praised for showing the inevitability of their class's downfall in the face of Soviet power, and their need to adapt to a new age. As one critic has put it: 'Bulgakov's *The White Guard* revives by means of the Turbin family chronicle the concrete story of lost monarchist illusions.'[12]

The central idea of the novel is the family in times of crisis. Man has 'made towers, alarm-bells and weapons for one purpose only,' Bulgakov writes – 'to

9 Information supplied by Dr N. Andreyev. See also 'Ot izdatel'stva' in the Paris edition, **166**, II. Page references to the English translation **168** will be given in the text. (The translation is taken from the edition of *Belaia gvardiia* in **2**, which differs slightly from the original **163**. In particular, Yulia Alexandrovna Reyss originally had the patronymic Markovna.)
10 **416** and **286**, pp. 147-8
11 **260**, pp. 46-7; **388**, pp. 81-3; and **401**, pp. 40-5
12 **217**, pp. 262-4; **424**; and **425**, p. 161

guard the peace of his hearth and home. For this he goes to war, which if the truth be known is the only cause for which anyone ought to fight' (p. 193). The Turbins live in their own 'world of comfort and security' (p. 38), which is threatened by the 'snow-storm from the north': the Revolution with its alien ideas and values. Only the Ukrainian hetman, backed by German power, seems capable of preserving their world, while the nationalist forces led by Petlyura – a more immediate danger than the Bolsheviks – seem little more than barbarians. Ultimately, only the Bolsheviks can provide order and civilization: the Turbins have no alternative but to accept their rule.

It is around the individual members of the family, and their friends, that the whole novel revolves. Its strength lies initially in the balance of these characters: Alexey, the peaceful doctor, caught up in events and trying rather ineffectively to do his part; his brother Nikolka, the young enthusiast with a sense of duty and loyalty to others; Yelena, the loving sister, disappointed in her marriage to Talberg, yet concerned above all with keeping the home intact. These are supported by their childhood friends: Shervinsky, aide to Prince Belorukov, opportunist, boastful, yet attractive in his grandiloquence; Myshlaevsky, the plain, efficient artillery officer, with his love of vodka and rough language, his contempt for the whole of the general staff; Karas, a very ordinary student become soldier. Later there arrives cousin Lariosik, gauche, lovable, unfortunate in marriage – and soon becoming excessively appreciative of the Turbin household. Even a minor character such as the maid Anyuta, with her nervous excitement in the presence of Myshlaevsky, is important in that she too serves to complement the richness and diversity of the family group. The various characters play different parts in the civic drama but the family circle, temporarily forced open by the events of the outside world, remains as strong as before – or stronger, in that Yelena's husband Talberg, who had introduced a foreign element into it, has left for good. As outside events become less urgent the personal element becomes once again stronger, and new relationships are established: Alexey with a woman who hid him from his pursuers, Nikolka with the daughter of a brave colonel he saw shot, Yelena with Shervinsky. But these relationships are such as to enlarge the family life, not diminish it.

Significantly, the most insistent leitmotifs throughout the book are those emphasizing all that is most permanent in the home: the cream-coloured blinds protecting its inhabitants from the world outside; the two clocks, one playing a gavotte and the other with its 'tonk-tank'; the chocolate-coloured books which they fear will be destroyed; Christmas and all that it implies; the stove with its tiles showing scenes from the life of Peter the Great (the 'Shipwright of Saardam') and the inscriptions written on it in chalk by Nikolka. The inscriptions must gradually be erased as some of the sentiments they express become inappropriate for the times, but the stove itself remains, unchanged, as a permanent symbol of the family. The leitmotifs conflicting with these, the snowstorm from the north and apocalyptic visions from Revelation (introduced first as the novel's two epigraphs), refer to external events and are more temporary in nat- ure. The more durable links should not be broken – which is perhaps what Bulgakov means when he writes: 'Never, never take the shade off a lamp. A lampshade is something sacred' (p. 29). It is worth noting that Alexey's new relationship with the beautiful and sadly sensual Yulia Alexandrovna Reyss is, as it were, authorized by the compatibility of the objects in her house (a portrait of a man with epaulettes, a cerise-shaded lamp) with those in his own back- ground.

The people in the Turbin circle share a realization of all that is valuable in the Russian past. Their cultural heritage is symbolized in part by the school they attended and which Alexey finds himself defending. Now the arguments over lit- erature, the mathematical problems, become part of what he has to fight for. As he wanders sentimentally through the corridors, he recalls incidents from the time spent there and particularly the janitor Maxim, who is still there trying to protect the property. But Alexey's nostalgia is for more than the days of his youth, it is for the Russia that once was, personified in a portrait of Tsar Alexan- der I and his troops at Borodino: 'Can you save this doomed building, Tsar Alex- ander, with all the regiments of Borodino? Why don't you come alive and lead them down from the canvas? They'd smash Petlyura all right' (p. 103). Alas, neither the troops nor the enemy are the same. The tsar has already been de- posed and murdered with his family. The present leader of the forces, the het- man, has fled; there is no one to defend. Myshlaevsky, as a last, futile gesture, requests permission to set fire to the school. It is refused, for the past, tarnished, ridiculous perhaps in new circumstances, must not be destroyed.

The family, certainly, are still living in the spiritual traditions of the nine- teenth century. Fundamentally hostile to the Revolution, they and their friends are inalienably attached to the monarchy: in their apartment they passionately sing the old tsarist national anthem, despite the possible danger. Myshlaevsky shouts out 'right!' in the theatre to the actor's words 'Russia acknowledges only one Orthodox faith and one Tsar!' (p. 49). These people represent the best of the old order, courageous, courteous, with a belief in honour: 'no one should break his word of honor, or life becomes impossible' (p. 171). But in these days 'Honor is to a Russian but a useless burden,' as Alexey recalls from *The Devils*, uncon- sciously comparing the Bolsheviks to Dostoevsky's fanatics. And in some ways, as the Soviet critic Lakshin points out, their ideas of honour seem old-fashioned in the changed world they live in, so that cousin Lariosik's speeches in praise of the family – 'Our wounded souls look for peace somewhere like here, behind cream-colored blinds' (p. 216) – sound like a mere parody, meaningless.[13] Communist criticism never tires of pointing out that this whole class is doomed, and it is right to dwell on the quixotism of the Turbins' attempt to preserve their values and style of living in a new age, to stress the historical inevitability of their failure. But the attempt had to be made nevertheless, for through their sufferings and struggles they undergo a kind of spiritual renewal (the process might be seen, as Lakshin suggests, as a 'retribution' for their privileged past), and this gives them strength for a new future.

Central though the theme of the family might be, the book is more than just a family chronicle. Two further leitmotifs throughout are the planets Venus and Mars in the sky: love and war. It is in the clash of these two elements, and the tension created by the conjunction of two opposing forces, that the novel's strength lies. The book is something of a *War and Peace* in miniature, with similar epic qualities and with a similar range of heroes – extending from the family circle into the whole of society – from the ordinary soldiers and citizens to the leaders themselves. One German critic even considers it as a parody (*sic*) of Tolstoy's work, pointing out that Bulgakov's heroes see the struggle in 1918 in terms of the war of 1812, but with their Borodino becoming a farce (he also indicates certain resemblances of Alexey Turbin to Andrey Bolkonsky and of Nikolka to Petya Rostov).[14] Although less vast in scope, the novel is within the same tradition as *War and Peace*, and the descriptions of the different companies of Petlyura's men as they advance towards Kiev remind us of Tolstoy's theory of the movement of peoples.

The clash of peoples, indeed, becomes a principal theme, only here there are three groups involved: the 'white guard' themselves, the Bolsheviks, and the supporters of Petlyura. Of these, the 'white guard' is the largest and most diversified. Apart from the immediate family and friends, it also includes two further 'positive' characters, the colonels Malyshev and Nay-Turs. The former is simply a good soldier, concerned for his men, carrying out his duty as long as he is able but unwilling to sacrifice lives in vain. Colonel Nay-Turs, whom Alexey has known since his days in the Belgrade Hussars, becomes the real hero and martyr of the White movement. Gruff, efficient, reminiscent in his speech of Tolstoy's Denisov, with tremendous strength of character and will, he finally gives his life for his men in a pointless but noble death. But Bulgakov does not allow this death to be forgotten: by showing him, in a prophetic dream of Alexey's, as a 'knight-crusader in paradise,' and by devoting an entire chapter to Nikolka's efforts to rescue him from the morgue and give him an honourable burial, he

13 **2**, pp. 18-21
14 **169**, pp. 331-45. A comparison with *War and Peace* is also made by **198**, p. 9.

emphasizes sacrifice and honour as positive values which, despite everything, have a central place in man's life.

Other members of the 'white guard' group, however, are by no means heroic, and it is one of the misfortunes of the Turbin family to find themselves, because of historical circumstances, the allies of so many people they cannot even respect. Their landlord Vasilisa, fearful of the least thing, miserly, hating his wife with all his heart, is the very antithesis of the Turbins living above, although his world too is similar to theirs. He and his wife are essentially comic characters, and when Vasilisa talks of his convictions that only the autocracy can save Russia, it sounds like a cruel parody of the Turbins' own, once sincerely held, beliefs. But the greatest scorn is reserved for the high-ranking officers of the 'white guard,' who are distinguished by self-interest, remoteness, and irresponsibility. Yelena's husband Talberg is the closest representative of this type, with his sense of political expediency and duplicity, suggested physically by his two-layered eyes, his rat-like appearance, and his insistence on talking of events as a mere 'comic opera' – excusing him from any show of decency towards those near to him. Others are hardly better. The hetman we see only in his German disguise as he flees the country. The commanding general, Belorukov, follows his example; Colonel Shchetkin deserts his post and drives to a woman's apartment, making no provision for his troops. General Makushkin, after being forced to issue boots against his will to Nay-Turs, simply gives up and goes home. About these and the other high-ranking officers the attitude expressed by the loyalist forces – Myshlaevsky in particular – is one of undisguised contempt.

'Away to the north and east beyond the furthest line of the blue-brown forest were the Bolsheviks. Only these two forces [Bolsheviks and Germans] counted' (p. 62). Ultimately, this is clearly true, but in the book the Bolsheviks are represented largely by the presence of their army and the armoured-train *Proletarian* in the last chapter: there is some justice in the claims of Bulgakov's critics that he did not give adequate treatment to them – if, that is, we are to judge the book on its equal distribution of 'political time.' In the immediacy of the struggle with Petlyura, the Bolsheviks of necessity remain in the background – but of that background one is constantly aware. They have their representatives, too, in a small group centred around one Shpolyansky, and in a heroic agitator whose escape these ingeniously arrange after he has spoken out publicly on the day of Petlyura's victory parade. But Bulgakov refuses to make Shpolyansky, the leader of the group, into the ideal communist hero. Playboy, poet, gambler, never lacking in money, lover of Yulia Reyss, he throws in his lot with the Bolsheviks, it would seem, more because he enjoys sabotaging the hetman's army (and because he thinks the victory of the Bolsheviks inevitable) than because of any personal devotion to the cause.

It is the other force which, at this moment in history, is the stronger, supported more by emotion than reason. Its leaders – Petlyura himself, his colonels Toropets, Kozyr-Leshko, and the colourful Bolbotun, popular heroes for the idea of Ukrainian nationalism they represent – are the true representatives of the majority of the people: not the Bolsheviks, whom they distrust as much as they dislike the Russian upper class in Kiev. The principal struggle in the book is indeed one of class, between the educated Russians with their values and culture and the more numerous but largely ignorant, resentful masses. Petlyura's attempt to seize power represents a rebellion of barbarian instinct over reason, a return to the forces of anarchy, which the intellectuals are right to fear. It is the old unending conflict between instinctive, animal man and civilization which (like the lampshade covering a naked light) should be kept intact. For when it breaks down even the educated behave instinctively, in their attempt to save these very values. Alexey, in a moment of anger, stuffs a newspaper into the face of the boy selling it – but immediately feels ashamed. (Later, when he is pursued, he kills a man, only to regret this in a more rational moment.) Nikolka behaves similarly towards a janitor. Petlyura's troops have no such hesitations, killing not only in battle but destroying ordinary citizens who might be considered their enemies. Two other characters, who make use of the breakdown of law and order to rob and plunder Vasilisa, are a manifestation of the same blind, animal force.

In many ways the book is concerned simply with human nature, unidealized. What is most frightening about the violence is that it is brought about not by evil personalities but by ordinary people behaving in a perfectly natural way. Support for Petlyura is general, even where it is unexpressed: in the newspaper boy or the taxi-driver who takes Alexey to the school. Others talk of it more openly: a beautiful market girl whom Vasilisa desires, with her defiance of the Germans ('we'll teach 'em it doesn't pay'), or an old man overjoyed to see Myshlaevsky because he mistakes him for a soldier of Petlyura's.

The people's attitude is often a basic one of satisfaction in taking revenge. 'Serve 'em right' calls out a voice at the funeral of some young officers, murdered in the night by peasants with Petlyura's men. Some boys whom Nikolka finds playing peacefully tell him that some shooting is 'our people, beating the hell out of the White officers,' getting even with them; again: 'Serve 'em right' (p. 168). Such attitudes emerge most clearly at the time of Petlyura's triumphant parade, as the Ukrainians delight in their own triumph, while the Russians watch uneasily.

'They'll touch the Jews all right, that's for sure ...'
'And the officers. They'll rip their guts out.'
'And the landlords! Down with 'em!' (p. 255)

(The heroic speech of the Bolshevik agitator at such a time, with its vision of a united, free world, is on a higher plane altogether.) To these people Petlyura becomes something of a god who will look after their interests, yet remains mysterious and remote. Even at this parade, no one knows where he is; he is everywhere and nowhere. From the beginning he has been shown to be equally mysterious, a myth; at the end he disappears as though he had never existed. The people are seized by an idea, of which they have no real understanding.

Bulgakov does not see anything noble in the people as such. They are basically ruled by self-interest and a narrow-minded distrust of all who are unlike themselves. The reforms which have been longed for by the peasants are predictably selfish: 'All land to the peasants. Three hundred acres per man. No more landlords ... No sharks from the City to come and demand grain. The grain's ours. No one else can have it, and what we don't eat ourselves we'll bury in the ground ...' (pp. 69-70). Many of the upper class are no better: the refugees concerned only with their skins; the forces who join the White general Denikin to attempt to recover their old status and property; the intellectuals who do not understand the peasants and hate them with all their soul, delighted when they are being robbed by the Germans: 'Serve them right! And a bit more of that sort of treatment wouldn't do 'em any harm either. I'd give it to 'em even harder. That'll teach them to have a revolution – didn't want their own masters, so now they can have a taste of another!' (p. 62). The Turbin family stand apart from the others not because they are any less concerned for themselves but because they represent the forces of education and civilization which – when upheld by the social system – hold in check man's instincts. Without these, human society reverts to a survival of the fittest: this seems to be Bulgakov's theme.

Yet his pessimism about human nature is counterbalanced by his belief, later more openly expressed in *The Master and Margarita*, that everything that happens is for the best. A belief, perhaps, that everything is God's will – for *The White Guard* is a profoundly religious book. At the end of it, Bulgakov contrasts the normal concerns of men with the innocence of a child, the Turbins' next-door neighbour, Petka Shcheglov. Petka has a simple dream, of a large, glittering diamond ball in which he can take delight. 'When grown-ups dream and have to run,' the passage continues, 'their feet stick to the ground, they moan and groan as they try to pull their feet free of the quagmire. But children's feet are free as air' (p. 296). But to pull his feet out of the quagmire, man needs simply to look up, to be aware of eternity. It is with this idea that the book concludes, in surely one of the most beautiful passages of Bulgakov:

The night flowed on. During its second half the whole arc of the sky, the curtain that God had drawn across the world, was covered with stars. It was as if a midnight mass was being celebrated in the measureless height beyond that blue altar-screen. The candles were lit on the altar and they threw patterns of crosses, squares and clusters on to the screen. Above the bank of the Dnieper the mid-night cross of St Vladimir thrust itself above the sinful, bloodstained, snow-bound earth toward the grim, black sky. From far away it looked as if the cross-piece had vanished, had merged with the upright, turning the cross into a sharp and menacing sword.

But the sword is not fearful. Everything passes away – suffering, pain, blood, hunger and pestilence. The sword will pass away too, but the stars will still re-main when the shadows of our presence and our deeds have vanished from the earth. There is no man who does not know that. Why, then, will we not turn our eyes toward the stars? Why? (p. 297)

The stars, the hill with its statue of St Vladimir and cross – even the ball that Petka has dreamt of – are obvious symbols of eternity. The related theme of immortality has been suggested throughout, in recurring images bound up with the Turbin family, the bearers of a spiritual tradition from one age to the next.

There are, however, more clearly religious references. The final chapter con-tains a passage from Revelation xx and xxi, one verse of which has already been selected for the epigraph: '... and the dead were judged out of those things which were written in the books, according to their works ...' Earlier the family's priest, Father Alexandr, has quoted Revelation xvi. 4: 'And the third angel poured out his vial upon the rivers and fountains of waters; and they became blood' – words which are repeated by another character later. These verses, dealing with the Last Judgement and the new heaven and new earth, clearly relate to the trials that have to be undergone at the time of the Revolution, and are reflected in the apocalyptic style of the book itself ('Great and terrible was the year of Our Lord 1918, of the Revolution the second'). Thus in a sense the Revolution becomes the Last Judgement, but beyond the suffering lies the new, better world. The events of the story take place at Christmas, the time when, for Christians, Christ is born anew; and this is too a time of rebirth for the Turbin family, which is deeply, yet unostentatiously, religious. Initially, Nikolka, grieving at the death of their mother, questions God's justice: '... God vouchsafed no answer, leaving Nikolka in doubt whether the things that happened in life were always necessary and always for the best' (p. 10). But Father Alexandr, who foresees the trials to come, maintains that one must never lose heart, and this view is justified by the events that follow.

The most remarkable affirmation of religious faith occurs when Alexey is on the point of death: indeed the suggestion is that he actually dies. Yelena's pray-ers for him are answered, and he miraculously recovers as a direct result of the coming of Christ: 'He appeared beside the open grave, arisen, merciful and bare-foot' (p. 277). Yet in the same way that Vasilisa parodies the family attitudes, another character, the poet Rusakov, represents a grotesque distortion of its religious views. After contracting syphilis – God's punishment, he thinks, for writing an anti-religious poem – he becomes an unreasoning religious fanatic. But Bulgakov has no time for narrow, doctrinaire religion, and Alexey tells Rusakov bluntly not to spend so much time thinking about God and to take bromide instead. Rusakov's political views are similarly extreme: he regards his companion poet, the Bolshevik Shpolyansky, as the precursor of the Antichrist, the Bolsheviks themselves as a horde of fallen angels, and Trotsky as Abaddon the destroyer. But this, the book indicates, is an incorrect view. Men shall simply be judged 'according to their works' (the second epigraph). Rusakov himself, after reading the passages from Revelation xx and xxi, finds peace as he reads xxi. 4: 'And God shall wipe away all tears from their eyes; and there shall be no more death, neither sorrow, nor crying, neither shall there be any more pain: for the former things are passed away' (pp. 295-6).

The key to the author's attitude towards religion is found in a prophetic dream of Alexey's (unfortunately omitted in the English translation). In it, Alexey sees Nay-Turs (before he has been killed) and one Sergeant Zhilin (killed in 1916), both now in paradise. Zhilin tells of how St Peter admitted all of his squadron to heaven, including the women who accompanied the men on their campaign – which causes Alexey to think of 'some woman's' black eyes. Zhilin tells too of Nay-Turs' later arrival there, accompanied by an unknown cadet whom he is unwilling to identify. In paradise he then saw a place prepared for the Bolsheviks who were to fall at Perekop in 1920; and asked God about this, as he had thought the Bolsheviks would be assigned to hell for their lack of belief. God's reply was that it did not matter, 'I am no warmer or no colder because of that' – all men are the same. In the final chapter it is again suggested that Bolsheviks will be welcomed into heaven: a sentry, momentarily falling asleep in the snow, sees Zhilin coming towards him.

In terms of the novel, the dream is prophetic in that Nay-Turs will indeed be killed, and Alexey will meet his woman with black eyes in Yulia. His request he has made to Zhilin, to 'join the heavenly brigade,' is almost granted: he will in fact die and be resurrected through his sister's prayers. Nikolka, we might note, will also descend symbolically to the underworld and return, in his mission to rescue Nay-Turs' body from the morgue: an explanation perhaps for the mysterious unknown cadet in the dream. (Yelena too *dreams* of Nikolka's death.) Paradise awaits us all when we are ready, we must conclude, and all will turn out for the best.

For Bulgakov (as for Tolstoy), the awareness of death and the afterworld gives meaning to life itself, and he constantly reminds us that this is not just a matter of current events. The permanency of places and objects is always being contrasted, often in an odd way, with transitory events: the statue of St Vladimir on its hill; that of Bogdan Khmelnitsky (the seventeenth-century hetman who united the Ukraine with Russia), which Petlyura's men are unable to desecrate; even an ordinary street-sign indicating a dentist's surgery. Mme Anjou's dressmaker's shop, now the headquarters of the Mortar Division, retains its lingering smell of perfume and delightful doorbell, which are incongruously out of place; a street, Malo-Provalnaya, acquires a mysterious significance for both Alexey and Nikolka. It is what is *behind* life that Bulgakov is interested in. His technique is one of alienation. In extraordinary circumstances the familiar becomes mysterious (in a way reminiscent of some of Gogol) and the reader can no longer make his usual assumptions about life. Characters seem to be strangely interrelated in an almost preordained fashion (Rusakov to Shpolyansky, to Yulia, to Alexey, for example). In that some of the minor characters are identified by description only ('the man in the mohair coat'), it is often left to the reader to make the connection with what has gone before: it only gradually dawns on us that Shpolyansky is a Bolshevik, that it is his mistress Yulia who rescues Alexey, or that the robbers of Vasilisa are men we have seen earlier on St Vladimir's Hill. As we realize this, we seem to be entering a world where all are part of one vast scheme and man's existence is governed by a kind of providence.

The novel is remarkably complex, partly because of this interplay of characters. There are many loose ends, which in the stage version are resolved: the fate of Shervinsky and Lariosik, for example. Yet in many ways the book is better because of these, it merges with real life where ends are not neatly tied. The budding love relationship between Alexey and Yulia, scarcely more than hinted at, is a masterpiece of understatement. As the critic K. Rudnitsky has pointed out, this is 'a book of impressions, not thoughts, an album of sketches from nature, not a finished picture – and here lies the secret of its charm.'[15]

Nevertheless, Bulgakov leaves us some memorable scenes in which he shows his sense of drama, notably in the two focal points, the school scene, where Malyshev is almost arrested by cadets angry at being told not to fight, and Petlyura's parade in Kiev. There are many others as vivid: the departure of Talberg, the pursuit of Nikolka and of Alexey, the hiding of their guns by Nikolka and Lariosik, the robbing of Vasilisa. Even such a minor event as the arrival of the comic Lariosik becomes a source of drama.

15 **461**, p. 129

Characteristic of the book's style is the mixture of this dramatic approach with picturesque, sometimes lyrical, description. Often this can be quite striking: one might think of the way the Germans in Kiev physically change in appearance after the emperor has been deposed – 'the color drained from every German officer, as the expensive material of their blue-gray uniforms was metamorphosed into drab sackcloth' (p. 71) – or of the facial expressions which are indicated by a comparison with the position of the hands on a clock – 'But at that hour the hands on Elena's face were showing the most depressed and hopeless time on the human clock-face – half past five ... Nikolka's face showed a jagged, wavering twenty to one ...' p. 184). Rarely, however, is a description allowed to go on too long without being brought down to the personal level, by interposed scraps of conversation: sometimes between Alexey and friends or members of his family, sometimes with no direct reference at all. This is particularly apparent in the parade scene, but also earlier, in Bulgakov's longish description of the events leading up to Petlyura's entry into Kiev (chapters four and five). The narrative is constantly punctuated by unknown people's conversation: '"No, he was an accountant." "No, a student,"' (of Petlyura); '"You can't mean it?" "I assure you he has"' (sprung from the Austrian army of Toropets). One 'omen' of events to come is described in a scene between the market girl and Vasilisa. Or Bulgakov simply writes in a conversational style of his own, without even indicating speakers: 'Wilhelm. Three Germans murdered yesterday. Oh God, the Germans are leaving – have you heard? The workers have arrested Trotsky in Moscow!! Some sons of bitches held up a train near Borodyanka and stripped it clean ... Petlyura. Petlyura. Petlyura. Peturra ...' (p. 74). It is not difficult in such writings to see the future dramatist.

The White Guard is a remarkable book. Varying between tragedy (death and personal loss) and hilarious comedy (in the characters of Vasilisa and Lariosik), combining personal stories with historical events, untidy, with loose ends and a multiplicity of characters, it is none the less a coherent, unified work of considerable power. Bulgakov may indeed not have understood events in a fully historical sense, but this is unimportant: as a description from the point of view of someone who lived through them it is an impressive achievement. Underlying it all is a belief in the importance of values, of the so-called higher things in life – and beyond. It is for this reason that the book deserves a valid place not only in Russian but in world literature, for although set clearly in a particular society at a particular time it relates fundamentally to the basic issue of permanent, moral values as opposed to the purely temporary, practical and political concerns of the moment. In an age of expediency and instant gratification of desires it is still as important to 'turn our eyes toward the stars.'

5

The playwright, 1925-26

The publication of *The White Guard* opened up for Bulgakov a new world which, if we are to believe what he says in *Theatrical Romance*, at first excited him, then quickly repelled him as he became aware of the pretentiousness of many literary circles. His novel had still only been published in part, and there seemed no likelihood that its conclusion would ever appear. But the two parts in *Rossiia* were read, and notably by the poet Pavel Antokolsky, who mentioned the novel to Boris Ilyich Vershilov, one of the producers of the Moscow Art Theatre.

The Art Theatre would come to play an enormous, and sometimes unfortunate, role in Bulgakov's career. Founded by Vladimir Ivanovich Nemirovich-Danchenko and Konstantin Sergeevich Stanislavsky in 1898, it had since its initial successes in the performance of Chekhov's plays become established as one of the most popular theatres in Moscow.[1] Its basic aim, from which it had never seriously departed, had been to introduce a new realism to the stage, in place of the stylized, declamatory manner of many theatres before the turn of the century, often still performing the Russian classics and translations of foreign plays – for the standard of contemporary plays of the time was at a low level. The Art Theatre had attempted to banish stage clichés and conventionalism in acting and provide instead a lifelike and unified performance, with greater emphasis on the role of the director and less on the individual 'star,' who was no longer to dominate the other parts. Audiences, long ready for a change in this direction, had welcomed Stanislavsky's innovations, which involved both the training of actors to 'live' their parts rather than recite them – the entire system which over the years was developed into his celebrated 'Method' – and a new realism in visual and scenic effects, which indeed had been the main attraction in many of the

1 For a detailed discussion of the theatrical background, see **485**.

theatre's early productions. Thus the Art Theatre had built up a reputation for its realistic performances of the Russian classics as well as of Chekhov and Gorky – and indeed in the first decade of the century it had taken over the artistic leadership of the country, remaining for many years the most innovative theatre. Stanislavsky, always anxious to find new ways, had encouraged experimentation, particularly in the theatre's separate studios, and the theatre itself had put on too a number of plays in the symbolist manner, with its productions of Leonid Andreev, Ibsen, Hauptmann, Maeterlinck, and Hamsun. But by 1914 it had essentially returned to productions where psychological realism – for which, after all, it had become best known – was the keynote, while Stanislavsky's pupils, Vsevolod Meyerhold and Yevgeny Vakhtangov in particular, developed their experimentation elsewhere.

Now, since the Revolution, the Art Theatre had been frequently accused (with many other of the 'academic' theatres) of being out of sympathy with Soviet reality, and after its return in 1924 from a two-year tour abroad (where unfortunately many of its members had stayed) it was forced to try to accommodate itself more to Soviet society. The result was that it desperately needed new, Soviet, plays: hence its interest in young writers of talent. Vershilov recommended *The White Guard* to the theatre's literary consultant, Pavel Markov. In the late summer of 1925 the theatre approached Bulgakov with the suggestion that he dramatize his novel for them. As it happened, he had already started turning the book into a play, and he gladly accepted the suggestion, beginning his life-long relationship with the Art Theatre. This first contact was thus quite fortuitous as far as he himself was concerned, but there is little doubt that he found this theatre most in accord with his own temperament. His own roots were in the realist tradition, and he had further come of age at a time when theatrical design was at its height in Russia: with the many painters of the 'World of Art' group who had spontaneously turned to set decoration as an art in itself, and with the brilliant décors of the Russian ballets of Diaghilev. Hardly surprising, then, that he attached great importance to visual and sound effects (he would perhaps emphasize these too much in some of his plays) and to the whole creation of atmosphere on stage. All this he found in the Art Theatre, which was associated above all with faithfulness to life; and, moreover, he must have been attracted to the theatre's insistence on authentic interpretation by the actor. What he could not realize at this time was that later, in some of his plays, he himself would come to stress atmosphere rather than character, and that the methods of the Art Theatre would by that time appear a shade too conservative.

For despite Bulgakov's own professed realistic tastes, he too – as had occurred in his prose writing – was clearly and inevitably influenced by the whole theatrical climate of the capital. He may have hated Meyerhold and his 'biomechanics,' but he could hardly ignore the fact that it was Meyerhold, both before and since the opening of his own theatre in 1923, who provided the whole sparkle and glitter of the age. Brilliant, dynamic spectacles followed one after the other: Mayakovsky's *Mystery-Bouffe*, Verhaeren's *The Dawns*, Crommelynck's *The Magnificent Cuckold*, Sukhovo-Kobylin's *Tarelkin's Death*, Ostrovsky's *The Forest*, Fayko's *The Teacher Bubus*, Erdman's *The Warrant*. Meyerhold saw the theatre above all as spectacle, with the actors demonstrating their roles as parts of a pattern – as in pantomime or the puppet show. Exaggerated, dynamic, full of movement, Meyerhold's productions also placed great reliance on 'constructivist' and totally unrealistic stage sets. Such a conception was not appreciated by Bulgakov, and no play of his would go to Meyerhold's theatre, which represented the extreme in avant-garde at this time. But Bulgakov's second and third plays would, significantly, go to other theatres where strict realism had been abandoned in favour of experimentation.

Less extreme than Meyerhold was Alexandr Tairov with his Kamerny Theatre. While he did not believe that the theatre should imitate life and was still concerned with each production as an aesthetic whole – building, too, 'constructions' and placing heavy emphasis on the role of music – he still stressed the individual actor and his special creativity. His recent productions had included Racine's *Phèdre*, Ostrovsky's *Storm*, and Chesterton's *The Man Who Was Thursday*. This theatre would indeed be suitable for Bulgakov at his most exotic and least realistic, in *The Crimson Island*.

On the other hand, Vakhtangov (who had died in 1922) had occupied a position somewhere between the avant-garde and the Art Theatre, insisting on the importance of both emotion in the actors and of special techniques. His theatre (the Third Studio, later the Vakhtangov Theatre) therefore valued the masterful actor and 'psychological' acting, while seeking too after sharp, expressive forms rather than necessarily real figures. Character interpretation was thus combined with expressionistic scenic devices – and this theatre too was most suitable for Bulgakov's second play, *Zoyka's Apartment*. Indeed, in that it allowed both for realism and for fantasy (its method has been referred to as 'fantastic realism'), for experimentation without the doctrinaire novelty of Meyerhold on the one hand or Stanislavsky's insistence on strict psychological realism on the other, this ought to have been Bulgakov's ideal theatre. (He did, in fact, offer it one other play, which was never performed, and was later invited to write his adaptation of *Don Quixote* for it.) This would perhaps be particularly true in the thirties, when the Art Theatre had become almost the established defender of traditional realism at a time when Bulgakov's plays were going beyond it – although it is true that in the thirties all theatres were restricted by a rigidly interpreted doctrine of socialist realism.

The different trends in the theatre reflected, of course, those in other literature, and again Bulgakov's position was essentially that of a realist with fantastic,
or at times expressionist, overtones. The tragedy of the Soviet theatre in the
twenties is that it indeed produced excellent directors and theatres, but no really
major playwright – nor has it done since. It did, however, produce a few fine
plays, including a number of Bulgakov's. For largely political reasons these would
not make the impact on Soviet theatre that they deserved (with the exception of
Days of the Turbins), but in retrospect we may see that here too Bulgakov deserves the highest place amongst his contemporaries, many of whom would be
reduced to writing political pot-boilers.

In a sense, then, Bulgakov started as a realist in the wrong age (for one who
was not of the 'proletarian' persuasion) and as a result problems with the Art
Theatre would be a major factor in the frustrations of his life. All this, however,
was unimportant for his first and most Chekhovian play which, with its greater
stress on individual characterization than some of his later ones, fitted in perfectly with the Art Theatre's customary manner of presentation. 'The White
Guard' was ready in September 1925. Vershilov took it to the theatre and I.Ya.
Sudakov, another producer, seized upon it immediately. Initial reaction was that
'the first talented play to depict the Revolution had been found.'[2] This was, in
fact, only the beginning of what turned out to be a long and difficult process,
and it was not until over a year later, in October 1926, that the play was performed, after innumerable changes had been made, many during the rehearsal
period. Nevertheless, the process was in many ways an enjoyable experience for
Bulgakov.

Markov, who became his lifelong friend, tells of how all those in the theatre
were struck by his elegance, his great charm and wit, his humour which at times
was penetrating enough to seem like sarcasm. Most outstanding to Markov was
Bulgakov's depth of observation, his penetration of other individuals' psychological makeup, and his 'greedy, inexhaustible interest' in life: 'In the bitterest
moments of life he never lost the gift of being surprised at it ...' The actors, delighted with the stories he could tell, welcomed him eagerly. From his school
days in Kiev he had nursed a passion for the theatre, and now he discovered he
had real talent, as writer, producer, even actor. Particularly outstanding was his
ability to act out the roles of his characters and to explain their lives off-stage as
well as on: 'He knew everything about each of the characters of *The Turbins*,
even if that man had only two or three lines.'[3] This had the most fortunate effect
on rehearsals and the whole spirit of the production.

2 **397**, p. 244
3 In **368**, p. 80. The account here is based on this article and similar descriptions in **3**,
   pp. 5-16.

Not that Bulgakov was always easy to get on with. He knew his heroes' lives so well that it was difficult to persuade him to make changes. Each line conveyed for him an exact meaning with relationship to a given character, and he was very sensitive to the 'rhythm of the sentence.' He could be upset by mistakes, or at times nervous, on edge. 'The drama,' Markov writes, 'was probably particularly close to him because it corresponded to his whole personality, always in a state of internal motion, never calm or dispassionate.'[4]

Later, he would become more disillusioned with the Art Theatre itself, while never losing his love for it – a process that is described satirically in *Theatrical Romance*. But at this stage, despite increasing frustrations, his relationship with it seems to have been reasonably happy. 'This is my world!' he exclaims early in his semi-autobiographical novel. And now, at last his financial problems seemed to be solved, even if he hardly became rich over night. We find a reference of Stanislavsky's to an advance made to Bulgakov of 1000 roubles on 15 July 1926, but later he would receive several hundred roubles a month in royalties.[5] One result, of course, was that he could give up writing feuilletons.

DAYS OF THE TURBINS

Genesis and development of the play
In *Theatrical Romance* Bulgakov tells of how the characters from *The White Guard* started to take on a life of their own, and of how he transformed the 'scenes' his mind conjured up into a play. But as it now stands, *Days of the Turbins* differs considerably from *The White Guard*. The one essential change is in the figure of Alexey, who is no longer a doctor only indirectly involved in events, but the colonel himself: in charge of the division defending the high school (taking over the original role of Colonel Malyshev) and dying there pointlessly (like Nay-Turs). Yelena and Nikolka remain largely as in the novel, but their young friend Karas has been replaced by the older, traditionalist Studzinsky. Shervinsky's role has been considerably expanded. Now aide to the hetman himself, he is more directly involved with historical events; he has assumed more of the character of the likeable liar, while his growing love affair with Yelena and eventual marriage proposal is one of the major issues in the play. Lariosik, who now arrives at the beginning of the action, is also a major character, touchingly comic, in the play unmarried, in love with Yelena and anxious to impress Myshlaevsky – who in turn becomes the main mouthpiece for the final acceptance of communism. Other characters have been omitted entirely: Vasilisa and Vanda, the Nay-Turs family, Yulia, Anyuta the maid, Rusakov, Shpolyansky and his group.

4 **370**, p. 228
5 **494**, p. 125, and **415**, p. 100

This transition, however, was by no means a simple one, and because of the political implications behind certain changes it is important to be clear as to what different versions existed. Bulgakov's original manuscript, written between June and September 1925 and still entitled 'The White Guard,' contained (according to one's way of counting) from twelve to sixteen scenes, was far too long, and essentially a simple dramatization of the book – although a few characters had been omitted. Alexey was still the doctor, who recovered at the end. His 'dream' was included in the form of a nightmare figure who discussed with him the fate of Russia and then showed him Bolbotun's troops approaching.[6] Malyshev and Nay-Turs were still there, and so were Vasilisa and Vanda. Shervinsky's character had already been expanded, however, as had his relationship with Yelena. And there was a new touch to Lariosik and Myshlaevsky, who developed a mutual liking for each other for all their difference in character. At the end, the characters sat and discussed what they were to do when the communists arrived. Despite its faults, according to Markov, 'in each scene there shone out [Bulgakov's] feeling for the theatre and in particular his feeling for the actor.'[7]

The Art Theatre sent a copy of the play for comment to the commissar for education, A.V. Lunacharsky, who in a letter dated 12 October 1925 to the vice-chairman of the theatre's board of directors, V.V. Luzhsky, criticized it severely – but on artistic, not political, grounds: 'I can find in it nothing which is inadmissible from a political point of view ... I consider Bulgakov a very gifted man, but this play of his is extremely untalented ... Not one average theatre would accept this play, precisely because of its dullness, arising probably from the complete lack of dramatic ability, or extreme inexperience, of the author.'[8] The theatre did not agree. A week previously Sudakov had already informed Bulgakov that Lunacharsky had no political objections to the play; the theatre had allotted parts, and rehearsals were to begin shortly, with Sudakov himself as producer rather than Vershilov.

In consultation with the theatre Bulgakov now began to make alterations and rewrite much of the play. Sudakov persuaded him to unite the roles of Alexey, Malyshev, and Nay-Turs, to make it shorter.[9] The dream was omitted at the insistence of Stanislavsky. Other characters were strengthened, notably Lariosik (now appearing in the first act) and Myshlaevsky, probably after Yanshin and Dobronravov had been allotted these roles.

6 187, folios 1-4; see also 291, pp. 317-18; 448, pp. 467-8; and 451
7 370, p. 226; see also on the various versions of the play, 359; 3, pp. 463-80; 438, pp. 38-65
8 188, folio 2487; also published with Sudakov's letter to Bulgakov in 448, p. 456
9 496, p. 38

For a number of changes were made in the theatre too. Originally, the older and more experienced actors had been cast,[10] but soon it became evident that the play was more suited to the younger ones, who were allowed to have their way, despite the misgivings of Stanislavsky and many others. It was a fortunate decision, and in years to come the play would be referred to as the 'new *Seagull*,' creating the reputations for these young actors – most of whom were between twenty-five and twenty-seven – in the same way as had Chekhov's play for an earlier generation. As early as 7 January 1926 preparations for putting on the play were announced in the newspaper *Vecherniaia Moskva*, and the rewritten play was read with a new complement of actors on 29 January.[11] The major work began on 24 February, the same day that a copy was sent to *Glavrepertkom*, the Main Repertory Committee under *Narkompros*, which was responsible for censorship of theatrical performances.

There were still many changes to be made, however, as rehearsals progressed. The version the theatre now had – the second, still entitled 'The White Guard' – differed considerably from that which was finally performed. For one, the scenes with Vasilisa and Vanda remained: they would go later when the play was still found to be too long (apparently, too, the actors who were to play them were rather weak). More important, whereas in the final version only Studzinsky is openly hostile to the communists, in this version this was not the case, and the last act in particular was far more pessimistic, the tone one of general resignation. Here, the Bolsheviks have not yet arrived, and those present sit down to discuss the situation and what they are going to do. Nikolka (not Studzinsky as in the final version) says that the Bolsheviks have put an end to Russia (p. 115) – adding later 'we had a Russia – a great power!' (p. 116).[12] Between these two sentences is a speech by Myshlaevsky, who shows a distinctly negative attitude towards the Bolsheviks as such. He talks of a card-table, which remains the same whatever is done with it: 'The time will come and it will return to its normal position, for it's not its nature to stand upside down.' So Russia too would

10 Originally: Alexey – Leonidov, Nikolka – Livanov, Lariosik – Zavadsky and then Verbitsky, hetman – Kachalov, Vasilisa – Tarkhanov. The final casting was Alexey – N. Khmelyov, Nikolka – I. Kudryavtsev, Yelena – V. Sokolova, Talberg – V. Verbitsky, Myshlaevsky – B. Dobronravov, Shervinksky – M. Prudkin, Studzinsky – Ye. Kaluzhsky, Lariosik – M. Yanshin, hetman – V. Yershov. The set designer was the talented N. Ulyanov.

11 **188**, folio 46. The following account is based on this and the variant of the play in folio 361. Changes have been marked on this in pencil to make it conform with the final version, folio 210. The 1966 version, which left out the hetman and Bolbotun scenes, is folio 1266. A translation into English, by William Blumberg, of the intermediate version also exists in **187**, folio 4. See also **270**

12 Page references to **3** are given in the text.

return to its former position, and the 'white guard,' 'crossed off the lists,' would no longer try to interfere, he says gloomily. There is then an interruption as Yelena's husband Talberg reappears, intending, in this version, to work with the Soviets; Vasilisa and Vanda also join the others. The end of the act emphasizes the mood of pessimism, as they start to play cards. 'I'll sit with you, Lena, forty days and forty nights, until everything ... gets back to normal,' Myshlaevsky says, 'after which I'll join the ration board.' Nikolka sings his cadets' song and Myshlaevsky makes his final speech: 'But no, for some this is a prologue, but for me – an epilogue. Comrade spectators, it is the end of the white guard. Non-party member junior Captain Myshlaevsky leaves the stage. I've been left holding the spades.' The ending is Chekhovian in spirit, with the stress on acceptance of the inevitable rather than joy for the future.

The preliminary work on the play went quickly and on 26 March it was shown to Stanislavsky in the foyer of the theatre. Markov recalls the anxiety with which the actors and author awaited Stanislavsky's decision, and the latter's demonstrative viewing of it: laughing out loud, crying, wiping his eyes. The protocols of the rehearsals note his general satisfaction, and from that time on he took an active interest, although he personally rehearsed only a few individual scenes – which for him was unusual. But the text still gave problems, not least to the theatre's own repertory committee. Bulgakov was asked to cut a scene showing Petlyura's men killing a Jew, and refused, stating that it was an integral part of the play. He also refused to change it to a three-act play, or give it the title 'Before the End.'[13]

On 25 June, Markov, Sudakov, and Luzhsky met with representatives of *Glavrepertkom*, who were unhappy with the play after seeing it in dress rehearsal.[14] V. Blyum, who would become a bitter critic of Bulgakov, accused it of being an apology for the 'white guard' movement; A. Orlinsky presented a detailed list of changes he would like to see made and which were, in theory, accepted by the theatre. The result of this was a conference on 24 August between Bulgakov, Stanislavsky, Markov, Sudakov, and Luzhsky, who together 'worked on the entire plan of the play, and established all the insertions and changes in the text.' The essential ones now made by Bulgakov for the final act were ready by 7 September. Myshlaevsky was made the positive character, and all negative aspects of him and the others were shifted onto Studzinsky. (In view of Trotsky's disgrace, too, 'the Bolsheviks' had to be substituted for all mentions of his name.) In its final version the play's ending is optimistic. Talberg, now wanting to take Yelena to join the Whites, is shown out. All celebrate, and outside the window they hear

13 **448**, p. 450; also quoted from the Art Theatre archives in **407**, II, p. 124
14 See **448**, pp. 460-1, for details

the 'Internationale' as the Red Army approaches. 'Gentlemen,' Nikolka says, 'this evening is a great prologue to a new historical play.' Studzinsky (not Myshlaevsky) replies: 'For some a prologue, but for some - an epilogue' (p. 122). It was presumably only now that the title was changed from 'The White Guard' to 'The Turbin Family,' with Bulgakov objecting, but eventually giving way - Stanislavsky used the new title on 12 September.[15] Sometime in the next few weeks this finally became *Days of the Turbins*.

Political debates and performance
The performance of *Days of the Turbins* was arguably the biggest theatrical event of the decade, and the debates over it reflect the intense struggle then being waged between art and politics. These events are consequently important not only for an understanding of Bulgakov's subsequent treatment but for the whole future course of Soviet literary policies. With the first full dress rehearsal in front of members of the public (17 September), doubts began to appear about the question of the play's acceptability as a whole. F. Mikhalsky, director of the Art Theatre's museum, recalls that 'The auditorium was divided into two camps - the play's defenders and its violent enemies. In the intervals heated arguments broke out, whistles were heard from the upper circles.'[16] After the rehearsal, at a meeting with the theatre producers, *Glavrepertkom* decided the play could not be performed as it stood, and the granting of permission for it was left undecided. The actors, who did not consider the play to be in any way counter-revolutionary, were dismayed. Various last-minute changes were made. To increase the propaganda element the 'Internationale,' which was to get louder and then die away again as the Red Army band passed by, was now to swell to a crescendo. On 23 September, prior to another dress rehearsal in front of representatives of the government, the press, and *Glavrepertkom*, the protocols note: 'At today's performance it will be decided whether the play passes or not.' The rehearsal began at 8:15 p.m. and went on until 12:32: finally, Lunacharsky, the most important of those present, expressed his opinion that the play would be passed. (An interesting sidelight is that at one of the dress rehearsals Meyerhold actually helped Stanislavsky by rehearsing the *audience* with him: where all the important people were to sit on opening night. Meyerhold, who continued to look up to Stanislavsky, better understood this kind of off-stage management.[17])

15 **494**, p. 143
16 **376**, p. 170
17 Information supplied to the author by K.L. Rudnitsky, an expert on the theatre and on Meyerhold in particular.

This, however, was only the beginning. Four days later, on 27 September, a discussion on the 'Theatrical Prospects of the Season' was held in the House of the Press on the Nikitinsky Boulevard. A. Orlinsky of *Glavrepertkom*, who was to become another of Bulgakov's bitterest critics, took the occasion to denounce *Days of the Turbins* on ideological grounds, claiming in particular that in the play there was not one representative of the working class.[18] On 2 October there was another public rehearsal in front of members of *Glavrepertkom*, and the same evening a further public discussion, on the theme 'The Theatrical Policies of Soviet Power,' took place in the Communist Academy. Once again, Orlinsky showed his bitter opposition to the play, but Lunacharsky, while criticizing it severely, stubbornly maintained that it was not harmful and should be performed. Bulgakov's enemy, Mayakovsky, who was against a policy of prohibition, agreed, thinking it was better the theatre should be seen for what it was.[19]

It was in fact the Commissariat of Enlightenment (*Narkompros*) under Lunacharsky, rather than *Glavrepertkom*, which finally decided the issue, maintaining that it was now too late to ban the play. Later Lunacharsky would complain that Orlinsky and Blyum had passed it initially and then 'when the theatre had already spent many thousands on it, and the actors had got to know their parts' they had tried to take it off, despite claims that they had used their influence with Bulgakov to make it more or less acceptable.[20]

And so, *Days of the Turbins* opened by default, on 5 October 1926 – with the theatre so nervous about the violence of the critics that Bulgakov himself was not invited to attend.[21] The young members of the theatre certainly justified themselves, as even the play's harshest critics agreed. Aware of playing people who, from the point of view of the new society, were enemies, they showed sympathy and understanding. Khmelyov, as Alexey, was interested in the 'downfall and inner collapse of that not numerous part of the "white" intelligentsia which believed in its cause.'[22] His performance was of a man who had gradually come to realize that all that he believed in was doomed, and was tense yet grimly assured in his own actions as a result. 'I cannot look at his eyes,' one critic was reported as saying angrily, 'I cry for him! Over whom! Over an enemy! He's a colonel after all! He's my enemy! But I cry over him.'[23] Dobronravov as Myshlaevsky was particularly successful in showing the plain, good-natured army offi-

18 **334** and **382**, p. 150
19 See **363** and **229**
20 **358**, VII, p. 511
21 **359**, p. 195
22 **327**, p. 382. For more on the actors, see **370**, pp. 144, 158; **254**; **275**; **308**; **344**; **397**; **438**, pp. 56-65; **496**.
23 **497**, p. 378

cer who becomes the communist sympathizer and, as time went on, the ending with his 'conversion' became more his scene. Yanshin, in the part of Lariosik which made his career, stressed the lyrical rather than the comic aspects of the character, actually against the wishes of Stanislavsky, who had tried to change this at dress-rehearsal stage and, faced with Yanshin's firmness, for once in his life had climbed down.[24]

The reactions of the audience were indicative of the arguments that would go on for several years. To some, the sympathetic portrayal of a White family was unthinkable, an outrage, but many of those present belonged to the same intellectual class as the Turbins and saw the play as a justification of at least their motives. According to one report, the audience stood up when the tsarist national anthem was sung. 'Feeling ran so high in the audience on opening night,' another account reads, 'that it required the intervention of the militia. Some shouted: "Nonsense! Counter-revolutionaries!" and others, "Thanks for the truth!" The women were hysterical; there were tears in the eyes of the men.'[25]

Lunacharsky had already made his position clear in an article that same day for the evening edition of the *Krasnaia gazeta* (reprinted three days later in *Izvestiia*). Bulgakov at least showed the inevitability of his heroes accepting communism, but the play lacked social background, and his attempt to show the sincerity of communism's enemies and to write an apologia of the White movement was unacceptable. None the less, the performance of such plays, which showed the position of those who would like to 'change the landmarks,' should be welcomed.[26] In the same issue appeared a letter from forty members of the Young Communist League (*Komsomol*), reprinted from that day's *Komsomol'skaia pravda*, protesting that the play placed a romantic halo around the whole of the 'white guard.'[27]

Other critical reaction was more violent. Orlinsky denounced the play in *Pravda* on 8 October and, four days later, in the theatrical magazine *Novyi zritel'*, where he coined the word 'Bulgakovism' (*Bulgakovshchina*). His colleague, V. Blyum, joined in with two very vituperative articles in the weekly journal listing theatre programmes. Other critics, who would make a career by criticizing Bulgakov, wrote similar articles. The play's heroes were 'so wretched, insignificant, elementary, colourless, and petty, their words and actions so vulgar, pallid, and boring, their souls and flabby characters so bare, that the question cries out: for whom and for what purpose is Bulgakov's play about them necessary'; this was

24 **516**
25 **415**, pp. 55-6
26 **358**, III, pp. 323-31
27 **452**

not a play but an 'irritating trifle,' an operetta, a melodrama, a middle-class vaudeville.[28] It was not only the critics who protested. The poet and playwright A. Bezymensky wrote an open letter to the theatre, complaining that it had insulted him by extolling his class enemy. Workers' groups wrote to the press demanding that the theatre answer the criticisms. The evening *Krasnaia gazeta* ran an enquiry amongst members of the public. The dramatist Lidia Seyfullina defended Bulgakov and attacked his critics at a discussion in the Polytechnic Museum on 25 October, but few present agreed with her.[29]

To judge from the press, everyone hated the play. But rather, the reverse was the case and it became the one great event of the theatrical season. N. Gorchakov has succeeded in recreating something of the whole atmosphere surrounding the play:

There was a long line of Muscovites at the ticket window in the evenings. That part of Russian society whom the Bolsheviks had termed 'former people' made their pilgrimage to the Moscow Art Theater. These were people who had lost relatives in the Civil War and in the Terror ... Such individuals hoped that this production heralded a peace between the Soviet regime and its enemies and an end to the terror of new repressive measures. They filled the auditorium of the Theater, eager to recognize with love and sadness the sufferings of individuals whom they held dear. Very often, after the scene with the White soldiers in the secondary school, some people in the audience would grow hysterical; the women would bewail their sons and husbands and some fainted, and the ushers would carry them out to the snow in the theater courtyard.

These were not playgoers but palmers, and their pilgrimage was to see a stirring miracle in a land of terror and 'class hatred' ... One could make a pilgrimage to this presentation, for it was filled with the miracle of Christian forgiveness; it called for extending one's hand to the defeated enemy of yesterday.[30]

It was precisely this view that was unacceptable. In another article in *Izvestiia*, Lunacharsky emphasized that the production was still an attempt to morally rehabilitate the Whites. There was another attack by Beskin.[31] And, in the meanwhile, the première on 28 October at the Vakhtangov Studio of Bulgakov's second play, *Zoyka's Apartment*, had only made matters worse.

28 **411, 412, 225, 226, 347**
29 **222, 333, 252, 417**
30 **288**, pp. 186-7
31 **358**, III, pp. 337-8; **220**

At the end of the year, on 22 December, a rather different première at the Maly Theatre attracted public attention: that of K.A. Trenyov's *Lyubov Yarovaya*, a play about a woman's break with her 'white guard' husband to become a communist. Lunacharsky suggested in *Izvestiia* nine days later that the play was to some extent an answer to *Days of the Turbins*.[32] Such a comparison was bound to be repeated, and in articles and discussions the plays became frequently linked (although their whole mood and approach was completely different). On 7 February 1927 an open discussion on the two plays was held in the Meyerhold Theatre where, unusually, Bulgakov himself was present. It seems to have been one of those occasions memorable enough to impress witnesses differently, for there is some disagreement among the most important accounts over whether Bulgakov spoke at length or said only a few words.[33] At all events, he was by that time infuriated with Orlinsky. Lunacharsky had begun by stating his position that while *Days of the Turbins* had many faults each person had his own road to communism (as Lenin had said): but artistically *Lyubov Yarovaya* was a better play. Then, Orlinsky had made his usual attack. The author of *Days of the Turbins* had shown a panicky fear of putting the masses – workers and peasants – on stage; there were not even any personal orderlies or servants. The characters were shown psychologically but not socially, although this had not been true of the book: Bulgakov, working for the Art Theatre, had adapted his social outlook accordingly. The name of the play had been changed in panic by the author.

Bulgakov then came up to the stage and, according to the *Pravda* report, told Orlinsky that every time he spoke out he said something that was not so. First, it was not the author who changed the name of the play, but the theatre, over his objections. Then there was the matter of the orderlies, which in reality had been unobtainable in Kiev at that time – and, in any case, to please Orlinsky he would have to have shown them ill-treated by Alexey. As for the servants, in a play where he had had to cut so much, there was just no room for them. The director had tried to persuade him to put one in, until finally, 'brought to boiling point, I wrote the sentence: "But where's Anyuta?" – "Anyuta's gone to the country." There you are, and I want to say that's no joke. I have a copy of the play with that sentence about a servant in it. I personally consider it of historical importance.'

There can be no doubt that Party members were seriously disturbed by the performance of plays such as *Days of the Turbins* and *Zoyka's Apartment*, which

32 **358**, III, pp. 344-6
33 See, in particular, **382**, pp. 150-1; **266**, pp. 81-2; **253**, **355**, **501**. For the minutes of this meeting, see **429**.

followed it, since these clearly invited audiences to question historical events and attitudes and were indeed a threat to Party authority. At a Party conference with the Agitation and Propaganda Department (*Agitprop*) of the Central Committee, held in May 1927 to consider the development of the theatre, both plays were discussed. Amongst those present were Lunacharsky and Bulgakov's critics Orlinsky, Litovsky, and Averbakh. Much of the discussion centred around whether the plays should have been allowed at all, with Lunacharsky still maintaining that *Days of the Turbins*, at least, had not been harmful. Orlinsky claimed some success for criticism in that the tsarist national anthem, which had originally been sung pathetically, was later sung with everyone drunk, 'discrediting' it; he also pointed out that the Art Theatre was afraid of younger spectators, who tried to stage protests against the play, and therefore it had stopped the sale of reduced-rate tickets.[34]

In fact, the theatre itself was doing very nicely in terms of box-office takings. The success of *Days of the Turbins* had been assured: some loved it, some hated it, but everyone wanted to see it. However, the play was not approved for the theatre's summer tour to Leningrad and there were doubts about the coming season – permission for it was not confirmed by *Narkompros* until 11 October. This was noted by Blyum, who congratulated Soviet power on the rehabilitation of the White officer-class and middle-class romanticism, and maliciously pointed out that the theatre's box-office takings had fallen off so much in the two months when the play was not performed that restaging it was a financial necessity.[35] (This was indeed so: Nemirovich-Danchenko's secretary, O.S. Bokshanskaya, notes in a letter to L.B. Bertenson that the restaging of the play which had 'fed' them the previous year would save the theatre from a serious financial situation.)

Criticisms continued, and as the play's second season ended it was decided to withdraw it as soon as there could be a new production at the Art Theatre.[36] By the beginning of 1929, with violent attacks too on his other plays, *Zoyka's Apartment* and *The Crimson Island*, not to mention his prose works, Bulgakov generally appeared to be the enemy of Soviet society. One critic even maintained that he had carried out a systematic five-year plan in literature, that of an 'internal émigré.'[37] When in March 1929 V. Ivanov's *Blockade* opened at the Art Theatre, *Days of the Turbins* was immediately banned, and *The Crimson Island*

34 See **455**, pp. 165, 365, 135, 432. Lunacharsky's final speech is given on pp. 227-44 and also published in **358**, VII, pp. 508-18.
35 See **340**, pp. 10-11, 14; **448**, p. 457; **470**; **421**, p. 87. Bokshanskaya's letter is in **187**, folio 77.
36 **398**
37 **401**, p. 51

at the Kamerny Theatre as well (*Zoyka's Apartment* having already been with-drawn).

Days of the Turbins, however, had already become known abroad, in basi-cally its second version with a few amendments: including the Vasilisa and Vanda scenes, with Talberg intending to join the Soviets, and with the less posi-tive ending.[38] It was performed in 1927 in Riga at the Theatre of Russian Drama and, in German translation, in 1928 in Berlin and Breslau. Later, the Prague Group of the Moscow Art Theatre performed the play, taking it to London, where it was a great success at the Kingsway Theatre. (One reviewer at least seems not to have realized that it differed from the Russian stage version, and concluded that Soviet censorship could not be so rigorous after all if the play had been performed in Russia.[39]) It was also shown successfully in Narva (1933) and in Warsaw.

And in the Soviet Union, too, *Days of the Turbins* was destined to continue on stage for many years. One person who did not seem to object to it was Josef Stalin – indeed the theatre records his attending fifteen performances. In a letter dated 2 February 1929 to the playwright Bill-Belotserkovsky deploring the lack of really Soviet plays, he pointed out that, on the whole, *Days of the Turbins* left with the spectator an impression favourable to the Bolsheviks: 'If even such people as the Turbins are compelled to lay down their arms and submit to the will of the people because they realise that their cause is definitely lost, then the Bolsheviks must be invincible and there is nothing to be done about it.'[40] The play was restaged in Moscow on 18 February 1932, apparently at his personal re-quest. (The details of this will be related in a later chapter.) The reception was tremendous: for months all the newspaper announcements for it – religiously collected by Bulgakov for the album he kept – stated 'All tickets sold.'[41] Various notable people are recorded as going to see the play; letters of thanks from dif-ferent groups appeared in the press. It was taken to Leningrad, where it enjoyed its 400th performance. Lunacharsky wrote a somewhat more favourable article in *Izvestiia*. Another critic, while pointing out the play's faults from a commu-nist viewpoint, wrote that Bulgakov 'sooner or later will turn ... to depicting the process of socialist construction.'[42] In 1935 the Art Theatre took *Days of the Turbins* to New York. It remained in the repertory until 15 June 1941, when the sets were destroyed in an air raid in Minsk, after a total of 987 performances.

38 See **20**. A copy of this rare edition is in the New York Public Library.
39 **360**, p. 714
40 **493**, p. 343
41 **187**, folio 77
42 **358**, III, pp. 473-85; **385**

In 1954, with recent criticism admitting that former judgements had been too harsh and that the Art Theatre had done a great deal of work with Bulgakov to 'overcome the incorrect tendencies' of *The White Guard*, a new production appeared at the Stanislavsky Theatre, with Yanshin in overall charge of the production and S.I. Tumanov as director. The following year, *Days of the Turbins* was published in Russia for the first time, and also performed at the Griboedov Theatre in Tbilisi with L. Varpakhovsky as producer. Two years after that it was performed in Novosibirsk.

By this time there had also been a number of performances of the play in English, the earliest being by the Yale University Dramatic Association (6-8 March 1934). In London it was performed at the Phoenix Theatre in 1938, when it received excellent reviews: 'I don't know of a play in London which is better written, better acted, or better produced.'[43] In 1960 it was produced on BBC television with Marius Goring as Alexey, and also on radio. In Czechoslovakia there was a production too, in 1964.

By the time of the première of the new Moscow Art Theatre production (also by Varpakhovsky) in December 1967, there were few even in the Soviet Union who any longer questioned the play's quality. Arguments centred around the performance rather than the contents, and there were inevitable comparisons with the past. Some months after its opening, the newspaper *Literaturnaia Rossiia* wrote enthusiastically: 'Let there be more of [Bulgakov premières], let our stage give life to an inimitable phenomenon in which there are hidden invaluable possibilities – the theatre of Bulgakov.'[44] The play remains in the repertory today, and there was a special celebration in 1976 marking the fiftieth anniversary of its première.

Today, the violent attacks on Bulgakov at the end of the twenties have been almost universally repudiated – although *Zoyka's Apartment* and *The Crimson Island* have never been published or restaged. The reasons for the attacks are various: the closeness of the time to the period of the civil war, the fact that the Art Theatre was considered very much the favourite of the bourgeoisie and far removed from the proletariat, the opposition of those more interested in the experimental theatre (Futurists, *Proletcult*, etc. – now referred to as 'formalists') who disliked the realistic methods of the Art Theatre. But undoubtedly the major criticism came from those who were associated with the Russian Association of Proletarian Writers, zealously promoting the social and communist purpose of literature. Bulgakov's critic Averbakh was one of the founder members of the RAPP, so was Lelevich, who maintained that literature should organize the

43 277
44 285; see also **463**, pp. 229-46; **190**; **365**; **465**; **314**, VI, pp. 183-4

consciousness of readers to one end.[45] Their views seem exaggerated today, and even by the end of the twenties it was necessary to keep them in check (RAPP was dissolved in 1932), but their influence was considerable. Since the sixties, the play has received the more serious criticism it deserves.

The play itself

One difficulty we must face in considering *Days of the Turbins* is the question of its different versions and the not infrequently expressed view that it was spoilt because of political considerations. In that many of the changes asked for by the Art Theatre were undoubtedly made to facilitate the play's being passed by the censor, and as a result the author's original idea was modified, we are certainly entitled to ask whether the play was not falsified and its impact weakened. We should, however, remember that as far as we know Bulgakov himself made the changes, often fairly subtle ones: achieving a difference of emphasis by a slight shift in roles, with many of the actual speeches remaining the same. Moreover, he had been changing the play in co-operation with the theatre (which was equally concerned with the technical matters of production) since it was first accepted for performance. The original version had been too long, too much an adaptation of the book, and quite unplayable: in this respect the author and his play had benefited from co-operation and it is rather pointless to complain that some passages are not as he originally wrote them. The real question is whether any of the earlier versions are artistically better than the final one.

This, I think, is not the case. We may perhaps regret the exclusion of the entertaining Vasilisa and Vanda scenes, but because of the length of the play they had to go anyway: Yanshin has further suggested that they would have unduly exaggerated the comic side of the work. As for the earlier ending, with the characters gloomily accepting the inevitable, this would seem, in 1926, too reminiscent of Chekhov and dramatically weak. The more positive tone, combined with a correspondingly greater emphasis throughout on the heroes' realization of the hopelessness of their position, makes for a stronger, yet not unnatural, conclusion. Furthermore, Myshlaevsky, the plain soldier and critic of the White generals, goes down rather more naturally as a new, rather naïve, communist sympathizer than as a monarchist nobly bearing his disillusionment, whereas the other characters who accept communism – Alexey having been killed – are reasonably apolitical anyway. In one respect only is the ending cheapened somewhat (at least in the current Soviet production): by the 'Internationale' increasing in volume as the actors turn to face the audience in a salute to the new society. One needs simply recall that in the first production this was a last-minute change and

45 See **478**, pp. 15, 23

that the original text called for the 'Internationale' to die away again as the military band passed by.

It is, of course, pointless to compare the play with the novel in terms of quality, for they are different works, but one cannot avoid some comparison for the sake of avoiding repetition. Of the main themes we found in the book, a number – the clash of peoples, the people themselves, religion and the meaning of life – have virtually disappeared; inevitably, because of the limitations of the stage. In the play, the central theme is that of the family itself and the opposition between the old order and communism, with the immediacy of the struggle with Petlyura as the essential historical background. The views of the family and their friends have changed little from the book, although the family drama has been strengthened by the inclusion of the romantic attachment of both Shervinsky and Lariosik to Yelena. All still believe in their culture and values and are sentimentally attached to Russia's past, of which the monarchy is the enduring symbol: the singing of the tsarist national anthem is one of the climactic points in the first act. As in the book, they show an undisguised contempt for the general staff and for Yelena's husband Talberg in his hasty escape. Their own nobility and courage is contrasted with the behaviour of the hetman himself, whom we see in the second act giving way with only the slightest hesitation to a German invitation to flee the country. Even Shervinsky, who has previously defended him, concludes that the hetman is an 'indescribable bandit.'

There is a nice balance between the historical and personal elements of the play. A few scenes relate either to one or to the other, but in the majority the family life of the Turbins is inextricably bound up with the contemporary events. The family tragedy, the death of Alexey and (in the play) the crippling of Nikolka, is the outcome entirely of historical circumstances; so too are Yelena's fortunes (that is, her husband's departure), the arrival of Lariosik, even the dinner in the first act before Alexey's regiment goes into action. The result is a striking conflict of mood, in that the drama of events alternates with comedy in the ordinary day-to-day relationships which, as in *The White Guard*, are preserved despite even greater hardships. Thus the play is correctly seen by most Soviet commentators as a tragi-comedy. Alexey, the one major tragic figure, and the more extreme Studzinsky are counterbalanced by the three comic characters of Shervinsky, Myshlaevsky, and Lariosik, with Nikolka and Yelena lying somewhere in between. The play never leans too far in either direction: Alexey will remind the others of the seriousness of the situation and later be mourned by them, while they will remind us that ordinary life has still to go on.

The strength of the play undoubtedly lies in the characters, a particularly happy combination of memorable and sharply distinguished types. No one individual is really central, not even Alexey, who because of his position and greater seriousness stands somewhat apart from the others. Very much the officer aware

of his responsibility, he is the only one with a real sense of history and understanding of events. Appropriately, it is he who in Act I explains to the audience
the historical situation – after refusing to drink to the hetman, whom he attacks
bitterly for not understanding it and not uniting the Ukraine against the Bolsheviks. It is he who expresses what is now, in the play, the major theme: 'In Russia, gentlemen, there are two forces: the Bolsheviks and us. We'll meet yet. I see
more threatening times. I see ... Well, never mind! We won't hold Petlyura back.
But then he won't come for long. But after him the Bolsheviks will come ...
Either we will bury them, or, more likely, they us. I drink to the meeting, gentlemen!' (pp. 48-9).

In many ways Alexey symbolizes the honourable side of the whole 'white
guard' movement, as becomes evident in the school scene (Act III), the climax
of the play both dramatically and psychologically. From the beginning, this
essentially tragic occasion has farcical overtones as close on the heels of the
cadets assembling prior to battle there appears the caretaker Maxim complaining
of the destruction of the school benches for firewood. Alexey appears, knowing
already that the situation is hopeless, that the cause has been betrayed by its
leaders. The drama already inherent in the book becomes the central point of
the play as the cadets try to arrest him for abandoning the struggle, and his
anguish explodes in the question 'Whom do you wish to defend?' Knowing further struggle is useless – on the Don as in Kiev – he takes upon himself not only
the responsibility in the given situation, but the historical responsibility too: 'I
am taking everything on my own conscience and responsibility, taking everything, I'm warning you, and, loving you, I'm sending you home. I have finished'
(p. 89). As the cadets depart, Maxim reappears, a kind of farcical parody of
Alexey himself, equally unconcerned for his own life and trying pointlessly to
save school property for a past director who will never return. As Myshlaevsky
and Nikolka in turn plead with Alexey to leave, he seems all the more determined to die – and is killed by a chance shot, becoming the rather pointless
martyr of a bygone age.

For the family, of course, his death is purely a matter of personal tragedy – to
his sister Yelena especially. Yelena herself is not an outstanding character, but
rather, with her red hair and simple charm, the centre around which the others
revolve, particularly her little group of admirers. 'She's pure gold!' Lariosik exclaims, to which Nikolka replies realistically, 'She's a red-head, Larion, a red-
head. A real misfortune!' (pp. 111-12). Nikolka, with his cadet songs and simple
enthusiasm, basically supports his brother Alexey in his views, but is far less
seriously inclined.

Indeed, for many of the characters politics is a secondary consideration, to be
taken into account principally when their own lives are affected. Thus the others
find it much easier to joke about events than Alexey. The three essentially comic

characters, Myshlaevsky, Shervinsky, and Lariosik, are a delightful mixture of differing types. Myshlaevsky with his love of vodka, his paternal affection for Yelena, and his lack of understanding of intellectual concepts, is something of the comic-uncle figure, yet honest and basically serious. In Lariosik he admires the other's naïve eloquence, his writing poetry, his timid enthusiasm; as Lariosik admires Myshlaevsky's apparent strength and manliness. Lariosik is almost the star role in the play, with his clumsiness, pathetic and touching love for Yelena, his desire to please. He has been compared with Chekhov's Yepikhodov ('twenty-two misfortunes'), but this is misleading for despite his awkwardness and constant getting into trouble he is by no means ridiculous, but rather a well-meaning and lovable person. He may come out with inappropriate comments and, after a little alcohol, become embarrassingly frank, but his essential good intentions shine through all his ineptitudes. Both Lariosik and Myshlaevsky are incapable of deceit, but the other character, Shervinsky, thrives on it. Boaster and extrovert, he is the first of a long line of likeable rogues in Bulgakov's plays, good-hearted but unconcerned for abstract conceptions of honesty. (Lunacharsky had a low opinion of him, holding that he did not fit into the Turbin family.) But despite his self-interest he is not without feelings of decency, which are very evident if one compares him with the far more contemptible Talberg.

It is the combination of these characters, the witty dialogue, and the mixture of comedy and melodrama that makes the play successful. Bulgakov also shows a superb sense of timing. Thus in the first act Yelena is anxiously expecting her husband Talberg, but the tension is heightened as first Myshlaevsky and then Lariosik arrive instead. In the final act, there is a reversal of the situation, with Talberg arriving just when he is *not* expected, at the very moment when the others are celebrating Yelena's engagement to Shervinsky (although here perhaps Talberg's appearance seems too artificial to be really convincing). During the dinner scene, a well-timed entrance is used as an ironic comment: Shervinsky, telling of the unexpected appearance of the allegedly murdered tsar at the German court, says 'the curtains parted and our sovereign came out' – whereupon Lariosik enters the room. Later Lariosik, drunk, falls asleep, coming to as Yelena and Shervinsky embrace, and saying 'Don't kiss – or I'll be sick': a hilarious conclusion to the first act.

Bulgakov shows his liking for irony elsewhere as well. A good example is in the first scene of the second act, where Shervinsky arrives on duty at the hetman's palace and is shocked to find that the other adjutant has abandoned his post (the telephone), making off in civilian clothes. Within a short time the hetman has gone too, in German uniform. Then Shervinsky himself follows suit in exactly the same manner as the other aide, so that it is the lackey Fyodor who answers the final telephone call.

Sound and other stage effects all have their importance in creating a particular mood: a clock playing a Boccherini minuet, suggesting the life of the family in more normal times; electric lights that go out, a rumble of guns in the background or the salute of guns at the end, immediately producing an atmosphere of unease; Yelena playing one chord repeatedly on the piano to signify her grief at Talberg's departure. Even the comical ringing of a stuck bell as Lariosik arrives adds to the tension until we know the cause. Music too is used to heighten the action – Shervinsky exulting in his success with Yelena with his own magnificent voice – or as an ironical comment in the songs that occur throughout, with words which are incongruously in conflict with actual events: after Alexey talks of meeting with the Bolsheviks, Lariosik sings that a thirst for meetings and everything on earth is useless; the cadets marching into the school to fight sing a love song.

Such devices may remind us of some of Chekhov's techniques, and indeed *Days of the Turbins* has often been compared with Chekhov's plays.[46] There are, of course, certain resemblances. Much of the atmosphere of the decline of one society and helplessness in the face of the future remains, although this is clearly more applicable to the second version, which was rehearsed but not performed. The play is also in the realist tradition of Chekhov, with people coming and going, eating, giving all the appearances of leading distinctly ordinary lives despite outside events. But *Days of the Turbins* is far more of a play of direct action than are Chekhov's plays, where the main drama is within the characters themselves. The characters in *Days of the Turbins* play an essential part in historical events, the outcome of which provides most of the action, whereas Chekhov's characters are largely incapable of looking beyond their own particular circumstances. This is the result, of course, of a difference in time, for by 1918 the urgent pressures of political events, of causes and conflicting forces, had replaced the general hesitation at the turn of the century to do anything at all.

Bulgakov was certainly aware of certain similarities of his work with Chekhov's, and indeed he deliberately parodies the earlier writer through Lariosik, who arrives with a collection of Chekhov wrapped in a shirt. Lariosik's last speech of the play repeats the final words of Sonya in *Uncle Vanya*, 'We will rest, we will rest.' But this remains a parody, and the play does not end here; instead there is a salute of guns, followed by the 'Internationale' as the Bolsheviks approach. *Days of the Turbins*, in its final version, represents an advance on Chekhov, and belongs to the new, revolutionary age.

For many years Bulgakov's reputation rested on this play alone, and its fame in the Soviet Union was based partly on its *succès de scandale*: as important as

46 See, in particular, **196** and **199**

the play itself are the arguments it created, its popular reception, and the hope it gave for pursuing a more liberal line towards those who had formerly opposed the Bolsheviks; also the new spirit it created in the Moscow Art Theatre. It is a part of Soviet theatrical history, a fact which overshadows simple considerations of quality. As a play in the realist tradition illustrating, without oversimplification, the problems that had to be faced in an age of transition, it hardly has an equal in the Soviet Union of those years. Indeed, most important, it is superbly representative of its age, and in this sense we must say it is a great play. Regrettably it was also virtually the last in which the positive qualities of the 'white guard' would be so honestly upheld.

6

Success and criticism, 1926-28

Life for Bulgakov at the time of *Days of the Turbins* was nothing if not exciting. Suddenly he found himself a literary celebrity, and for a change he was not short of money. Indeed, he is reported as saying that he did not know what to do with it and as hesitating over whether to buy a carpet for his study: was a writer really entitled to one, and would it not lead to difficulties with his tax inspector?[1] After moving to Obukhov Lane, Bulgakov and his wife had moved twice again, first to No 4, Maly Lyovshensky Lane and then to a larger apartment, No 6, at 35a Bolshaya Pirogovskaya Street. They had managed to travel a little, too: in 1925 they had been in the Crimea together with the poet M. Voloshin (as a result of which a number of feuilletons were published in the evening *Krasnaia gazeta*), and also in Tbilisi. But now they planned a trip abroad, to Paris. They got as far as obtaining French visas before they learned that their Russian exit visas had been refused.

Bulgakov's literary attitudes had not escaped the notice of the police. On the day of the dress rehearsal of *Days of the Turbins* he was interrogated by them, and some months earlier his flat had been searched. Some diaries were taken, which were later returned, and also the manuscript of 'Heart of a Dog,' which was not. Later the police, remarkably, would leave Bulgakov alone: references to searches of his flat in the thirties are incorrect. But the impression left on him by this one occasion was strong enough for him to decide not to keep a diary in future – he destroyed those for the years 1921 to 1926, except for a few pages – and instead he started sending 'autobiographical' letters to his friend Pavel Sergeevich Popov, possibly with an eye to their publication at a later date. (After Bulgakov's death, Popov made use of them to write a biography which, however,

1   **382**, pp. 151-2

has never been published.[2]) His precautions were sensible, for Stalin was by now gradually eliminating all opposition to his personal rule (his 'enemies,' Trotsky and Kamenev, were in October 1926 expelled from the Politburo) and virtually any intellectual might be considered a potential enemy, let alone a non-conforming one.

But if Bulgakov was suspect to the more orthodox communists (and to some of the more socialist-minded writers too: Gladkov complained to Gorky that Bulgakov made too much show of his 'culture'[3]), he none the less enjoyed considerable success with the general public. 'M. Bulgakov has become one of the most popular prose writers precisely because of his scepticism,' we read in one article.[4] Some people wondered whether his popularity had not gone to his head, for it was about this time that he took to wearing a monocle, which was interpreted as a sign of arrogance, particularly by his former comrades in *Gudok* – who immediately put up a photograph of him wearing it on the board 'Sobs and Sighs.' One day Bulgakov came into the office, saw it, and burst out laughing – but he stopped wearing it from then on.[5] According to his wife, the whole thing was just a joke.

Still, he had some cause to be proud of his success. In *Theatrical Romance* his narrator's name (Maxudov) appears on a poster alongside those of Aeschylus, Sophocles, Lope de Vega, Shakespeare, Schiller, and Ostrovsky. On the posters advertising *Days of the Turbins*, Bulgakov's name was indeed in similarly illustrious company. One reviewer, commenting on this, wrote somewhat sarcastically: 'Bulgakov after all is the hope of the Russian theatre; there is no theatre which would not prepare to put on his play. From the Art Theatre to the Kamerny by way of the Third Studio lies the triumphal road of this playwright. Theatres which have not received his plays feel punished like children without a dessert.'[6] But for all of this, it was still to the Moscow Art Theatre, where he acquired the jocular title 'knight of art,' that Bulgakov would become most devotedly attached.

One again wonders perhaps why the Art Theatre should have suited him so well, when some of his plays might have benefited from a freer, more modern style and a less rigid interpreter than Stanislavsky. By ten years after the première of *Days of the Turbins* Bulgakov was himself disillusioned with the theatre

2 In 187, folio 556. The foregoing is based on a conversation with K.L. Rudnitsky and on 379, pp. 151-2, 162.
3 293, p. 30
4 442
5 261, pp. 75-6
6 242, p. 8. *Zoyka's Apartment* was being produced at the Third Studio (renamed the Vakhtangov Theatre that year); *The Crimson Island* was destined for the Kamerny.

- realizing, perhaps too late, that a strictly realistic approach was not entirely appropriate to plays whose focus was not character as much as a hyperbolic expression of theme. And he did, of course, try the other theatres: *Zoyka's Apartment*, his next play, would certainly have failed at the Art Theatre. But the experimental theatre as such remained not to his taste. He had even poked fun at Meyerhold in 'The Fatal Eggs,' writing that he 'died, as everyone knows, in 1927, during the staging of Pushkin's *Boris Godunov* when a platform full of naked boyars collapsed on him ...': a sentence that Meyerhold would often recall with some irritation.[7] Yet, although their relations were not amicable (partly because of the mutual dislike of Bulgakov and Mayakovsky), Meyerhold did take some interest in Bulgakov - hardly surprising perhaps, since he was at that time desperate for new plays. In 1927 he wrote to him inviting him to give a play to his theatre, and was disappointed when he learnt that none was available. Sometime later he actually took Bulgakov to visit his theatre, but nothing ever came of it.[8] Whether, of course, Bulgakov could have reconciled himself to working with Meyerhold, whose conception of the theatre minimized the importance of both author and individual actors, is most unlikely.

ZOYKA'S APARTMENT

At the same time as Bulgakov had been working on *Days of the Turbins*, he had also been writing his second play. In 1925 producer A.D. Popov and actor V.V. Kuza from Vakhtangov's Third Studio had visited him in his house on Obukhov Lane, with the suggestion that he should write a comedy for the theatre. Some time after this Bulgakov read in the evening edition of the paper *Krasnaia gazeta* of how the police had discovered a gambling den disguised as a dressmaker's workshop in the apartment of a certain Zoya Buyalskaya.[9] In *Theatrical Romance* he again indicates how *Zoyka's Apartment* developed in his imagination. As he later told his (third) wife, it was written down in five days.[10]

The play was to have been ready for the 1925-26 season (before the première of *Days of the Turbins*), but the theatre was hesitant, there were probably a number of changes, and a fresh start was made for the beginning of the next season.[11] The action takes place in the twenties, during the NEP. Zoya Denisovna Pelts (Zoyka), with her lover Obolyaninov, maid Manyushka, and cousin Ametistov, open a 'sewing-shop and school,' in reality a brothel. They are supported by

7 8, p. 86, and 517, p. 460
8 I am indebted to K.L. Rudnitsky for this information. See also 380, p. 425
9 From an unpublished letter of L.Ye. Belozerskaya to the journal *Teatr*, 1971
10 9, p. 97
11 529, p. 165

the corrupt commercial director of a metals trust, Goose, until he discovers that the girl he loves, Alla, is working as one of the 'models.' Also involved are two Chinamen, Gandzalin (nicknamed 'Gasoline') and Cherubim, so called because of his deceptively angelic appearance. Cherubim finally murders Goose for his money and escapes with Manyushka, his mistress. Ametistov makes off too, but Zoyka and Obolyaninov are arrested.

Alexey Popov's immediate problem as producer was just how the play should be interpreted – for he soon discovered it was a little more than the satire on life under the NEP he had expected: 'it turned out that there was no real satire, no power of revelation, no clarity of ideas in the play. Rather, it was a lyrical-criminal comedy.'[12] His solution was to dwell on the grotesque side of the play, with sets by S. Isakov that drew on the techniques of the German expressionists. In a press interview two days before the opening, nervous after the reaction to *Days of the Turbins*, he tried to present the play as a kind of exposé. '*Adventurism, sordidness* and *depravity*: that is the fare of *Zoyka's Apartment*.'[13]

The play opened on 28 October 1926 to a delighted audience, although a number of critics claimed that this was largely because it consisted of the bourgeoisie and nepmen who wanted to mock at everything Soviet. But theatrically, too, the play was an undoubted success, not least because of the fine acting. M. Knebel in his memoirs recalls the brilliance of Ts. Mansurova as Zoyka and R. Simonov as Ametistov, and the atmosphere created by Isakov's sets.[14] (A nice satirical touch, too, was that Goose was made up to look like Lunacharsky.) It is worth quoting in full Knebel's description of the orgy in the last act – including a mysterious 'dead body' as one of the guests – before the murder and arrest.

Huge, exaggerated bows decorated the walls of the 'workshop,' mannequins and luxurious fabrics created the impression of 'business' on a European footing. Then this 'working apartment' changed its appearance and rhythm – there began the night demonstration of living models. I remember how against the background of the furious activity of Zoya and Ametistov, the mysterious appearances and disappearances of ladies and their partners, there came the entrance of the 'dead body,' called Ivan Vasilievich. The 'dead body' was played by B. Shchukin. Looking round dejectedly, he went over to the Chinaman Cherubim, busy with the clandestine sale of cocaine, and invited him to a waltz. It was not just a matter of the gay humour of the performance, but of the note of true drama

12 **439**, p. 118; see also **406**, II, p. 316
13 **534**; see also **371**, p. 155, and **528**
14 See **329**, pp. 425-6, for this and the following. The other roles were: Cherubim – Goryunov, Gandzalin – Tolchanov, Alliluya – Zakhava, Goose – Glazunov, Obolyaninov – Kozlovsky, Manyushka – Popova, Alla – Orochko.

that the producer Popov and the actor Shchukin found in that humour. The dance of the eternally sad 'dead body' with the mannequin, Shchukin's tears in the moment when he understood that his arm was embracing not a woman but a torso on a wooden support: this was a moment of real tragi-comedy. 'Get away from me,' Shchukin said, turning to the male and female 'consolers,' and walked away. And despite the fact that this was no more than the 'dead body' of some Ivan Vasilievich, it seemed that in it there lived something real, human.

The play was sufficiently popular for it to be performed almost immediately in Kiev, Sverdlovsk, and Baku as well; attempts were made to stage it at the Leningrad Bolshoy Dramatic Theatre, in Rostov-on-Don, Saratov, and Tbilisi. In 1928 it was performed at the Theatre of Russian Drama in Riga,[15] and in 1929 it was translated into German and published in Berlin.

Nevertheless, the critics' reactions were by now predictable. Most praised the acting and the work the theatre had done, but considered the play little more than pornography. Litovsky, writing under the name of Uriel, said it was a 'talentless, wearisome trifle.'[16] Bulgakov's enemy Orlinsky attacked him bitterly in *Pravda*. The author wanted to resurrect the old régime, he said, for which all the characters in *Zoyka's Apartment* were nostalgic; he was a right-wing conservative in literature: 'The play is more than pitiful in its lack of talent and depth.'[17] Another critic pointed out that Bulgakov tried to bypass Soviet power and the Communist party, but that the people could put up with such a play after *Days of the Turbins* – and suggested, quite absurdly, that the row about *Days* had forced the theatre 'to undertake a heroic struggle with the author and give the comedy the comparatively inoffensive form in which it is now being played.'[18] In an article the following year devoted to Bulgakov, the notorious Zh. (Yakov) Elsberg neatly summed up the critics' main quarrel with him. He had two tendencies: 'of reducing what was important to a farce, and making farce important. This corresponds to the "ideology" of the philistine, for whom the fate of his own petty "I" is important and unshakable but the Revolution is a stupid, senseless, and transient farce.'[19]

In the Party conference of 1927 on the theatre – much of which was devoted to *Days of the Turbins* – *Zoyka's Apartment* was also mentioned, and again we

15 **170**, pp. x, xvii, and **354**, p. 245
16 **506** – reprinted in **356**, pp. 228-30; see also **527** and **386**
17 **413**
18 **228**. The critic suggests that this was the reason for delaying the play by a year – although the fact that *Days of the Turbins* opened a mere three weeks before *Zoyka's Apartment* makes this clearly impossible.
19 **260**, p. 47

find evidence of the confusion that prevailed amongst the censors. This time Lunacharsky had from the beginning been against allowing the play, but others, including Orlinsky, had not been positive enough, despite Lunacharsky's warnings that they would again burn their fingers. The play nevertheless managed to survive for all of two seasons and part of a third – two hundred performances – before it was taken off early in 1929.[20]

It is indeed surprising that, with its obvious uncommunist subject, *Zoyka's Apartment* should have been performed at all. But it was not the only play of its type in Moscow. Under the NEP period such circumstances as those shown in the play did indeed exist, and had been portrayed in other works.[21] But *Zoyka's Apartment* had no positive heroes, and furthermore, according to Knebel, some of the actors tended to idealize the essentially negative roles – Goose and Alla in particular. Some of the villains were quite likeable: from a communist viewpoint, this was indeed an immoral play. More important, of course, Bulgakov's whole position was judged to be that of a writer spiritually bound to the old order, an 'internal émigré.' *Zoyka's Apartment*, with its heroes who all want to escape abroad, whether they were idealized or not, could only confirm this opinion. Since its ban, the play has never again been performed, or published, in the Soviet Union (despite the fact that it was announced for publication in 1968 in the journal *Baikal*[22]).

Zoyka's Apartment was also performed in Belgrade (badly, Bulgakov thought), and in the mid-thirties there came the possibility of a performance in Paris: by August 1934 Bulgakov was writing to its French translator, Marie Reinhardt. He now made corrections to his hastily written earlier manuscript, polishing it but also toning it down – hoping vainly for another production in the Soviet Union. (A few changes were also made in the names of minor characters: in particular, Alliluya, chairman of the house committee, became Portupeya – probably because the first name was too close to that of Stalin's wife.) Some problems arose too because of textual changes made in the French version, and Bulgakov felt obliged to ask his brother Nikolay, living in Paris, to see there should be no 'distortions or fabrications of an anti-Soviet character and, consequently, completely unacceptable and disagreeable to me as a citizen of the USSR.' (He later wrote again, to protest about Goose being labelled a Jew, contrary to his intentions.)[23] *L'Appartement de Zoïka*, in an adaptation by Marie Reinhardt and Benjamin Crémieux, opened at the Théâtre du Vieux-Colombier in Paris on 9 Febru-

20 **455**, pp. 232-3, and **379**, p. 151
21 See on this **170**, pp. x-xix; **450**; and **9**, pp. 97-103
22 **306**, p. 342
23 **352**, p. 137

ary 1937. It was reasonably successful but with at least one critic commenting on the corrections made 'to take into account the sensibilities of those sympathetic to the Soviet Union!'[24]

Criticism of the play in recent years has tended to be brief and less harsh, although *Zoyka's Apartment* is still regarded as a weak work, as might be expected for a play which has not been accepted despite the rehabilitation of its author. Typical are the views of A.O. Boguslavsky, who finds it neither a satire nor a tragi-farce, but rather a mixture of a vaudeville review, complete with 'strip-shows and eccentric dances,' and the tradition of the bourgeois detective story.[25] The most detailed discussion of it has been given by K.L. Rudnitsky, but he too finds it has many faults.[26]

As with *Days of the Turbins*, we have first in any discussion of *Zoyka's Apartment* to deal with the relative merit of texts.[27] Bulgakov's own 'final version' of 1935 is clearly superior from the point of view of deletions made for the sake of removing over-lengthy and rather pointless dialogue. But at the same time one cannot help regretting many of the changes made in it to improve the play's acceptability. A great deal of the satire has disappeared, particularly that which is more risqué both politically and sexually. A number of speeches have not only been shortened but weakened, their impact lessened, and some of the detail useful in any interpretation of the play removed. Thus the final version is tidier but less forceful, leaving the impression of something not quite complete. As a result, the play loses in clarity: here, whatever one's suspicions, one is not really certain whether Zoyka's workshop is a brothel or simply a clandestine nightclub. The role of the 'dead body' in particular has been reduced so much that it loses all purpose, and much of the point of the final act is obscured.

The original version is more explicit in every way. In a scene where various dresses are demonstrated for Goose, there is a picture of a naked woman, which he admires and wants to buy. As the demonstration proceeds he asks for more revealing dresses to be shown and ends up with one model sitting on his knee and kissing him. In the final act, with the orgy and the 'dead body,' there is more drinking and singing and an auction for a kiss from one of the girls – with the purchaser, a homosexual, becoming disappointed because he thought he had been bidding for a boy. There are more references to cocaine and other drugs, to the bribing of the house committee chairman Alliluya, and to the extent of

24 **353**, p. 142
25 **466**, p. 263
26 **502**, p. 734, and **395**, p. 33. For a detailed discussion, see **461**, pp. 133-5.
27 See, for the final text, **4**. The earlier version is published, incomplete, in **171**; issue number and page references to this version appear in the text. A type copy of the 1926 version also exists in the Leningrad Public Library, and it has appeared in German as **173**.

Goose's corruption. There are more specific allusions to political figures or attitudes: a picture of Karl Marx, Ametistov's making money by selling pictures of 'our Party leaders,' and mentions of Kalinin. There is a great deal more emphasis on the past, largely in the nostalgia of Zoya and Obolyaninov; more of the characters talk about going abroad, the delights of Paris, and the ways of getting visas or taking money over the border. And finally the ending is more tragic, with Zoyka taking farewell of her apartment as opposed to the farcical conclusion to the 1935 version. All in all, then, one must prefer the earlier version – from which it is always possible to remove excess verbiage in any theatrical presentation. Our discussion will be based principally on the 1926 text.

The general theme of the relationship to the new Soviet order of people spiritually tied to the old is common to all four of Bulgakov's plays written at the end of the twenties. In *The Crimson Island* the treatment is pure burlesque. In *Days of the Turbins* we see those of the old order who come to accept communism and live under it; in *Flight* those who emigrate and long for their native land; in *Zoyka's Apartment* those who remain, and long to emigrate. In *Days* and *Flight* the heroes act honourably in accordance with their ideas. But in *Zoyka's Apartment* the characters cling only to the externals of aristocracy, while any nobility of character has long since disappeared: in the whole play there is not a single person who is in any way admirable.

All the major characters, Zoyka, Obolyaninov, Ametistov, Alla, Cherubim, long to go abroad, to Paris or Shanghai. The theme of escape is hammered home time and time again by two songs, lines of which occur as leitmotifs throughout: 'They remind me of another life and a distant shore' (from Pushkin's 'Don't sing to me, my beauty') and 'we will leave the place where we have suffered so.' Paris for these people is like the symbol of Moscow for the characters of Chekhov's *Three Sisters*: remote yet eternally desirable, the place where the splendour of their lives will be restored. 'No one will know how Alla worked as a model ...' Zoyka says when she tries to seduce her into joining the enterprise. 'In the spring you will see the Grands Boulevards! In the sky above Paris in spring there is a lilac sheen, just like this ...' (no 97, p. 84) and she shows her a lilac-coloured dress. Alla's longing for Paris is then shown symbolically as she seizes avidly on the lilac dress when Zoyka offers her one. Yet the triteness of these characters' conception of the foreign capital is epitomized in Goose's remark that the club's manager Ametistov has brought Paris to the Moscow apartment (no 98, p. 74): the city is not real, but an ideal of which they themselves have little realization except for this outer glitter which they try to imitate.

For Zoyka and Obolyaninov we can perhaps feel some sympathy in their desire to get away. Obolyaninov, an aristocrat, cannot reconcile himself to the loss of his title, Zoyka to her new position and the fact that she has holes in her stockings, whereas formerly she never even wore a pair more than once (no 97, p. 62). If Zoyka is the more practical of the two, it is Obolyaninov who, in his longing for an irretrievable past, is the more eloquent spokesman for the old order. Through him Bulgakov satirizes the Soviet tendency to judge everyone in terms of his 'former' position. After being called a 'former count,' he sees on display a 'former chicken,' changed by Soviet power; he concludes that 'former tigers' will become elephants, probably, and that he himself is no longer 'Pavlik' but only 'former Pavlik' (no 97, pp. 69-70) – as though his entire personality has disintegrated. Yet such moments, when we sympathize with his lack of compre-hension of the new and hostile world, are comparatively rare: more often we find Obolyaninov pathetic with his absurd aristocratic pride, his contempt for everyone in Moscow, and his constant repetition of the refrain about another land. He is indeed a 'former' person in the sense that he is not interested in life or in other people but only in the way he has been insulted – but like Turge-nev's Pavel Petrovich he prefers to think of this more in terms of an attack on some abstract and aristocratic principles. Thus he takes refuge in the dreams in-duced by drugs: at least no less real than his memories of the past.

This, however, is but one side of the play, for the aristocrats become allied with petty crooks, who have quite different motives – and all become more deeply involved in crime as the play progresses. Goose, Alliluya, and Manyushka are just concerned with making money, wherever they are; Ametistov, crook and opportunist, wants to go abroad not to retrieve his past but because it is some-where else he can try his fortunes, possibly with less likelihood of being arrested. In his letter to Marie Reinhardt, Bulgakov describes him as unprincipled, bold, decisive, and impudent – but extraordinarily attractive; dreaming of the rich life and of opening a gambling house; telling lies in a magnificent, talented, theatrical manner and showing off with phrases in French which he pronounced mon-strously. With his pretence in front of Alliluya of being a Bolshevik (who has left the Party because it had lost its purity of line!) or of being an aristocrat in front of Obolyaninov; with his sense of style as manager of Zoyka's enterprise and yet his easy familiarity towards everyone – he is the major source of comedy in the play. Not only is he one of a line of such types in Bulgakov's work, he has also been described, by at least two Soviet critics,[28] as the forerunner of Ilf and Pet-rov's scoundrel Ostap Bender.

Also comic characters are the corrupt and officious house committee chair-man (who takes his origin from Vasily Ivanovich of 'A Lake of Home-brew' and will also become a stock character in Bulgakov), and, on the surface at least, the

28 **461**, p. 134, and **354**, p. 245. Bulgakov's letter to Marie Reinhardt is quoted from the latter, pp. 245-6.

two Chinamen with their absurd and stereotyped speech. As the American scholar Ellendea Proffer has pointed out, there is almost something Molièrian about the play (although the didactic tone of Molière is lacking): people eavesdropping and hiding in cupboards, a pretty maid confidante, and a hypocrite such as Alliluya.[29] Some of the characters' names add to the amusement too: Goose (appropriate), Cherubim (ironical), Alliluya (or Portupeya – meaning 'sword-belt'), Ametistov (meaning amethyst), Gasoline.

In all of this there is a great deal of fairly obvious satire on life at the time of the NEP. The opening of the play, with its shouts of 'We buy primuses!' 'We sharpen knives and scissors!' and 'We solder samovars!' is reminiscent of that better-known satire on the period, Mayakovsky's *Bedbug*. It is a society where money and pleasure have become all important. 'A man who earns 2000 roubles a month cannot be vulgar,' Ametistov tells Obolyaninov. '... Who plays the piano? You, but Goose dances' (no 98, pp. 56-7). Bribes, drug-taking, sexual indulgence encouraged by such wicked Western inventions as the foxtrot are a natural result of this. As Rudnitsky has expressed it: 'Bulgakov too soberly and too truly appraised the might of the victors to see the nepmen as a new and real historical power ... In the nepmen he saw only the scum of history.'[30]

Apart from the NEP, however, there is also some satire on communist institutions and living conditions: 'Under Soviet power bedrooms aren't allowed ... The house committee is an unslumbering eye ... You see, I have a briefcase. This means I'm an official person, immune. I can go in anywhere': all this Alliluya tells Manyushka, and then tries to kiss her (no 97, pp. 58-9). 'In the USSR fleeing is not allowed,' a fat policeman says near the end. 'Everyone must be in his right place' (no 98, p. 86). And Ametistov (of course) shows downright disrespect towards the authorities, particularly when he talks about selling pictures of the leaders: 'if it were not for them I'd have died of hunger ... I sold them for twenty kopecks each! ... Comrade, buy a leader!' (no 97, p. 94).

Yet if *Zoyka's Apartment* is ostensibly a comedy, it has also elements of pathos and a plot which is more closely akin to the melodrama: providing for some difficulties of interpretation. The Soviet labels of 'tragi-farce' or 'satiric melodrama' are still perhaps the best descriptions of its genre, and we might like to add to these a further suggestion that it is a black comedy ahead of its time.[31] For something suddenly seems to go wrong for those involved in the enterprise. Zoyka, Obolyaninov, Ametistov, Manyushka, all basically harmless enough, become entangled in real evil, with which they cannot cope. As amateurs, they suc-

29 **450**, p. 284
30 **461**, p. 134
31 See fn 21 above

ceed in entering the criminal world and then find they cannot keep it within the bounds of their own, admittedly somewhat broad, sense of morality. 'This was not in the programme!' Ametistov exclaims when he finds that Goose has been murdered (no 98, p. 83). Now they have become the victims of the sinister Cherubim, although they have only themselves to blame. Cherubim is the real villain of the play, and it is the tatooed dragon on his chest, making him 'terrible and strange,' that represents his character, rather than his angelic appearance which deceives everyone. He is, of course, a ruthless and less naïve version of the coolie in 'A Chinese Story,' written shortly before *Zoyka's Apartment*: his real name is virtually the same (Sen-Dzhin-Po rather than Sen-Zin-Po) and like his prototype he has an angelic smile and kills unhesitatingly for the sake of reward – here for the money and the girl Manyushka. Cherubim is dangerous not so much because of his fiery temper, but because of the cold-blooded purposefulness that lies behind it, evident in Act III when, interrupted in a fight with Gasoline, his rival for Manyushka's affections, he locks him in a wardrobe to stab him later (only to find him gone). Thus his later stabbing of Goose is unexpected only because the spectator, like the characters in the play, has failed to see Cherubim as really evil and has been seduced by the apparent comedy in front of him. But the murder is just a part of the evil with which these people are now involved, although it is a fitting culmination to the scenes of drunken revelry and despair which precede it. The couples dancing, an opium smoker, the auction of a kiss, create an atmosphere not of happy abandon but of weary futility: debauchery is shown to be sordid, not funny. Hence the main reason for treating this play not as a simple comedy, where the final act would be out of place, but as a grotesque and sinister farce, a kind of twentieth-century morality play.

The tone for much of this final act is set by the mysterious 'dead body' who, unable to find a woman to dance with, first mistakes Cherubim and then a mannequin for one, and then is offended at everyone and everything, despite the efforts of his friend Robber and the others to cheer him up. He has a sobering effect upon all of them: he alone welcomes Goose's argument with Alla and the final arrests as a diversion from the boredom of the evening's entertainment. The extraordinary thing about this 'dead body' is that he behaves exactly like a living person and is accepted by the others as such (he is referred to as Ivan Vasilievich) so that, were it not for the name used for him in the list of characters and directions, there would be no reason for considering him anything but another guest. It is difficult to know exactly what Bulgakov meant by giving him this name, although his overall role in the act is clear. He seems to have a certain relation with Ametistov, whom he recognizes as someone from Voronezh (no 98, p. 71): Ametistov too has been in the dead body's home town of Rostov-on-Don, and has as one of his pseudonyms Vasily Ivanovich, the dead body's name and patronymic reversed. In that Ametistov is supposed to have been shot for his crimes in Baku, one might perhaps interpret the dead body as his ghost or double: lugubrious and unfortunate (appropriate for a dead man) as Ametistov is gay and successful – and introducing into the play the idea of final retribution for one's crimes. Other possibilities are that he foreshadows the murder of Goose or that the others in the apartment are hardly alive either, so that they quite naturally treat the dead body as one of themselves. (This would seem to be confirmed by a sentence from the stage direction which opens the act in the 1935 version: '*The mannequins stand smiling, one cannot make out if they are alive or dead.*')

The whole final act, in fact, is nothing but a grim nightmare. But this too has been foreshadowed by earlier scenes, notably the steamy Chinese laundry and opium den in the first act and the evening demonstration of dresses for Goose. There is a steady progression, the slow descent of the characters into hell, where they are forever condemned to their futile existence. (We might contrast them with the Turbins in *The White Guard*, who after the Last Judgement of the Revolution embark upon a new life.) The foxtrot in the last act takes on a 'hellish character' and one of the guests says that in it there is 'something infernal'; later the dead body refers to the 'devilish boredom' at the party (no 98, pp. 69, 70, 86). The play has opened with a flaming sunset, an aria from *Faust*, and a reference, in the later version, to a 'hellish concert.'

In their own closed world the characters are cut off from life outside and instead live in a bustle of mournful and senseless activity. It is the atmosphere of darkness and smoke from the Chinese lamps, both in the laundry and in the apartment, that gives the play its particular quality. In it, there move people with the incongruous names of Alliluya and Cherubim. Zoyka herself, significantly, is referred to on several occasions as either the devil or as someone in league with him. We might note that her apartment is set on Sadovaya Street, presumably the Pigit House again, where Bulgakov had actually lived: here too Bulgakov would later locate the apartment occupied by the devil in *The Master and Margarita*. The suggestion that Zoyka in her machinations can be compared with Woland, and the final act with Satan's Ball in that novel, is a valid one, provided we do not take the parallel too far.[32] (Bulgakov's early novel about the devil, that would eventually develop into *The Master and Margarita*, was written not long after *Zoyka's Apartment*.)

There is, of course, no real character study in the play, nor indeed is there a central character with whom the spectator can identify. The people before us might excite our pity, but hardly our sympathy. But, as elsewhere in Bulgakov,

32 See fn 21 above

the strength of the play lies not in its characters but in its atmosphere, and thus Popov's decision to exaggerate the grotesque and treat the characters satirically would seem reasonable. The text provides many opportunities for such a treatment: stage settings based on an expressionist technique (as were those of Isakov), scenes which dissolve into each other in an almost dreamlike way, and altogether a strident tone are clearly appropriate. The use of music is particularly striking in this play. The two song leitmotifs noted earlier, except as repeated by Obolyaninov, are sung by a mysterious voice off-stage, as a direct commentary on the action (often after a reference to going abroad). Another song 'It was evening, the stars were shining' is used to announce the arrival of Ametistov, who then hums it to himself when he has discovered Goose's murdered body and knows that he must leave. The final act is full of raucous drunken singing to the accompaniment of Ametistov on the guitar and the foxtrots played by Obolyaninov on the piano.

Everything in *Zoyka's Apartment* is mysterious, not what it seems on the surface. One of the registered inhabitants of the apartment does not exist, he is a 'mythical being' (no 97, p. 60). A workshop is really a brothel, a laundry an opium den. Strangers from the police seem menacing and oddly inept: on stage they were made to look like bandits. We are back to the whole question of what life is beyond mere appearances, back to the world of Gogol with scenes that are familiar yet unfamiliar. *Zoyka's Apartment* is not the best but perhaps one of the most interesting of Bulgakov's plays, and unique amongst his 'comedies' as the only one which makes a nightmare out of everyday Moscow life, rather than involving past or future. This particular atmosphere will be repeated, more effectively, in the play *Flight*, where the scenes themselves are labelled 'dreams.' Less successful in terms of plot and character interest, *Zoyka's Apartment* none the less approaches *Flight* in its technique and style, representing a certain turning away from the realistic approach of *Days of the Turbins*. Regrettably, however, this was only temporary; for Bulgakov, after the twenties – with the limitations of working as a paid employee of the Moscow Art Theatre – was hardly in a position to continue such experimentation.

THE CRIMSON ISLAND

On 25 March 1927 the editor A.N. Tikhonov wrote to Gorky that Bulgakov was trying to have his play *The Crimson Island* performed, but without results.[33] This play would in fact open only twenty-one months later – and would close again almost immediately – during which time Bulgakov wrote another play, *Flight*, and worked on it in the Art Theatre.

33 **195**, p. 164, and **40**, p. 30

The origin of *The Crimson Island* goes back to 1924, when Bulgakov had published in *Nakanune* a feuilleton with the same title, and subtitled 'A novel by
Comrade Jules Verne translated from the French into Aesopian by Mikhail A.
Bulgakov.'[34] On a desert island an aristocracy of white 'arabs' (*arapy*) is overthrown by the oppressed red 'ethiopians' (*efiopy*) after the king, Sizi-Buzi, has
been killed by a volcanic eruption. A 'double-dyed' arab, Kiri-Kuki, rules for a
time but is then thrown out and joins his European friends under Lord Glenarvan, who was exploiting the island. Their attempts to reconquer it, however, fail
because of a plague that has broken out there.

It does not need much perception to see that this is a lighthearted burlesque
on the Revolution (the volcanic 'eruption') and the civil war, with Sizi-Buzi
representing Nicolas ii, the white arabs the aristocracy, the double-dyed ones the
liberals, the ethiopians the proletariat, the plague communism, and so on.[35] It is
simple and witty, with a number of humorous touches, such as the absurd telegrams about the situation which 'astound the world,' the stereotype figures of
the capitalists, and the ludicrous disguises of well-known figures. Kiri-Kuki
(Kerensky), for example, is described as a drunkard and loafer who, sitting on
his barrel, sways first right, then left. The parody on Jules Verne's works, with a
number of his heroes included among the Europeans, adds to the fun.

The play based on the story is more complicated. Bulgakov takes the same
subject matter, expands it, and makes of it a play within a play, entitled *The
Crimson Island. The dress rehearsal of a play by Citizen Jules Verne in Gennady
Panfilovich's theatre, with music, a volcanic eruption, and English sailors. In four
acts with a Prologue and Epilogue.* Originally it also bore the further subtitle 'A
dramatical pamphlet.' It opens with a prologue in the theatre, where the director, Gennady Panfilovich, and his company prepare to put on a rehearsal of a
new play by one Dymogatsky (whose pseudonym is Jules Verne) so that the censor, Savva Lukich, can pass judgement on it. The play – similar to the story, but
with a few differences in the characters (in particular there are two positive
heroes, Kay-Kum and Farra-Tete, representing Lenin and Trotsky) – is then put
on, with the censor arriving in time to take part himself in the final act with the
others. It ends with the defeat of the Europeans by the islanders, but this does
not please Savva Lukich, who bans it (in the epilogue). So it is rewritten to
include an international revolution, with the English sailors revolting against
their capitalist masters.

34 **105** and 8, pp. 217-36
35 Strictly speaking, both the story and the play are low burlesque, and it is this term I use
to refer to genre. However, at times I shall also use the term 'allegory,' in the broader
sense of the word ('a story in which people, things, and happenings have another meaning' – *Webster*). Although this is not precise in literary terminology it would seem to be
the most suitable word to refer to certain aspects of the works.

The main satirical thrust of the play obviously concerns the censorship - and appropriately, *Glavrepertkom* did indeed make a number of cuts before allowing the play for performance.[36] For the Kamerny Theatre, which was to stage it, *The Crimson Island* represented, in producer Tairov's conception, a continuation 'along the lines of the harlequinade, that is, along the lines of the grotesque exposure of ugly phenomena in life and the satirical revelation of their essential narrow-mindedness.' It was important, he thought, 'finally to reveal by way of self-criticism the falsity of ... techniques [of theatre and censor], unfortunately still not completely eradicated up to the present day.' The theatre wanted to get rid of these by satire, and 'to highlight the uselessness of this time-serving attitude which was prepared at any time to combine Jules Verne with the Revolution, constructivism with naturalism, lack of culture with ideological qualities, and so on.' This was a noble - if somewhat naïve - aim and furthermore the play was 'self-criticism' for the theatre, which itself had been sufficiently wary of Bolshevism to stage a number of propagandistic caricatures of former Russia and the world outside the Soviet Union.[37]

Later, a member of the theatre's artistic council maintained that *The Crimson Island* had been forced through by Tairov and that the troupe of the theatre had not voted on it,[38] but shortly before the opening one critic surprisingly gave qualified support to the play, expressing views similar to Tairov's own. According to Pavel Novitsky, *The Crimson Island* was 'an interesting and witty parody. Parodied is the revolutionary process, the revolutionary lexicon, and the techniques of Soviet tendentious-precocious drama.' The critic pointed out how the revolutionary leaders had 'honest frank faces and ideological eyes,' and how all fawned before the all-powerful Savva Lukich, who sat on the former tsar's throne (on stage) like the 'ominous shadow of the Grand Inquisitor, suppressing artistic creation, cultivating slavish, fawningly absurd, dramatic clichés, and effacing the personality of the actor and writer.' But he warned that the play's producer should have a lot of tact, and that the play would be too risky for provincial audiences. One should also guard against being too much carried away by its 'exotic and satirical paper roses.'[39]

The play opened on 11 December 1928, in an elaborate production by A. Tairov and L. Lukyanova.[40] The actors were good, but the one thing that impressed everyone was the costumes and exotic sets designed by V. Ryndin. The

36 The uncensored version (with its subtitle 'A dramatical pamphlet') is in **186**, *fond* 2030, *opis* 1, folio 247.

37 **209**; see also **288**, p. 234

38 **508**

39 **396**

40 **319**, pp. 207-8; also **9**, p. 247, n2. Page references to **4** will appear in the text. The cast was Dymogatsky - Ganshin, Gennady Panfilovich - Arkadin, Savva Lukich - Viber.

latter consisted of a mixture of constructivist and pictorial elements: the ship taking the Europeans to the island was constructivist, the exotic flora of the island and Lord Glenarvan's castle were created by decorative painting. Prominent in the scenes on the island was the smoking volcano, and adding to the overall impression was a clever musical arrangement 'which illustrated the performance and ironically accentuated the stage situations.'[41]

The public enjoyed the play, but not so the critics, who congratulated the theatre on the technical matters of production but raised their usual howls of protest at the play itself. *Komsomol'skaia pravda* thought the play was boring and that its political malice was quite without effect: Bulgakov was 'fashionable' and the production was mere 'speculation on this odious name.' *Pravda*, a few days later, came out with a similar article.[42] 'The malice of the middle-class Bulgakov,' we read elsewhere, 'overcame the artist Bulgakov ...' He was accused of wanting to get his revenge on the Repertory Committee and to mock at everything Soviet, although in fact the play was comparatively harmless: 'there did not ensue any "eruption of the volcano." A slight puff of smoke, typical of Bulgakov, was given off, in places there "erupted" cunning words about the oppression of "holy art,"' but generally the play was disappointing.[43] More seriously, another critic, Ilya Bachelis, in a longish article where he called *The Crimson Island* 'a lampoon on the Revolution,' took issue with the whole question of freedom of creativity, which he quite correctly accused both Bulgakov and Tairov of demanding[44] – and indeed, at a time when increasing efforts were being made to control freedom of creativity, an attack on the censorship itself could only be seen as provocative.

In February the Repertory Committee itself was criticized by Stalin (in his letter to Bill-Belotserkovsky) for the mistakes it made in allowing such plays: *The Crimson Island* and 'the really bourgeois Kamerny Theatre' were mentioned specifically.[45] The authorities were quick to take the hint. First *Zoyka's Apartment* and then, in March 1929, *Days of the Turbins* and *The Crimson Island* were taken off, the latter apparently after only four performances.[46]

The play has not been performed in the Soviet Union since that time, neither has it been published there. In later criticism the general tendency has been to

41 **504**, p. 11, and **202**. For pictures, see **319**, pp. 139-40.
42 **224** and **206**
43 **259**, **511**, **526**
44 **208**, pp. 107-8
45 **493**, pp. 343-4
46 **9**, p. 247, n 3. The actual date of the last performance of *The Crimson Island* is in some doubt but the major papers all announced its withdrawal, with that of *Days of the Tubins* and *Zoyka's Apartment*, in early March 1929.

mention it only briefly, although two articles have compared it, interestingly, with Mayakovsky's *The Bathhouse*, which ran afoul of the critics in 1930. One of them suggests that whereas Mayakovsky (in his play's third act) showed himself against the bureaucratic leadership of art, Bulgakov was against the whole concept of *Party* leadership: *The Bathouse* affirmed communist principles of art, *The Crimson Island* denied them.[47] The other – by Rudnitsky, who talks too of Vishnevsky's *The Last Decisive* – is far more sympathetic, concluding that all three playwrights were moved by dislike of naïve propaganda plays and ignorant theatrical law-givers. His views, in fact, echo those of Tairov and Novitsky. Bulgakov 'came out against the coarse and ignorant interference in the life of the theatre by zealous administrators, who had just banned his play *Flight* from the stage.'[48]

The play has been performed once in the West. *L'Ile pourpre*, in a French adaptation by Georges Soria and production by Jorge Lavelli, opened at the Théâtre de la Ville in Paris on 17 February 1973, but it was not received with a great deal of enthusiasm. The play was considered too long; the best parts were the prologue and the epilogue with what was in between rather wearisome, nor was there much in the way of character; the form of a 'play within a play' was exploited clumsily, 'to the extent that the adventure of the natives swallows up the protestations against the censorship.'[49]

Such criticisms are interesting in that they do reveal some of the play's weaknesses – and also indicate that the Soviet critics of the twenties who found the play boring were not entirely alone. *The Crimson Island*, with its four acts in addition to the prologue and epilogue, does indeed need drastic cutting on stage to prevent it from becoming tedious. But much depends on the manner of presentation. It surely has to be played very fast, almost in the style of a slick music-hall sketch, with considerable exaggeration on the part of the characters and at the same time a certain lightness of touch: to make of it a serious problem-play is a mistake. In its style *The Crimson Island* is unique amongst Bulgakov's plays. Partly because of this style, and because of the play's absurd names and situations, it is easy to underrate it; all the more so because of the natural tendency of critics, Soviet and Western alike, to assume that the play's one serious issue, the censorship, is at the same time the play's sole purpose. If this were so, then all of the play within a play would indeed be a long and boring way to make a short point. But the play is, in addition, a satire on the theatre, a parody of other literary works, a burlesque on the Revolution, and not least an exotic

47 **378**, pp. 242-53
48 **461**, pp. 135, 137; see also **314**, III, p. 571
49 **248**

comedy of fictitious life on a desert island and in a lord's castle: Dymogatsky's creation is in no way secondary to the main action but an essential part of it. Rather than being an over-long development of a single theme, the play if anything tries to do too much – and possibly succeeds.

Let us first examine the action 'in the theatre' (as opposed to that 'on stage': Dymogatsky's play). In these parts of the play the approach is largely satirical. The life of the theatre is shown to be chaotic and disorganized, as opposed to the 'magic' created on stage: in this respect the play is a precursor to *Theatrical Romance*. Money is short, so backdrops have to be cut up to patch others; a cabin from *Uncle Tom* must be used instead of a wigwam. The director is constantly interrupted by telephone requests for free tickets. Author Dymogatsky is three days late bringing in his play, ruining the production schedule, but it is still seized upon avidly because of the need for something contemporary. Everything is a rush, confusion, with no time even to learn the parts, and yet 'The theatre is a temple,' as the director constantly repeats, parodying an attitude consciously fostered by the Art Theatre and others. One can suppose that much of this stems from Bulgakov's personal experience.

Included within the satire is the most important single issue, the censorship. Corrections must be made to Dymogatsky's play (some have been made already): the first stage involves the cuts made by the theatre itself in anticipation of the censor's requirements. 'What if it isn't ideological at all?' the director asks the play's author. 'Bear this in mind, in case of anything at all, I'll cross it out mercilessly, I have to save my skin here' (p. 86).

The second and most important stage of the censorship is represented by Savva Lukich himself, who in accordance with accepted practice has to see a dress rehearsal of the play before it can be approved. Savva is above all a figure of power. The stage is filled with unnatural red light when he arrives; when he takes part in the play, he too is respectfully greeted by the arabs, and the orchestra has to play a revolutionary song for the English sailors instead of 'It's a Long Way to Tipperary.' Later 'he sits on the former throne so that he rules over the Island' (p. 174); in the epilogue he 'sits on the throne above the crowd' (p. 181). The parallels – extended from Dymogatsky's play to its theatrical setting – are clear: the monarch has been replaced by the censor, and the ban on the play has all the authority of a royal edict. (It is worth noting that the relationship of Gennady Panfilovich to Savva Lukich foreshadows that of Molière to Louis XIV in Bulgakov's later play about the theatre and censorship. Louis XIV, too, like Savva Lukich, loved to appear on stage.) Dymogatsky's reaction is to protest the ban: 'And now an ill-boding old man appears ... and in one sweep, with one stroke of his pen he kills me ...' His speech that follows is a slightly modified quotation from Griboedov's *Woe from Wit*, making it clear that Dymogatsky equates the censors with the oppressive officialdom of the early nineteenth century: 'And who are the judges? Because of their antiquity, their hostility towards free life is implacable. They find their judgements in forgotten newspapers from the time of Kolchak and the conquest of the Crimea!' (p. 184). Such a comparison was almost unforgivable from a Soviet point of view – and particularly since it was the type of speech that, a few years earlier at least, might have brought the audience to its feet in applause.

The solution to the theatre's dilemma, the changed ending, is then offered by the director without even consulting the author. 'But perhaps the citizen author does not wish an international revolution?' Savva Lukich asks. 'Who? The author? Doesn't wish it?' Gennady Panfilovich replies. 'I'd like to see the man who doesn't wish an international revolution!' (pp. 186-7). (The majority are, in fact, against it.) So the revised version is played, and passed (but for Moscow only, as had happened for Bulgakov's plays), and now its author is deliriously happy: thus the third stage of the censorship, with the author himself corrupted for the sake of seeing his work performed. (Bulgakov knew the situation well, and humorously places himself in the same position as Dymogatsky by twice alluding to himself in the play: in references to *Zoyka's Apartment* and *Days of the Turbins.*)

It is hardly surprising that the issue of censorship has most caught the attention of the critics. But the success of the play as a whole still rests on the question of how successful is the play within a play in its own right. If, as Rudnitsky suggests, Bulgakov's satire is directed also at Dymogatsky, who 'composed a ridiculous, non-sensical play' consisting of 'all kinds of absurdities drawn out over four acts,'[50] then the major part of Bulgakov's play itself is ridiculous and non-sensical, and *The Crimson Island* fails.

Dymogatsky's play, however, turns out to be extremely entertaining. It is first of all a parody, consisting of a number of elements taken from different sources. On a minor level, the actors repeat lines not only from Griboedov but from Sumarokov's *The False Dimitry*, Chekhov's story 'Gooseberries,' and Gogol's *The Inspector General*; a scene between Kiri, the maid Betsy, and Lady Glenarvan is reminiscent too of Khlestakov's declarations of love in the same play. But rather more obviously, Dymogatsky's play parodies allegories on the Revolution such as Mayakovsky's *Mystery-Bouffe* and the writings of Jules Verne. The Europeans in Dymogatsky's play are dressed in costumes taken from illustrations of Jules Verne's books and use something of the exaggerated style of language expected of them: such as Hatteras, the resurrected valiant explorer of the polar seas, from *les Aventures du capitaine Hatteras* (1866), or Paganel, secretary of the Paris Geographical Society, from *les Enfants du capitaine Grant* (1868). Most of us have some vague ideas about Verne's heroes and can enjoy seeing these types represented comically, even if we are not familiar with his books in any detail. (Also from *les Enfants du capitaine Grant* are Tohonga, and Lord and Lady Glenarvan – intrepid adventurers in South America. Servant Passe-partout is the manservant of Phileas Fogg in *le Tour du monde en quatre-vingt jours*, 1873.) There is nothing particularly significant about the choice of characters from Verne, apparently a favourite of Bulgakov's,[51] nor anything surprising about combining them with an irreverent allegory on the Revolution. For essentially Bulgakov is using them at the same time to parody the capitalist world as well – and for this purpose, Verne's exaggerated, larger-than-life figures are peculiarly appropriate.

With the natives on the island, however, we are involved only in the allegory, which for any audience is more immediately understood than the more literary elements which make up parody. What is important for the spectator is his enjoyment at seeing oddly dressed primitives with comic-opera names acting out, with the same seriousness but on a far more trivial level, the events which had shaken Europe following the Russian Revolution. The allegory is essentially a good one, but it differs from a play such as *Mystery-Bouffe* by trivializing the events rather than elevating them: hence its political unacceptability. (In this sense too it might be considered provocative.) Its broad outlines need no elaboration, but there are a number of interesting details. The volcano, which kills Sizi-Buzi II together with his harem and half the arabs, had been dormant for three hundred years – the period of the Romanov dynasty; Sizi himself is described as 'a stupid villain on the throne' (p. 92). After the play has been banned, the actor playing him still expresses certain monarchistic sentiments, but at the end, as he disappears into hell, it is suggested he is only an imposter, as he repeats False Dimitry's speech from Sumarokov's play: 'I'm disappearing ... go to hell, my soul, and be a prisoner there for all eternity' (p. 189). The 'positive' natives, of course, have become atheists; instead of slaving in factories they are occupied sowing maize, finding pearls for Sizi, and gathering turtle eggs. After the eruption, they come in with red flags; elsewhere there appears a red light: obvious symbols which are in evidence throughout quite apart from the use of 'crimson' in the title. Thus Kiri-Kuki (who is elsewhere symbolized by a suitcase he carries with him everywhere) decks himself in crimson feathers and renames the island 'Crimson' to indicate his pretended change of allegiance; the arabs, too, instantaneously lose their own feathers and begin to sprout crimson ones, while their lanterns change from white to pink. At the end of the revised

51 See **349**, p. 116

version the sailors all wave red banners with the inscription 'Long live the Crimson Island!'

But the strength of the play as a whole is neither in the parody nor in the allegory, however amusing these might be. *The Crimson Island* is based on a kind of humorous fallacy, which the spectator accepts and enjoys with all its incongruities. The whole thing is unbelievable – even the action in the theatre, for actors who have not seen their parts can hardly, as here, put on a dress rehearsal immediately, with prompter or (as in fact is the case) without. But this does not matter, for we are not concerned with realism so much as with the theatre as demonstration, an approach that was particularly dear to the heart of Tairov. Dymogatsky's play, of course, is not meant to be believable. The inhabitants of the island are not real natives at all but Europeans in fancy dress: acting, thinking, and speaking like Europeans, except that they are in odd surroundings. Thus there are both anachronisms and deliberate transferrals of concepts to places where they are inappropriate. Kiri gives Lady Glenarvan a parrot as a decoration for her drawing room although, since at this time he has not left the island, we would hardly expect him to know what a drawing room is; earlier he has said he is 'registered' on the island (an 'uninhabited' one), and elsewhere he styles the guard the 'People's Honoured Arabs' (p. 124) – both concepts applicable only to the Soviet Union. Similarly the arabs address their superiors in a manner suitable to soldiers in the Russian tsarist army, and Sizi's wigwam becomes a 'court.' As for the Europeans, they are none other than the actors of Gennady Panfilovich's theatre transformed, except that they are not really very good actors, just playing themselves most of the time. Gennady Panfilovich, imperious, demanding, changes little when he becomes Lord Glenarvan, and even repeats his personal catch-phrase 'The theatre is a temple,' but substituting 'a man's home' for 'theatre.' In the theatre and in the play he is equally jealous of his wife, the 'grande coquette' who, as Lady Glenarvan, is as attracted to Kiri-Kuki as she is in real life to Dymogatsky – but on stage she can have an affair with him (a nice piece of wish-fulfilment, until it is interrupted by her real-life husband). Her servant Betsy dislikes her as much on stage as the actress playing her dislikes Gennady's wife in reality. Dymogatsky/Kiri-Kuki (a further manifestation of Bulgakov's 'likeable rogue') is the pivotal figure in both parts. Metelkin, Gennady's obsequious assistant, is appropriately both servant and a parrot in the play; Sizi-Buzi in life is a monarchist. Even Savva Lukich insists on entering into the spirit of the play and, as we have noted, becomes part of the allegory.

There are, perhaps, certain philosophical and psychological overtones here, concerning the whole issue of personality and reality as opposed to play-acting. At all events, we find a deliberate confusion between 'real life' (as represented by the actors) and 'play' (the characters they represent). Hardly surprisingly, there are several occasions when the action of the play is interrupted for 'characters,' momentarily, to become 'actors' again, and in the epilogue this situation is reversed, with the actors retaining their names as in the play – and of course costumes too – rather than reverting to their original roles. Thus ultimately the play is a satire on human foibles: we have not two plays but only one, about absurd behaviour, which on stage or off seems perfectly normal.

Nevertheless, for all the serious implications of such a theme (and for all Bulgakov's other comments about the play's being 'a pamphlet against the censorship'[52]), *The Crimson Island* remains a light-hearted farce whose main attraction is the simple fun and nonsense that runs throughout. It is also a superb theatrical *spectacle*, where what is created on the stage is described as 'magic.' Thus we may take a typical stage direction: *'The sun is burning, the tropical island sparkles and shimmers. On the branches monkeys and parrots are flying.* Sizi-Buzi's *wigwam at the foot of a volcano, surrounded by a palisade. The ocean in the background.* Sizi-Buzi *is sitting on a throne surrounded by odalisques from his harem. Beside him there stand, wearing white feathers, the sparkling* Likki-Tikki, Tohonga, *and a row of arabs with spears'* (p. 99). At night, there is a moon in the sky, and ships arrive on the stage: on the first occasion lowered from the sky as though crossing over a large expanse of blue. Gennady Panfilovich is right when he says of the volcano, 'an eruption's a good thing! A classy thing! The public loves such things' (p. 87). The volcano emitting smoke and glowing ominously clearly has pride of place on the stage, but equally important are the talking parrot and other pieces of exotica. Music further contributes to this atmosphere, with the orchestra under Likui Isaich playing a major part, however incongruous his selection of works might be. There are marches, fanfares, trumpet calls, rolls on the drums. Lady Glenarvan sings a romance. The sailors, as they arrive and depart, sing either 'Over the seas. Over the seas' (a refrain which is later taken up by the parrot) or 'It's a Long Way to Tipperary.' For the ending of Dymogatsky's play a huge choir sings a song of triumph to orchestral accompaniment.

In all of this, as part of the fun and nonsense, there is a great deal of slapstick: the volcano seems to move itself into place, a banana tree is put down on top of Dymogatsky, or a backdrop of a Gothic cathedral, patched up with bits of the Kremlin, is lowered by mistake. A telephone stops ringing when Gennady answers it verbally without even lifting the receiver; there is a tremendous splash as Kay-Kum and Farra-Tete jump into the sea. Other absurdities abound: Glenarvan and Paganel planting English and French flags respectively and arguing over possession of the island, the parrot mimicking everyone idiotically, Kiri-Kuki

52 **306**, p. 343

claiming to have hit himself against the volcano or deducting ten shillings from ten shillings by taking nought from nought and one from one. These and similar inanities are just very funny.

The ending is a climax of exuberant nonsense. Dymogatsky's revised play finishes with the triumphant chorus, Sizi-Buzi makes his descent into hell, and Savva Lukich announces the play is allowed. This is then illustrated graphically. '*A thunderous outburst of enthusiasm, a most terrifying commotion takes place. The backdrop goes up. There appear flashing lights and mirrors, wigs on their stands.*' In the joy that follows, the author in his rapture combines totally incongruous ideas ('How glorious is our Lord in Zion ... Oh it's a long way to Tipperary') while the orchestra takes another path again and plays from *The Barber of Seville*. Arrangements are made to sell tickets and '*on the ship, on the volcano, in the audience flare up the fiery letters: "The Crimson Island – today and every day!"*' To conclude a 'revolutionary' play the author and Savva Lukich exalt – outrageously – in the words of the Russian version of the Lord's Prayer:

Kiri-Kuki. Today, for always, and for all time.
Savva. Amen! (pp. 189-92)

The Crimson Island is a long and reasonably well sustained farce – although it could certainly be cut in places to eliminate more tedious passages. Bulgakov has taken elements of different genres and fused them together into a comedy show, which certainly includes a number of serious ideas such as the question of censorship, but which should not itself be taken too seriously. Played as such it is brilliant, while as a serious theatrical drama it must obviously leave much to be desired: we should not try to make of it more than it is and run the risk of appreciating it less. *The Crimson Island* was an experiment in form that Bulgakov was not to repeat, and, except for its length, he showed considerable skill in handling it. No one can pretend it is a great play: rather we should perhaps judge it on the level of a witty script for comedians – or of a television special which, were such levity possible in the Soviet Union, might be performed on the anniversary of the Revolution.

The mature dramatist, 1928-30

In his feuilleton 'Red Crown (*Historia morbi*)' of 1922, Bulgakov had treated the themes of war and hangings, of sickness caused by guilt and intensified by apparitions of a dead soldier; the narrator had also wondered whether the responsible general was haunted in the same way. In 1926-27 Bulgakov was to turn to the career of General Slashchov, the brilliant but eccentric defender of the Crimea at the age of thirty-four, subsequently accorded the honorific title 'Krymsky' (Crimean). As the writer Dmitry Furmanov indicates in an introduction to Slashchov's book, *The Crimea in 1920*, its author was noted for his brutality.[1] He was also a drug addict and alcoholic, in many ways unreliable, as Baron Wrangel too has pointed out in his memoirs. Even Slashchov admits that there was a general feeling he was suffering from upset nerves if not actual madness. Wrangel he saw as his bitterest enemy, claiming that Denikin, whom Wrangel had replaced as commander-in-chief, had been slandered by the influential bishop Veniamin; he also complained of attempts to discredit himself, particularly after his summary execution of a Colonel Protopopov. Two things stand out about him, that he was indeed sick to the point of being unbalanced and that he was a brilliant general.

In his book, Slashchov described his successful defence of the Crimea against the Reds in the first quarter of 1920, followed by his occupation of the mainland, the Northern Tauride. When in October the whole front collapsed, Slashchov's army was forced to withdraw from the mainland to the Crimea once more, and from there it embarked for Constantinople. Once there, Slashchov left the army and, threatened with a military 'court of honour' by Wrangel, wrote a

---

1 **484**, p. 3; see also **521**, pp. 124, 152, 156, 257-8, and Slashchov's later book **483**

defence of his actions entitled *I Demand a Trial by the Public* (where he referred again, amongst other things, to his execution of Protopopov). Later he returned to Russia, where incredibly he was pardoned and served in the Red Army, until in 1928 he was killed by a relative of a man he had shot in the Crimea.

Slashchov's book must have made fascinating reading for Bulgakov. According to his wife, maps were spread out on the table and the campaigns followed in detail. Slashchov himself was the perfect figure around whom to develop the themes of 'Red Crown.' The result was the play *Flight*, with its central character, General Khludov, based on Slashchov; Wrangel appears as the commander-in-chief, and Veniamin as the archbishop Afrikan, while Slashchov's execution of Protopopov may have suggested that of the orderly Krapilin. But the historical account was further combined with another element.[2] Earlier, Bulgakov's wife had described to him some of her experiences abroad. 'All that should be written down,' he had told her, and jotted down in pencil a rough plan for the kind of book that could be written: with the idea, she recalls, that she herself should write it. In particular, she described to him, sometimes while playing cards, the atmosphere of Constantinople, where there was a famous 'menagerie,' apparently run by the former humourist Arkady Averchenko. All these elements went into the play.

In April 1927 Bulgakov signed a contract with the Moscow Art Theatre for the play, which at this time is referred to as 'Serafima's Knight' or 'The Outcasts.' It was completed the same year. An early variant gives different titles to the scenes and divides them into five acts instead of four, but otherwise changes involve only one name and the elimination of unnecessary dialogue.[3]

The play's four acts each consist of two scenes which Bulgakov entitles 'dreams.' The background is the withdrawal of the Whites from the Northern Tauride and the Crimea in 1920, under General Roman Khludov. Retreating with him are the free-wheeling Cossack general, Charnota, and his mistress Lyuska; also two civilians, Golubkov and Serafima, wife of the assistant minister of commerce, Korzukhin, who abandons her to save his own skin. After reaching Constantinople, the heroes are reduced to living in a state of penury, until Charnota succeeds in winning a large sum of money from Korzukhin in Paris. Khludov, a sick man haunted by visions of the orderly he has hanged, finally decides to face up to his past by returning to Russia, as do Golubkov and Serafima.

Bulgakov had written many of the parts of *Flight* with the actors of the Moscow Art Theatre in mind, particularly those who had been in *Days of the Tur-*

2 The following is based on a personal conversation with L. Ye. Belozerskaya and on her unpublished memoirs.
3 Typewritten copy in **189**; see also **187**, folios 123, 126, 143, and **186**, *fond* 656, *opis* 3, folio 330

bins. As the play progressed, he read it at night to his friend Yanshin (Lariosik) whom he intended to play Golubkov, and to Sokolova (Yelena) who was to play Serafima. Khludov was to be played by Khmelyov, the former Alexey Turbin; Charnota was for Dobronravov (Myshlaevsky), Lyuska for Androvskaya.

The Art Theatre accepted *Flight* in early January 1928.[4] A copy was sent to *Glavrepertkom*, who in a resolution of 9 May found it unacceptable in that it idealized its White heroes rather than stressing the historical rightness of the Revolution, and 'declared itself against its inclusion in the repertoire of the Moscow Art Academic Theatre.' The theatre seemed to feel, however, that *Glavrepertkom*'s objections could be overcome, and continued discussions with them. When in October the play was read to the other members everyone was enthusiastic, including the great Gorky who was also present.[5]

The support *Flight* enjoyed is apparent from the minutes of a meeting of the theatre's Artistic Council on 9 October, under the chairmanship of Nemirovich-Danchenko. Markov and Sudakov reported that *Glavrepertkom* were now demanding only a few minor changes such as strengthening of the role of Baev, the one Red soldier in the play. V.P. Polonsky, critic and historian, then gave his opinion that *Flight* was 'one of the most talented plays of recent times' and should certainly be performed: 'We must give Bulgakov the chance to become a Soviet playwright.' A particularly strong viewpoint was put forward by Gorky:

I do not see on the part of the author any idealization of the White generals. This is a magnificent play, I read it three times and read it again to A.I. Rykov and other comrades. It is a play with a deep, cleverly hidden satirical content. I would like to see such a thing put on by the Art Theatre ...

...

Flight is an excellent work, which will be damned successful [*budet imet' anafemskii uspekh*], I assure you.

A.I. Svidersky, the head of the Chief Administration for Artistic Affairs (*Glaviskusstvo*), liked the play too, and thought that the theatre should surely put on things which gave rise to discussion. Nemirovich-Danchenko summarized the proceedings. His misgivings had been dispelled: 'When *Glavrepertkom* see the play on the stage, they will hardly object to its performance.' *Pravda*, reporting

---

4 **379**, p. 169, n 2. *Glavrepertkom*'s resolution is published in **448**, pp. 461-2.
5 **376**, p. 110, and **368**, pp. 82-3. Some of what follows is based on this latter article, also on **188**, folio 3694. The minutes of the meeting are published in **448**, pp. 462-5; also partly in **372**, pp. 388-90.

on this meeting two days later, announced that *Glavrepertkom* had sanctioned the play for rehearsal with a few changes.[6]

Rehearsals had already begun the day after the meeting, with Nemirovich-Danchenko appointed producer and Sudakov, Litovtseva, and Stanitsyn assistant producers. Sets were to be by Dmitriev. Not all the parts were distributed in accordance with Bulgakov's original conception: Kachalov was now to play Charnota and Tarasova, Serafima.[7] As previously, Bulgakov helped by demonstrating the parts. For a time at least *Flight* was rehearsed in the foyer of the theatre.

But many of the members of *Glavrepertkom* were still unhappy about a play which 'gave an incorrect conception of the civil war in Russia.'[8] Stanislavsky and Nemirovich-Danchenko, however, approached Lunacharsky and Svidersky, who both were strongly in favour of the play and thought any faults could be rectified before the dress rehearsal. One of the opponents of the play recalls that the matter went to the collegium of *Narkompros* and the play was discussed several times: 'Every time I had to speak out against the viewpoint of Anatoly Vasilievich [Lunacharsky].' Svidersky, too, at a plenary meeting of the Central Committee of the All-Russian Union of Art Workers, repeated that *Flight* was one of the best plays he had read and it would produce an outstanding impression on the worker.[9]

But now it was the critics, infuriated by the news of the impending production, who took up the issue. A fierce debate began over whether *Flight* should be performed or not. The most virulent attack was by Ilya Bachelis in *Komsomol'-skaia pravda* on 23 October. He pointed out that although *Glaviskusstvo* under Svidersky were in favour of the play, *Glavrepertkom* – with whom he agreed – were largely against it. There could be no room in the administration of theatrical life for policies of tolerating, let alone patronizing, the 'white-guard exercises' of people like Bulgakov. Whereas *Days of the Turbins* had tried to justify the middle category of officers, *Flight* did so with the generals: Bulgakov wanted to forget the past and reconcile the people with the 'white guard' movement.[10]

The next day, 24 October, *Pravda* reported on a meeting of the Artistic-Political Council of *Glavrepertkom* with the representatives of various political and trade-union organizations. The speeches contained all the old arguments against showing sympathy for the Whites. As a result of this meeting the council

6 383
7 188, folio 7; see also 3, p. 470
8 For this and what follows, see 456, pp. 154-5.
9 Quoted from 525 in 263, p. 101
10 207

of *Glavrepertkom* now changed its mind once again, and decided unanimously that the play should be banned.[11]

Surprisingly, this was not the end of the matter. The diary of the rehearsals makes no reference to a ban at all: the theate clearly did not consider *Glavrepertkom*'s decision as final – perhaps again counting on intervention from elsewhere, for one of the real difficulties of censorship was the many different bodies involved. According to Yanshin, Gorky also strongly urged the theatre to carry on with the play.[12] Debates continued, with the theatre finding some unexpected sources of support. An interesting case involved an S. Kanatchikov, who was the representative of the Russian Association of Proletarian Writers (RAPP) on the Federation of Organizations of Soviet Writers (FOSP). Reporting on the FOSP meeting to the Party members of RAPP's secretariat, he praised the play and told of how Vs. Ivanov had suggested printing extracts from it in the twelfth issue of *Krasnaia nov'*, for which there was no material; he had voted for this. Alas, he was labelled a 'free-thinker,' and accused by the playwright V. Kirshon of voting for a counter-revolutionary play. A unanimous decision was taken 'to ask the Central Committee to relieve comrade Kanatchikov from representing RAPP at FOSP.'[13]

On 13 November another important meeting of *Glavrepertkom* took place.[14] The deputy head of *Agitprop*, Kerzhentsev – who had frequently clashed with Lunacharsky because of his extreme left-wing (*Proletcult*) persuasions in art – attacked the artistic councils in the theatres for not themselves protesting about *Flight*. Averbakh and Kirshon attacked the play's defenders. Yet there were still plenty of these, and later the critic Litovsky was to accuse such people of applying petit-bourgeois pressure on the theatre.[15]

By January 1929 Litovtseva was in charge of producing *Flight* (Nemirovich-Danchenko, for a while otherwise engaged, intended to return to it later).[16] The last entry in the rehearsals diary is for the 25th. In December *The Crimson Island* had opened, with the resulting scandals: clearly it was simpler to prevent a play's appearance than to take it off after its performance. By 30 January *Flight* too had finally been banned, except that there remained a possibility, if Bulgakov would agree to fundamentally change the play, that it could still be considered again.[17] This Bulgakov refused to do: which, from the point of view of the

11 **490**
12 **448**, pp. 465-6
13 See **478**, pp. 209-11
14 **407**, I, p. 580; **313**, p. 2; **205**. On Kerzhentsev, see **276**, p. 304.
15 **356**, p. 94
16 **278**, p. 421
17 **343**, p. 307

censors, had been the whole trouble all along. 'For a long time, even before my work in the Repertory Committee,' Litovsky has written, 'there dragged on this story of the permitting and forbidding of *Flight* by the organs of control, but Bulgakov stubbornly refused to change the play.' He would not 'introduce the minimum necessary alterations which would have made this play acceptable.'[18] In February the theatre's ally Svidersky was replaced as head of *Glaviskusstvo* by L.L. Obolensky.

Stalin also expressed his feelings about the play in his famous letter. It was, he said, an attempt to justify or semi-justify 'white guardism' and hence an anti-Soviet phenomenon. He would not, however, object to it if Bulgakov added one or two more scenes to depict 'the inner social mainsprings of the civil war in the USSR,' so that it should be understood that the Bolsheviks had ejected those who were 'honest' in their own way because 'they were sitting on the necks of the people.'[19]

For Bulgakov the ban, followed by that of his other plays, was a tremendous blow. Yanshin reports how at first he would joke about it, but then started, as though deliberately, to emphasize his old-fashioned appearance as a kind of protest: 'There, you wanted to see me like this ... so there, here you are ... that's how I am.'[20] It was a blow too for the theatre, and far from boldly 'admitting its mistake' and 'renouncing the play' as one Soviet critic has written,[21] it continued in its attempts to stage it.

Four years later, late in the 1932-33 season (after the restaging of *Days of the Turbins*), it began rehearsals once again, with Khmelyov again to play Khludov.[22] General discussions on the characters and the early scenes, under the producer Sudakov, began on 10 March 1933 and continued until 21 April. Stanislavsky wrote on 15 April to Yenukidze, president of the Commission of Management of the Bolshoy and Art Theatres, that *Flight* would perhaps be given that season. On the 27th Sudakov reported having several fruitful discussions with him and Litovsky. Bulgakov agreed to a number of changes in Khludov's portrayal, who, in particular, was to shoot himself rather than return to Russia.[23] (There has been talk too of a variant of the play containing a 'ballad of the pistol' as a counterpart for the 'ballad of the dollar': a song of praise to the dollar by Korzukhin.) In July it was even announced that the play would be taken to Leningrad

---

18 **357**, p. 232, and **356**, p. 17. Svidersky's replacement is mentioned in **379**, p. 171, n 2.
19 **493**, p. 342
20 **448**, p. 466
21 **200**, p. 148
22 Sokolova would now be Serafima and Prudkin – Golubkov.
23 See **448**, p. 466, and **379**, p. 169, n 2. The following is based on **188**, folio 8.

in January of the following year.[24] But matters dragged on, and by October we find in the diary only various entries concerning the music for the play: the last on the 15th. In March 1934 Stanislavsky wrote to Nemirovich-Danchenko, agreeing that *Flight* would not be allowed.

Thus for the time of Bulgakov's life the play was not performed. He would turn to it again when writing his opera libretto 'The Black Sea' - but this was not produced either. *Glavrepertkom* gave permission for *Flight* to be printed in 1940, after Bulgakov's death, but it still remained unpublished.[25] Fifteen years later, in 1955, N.P. Akimov, main producer of the Theatre of the Lensoviet, announced that *Flight* would be their second new play in the forthcoming year, and in honour of the production the writer V. Kaverin, the initiator of Bulgakov's rehabilitation, devoted to the play a large part of an article on Bulgakov's dramatic works. But the production did not take place, nor did a proposed one for 1957 by R. Simonov and A. Abrikosov of the Vakhtangov Theatre.

Ironically, after many of Bulgakov's plays had been allowed for Moscow only, *Flight* was to open first of all in the provinces: at the Gorky Dramatic Theatre in Volgograd (Stalingrad) in March 1957.[26] The audience gave the play a warm reception, and general reaction to the acting was favourable. The major review talked of the history of the play and the previous attacks of the RAPP critics. But 'In our days ... M. Bulgakov's thoughts have found their historical confirmation and his play can hardly give rise to objections.' Bulgakov, the critic said, mocked those who acted against the Revolution, but showed the tragedy of the individual situation of those who were objectively honest. In April and May the following year the play was also performed in the F.E. Dzerzhinsky Central Club in Moscow.

Flight's rehabilitation was confirmed when it opened on 27 June 1958 at the Leningrad Academic Pushkin Theatre, in a production by L. Vivien with sets by A. Bosulaev. The moving force behind the production was the outstanding actor Nikolay Cherkasov, who very much wanted to play Khludov.[27] He gave to the part all the brilliance for which he had become famous in his many performances as Don Quixote (in Bulgakov's play performed in 1941, and in the Soviet film of 1957, amongst others). In the second scene, Khludov's headquarters in the waiting room of a station (presumably Dzhankoy) in the northern Crimea, he looked 'like a man in the grip of a nightmare. In the abrupt way he pronounces the

24 **231**; see, further, **494**, pp. 336, 371
25 Noted in **186**, *fond* 656, *opis* 3, folio 330. For what follows, see **437**; **325**, p. 71; **390**; and **426**.
26 N. Pokrovsky, producer; N. Medovshchikov, set designer; V. Klyukin as Khludov; K. Sinitsyn as Charnota. For the following, see **203**.
27 **431**, p. 6

words of the part, you feel the collapse of the white-guard movement.'[28] In the final scene he walked towards the audience from the back of the stage and fell to his knees, bending his head to the ground before the idea of Russia. But despite Cherkasov's performance, the production as a whole was disappointing, and the theatre failed to find the overall tone for the play. At least one critic thought its revival was unnecessary.[29]

Flight had to wait until 1967 for a professional Moscow production, by which time it had been published in two separate collections of Bulgakov's works and had received serious consideration from a number of critics, none of whom seemed to have any doubts that it was a completely acceptable play. A. Goncharov's production opened at the Yermolova Theatre on 22 March 1967, with I. Solovyov as Khludov and L. Gallis as Charnota. There was an interesting new element, with Golubkov as a narrator reading Bulgakov's directions at the beginning of each scene.[30] The excitement in Moscow was tremendous: 'Every time *Flight* is on, the Yermolova Theatre is besieged by a huge crowd of people wanting to get in to the show,' Rudnitsky wrote. Criticism generally concentrated on the actual performance rather than on any questions of acceptability.

Today, *Flight*'s rehabilitation is complete. It was also produced in Irkutsk in 1967, and in Odessa, at the A. Ivanov Russian Dramatic Theatre, a year later. (Unfortunately an intended production by Stanitsyn at the Moscow Art Theatre in 1973, with Yefreymov as Khludov, was abandoned.) A film of it – a poor one, emphasizing the civil war scenes and including Red Army general Frunze's crossing of the Sivash – was made in 1970.[31] Abroad, it has been performed in Prague (1959), Bydgoszcz in Poland (1960), Paris, at the Théâtre des Amandiers, Nanterre (1970-71), and in a particularly brilliant performance at the Bristol Old Vic, directed by Val May, designed by Alex Day, and with John Bennett in the role of Khludov (March and April 1972). *Flight* 'emerges as one of the few masterpieces of Soviet theatre yet to reach the British stage,' one critic wrote. '*Flight* is the work of an author who still believes he can get away with the undisguised truth ...'[32]

It has been suggested that *Flight* is a continuation of *Days of the Turbins*, and there are indeed certain similarities. The White officer class is again portrayed, but this time we are dealing rather with the general staff, so much hated in the earlier book and play, with the hetman reincarnated in the commander-in-chief. Khludov is to some extent reminiscent of Alexey, Korzukhin of Talberg (Lyuska

28 **514**, p. 326
29 **321**. For a general account of the production, see **406**, III, pp. 250-3; also **489**, p. 283.
30 **535** and **405**. For what follows, see **464** and **463**, pp. 246-58.
31 **487**, pp. 59-60; **399**; **238**
32 **520**

calls him a 'little rat'), Charnota of Myshlaevsky, Golubkov of Lariosik or Nikolka. But the historical circumstances and motivations of the characters are different. It is a continuation only in the sense that it represents a later stage of the whole 'white guard' movement, both in terms of the struggle and of its moral collapse.

This is personified in the career of Roman Valeryanovich Khludov who, although appearing in only four of the eight 'dreams' (the four that are the most serious), is the major tragic figure of the play. Like the White movement itself, he has fallen from high-minded belief in a cause to the role of a cynical but apparently necessary hangman, now forever associated with the black sacks of the bodies hanging on the street lights around his headquarters. 'Who would have done the hanging? Who would have done the hanging, Your Excellency? ' (p. 49),[33] he asks the commander-in-chief, whom he hates for getting him involved in a cause which is hopeless. Now, a disillusioned fanatic, he feels (in the words of the Art Theatre rehearsals diary for 1932-33) 'the shame of war, confusion, perplexity, wounded pride, conscience, and malice.' His responsibility is not even limited to his own actions, but to the scope they have given to his less conscientious subordinates. Thus one Colonel De Brizar, with his simple enjoyment of hangings, his madness resulting from a wound, and the exaggerated hopes for victory he expresses to the commander-in-chief, is a cruel parody of Khludov himself. So too is the sinister Tikhy (meaning 'quiet'), the head of counter-espionage, who uses his power for his own financial advantage. Khludov is above such behaviour, but tragically becomes associated with it, and his basic honesty will not allow him to shirk the entire responsibility.

'So – all that I did was quite useless,' he finally concludes (p. 103). The process of this realization is one of the main themes in the play and when we first see Khludov he functions automatically, although he realizes the futility of the hangings he orders. Whereas everyone is fleeing to get 'under the wing of Roman Khludov,' he is as powerless as they; until the end, when he can, on a purely personal level, indeed take Serafima under his wing while Golubkov and Charnota go off to Paris to get money from Korzukhin. Until then he is tormented by the thought that he is not loved (for all his undoubted good intentions): 'Love is what we need, nothing can be done in war where there is no love! ... Nobody loves me' (p. 43). Khludov is a lonely man, as is emphasized in the station waiting-room of the second scene, where he sits apart from the others. Even at the end, he returns to Russia alone, not with Golubkov and Serafima. His inner despair is barely disguised by his cynicism and bitter dislike of hypocrites such as the archbishop Afrikan, Korzukhin, or the commander-in-chief. On such occa-

33 Page references to 39 are given in the text.

sions he can be amusing, even witty. For Khludov himself is no hypocrite, and even early in the play retains a fundamental decency. Thus, once orders have been carried out, he can be reminded by the station-master and his family of the troubles of ordinary men and the joys of children; or he can sufficiently respect the honest Golubkov to try to find out what has happened to Serafima after she has been arrested by counter-espionage and dramatically rescued by General Charnota.

It is similar with the orderly Krapilin, whom Khludov remembers rather than the others he has hanged because he is able to respect him for his honesty in telling him what he thinks of him. In a way Krapilin becomes his double, acting out the two sides of Khludov's nature, telling him 'eloquently' (because it is true) that he is a jackal, a hangman, but then relenting in a sudden awareness of the surrounding circumstances: at which point Khludov has him hanged in a burst of self-revulsion. As he prepares to leave the station, Khludov asks himself: 'What is this illness of mine? Am I really ill?' and seeing the hanging body of Krapilin, he affirms, 'I am ill, I am ill. But what of, I do not know' (pp. 54-5). From this point on Krapilin becomes the personification of Khludov's guilt, appearing next when Khludov catches sight of the dark sacks covering up the chandeliers in the palace in Sevastopol where the commander has his office, reminding him of bodies he has had strung up. A little later, in the presence of Golubkov, Khludov tries to justify himself to the apparition, but it is to himself he is talking, to his better self whom he has almost destroyed, and to whom Golubkov is now appealing as well. Khludov's own moral crisis is the outcome of the struggle between his noble aims and the role of hangman he has adopted as the means to bring these about – and the result is a kind of schizophrenia: 'My soul is split in two, and words come through to me faintly as though down through water into which I am sinking like lead, and these two, both of them [Golubkov and Krapilin], the damned limpets, swinging on my feet, pulling me down into the darkness, and the darkness draws me' (p. 70).

Golubkov is wrong at this point in calling Khludov mad, he is simply a man burdened beyond his capability, and the only solution is for him to make his proper expiation. Krapilin is not the cause of Khludov's sickness – Khludov is sick from the beginning – but rather the means of his recovery. Khludov's final return to Russia is thus not a desire to die but a necessary pilgrimage to confront his own past: 'I remember armies, battles, snows, lampposts, and on the posts – lights,' he tells Serafima. 'Khludov will go back under the lights' (p. 106). It may be that, as Charnota says to him, 'you will live for just so long as it will take to haul you off the steamer and put your back against the nearest wall,' but it is the only way that his guilt, in the guise of Krapilin, will finally leave him.

With Khludov, of course, are fleeing thousands of others, few of whom will ever return to Russia. The Russian title '*Beg*' is difficult to translate for in general it means 'running,' also 'race'; thus it can be applied to the concept of 'flight,' which still seems the most appropriate English word. In the eyes of the arch- bishop Afrikan this flight is heroic, comparable to that of the Israelites out of Egypt, to which there are a number of references. But this comparison with the Exodus turns out to be ironic. When Afrikan prays for deliverance before a pic- ture of St George and the dragon in the station waiting-room (compare the pic- ture of Alexander I in *Days of the Turbins*), Khludov breaks in sarcastically to say he has no call to trouble the Almighty: 'now the water in the Sivash has ebbed away ... and the Bolsheviks have crossed it like a ballroom floor: St George is laughing at us!' (p. 49). It is the Bolsheviks for whom the waters have parted, the Whites who will have to be herded into ships to avoid the approach- ing flood: 'Noah's Ark,' as the colonel De Brizar more accurately describes it.

The image of water is linked with the play's central symbol, introduced by Khludov in a dialogue with the commander-in-chief. He tells of how once in his childhood he went into the kitchen at twilight and found the stove covered with cockroaches which ran away as he struck a match. And the present circum- stances are similar: 'darkness and rustling – I look and I wonder: where are they all running to? Like the cockroaches – into the slop-pail. Down from the kitchen table – plop!' As the commander says he is going to a hotel, Khludov forces the comparison home, asking 'Nearer to the water?' A short time later Khludov tells Golubkov that the commander has left: 'The slop-pail. He has passed on into oblivion – for ever' (pp. 66-8). The nature of this flight, then, is comparable to cockroaches running to the water: a chaotic stream of people running to save their own skins or in some cases for no very clear reason at all. At one time Bul- gakov even thought of giving the play the title '*Tarakanii beg*': a flight of cock- roaches or, in the other sense of *beg*, a cockroach race. And this is what we find in Constantinople, where we see actual cockroach races, on which Charnota squanders his money.

While this image of scurrying cockroaches relates to almost everyone in the play, it is Charnota who most clearly personifies this futile movement. He is fas- cinated with the races and, perhaps significantly, the name of a cockroach he backs to win but who is 'running out' is Janissary, in former days a soldier in the Sultan's army. For Charnota too is 'running out,' no longer certain which way to run or whether to run at all. 'Run away perhaps?' he asks himself. 'But where, if I may ask, Grigory Lukyanovich, would you run to? You're not in Tauria here, there's nowhere to run to' (p. 80). Shortly afterwards he considers going on to Paris, Berlin, or even Madrid. He, like the others, is by now trying to run only from himself. In Constantinople, living in a house with a reservoir in the court- yard, he has already reached his metaphorical bucket of water; and not for noth- ing does his former mistress Lyuska, who flees to the rich Korzukhin in Paris, say she has dreamt of cockroaches the night before he turns up there. Whereas at the end of the play Khludov says 'I'm not a cockroach, I do not intend to swim around in the slop-pail' (p. 106) and returns to Russia, Charnota symbolically continues his flight by running off with his money to the cockroach races again.[34]

This is the real tragedy for Charnota, who throughout is paradoxically the major comic figure. For in *Flight*, tragedy and comedy are not mutually exclusive, but rather different sides of the same coin. Charnota has a zest for life that makes him little aware of the problems that burden the others, but because of this he is denied their ultimate salvation. Functionally, he is the comic foil to Khludov, whom he is quite incapable of understanding. Thus he waltzes through the war with his military band, swearing or laughing vigorously, or rescues Serafima from counter-espionage with no real thought of the consequences of his actions – in fact getting thrown out of the army as a result. Interestingly, the rehearsals diary contains the remark that he is not a real general at all, that he got his promotion from Wrangel or perhaps even promoted himself: 'a free-thinking hooligan, but irreplaceable in a campaign.' 'I'll sell my trousers, I'll sell anything, only not my revolver!' he tells Lyuska, who replies that it takes the place of his brain (pp. 83-4). Fighting, playing cards, betting, all are part of the gamble that is his entire life. His moment of greatest glory, the funniest scene in the play, is when he fleeces Korzukhin at cards, the whole time ludicrously attired in lemon-coloured underpants because he has sold his trousers. But in the end result he is a loser, as is Lyuska too. Another comic figure, she reflects his fate: loving the danger and glory of war but forced by circumstances to opt for comfort in marriage to a person she loves as little as Charnota loves his new life abroad.

In others who are part of the flight abroad, comedy is combined with satire, and tragic overtones are almost entirely lacking. Korzukhin is one such figure, a comic scapegoat for the more obvious evils of a capitalist society. In a sense he is the victim of the others: first of Khludov who, at the station, takes pleasure in burning the furs Korzukhin intended to transport abroad; then of the commander-in-chief, who is furious with him for an article in a paper he edits; and finally of Charnota, who wins from him at cards far more than the money he has refused to give Golubkov. Yet ultimately he remains untouched by such set-backs, for the Korzukhins are the world's spoilt children (Lyuska treats him accordingly) with enough money and influence to live in comfort wherever they find themselves. While we may delight in his discomfiture, there is no real malice in Bulgakov's portrayal, and unlike Talberg of the *Days of the Turbins* Korzukhin has a certain style of his own. Indeed, there is something rather attractive about

---

34 See also on this **198**, pp. 23-4, and **418**, p. 258

his frank, even naïve, belief in the power of wealth, as represented by his safe which opens to the ringing of alarms and the flashing of lights, and his 'ballad of the dollar.' This 'ballad' is a delightful piece of bombast, comic only because of its subject, reminiscent in its style to Satin's famous speech on man in Gorky's *Lower Depths* – to which it might be seen as an irreverent reply.

Other figures are less attractive. Archbishop Afrikan, for all his religious pomp and speeches filled with biblical quotations, is concerned only with the saving of his own skin: 'strives for the good life' and is a good actor, as the re- hearsal diary notes. The commander-in-chief, the notes suggest, 'looks at himself as the weapon chosen by God to save Russia.' Yet at a time of disaster his main concern is to complain that a newspaper has compared him with Alexander the Great. The absurdity of his question as to whether he looks like Alexander is emphasized by De Brizar's diffident but senseless reply: 'I regret, Your Excel- lency, but it is a long time since I last saw a portrait of His Majesty' (p. 62). As Khludov puts it sarcastically in a direct quotation from Gogol, infuriating the commander: 'Alexander of Macedonia is undoubtedly a hero, but why break the furniture?' (p. 67).

Yet the main plot of the play concerns none of these figures, and paradoxi- cally not even the real 'hero,' Khludov. Essentially, *Flight* is the story of Golub- kov and Serafima, the lyrical figures who move through a changing landscape until they find their future in their own country once more. The play begins and ends with them; Golubkov is present in seven of the eight scenes, Serafima in five – a record shared only by Charnota, their most constant companion. It has further been pointed out that the name Golubkov, if we substitute an 'a' for the first 'o' (as it is pronounced in Russian) is an anagram for the name Bulgakov.[35] It is completely logical that the Moscow production of *Flight* should have had Golubkov read Bulgakov's stage directions, for in a real sense he is the narrator. The whole of *Flight* represents a dream, dreamt by Golubkov and Serafima: or, in a formal sense, a succession of eight dreams which merge one into another (technically by the dimming of lights rather than the use of the curtain). On two occasions Golubkov refers to dreams, at the very beginning – 'You know, there are times when I really begin to think I am dreaming' (p. 28) – and in Paris – 'I am dreaming, I have dreamt my whole life' (p. 93). In the course of their 'flight through the autumn darkness' he and Serafima meet various figures, some comic, some tragic, some just terrifying. But they themselves are in this situation largely by accident: Golubkov because, as a university professor, he finds it impossible to work in St Petersburg (as though it were more possible under the retreating Whites), Serafima because her husband is running too. Their flight is as senseless as many dreams are, so that finally their one desire is to wake up. 'It never was, never; it was a bad dream!' Golubkov says in his final speech, 'Forget it, forget it! A month will pass, we shall arrive, we shall have come back home, and then the snow will fall and blot out our tracks ... Let us go, let us go!' (p. 110).

We do not, of course, see this awakening. The 'unreality' of the past, of situations lived through, and indeed of life itself, is what interests Bulgakov. The theme of what is 'real' is present in many of his works: to show this as being everyday life in the Soviet Union would not suit his purpose. The play relates to historical events, with references to actual places important in the civil war and the emigration, but the scenes themselves seem to take place in a vacuum so that, as has been suggested by one critic, the stages of the flight represent a state of mind rather than an actual place,[36] and are deliberately given a mysterious, nightmarish quality. The scene of the cockroach races, in particular, is like a grotesque children's pantomime, with the owner, Artur Arturovich, appearing and disappearing like Punch in a 'Punch and Judy' show.

Related to this is the lack of permanency in the lives of the major characters, who go through disturbing dreamlike yet credible transformations, Golubkov from assistant professor to player of a barrel-organ, Serafima from important lady to pauper. In the first scene we see – taking refuge in a monastery – a chemist and a comical pregnant woman, apparently near to delivery. When the Reds have left it is revealed that the chemist is the archbishop Afrikan, while the woman becomes an equally comical General Charnota. (Both Slashchov and Wrangel mention a Korsunsky monastery in their memoirs, and the latter also tells of an occasion when two White officers were disguised as nuns.) Later, Charnota is transformed into a street-hawker in Constantinople, where he longs for his glorious past. 'I can't sell rubber devils! I'm a soldier!' he tells Lyuska (p. 83). She too goes from campaign-wife, to prostitute, to wife of the rich Korzukhin – who is concerned with forgetting the past, particularly the Crimea, which 'was overrun by all those half-crazed generals' (p. 93). Khludov's transformation, after his power and position in the army, to a sick grey-haired man is particularly pathetic. 'But do you remember – night, general headquarters ... Khludov – the monster, Khludov – the jackal?' he says to Serafima, somewhat regretfully. The past becomes remote, no more than the accidental path by which one has reached one's present position in life. Yet one is bound to this past and has to pay for it, as Khludov recognizes only too clearly. Thus an entire past life is reduced to a number of impressions of memorable scenes (or dreams): the darkness of the monastery, where monks appear and disappear through the

---

36 475, p. 78. This article deals interestingly with a number of the leitmotifs and technical details of the play.

floor; a station waiting-room with its huge windows; or Constantinople with its carousel of cockroach races and the muezzins calling to prayer (this 'terrible city,' comparable to the Moscow or ancient Jerusalem of *The Master and Margarita*).

This whole unreal atmosphere, similar to the closed world of *Zoyka's Apartment* yet more immediate to the spectator's own experience, is to a large extent created by visual symbols which can be most striking in a stage production. In addition to the black sacks, the cockroach races, the picture of St George, we might note portrayed on stage a glowing needle used for torture by the counter-intelligence section, or the lights of railway signals and street lamps outside the waiting-room, referred to as 'moons.' 'Don't you remember? The frost, the windows, the station lamp like a pale blue moon,' Golubkov says to Korzukhin (p. 93); Khludov too asks Krapilin how he alone broke himself off 'from that long line of moons and lampposts' (p. 103). Yet the overriding leitmotif is the darkness which is the background of the first two dreams and into which everything dissolves at the end of all the others, which themselves take place at twilight (dreams three and four) or at the time of the setting sun (the last four dreams). Darkness is the time of sleep and dreams. It can be symbolical of death, or non-existence. It can denote evil as opposed to the light (as in *The Master and Margarita*). Twilight is also the time when Khludov as a child discovered the cockroaches, which then ran to the water. All are appropriate to the themes of this play.

Sounds, too, have a similar impact: the monastery is typified by the chanting of monks, the terrible station by the chatter of the telephone operators and the clanks and groans of the armoured-train, Constantinople by a whole orchestra of noises, from the dripping of a fountain and the chanting of the muezzins. '*A strange symphony*' is our first impression of the town. '*Someone is singing Turkish refrains intermingled with the Russian "Separation" on a street-organ, the moaning cries of street vendors, the rattling of trams.*' As he complains of the horrible city, '*Constantinople groans over* Charnota' (pp. 73-4). He himself is symbolized by the waltz (or in Constantinople a strident march) that accompanies him; Korzukhin by his safe with its bells and music. The play is simply full of noise – songs, gunfire, the clatter of horses' hooves – which achieves an effect of unease, tension: the dominant mood of the play. At times, too, all noise ceases, to allow us to become aware of it in the silence that follows.

In fact at times stage directions seem as important as the text, and many of them are clearly meant to be read, particularly those that introduce each dream. These are preceded by epigraphs, only four of which (from popular songs, from *Queen of Spades*, and from the Bible) appear to be quotations. Rather they are used in the same way as chapter headings, giving some indication of the contents to follow: 'I dreamt of a monastery,' 'My dreams are becoming more and more like nightmares,' 'A needle shines through my dream' (epigraphs to the first three dreams). The directions that follow are frequently descriptive of a general situation that is impossible to portray on stage. This is particularly true of the second dream: *'There has been a fierce frost, unprecedented for early November in the Crimea. Sivash, Chongar, Perekop, and this station are icebound ... The front-line staff has been quartered at this station for three days and three nights, and for three days and three nights it has not slept but continues to work like a machine. Only an experienced and keen observer might notice the shadow of anxiety in the eyes of all these people'* (pp. 40-1). Such writing is appropriate to the novel: Bulgakov, it seems, cannot resist telling a story and supplying such literary details.

With its many formal devices, its emphasis on atmosphere and psychological states, the play is very far from straight theatrical realism, for all its solid basis in the events of the civil war. Nor is it a tidy, well-balanced play theatrically, for it falls into two distinct parts, in Russia and abroad. Rather it is a headlong movement in one direction until this comes to a halt, reflecting the nature of the flight itself. In genre it is described most simply as a tragi-comedy, but even this is not really satisfactory, for it is more a simple mixture of tragedy and comedy from the beginning. As Kaverin has put it: 'At times in front of you there is a psychological drama, at times a phantasmagoria, almost going beyond real conceptions of the surrounding world. Perhaps it would be most accurate to call this work a satirical tragedy. Or perhaps a satirical comedy?'[37]

From the point of view of theatre, *Flight* is difficult to characterize, for it transcends theatrical forms, reflecting in semi-realistic manner certain aspects of life itself. Concerned (just as much as *Days of the Turbins*) with a particular society at a particular time, it none the less has greater universality. Watching it, one has the impression that this is simply truth, a part of life with all its complexities; that the play is about man with all his strengths and weaknesses – this represented above all in Khludov, who is, as all of us, guilty although honest. His dilemma is a real one, involving the terrifying consequences of taking responsibility. Thus his enemies might regard him as a modern Macbeth – but he is one who has been motivated, not by desires of personal glory but by a cause in which he believes; one too who, after seeing Banquo's ghost, stops in his tracks and tries to expiate his guilt. The other characters, too, are recognizable in any society, with problems which all may potentially face. For this reason – combined with the atmosphere created by its theatrical effects – the play is unforgettable. As one British critic has written, 'all human fleeing life is there; it's a world which one cannot easily forget or ignore.'[38]

37 **325**, p. 73
38 **400**

For Bulgakov, *Flight* represents the height of his achievement as a playwright. In Russian theatre it stands out as unique, and is already assured there of a permanent place. The same should be true of world theatre, once the play has had time to become better known than at present.

REJECTION AND DESPAIR

In the years at the end of the twenties, Bulgakov and Lyubov Yevgenievna took full advantage of the cultural life of the capital, and had many friends in the theatrical and literary world.[39] They particularly looked forward to theatrical premières and saw most of the new plays, which they would discuss with interest. Bulgakov even developed his own terminology to describe the plays they saw: 'boringly gay,' 'waltz with figures,' and so on. (Surprisingly, he was not particularly attracted to the cinema, which he pretended not to understand. His wife recalls one occasion when he kept asking 'who had walloped whom, the good guy – the bad guy or vice versa?' so that two ladies in the audience, not understanding the joke, insisted she should explain it to him.) Concerts and the opera were a great source of pleasure, for he had never lost his love of music. He still played the piano well, and liked to sing to himself a particular aria from *Aïda* which, with *Faust*, was his favourite opera. Frequently there were singers and musicians in the Bulgakovs' flat, and on occasions their friends would put on impromptu concerts. 'I particularly appreciate music which helps me to think,' Bulgakov used to say. His love for music is reflected in his works and the composers' names he uses for many of his characters.

One frequent visitor at that time was the artist N.A. Ushakova-Lyamina, who often drew Bulgakov, and in fact had included a picture of him fetching firewood, complete with monocle, in an illustrated book about cats, *Muka Maki*, in 1927. Both Bulgakov and his wife loved animals and had various cats until 1929, when they acquired a dog, which Bulgakov named Bouton after Molière's servant in the play he was now writing. (He would include a description of how he had obtained the dog in the play *Adam and Eve*. The sign 'Bouton Bulgakov – ring twice' was pinned on the door.) Animals too are frequently mentioned in Bulgakov's works: Pilate's dog in *The Master and Margarita* was given Lyubov Yevgenievna's nickname, Banga.

It was about this time that Sergey Yermolinsky began coming to the apartment, to visit a young girl who was staying there, M.A. Chimishkyan, whom the Bulgakovs had met in Tbilisi. Later, she would become his wife, and Bulgakov

39 The following is based on conversations with L.Ye. Belozerskaya and on her unpublished memoirs.

his lifelong friend. Yermolinsky has written of the comfort and slightly Bohe-mian atmosphere he found there, of the many guests, and of how sometimes Bulgakov would leave them and shut himself away in his study to work: when everything else just ceased to concern him.[40] He mentions the extraneous and casual nature of Bulgakov's friendships, and indeed we find other similar refer-ences – his friendships appear to be almost inconsequential – reminding us that despite Bulgakov's great charm he was essentially a reserved, even shy, man, for whom anything that prevented him from writing was something of a nuisance. Although he would write at all times of the day – not, however, sitting down to do so regularly at precise hours – he particularly liked to write at night, when everything was quiet. 'He would write in his large, very characteristic handwrit-ing, without pressure, in thick notebooks and for the time being there were no encroachments upon his work – no interference, no one looking over his shoul-der.' There were times too when he was idle, for he worked in bursts of energy and then would be exhausted.

The year 1929 was when he wrote *Molière (A Cabal of Hypocrites)*; the pre-vious year he had started on a novel about the devil (possible titles: 'The Black Magician' or 'The Engineer's Hoof') which, years later and greatly transformed, would become his masterpiece, *The Master and Margarita*. Also in 1928 he had written an introduction to a novel by his old friend Yury Slyozkin, showing, albeit in ironical terms, his distinct lack of enthusiasm for the other's concern with an entirely imaginary world of sentiment: for Bulgakov literature had to be concerned with actual life, not just beautiful stories.[41] He was always con-scious of the responsibility of being a writer, and disliked those who took it less seriously or were less than honest. E. Mindlin relates how once at an open dis-cussion Bulgakov had made fun of a writer from Kharkov who had written a love scene with the couple whispering 'sweet nothings' about the international revolution and singing to each other the 'Internationale.' Bulgakov maintained that the fact that there had been a Tolstoy in Russian literature obliged every Russian writer to be mercilessly strict towards himself and to others. It obliged him: 'To complete truth of thought and word ... To utter sincerity. To knowing why and for what end you are writing! To a merciless intolerance towards every untruth in your own compositions! That's what the fact that there was a Lev Tolstoy in Russia obliges us to!'[42]

The violent critics of the RAPP, concerned only with the social purpose of literature, had of course no use for such idealism. Writers such as Blyum could

40 **266**, p. 82. See also, for what follows, pp. 89, 87.
41 **522**, pp. 85-9
42 **382**, pp. 154-5

even maintain that satire could no nothing but harm towards the cause of social-ism. In the article he published in February 1929, 'The Right-wing Danger and the Theatre,' he is concerned solely with Bulgakov's class attitude. Central to the article is a cartoon showing Bulgakov as a chef (complete with monocle) serving up a dish of puppet officers and aristocrats; the smell from this rises diagonally across the whole page and in the top corner an honest citizen is holding his nose. The caption reads 'Playwright Bulgakov with his concoctions.'[43] Blyum was but one of many; despite Bulgakov's popularity, he had enemies on all sides. When Mayakovsky's *The Bedbug* opened on 13 February 1929, Bulgakov was to find his name included in it in a dictionary list of 'obsolete' words.

For the relative artistic liberalism of the twenties was drawing to an end. The New Economic Policy had ended in 1928 and been replaced by the first five-year plan. The first sabotage trials had been held, Trotsky had been expelled first from the Party, then from the country. Forced collectivization of agriculture was on its way, so was the cult of Stalin and absolute subservience to the offi-cial line. And Bulgakov was not very good at conforming. As his album of criti-cal articles grew he became more and more impatient, more irritable, and more suspicious. He began to sleep badly and to develop a nervous tick of jerking his head and shoulders. And now all his plays were banned, his books were removed from the libraries. As a writer he was indeed in a difficult position. Outstand-ingly honest, he was unable to praise his society without qualification, as the critics demanded, nor could he hide his belief in the freedom of the artist or in values which at this time seemed no longer relevant. As the critic R. Pikel put it, exulting after the banning of Bulgakov's plays: 'His talent is as obvious as is the socially reactionary nature of his works ... *The withdrawal of Bulgakov's plays* signifies a thematic sanitary cleansing of the repertory.'[44] It was the beginning of a decade of repression that not all would survive, and a number of Bulgakov's enemies would themselves perish in the purges that would take place, Pikel, Averbakh, and Kirshon amongst them. Yet paradoxically, as far as his writing was concerned, Bulgakov still managed at times to express a certain optimism, which in the long run was justified. 'I don't believe in hiding a light under a bushel,' was one of his favourite sayings: sooner or later it would be possible to say what one wanted.

On a practical level, with his plays withdrawn he was again short of money. A thousand roubles, the advance he received for *Flight*, had to be repaid to the Art Theatre: this was the agreement if a play should be banned before perform-

43 227
44 430. A fascinating account of Pikel's subsequent fate, as a somewhat unwilling employee of the NKVD (the acronym of the secret police at that time), is given in **414**, pp. 82-177.

ance.[45] Furthermore, he had not received payment for his works taken abroad and published without his permission: *Days of the Turbins* and *Zoyka's Apartment* in Berlin, *The White Guard* in Riga. (The publication of the first of these was the subject of a long correspondence between Bulgakov and the former publisher of *Rossiia*, S. Kagansky, who claimed unjustifiably that he was Bulgakov's authorized agent.)[46] By 1929 Bulgakov's financial position was such that he was obliged to accept 5000 roubles from his friend Veresaev.[47]

That year, however, brought even further troubles. In February, at a reception where he had been playing the piano, he met the woman who would eventually become his third wife, Yelena Sergeevna Shilovskaya (née Nyurenberg), a friend of his wife's.[48] Two years younger than Bulgakov, she had spent her childhood in Riga, in a family which was devoted to the theatre. Her father, a tax inspector, had written theatrical reviews for the journal *Teatr i iskusstvo*, while her older sister Olga, after initially wanting to become an actress, had become Nemirovich-Danchenko's secretary in the Art Theatre (O.S. Bokshanskaya). For Yelena Sergeevna, Bulgakov would begin in September 1929, in the form of letters, his autobiographical manuscript 'To a Secret Friend,' the basis for his later *Theatrical Romance.* His secret relationship with her and the strong physical attraction that existed between them would later be reflected in that of the Master with Margarita. But now the problems seemed overwhelming. Bulgakov was a poor writer who could not be published, while Yelena Sergeevna, as the wife of Lieutenant General Ye.A. Shilovsky, chief of staff of the Moscow Military District, was a member of the Moscow élite. Divorces for both of them at that time would involve too many people and cause too many problems. Regretfully they decided there was nothing that could be done, and for a time agreed to stop seeing each other.

It was a low point in Bulgakov's career, and in July 1929 he drafted a letter to Stalin, Kalinin, Svidersky, and Gorky.[49] In it he spoke of the banning of his plays, the police interrogation and search, his earlier request for a short trip abroad which had been refused, the campaign of the critics against him, and the

45 See **188**, folio 7715
46 **352**, pp. 135-7. The versions are **20**, **173**, and **167**.
47 **346**, p. 254. The author apparently received this information from Bulgakov's widow.
48 I did not have the fortune of meeting Yelena Sergeevna before her death in 1970. Information in this chapter is based on conversations reported to me by L.Ye. Belozerskaya, Irina Ivanovna Bulgakova-Koeppen, Miss Avril Pyman, and M. Michel Vassilieff; see also **9**, p. xvii; **40**, p. 33; and **345**, p. 638. For 'To a Secret Friend,' see **245**, pp. 226-7; **177**; **491**, p. 93.
49 For this and the following three letters to Yenukidze and Gorky, see **379**, pp. 151-4. Two are also in **448**, pp. 450-1.

unauthorized publication of his works in Berlin and Riga. His wife too, he said, had asked to go abroad, to put his affairs in order, and been refused. His manuscripts had not been returned by the GPU; he had been refused permission to send *Flight* abroad: 'Towards the end of my tenth year [as a writer], my strength has given way, and without the means of existence, persecuted, knowing that within the boundaries of the USSR I may neither be printed nor performed any more, reduced to a state of nervous disorder, I turn to you and ask for your intercession with the government of the USSR to exile me beyond the borders of the USSR together with my wife L.Ye. Bulgakova, who joins in this petition.'

The letter was probably not sent, although we cannot be absolutely certain, but on 3 September Bulgakov wrote a shorter letter to Yenukidze, stressing that as a writer he was condemned and unable even to pay his taxes, and again asking leave to go abroad with his wife 'for the period which the government of the Soviet Union will find necessary to allot me.' The same day he wrote to Gorky asking for his intercession: 'My fatigue and despair are without limit. I cannot write anything ... Why keep a writer in a country where his works cannot exist? I ask for a humane resolution – to let me go.' Receiving a request from Gorky for a copy of his letter (through the writer Zamyatin – who also requested to go abroad, and was finally allowed to do so in 1931), he repeated its contents in another letter on 28 September, adding that not a line of his was being printed, that he had no work and not a kopeck of author's honorarium. 'In a word, everything written by me in ten years of work in the USSR has been destroyed. There remains only to destroy the last thing remaining – myself.' Nothing came of these applications.

In the meantime, despite his growing depression, Bulgakov finished his play *Molière*, and read it to the Art Theatre. Although it was received well, we find Leonidov writing on 30 January 1930 to Stanislavsky (who spent a year and a half in Nice after his first attack of angina pectoris) that nothing could be done about it at the time because of the theatre's greater need for contemporary plays. Stanislavsky hesitated, answering that it was very interesting about Bulgakov's play ('Won't he give it to someone else? That would be a pity') and that the artist Golovin should do the scenery for it. But on 18 February the play was in any case banned by *Glavrepertkom.* [50]

'A profound depression came over me, and strange premonitions. I began to be afraid of the dark. In short, I was slipping into psychic illness': Bulgakov's description in *The Master and Margarita* would seem to refer, with only slight exaggeration, to his own nervous state at this time. In a mood of despair, he sud-

[50] See **343**, pp. 323, 333, and **494**, p. 224. In his letter to the Soviet government Bulgakov erroneously writes that *Molière* was banned on 18 May rather than 18 February.

denly burnt the bulk of his novel about the devil: tearing the manuscript vertically and keeping only the left-hand third of the pages, all that remains in the
archives.[51] He also destroyed the drafts of a novel 'Theatre' (possibly the genesis
of *Theatrical Romance*, written on the basis of his 'To a Secret Friend') and a
comedy (probably an early version of *Bliss*). At this time he would sometimes
speak of literary suicide, and there exists too a draft of a suicidal poem. It was
Yelena Sergeevna who finally persuaded him to write to Stalin himself, and he
did so with the intention, she has recalled, of actually committing suicide if he
did not receive a favourable reply. Although his wife at the time disputes this,
according to Yelena Sergeevna he owned a gun, illegally, which she had taken
from him, saying it would be less dangerous for a person with her connections.
Afterwards, they went together to throw the gun into a pond not far from the
Novodevichy Monastery.

On 28 March 1930 Bulgakov sent a letter to the Soviet government in the
person of Stalin himself and, apparently, to seven others including Lunacharsky.[52] Once again, there exists some doubt as to whether the published text is
that which was actually sent, although the available copy is undoubtedly in Bulgakov's writing. Possibly it is a first draft, as Bulgakov's sister Nadya maintained;
it is also very long, whereas according to Lyubov Yevgenievna her husband followed the advice of a friend, who told him that letters to the government should
be particularly brief. But at all events a letter was sent, whether or not it contained all the ideas expressed in Bulgakov's original.

In this he spoke frankly of his inability to write a 'communist play': he had
not even tried to do so, 'knowing full well that such a play would not work out
in my case.' He stated that of 301 reviews devoted to his works, three had been
favourable and 298 hostile, and he gave examples for the purpose of showing
how the press and repertory authorities had '*with unusual fury* proved that the
works of M. Bulgakov cannot exist in the USSR. And I declare,' he continued,
'that the Soviet press is *quite right.*' Referring to *The Crimson Island*, he
affirmed that in it he did indeed appeal for freedom of the press, to do so and to
struggle with censorship being his duty as a writer. He himself had become a satirist, yet Blyum had said that satire was not needed in the Soviet Union: 'Am I

---

51 I am indebted to Lev Shilov and to Marietta O. Chudakova, who works in the Manuscript
Division of the Lenin Library, for this information. See too her **245**, pp. 219-20. Bulgakov refers to this, and the other works destroyed, in his letter to Stalin. The quotation is
from **100**, p. 162.
52 This information, and that about the draft of the poem, was supplied by K.L. Rudnitsky.
The letter is translated, somewhat inaccurately, in **184**. For the Russian text, see **183**.
There is some confusion in the different sources over the number of reviews of Bulgakov:
301 and 298 hostile, or 300 and 297 hostile.

conceivable in the USSR?' he asked. He also defended his honest account of the intelligentsia in *Days of the Turbins*, *Flight*, and *The White Guard*. Now all his works were banned; as a writer he was destroyed. Thus he asked the Soviet government to let him leave, or failing that to find him work in the theatre (more specifically, in the Moscow Art Theatre[53]) as a producer, as an extra, or even a stage-hand. 'And if even this is impossible, I ask the Soviet Government to do as it thinks fit with me, but at least to do something with me, because I – a dramatist who has written five plays, who is well known in the USSR and abroad, and who is available at a moment's notice – am afflicted by misery, penury, and ruin.'

The letter was answered three weeks later. On 18 April (four days after Mayakovsky's suicide) Stalin personally telephoned Bulgakov. He was alone with his wife at the time, and she listened in on the extension earpiece. Told by Bulgakov of the conversation afterwards, Yelena Sergeevna noted down its essence in her diary:

'We have received your letter. And read it with our comrades. You will have a favourable answer to it. Perhaps we really should let you go abroad? So we've made you very tired of us?'

'I've been thinking a great deal recently as to whether a Russian writer can live outside his native land, and it seems to me that he can't.'

'You're right. I don't think so either. Where do you want to work? At the Art Theatre?'

'Yes, I would like to. But I spoke about it and was refused.'

'Well, put in an application there. I think they will agree ...'

Bulgakov thus turned down his one and only opportunity to leave the country. But Stalin had been willing to give him some protection – which would be valuable in the years to come.

Almost immediately, Bulgakov began working on an adaptation of Gogol's *Dead Souls* for the Art Theatre, in consultation with the producer, V.G. Sakhnovsky, but he did not actually join the theatre at this time. Indeed, shortly after Stalin's telephone call he was visited by F.F. Knorre and N. Kryuchkov with an offer of employment from the so-called Theatres of Working Youth (known by their initials, TRAM). These theatres, of which there were about seventy by 1930, were an attempt to involve the proletariat in theatrical enterprises of an amateurish nature, with the main emphasis on simple propaganda

---

53 This particular sentence does not appear in **183** but is quoted in **352**, p. 138. The extract that follows from Yelena Sergeevna's diary is quoted on p. 139 of the same article.

plays. With their assumption that there was no real need for mastery and their isolation from the professional theatre, yet with their pretensions at creating a new kind of 'TRAM' drama, they must have been totally alien to Bulgakov. But he nevertheless accepted the offer, and was formally employed as of 1 April.[54] With Knorre and Kryuchkov he then went to the south to become acquainted with TRAM's work, staying in the Pension Magnolia in Yalta (from where he wrote in July to his fellow dramatist Natalya Venkshtern of 'boredom so monstrous you can find it only in dreams').

He returned to Moscow on 3 August, when he was finally appointed producer at the Moscow Art Theatre. On 6 August he wrote to Stanislavsky (who was still abroad) to express his pleasure at the appointment.[55] Stanislavsky too was delighted. On 2 September he wrote from Badenweiler to the theatre director, M.S. Geytts: 'We place great hopes in Bulgakov. You will see he may make a producer. He is not only a writer, but an actor as well. I am judging from the way he demonstrated to the actors at rehearsals of *The Turbins*. Really he produced it, at least gave those sparkles which glittered and created the success of the spectacle.' And welcoming Bulgakov in a letter two days later he repeated that he had felt in him both a producer and an actor: 'Molière and many others combined these professions with literature!'[56]

At least now Bulgakov had the means to exist and was able to continue work in the theatre. Some aspects of this he would enjoy, but basically it was the beginning of a frustrating time in his life, as he would gradually come to realize the difference between Stanislavsky's and his own ideas. His growing nervous condition did not improve. Nor did his public image: in a handbook on Soviet writers published that year he was referred to as belonging 'to the right wing of our literature, being one of the neo-bourgeois writers.'[57] But generally he was not so much in the news: at the beginning of the thirties the controversies around Bulgakov were largely forgotten.

---

54 See **187**, folio 521, from which it appears that his employment was backdated to the beginning of the month. See also **449**, p. 560, and **186**, *fond* 2050, *opis* 1, folio 197. Information also supplied by L.Ye. Belozerskaya.
55 Quoted from the Theatre Archives in **2**, pp. 35-6
56 **494**, pp. 269, 270
57 **499**, p. 45

8

The Moscow Art Theatre, 1930-32

The first years of Bulgakov's employment at the Moscow Art Theatre were largely devoted to the production of *Dead Souls* and, unfortunately, were typical of the frustrations that he would continue to endure. Work on the play began in 1930 and dragged on over two years, with a great deal of rewriting. But at this stage of his relationship with the theatre Bulgakov was more accommodating than he would be later: perhaps because he desperately needed the work, perhaps because *Dead Souls* was after all only an adaptation from Gogol and not an original work. Even after entering the theatre Bulgakov continued to work for TRAM in the evenings as well, acting as reader for plays submitted.[1] It was something he hated, and one can only assume that he was obliged to accept it for financial reasons. He endured it until 15 March 1931, then resigned. Three days later he wrote to Stanislavsky that he just could not cope with TRAM work and asked him to include him amongst the actors at the Art Theatre as well as on the production side.[2] In a further letter to Stalin on 30 May, he said he left TRAM because his brain 'was ceasing to function.'

But he still worked desperately, writing at night, and starting once again to make plans for his novel about the devil, now referred to as 'Consultant with a Hoof.' He further undertook a production of Natalya Venkshtern's play *Solitary* for the Theatre of the Institute of Health Education, to be finished by July. He was already close to a state of nervous exhaustion: 'I overtaxed myself ... I am exhausted ... Now all my impressions are alike ...' The reason for writing to Stalin again was to ask permission to go abroad to recuperate from his ill-health:[3]

1 Information supplied by M.O. Chudakova; see also **449**, p. 560, and **187**, folio 521.
2 **188**, folio 7714; also translated in **449**, p. 560
3 The letter is published in **379**, pp. 154-7.

Since the end of 1930 I have been suffering from a severe form of neurasthenia with fits of terror and anguish of heart, and now I've had it. I have ideas in me but I have not the physical strength or the conditions to carry out the work. The cause of my illness is quite clear to me: in the wide field of Russian literature in the USSR I was the only literary wolf. I was advised to dye my skin ... I was treated life a wolf too ... I am not malicious, but I am very tired and at the end of 1929 I collapsed.

...

The cause of my illness is the persecution of many years and then silence.

He had no desire to emigrate, he said, but needed to see the world and then return. His wife had to go with him for he was seriously ill: 'I suffer from fits of terror when I am alone.' He concluded by saying that his dream was to be summoned personally to Stalin. As far as is known, his letter remained unanswered.

Paustovsky relates how Bulgakov would invent stories about a meeting with Stalin, who would provide him with new clothes and express his concern that the theatres were not putting on his plays[4] – despite Bulgakov's strained nerves he could still be humorous. The actors in *Dead Souls* continued to respect him highly, and he showed his usual brilliance in directing them; he even substituted for them when they were sick. His love for the theatre remained with him, and according to Yanshin he seriously considered acting himself – as his letter to Stanislavsky had indicated. Later that year he would write to Popov: 'I hope ... it will become clear that I am conceivable only on the stage ...'[5] But above all he was tired. In July he and his wife went on holiday to Zubtsov, visiting Natalya Venkshtern, whose play he had been working on. 'My plan?' he wrote to her: 'To sit ... alone and write, enjoying elevated literary conversations with you. Outside of writing, I'll lead a bare type of life: dressing-gown, slippers, sleeping, eating ... We'll *entertain* each other with *gay* stories.'[6] By the end of August he had completed another play, *Adam and Eve*. Then he began work on a further adaptation, of Tolstoy's *War and Peace*, which would be finished the following year. That autumn Stanislavsky started to take a hand in the production of *Dead Souls*. And now there was good news, for Bulgakov's play of 1929, *Molière*, was finally put in the repertory of the Art Theatre (although its production would drag on disastrously for four years).

However quiet and lonely Bulgakov's life now was, he himself was still appreciated in the theatrical and literary world. In December 1931 Nemirovich-

4 **419**, pp. 64-6
5 **379**, pp. 162-3
6 **186**, *fond* 2050, *opis* 1, folio 197

Danchenko wrote: 'Of all those writing for the stage I at present feel a real play-wright only in three: Bulgakov, Afinogenov, and Olesha.' On 4 February Gorky in a letter to Markov suggested for the fifteenth anniversary of the Revolution a satirical survey of the most characteristic events of European life: 'I have several ideas and themes which I would like to present to the attention and judgement of our talented playwrights: Bulgakov, Afinogenov, Olesha, and also Vsev. Ivanov, Leonov, and others.'[7]

The year 1932 began well. In January permission was granted for the restag-ing of *Days of the Turbins*, the result (according to the actor Leonidov) of Stalin's intervention after being asked if the play could really not be performed. For Bulgakov 'a part of his life was restored.'[8] On 15 or 16 January (Bulgakov mentions both dates) the theatre telephoned to tell him the news. 'It's unpleas-ant for me to admit,' he wrote to Popov on the 25th, 'that the news over-whelmed me. I became physically unwell. Joy sprang up, but immediately so did my melancholy.'[9] He then told Popov a delightful story, written with all his cus-tomary humour, of how the new domestic help, a simpleton, had foreseen that the play would be performed just a few minutes before the call. According to Sergey Orlovsky, who worked in the theatre, at Stalin's request the play was then put back on the stage within four days so he could come and see it, and cer-tainly Bulgakov is recorded as attending a rehearsal on 20 January.[10]

The public opening was a month later, on 18 February. 'All the way from the Tverskaya to the theatre,' Bulgakov wrote to Popov, 'there stood male figures murmuring mechanically "do you have a spare ticket?" It was the same in the direction of the Dmitrovka.' Bulgakov watched the play from the wings. After-wards there were twenty curtain calls. He himself did not go out, having decided against it when a messenger arrived from Stanislavsky with the obvious intention of advising him not to. 'There was no particular wisdom in this decision. It was a very simple decision. I want neither tributes, nor curtain calls, generally I want nothing except for the love of Christ to be left in peace, to be able to take hot baths and not think every day of what to do with my dog when the apartment lease expires in June.'

By April, when this letter to Popov was written, Bulgakov's weariness and de-pression had caught up with him again. He was becoming more frustrated with the work on *Dead Souls*, which was now entering its final phase. And then there

7 **278**, p. 444, and **293**, p. 30
8 **491**, p. 97; see also **342**
9 For this and subsequent letters to Popov, see **379**, pp. 163-7.
10 **415**, p. 86, and **188**, folio 77. The latter is the rehearsal diary for *Dead Souls*, where Bulgakov is recorded as absent to attend the rehearsal of *Days of the Turbins*. Stalin is not mentioned there – but we would not necessarily expect him to be.

had been problems with *Molière*, which had been temporarily 'killed' by his 'fellow dramatist,' Vsevolod Vishnevsky: Bulgakov wrote bitterly about him to Popov. (Vishnevsky, considerably more sympathetic to the communist cause, made it his business to attack other 'erring' writers and critics too – such as Averbakh and Kirshon – and had also written unfavourably on the renewal of *Days of the Turbins*. In a parodistic prologue to the first variant of his *Optimistic Tragedy*, the Turbin brothers appear amongst other stage characters he condemns.[11])

None the less, Bulgakov still was able to sign a contract for a biography of Molière in book form, and *Days of the Turbins* had come to stay: for many years he would be remembered at least as the author of this play. *Dead Souls* opened at the end of the year. And 1932 was notable for Bulgakov in another respect, for it was now that he finally divorced his second wife, Lyubov Yevgenievna, and in October married the woman he had met three years previously, Yelena Sergeevna Shilovskaya: the inspiration for his heroine in his greatest book.

DEAD SOULS (adaptation)

Bulgakov began to discuss an adaptation of *Dead Souls* with the producer Sakhnovsky and literary consultant Markov in April 1930, apparently because the adaptation on which he was expecting to work as assistant producer was sadly inadequate: 'I understood that while yet on the threshold of the theatre I had come to grief – they had appointed me for a non-existent play ... In short, it was up to me to write it.'[12] But all along he had his doubts: '*It is impossible to make an adaptation* of *Dead Souls*,' he later wrote to Popov. 'Take this as axiomatic from a man who knows the work well.' He began work the next month, while discussions with Sakhnovsky (and for a while with Markov) continued. These were supplemented by a great deal of research, which involved reading Gogol's letters (including his *Selected Passages from Correspondence with Friends*), various contemporary documents, articles, and letters by Belinsky, Herzen, Chernyshevsky, and Zhukovsky.

In its final form, the play begins with a prologue where Chichikov, talking to the secretary of the trusteeship council, gets the idea of purchasing from other estates serfs who had died ('dead souls') but who, for official purposes, are counted as alive until the time of the next census. He can then mortgage his

11 See **407**, II, p. 35
12 **491**, p. 97. For other details, see **9**, pp. xx, xxvi, n 8, and **471**. Much of what follows
   is based on Sakhnovsky's statements, in this article, in **473**, pp. 201–77, and in **472**.
   Versions of the text consulted are in **188**, folios 4, 13, 17, 338, 640, 948.

estate on the basis of an apparently large number of serfs, whom he has acquired at bargain rates. The play then follows the main events of Gogol's story in Part I of the book (but with some change in the order and content of the scenes): Chichikov's introduction to the landowners and officials in a provincial town, and his visits to Manilov, Sobakevich, Plyushkin, Nozdryov, and Korobochka in turn; followed by a ball at the governor's, where Chichikov's secret is revealed by Nozdryov. The conclusion is based on Part II of Gogol's novel: Chichikov is arrested in his room as he is preparing to leave, but once in prison he manages to bribe his jailors and the police captain, and make his escape.

Bulgakov's original conception differed from the final version in a number of respects. Despite his hesitations over the adaptation as a whole, he seriously attempted to capture the spirit of Gogol in a reasonably free and original manner. Sakhnovsky, it seemed, encouraged him. The prologue was at first to take place in Gogol's beloved Rome, with him standing and writing *Dead Souls* or dictating it to Annenkov. But then Bulgakov changed his mind and set it instead in a Russian inn (although some suggestions of Italy were still to remain in the original sets).[13] The main feature of the original version was a narrator, Gogol himself, referred to as 'the first character in the play,' appearing at the beginning to introduce Chichikov, and in many of the subsequent scenes to give Gogol's own thoughts on life. There were, too, a number of other scenes or incidents which were later eliminated. As in Gogol, a police captain was to appear in time to rescue Chichikov from being beaten by Nozdryov. The scene with Korobochka was to begin with Chichikov's arrival at her house in a storm: this was considered particularly important and was to include a whole concert of barking dogs (which Bulgakov and Sakhnovsky worked on with gramophone records at home). In the ball scene there was to be a certain amount of 'devilry,' with Chichikov running away and the others looking for him all over the place, even in the chandelier, really thinking he was a devil; then Korobochka would come in, asking the current price of dead souls.[14] And Gogol's mysterious Captain Kopeykin was actually to appear in the interrogation scene (after the postmaster, played by Yanshin, had related his story), with the public prosecutor dying soon after. As a finale, the narrator was to read Gogol's famous description of the departing troika. Its bells would be heard, joined by other bells coming in from all sides; there was to be a loud thundering of the troika, and a voice singing the coachman's song. A choir and an organ would take this up, all rising to a tremendous crescendo, and then dying away again.

13 See also **377**, p. 167. For the narrator's passages in the original version, see **380**. This contains a detailed account of progress on the play and of the influence of Meyerhold on the original conception; also a valuable textual comparison with Gogol's works.
14 See the versions of the play in **187**, folios 164-7. Other information is based on personal interviews and on **308**, p. 180.

The play was read to the theatre on 2 December 1930 and rehearsals of this early version started soon after.[15] There followed a long and trying experimental period, with scenes added and then cut again as the play was found to be too long: an entry in the rehearsal protocols on 8 January 1931 records sixteen scenes and a prologue and an epilogue, compared with only twelve and a prologue in the final version. And there were long discussions over the role of the narrator (to be played by Kachalov). It gradually became evident, however, that there was a real conflict about what the play was trying to do, and this became more acute as rehearsals continued throughout 1931. Bulgakov and Sakhnovsky were concerned with the more fantastic, universal side of Gogol, rather than with the strictly realistic. Nor was the text the only problem. Almost as important was the stage set, to be designed by V.V. Dmitriev. First, the deadlines for viewing the model had to be extended. Then, when the mock-ups for the third and fourth acts were ready, they were not to the liking of Stanislavsky, who on 18 February had a three-hour discussion about them with Sakhnovsky. In April this was twice repeated. Already it was becoming apparent that the production would have to be delayed.

The main problem was that Dmitriev, whose sketches Bulgakov approved, also departed from Stanislavsky's ideas of theatrical realism, attempting to show the personality of the characters through their homes and possessions and to emphasize Chichikov's acquisitive passion: filling the stage with objects of all kinds, with symbolical significance.[16] According to Sakhnovsky, 'From all this material Dmitriev created some monstrous pieces of furniture of a type of its own ... The furniture and objects were distorted and exaggerated. Every object seemed to have its own kind of misshapen appearance ...' A great deal was done, too, using different planes of action on stage, and many accused Dmitriev of being too much under the influence of the 'formalist' theatre – referring to Meyerhold's controversial 1926 production of Gogol's *Inspector General.* To suggest something of a dreamlike, unreal atmosphere Dmitriev had the sets painted with blurred edges, so they seemed to fade away into an indistinct mist – which turned out to be distracting. He tried having different colours for different scenes. He then tried painting in the corners again, making them seem to appear from behind curtains, which formed a 'framework' for the setting.

The more fundamental problem, of course, lay with the theatre itself. It had grown up on the basis of a strong realistic tradition, and its members were simply out of their depth when it came to techniques involving 'grotesqueness and eccentricity,' which they did not understand: *Dead Souls* had, by one means or another, to become a 'realistic' production.

15 **270**, p. 752, and **188**, folios 76-8
16 **246** and **510**, pp. 220-2

Bulgakov constantly attended rehearsals throughout 1931, and so on occasions did Stanislavsky. With the beginning of the new season in September, however, concerned that the overall tone for the play had still not been found, Stanislavsky began to take it in hand and impose his own ideas upon it – often rehearsing the actors at his flat, for he was ill at the time. And to add realism to the production the theatre concentrated on acquiring genuine period furniture, consulting old drawings, borrowing from museums, and even buying a great deal at auctions: there are endless lists of stage properties and diagrams in the rehearsals protocol for this period. In October *Sovetskoe iskusstvo*, reporting on the rehearsals, emphasized that the theatre regarded *Dead Souls* as a real portrait of the age of Nicolas I and considered that Gogol was trying to show real, live people.[17]

These were exactly Stanislavsky's ideas, and Sakhnovsky was not able to stand up to him. Stanislavsky went about the business with his usual thoroughness, analysing the characters, directing exercises – even spending four hours with Toporkov (Chichikov) on one line at the first rehearsal.[18] He insisted that the image of Gogol's Russia should be 'created by the performances of the actors themselves, and not by external production techniques.' At first Bulgakov seems to have deferred to him as someone with greater experience, and even wrote on 31 December 1931 to express his pleasure at his coming to a rehearsal of the ball and supper scenes at the governor's: 'I do not worry about Gogol when you are on the stage.'[19] Yet it was certainly not easy for Bulgakov to give up his strongly held views. He had loved Gogol ever since his childhood, although he had only gradually come to understand him as a 'genius with his bitter laughter at the imperfection of human society and human relationships.'[20] And now he cannot have enjoyed seeing the book he knew and loved, whose whole atmosphere he had at least tried to capture, made into a routine realistic production with its principal emphasis supposedly on the ills of nineteenth-century Russia. In this case his own stage sense was accurate. *Dead Souls* is indeed a case of a play spoilt by the theatre, by Stanislavsky in particular. It was one more stage in Bulgakov's growing bitterness against all those who failed to appreciate or understand him as a writer. On 7 May 1932 he wrote wearily to Popov: 'So, dead souls ... In nine days time I shall be forty-one. It's monstrous! And so towards the end of my work as a writer I am forced to write adaptations. I look at my shelves and am horrified: who, who shall I yet have to adapt tomorrow? Turgenev, Leskov, the

17 **374**
18 **403**, pp. 320-1
19 Quoted in **460**, p. 425; also in **377**, p. 168, and in **448**, p. 455. **477**, p. 198, also indicates Bulgakov's warm respect for Stanislavsky at this period.
20 **372**, p. 387

Brockhaus-Efron Encyclopaedia? Ostrovsky? But the latter, fortunately, adapted himself, evidently foreseeing what would happen to me.'[21]

The last stage of the work (by which time the number of scenes had been reduced), with rehearsals at last underway in earnest, began after a dress rehearsal in April 1932, but a further dress rehearsal was postponed until November. It was now that the final textual changes were made, and Dmitriev, meanwhile, was replaced as designer by Simov, who provided the required realistic décor.

The play opened as the first new production of the season, before an audience of school children, on 23 November,[22] nearly two years since the first reading. Reaction to the subsequent performances was mixed. In terms of simple, realistic theatre the play was undoubtedly successful, and according to one critic received a public ovation. The actors came in for their share of praise, particularly Moskvin as Nozdryov, who was considered to be outstanding. Plyushkin, played by Leonidov, became almost a tragic figure, yet a typical miser, like a bird of prey. Toporkov as Chichikov was not quite so successful, managing only, as the critic from *Vecherniaia Moskva* indicated, to show him as a rogue and swindler. The same critic, however, took a very favourable view of the play as a whole.[23]

Almost immediately other reviews began to express doubts – although for the first time there was no personal attack on Bulgakov. Beskin stressed that the main fault was lack of social background, saying that the laughter was of the wrong kind; other critics, while praising the acting, predictably took a similarly strong social line. The whole aim of the production, wrote the notorious RAPP critic Vladimir Yermilov, was to show that Chichikov too was a human being, whereas properly performed the play could have been a powerful weapon of struggle: 'To be closer to Gogol, one must be closer to our contemporary life.' There were a number of public discussions of the play, one in the 'Hammer and Sickle' Factory, with Sakhnovsky, Toporkov, and Kedrov (Manilov) taking part. Most present attacked it, although the editor of *Rabochaia Moskva*, which had organized the discussion, maintained that it was still a lively illustration to the book.[24]

There were, however, a number of reviews which treated the play more seriously from the artistic point of view and pointed clearly to its undoubted weaknesses: that it was too much an illustration of individual scenes from the book;

21 Quoted in **266**, p. 89, and **2**, p. 31
22 Various dates have been given for the première. According to newspaper reports, there were closed performances on 23 and 28 November and 1 and 4 December, with the official première on 9 December. (I am grateful to Miss Lesley Milne for this information.)
23 **505**, p. 70; **301**, p. 375; **300**
24 **219**, **264**, **318**, and **513**

for someone who had not read this there were no links between scenes; characters too were episodic; and there was none of Gogol's sad laughter.[25] The most substantial of such criticisms, by D. Talnikov, maintained that there *were* no successful adaptations and that even Gogol himself could not have made a successful one of *Dead Souls*. The Art Theatre had provided a perfect example of this in producing material that was dramatically weak and furthermore had not been overcome theatrically, although this was hardly the fault of the adapter. Gogol's whole style of 'grotesque' rather than 'everyday' realism was absent: indeed Gogol was foreign to the realistic methods of the Art Theatre, which had also been wrong to abandon the narrator. Dmitriev's exaggerated sets, Talnikov thought, would have been better than Simov's realistic ones. Chichikov should have been shown more as a symbol, a man who was found everywhere – in Captain Kopeykin and in Napoleon too. The play was too realistic, and Meyerhold's production of Gogol's *Inspector General* had been far better.[26]

It must have been frustrating for Bulgakov to read this, for here basically were his own ideas, which had been worn down by the insistence of the theatre. It was in fact a total justification for his original conception or, at a more remote stage, for his conviction that it was impossible to dramatize *Dead Souls* at all. Andrey Bely (whose book on Gogol was published two years after) wrote a similar article, complaining at the lack of Gogol's 'lyrical digressions,' at the omission of symbolically significant details such as the story of Captain Kopeykin. He too compared the play unfavourably with Meyerhold's production. (Yermilov, in a second article, took exception to some of Bely's remarks and stressed again that there should be more in terms of content and ideas from a proletarian viewpoint: 'Gogol's truth has become part of the truth of the proletariat,' and it was this truth that was expected of the theatre.)[27]

None the less, in terms of the public, *Dead Souls* was a highly successful production and remained as standard fare in the Art Theatre repertory until the late sixties. By the end of 1958 it had already seen 696 performances. In 1965 the theatre took it to the Aldwych Theatre in London, and to New York, where it received mixed reviews. 'Cries out for more adventurousness on the part of the adapter,' one writes. Another: 'this production is a glorious example of the Moscow Art Theater's amazingly broad-based performing skill.'[28]

On 23 August 1952 a new production by M.V. Chezhegov opened at the Comedy Theatre in Leningrad. Interestingly, the narrator was restored, replacing

25 See, for example, **384**
26 **498**
27 **212, 265**
28 **230**, p. 27, and **307**

the prologue by reading from Gogol, and also reading a number of his 'lyrical passages' throughout.[29] The play was published in the West in 1964, together with *Ivan Vasilievich*, in Munich. In Russia a number of individual scenes have been published in collections for theatrical groups, but it has not appeared in its entirety.

In that *Dead Souls* is purely an adaptation of Gogol and hardly a play in its own right, it is difficult to discuss it on its own merits. Indeed, a main consideration frequently stressed by Sakhnovsky and others was that there should not be a single line which did not occur in Gogol. Whether, however, there is any particular merit in this is debatable, depending on how much importance we place on originality in an adaptation of another's work. As a direct representation of Gogol's major scenes on stage this adaptation is largely successful: in making what might have been an almost mechanical transfer from book to play, Bulgakov has shown considerable skill. Inevitably, he has had to condense or combine scenes of the original, or transfer speeches to different scenes, but the only falsification of Gogol to any degree is the ending, Chichikov's arrest and escape from prison, which is carried out by the characters in the town instead of the totally different characters in Part II of the book.

One cannot, of course, help but regret the omissions forced upon Bulgakov: Chichikov's arrival at Korobochka's and her appearance at the ball, the police captain coming to arrest Nozdryov, Captain Kopeykin. A scene depicting the dead souls themselves, as Chichikov reads over the lists of them, might also have added to the production. But such omissions can hardly be blamed on Bulgakov, who might indeed have produced a more interesting version had he been more able to go his own way and develop the fantastic side of Gogol – and in a theatre other than the Moscow Art Theatre. But this conflicted totally with the ideas of Stanislavsky, who is reported as saying:

The production must give a picture of Russia under Nicolas, genuinely as reflected by Gogol but in the interpretation of contemporary Soviet theatre. The social meaning of Gogolian satire must resound so that Gogol's poem should be close, comprehensible, and convincing to the Soviet spectator.

Dead Souls is one of those productions which build for the theatre the foundations of socialist realism.[30]

Such a view was undoubtedly coloured by political considerations.

Ultimately, we can add little to Talnikov's criticisms and we may agree with him that there are probably no entirely successful adaptations. Yet for all this,

29 **474**
30 **472**, p. 18

Dead Souls is effective in terms of its limited aim, as an accurate and unadventurous adaptation, to which Bulgakov brought his skill as a dramatist, while being denied the use of his own particular type of insight. In his own career, the play is significant more because of the frustrations it caused him – which would soon be repeated with an original work of his own – than as part of his literary achievement.

WAR AND PEACE (adaptation)

In September 1931, while work on *Dead Souls* was still going on, Bulgakov began his adaptation of *War and Peace*, for which he had already signed a contract with the Bolshoy Dramatic Theatre in Leningrad. But, not yet disillusioned with the Moscow Art Theatre, he hoped that it would also be accepted there and had suggested this to Stanislavsky on 30 August, pointing out that he had turned to the other theatre solely for financial reasons. 'It would be advisable for you to raise the question of a contract for *War and Peace* MOST URGENTLY,' he insists. 'I repeat: an iron necessity now governs my contracts.'[31] The Art Theatre certainly showed interest: Stanislavsky had in fact been interested in performing an adaptation of *War and Peace* as early as 1910. But Bulgakov's basic approach did not satisfy Nemirovich-Danchenko, who had his own ideas about producing the novel in the theatre, and wanted its author shown in a new way rather than having a routine adaptation. On 7 October he wrote: 'How will he develop all the stories? My plan was: three plays, complete, separate. Rather as I made *Nikolay Stavrogin* from the novel *The Devils*.'[32] Bulgakov did not adopt Nemirovich-Danchenko's suggestion of three separate plays. *War and Peace* was completed on 2 February 1932, but the performance never took place, nor has it ever been published in its entirety. (Three years later, Stanislavsky expressed interest in another adaptation by N.M. Alpers, but nothing seems to have come of this either.[33])

Bulgakov's adaptation begins after Pierre Bezukhov has already prevented the seduction of Natalya Rostova by Anatole Kuragin: covering, in terms of Tolstoy's novel, only the events of 1812 and ending with the victory of the Russian soldiers under Kutuzov over Napoleon. More than anything else, the play bears witness to the impracticality of the task itself. It is clearly impossible to show on stage more than a small part of the book, and to do this at all Bulgakov needed

31 See **187**, folios 206-8, and **188**, folio 7715; also **162**. The date of completion of the play is noted on the manuscript in **187**, folio 208.
32 **278**, p. 442
33 **494**, pp. 406-7

thirty scenes, which are of necessity short and depict only certain highlights. With 115 characters (plus narrator) to be included in a brief space there is no time for real character development: people are simply represented on stage and the viewer is left to make his own mental association with those figures he already knows from his reading of Tolstoy. Except for Pierre and Natasha, the characters appear only briefly. Even Prince Andrey occurs in only four scenes, while some of the secondary figures have no more than a few lines: Hélène, Anatole, Denisov, Karataev. Bulgakov thus relies very heavily on the audience's knowledge of the book itself, using the narrator where necessary to read some of Tolstoy's descriptions. (In the occasional scene he says more than the characters themselves or – an interesting technique – in scenes involving French acts as a kind of interpreter.)

Considering the tremendous difficulties of the task, Bulgakov's adaptation is remarkably competent. He has shown considerable skill in his selection of incidents and was wise enough to limit the scenes to those of one year, omitting not only the historical events but the whole story of Pierre's disastrous marriage with Hélène (who appears only briefly at the beginning), Pierre's duel with Dolokhov, Prince Andrey's courtship of Natasha, and Anatole's attempted seduction of her. Basically, he has taken a few key chapters – occasionally changing their order slightly – and reproduced the events and the dialogue in them with painstaking accuracy, if with necessary abbreviation. In this sense, the play is certainly faithful to Tolstoy. Nevertheless it still remains little more than an outline sketch which only serves to suggest Tolstoy's novel to the viewer. Again, one should not blame Bulgakov for this, except perhaps for attempting an impossible task. Few adaptations are really created anew by the adapter – in which case they may become almost independent works in their own right. Bulgakov chose to remain close to Tolstoy, as he had to Gogol, and limit himself to a competent if somewhat mechanical reproduction of a great original.

ADAM AND EVE

In the autumn of 1930 the Red Theatre in Leningrad, a young company badly in need of good plays, approached Bulgakov to write a play, allowing him choice of theme and paying him, at his insistence, a non-returnable advance.[34] (It further paid his way to Leningrad to acquaint him with the theatre and the city, which he had not previously visited.) By the next year he had completed *Adam and Eve*, in which Leningrad itself was shown as destroyed by a future war. He also

34 An account of this, with interesting descriptions of Bulgakov at the time, is found in **477**. His own letter to Stanislavsky on the subject is in **188**, folio 7715.

offered the play, in Moscow, to the Vakhtangov Theatre which, according to Bulgakov's letter to Stanislavsky on 30 August 1931, 'signed a contract with me as a matter of urgency without knowing a single letter from the play.' He would have preferred to offer it to the Art Theatre, he explained, but he was desperately short of money, could not wait until the Art Theatre would have decided on the play, and – if the play should be banned – could not repay the advance as the theatre's contracts demanded: 'I am constantly under the threat of being banned. An unthinkable clause! ... That's why my play went urgently to the Vakhtangov Theatre.'

The play was indeed not performed. The Red Theatre itself realized that it would be impossible, and when it was read to the Vakhtangov Theatre the commander of the armed forces, Ya.I. Alksnis, who had been specially invited, gave his opinion that the play could not be staged precisely because it showed the destruction of Leningrad.[35] Undoubtedly the censors found other reasons too. *Adam and Eve* has never appeared, on stage or in print, in the Soviet Union, and in works dealing with Bulgakov has received only brief mention.[36] Until its 1971 publication in Paris, in what seems to be a slightly later version, it was virtually unknown. The same year the apparently earlier text appeared in English translation.[37]

The play is set against a background of war, with six characters – Adam Krasovsky and his new bride Eve, a pacifist professor Yefrosimov, hooligan Markizov, writer Ponchik-Nepobeda, and fighter-pilot Daragan – surviving a gas attack, thanks to an invention of Yefrosimov. He, however, clashes with Adam and Daragan because of his pacifism, but Eve (for whose love Markizov and Ponchik have also been competing) falls in love with him and abandons her husband. The play ends with the war over and the discovery of other survivors. There are a few slight changes in the later version. 'The town' has been substituted for 'Leningrad,' a few characters at the end have been cut, and so too have some of Daragan's descriptions of air battles (which, interestingly – in 1931 – make it clear that the Germans are considered the major enemy); some of the pacifist and anti-ideological arguments have been shortened and weakened. And a few lines have been added at the end to return us to Adam and Eve's apartment and indicate that the whole story of death and destruction was only a dream. Such an ending weakens the play and is best ignored as an unsuccessful attempt, along with the other changes, to make the play more acceptable for production.

35 From L.Ye. Belozerskaya's unpublished memoirs
36 Notably **407**, II, p. 134
37 **4**, pp. 5-77, and **11**. Page references to the former appear in the text.

Adam and Eve is one of two plays by Bulgakov to relate specifically to an imaginary, future world, although it had been foreshadowed in some respects by his early tales of fantasy, notably 'The Fatal Eggs.' The previous year he had started another play set largely in the future, *Bliss*, which would only be taken up again later and then transformed into its counterpart about the past, *Ivan Vasilievich. Adam and Eve* is at once more serious and less fantastic than these plays, containing little which is inconceivable; in a sense it is even prophetic. Ten years after *Adam and Eve* Russia was at war with Germany, resulting in tremendous destruction (even if not as great as that forecast in the play): 1,300,000 people would die in Leningrad itself. Bulgakov's concerns expressed here were very much a result of a growing awareness of the horrors which threatened to overtake Europe. The weapon he so much fears, of course, is gas, as is appropriate to the thirties. Nowadays one would expect such massive destruction as the result of an atomic war, but the difference is not great: *Adam and Eve* is all too relevant to today's age.

This is the most intellectual and literary of Bulgakov's plays, relying heavily on arguments expressed by characters who themselves tend to be stereotypes or somewhat colourless (such as Eve). Adam is the typical conscientious communist, Daragan the militant one. Markizov is the likeable rogue, Ponchik the opportunist writer, Yefrosimov the absent-minded professor taken to the extreme. But a number of these depart from the stereotype in certain respects: Yefrosimov, for example, is considered by the others to be the 'mad scientist,' but ironically because of his pacifism rather than any desire to rule the world. Nor does a certain weakness of characterization mean that the play is inneffective theatre, for the situation itself and the formal devices employed to increase tension are quite sufficient to sustain the viewer's interest and horror at what could be an entirely realistic situation.

The play begins with an assertion of the beauty of life, which is contrasted with war throughout, and is here represented by music and departure for a holiday. '*Faust* today, and tomorrow evening we go to Cape Green!' Adam says. 'I am happy! When I was standing in line for the tickets, I broke out in a hot sweat all over and I understood that life was beautiful!' (p. 7). But his and Eve's happiness is interrupted by a succession of extraordinary events, which dramatically demonstrate the total peripeteia that their lives are about to undergo. A stranger, Yefrosimov, jumps through their window (to avoid a fight with hooligan Markizov). A brick comes hurtling after him. He insists on 'photographing' everyone with his 'camera.' There are arguments, more strangers, then catastrophe, death, which soon 'flies in pieces in the world, sometimes screaming in unknown languages, sometimes sounding like music!' (p. 34). The simple happiness of the beginning is gone, poisoned not just by gas but by the actions of men. Later, simple life and joy in it will return, with the suggestion that the earlier happiness was false anyway, as Eve comes to a deeper understanding of what is important: 'the forest and the singing of the birds, and the rainbow, this is real, but you with your frenzied cries are unreal' (p. 59). The permanent world of things is contrasted with man's uneasy hostility in it, an idea affirmed by Yefrosimov a little later. Man's true desires, as stated by Eve, are simple: 'a little house in Switzerland and – ideas, wars, classes, strikes be damned.'[38]

But Daragan and Adam have greater faith in an idea, and ideas are shown as a cause of war, which is seen as tragic, not noble – particularly in an age where individual acts of heroism are meaningless. As we are reminded by the first epigraph to the play (a quotation from a book entitled *Military Gases*, which Bulgakov consulted), 'The fate of dare-devils who thought that in gas there was nothing to fear has always been the same – death!' (p. 6). As Eve says, not one of these men should be still amongst the living, but the 'great magician,' Yefrosimov, whom they wish to kill, has brought them back from the next world.

The apparatus which has saved them is in fact a symbol of all that Yefrosimov stands for, the antithesis to the destruction that the others seek. Ideologically, the play presents the conflict between him as the broad-minded pacifist and those who believe in fighting for the victory of a cause, the committed communists. Thus early in the play, when Adam says there will be a war because the capitalist world is filled with hate for socialism, Yefrosimov replies that it could equally be because the communist world hates capitalism, and that when hatred and the use of weapons is actively encouraged, on either side, a conflict is bound to result. For Adam, the ends justify the means, since 'on the side of the USSR there is a great idea,' while for Yefrosimov, who questions the ends, the means are the greatest source of danger (pp. 14-16). Hence, together with his pacificism, he fears the scientists, who experiment for the pleasure of it and then abdicate the responsibility for the use of their inventions. 'I am afraid of ideas,' he repeats: 'Each one is good in itself, but only until the moment when some old professor arms it with technology.' The old man will provide the means of destruction, then say simply 'I did what I could. The rest is your affair. Ideas, clash!' (p. 16). We might compare this with the scientists of Bulgakov's earlier stories, unleashing destructive forces which they cannot control.

---

38 In the earlier text only: see **11**, p. 210. In these ideas one is perhaps reminded of Rilke's '... Siehe, die Bäume *sind*; die Häuser, / die wir bewohnen, bestehn noch. Wir nur / ziehen allem vorbei wie ein luftiger Austausch. / Und alles ist einig, uns zu verschweigen ...' (from the second of his *Duineser Elegien.*)

At a deeper level, we might see the play as a plea for objectivity, in the sense of applying the same criteria to communism as to its enemies: which runs counter to the communist view that communism itself is historically objective and hence the sole source of truth. Neither Adam nor Daragan, with their commitment to the victory of communism, can be sufficiently objective in its true sense to understand Yefrosimov's arguments (which would be unacceptable in the Soviet Union even today). His idea of giving his anti-gas device to all nations at once rather than just the Soviet Union is unthinkable to them. Daragan's only consideration here is to gain the advantage over his enemies: this he accepts as unquestionably as, after the attack, he accepts the necessity for revenge by dropping a bomb on them. When he later discovers Yefrosimov has destroyed his bombs, he can see this only as treason, not as an attempt to save humanity. Adam differs from Daragan only in wanting to see justice, with Yefrosimov tried by a proper court rather than being shot on the spot. To both it is heresy when Yefrosimov says he is just as indifferent to communism as to fascism (a statement that in the later version was replaced by a rational argument against the use of a weapon that could threaten all mankind).

These probably come close to Bulgakov's own feelings, and indeed one suspects that this play reflects a number of his deepest personal convictions, expressed somewhat uncharacteristically in the form of open argument – as though suddenly all his frustrations at the society he lived in had burst out in the character of Yefrosimov. There are certain similarities between Bulgakov at this time and his pacifist hero: the professor's extreme nervousness, his isolation from the world in his laboratory, his disillusionment with men and love for a dog (which had been suggested by Bulgakov's dog Bouton), even his love for another man's wife. In the play the author never adjudicates between the different views, but Yefrosimov is clearly the victor in that neither of the others proposes any rational arguments to counter his own. He is shown as an individual carrying out a one-man struggle against an uncomprehending state as represented by Adam. He is victorious only because in conditions of total war the state apparatus is destroyed or ineffective, and the struggle becomes a personal one.

Indeed, the whole play evolves in purely personal terms, and it is here that its main interest lies. The terrors of war are first discovered as Eve wanders through the ruins of a Leningrad department store, almost out of her mind, a scene which comes close to real tragedy. With the immediate society around them destroyed, the characters are thrown back on themselves and the basic need for a society of other people. Ostensibly, Adam and Daragan are concerned with the survival of communism as such, but in the circumstances in which they find themselves this is nonsense. Nevertheless, the idea is still advantageous to them, for it is as a representative of communism that Adam can take power in this now independent community; as a fighter for communism that Daragan can do what, as an individual, he feels like doing: drop bombs on his enemies. In the attitudes of these two, as they follow their own primitive instincts (backed by the acquiescence of Markizov, Ponchik, and, initially, Eve), we find precisely those human factors that have led to wars throughout history. Their fury at their enemies and near murder of Yefrosimov for thwarting their plans express in a microcosm the holocaust that is going on all around them: war is seen to be the result of human imperfection and irrationality rather than just the clash of great ideas which, more exactly, are the cause of the anger leading to war.

It is not surprising, then, that on a more down-to-earth level the struggles amongst the characters themselves revolve largely around their love for Eve. For these are simply humans in conflict, and in this new primitive society they are engaged in the basic struggle for possession of the one available female. Eve here is just 'woman,' with the others attempting to become her Adam, 'man.' Neither in love nor in war do they behave rationally, but instead follow their own instincts – except for Yefrosimov, who in the final count is more a man of ideas than the others, and to some extent stands above their primitive passions. In that he is the one eventually chosen by Eve as her 'new Adam,' civilization might be said to triumph over chaos, suggesting a new evolution of mankind.

Yet Yefrosimov, initially, is hardly an admirable character. Irritably nervous, ill at ease in human society, and afraid even to show his love for Eve, he lacks the humanity which civilization needs in order to flourish. For all his pacifism, he loves no man but only his now dead dog Jacques who, unlike humans, has never hurt anyone. Despairing at human cruelty, he has withdrawn from the world to his laboratory. But 'It is not good that the man should be alone,' as Markizov reads from a torn and incomplete Bible he has found after the destruction; 'I will make him an help meet for him' (Genesis ii.18). The title *Adam and Eve* is appropriate, if misleading, for the play concerns man and woman coming together out of chaos and the foundation of a 'new' human society – hinted at in its last speeches. Eve is 'born' of Yefrosimov's ideas, but it is not until he becomes the 'true' Adam that the biblical story is recreated: until their union neither of them is complete, neither really human. It is now that Eve reveals to him, in Platonic terms, that they were really created as one being: 'It turns out that we are completely alike, one soul, cut in half ...' Her former husband Adam was 'first man' in the old society, but now appears inhuman, an impostor: 'I see that my husband has stone jaws, is warlike, and an organizer. I hear war, gas, plague, humanity, we'll build cities here ... we will find human material! ... But I don't want human material, I want simply people, and more than anything else, one person.' Now Eve, the 'progenitress' as Yefrosimov has called her, will build a new world with him. 'I am the woman Eve, but he is not my Adam. You will be Adam!' (pp. 71-2).

The link with the story of man's creation is made throughout the play, but it is further connected through the play's second epigraph (from Genesis viii.21-2) to the story of Noah's Ark, the end of the flood and God's wrath, and the beginning of a new life. Again in Bulgakov, we have in religious terms the idea of destruction and chaos followed by rebirth, as we have seen already in *The White Guard*, *Days of the Turbins*, and *Flight*. In *Adam and Eve* something of the same suggestion is also made visually, with the scenic representation of heaven and hell in the second act: '*In the huge windows of the department store are heaven and hell. Up above, heaven is lit by the early morning sun, but hell beneath is lit with a large rich glow. Between them there hangs smoke, and in it is a transparent quadriga over the burned ruins. There is a genuine dead silence*' (p. 30). The quadriga, a two-wheeled chariot drawn by four horses, is surely symbolical of the apocalypse.

It is clear that, from a communist viewpoint, the play is unacceptable. Not only does it run counter to the whole idea of commitment to a cause but, more important, its communist characters, Adam and Daragan, are openly criticized rather than being made into positive heroes. Furthermore, the whole theory of socialist realism is bitterly satirized in the character of Ponchik-Nepobeda. He is a strictly comic, even absurd, figure, with outlandish pretensions that have been encouraged by the literary canons of his society. The satire centres around his novel, a typical piece of bad socialist realism, which he insists on reading over and over again to the despair of the others. Ponchik has written a bad book because it is made up of standard phrases and images, clichés typified by expressions such as 'rang out over the strip of land.' Originality has been replaced by the demand to show the country in a certain way, so that virtually the same first paragraph as Ponchik's is produced by another author, simply because he and Ponchik were together on a writers' excursion to a collective farm. It is not surprising that Markizov, trying to write a book of his own and anxious to learn, after a few genuine moving sentences copies this same style – but is then accused by Ponchik of plagiarism. But where there is no originality the word 'plagiarism' loses its meaning: such novels devoid of artistic merit were produced by the hundreds to meet the requirements of socialist realism. 'Explain to me why literature is always so boring!' Markizov demands (p. 48). Ponchik, in a rare moment of honesty, admits that the novel is valueless and destroys it. But later, when other people appear, he regrets this, for Ponchik-Nepobeda is the typical timeserver: not entirely unjustly does Markizov refer to him as the snake from the Adam and Eve story. His grovelling attitude, concern only for his personal safety, combined with his pretentiousness as a writer, are one of the main sources of humour in the play.

But Ponchik is important in another way, for into the mouth of this comic character Bulgakov has put a number of other ideas which it would have been inadvisable for him to express seriously. Thus a speech where Ponchik begs forgiveness from God for working for the *Atheist Journal* appears hilariously funny and provides welcome comic relief – unless one decides to take it seriously, when its tragic implications become apparent. (In exaggerated form it could even reflect something of Bulgakov's own attitude, and his despair at this stage in his life.) 'I worked for the *Atheist* because I was frivolous. I'll tell you alone, Lord, that I'm a believer to the marrow of my bones and hate communism ... Look down, O Lord, on your perishing slave, Ponchik-Nepobeda, save him! I'm orthodox, Lord, and my grandfather served in the consistory ...' (p. 39). Ponchik is most eloquent when talking of Europe – 'where there are cities and civilization, where there are lights!' (p. 65) – which leads into a denunciation of communism for having upset the world and the values of civilization, and for having destroyed Russia. 'It's done for, praise be to God, your communism is! And even though it's done for, it's left us its visionary, wearing a gendarme's uniform.'[39] All of this can, of course, be seen as satire on the type of man who, when things go badly, immediately starts looking for better things elsewhere: Ponchik remains a comic, and negative, character. But what he actually says can be taken seriously – a fact of which the Main Repertory Committee was certainly aware.

Functionally, the foil to Ponchik is Markizov, who engages in discussions with him, tries to learn from him, and is rival to him in claiming Eve's attentions. The two of them together act as a pair of buffoons, providing relief from the seriousness of the action and, at the same time, making a mockery of Adam's noble ideas of an ideal, communist society. Thrown out of his union for hitting someone, a hooligan, drinker, and seducer, Markizov is hardly an ideal example of a working man. This, combined with his ludicrous appearance, his odd respect for those who know more than he does, and his sometimes inappropriate attempts to imitate them, makes him a figure of fun to delight any audience. Yet at the same time he is rather pathetic and likeable, anxious to learn and be seen to be as good as anyone else. 'I have weak eyesight, and besides, I'm no worse than other scholars,' he replies when Eve asks why he has started wearing blue pince-nez (p. 53). When he starts to write a journal and then a novel, his style may be pretentious, but at times he is moving, sincere. Unlike Ponchik, who in this respect is less intelligent, he understands Eve when she tells him she wants only friendship, and accepts the situation sadly but with the same good grace as when, after the attack, he has had to have his leg amputated. If in some ways he is related to Ametistov in *Zoyka's Apartment*, there are nevertheless qualities in him which remind us of Lariosik.

39 Again, in the earlier text only. See **11**, p. 207

Like most of Bulgakov's plays, *Adam and Eve* places a certain reliance on the use of leitmotifs and symbols. Cape Green is used to signify the place of safe haven and rest – so that even after the destruction Adam can symbolically give his old tickets for Cape Green to Eve and Yefrosimov. Animals are associated with Yefrosimov, first his dog who is killed, then a cock with a broken leg that he cares for. Sound effects too are particularly important. Guns, rockets, cars, airplanes, all combine to create an atmosphere of unease, tension. Act I, where Yefrosimov is anxious about his dog Jacques, is marked by dogs howling in anticipation of dire events and then becoming silent as they are killed. It is also accompanied by the music of *Faust* on the radio and Markizov's accordion outside. But *Faust*, after beginning 'sonorously and gently,' changes to a march, then rises in a crescendo to its famous Soldiers' Chorus, 'We will not shame the glory of the fatherland,' before a sudden silence ensues as the music on the radio breaks up and life ceases: an appropriate background comment on the fate of dare-devils. In the following acts the radio becomes all-important as first various trumpet blares and martial music are heard, and then once more all are left listening to the silence, with only Markizov's accordion left to provide odd snatches of music.

Some of the stage directions, like those in *Flight*, are intended more for the reader than the spectator. Yefrosimov is described as having '*a fog over his eyes and little candles in the fog*'; his '*irreproachable linen shows that he is a bachelor and never dresses himself, but that some old woman, certain that Yefrosimov is a demi-god and not a man, irons, presses, reminds him of things and gives him everything in the morning*' (p. 9). But some are realizable and can produce significant visual effects: the lamp with the thick shade, under which '*it is pleasant to play patience, but any thought of patience is excluded as soon as Yefrosimov's face appears by the lamp*' (p. 7), although it becomes cozier when Ponchik seats himself there. Not as striking as *Flight* in its visual effects, the play none the less has a second act with considerable scenic possibilities: the ruined department store in Leningrad, complete with dead customers, trampled packages, and a tram that has run into the store; and with heaven and hell in the windows alongside.

Adam and Eve is a well-constructed play with nicely balanced characters and dialogue which is both entertaining and convincing. Its one fault, perhaps, is that it is too intellectual, with characters who do not move us as individuals. The viewer experiences little of the emotional involvement associated with plays such as *Days of the Turbins* or *Flight*. But seen as a piece of anti-war propaganda it is frighteningly effective. And for all its commitment to a pacifist attitude, the intellectual arguments do not outweigh dramatic considerations, since the entire action is a demonstration of the ideas expressed. The happy ending, with Daragan showing nobility and willingness to forgive Yefrosimov for his treachery, perhaps rings rather false, as though it had been provided largely with the aim of showing communist magnanimity. But despite this, it remains a most interesting play, in which Bulgakov reminds us once again that he is concerned with the problems of mankind and not just those of his own country. Regrettably, from a Soviet viewpoint it is the least acceptable of his plays: for all Bulgakov's probable attempts to disguise or minimize some of the views expressed, it remains simply unplayable in the Soviet Union.

The Moscow Art Theatre, 1932-36

Bulgakov and Yelena Sergeevna were married on 4 October 1932, and he became the guardian of her five-year-old son, Sergey (who was later to become the assistant director of the Gogol Theatre in Moscow). It marked the end of a difficult time for both of them, and indeed they had said little to anyone until they knew their marriage would be possible. It would make for a distinct improvement in Bulgakov's personal happiness, although there was the immediate problem of where they were going to live. Over a year later they still had not been able to move into a new flat and on 17 October 1933 we find Bulgakov writing to Veresaev of his depression: 'It is a long time since I have been as perturbed as now. Insomnia ... in my declining years I've landed up in someone else's living space.'[1] But finally they were able to move to flat 44 at Nashchokinsky Lane (now Furmanov Lane), no 3/5, where they would spend the rest of their lives. 'Writers live above and below and behind and in front ...' Bulgakov wrote enthusiastically to Veresaev on 6 March 1934, 'I'm happy that I have got out of the damp pit of the Pirogovskaya. And what bliss not to travel by tram!'

There is no doubt that Yelena Sergeevna was a fortunate influence on Bulgakov – and indeed that this was the happiest of his three marriages. In a dedication to her on a copy of his 'No 13 – the Elpit House – Workers' Commune' he wrote: 'A souvenir for the collection of the woman who alone was my inspiration, to my wife Yelena Sergeevna. This story relates to the old period of my life. M. Bulgakov. Moscow, 17-XII-1933.'[2]

Yermolinsky has given an interesting account of his first visit to the new apartment, where everything was neat and orderly, bearing the mark of Yelena Sergeevna's efficiency and charm, which caused him to fear that Bulgakov had

1 For this and the following letter, see **379**, p. 161.
2 **187**, folio 274

become a bourgeois. But he was soon reassured by the sight of him coming out of the bathroom in his old knitted nightcap and dirty-lilac dressing gown:

He was just as I had known him before, and yet different too – the nervous tension which had struck one in recent months and which disturbed me had disappeared. As though his affairs had immediately taken a sharp turn for the better; dangers and threats had passed and at last life had entered upon a peaceful course.

...

Their house, as though to spite all the hostile elements, radiated happiness. Although perhaps there may have been only debts in a rather cloudy future. The lady of the house was energetic and irrepressibly frivolous. And life ceased to be fearful.[3]

Not that their marriage would always be an easy one. Yelena Sergeevna was used to life in high society, was even somewhat spoilt. Attractive, sexually provocative even, she was accustomed to having her own way. For a long time she did not really understand her husband: he opened up for her, she would say later, 'a new world' – which perhaps she only truly appreciated after his death. In the first years of their marriage she tried to make him more sociable, wanted him to receive other artists – in fact wanted to make him into a great Russian writer, who could live a life of success. Religion, which was important to him, for her was 'unfashionable.' To some extent there was a clash of two personalities. Yet the marriage worked, and in many ways she was able to protect him. Fearful lest her former husband should use his influence to take revenge on Bulgakov, she would invite all the important people to their apartment, despite his protests. Above all, she managed to bring into his life the confidence and stability, and gaiety, that he so much needed – even if she showed a certain possessiveness, protecting him even from the members of his own family.

In other ways, there was no great change in his life. Apart from his writing, he enjoyed skiing in the winter and playing tennis in the summer – although generally was no great sportsman. He continued to follow the careers of other writers he had known, and maintained his interest in literature in general. His library contained a good selection of Russian nineteenth-century authors and a mass of now-forgotten works of his own day. Among the writers he knew and liked were Molière, Hoffmann, Saltykov-Shchedrin, Babel, Lunts, Zamyatin, Sukhovo-Koby-

---

3 **266**, pp. 85-6. What follows is based on Irina Ivanovna Bulgakova's recollections of meetings with Yelena Sergeevna.

lin – and, of course, Gogol.[4] 'I sat ... two nights over your Gogol,' he wrote to Veresaev after the publication of his book on Gogol in 1933. 'Heavens! What a figure! What a personality!'[5] Towards Chekhov he was relatively indifferent; he did not like Pilnyak. Of the Russian philosophers he read Solovyov, but not Shestov. Literary criticism and theory did not interest him, but he loved browsing through biographical materials or old magazines. Simplicity, for Bulgakov, was the hallmark of good writing. The actor Toporkov recalls how once Bulgakov advised him to turn into a story an amusing incident he had just related. It was not a question of knowing how to do it: 'write it as you were telling it just now.'[6] Another would-be writer, who was working as a chambermaid in the Astoria Hotel in Leningrad, has also described meeting him once when he stayed there. Asked to read a story she had written, he advised her 'write about what you know and have seen. In front of you there stands a writer ... in crumpled white trousers and with ruffled fair hair. Just describe him that way.'[7]

Bulgakov also managed to travel a little in these years. In Leningrad in 1933 he had met for the first time the poetess Anna Akhmatova, who became an ardent admirer of his works and later one of the Bulgakovs' dearest friends. On a summer trip to Yalta the same year he had met Chekhov's sister, Maria Pavlovna.[8] And in 1934 he made a further attempt to get abroad, for two months, with Yelena Sergeevna (partly in connection with his continuing work on Molière).[9] 'I must – I have the right to – see the world,' he told Veresaev on 24 April, 'if only for a short time. I test myself, I ask my wife if I have that right. She answers – you have.' Two days later he told Popov he had put in his application, saying that he had long 'dreamt of the Mediterranean waves and the Paris museums, and a quiet hotel, and no one who knows you, and Molière's fountain and, in a word, being able to see all this ... Oh, if only it would come true! Then you can prepare another chapter – the most interesting one.' On 1 May he wrote the, by now, obligatory letter to Gorky asking him for his support, but emphasizing that he must be back by the autumn, for the continuing work in the theatre on the production of Molière.

Once again, permission was denied him. On 11 June he wrote yet one more letter to Stalin expressing his sense of bewilderment that no one seemed to be-

4 Information supplied to me by M. Michel Vassilieff from a conversation with Yelena Sergeevna. See also 266, p. 91, for this and the following.
5 379, p. 160
6 157, p. 97; reported also in 491, p. 100
7 441
8 449, p. 561, n 11, and 418, p. 273
9 For this and the following, see 379, pp. 161-2, 168, 157-8.

lieve him when he said he would return to Russia after two months: '... why, intending one thing, should I request something else? ... Having intended [in 1930] a permanent departure ... I did not ask then for a two-month trip.' Bulgakov was perhaps naïve, but he had been brought up to a sense of honesty which, even in Stalin's Russia, he expected to be recognized. 'I can't get used to it,' he once told Yermolinsky: 'although I should do ... I'm afraid, afraid at every manifestation of distrust for myself, or when I run across suspicion, carping at every word I write. But perhaps that is not only my misfortune?'[10] He remained an extremely sensitive person, afraid of outside criticism – not without reason, perhaps, in the increasingly repressive and dangerous atmosphere of the thirties. For Stalin's great purges were just beginning. The poet Mandelshtam, who also had an apartment on Furmanov Lane, was in 1934 arrested and exiled – there is an account of Yelena Sergeevna bursting into tears when told the news by Akhmatova.[11] Yet for Bulgakov himself, even at such a time, there remained a sense of disappointment at his inevitable lack of recognition and literary isolation in this society. He was not even invited to attend the First All-Union Congress of Soviet Writers, held from 18 August to 1 September that year. Two years before, the various competing literary and artistic associations had been abolished. The theory of socialist realism was now loudly proclaimed and a new Writers' Union established, to which even Bulgakov would have to belong. Conformity, not originality, was demanded of a writer.

As for his idea of going abroad, he finally seems to have become resigned, for a year later, on 26 July 1935, he wrote to Veresaev: 'They have refused me a trip abroad (You, of course, will throw up your hands in amazement), and instead of the Seine I have landed up on the Klyazma. Well, it's a river too.'[12]

Yet despite such frustrations the years at the beginning of the thirties continued to be most productive for Bulgakov. True, a projected play about the French Revolution, to be ready by 1 February 1933, came to nothing and he was obliged to return an advance of 1500 roubles received from the Theatre for Children.[13] But now his most immediate interest was the figure of Molière. After writing his play, he had engaged in further research which produced three other works: *Half-witted Jourdain* (a light comedy based on *le Bourgeois gentilhomme*) in 1932, an ambitious imaginative biography, *Life of Monsieur de Molière*, written in 1932-33, and a Russian translation of *l'Avare*, completed in 1936.

10 **266**, p. 92
11 **366**, p. 39
12 **234**, p. 162
13 Contract in **187**, folio 538

In late 1932 or 1933 he had also started working again on the novel which was to become *The Master and Margarita*, telling Veresaev on 2 August: 'The devil has taken hold of me. Already in Leningrad and now here, stifling in my horrid rooms, I starting scribbling page after page again of that novel of mine which was destroyed three years ago.'[14] By April 1934 he had completed another play, *Bliss*. And as a result of keeping up his various business contacts he turned to a type of work which was new for him - writing film scenarios - while at the same time still dreaming of his novel. On 26 June he wrote to Popov: 'I am writing *Dead Souls* for the screen and I'll bring the completed thing with me. Then the fuss over *Bliss* will begin. Oh, how much work I have! But in my head there roams Margarita and a cat and flights through the air ... But I am still weak and run down. Although certainly I'm getting stronger every day.'[15]

June 1934 also saw the five-hundredth performance of *Days of the Turbins*, which was marked by an official letter of congratulations from Sakhnovsky on behalf of the theatre.[16] Sometime later *Days of the Turbins* went on tour to Kiev, with Bulgakov delightedly showing the cast the various places of relevance to the play. 'I watched the lights on the river,' he wrote, 'and remembered my life. When I walked in the parks by day a strange feeling came over me. My country! Sadness, sweetness, alarm! ...'[17]

In October he started collaborating with his friend Veresaev on an ambitious play about Pushkin, later to be entitled *The Last Days*. At the same time he was still involved in the Art Theatre. Nearly two years previously, in December 1932, work had started on *The Pickwick Club*, an adaptation from Dickens by Natalya Venkshtern, an old friend (her original plays had had a similar fate to his own and had been banned).[18] She had done a great deal of research on Dickens and had shown Bulgakov her adaptation, possibly benefiting from his experience - he too made various notes from Dickens' book and its Russian translation. He was appointed assistant producer for the play (under Stanitsyn, producing his first play at the Art Theatre) and apparently begged the theatre to be allowed to act in it too, 'since he wanted to get closer to the whole theatrical workshop.' He was given the small part of the president of the court, and by October 1934 the work was in its final stages. The play opened with considerable success on 1 December, and remained in the repertory for many years, being performed as

14 **379**, p. 161
15 **491**, pp. 98-9
16 **372**, pp. 399-400
17 **448**, pp. 455, 471
18 For the following, see **446**, p. 447; **415**, pp. 74-5; **270**, p. 752; **188**, folio 110; **368**,
   p. 80. Information also supplied by L.Ye. Belozerskaya.

late as 1957. (It would later become noted for bringing into prominence the 'third generation' of actors, as *Days of the Turbins* had done for the second.) Bulgakov played his role with distinction and obvious enjoyment, and was convinced that the experience helped him a great deal as a dramatist. It is the only time he is recorded as having actually acted on the public stage.

But by 1935 there were more frustrations, involving bitter arguments with Stanislavsky over *Molière*, and unpleasant disagreements with Veresaev about their play on Pushkin: it seemed that his writing brought nothing but problems. In the summer he transformed his comedy *Bliss* (not performed) into another play, *Ivan Vasilievich*.

THE FILM SCENARIOS

Bulgakov had worked with a film scenario as early as May 1932, changing the dialogue for 'The Fishermen's Revolt' at the request of its production studio *Mezhrabkomfil'm*.[19] In 1934 he completed two scenarios of his own, and became involved in the noisy world of film directors – which Yermolinsky suggests was probably something of a strain.[20]

'Dead Souls' was the first of these, intended for *Mosfil'm* (then the First State Cinema Factory, *Goskinofabrika*). In this production, which he discussed with the two directors Vaisfeld and Pyrev, Bulgakov apparently hoped to realize his original intentions for the stage adaptation but once again, because of the demands of others, was unable to do so. The scenario appears to have gone through several variants, a third one of which is dated 12 August 1934. I.A. Pyrev, it would seem, worked on this again later – after L. Trauberg's film of 1960 – producing a corrected version in 1965.[21] But the scenario itself remained unused.

On 15 August Bulgakov started on a version of Gogol's *The Inspector General* for *Ukrainfil'm* (VUKFU), in collaboration with the director Korostin, who possibly wrote more of it than Bulgakov.[22] (They were not alone in their endeavour: another scenario for it was written by the well-known director and writer, V.B. Shklovsky, at about the same time. A Czech film too had been made the previous year. Ultimately the only Russian films actually made of *The Inspector General* were the one of 1916 and V. Petrov's production of 1952.) It is worth looking briefly at Bulgakov and Korostin's scenario (which had four variants), as an interesting and imaginative interpretation of Gogol: generally, they have

19 **187**, folio 537
20 **266**, p. 89
21 Information supplied by M.O. Chudakova; also in **446**, pp. 447, 446.
22 **40**, p. 42; see also **407**, II, p. 142; **215**

made good use of a medium which obviously allows for greater freedom of presentation than does the stage.[23] Thus, for example, Bobchinsky and Dobchinsky are shown on their excursions around the town, and Judge Lyapkin-Tyapkin is seen visiting Dobchinsky's wife while his dogs keep her husband outside. The mayor, who has been concerned about the 'extraordinary rats' in his dream, sees a huge rat first and foremost when he looks through the keyhole of Khlestakov's room. Later, when his daughter is to marry Khlestakov, he strides about the town as the merchants bow before him. Khlestakov too, mistaken for the inspector, is seen in triumphal parade through the streets and then on his visits to the prison, school, and charity institution. His imagined life in St Petersburg is shown. There is more detail, too, on the intrigues involving minor characters.

More important are those occasions where the authors radically depart from Gogol, as in the scene where Khlestakov attempts to seduce the mayor's wife, dragging her away to his room while the mayor, at first angry, decides it is expedient to allow it to happen nevertheless. But nothing does happen: in the bedroom Khlestakov is so terrified by the woman's passionate advances that he runs away from her, and finally falls asleep. The most significant change concerns the real inspector, whom we see at intervals speeding in his troika to reach the town (and, on one occasion, remembering how he had given an important person a bribe himself before he reached his present position). After Khlestakov's departure and the realization that he was an impostor, there is the same 'mute scene' that ends Gogol's play, but it is followed by the arrival of this real inspector. In despair, the officials collect as much money as they can amongst themselves, and the mayor takes it to him as a bribe. Finally he emerges, giving a sigh of relief: 'He took it!' – the final words in the film.

This is an interesting reinterpretation, and one which certainly could have made for a worthwhile film. Alas, it was never produced. Bulgakov's work for the cinema was without particular importance, but even here his original mode of thought and customary humour were apparent. Later he would regale the actor G.G. Konsky with a story of how once someone phoned from *Sovkino*, wanting a story for a film. By that evening he had made up a scenario: 'The zoo burnt down in some provincial town. And they decided to resettle the animals that were unharmed in the apartments of those who had extra room. So they put a boa constrictor into the house of one citizen. But it turned out that there was such an atmosphere in the house that the boa constrictor could not stand it, and crawled away on the third day. That's all.' The film studio never phoned back to him.[24]

23 The scenario was published in a limited edition, **156**. One copy is in **189**.
24 See **269**

HALF-WITTED JOURDAIN

While rehearsals of the play *Molière* – along with the discussions – went on end-lessly, Bulgakov continued working on the French dramatist. The play *Half-witted Jourdain* was essentially a reworking of Molière's *le Bourgeois gentil-homme*: the story of a bourgeois with absurd pretensions of being an aristocrat. Written in 1932 for the Theatre-Studio of Yu.A. Zavadsky, it was not performed until some forty years later, when it enjoyed considerable success at the Theatre of Young Spectators in Krasnoyarsk.[25] It was published in the collection of *Dramas and Comedies* in 1965.

In some ways it is the most puzzling of all Bulgakov's plays, in that it is neither a translation of Molière nor an independent work. However well it may be written, it adds little to *le Bourgeois gentilhomme* itself – although it does shorten it, cutting out some of the material less essential to the plot, and in par-ticular the rather tedious 'ballet' of the original involving the Turkish ceremony – in his *Life of Monsieur de Molière* Bulgakov calls this an 'intermezzo that spoils a fine play' (p. 214).[26] *Half-witted Jourdain* cannot perhaps be taken too seri-ously. Rather, we should regard it as an exercise, of value largely to Bulgakov himself. As K. Rudnitsky has indicated, both this and Bulgakov's subsequent translation of *l'Avare* were almost certainly a means for him to understand the technique of a dramatist he so much admired. *Half-witted Jourdain* 'was an attempt – witty and original – to resurrect and bring together, in one composi-tion, the most lasting, perhaps the most eternal, comic techniques which were used by the genius Molière, and at the same time to resurrect the atmosphere of a performance in Molière's time.' An analysis of these techniques themselves is beyond the scope of this book, but it is worth noting exactly what Bulgakov has done with Molière's original.

Half-witted Jourdain is a play within a play, beginning with the preparations by Louis Béjart of Molière's troupe to stage *le Bourgeois gentilhomme*. This comic introduction itself sets the tone for what is to follow: there is a certain amount of amusing 'business' on stage, and some of Bulgakov's own dialogue is indeed reminiscent of Molière's style. (The members of the theatre are identified with the real actors in Molière's troupe by name and, in as far as is possible in a short introduction, by well-known characteristics: Hubert by his playing female roles and Louis Béjart by his limp.[27]) The play as now performed follows closely the scenes of the original with a few slight changes in their order and with differ-

---

25 For this and subsequently, see **462**, p. 87.
26 **96**. Page references are given in the text.
27 In fact, according to Bulgakov's *Life of Monsieur de Molière*, Louis Béjart retired shortly before the performance of *le Bourgeois gentilhomme*.

ent divisions between the acts. Bulgakov keeps strictly to Molière's plot and generally to his individual motifs – but only rarely is there a direct translation. In most cases he paraphrases individual scenes, writing them anew on the basis of Molière's material and trying to keep Molière's style. He also makes a number of small additions: Jourdain's dance and music masters giving the fencing master a thrashing; the performance of a short scene from *Dom Juan*; Jourdain trying to use his newly acquired 'philosophy' to pretend he has not been disgraced in front of the marquise he is courting, then trying to sing and dance to take his mind off it.

Often Bulgakov adds some comic buffoonery of his own. Madame Jourdain, learning of her husband's treachery, exclaims: 'The scoundrel! It's not yet twenty-four years we've been married, and he's already stopped loving me!' (p. 308). Later, the servant Brindavoine refuses to come to her because it is the end of the first act.[28] When Jourdain is with his marquise, Brindavoine rushes in to put a cold compress on his head; then, as dinner begins, Madame Jourdain suddenly appears sitting on a table which flies up out of the floor. At one point Bulgakov cannot resist a jibe at some of his own colleagues. 'We are true men of art,' the dancing master says, 'and so serve with our art whoever pays us money, without getting into long discussions' (p. 329).

Half-witted Jourdain is a successful imitation – rather than adaptation – of Molière's play, the style and atmosphere of which Bulgakov has captured very well. Indeed, one has the impression of reading a Molière text, even though someone familiar with the original will realize the two do not correspond. Bulgakov's major change has been to emphasize the more farcical elements of the play – and in doing this, he has created his only pure farce. It bears witness to his skill as a playwright, but it remains a dramatic exercise, a curiosity, which can hardly be compared with his original works.

LIFE OF MONSIEUR DE MOLIÈRE

Far more important than *Half-witted Jourdain* is Bulgakov's ambitious biography of Molière. After writing his play he continued his research, not only becoming thoroughly acquainted with his hero but also able to sense the whole spirit of Molière's age. 'I no longer remember how many years it is,' he wrote, 'counting from the beginning of my work on the play, even, that I have been living in the ghostly and fairy-tale Paris of the seventeenth century.'[29] In June 1932

28 Quotations are translated from 1. Bulgakov has combined Molière's two servants into
   one, taking his name from *l'Avare*.
29 For this and the following, see 2, pp. 31-2, and 245, pp. 231-2.

he signed a contract with the series 'Lives of Outstanding People,' and worked on the book for the remainder of that year and the following spring. With typical care, he wrote to Paris for information, asking even for a detailed description of Molière's statue, which would occupy but a short paragraph in the book. His brother Nikolay, living there since 1929, responded with various materials.

The complete biography was sent to A.N. Tikhonov, the editor of the series. His negative reaction is described by Bulgakov in a letter to Popov dated 13 April 1933:

My narrator ... is called a free and easy young man who believes in magic and devilry, has occult powers, likes risqué stories, uses doubtful sources, and, worst of all, has a tendency towards royalism. But this is not all. In my work, in T's opinion 'there show through, transparently enough, allusions to our Soviet reality'! ... T writes that instead of my narrator I should have 'a serious Soviet historian.' I told him that I am not a historian, and refused to change the book.[30]

Gorky, who had founded the series, for once did not support Bulgakov, writing to Tikhonov on 28 April to express his agreement with him and complaining of the book's lack of seriousness: 'It is necessary not only to supplement it with historical material and give it a social significance, but to change its "playful" style.'[31] According to Lyubov Yevgenievna Belozerskaya, Bulgakov's former wife, who was now working in the editorial office of 'Lives of Outstanding People,' Gorky privately told Tikhonov: 'Of course it's talented, but if we print such books we might get it in the neck.'[32] (This was indeed likely, for despite Bulgakov's disclaimer one cannot fail to see in the book implications, at least, for his contemporary Soviet society.)

Twenty-nine years later, in 1962, *Life of Monsieur de Molière* was published in the same series that had once refused it, with an afterword by Kaverin justifying it, and a foreword by G. Boyardzhiev pointing to some of its faults: particularly its emphasis on Molière's servile attitude towards Louis XIV. The Soviet scholar Lakshin, reviewing the book, was more enthusiastic, disagreeing with Boyardzhiev and to some extent comparing Molière's life and Bulgakov's own.[33] The book was reprinted in the *Selected Prose* edition of 1966, and translated into English in 1970.

30 **379**, p. 167. Gorky's letter to Tikhonov and his private comment are also reported on
   p. 174, n 48.
31 **297**, pp. 63-4
32 From L.Ye. Belozerskaya's unpublished memoirs
33 **95**, pp. 225-32, 5-8; **335**

Life of Monsieur de Molière, despite its abundance of detail based on an impressive amount of research, is not a scholarly work as such; rather Bulgakov has used his right as a creative artist to show his own interpretation of Molière's life. One may perhaps argue over his thoroughly eclectic use of his sources (some of which he indicates) and his unhesitating reliance on certain of those whose accuracy is open to question.[34] But this is more appropriately left to the Molière scholars: in broad terms, the book is accurate enough and Bulgakov's interpretation is convincing. Interestingly, as Rudnitsky has pointed out, a book written after Bulgakov's play about Molière comes to read more like a preface for it.[35]

As background for his story, Bulgakov tries to convey the whole atmosphere of seventeenth-century France. Part of this involves the historical circumstances: he records, for example, the main events preceding the birth of Louis XIV, the details of the *Fronde* in opposition to Cardinal Mazarin (including some of its participants), the wars in which Louis XIV took part. As important is his picture of the society at that time. Descriptions of the comic actors whom the young Jean-Baptiste Poquelin saw at the Hôtel de Bourgogne as a boy, of the high tragedy of the Hôtel du Marais, are followed by the street scenes of the market round the Pont Neuf and the St Germain fair, complete with merchants, rogues, wandering players of all kinds. In later chapters, Bulgakov will show that he has an excellent knowledge of conditions for strolling players in provincial towns, that he is well acquainted with the actors and methods of the Italian troupe, and with the history of the Petit Bourbon Palace, which was to become Molière's first established theatre. He can describe the salons of Madame de Rambouillet and Madeleine de Scudéry, what was said there and by whom – the whole atmosphere that was the background for Molière's play *les Précieuses ridicules.* Many scenes are brought to life by the inclusion of small but typical details: in an early chapter Bulgakov mentions particularly a patent medicine called 'orviétan,' sold by a certain Cristoforo Cantugi and which soon became a fad over the whole of Paris. A constant feature of the narrative is Bulgakov's love for telling a little story, interesting for its own sake. Thus we find details of the various people who identified themselves with those Molière ridiculed in his plays (such as the Duc de la Feuillade, who intentionally humiliated Molière as a result). We learn of how a group of Molière's friends, when drunk, decided to drown themselves, but Molière prevented it by persuading them to wait until they were sober. We

34 For some of the sources Bulgakov has clearly used, see 235. I am grateful for the comments of Professor D. Fletcher and of Mr Prem Benimadhu, a Molière expert, who points out that Molière's being a student of Gassendi is now generally discounted, and that Bulgakov overlooks the importance in Molière's life of the historian and philosopher, La Mothe le Vayer. He also fails to mention Molière visiting the various 'cabarets.'
35 462, p. 88

are told the story of the forced marriage of Count Philibert de Gramont to an English Miss Hamilton, whom he had seduced – which 'may have prompted' the writing of the play *le Mariage forcé*. Or, on a more general problem, there are a number of anecdotes about the state of French medicine, which Molière frequently mocked in his works.

Bulgakov's style of presentation is what most distinguishes him from the scholar. As earlier in *The White Guard*, he shows his liking for inventing dialogue, which gives immediacy to the scenes described. The book is full not only of conversations, but of the thoughts, even the dreams, of individual characters. This, clearly, is not historical fact, but a fictional interpretation of it, fictionalized biography – imaginative rather than falsified, and written above all as a story to entertain the reader. Bulgakov's principal technique involves linking together a number of short scenes which in their totality give the impression of a theatrical spectacle[36] – in which, of course, Molière is the principal actor. Central to such a technique is the device of frequently shifting viewpoints. The reader is constantly encouraged to picture the scene before him, as though he himself were present, and then to enter the minds of various characters in turn.

This is particularly evident in what is perhaps the most vivid chapter, describing the troupe's first performance in front of the king's brother, Philippe d'Orléans (pp. 85-94). At first Bulgakov places the reader as a pure observer in the midst of the preparations: 'During the latter part of October, uncommon excitement reigned in the huge Salle des Gardes, also known as the Hall of the Caryatids, in the Old Louvre Palace. The air was filled with the screeching of saws, the deafening tattoo of hammers in the hands of theater builders. A stage was being constructed in the hall, then mounted with the necessary equipment.' Then, when Molière appears, there is a shift to his viewpoint: 'In the midst of all these, a homely, grimacing man, his caftan sleeves smudged with paint, was rushing about nervously, now shouting, now pleading with someone ... Besides, he began to stutter, and this always terrified him.' As the day of the performance approaches, the narrator himself addresses the reader: 'It must be said that from the moment he entered Paris the director acted wisely ... Who was helping him? Uninformed people thought that it was Prince Conti. But you and I know that the God-fearing Conti had nothing whatsoever to do with it.' Then again we become observers, as Molière addresses Philippe, until suddenly we see the scene through Philippe's eyes: with his own thoughts about the man in front of him, and then about the members of the troupe as they are presented. With the news that the king will see the performance there is a further shift to Molière's feelings of anxiety. For the performance itself, the scene is set anew for the observer,

36 See **2**, p. 32, and **335**, p. 252; cf. also Uspensky's discussions on viewpoint in **507**

then we return to Molière and his fear as he sees the king and the actors of the illustrious Bourgogne troupe. As a tragedy is performed, badly, we are given the thoughts of the bewildered audience. A similar technique is continued for the comedy which is then played, successfully, with the narrator entering various people's minds – except that of the king, whose royalty is emphasized by his being seen only from the outside, at the end of the play 'still wiping his eyes, as though crying for the loss of someone near and dear.'

Bulgakov was right to refuse the suggestion that his narrator should be 'a serious Soviet historian' – who would, undoubtedly, have written a totally different book. Bulgakov's narrator is ubiquitous, capricious, and argumentative, a character in his own right, who makes use of simple artistic insight to enter into the minds of those he is studying. He can record in detail private conversations between Molière and the king. He can observe Molière talking of his marital and other problems to his friends Chapelle and Boileau in the park at Auteuil (pp. 221-4): even if, we may note, Bulgakov was not responsible for inventing this particular scene.[37] As Kaverin points out, the book reads like a monologue – in which the narrator engages the reader in conversations, asks rhetorical questions, shows a love of exclamations, and at times is quite facetious.

From his somewhat privileged position, this narrator can further allow himself to argue with the evidence of Molière's contemporaries and other authorities. There were some who said that Molière had depicted his own father in the miser Harpagon, but 'I refuse to believe these empty gossip-mongers! The dramatist Molière did not malign his father's memory, and I will not malign it either' (p. 9). There were some who said his stepmother ill-treated him and was later depicted as Béline in *le Malade imaginaire*: 'I believe all this to be untrue' (p. 13). Often, one feels, such comments are more ironical than serious, for at such times the narrator adopts the role of an ardent admirer, who refuses to believe any ill of his hero. Here Bulgakov is perhaps laughing at himself, for Molière is very much his own hero too ('I, who am never to see him,' he concludes in his final sentence, 'send him my farewell greetings'): his admiration for him is felt on every page, without the need for arguments in his defence. But on occasions the narrator serves as a useful vehicle for the author, sometimes as though in jest, to express views of his own: on the stupidity of provincial censors (not understanding Corneille but demanding a copy of his play anyway), on taking one's themes from other authors, on the Aristotelian rules of unity, and, very occasionally, on the quality of particular plays by Molière.

Bulgakov is concerned with the fate of each individual play (even noting rather tediously how much each brought in, in terms of box-office revenue each

37 Kaverin's comments are in **95**, p. 228.

season) but generally the book is not a literary discussion of them, nor even a portrait of Molière the creative artist. Molière's creativity, as perhaps is appropriate for a pre-romantic age, is taken for granted, seen simply as part of his trade of comedian. It is the problems Molière encounters that interest Bulgakov: his early struggles to pursue his chosen career, his difficulties in performing the plays he wants, and his slowness in coming to an understanding of his own calling – as Lakshin has put it, Bulgakov's purpose is to show the progress of Molière's talent and its struggles with the world around him.[38] Hence, for example, the discussions of Molière's obstinate love for playing tragedy, in which he and his troupe were destined to failure, and lack of appreciation of comedy, where their true strength lay. But more important is the whole picture of Molière, for all his unshakeable dedication to his chosen career, as an ordinary human being coping with life as best he can: quite the opposite of the romantic idea of the artist as being far removed from the masses.

The form of the book is that of a chronicle of Molière's everyday life, in which each significant fact is recorded. Part of this chronicle has as its purpose to detail all those who in one way or another were important to Molière: his grandfather, Louis Cressé, who introduced him to the theatre; the members of the Béjart family, with whom he was associated for most of his life; his friend Claude-Emmanuel Chapelle and tutor Pierre Gassendi; Georges Pinel, who helped him get money from his father, and then became an actor himself; the Prince de Conti, who patronized him; the barber, Maître Gély, whom he assisted in his shop; his enemy Lysidas de Visé, who wrote a play mocking him; the great playwrights Jean Racine and Pierre Corneille. (These too, we might note, are seen in purely human terms rather than as men of genius: Corneille, at the time of his collaboration with Molière on *Psyche*, is just an old man in need of money.) Equally important are the actors and actresses of Molière's troupe, whose entry into his theatre, performances, departure, or death are all lovingly recorded.

An important part of this chronicle, too, concerns Molière's purely private and personal life, from the house where he was born (described in smell as well as appearance), his school, his various loves, disappointments, to his final collapse and death. The major problem on this personal level is that of his marriage to the actress Armande Béjart, brought into the theatre at the age of ten with the name of Menou and apparently the younger sister of Molière's early mistress Madeleine. In considerable detail Bulgakov discusses the mysterious birth of Armande, and on the basis of existing (if conflicting) evidence and his own deductions concludes that she is really Madeleine's daughter. His arguments are logical and convincing. But he is cautious over whether Molière himself could have been

38 **335**, p. 253

her father, as rumour had it. He avoids judging the issue on insufficient evidence and, in contrast with his earlier play *Molière*, does not exaggerate the importance of this possibility. Certainly, Bulgakov points out (again in contrast to the play) that Molière was able to convince the king that the rumours were without substance. Similarly, the story of Molière's attachment to Michel Baron, the young boy he brought up with so much devotion and who later was said to have deceived him with Armande, occupies a significant but comparatively minor place in the book.

It is this picture of Molière as an ordinary person which Bulgakov contrasts with the immortality of his works. Indeed, this whole theme is introduced, along with both the narrator and the hero, in a highly original prologue, which sets the entire tone for what is to follow. This consists of a conversation with the midwife who is about to deliver a very mortal Jean-Baptiste Poquelin into the world. 'You must realize that three centuries hence,' the narrator tells her, 'in a distant country, I shall remember you only because you held the son of Monsieur Poquelin in your arms' (p. 2). He indicates that Molière will become famous in many lands, even more so than the Sun-King, Louis XIV; that others, whom the midwife has never heard of, will write about him or be influenced by him: he mentions Griboedov, Pushkin, and Gogol. He talks of how Molière's plays will be performed by future generations, and how plays will be written about him too (one thinks, of course, of Bulgakov's own play). Finally, he again stresses the immortality of Molière, before returning to the personal level, to the midwife who is about to deliver what for her is a perfectly ordinary baby: 'Be careful, then, I beg you! Tell me, did he cry out? Is he breathing? ... He is alive!' (p. 7).

The theme of immortality has an important place in Bulgakov: we have seen it earlier in *The White Guard* and later it will appear in *The Master and Margarita*. In this first chapter Bulgakov also contrasts Molière with Louis XIV, who regards only himself as immortal and is blind to the 'true immortality' of the other. The relationship between the two makes one of the most interesting topics in the book and, despite Louis' 'blindness,' Bulgakov does not allow us to underestimate the very real part he played in Molière's career. To talk only of the evils of autocracy and of Molière's 'servile attitude,' as do some of the Soviet commentators, is to ignore the fact that Louis was largely a positive influence, establishing Molière in Paris and also giving him commissions – to say nothing of protecting him from his enemies. In trying to please the king Molière was only following in the paths of other artists before him. He is perhaps amusing in his antics to stay in the king's good graces: writing flattering prologues; adding a character to a play at the king's suggestion, or adding ballets so that the king could dance in them; inviting him to be godfather for his son (named Louis). But this enabled the genius of Molière to survive, and for Louis Bulgakov shows respect. While mocking his worldly ambitions, he admires his strength and decisiveness, combined with his unfailing courtesy - qualities which are shown to their best advantage in the story of his treatment of Fouquet, his superintendent of finance who converted treasury funds to his own use. Nor is Louis' image tarnished by the obsequiousness with which his courtiers treat him, for he stands above such triviality. With his favourable attitude towards Molière, whose plays he has the wit to honestly enjoy, he becomes a second hero of the book. It is true, of course, that his protection of Molière is arbitrary, and can be withdrawn towards the end of Molière's life in favour of the composer Lully. But there is a sense in which even Louis is immortal, as patron not of Molière alone but of all those great artists of France's glorious age, of which Louis has deservedly become the symbol. There are several occasions when Molière is shown in conversation with Louis, who for the most part appears as his beneficent patron: it is Molière's enemies - the insulted aristocracy, bourgeois, priests, doctors - rather than the king who try to limit his creative freedom.

There is clearly a parallel between Molière's relationship with Louis xiv and that of Bulgakov with Stalin: in the interest taken by the ruler, in the playwrights' petitions for various favours, and in the protection they both received. It is true that the similarities are superficial, for Stalin's assistance to Bulgakov was of the slightest and it is ludicrous even to compare him with Louis xiv in his patronage of the arts. (As symbols of their respective ages, there could hardly be a greater contrast!) Nevertheless, as Lakshin points out, one 'gets the feeling that the life of Monsieur de Molière has a greater relationship to the life of citizen Bulgakov than it seems at first.'[39] Bulgakov's interest in the other stems not so much from the fact that their lives were similar in any detail, but from Molière's being a great dramatist who exemplified a persistent struggle for creative freedom - which was to remain Bulgakov's major concern. It is here, of course, that we find one undoubted reason for the book's not being publishable in the Soviet Union of the thirties, where the parallels to that particular society and Bulgakov's plea for artistic freedom would have been only too readily understood.

For the fate of Molière's more important satirical plays also reflects that of Bulgakov's own: delighted audiences, followed by the ire of those who are satirized, and, where the group is sufficiently powerful, the prohibition of the play in question. Again, questions of censorship arise. To make it acceptable, *les Précieuses ridicules* has to be 'mutilated' by the author, who understands that 'spoiling it' will nevertheless not destroy its basic idea. It was a technique with which Bulgakov himself was familiar: some two years after writing this he would be

39 **335**, p. 254

making changes to *Zoyka's Apartment*, partly for the same reasons. We are reminded of critical reaction to this play too by one De Visé, who (writing of *l'Ecole des femmes*) 'wished first of all to say that the comedy could not succeed, but this he was unable to say, since it was a magnificent success. Therefore, de Visé said that the comedy's success was merely due to the excellent performances of the actors, which shows that de Visé was not a fool. He went on to state that he was grieved by the multitude of ribaldries in the comedy, remarking, by the way, that the plot was poorly constructed' (p. 153). The story of the ban on *Tartuffe* runs over several chapters and epitomizes the struggle between those who thought Molière dangerous and his own stubbornness. When finally the king gives his permission for the performance, the narrator exclaims in another heart-felt cry (thinking perhaps of the restaging of *Days of the Turbins*): 'Who will explain to me why a play that could not be performed in 1664 and 1667 could be performed in 1669?' (p. 203).

We should not take the parallels between Bulgakov and Molière too far. Bulgakov's interest in him stemmed possibly from a feeling that they shared similar problems, but he goes beyond this, trying to understand the whole life of the other – which was in no way like his own. But it is Molière's ultimate success in his endeavours, despite all his difficulties, that provides the basis of optimism on which the whole work rests – which, of course, coincides with Bulgakov's own optimism regarding the survival of true works of art despite even the severest contemporary criticism.

Life of Monsieur de Molière exhibits a tendency of Bulgakov in the thirties to express his ideas through the lives or the creations of others rather than in pure fiction (with the notable exception of *The Master and Margarita*). Yet this is still a creative biography, which we read for Bulgakov as much as for Molière. It is indeed a remarkable book, whose subject provides universal interest and whose style and approach gives it all the appeal of pure entertainment. Perhaps because of a certain hesitation over its form, it has not been fully appreciated. To those who might complain that it is neither one thing (biography) nor another (fiction) one may legitimately reply that it is both biography and fiction, and is successful on either level. In the opinion of this author, *Life of Monsieur de Molière* deserves far greater recognition than has so far been the case.

THE MISER (translation)

The final work in the Molière group was not written until a few years later, at the time when Bulgakov's play itself was about to open. 'Not counting *Molière*, which is to appear this month,' Yelena Sergeevna wrote on 4 January 1936 (to V.Ye. Volf, director of the Red Leningrad Theatre), 'not counting *Ivan Vasilie-*

vich at the Satire Theatre, he has taken in addition an urgent job - the translation for Academia of Molière's *The Miser* and he is translating at nights.'[40] The translation was published, without attracting much attention, in the third volume (1939) of a four-volume collection of Molière's works, and republished in 1952 in a volume of selected comedies by Molière. It follows the original closely, although with normal rephrasing at times. One misses, perhaps, the eloquence of the seventeenth-century French, for the Russian is far more direct: a sentence such as 'elles ne sont pas fort accommodées' is translated as 'they are poor'; 'Oui, je conçois assez, mon frère, quel doit être votre chagrin' as 'Oh, how well I understand your sadness!' But generally the translation is accurate and competently rendered into a good modern Russian.

MOLIÈRE OR *A CABAL OF HYPOCRITES*

History of the play and performance
Between 1934 and 1936 Bulgakov wrote three plays, *Bliss, Ivan Vasilievich*, and *The Last Days*. But these years are important most of all for the Art Theatre's work on *Molière* against the background of the author's increasing frustration and arguments with Stanislavsky: the whole process which completed Bulgakov's disillusionment with the theatre and led finally to his resignation. It is to the whole story of this production - which dates from some years earlier - that we must now turn.

Bulgakov had started on the play in October 1929,[41] dictating much of the text, as his wife Lyubov Yevgenievna recalls, striding about the room and playing all the parts himself. She had initially helped him to translate various biographies, but it is obvious from the text that Bulgakov was not concerned with a purely historical presentation. One has only to compare the play with his own *Life of Monsieur de Molière* to see that it is essentially fiction based on certain details from Molière's life which are brought together with comparatively minor concern for their accuracy or chronology. Whereas the major characters are identified by name with actual figures (Molière, Louis XIV, Madeleine and Armande Béjart, the actors La Grange and Du Croisy), others, although based on real people, are given fictitious names. Thus the Archbishop of Paris is called the Marquis de Charron rather than Hardouin de Péréfixe as in real life; the curé of the church of St Barthélemy, Pierre Roullé (who demanded that Molière be burnt

---

40 **187**, folio 223. This letter makes clear that both **306**, p. 347, and **40**, p. 43, are in error with their dates of 1933 and 1935.
41 **9**, pp. 351, 358. Some of the information that follows is from L.Ye. Belozerskaya's unpublished memoirs.

for his play *Tartuffe*), has simply become Father Barthélemy. Molière's protégé, Michel Baron, has become Zacharie Moirron.[42] Some characters are simply invented, notably Molière's servant Bouton and a vicious musketeer (who may, however, have been suggested by the Duc de la Feuillade).

The play deals basically with the change of Molière's fortunes in regard to the king; from a successful stage performance in front of him at the beginning to Molière's death on stage, in a theatre packed with his enemies, at the end – after *Tartuffe* has been banned and the king's patronage withdrawn. The villains are the members of the secret Cabal of the Holy Writ, Archbishop Charron in particular, who conspire to cause Molière's downfall; also their tool, the Marquis d'Orsigny (the musketeer), known as 'One-Eye' or, from a phrase he constantly uses, 'Start Praying.' Molière's unfortunate marriage to Armande Béjart, her flirtations with Moirron, and the latter's denunciation of Molière after being thrown out of the company, all form an important part of this somewhat complex play.[43]

Originally entitled *A Cabal of Hypocrites*, it was read first of all to the Bulgakovs' friends, the Lyamins. At the second reading, in Bulgakov's apartment, Markov, Moskvin, Stanitsyn, Yanshin, and Olga Knipper-Chekhova of the Art Theatre were all present. It was formally read to the theatre in January 1930 and, we may recall, rejected in February because of the need for contemporary plays.[44] However, a year and a half later, on 30 September 1931, Bulgakov sent a copy to Gorky and, probably as the result of his favourable assessment, it was put into the Art Theatre repertory shortly afterwards. Not only did it then receive official permission, but Bulgakov was also allowed to send it to the Fischer Publishing Company in Berlin.[45] Then in February or March 1932 it was 'killed' by Vishnevsky, 'who stabbed me in the back with a Finnish knife and with the public standing silently by' – only to be officially put into production again on 31 March, with N. Gorchakov named producer. (Gorky, delighted, further assisted Bulgakov by sending Fischerverlag his recommendation for the play, calling it 'a very good, artistically made piece, in which every part gives solid material for the performer.' Bulgakov, he went on, had 'written an excellent portrait of Molière in his declining years. Of Molière tired from the mess of his personal life and from the burden of his glory. Just as well, boldly and, I would say, beautifully is the Sun-King presented ...') Nothing further was done

---

42 An alternate version of Baron's name was Michel Boyron; Bulgakov's invented name could also have been suggested by that of Madeleine Béjart's first lover, Mormoiron.
43 There is one variant, with a few minor changes, in **188**.
44 See chapters 8 and 9
45 For this and the following, see **448**, pp. 451, 457, 472; **294**, p. 171; **195**, p. 166; **295**, p. 206; **379**, p. 164; **270**, p. 752; **3**, p. 473.

on the play that season. In October its impending production was announced in
Sovetskoe iskusstvo, with the artist P.V. Vilyams also named as set designer.[46]
Despite a few desultory rehearsals and the preparation of sets, however, there
was still very little accomplished, and by 15 April 1933 we find Stanislavsky
writing that a dress rehearsal by the end of that season too was impossible.

For some years now, in fact, Stanislavsky had been ill and, since 1931, was
under the care of a permanent nurse: the result of several heart attacks. He remained a severely sick man for the rest of his life – which had a bearing on the
events that followed. That summer he departed for Nice and then, as he was
about to return in the winter, had another severe attack of angina pectoris,
which caused him to remain abroad for the winter as well. In March 1934, still in
Nice, he wrote to Nemirovich-Danchenko to say that he had not done very much
on *Molière* at all. 'The role of Molière has had a strange fate,' he concluded.
'Two actors latched onto it straight away: Moskvin and Tarkhanov. Now both
have cooled towards it. What is the matter?'[47]

Bulgakov, who was assistant producer, was getting impatient at the delay –
not surprisingly for the play had now been written over four years previously.
But after Stanislavsky's return to Moscow in autumn 1934 rehearsals began in
earnest. Gorchakov has left a detailed account of the discussions between Stanislavsky, Bulgakov, and himself, also of Stanislavsky's work with the actors.[48]
Much of the same material remains in the Theatre Archive – fortunately, for
Gorchakov's chronology is somewhat inaccurate.

Initially, Stanislavsky had a long discussion with Gorchakov to express his
doubts about the whole conception of the play. His main concern was that
Molière was shown as an ordinary person rather than as a man of genius, and
always as defeated. Gorchakov pointed out to him that Bulgakov had 'suffered
so much waiting for this production that the slightest remark about the text of
the play makes him literally shake with anger' (p. 354). So Stanislavsky, fearful
lest open criticism might cause Bulgakov to withdraw the play completely, decided to let rehearsals go ahead, but gave instructions that only the play's broad
outlines should be dealt with. Bulgakov was to work with the actors so that he
would come to understand what was required. 'In other words,' Gorchakov
asked him, 'the only purpose of this kind of rehearsal is to convince Bulgakov of
the necessity for further work on his play.' 'Exactly,' replied Stanislavsky. 'This

46 **494**, p. 303, and **457**
47 **494**, pp. 336-8, **374**
48 **291**, pp. 532-56. Page references in the text are to the abbreviated English version **292**,
    pp. 353-91. This needs to be used with caution, and on occasions I have preferred to
    make my own translation. A good acount of this material but with inaccurate dates
    appears in **9**, pp. 351-9. See also **188**, folios 85 and 1332

is my purpose. But neither the actors nor Bulgakov should be aware of this' (p. 358). It was this initial dishonesty of Stanislavsky's which was responsible for many of the later troubles.

So rehearsals began in late 1934,[49] with Gorchakov reporting every day to Stanislavsky in his flat at No 6, Leontievsky Lane. Stanislavsky was still too ill to come to the theatre or manage rehearsals, so it was several months before he could see the production, and in the meantime not all the actors liked this new method of work, which meant largely improvisation around a few key scenes. Neither did Bulgakov, who claimed, not unnaturally, that his scenes were linked together by a logical sequence, and should be played that way.

The first showing to Stanislavsky took place in his own apartment on 5 March 1935, and is recorded in considerable detail both in Gorchakov's account and in a special protocol of Stanislavsky's comments. After expressing general satisfaction, Stanislavsky went on to say that he still did not see Molière as a man of talent. 'I, as a spectator, want to know what constitutes the greatness of the man. You are showing me a life, but not an artistic, creative life' (p. 360). Bulgakov objected that it was impossible to bring out Molière's genius any more than he had already done, or to include Molière's *Tartuffe* in the play. But Stanislavsky wanted to see him writing, and disagreed with Bulgakov that Molière was unaware of his importance. There was too much in the play about Molière's personal life and his love for Armande. More important was his exposing the vices of his society, for which he had to rely on the protection of the king. As Stanislavsky expounded on the Molière he would like to see, Bulgakov defended his own conceptions and his idea of showing Molière as an ordinary man: his work on it was finished, he said. Stanislavsky still wanted him to make alterations. 'It will be very difficult for me to do this,' Bulgakov replied. 'After all, work on the play has been dragging on for nearly five years.'

The essential differences between Bulgakov and Stanislavsky were never overcome. Following this rehearsal, there took place a number of others on individual scenes. On 14 April Bulgakov indicated a couple of minor changes he would make, but there was still some dissatisfaction with his stage directions, causing Stanislavsky to comment again to Gorchakov that Bulgakov should be persuaded to make other changes. He added – rather late, one feels – that there was much in the play that was historically false. The next day Bulgakov was absent, and Stanislavsky, at his apartment as usual, decided to rehearse the scene of Moirron's attempted seduction of Armande, asking for a careful record to be kept and sent to Bulgakov later. In this scene Stanislavsky had Armande and Moirron

49 Gorchakov reports Stanislavsky, at a rehearsal that can be identified as that of 5 March 1935, as saying rehearsals had only been going on for three months.

actually rehearsing with each other from Molière's *Dom Juan*; and then he added a short scene where, after Molière had returned and driven out Moirron, he sat down at his table to write. 'Oh, what Bulgakov will do to us for this!' Livanov (playing Moirron) exclaimed at one point.

The rehearsal which turned out to be most crucial took place at Stanislavsky's flat three days later. It began well, with Gorchakov telling Stanislavsky that he and Bulgakov had been working together on the scene of Armande and Moirron, and that Bulgakov had asked for four days' leave to write a new text for that scene. Profiting once again from Bulgakov's absence, Stanislavsky then went on to rehearse the scene of the Cabal, making more changes, to be recorded in the protocol. It was this that turned out to be the last straw.

Bulgakov read the protocol on 22 April, after his four days' leave, and recorded in it that he categorically refused to make any more changes. The same day he wrote essentially the same thing to Stanislavsky: 'the changes noted in the protocol for the Cabal scene, and also textual alterations noted earlier for other scenes, violate once and for all, as I have become convinced, my artistic intentions and lead to the composition of some new play, which I cannot write as I radically disagree with it.'[50] Four days later Bulgakov noted in the protocol that overwork had brought on neuralgia and therefore he asked for two weeks' leave.

Reluctantly, Stanislavsky decided to continue rehearsals using Bulgakov's text as it was. The 1934-35 season came to an end with him still devoting his main attention to work on the individual roles – at times using extracts from Molière's plays, and still expressing regret that Bulgakov had refused to include any in the play itself. For the summer of 1935, Stanislavsky went to a sanatorium near Moscow and stayed until the beginning of winter. On his return, he was still dissatisfied with the play and, according to Gorchakov, became more and more despondent, refusing to allow it to proceed to dress rehearsal. His criticism remained what it had always been: 'Bulgakov wrote a play not about the greatness of Molière's ideas nor about his tragic fate, but instead about the personal misfortunes and mishaps of an ordinary writer' (p. 388). After Gorchakov had tried for a final time to persuade Bulgakov to make changes, and failed, Stanislavsky told Gorchakov to release the play on his own authority and withdrew from the production.

One cannot perhaps be too hard on Stanislavsky, whose major fault – as he came to realize – had been to try to produce the play at all when he was not in agreement with its basic conception. Bulgakov had not wanted to call the play *Molière* in any case and did not think of his plays as having any particular histori-

50 **188**, folio 7718; published in **448**, pp. 452-3

cal significance, whereas Stanislavsky was concerned with issues such as his responsibility to the French nation[51] – and of course the doctrines of the age demanded of the theatre a proper interpretation of history. Stanislavsky's own success in the past had been too great for him to simply allow an author to go his own way; at his age (seventy-two in 1935) and with his ill-health it was hardly surprising if he was over-dogmatic in his views. Neither he nor Bulgakov was really capable of understanding the viewpoint of the other and an increasing hostility between them was the result. Bulgakov started to have frequent periods of depression, and became suspicious of everyone; whereas Stanislavsky started work in 1936 with an experimental group on a production of Molière's *Tartuffe*, which was staged in 1939, after his death.

After watching a rehearsal of *Molière* on 31 December, Nemirovich-Danchenko took over the production. At a discussion of the play on 12 February, three days prior to the première, he expressed strong support for the play, giving credit to those who had worked on it before him, but pointing out that the long delay in its production – although beneficial – had been due to a lack of organization on the part of the theatre. He stressed too his high opinion of the author as an exponent of dramatic technique, adding that he thought the attacks on him were the result of misunderstandings.[52] Gorchakov, too, defended the play, in an article which appeared in *Literatúrnaia gazeta* on 10 February. But the following day Bulgakov's old enemy Litovsky attacked the play in *Sovetskoe iskusstvo*, saying that it was no more than a light historical melodrama, a 'gala performance, a cultured performance, but unfortunately based on very weak material.'[53]

After nearly 300 rehearsals, *Molière* opened on 15 February 1936. It was a brilliant production, with music by the composer Glier and lavish sets by P.V. Vilyams (who in later years would be criticized for his love of luxurious settings):

All the props for *Molière* were gloomily symbolic. Theater costumes were hung on the racks, thrown across the railing, and piled on the floor in Molière's dressing room. They were like broken dolls, with the terrible grins of masks from the *commedia dell'arte*. Frightful and monstrous masks decorated the faces of the clowns painted on the portals. In the scene at the court of Louis XIV, monstrous and gilded caryatids replaced the clowns and the dolls. In the scene of the 'Cabal of hypocrites,' the colors, figures, and costumes were filled with a gloomy mystery.[54]

51 Based on a personal conversation with M.M. Yanshin
52 **278**, pp. 485-6, and **372**, pp. 398-9
53 **290**, and **356**, pp. 327-30
54 **288**, p. 329; see also **298**, p. 617

According to one source the play was a success with the audience, but Gorchakov states that public reaction convinced Stanislavsky and Nemirovich-Danchenko that the play had failed. At all events, the criticism soon began in earnest.

The play was performed for the last time on 4 March. On 9 March *Pravda*
published a violent attack entitled 'External Brilliance and False Contents.'
Molière, it claimed, was not only a bad play, but an incorrect interpretation of
what could have been an interesting historical theme – which Bulgakov had managed to spoil. The main line of the play was Molière's marriage to his own daughter, but since Bulgakov could not completely get around social issues something
was shown too of Molière's struggles with the church. However, Louis xiv's banning of *Tartuffe*, instead of being necessitated by the class struggle, was shown as
pure caprice. Bulgakov, 'taking refuge in historical settings,' was trying 'to force
through a reactionary view of artistic creativity as "pure" art.' The theatre, the
article went on, had concentrated on the external glitter of the performance,
abandoning the principles of realism. 'This false, worthless play cuts decisively
across the whole creative line of the theatre and puts it in a false position with
respect to the spectators ...' Such plays were not needed, but rather those that
were 'full of ideas, realistically full-blooded, and historically true.'[55]

After reading the article, Bulgakov apparently called his wife and said 'You
understand what this means? It's finished with plays.' And he immediately took
her out to buy some history books so he could enter a competition he had read
about a few days before, to write a history textbook for secondary schools. The
same day he went to see Yermolinsky, to ask advice about money matters, for if
Molière was not to continue he would once again be in financial troubles.[56]

The next day there appeared an article by B. Alpers entitled 'The Reactionary
Conjectures of M. Bulgakov': Molière was pitiful and cowardly, his creativity unconscious; Molière's image was 'dethroned by a contemporary dramatist in order
to prove a false and reactionary thesis.' Other articles appeared attacking Bulgakov and agreeing with that in *Pravda*. That year, 1936, represented the height of
reactionary attitudes towards the arts, and on two occasions, 14 and 26 March,
even Meyerhold (himself under pressure at this time in his life – he would 'disappear' three years later) attacked both the lavishness of the production and its
faulty material. Yanshin, too, who had played Molière's servant Bouton in the
play, was evidently persuaded to write a 'self-criticism' of the production, saying
that what was most at fault was the 'incorrect text, which distorted historical
reality' – although he went on to say that all of those involved were as much to
blame as Bulgakov.[57] (Yanshin claims that his words were misreported, but none

55 **512**
56 **339**, pp. 59-60, and **266**, p. 84
57 **194**; **402**; **373**, pp. 344-5, 355; **309**

the less they led, hardly surprisingly, to Bulgakov's becoming increasingly cold towards the man whom he had trusted as a personal friend.)

Molière was withdrawn after only seven performances. Work which had started on a Leningrad production at the Bolshoy Dramatic Theatre was stopped.[58] So was the work on *Ivan Vasilievich*, although it was already in the dress rehearsal stage and due to open at the Theatre of Satire a week later. Prospects vanished for the performance at the Vakhtangov Theatre of Bulgakov's play about Pushkin, *The Last Days*, which had been finished the previous September.

Once again, all Bulgakov's hopes had collapsed. Angry at the Art Theatre, bitter above all with Stanislavsky, he finally resigned.

Later criticism of the play tended to support Stanislavsky's views and it received little serious discussion until after its publication in 1962 in the volume of Bulgakov's *Plays*, and in 1963 in *Dramas and Comedies*. Once again, it is K. Rudnitsky who has written most interestingly about it.[59]

The play has been performed on several subsequent occasions in the Soviet Union, in Kaunas in the mid-sixties, and twice in Moscow in 1967. Its major production, by A. Efros with A. Pelevin as Molière, was in February at the Theatre of the Lenin Komsomol – complete with a fashionable vocal and instrumental ensemble which performed the music of Molière's age. The production was not particularly outstanding and was soon taken off – apparently because of the over-enthusiastic reaction of the audience to such sentences as 'I hate the king's tyranny.'[60] At about the same time it was put on for two or three evenings by students of the Shchukin Theatrical Institute as their graduation exercise in what was, it seems, the best production of all but was seen by very few. In 1973, to mark the 300th anniversary of Molière's death, the play opened at the Gorky Dramatic Theatre in Leningrad, in a highly professional production by S.Yu. Yursky, who also played Molière. But regrettably the producer agreed with Stanislavsky rather than Bulgakov: showing extracts from Molière's plays at the beginning of each of the production's two acts, and having Molière not only writing on stage but directing a rehearsal – just what Bulgakov had not wanted.

Molière has also been performed in English by students of the Rose Bruford College of Speech and Drama, at the Shaw Theatre in London in 1972, where the director, Jean Benedetti, apart from adding incidents from Bulgakov's own life to make clear the parallel between him and Molière in their relationships to Stalin and Louis XIV, also adopted Stanislavsky's idea of having the actors per-

58 **266**, p. 84, and **294**, p. 171

59 **461**, pp. 138-41; **462**

60 **404**, **312**, **280**. For the most detailed account of the performance, see **463**, pp. 263-85; for that at the Shchukin Institute, see **284**.

form a large chunk from *Tartuffe* in the middle of the play. Reviews were some-what cool. 'Over-identification with Molière leads him to falsify the Frenchman's life to accommodate his own tragic experience,' one critic wrote. Another said it was 'a rattling good melodrama, with some scenes of extraordinary theatrical flair: but it has neither the personal nor public insight to qualify as a political tragedy ... Plot construction is rough and ready.'[61]

The play itself

From the outset we must admit that there is some justice in the criticisms that have been made of this play. While we need not agree with Stanislavsky and can readily accept Bulgakov's picture of Molière as an ordinary man unaware of his significance, it is more difficult to reconcile the events in the play with his actual life, which Bulgakov virtually rewrites, exaggerating the element of persecution and the importance of Molière's marriage. Nor is this in any way made clear for the viewer not familiar with Molière's biography who, on learning that the truth is somewhat different, is liable to feel with some justification that he has been cheated. One's view of the play will thus depend first of all on how much one feels the author is justified in radically changing history for his own purposes.

Apart from small matters of detail and chronology, and the change of certain names, the play departs from fact in a number of ways. The pivotal issue of Molière's marriage to his own daughter is at the best unproved: many Molière scholars regard it as pure slander. Madeleine Béjart did not, as in the play, leave the troupe after the marriage nor did Armande leave Molière as a result of the intervention of the Archbishop of Paris. An affair between Armande and Baron (perhaps with reason given a different name by Bulgakov) is similarly specula-tive: Baron was driven out of the troupe earlier at Armande's insistence and re-turned later, without denouncing Molière to the king in the meantime. Louis XIV did not withdraw patronage from Molière on the grounds of his supposed incest, which Molière convinced him was untrue; nor did he ban *Tartuffe* after having allowed it, rather the reverse: he finally allowed it after others had forced a ban. Molière himself, although subjected to some harassment and certain scenes of violence in the theatre, was not, as we have here, persecuted to the ex-tent of wanting to leave the country, was not nearly killed by a deliberately vici-ous d'Orsigny, and died only several years after the controversies over *Tartuffe*: after a performance, not on stage. Thus the cause of his death, as recorded by actor La Grange in the last speech of the play, was not 'the disfavour of the King and the black Cabal' (p. 284),[62] except to the extent that this probably had con-tributed in a very general way to his ill-health.

61 **223** and **519**
62 Page references to **3** will be given in the text.

It is true that certain other scenes are based loosely on known or reported events from Molière's life: such as the discovery of the urchin Baron hiding in the 'magical' harpsichord of a charlatan (Raisin in real life), or Molière's having supper with the king – based on an incident known as the 'en cas de nuit.' As 'valet de chambre tapissier du roi' Molière did indeed have the right to make the king's bed, as referred to in the play, and insisted on exercising it; musketeers and other soldiers, after their privilege of receiving free tickets had been withdrawn, did indeed break into the theatre and kill a porter (causing the actor Hubert to dig a hole in the theatre wall and get stuck in the process of trying to crawl out). But these last events took place nine years before Molière's death – even if other scenes of rowdiness occurred on occasion, as was normal in a violent age. The Cabal of the Holy Writ is also based on fact, on the secret Compagnie du Saint-Sacrement, referred to popularly as the 'Cabale des dévots,' and whose efforts to have *Tartuffe* suppressed were strongly supported by the Archbishop of Paris. But it was not nearly as powerful as it is shown in the play; at the time in question it had fallen into disrepute, was suspect to many laity and clergy alike, and was dissolved the year after the original ban on *Tartuffe*.[63]

Generally speaking, then, a number of events from different times of Molière's life have been brought together, reinterpreted, and combined with material that is fictitious or dubious. Undoubtedly, some of the changes were a result of Bulgakov's having to fit a relatively ordinary life into a dramatic framework, but we may tend to agree with one Soviet critic that in doing this he 'has allowed himself to be too carried away by the vicissitudes of fate, by the element of melodrama'[64] – even if, we might add, it is good melodrama. Furthermore, if the aim of the play is to show persecuted genius, then its impact is surely weakened by the knowledge that, however accurate some of the individual details, in totality Molière's life was not really as shown in the play – except perhaps on a purely psychological level. One could perhaps see Bulgakov as attempting to represent all those events, real or imagined, which were part of Molière's consciousness before his death, but the problem then arises that the style is largely realistic: there is nothing to suggest that we are dealing with Molière's psyche.

Bulgakov was of course thoroughly familiar with Molière's biography and must have had a reason for making the various changes. It has been suggested that he falsified Molière's story to make it seem closer to that of his own life – and one can make the obvious parallels between Louis XIV and Stalin, the Cabal and the orthodox communists, the reactions of critics to Molière and Bulgakov alike. Or he may perhaps have seen Molière as representative of any writer, whose real life was therefore relatively unimportant. Another possibility is that

63 See **235**, pp. 185-7, 233-5; and **193**, pp. 384-410
64 **322**, p. 193

he was more interested in showing the effect of Molière's genius on others – as he would later do in *The Last Days*, where his hero Pushkin never actually appears on stage at all – with the precise details of his life correspondingly less important. Yet if such was Bulgakov's purpose, he has still not quite succeeded, for the character of Molière is essentially too strong to be thus confined. We are, then, left in some uncertainty over Bulgakov's intentions. We simply have to accept his unhistorical Molière and admit, with his critics, that he may have shown some lack of judgement in allowing the play to revolve around the dubious issue of Molière's possible but unlikely incestuous marriage.

It is, of course, fair to point out that the prominent place given to Molière's unhappy domestic situation only reflects its importance to him personally. It was one of the major factors involved in the tragedy of his declining years, and it is in his relationship with Armande that he is seen as most human, as fallible as the Sganarelle in his own plays – as whom he is made up at the time of his first appearance. The figure of Sganarelle appears in seven of Molière's plays and is usually the jealous bourgeois of forty: in love with a young coquette, or seeking domestic happiness in vain. The relevance of this to Molière immediately becomes clear when he asks Armande 'You won't deceive me?' just after Bouton has pointedly asked how old he is (p. 228). In his personal life, Molière is shown as no wiser than anyone else.

As Rudnitsky has pointed out, however, the underlying theme of the play is that creation is stronger than the creator.[65] Molière, as Bulgakov intended, struggles simply for happiness without realizing his own significance. But part of this struggle is also to write what he wishes, as an artist, and to have his plays performed. In this he resembles any artist, and in the last act, in nightcap, underwear, and dressing-gown before a performance, he is reminiscent of Bulgakov's other eternal artist, the Master. His death on the stage in his own play, human though it might be, 'is as though surrounded by his immortality, by that reality of unyielding art which is stronger and more endurable than yielding and tired human flesh.'[66] We thus have the same basic theme as in *Life of Monsieur de Molière*. It is his creativity, as well as the man himself, that the others respect and love.

The actors and actresses in his troupe also share in his personal tragedy, even Armande and Moirron who are partly to blame for it. So of course does his early mistress Madeleine, Armande's mother, who knows the truth about his marriage; so does his true disciple La Grange, who becomes his biographer and, in the play, 'narrator' of his life by means of his *Régistre* (one of the major sources for

65 **462**, p. 88
66 **461**, p. 141

Molière's biography). Yet closer to him than any is his servant Bouton, his own creation, representing the voice of plain, down-to-earth practicality which Molière chooses to ignore. Bouton expresses his master's own hesitations or, when unheeded, attempts simply to look after his master's interests – as when he tries in the first act to distract One-Eye from paying too much attention to Armande – 'It's started. Oh, my frivolous maître!' (p. 230), or later to minimize the importance of Moirron's taking Armande into his room. The relationship between Bouton and Molière (like that of Sancho Panza and Don Quixote – a theme Bulgakov would take up later) is one of love, as Bouton finally points out to Molière, who denies it. Bouton has served his master for twenty years, and at the end of the play there is nothing more touching than his simple answer to La Grange's question as to why he does not go now to his dead master: 'I don't want to.' Without Molière to command him, it is pointless.

For most of the play, Bouton is the major source of comedy, and a comic foil to Molière. Indeed with the logical absurdities he uses to answer Molière's anger he might be taken for a Molièrian character himself, the typical servant replying to his master.

Molière. You're lying, by your eyes I see you're lying!
Bouton. Sir, in order to lie, one must at least say something. But I haven't said anything yet. I took off my shoes since ... Will you please see the nails? Shoes with metal plates on them, may they be damned ... (p. 249)

But he also becomes a humorous parody of Molière himself, which he seems to realize when he insists 'I myself have a tragic fate' (p. 269). In the last act, afraid for his skin after his master's forthrightness, he shouts his loud praises of the king: aping what Molière has himself done during the whole of his time at court. Molière's reaction 'God, what a talentless fool!' applies not to the uselessness of Bouton's action but to his abilities as an actor: Molière himself was able to say essentially the same far more brilliantly.

This is indeed how the play opens, with Bouton listening in awe at Molière's talent for flattery: 'Oh, what a mind! He was clever enough to call him the Sun.' 'I am a comedian, an insignificant role,' Molière ironically continues, 'But I am famous because of acting in your time, Louis! ... Great! ... French!!! ... King!!!' (p. 221). More central than later in *Life of Monsieur de Molière* is the theme of Molière's relationship with the king, and there are indications even at the beginning, as Rudnitsky again suggests, that Molière hates his role of flatterer.[67] Only at the end, in a dialogue which expresses the ideological basis of the play, does he openly reveal his own feelings:

67 **461**, p. 139

All my life I licked his spurs and I thought only one thing: don't crush me. And now, just the same – he's crushed me. Tyrant!

...

But after all, Bouton, why was it? Because of *Tartuffe*. Because of that I humiliated myself. I thought I would find an ally. And I found one! Don't humiliate yourself, Bouton. I hate the king's tyranny! (pp. 273-4)

Such words express any artist's dilemma in an age of repression and, of course, can equally be regarded as a commentary on Bulgakov's own age under Stalin – as they most certainly were understood.[68]

But again, any direct comparison between Louis XIV and Stalin is very much in Louis' favour. Louis is not really shown as a tyrant, but simply as a man of power, whose word is law, but who until he learns about Molière's scandalous marriage shows more sympathy towards him than he does to his enemies. Like Molière, he has his own shadow, a jester called the Just Cobbler, who apes his power on a purely symbolical level and pronounces the occasional word of wisdom, asking the king, for example, whether it is true that no kingdom can exist without denunciations. Louis stands far above his courtiers, and is shown intelligently dispensing a kind of rough if arbitrary justice: giving only a light prison sentence to a man who has cheated him at cards, and allowing him to keep his winnings; protecting Molière despite the pleas of his enemies; refusing Moirron, whom he clearly despises, a position at the Bourgogne Theatre because he is a bad actor but offering him work in the secret police. Yet essentially he too is a figure of comedy, too dignified even to play his own hand at cards, and exquisitely polite because of his assurance of power: preceding his orders with the words 'if it is not too difficult for you' or apologizing for interrupting a hilariously funny spitting match between One-Eye and Charron after a quarrel in his own reception room. Because of this, his final treatment of Molière is perhaps unconvincing: it is difficult, given the quiet power and authority he shows, to imagine him seriously concerned that Molière blasphemes against religion in his works, or is a criminal and an atheist.

The real conflict, however, is more between Molière and his enemies in the church, the Cabal of Hypocrites (the title that Bulgakov himself chose for the play). We can perhaps see the play as consisting of two elements: Molière and his basically innocent if unhappy personal life, as opposed to the Cabal, which does everything possible to vilify him, using anything which serves their purpose as

---

68 In a conversation with M. Michel Vassilieff, Yelena Sergeevna reported that none the less Stalin supported the play's performance but had been persuaded to change his mind by Litovsky.

evidence, true or false (and notably the scandal surrounding his marriage). This requires, however, considerable emphasis on the power of the Cabal throughout the play, which in practical terms depends on the character in whom it is personified, Archbishop Charron. Except for him, it consists only of shadowy, mysterious figures, and indeed its strength lies in their very anonymity. Bulgakov well succeeds in creating the sinister atmosphere of repression that it represents, but it is perhaps significant that in his conversation with Stanislavsky he expressed concern over the scene of the Cabal in particular – and over the archbishop. Charron is admittedly a real figure of power and a worthy opponent to Molière: but there is a danger of his impact being weakened by Bulgakov's introduction of another major adversary to Molière in the figure of One-Eye, a mere buffoon of no real account, the stereotype of the bold and dangerous musketeer. (However, with his ridiculous repetition of 'start praying,' there are very real possibilities for comedy in this role.) Although simply an instrument of the Cabal, he tends to overshadow Charron since to Molière he represents the more immediate danger. The success of any production depends in large measure on achieving the right balance between these two characters.

Other characters, namely the actors of Molière's troupe, tend with the one exception of Moirron to be episodic and show little development. Madeleine, La Grange, Du Croisy, even Armande, although competently drawn, simply represent historical figures: the disadvantage perhaps inherent in a pseudo-historical play. Generally, *Molière* is a play of superbly developed situations rather than character, and its real strength lies in the atmosphere created. Bulgakov's mastery of stagecraft is apparent from the first scene. The backstage of the theatre – the place where real and fictitious life meet – gives ample scope for creating theatrical alienation, as was exemplified in Vilyams' original grotesque sets. Both sides of Molière's life are suggested simultaneously. In his dressing room there is a multitude of lights, suggesting the magnificence of the occasion; in the other there is only a crucifix with a lamp in front of it and, on the table, a lantern with a green glass shade: under this sits La Grange, whose function in the play will be to record the tragic events in Molière's life. Molière then appears in the guise of Sganarelle, with an exaggerated wig, a caricature helmet, and a false lilac-coloured nose with a wart on it. Motifs introduced at the beginning all have their part in the action that follows. While Molière is engaged in a comic argument with Bouton, La Grange begins to silently cry to himself, indicating in almost Chekhovian fashion the tragedy that is to come. Later, when Molière goes to kiss Armande, Sganarelle's nose gets in the way. He then leads her to the crucifix to swear that she loves him.

The contrast of light and darkness, evident here, comes to be particularly important in creating a mysterious, even threatening, atmosphere. As Molière tells

Madeleine he is to marry Armande, all the lights in the theatre go out. When Molière has left, La Grange returns with his green lantern – we now see it is his leitmotif – learns from Madeleine that she has failed to prevent the marriage, and records its event in his *Régistre*. He takes the lantern away and there is again darkness until the figure of the boy Moirron mysteriously emerges from the harpsichord that has stood on stage all this time. Another light, as Molière returns. Whereas Act I alternates between light and darkness, in Act II the light predominates, since it opens with Louis, the Sun-King, and his court. As the king goes to bed, the lights are of course extinguished, dark figures of musketeers take up their guard, and mysterious voices echo all around: 'The king is asleep!' Then *'the palace dissolves in the darkness and disappears ...'* and it is suddenly daylight again in Molière's flat (p. 245). We are reminded that *Molière* was written only two years after *Flight*, which it resembles in its effects.

As too in *Flight*, the play is full of sounds, noises – some of which serve as a comment on what has just been said. In the first act there are three occasions when thunderous applause is heard as the audience follows the lead of the king – on the final occasion it emphasizes Molière's prognostication about having to suffer because of his marriage. There is music from the harpsichord, a triumphal march as the king departs; in the second act a trumpet flourish, and a song from Armande and Moirron with harpsichord accompaniment.

It is Act III that is most remarkable for the atmosphere created by theatrical and symbolical effects. In the first two scenes, the most visually dramatic in the play, darkness again predominates: '*A stone cellar lit by a three-candled candelabra. A table covered with red cloth, on which is a book and some manuscripts or other. At the table sit the* Members of the Cabal of the Holy Writ *in masks; in an armchair, separately, without a mask, sits* Charron. *The door opens, and two men in black, of sinister appearance, lead in* Moirron *with hands tied and a blindfold over his eyes*' (p. 251). The whole atmosphere here is one of secrecy, mystery. The scene finishes, after the interrogations, with Charron saying 'Let us pray' (*pomolimsia*), which reminds us of One-Eye with his constant repetition of 'start praying' (*pomolis'*) – as though Charron were saying they all should rely on him to be their executioner. This is followed by the singing of the monks in prayer as the scene gives way to an immense dark cathedral, with two candles in the archbishop's confessional, and two unknown figures whispering about *Tartuffe*. Again there is unrelieved darkness as Madeleine is brought to confess, but in the background is a sonorous organ and even a choir, which are used as a direct accompaniment to Madeleine's – and then Armande's – dialogue with Charron.

Structurally too the play is impressive. The first act is remarkable for the way that different essential threads in the story of Molière are interwoven: the patronage of the king, the coming disastrous marriage of Molière and Armande, the introduction of Zacharie Moirron and of Molière's later enemy One-Eye. The last act (again in a way reminiscent of Chekhov) is a complete reversal of the situation at the beginning of the play. There, Molière had gained the approval of the king and was prepared to flatter him. By the end he has lost the king's approval, his flattery changes to curses, and he is in fear of his life – to the extent of symbolically hiding himself by huddling up in his blanket. Before, he was preparing for success in the theatre, now instead he prepares to leave Paris. Moirron, Molière's discovery of Act I, has in the meantime betrayed him, and now returns to defend Molière and then commit suicide. Details are repeated from the first act to make the contrast more vivid. As earlier, Molière is again seen arguing with his servant Bouton, whom he even gives money for a shirt he had torn in the first act. Almost delirious, he recalls Madeleine, who has died, as though she were still alive. Bulgakov changes a date slightly to emphasize the comparison: formerly on 17 February (rather than the actual 20 February 1663) Molière was happy to be with Armande, whom he was to marry that night; now it is 17 February ten years later, Armande has gone, Madeleine is dead, and that night he will die himself. In the theatre, too, the décor – with the dressing-rooms, crucifix and lamp, green lantern – is exactly the same as before. With a comic nose, Molière even looks the same. The actress Rivale is still running around half-naked as before. The theatre is again overcrowded, the audience is similarly noisy: but instead of applause there are now howls of derision from the musketeers who have murdered a porter. One-Eye had previously brought money from the king to show his appreciation but now, at the news that he is in the theatre, Molière hides under Moirron's cloak; when the performance continues, One-Eye seats himself on the edge of his box threateningly close to the stage.

Bulgakov has picked up all the threads from the beginning, but tied them around Molière's own neck, as it were. There then follows the conclusion of the play, the performance of a scene based on *le Malade imaginaire*, with a crowd of doctors of terrifying appearance chanting around the man who, ironically, is very sick indeed. For the climax, as Molière falls and the confusion increases, Bulgakov draws a nightmare scene of Molière being ritualistically hounded on all sides. Then, as though in parody of his triumphal exit in the first act, Molière is carried off. To quell the audience the lights are turned off: again the darkness, then the crucifix is illuminated; then La Grange, as before, appears with his green lantern to make his final entry in the *Régistre*.

This type of action gives great possibilities for any imaginative interpretation. The whole play is a hyperbole of Molière's life, and needs to be played as such – as a nightmare experience of the central character, perhaps, avoiding as far as possible a too realistic presentation of individual scenes. Or it could be performed as a psychological drama, as a grotesque drama of the absurd. Regrettably we are still waiting for such a production, and so far, treated in a straightforward manner, the play has not fully succeeded. Until that time we must reserve judgement on its overall quality. *Molière* (or, to give it the title Bulgakov intended, *A Cabal of Hypocrites*) is undoubtedly a most difficult play, both to interpret and to perform. It has certain inherent problems which cannot be entirely overcome; but its whole conception and stagecraft are such that it deserves to be considered at the very least a noble failure, an undertaking which Bulgakov was right to attempt, and a challenge to any theatre.

10

Plays of the mid-thirties

In Bulgakov's letter to Stalin of 1930 he mentioned a comedy he had destroyed: probably the first draft for *Bliss*, which he began that year.[1] The play was taken up again in May 1933 for the Leningrad Music Hall, and completed in April 1934, when it was also given the subtitle 'Engineer Reyn's Dream in Four Acts.' It involves a visit to the year 2222 of Engineer Reyn with his house manager, Bunsha-Koretsky, and a thief, Yury Miloslavsky (his name taken from the title of M.N. Zagoskin's historical novel). In a rational and pleasant society they are made welcome, particularly by the People's Commissar for Inventions, Radamanov, whose daughter Avrora falls in love with Reyn. But Reyn is expected to give his time machine to the society, and then it is decided that the three of them are dangerous and should be 'cured' of their harmful tendencies: so they escape back to the twentieth century, taking Avrora with them.

In a letter to Popov on 10 July 1934 Bulgakov told him of a meeting, in the Astoria Hotel in Leningrad, with the director who was to produce the play, who had dinner with him, 'didn't say a single word about the play and then it was as though the earth had swallowed him up, he was no longer there!'[2] *Bliss* was apparently banned outright, and has never had a stage production.

The following summer, 1935, Bulgakov rapidly completed another play, *Ivan Vasilievich*, by taking basically the same material as in *Bliss* and reworking it, in three acts instead of four, and with the time machine used this time to travel into the past. The main characters remain the inventor, now with the name of Timofeev, the thief Miloslavsky, and the house manager Bunsha-Koretsky, whose

1 **407**, II, p. 135. Confirmed by L.Ye. Belozerskaya. See also **446**, p. 258
2 **491**, p. 99

name and patronymic are now Ivan Vasilievich. Reyn's neighbour, Mikhelson, whose room Miloslavsky was in the process of robbing at the beginning, has become Anton Semyonovich Shpak, and a female neighbour has been made into Bunsha's wife, Ulyana Andreevna. In this play we also see Timofeev's wife Zinaida, who is in the process of running away with a film director, Yakin.

The first act contains a great deal of dialogue which is closely similar to that of the earlier play. But here Ivan the Terrible is released into the twentieth century, where he causes considerable confusion in Timofeev's flat, while Timofeev himself goes to find a key necessary for his machine. Meanwhile, Miloslavsky and house manager Bunsha have landed up in Ivan the Terrible's palace, where they too cause confusion – but fortunately Bunsha is so like Ivan in appearance that for a while they deceive those at his court. Finally Timofeev gets everyone back to his right century. He then wakes up: it was all a dream.

Ivan Vasilievich was accepted in 1935, and rehearsals started at the Theatre of Satire in Moscow.[3] By March 1936 it had reached dress rehearsal stage, when, a week before its opening, the 9 March article attacking *Molière* appeared in *Pravda*. As a result *Ivan Vasilievich* was also taken off, and little more was heard of it until it was published abroad, with *Dead Souls*, in Munich in 1964. In 1965 it appeared in the Soviet edition of Bulgakov's *Dramas and Comedies*. (*Bliss* was published in the Tashkent *Zvezda vostoka* the following year.)

In 1966, with the 'rehabilitation' of Bulgakov already well underway, *Ivan Vasilievich* was finally put on in Moscow by D.A. Vuros at the Theatre-Studio of the Cinema Actor. Reviews were only average, but the play was a success with the public as a rather ordinary light comedy. In the 1966-67 season it was also performed in Irkutsk, Tashkent, and Omsk – as well as having another Moscow production at the Central Theatre of the Soviet Army. It has played too in Baku, Kharkov, and Kiev. As of 1974, it was still in the repertory of the Cinema Actors, and in 1971 Leonid Gayday started working with Vladlen Bakhnov on a film scenario for it.[4] The result was a surprisingly good light comedy film entitled *Ivan Vasilievich Changes Profession*, which remained remarkably faithful to Bulgakov's text. In a comparatively short time, the play has thus become one of Bulgakov's most popular, if entirely inoffensive, productions. It has been translated into French, but not so far into English.

Ivan Vasilievich, then, grew out of *Bliss*, which, although outwardly similar, is a very different play, both more serious and less successful in dramatic terms – whereas the later play is a highly professional light comedy and little more. The impetus for *Bliss* was provided by Mayakovsky, whose play *The Bathhouse*,

3 **1**, pp. 593-4
4 See **463**, pp. 258-63; **210**; **487**, p. 58; **467**; **479**; **375**; **500**

equally involving travel to the future in a time machine, opened – if only for a short time – in 1930: Bulgakov in fact has his inventor living on 'Bathhouse Lane.' In *The Bathhouse* itself we do not actually see life in the future, which had already been shown in Mayakovsky's earlier play *The Bedbug* – as ordered, regulated, and totally sterile. Here the negative hero, resurrected from the past, becomes a danger to the new way of life with his old vices and attitudes, and yet our sympathies remain with him rather than the new. To the future age of *Bliss* the three men from the twentieth century (who also have our sympathies) represent a similar threat, although it is not as great, nor is the society itself as inhuman as that of *The Bedbug*. Bulgakov, as it were, tries to give a different picture of the future, less fantastic and more acceptable than in Mayakovsky.

Compared with that of *The Bedbug*, the communist society of *Bliss* is indeed rational and humane. There is little in the way of dehumanizing technology, although many past deficiencies have been overcome: there are no thefts (until Miloslavsky arrives), no bureaucracy. An Institute of Harmony ensures smooth relationships – even if its director, Savvich, is himself unable to win the love of his 'ideal' partner, Avrora. For the people in this society are still human and imperfect, quarrelling, falling in love inappropriately, being coquettish, kissing (whereas in *The Bedbug* even handshaking is considered unhygienic). They are, in fact, ordinary, unchanged human beings in a society which has simply been better organized, to the benefit of all. The fact, however, that not only the three from the twentieth century but also a woman living in the future reject such a pleasant existence raises the question as to whether men really want a well-organized society at all – and this at a more fundamental level than in *The Bedbug*, since the future as shown cannot be as easily dismissed as pure fantasy.

What, then, is wrong with this society? Not that it is inhuman, but that it is boring, like Dostoevsky's Palace of Crystal. Avrora, who lives there, wants to leave for a more dangerous life: 'I am bored with these columns, I am bored with Savvich, I am bored with Bliss! I have never experienced danger, I don't know what kind of a taste it has!' (p. 104).[5] 'Bliss,' the name of the part of Moscow these people inhabit, is clearly ironical, but we can interpret it too on a religious level, as being a kind of man-made Garden of Eden, against which Avrora, like Eve, rebels in the name of experience. Radamanov's secretary Anna, too, is shown as attracted to the ways of Miloslavsky by the very fact of his being a criminal. He too is bored here – visiting a museum and shedding 'tears of tender emotion' in front of the figure of a policeman, who has given meaning to his profession of thief. Even the unenterprising Bunsha joins with him in recognizing this boredom. And if simple human desire for excitement in life has been lost in

5 Page references in the text are, for *Bliss*, to **12**, for *Ivan Vasilievich*, to **91**.

the rationalism of the new age, so too has an element of freedom. Such Dostoevskian concerns are clearly inadmissible for the communist, whose main purpose is indeed to build the perfect society: it is hardly surprising that *Bliss* has not been performed. In the new world Miloslavsky asserts his desire for independence by continuing to steal, Reyn (unlike Mayakovsky's inventor in *The Bathhouse*) by wanting merely to keep his own invention rather than giving it up for the benefit of others. But, as in *Adam and Eve*, science in Bliss is expected to support an 'idea,' even if here the 'idea' is a worthy one: Radamanov cannot allow Reyn to go his own way because of the possible trouble it would cause. Neither can Savvich allow three free-thinkers to disrupt the harmony of society. This inevitably leads to force, as the three of them are to be 'cured' against their own wishes: as effectively, no doubt, as the inventor in Zamyatin's *We* is also cured, ostensibly for his own good.

On another level, Bulgakov uses *Bliss* to satirize certain aspects of life in his own time. The centre of the satire is the idiotic house manager, Bunsha-Koretsky: a descendant of Vasily Ivanovich in the feuilletons, of Alliluya/Portupeya in *Zoyka's Apartment*, and Ponchik-Nepobeda in *Adam and Eve*. With his petty officiousness (which he believes is necessary for the survival of the state) he is a major source of comedy in the play, the typical narrow-minded bureaucrat. Thus, for example, despite his pretensions to culture, which cause him to go to 'useful' lectures (on venereal disease) which he does not understand, he shows not the least sense of wonder when Reyn's machine actually works, but merely denounces him to the police for 'making without permission a machine out of which a tsar appeared' (p. 80). He is typical of a parvenu class, that believes it only need learn facts rather than understanding and appreciating life itself – for which questioning, rather than blind acceptance, is necessary. He is therefore unable to understand the new society's difference of approach, with its lack of trade unions, police, or documents. So he insists on writing reports that are no longer needed; rather than recognizing its advantages, he is merely suspicious of a place where they wear dress coats, hold balls, and just enjoy themselves. 'Socialism is not at all for the purpose of enjoying oneself' (p. 86). In new circumstances, he mindlessly continues to behave in the same old way, warning Radamanov of a possible 'deviation' in his theories, writing official complaints about the Institute of Harmony, denouncing Avrora and Reyn for kissing each other. We find then yet another indictment of the kind of man to whom the Revolution had given power: unimaginative, unintelligent (he is only suspicious of Miloslavsky long after it is obvious he is a thief), and accepting without question that the state should do everything for him – even, here, wanting it to find him a wife.

Miloslavsky (reminiscent of Ametistov in *Zoyka's Apartment*) is his perfect foil, with his impulsive stealing, his lies, and his likeable charm: a further demonstration of Bulgakov's theme here that criminality is more interesting than a dull, rational life. It is clear that he considers himself an artist – although when called upon to recite he can barely stutter out the first two lines of Pushkin's 'Poltava' (which he has read in Mikhelson's flat and which become a kind of leitmotif for him). But in life itself he is a genuine actor, who almost believes in his own lies. His sense of style is clear from his whole-hearted enjoyment of each situation which presents itself – which he takes to extremes as when, for example, for a dance, he demands that a tune popular in the twentieth century be played to the accompaniment of a cannonade and bells. In contrast, Reyn, ostensibly the hero of the play, is a colourless and uninteresting individual.

But despite the comedy the overall tone of *Bliss* is serious. Like *Adam and Eve* it is an intellectual play, but the arguments are not so incisive, the issues not so clear. Nor does the action arise directly out of the issues to the same extent, and ultimately we find it is a somewhat laboured demonstration of the theme. For the society we are shown is intended to be dull and, regrettably, so too are many of the individual scenes. The play is most interesting, perhaps, from the point of view of being Bulgakov's answer to Mayakovsky – but it does not share the advantage of the originality of *The Bedbug* and *The Bathhouse*, which ultimately are both better plays. In *Ivan Vasilievich* it is precisely the comic elements which have been strengthened, to the exclusion of any serious theme. By allowing Miloslavsky and Bunsha to go back into a period of history with which the viewer is familiar and by following the escapades of Ivan the Terrible in the twentieth century Bulgakov has created far more possibilities for comic situations.

Thus whereas *Bliss*, although subtitled a dream, is not shown to be one on stage at all, in *Ivan Vasilievich* a conventional 'dream technique' is used, with Timofeev falling asleep at the beginning and waking at the end. A rational explanation is provided for his dreaming of Ivan, since he hears a programme about him on the radio – which in the dream becomes the time machine. (The theme of Ivan is further used as a leitmotif, before his actual appearance, by Miloslavsky who, in Shpak's room, reads Alexey Tolstoy's poem about Ivan, 'Prince Mikhailo Repnin,' instead of 'Poltava' as in *Bliss*.) There is nothing 'real' about the play at all in fact: all treat incredible situations as though they were part of one huge, but quite normal, joke. *Ivan Vasilievich* has become a first-class, if essentially harmless, light comedy, revolving largely around the physical resemblance between Bunsha and Ivan.

In this play Bunsha continues to be the officious, party-minded house manager: indeed he pronounces a number of the same speeches. The element of satire remains when Bunsha returns to the past and, disguised as Ivan the Terrible, once again reveals his narrow-mindedness and inability to come to terms with a new situation: refusing to sign papers for which, as house manager, he has no authority, or talking about trying to introduce co-operatives. Yet here another dimension is added and the satire becomes sharper, as Bunsha under the influence of alcohol shows distinct monarchistic tendencies. As one Soviet critic has pointed out, Bunsha is a petty tyrant in real life and only reveals his true colours when he replaces Ivan: 'In front of our eyes the domestic tyrant grows into a state tyrant.'[6] But the essential comedy lies in the incongruity of the whole picture of Bunsha as Ivan, for there could be no greater contrast: Bunsha is basically a coward, both in the sixteenth century, where he is afraid of everyone, and in the twentieth, where he is afraid of his wife.

The foil to Bunsha is again Miloslavsky, who now becomes the comic hero of the play. (In *Bliss*, after the same opening, he had remained solely as a likeable thief with comparatively little part in the main action, which was left to Reyn.) To his earlier characteristics are added in Act III his enterprise and resourcefulness as 'Ivan's' secretary, which save both him and Bunsha from a difficult situation. If the motive of most of his actions remains theft, there is as much comedy too in his easy lies (which now serve a real purpose), and in his colloquial manner towards those at Ivan's court. Characteristically for this play, he too treats everyone exactly as though they were twentieth-century figures in absurd costumes – and this dream world is highlighted by the mention of his 'double,' a sixteenth-century Prince Miloslavsky who has been hanged shortly before. Whether Miloslavsky is complaining of the treatment of thieves at Ivan's court –'If you want to know, Fedya, you have to treat thieves gently' (p. 60) – giving away land to Sweden to the horror of all, or robbing both the Swedish ambassador and the patriarch, he remains a delightful character, the strength of the whole play.

There are further comic elements too which are not found in *Bliss*, involving Timofeev's actress wife Zinaida and her manner of treating all situations – leaving her husband or entertaining a lover – as though they were simply a film script. Her indignation when others do not react in the proper way only adds to the comedy. When Ivan the Terrible enters her life in the twentieth century, the whole situation becomes even funnier, with characters again judging the others purely in terms of their own preconceived ideas. Thus when Zinaida and Yakin find Ivan in Timofeev's absence, they immediately assume he is an actor: Yakin even offers him a contract to play the part of himself. Realizing the truth, they show no more sense of wonder than does Bunsha, but egoistically treat the whole matter as an unimportant interlude in their own lives.

6 479, p. 72

Ivan himself is somewhat tamed by the twentieth century, largely by the fact that no one really takes him seriously. In his confrontations with the modern world and the many things he does not understand – gramophones, telephones – he too transfers his conceptions and values from a different age. First, he assumes Timofeev's 'boyarinya' is not with him because she is in church. Then, while he is alone, Bunsha's wife Ulyana Andreevna comes and bangs at the door, he makes the sign of the cross and the knocking ceases; she then starts shouting, so Ivan again makes the sign of the cross and she stops: 'What the cross of life will do!' he says. Then Zinaida comes, he makes the sign of the cross again, but she just walks straight in the door. Later in the play he (appropriately) thinks Ulyana Andreevna is an old witch – whereas she merely thinks he is her husband who has got drunk, until he tries to beat her. Such misconceptions on the part of almost everyone can be very funny, and with them too Bulgakov shows he is a master of entertaining dialogue and witty character drawing. Some of this had already been developed in *Bliss*, but here, by the elimination of other material, Bulgakov has concentrated and added to the comedy.

We can perhaps trace here a direct line of development from *Zoyka's Apartment*: the serious tragi-farce gives way to the intellectual utopian problem play (*Adam and Eve*), which in turn is replaced by the comic, yet still serious, utopian play (*Bliss*), to become finally, in *Ivan Vasilievich*, the purely satirical situation comedy lacking in any serious ideas. Neither *Bliss* nor *Ivan Vasilievich* can be compared with Bulgakov's masterpieces. Despite the possibilities for theatrical effects – the time machine itself, unexpected and startling appearances – there is none of the atmosphere which characterizes *Flight, Molière*, or even, to take one of the direct predecessors, *Zoyka's Apartment*. But in *Ivan Vasilievich* Bulgakov has understood the limitations of *Bliss*, admitted the difficulties of turning a utopian play into a serious work, and concentrated instead on technique, making it into a good divertissement which the audience can simply enjoy. In it, there are no heroes as such, for even Timofeev has little concern with anything except his invention. The central character is a crook, the rest are tyrannical, stupid, or simply immoral and self-centred. Yet all this is treated very lightly: there is none of the bitter exposure of human greed and stupidity that we shall find in *The Master and Margarita*. One Soviet critic in particular has tried to make *Ivan Vasilievich* into a serious play, claiming that it shows the 'vulgar triviality [*poshlost'*] which suffocates the honest, good man in waking life.' He goes on to say that there should be shown a real conflict between Timofeev's enthusiasm for his machine and his family life.[7] But such a view surely makes the play more weighty than it is, for the charm of *Ivan Vasilievich* lies in its being good satirical comedy which needs little interpretation. As another critic has expressed it, 'This is not the best creation of a talented author but nevertheless a work which has on it the stamp of professional mastery, which is witty and gaily mischievous.'[8] Hardly a major work, for the Russian viewer at least it is one play by Bulgakov that can be enjoyed without the worry of possibly unacceptable ideological overtones.

THE LAST DAYS (ALEXANDR PUSHKIN)

At the beginning of October 1934 Bulgakov told his wife he had decided to write a play about Pushkin: 'Of course,' he added, 'without Pushkin' – for he considered it impossible to show Russia's national hero successfully on stage. On the 18th Bulgakov went to see his friend Veresaev, a Pushkin authority, with the suggestion that they should work on the play together, with Veresaev collecting the historical materials and Bulgakov writing the text. Veresaev agreed enthusiastically, and they both set to work. A first contract with the Vakhtangov Theatre was signed on 17 December.[9] It seems that even during the initial stages there were some disagreements (Veresaev particularly regretted the exclusion of Pushkin himself) and as the work progressed they would become more significant; they are reflected in a lengthy correspondence between them throughout the summer and autumn of 1935.[10]

Bulgakov's notebooks for the play show the amount of research that went into it: the sources used, the composition of the characters, the historical detail.[11] The credit for a great deal of this must clearly go to Veresaev, even if the actual choice of materials, interpretation of some of the characters, and composition of the play are due entirely to Bulgakov, who fought stubbornly with his colleague to write the play as he conceived it. But unlike *Molière* (over which Bulgakov was arguing with Stanislavsky during the same period) *Alexandr Pushkin*, as it was initially called, was based more firmly on historical fact: it could hardly be otherwise when the details of Pushkin's life and death were so well known to the majority of Russian theatre-goers.

As Bulgakov intended, Pushkin himself does not appear in the play, except as a shadow in the distance or a body carried across the back of the stage. The action takes place at the beginning of 1837, when Pushkin is heavily in debt and receiving anonymous letters indicating his wife Natalya Nikolaevna is having an

8 **210**

9 For this and similar details, see the versions of the play and the various contracts in **187**, folios 218-25, 242-3.

10 **234**

11 Published in part in **444**. The date for the first version is given on pp. 431 and 444.

affair with a French officer, Georges D'Anthès. This leads to Pushkin writing an insulting letter to D'Anthès' adoptive father, the Dutch ambassador Baron Heeckeren, and a duel between D'Anthès and Pushkin, who is killed. Important in the play too are Pushkin's friends, the members of the society he lived in, the tsar Nicolas I and his police, and finally an invented character, Bitkov, a spy in the guise of a clock repair-man in Pushkin's own house. There exist few significant variations from the play's final version. From Bulgakov's notebooks we know that originally the duel scene was longer, with the countess Vorontsova, one of Pushkin's supporters, appearing with her husband and wanting to stop the duel; that the poets Benediktov and Kukolnik, and then the French ambassador, were to appear among the crowd outside Pushkin's apartment to pay their insincere homage to the dead Pushkin.[12]

The first draft was finished by 27 March 1935, and on 16 May a further contract was signed with the Red Theatre in Leningrad. On 18 May Bulgakov read the play at home to Veresaev and his wife, and to L.P. Ruslanov, I.M. Rapoport, B.Ye. Zakhava, and A.O. Goryunov of the Vakhtangov Theatre. It was now that the serious disagreements would begin. Veresaev wrote to Bulgakov expressing concern over a number of points which had not been changed before this reading: in particular he did not like a scene where D'Anthès, thinking of the duel, fired at a picture in Heeckeren's apartment. Generally he gave expression to what was obviously a mounting frustration with the partnership. Bulgakov answered the next day, pointing out that he had in fact made many changes at Veresaev's request, refusing only when they were theatrically impossible. D'Anthès' firing at the picture he defended as being reminiscent of Silvio in Pushkin's story 'The Shot.'

Veresaev was for the moment convinced, for on 22 May he telephoned Bulgakov asking him to forget his letter. After another reading to actors of the Vakhtangov Theatre on 2 June, presumably because of his further doubts, he wrote suggesting that it was really impossible for two people to work on a play and that he should step down as co-author. Bulgakov greatly appreciated this letter and when he met Veresaev in the summer asked him to give various additions for a couple of scenes. He would then 'iron out' the play and send it to Veresaev to see if he would still like to sign it with him or not.

But by late summer Veresaev was again unhappy with the play, having tried to rewrite everything as he thought it should be written. 'Perhaps the result will be two plays which it will be quite impossible to reconcile, or perhaps somehow we'll manage to agree,' he wrote on 1 August. So their disagreement began once more. Bulgakov's reply was a frank criticism of Veresaev's version. 'You went

12 **444**, pp. 438-43

over all the knots in the play which I had tied with such care - over just those places where I had avoided a frontal attack - and with greatest accuracy untied all those knots, after which all the clothes fell off the heroes; and everywhere where the play was subtle you put thick dots on the "i"s.' This letter is interesting in that its details reveal Bulgakov's concerns with the subleties of stage production. Veresaev's version, he wrote, was unplayable 'Because what you are writing is *not a play*.' Finally he asked Veresaev to return to his intentions expressed in his July letter, allowing him to amend the play as necessary - it was, he stressed, already ready - and then decide whether to sign it with him or not.

Veresaev's answer on 22 August was bitter, accusing Bulgakov, significantly, of being blind to the social side of Pushkin's story. 'This blindness was strong in you previously as well but now, befogged by the praises of your admirers, it is even more difficult for you to feel the defects of your play in this respect.' An example of this was the scene between Nicolas and the older poet Zhukovsky, with the tsar angry at Pushkin only because he was wearing a dress-coat instead of his uniform. He suggested that the theatre should decide between the two versions. 'And I reserve the right, as far as is possible for me, to fight for the removal from your fine play of often surprisingly unnecessary breaches of historical truth and for the strengthening of its social background.'

In a sense, of course, Veresaev was right when he accused Bulgakov of being unconcerned with social issues, for considerations of artistry had always been more important to the latter than 'correct' historical interpretations: hence his very unacceptability in this communist society. Veresaev's own writing - which did not include plays - was in accordance with his marxist convictions, whereas Bulgakov was a playwright of intuition.

Both Bulgakov and Veresaev were now exhausted and angry from their arguments. For Bulgakov, all this had been going on at the same time as his struggles with the Art Theatre over *Molière*. The remainder of his correspondence with Veresaev concerns largely practical matters, although Veresaev abandoned his idea of having the Vakhtangov Theatre decide between the two versions. An agreement was signed, stipulating that royalties be divided between the two of them. Bulgakov completed the play on 9 September and sent Veresaev a copy the next day. *Glavrepertkom* approved the play on the 20th. On 9 October *Literaturnaia gazeta* announced that B.Ye. Zakhava of the Vakhtangov Theatre was to produce *Alexandr Pushkin* in 1937 to celebrate the hundredth anniversary of Pushkin's death, and that rehearsals would begin soon;[13] on 6 December another contract was signed with the Theatre of the Red Army of the Ukraine in Kiev. Two weeks later, on the 19th, Veresaev formally withdrew from the partnership.

The play would not, however, be performed at this time. On 10 March 1936 the Vakhtangov Theatre indicated that the production was underway,[14] but the previous day *Pravda* had attacked *Molière*: as was the case too with *Ivan Vasilievich*, *Alexandr Pushkin* was withdrawn (although by as late as that September its Leningrad production was still being announced for the next year – and again Bulgakov managed to keep his advance[15]).

It would be another three years before there was a new possibility for its performance. *Alexandr Pushkin* received a further approval from *Glavrepertkom* on 26 June 1939,[16] and on 24 October the Artistic Council of the Moscow Art Theatre met to discuss the play. In fact, the Art Theatre had been interested in it all along: as early as 20 June 1935 Sudakov had written to Bulgakov asking for a copy so that the theatre could work on it at the same time as the Vakhtangov Theatre, but Bulgakov had replied that he was bound by contract. Now everyone was enthusiastic, Stanitsyn in particular. It was decided to produce the play the following year, and a contract was signed on 22 January 1940. The play would be called *The Last Days*; Stanitsyn and Toporkov, who played Zhukovsky and Bitkov respectively, were appointed producers.

Bulgakov himself was by now seriously ill and would not live to see the production. Work on it did not actually begin until 15 December 1940, nine months after his death.[17] Again, it was some time before rehearsals really got underway, although soon there was an additional incentive: Germany invaded the Soviet Union on 22 June 1941 and a play about the Russian national hero could be counted on to appeal to patriotic feeling. It was Nemirovich-Danchenko who was to oversee the production and finally release it – Stanislavsky having died in 1938 – and indeed it was the last play that he worked on, for he too died a mere two weeks after the opening. Nemirovich-Danchenko worked with the actors mainly after seeing the play's dress rehearsal on 12 March 1943. Above all he insisted that he wanted to feel the tragedy of Pushkin, to feel the spirit of the poem 'Winter Evening' with its opening line 'The storm covers the sky in darkness ...' The final scene – of those travelling with Pushkin's coffin, at a stationmaster's cottage – he emphasized, had to be particularly strong: and he has been held in esteem in the theatre ever since for insisting that real steam should issue from the samovar, to give the idea of the bitterly cold night.[18]

14 **192**
15 **454**, and **477**, p. 200
16 Noted on a manuscript of the play in **189** and **187**, folio 218. See also here, for further details, folios 244 and 556.
17 **270**, p. 753
18 See, for a more detailed account of the rehearsals, **278**, pp. 564, 578-83; **392** and **393**; **406**, II, p. 560; also typescripts in **188**, folios 17, 18, 1163, 1187.

The Last Days opened on 10 April 1943, and was an undoubted success with the audience.[19] Once again P.V. Vilyams' sets were particularly effective. The stage was separated from the audience for the whole show by a tulle curtain which, when illuminated from behind, was transparent and made everything seem as though in a mist; if it was illuminated in front, nothing could be seen behind. 'On the tulle appears a hazy sky, clouds move across, a wind starts to howl. Then the clouds seem to melt, and behind them emerges a scene the edges of which also dissolve in the darkness without having a sharply defined frame.' The first scene opened with 'Winter Evening' sung by Alexandra Goncharova, the lights in Pushkin's living room became visible, then the room itself. The comfort of Pushkin's apartment and elegance of the rich eccentric Saltykov's in the second scene were followed by a ball in the lavish winter garden (complete with fountain and flying birds) of the countess Vorontsova, before there appeared the dark government office of the secret police, the Third Division: shown by Vilyams as in a vaulted basement, with a gloomy green as the dominant colour. The duel scene, with its snow-drifts and hump-backed bridge, was equally impressive, while most found that the best were the last two scenes: the night on the Moyka in front of Pushkin's house and the bleak country station.

The critics all agreed on the excellent acting and production, but the play itself they regarded as a noble failure. *Literatura i iskusstvo* came out with three articles on 24 April, one of them by the writer Konstantin Fedin, who subjected it to fair criticism but maintained that no theatrical techniques could really make up for the absence of Pushkin himself, who created history as well as being crushed by it.[20] Other articles, concerned as always with social issues, pointed out that Pushkin's family concerns should have been shown as the result of the national struggle rather than the reverse, and that there was too much emphasis on Pushkin's fate rather than on his struggle; Bitkov, one of the most successful characters created by Bulgakov, became the hero.

Despite the critics the play remained in the Art Theatre repertory for thirteen years, until 1959, with over 240 performances. In 1949 it was also performed at the Polish State Theatre in Warsaw. It was published, together with *Days of the Turbins*, in 1955, and later in Bulgakov's two collections of plays in 1962 and 1965. Kaverin, talking of the 1955 publication, defended the play, and so later, in her book of recollections, did Vera Smirnova, disagreeing with Fedin's article. Rudnitsky also wrote favourably of it, and in a comparison of literary works

19 The actors were: Natalya – A. Stepanova, Alexandra – S. Pilyavskaya, D'Anthès –
   P. Massalsky, Nicolas – Kachalov. See 3, p. 477. Quotations from the play are also
   translated from this edition. Page references are given in the text. For the details on
   the production that follow, see 298, pp. 619-20.
20 273 and 274; see also 394 and 302

about Pushkin it has received highest honours.[21] More recently, on the occasion of the 175th anniversary of Pushkin's birth, it has had two further productions. It opened at the Moscow Pushkin Dramatic Theatre on 29 May 1974, in a production by B.N. Tolmazov, with rather bare sets by V.Yu. Shaporin. The theatre decided to cope with Pushkin's absence by the simple expedient of putting him back in, having him appear constantly on stage, often to the accompaniment of a voice in the theatre reading his poems, and even fighting the duel with D'Anthès (whose shot at the picture was omitted). The audience's reaction was less than enthusiastic. A new production of the Moscow Art Theatre under Stanitsyn (who again played Zhukovsky) opened on its summer tour to Leningrad ('Pushkin's town') on 6 June 1974. Interestingly, the sets were once more those of P.V. Vilyams. Pushkin, again, appeared on stage.

As a biography of Pushkin at the end of his life, *The Last Days* is basically historically authentic, even if there are a number of necessary inaccuracies in minor details and in the chronology. The incident of Pushkin's being improperly dressed, for example, had taken place two years previously; D'Anthès had flirted with Natalya at dinner at Vorontsova's ball rather than coming to her in the garden, as in the play; Heeckeren did not himself go to the scene of the duel; and so on. Some scenes are clearly invented: a reception at the rich Saltykov's, the office of the Third Division, the scene in the station. So too are certain characters: Bitkov and, another spy from the aristocracy, Bogomazov. But such minor departures from fact, necessary dramatically, are insignificant and do nothing to alter the story of Pushkin's last days, which are faithfully represented.

In many ways *The Last Days* is a development from *Molière*, to which it is thematically similar: both concern the relationship of the artist to his society, creative freedom, censorship, and the devices of the artist's enemies to silence him. But where in *Molière* we are shown the man and not the artist, in *The Last Days* the situation is reversed, with the man absent and the artist present in his frequently quoted poems. Thus in the earlier play one has to decide whether one can accept an unhistorical Molière; here it is a question of accepting an historical but absent Pushkin.

Bulgakov was probably right in thinking that no representation on stage of a character as well known and loved in Russia as Pushkin could be entirely successful. To exclude the central character entirely was certainly a bold experiment but it was also a logical solution to a dilemma that other dramatists did not take seriously enough. Pushkin here is shown largely in his effect on others. The plot surrounding him, the hatred of his enemies, the love of his friends, the indifference of society – all this replaces the figure himself, and the success of the play is

21 See **325**, pp. 69-70; **489**, pp. 100-2; **461**, pp. 141-2; **348**, pp. 177-8

therefore made to depend on the total image of the man and his age. In this Bulgakov has undoubtedly been assisted not only by a Russian audience's familiarity with the poet (for whom each individual can supply his own image) but also by its knowledge of many of the other characters and circumstances surrounding Pushkin's death: Fedin is right when he says that this is not a play in the usual sense but rather an illustration of Pushkin's biography.[22]

We are, of course, still aware of Pushkin's physical presence in the background. In the first act we hear him come into the apartment and his sister-in-law Alexandra actually addresses him; D'Anthès, paying court to Natalya, listens at his door to be sure that he is asleep. In Act II he is a dark figure standing at a distance, who causes the tsar's displeasure for not being in uniform. In Act III we only hear the shots of the duel from a distance, but at the end of the act Pushkin is carried, wounded, across the back of the stage into his study. In the final act it is his dead body which is taken first from the apartment, then on the long journey to its burial place. But more important is the fact that the entire drama revolves around him: in a very real sense the poet remains central, present in the consciousness and conversations of the others at all times. As Rudnitsky puts it, 'It is as though Bulgakov asks each of the characters of the play: "How do *you* understand Pushkin?"'[23]

In his age, of course, Pushkin was a political as well as a literary figure although, as in the case of Molière, his downfall was brought about by a whole complex of circumstances. The villains in *The Last Days* are his political enemies, the tsar himself, Benkendorf (head of the Third Division), his deputy Dubelt, and to a lesser extent their paid servants Bogomazov and Bitkov. 'The downfall of the great citizen came about,' an officer says in the crowd near the end, 'because in this country unlimited power is entrusted to unworthy people, who treat the populace like slaves' (p. 353). Pushkin's own subservient position is in fact subtly underlined in the ball scene by the presence of a negro page to Nicolas, reminiscent of Pushkin's ancestor Hannibal, servant to Peter the Great: Pushkin himself is several times referred to as 'the African' or 'the Arab.' Nicolas' imperious tone to another Gentleman of the Bed-Chamber – the rank he has given Pushkin – for using an incorrect form of address shows how exacting autocracy can be.

Unlike Louis XIV, Nicolas has no respect for the artist's talent; nor does Pushkin attempt to court his favours. Nicolas 'assists' Pushkin purely for his own ends, so that he can control him and also have the pleasure of his wife at court. Nicolas is shown, however, not as an evil autocrat but as a man with his own pro-

22 **274**, p. 441
23 **461**, p. 141

blems, acting in accordance with what he believes is right and good for Russia. 'No one knows or will ever understand what a heavy burden I am fated to carry!' he tells Natalya quite sincerely (p. 310). Because of his own position and concept of authority, he cannot understand Pushkin, with his lack of gratitude and almost treasonous writings: thus he is genuinely indignant at the other's lack of respect for him in not wearing his uniform when required to do so, or at his writing a history of Pugachyov, a man who for him was simply a scoundrel. 'He has no heart,' he tells Zhukovsky (p. 313). Bulgakov, however, only hints at the popular view of Nicolas' direct involvement in Pushkin's death by not preventing the duel (in his vague words to Benkendorf, 'he will not die as a Christian'): it is left to Benkendorf to suggest more positively that the police should go to the wrong place.

Benkendorf and Dubelt are, in contrast to Nicolas, far more sinister, the one an efficient fanatic carrying out a task he unquestioningly believes in, the other simply doing his job and cynical enough about it to link himself with those men who bought Christ's execution (he pays his spies the 'thirty pieces of silver' given to Judas Iscariot: thirty roubles to Bitkov, thirty chervontsy – ten-rouble pieces – to the more aristocratic, ubiquitous Bogomazov). It is, of course, not difficult to equate the tsarist secret police with its Soviet equivalent, and once again we can see Pushkin's struggle as representative of that of any artist, in any age, against political repression.

But Pushkin's actual downfall is brought about not only by his political enemies but by his whole family situation – although this in turn is the result of the life at the St Petersburg court. In contrast to *Molière*, there is no need to falsify the details, for the situation itself – a wife who is a favourite of the tsar, a scandal caused by a French officer, anonymous letters, an idolizing sister-in-law, debts Pushkin has incurred to keep his wife at court – is full of drama. The only solution for Pushkin would be to leave St Petersburg, which he could not do without the tsar's permission, even if his wife were willing to go: a situation which is made clear by Pushkin's old servant, Nikita Kozlov, at the beginning of the play. Natalya herself is shown sympathetically, wanting success and the life that only St Petersburg can give her. 'It's not my fault! I swear it's not my fault!' she exclaims when Pushkin is brought in wounded (p. 344). Her relationship to D'Anthès is ambiguous: she is half frightened of him, half desirous of his attentions. Life is not easy for her as the wife of a great man whose poems she is unable to appreciate: 'Why has no one ever asked me if *I* am happy? People can only demand things of me. But has anyone ever felt sorry for me? What more do you need from me? I bore him children and my whole life I hear poems, only poems' (p. 342). In her final desire that Pushkin should be saved when it is too late, she becomes almost a tragic figure. As Zhukovsky says, 'They'll tear her to pieces now, tear her to pieces' (p. 348). With her sense of duty in conflict with her desire for social success she is a convincing and not unlikeable character.

The other major character in the Pushkin drama is D'Anthès himself, Pushkin's killer. The idea of death is associated with him from the beginning; for as Natalya tells him, this is what it would mean if he were caught in Pushkin's house. But D'Anthès regards it light-heartedly: 'Chaque instant de la vie est un pas vers la mort.' Ironically, of course, it is not his own death which will result from the situation but Pushkin's. 'They will put me on a gun-carriage and take me to the cemetery,' he says, in words which will refer to the other. 'And there'll be a storm too, and nothing will change in the world' (p. 297). Psychologically, D'Anthès kills Pushkin from the moment he decides to fight: throwing a music box belonging to Heeckeren on the floor and, not even aiming, shooting at a valuable picture – things he cares about as little as he does about Pushkin's poetry. Whereas Silvio, in Pushkin's 'The Shot,' has done likewise in order to spare his victim, D'Anthès shows no such mercy because basically he is indifferent. 'What are you doing?' his adoptive father Heeckeren asks in horror, in words which can be understood in a broader sense to apply to D'Anthès' whole involvement with Pushkin. The shot at the picture is the climactic point of the play, merely echoed by the faint sound of the two actual shots in the dual scene that follows.

In these and other of Pushkin's enemies – the homosexual Heeckeren, to whom Pushkin's challenge is sent, the vicious author of the anonymous letters, Dolgorukov – we are presented with a collection of individuals concerned largely with trivialities. As illustrations of the historical figures they represent these characters are undoubtedly successful. But as important is the world of high society to which they belong: shallow, concerned with the niceties of behaviour rather than with individual merit. 'One cannot believe,' Stroganov says of Pushkin's letter to Heeckeren, 'that this is written by a Russian aristocrat. Oh, what an age! What licence!' (p. 334). The representation of this entire society unappreciative of Pushkin, who was alien to it, is one of the major aims of the play. Herein lies the importance of the remarkable second scene, where two writers who fit perfectly into society (and had both been criticized by Pushkin), Kukolnik and the currently fashionable Benediktov, are received at Saltykov's, a man of outrageous manners and exaggerated self-importance. It is the funniest scene in the play. As Saltykov's two sons from the Preobrazhensky regiment stand smiling idiotically every time Kukolnik tells them to do something, there takes place the most absurd conversation, in which Saltykov reveals his only real comprehension of books – collectors' pieces, which should not contain typographical errors and which 'are not printed so as to be touched by human hands.' And yet such a man can aspire to social and even literary leadership, can patronizingly call the tsar '*le grand bourgeois*,' while Pushkin can be called to account for his 'unpatriotic writing.' The whole futility of this type of society is epitomized by a discussion as to whether Pushkin or Benediktov is the better poet (Benediktov has already recited one of his poems, allowing the viewer to form his own conclusions), while Saltykov's servant Agafon stands poised on a step-ladder with a book of Benediktov's, waiting for his master to decide whether to substitute it for Pushkin's works on the shelf he keeps for the 'first' poet. There he remains until, after Benediktov has also been criticized, Saltykov orders both his and Pushkin's books to be removed. The triviality and pretentiousness of these discussions is what stands out most.

There are few heroic characters in this play. As individuals, the majority of them are pursuing their own ends: wanting the favours of a woman (the tsar, D'Anthès), wanting love and success (Natalya), money (Bogomazov, Bitkov), the elimination of an enemy (Benkendorf, Dubelt, Heeckeren, Dolgorukov). Ultimately it is this which brings about the destruction of genius – although we should note that Pushkin himself, with his desire for revenge, is equally human in this regard. Even the motives of Pushkin's allies, such as Alexandra, are questionable, and the other positive characters, Vorontsova (who twice stands up for Pushkin) and Zhukovsky, are quite powerless. All Zhukovsky can do on the occasion of Pushkin's death is sit down and write a poem: then he is immediately forced to compromise on the handing over of Pushkin's papers.

Yet the power of poetry as such is one of the underlying themes of the play, for Pushkin and Zhukovsky have survived where the Benkendorfs and Dubelts have not. More than anywhere else, Pushkin's presence is felt in his works themselves – two of the scenes, D'Anthès shooting at the picture and the final scene in the post-station, are even deliberately reminiscent of stories from *The Tales of Belkin*. Pushkin's poems are frequently quoted, often as a commentary on the events or situation: 'Temporal Power' by the police chief Dubelt to indicate Pushkin's opposition to autocracy (also two further anti-monarchist lines incorrectly attributed to him); four lines from 'It is time, my friend, it is time,' to indicate his desire for peace despite lack of happiness. *Eugene Onegin* is used by Zhukovsky and Alexandra to tell their fortunes: with one stanza, on the pleasures of cuckolding a man and then subjecting him to a duel, ironically reflecting not Pushkin's attitude but that of his opponent, D'Anthès, towards him. (Only the first two lines 'With an insolent epigram/'tis pleasant to enrage a bungling foe,' and then the ninth and tenth lines 'Still pleasanter – in silence to prepare/an honourable grave for him'[24] are quoted, and are twice referred to again by Natalya in her remorse after Pushkin's death.) Most important of all, however, is

24 453, I, p. 251

Pushkin's poem 'Winter Evening,' which sets the mood for the whole play – be-ginning and ending it as well as being quoted on three other occasions. Its theme, of the storm covering the sky with darkness and twisting whirlwinds of snow, is taken up in the play itself: three of the four acts take place while a blizzard is raging outside, and the characters constantly refer to the terrible weather. This storm of course can be taken symbolically to indicate the one that is the subject of the play, that raging around Pushkin himself.

Central to this theme of the power of poetry is Bulgakov's invention, Bitkov. When we see him with Dubelt, he appears as a man just doing his job for money. But as a spy in Pushkin's house he is affected by Pushkin's poems to the extent of becoming his advocate: learning his poems so he may report them, but re-membering them because he loves them. For the last few months of Pushkin's life, Bitkov becomes his constant, if unseen, companion (somewhat like Molière's Bouton), who helps when he can. As he shares in Pushkin's last journey, he tries to understand what it was all about – not very successfully perhaps, but in his bewilderment we feel not only the voice of simple reason (why did this man have to die?) but the force of these poems that the authorities so much feared: 'And because of those poems there's no rest for anyone ... not for him, not for the authorities, not for me, God's servant Stepan Ilyich' (p. 357). He had been with Pushkin, every day except for that of the duel. But now he 'can't go to their house anymore' – the place where clearly he personally had benefited, had come to know a different and better life. Unlike the aristocrats who dominate the play, Bitkov is representative of the common man, Pushkin's natural ally, who just loves his poems; at one with the people clamouring outside the apart-ment and a student who reads Lermontov's 'Death of a Poet.'

As Nemirovich-Danchenko indicated in his comments on the play, the final scene is particularly important: the end result of a progression which one is tempted to interpret as Pushkin's own descent from fame into the isolation of death. 'There is something tragic in that after we have seen a cosy apartment, a palace, the rich house of Saltykov, the play finishes with the worst of peasants' cottages. In this Bulgakov shows a kind of extraordinary depth. The glitter of St Petersburg, the magnificent flat, the palace, the ball, and so on – and suddenly a wilderness ... a sooty ceiling, tallow candles ... bitter cold ... and some gendarmes. It's Pushkin they're carrying.'[25] The emphasis on secrecy – no one must know the identity of the body – gives an air of furtiveness to the scene. Yet the fact that this is still Pushkin is subtly emphasized by the setting itself, that of his own story 'The Station-Master.'

25 **393**, p. 341

We do indeed see what Pushkin represented for the different individuals in this society, not forgetting Zhukovsky and Vorontsova, his most eloquent supporters. But whether this is really sufficient to make up for the lack of Pushkin himself must still remain an open question: as in the case of *Molière*, a great deal depends on the skill of the theatre. And one cannot help feeling here that Bulgakov tries to compensate for Pushkin's absence by his usual skill in managing visual and technical effects (which, in the original production, with Vilyams' lavish sets, were certainly exploited to the full). Again he makes use of his favourite technique of alternating light and darkness, in scenes which dissolve into each other. Darkness, in fact, is the dominant mood, for only two scenes (at Saltykov's and at Heeckeren's) take place in full daylight, the rest being set in the evening or at night, or as the winter sun is going down (the duel and Pushkin's return). But the darkness is constantly illuminated by the appearance of actual lights, often candles, within it – a feature which gives remarkable unity to the play. In Vorontsova's garden the candles of the first scene are replaced by lights in the bushes, and these too are extinguished at the end. Candles then appear from out of the darkness behind green screens in the office of the Third Division. Later, when Pushkin is brought home wounded, Bitkov appears with a candelabra, while a maidservant carries a candle. In the next scene it is Zhukovsky who has a candle, to put the seals on the doors of Pushkin's study – an action repeated a little later by Dubelt with a candelabra. On the Moyka outside, the street lights shine in the darkness instead, as do the lights from Pushkin's windows. In a remarkable transition to the next scene these go out before yet another appearance of candles as they move ahead of Pushkin's coffin, while a choir sings in the background. Then this becomes the howling of the storm before a candle appears in the desolate postal station. Lanterns approach, the stationmaster brings a light, and his wife lights a candle in another room. This constant leitmotif of light shining in the darkness can obviously be seen as symbolical of Pushkin himself. Visually the play is impressive, but one might still wonder whether, in the physical absence of the hero himself, it is not rather empty glitter.

There are, too, various leitmotifs in the play, apart from the storm and howling of the wind that occurs throughout. Clocks are constantly present, to be repaired by Bitkov, to strike at appropriate moments, even to strike thirteen on the day of Pushkin's duel. In Heeckeren's flat these are replaced by the music box he delights in, part of his world of things which he loves 'like a woman loves rags,' while ominously guns hang on the wall. As in Bulgakov's other plays, *The Last Days* is full of noises: door-bells ringing, people knocking, students shouting, the all important gun-shots. There is music in the song setting of Pushkin's poem, the orchestra for the ball, the soft choir after Pushkin's death.

These elements make *The Last Days* a remarkable play of atmosphere. It is also a convincing picture of Pushkin's age and those people who surrounded him. Indeed it is a play of many qualities: less dramatic and forceful than *Molière*, which in many ways it resembles, it is nevertheless a masterpiece of technique, in which – unlike *Molière* – all the tones and characters are delicately balanced. Is this sufficient? To make it a good play, one that is indeed more easily playable than *Molière*, the answer is yes: in terms of good theatrical writing and technique it is of the highest order. But to make it an outstanding play, regrettably no, for atmosphere cannot replace tragedy, which must be embodied in a living person. The idea of Pushkin is there in all its force but, for the spectator to truly identify with it, it still needs to be personified on stage. *The Last Days* is another experiment, although very nearly a successful one. In terms of Bulgakov's development as a dramatist it is vital, for it shows him endeavouring to reach after new possibilities – and it would lead to his masterful adaptation of *Don Quixote*. But ultimately we might agree with the Soviet critic who said that the play was one of the 'most subtle, thoughtful, and artistically sensitive productions of the Art Theatre ... But it is impossible to create tragedy where there is no tragedy. And there is none in Bulgakov's play.'[26] None the less, for all its modesty it remains a work of considerable craftsmanship.

26 **257**, p. 93

11

The Bolshoy Theatre, 1936-38

Bulgakov resigned from the Moscow Art Theatre in 1936 angry and bitter over the handling of his plays and their lack of success. But he still agreed to perform one more task for the theatre, signing a contract on 22 May to translate Shakespeare's *The Merry Wives of Windsor* and make revisions to it, including some scenes from *Henry IV*. This production was announced for the following year but Bulgakov did not complete the work and returned his advance to the theatre on 16 October.[1] A week and a half earlier, on the tenth anniversary of the première of *Days of the Turbins*, he had written to Popov:

I am sitting at my ink-well waiting for the door to open and a delegation to appear from Stanislavsky and Nemirovich with an address and a valuable presentation. In the address will be mentioned all my mutilated or ruined plays and a list will be cited of all the joys that they, Stanislavsky and Nemirovich, gave me for ten years in the Art Theatre Passage. The valuable presentation will consist of a large saucepan of some noble metal (for example, copper) filled with that same blood that they drank from me in the course of ten years.[2]

Articles in the press, he would later write, had also shown him 'with indisputable clarity' that it was pointless for him to compose further plays and present them to the dramatic theatres.[3]

After his resignation he was invited to become a librettist and consultant for the Bolshoy Theatre, a post that he occupied for the rest of his life. The details of his employment there are not well documented, but it would seem that,

1 **187**, folio 539; see also **221**
2 **379**, p. 168; also quoted in **448**, p. 453
3 **379**, p. 159

although he wrote four libretti and worked on several others as a consultant, the work was not particularly onerous. Nevertheless, he performed it conscientiously. B.A. Mordvinov of the theatre has related that he was involved in practically all the new productions there, and that his comments were always valuable, although he tried to remain in the background as much as possible. Sometimes he would be seen sitting making notes in a corner or walking nervously up and down the aisles of the auditorium with some thoughts that were bothering him, although he would only give his criticisms when questioned – 'and in the end result everything he expressed always gave something very important and really deep in a theatrical sense.'[4] Both Mordvinov and later Leontiev remembered that for the five years of his work as literary consultant Bulgakov showed great tact with the playwrights and script-writers who brought their synopses for possible opera and ballets. 'Those materials which went to Bulgakov for his professional opinion returned imbued with the great experience and good advice of a dramatist.'[5] There were undoubtedly some aspects of this work that Bulgakov enjoyed, for he had always loved music and the opera in particular: Yermolinsky tells us that, as a member of the theatre, he would often go to performances of his favourite *Aïda* in an old-fashioned production dating from before the Revolution. When he was writing his libretti, he imagined himself to be the composer, the singer, the conductor. 'He sang the arias, choosing a suitable tune, accompanying himself on the piano, or imagined the orchestra playing the future overture to his opera, and conducted it in an inspired fashion. He played about, enjoyed himself.'[6]

But none the less, the work of a librettist with its limited possibilities for independent composition must have been something of a let-down for him. His own works, it seemed, were condemned to the drawer; and in 1937 he wrote ironically to Popov of those well-wishers who tried to console him with the thought that they would be published after his death.[7] He did not abandon his own writing entirely, although it was two years before he wrote another play. In 1936 he took up again the work which would become *Theatrical Romance*, in which he would give expression both to his frustrations at the Art Theatre and, at the same time, to all his love for theatrical life. He also started writing the school textbook for secondary schools, the competition for which he had seen announced just before the opening of *Molière*. He spent several months on this 'History Course of the USSR,' completing about a hundred pages covering Russian history from early times to those of Peter the Great. But in the summer he started to get bad headaches, which forced him to interrupt it, and afterwards

4 **372**, p. 394
5 **187**, folio 556
6 **266**, pp. 90, 89
7 **379**, pp. 168-9

he did not return to it – in any case, it is unlikely that he could have competed successfully with professional historians.[8] In 1938, after laying aside *Theatrical Romance*, unfinished, he at last wrote another play, an adaptation of *Don Quixote*.

Bulgakov was not poor at this period of his life, for besides his salary from the Bolshoy there were still the royalties from *Days of the Turbins* and *Dead Souls*. And even when his plays had not been performed he had still received, from various theatres, advances which he was not usually asked to return. But in the thirties there were more worrying issues than one's financial position. Bulgakov could hardly help being aware of the general atmosphere of the age. It was a dangerous time for writers whose works fell under suspicion, and his own position was at best a precarious one. For some years now he had been under considerable nervous strain, and it is hardly surprising that now his fears increased, that he became suspicious of everyone, melancholic, shut up within himself. An acquaintance of his brother Nikolay visiting Moscow in these years recalled a long conversation with him, when Bulgakov covered up the telephone with his coat in case there should be a microphone there: a sensible precaution.[9] Yet despite his fears he was not subjected to any harassment on the part of the police, or even searches, in the thirties, and because of this it has been suggested that it was Stalin personally who protected him from the great purges. He was sufficiently aware of this possibility to write to Stalin (in February 1938) on behalf of the playwright Nikolay Erdman, requesting that he be allowed to return to Moscow from his 'exile.'[10] Alas, it was in vain.

Mandelshtam, too, returned to his flat on Furmanov Lane in 1937 after his exile, only to be ordered away from the city again in June, before his arrest the next year. There were all too many similar cases and in a very real sense Bulgakov was lucky, even if as far as his writing was concerned it brought him little consolation.

But now there was another problem. While everyone congratulated him on his good health and he himself confirmed it, in reality he began, as a doctor, to recognize disturbing symptoms. In a short time he would be very ill indeed.

THE OPERA LIBRETTI

Bulgakov's employment at the Bolshcy Theatre lasted until his death in 1940 and his libretti were written at various times during that period, but it will be convenient to discuss them here.

8 **339**, pp. 59-60. I am also grateful to L.A. Shilov for some of the information here.
9 Told to me by Bulgakov's cousin, C.P. Bulak
10 **379**, pp. 159-60. For the following, see **367**, pp. 630-1.

The first of them, 'Minin and Pozharsky,' was commissioned by the Bolshoy on 17 June 1936, apparently on the orders of Stalin;[11] the music was composed by Boris Asafiev. The opera is set in 1611-12, during the war of liberation against Poland. Minin and Prince Pozharsky lead the citizens of Nizhny Novgorod against the Poles occupying the Moscow Kremlin and holding Pakhomov, brave fiancé of Minin's daughter Maria, in captivity. An attempt of a Polish captain Zborowski to murder the two leaders fails, and the Cossack troops, who refuse to fight with the Russians because they have not been paid, go into action when the Poles insult them by offering them a reward of looted icon-frames. The Russians drive out the Poles and rescue Pakhomov.

Th libretto was completed on 25 December 1936 and the official hearing of the opera took place two days later. It was accepted for production in the current season and details were published in the press the following June. But then a complication arose when the same year permission was also given for a new production of Glinka's *Ivan Susanin* (a new title for his *A Life for the Tsar*, which was no longer appropriate). Since 'Minin and Pozharsky' and *Ivan Susanin* were both about the war with Poland of 1609-12, the theatre had to decide whether to abandon one of them or show two different operas on essentially the same subject. Bulgakov, it seems, was invited to work on the new Soviet libretto for *Ivan Susanin* too (to replace the original 'monarchistic' one of 1836 by Baron G. Rozen), together with the poet S.M. Gorodetsky; but he refused, although later he would agree to correct Gorodetsky's version,[12] extracts from which were published in September 1937. The theatre, in the meantime, delayed in making a firm decision on 'Minin and Pozharsky.' In October we find Kerzhentsev, chairman of the Central Committee on the Arts, expressing some dissatisfaction to Asafiev about the libretto, but hoping that the opera would nevertheless be performed in the autumn of 1938. Two months later, he wrote: 'I read over Bulgakov's libretto again and consider that basically it is not bad at all, but it is schematic and needs considerable additional work.' Preparations for the production of 'Minin and Pozharsky' continued, with Bulgakov assisting, and in January it was announced that it would be put on in the first half of 1939.[13]

But finally it was decided to cancel it, and go ahead with *Ivan Susanin*. According to Leontiev (once again echoing Mordvinov), Bulgakov then calmly started to work on *Ivan Susanin* – 'without any self-interest or hurt feelings as an author ... making comments, giving advice, bringing to it the colossal store of

11 Told to M. Michel Vassilieff by Yelena Sergeevna. For further details on this opera, see 93; **186**, *fond* 656, *opis* 5, folio 9966; **187**, folio 540; also **491**, p. 87.
12 Told to L.A. Shilov by Yelena Sergeevna; see also S. Gorodetskii, '*Ivan Susanin*. Otryvki iz libretto,' *Sovetskoe iskusstvo*, 5 Sept. 1937
13 **458**

knowledge which he had accumulated for "Minin and Pozharsky."[14] It opened on 21 February 1939; his own opera was never performed.

It is difficult to judge how successful 'Minin and Pozharsky' would have been. The libretto, as Kerzhentsev pointed out, is very schematic: a straightforward dramatization of individual scenes with little real development. It is full of exclamations, dramatic statements and gestures, and its sole motive for action is fierce patriotism of a very basic kind. Only in the scene of the would-be assassin Zborowski's death, where the Russians respect his brave spirit, and in that of the insulted Cossacks, does the work become involved in any real psychological insight. But then we may not be justified in applying literary criteria to an opera at all, which can only be judged in its entirety, with its music in first place.

In April 1937 Bulgakov completed a second libretto, 'The Black Sea,' on a similar theme to that of his play *Flight*. In it, Serafima becomes Olga Andreevna Shatrova, arrested by Wrangel's counter-espionage for hiding a member of the revolutionary committee; Golubkov is her husband trying to save her from the White commander-in-chief, who is reminiscent of Khludov; Colonel De Brizar becomes Colonel Bregge. The main action involves the conflict in the Crimea, and a new hero is introduced: the Red front commander Mikhaylov, clearly based on Frunze.[15] On 20 April *Literaturnaia gazeta* announced that S.S. Pototsky was writing the music for the opera, but in fact nothing came of it - possibly because two weeks previously Pototsky himself had been violently attacked in the journal *Muzyka*.

Nor was Bulgakov's next attempt any more successful. In November it was announced that he was writing a libretto (begun 'urgently' seventeen months earlier) for 'Peter I,' which would include Peter's victory at Poltava, his great reforms, and his struggle with the tsarevich Alexey. For the music, the Bolshoy was commissioning 'one of the most outstanding Soviet composers.'[16] (The obvious choice for this would have been V.V. Shcherbachev, who had been offered a libretto on the subject by N. Vinogradov as early as 1924, and who later wrote the music for the film *Peter the Great*.) Again, nothing happened. The same year Bulgakov helped edit the text of the arias and choruses for A.G. Preys' libretto 'Mother,' which was to be performed in December 1938 to the music of V. Zhelobinsky. And in 1938 he started work too on a libretto for 'War and Peace,' but got no further than the outline plans for the first two scenes, which take up nine smallish pages of his notebook.[17]

14 **187**, folio 556
15 **407**, II, pp. 131-2; also **328** and D. Kabalevskii, 'Tsinichnaia khaltura,' *Muzyka*, 6 April 1937
16 **410**. For the date of commencement, see **245**, p. 242.
17 See **326** and **187**, folios 545, 209, 210

Bulgakov's only libretto to enjoy any measure of success – and even that was very slight – was his one-act 'Rachel,' written in 1938 on the basis of Maupassant's story 'Mademoiselle Fifi.'[18] It is set during the Franco-Prussian War, when a prostitute, Rachel, after patriotically killing a German officer, Von Eyrik, asks help from a priest, Chantavoine, who hides her in the belfry. Here she deceives the soldiers by hiding in the bell itself, holding on to the clapper. Finally the Germans are forced to depart, and Chantavoine has to ring the bell for Eyrik's funeral, which he does with great joy: the bell peals out and a choir sings a hymn of victory.

The music for this was originally to be written by I.O. Dunaevsky, with whom Bulgakov had some correspondence in the winter of 1938-39. His main fear was whether in fact Dunaevsky would actually do anything about it. 'Write, write!' he encouraged him on 26 January. In sending this letter for her husband, Yelena Sergeevna added her own comments:

Will 'Rachel' really be another superfluous manuscript, buried in a red chiffonier? And will you, too, really be just the next person to disappear like a shadow from our lives?

We've already had many such cases. But for some reason I believed in you. Was I wrong?[19]

It is perhaps an indication of the extent of the Bulgakovs' despair that they were now so anxious about a libretto, something trivial when compared with Bulgakov's major works. Dunaevsky did not write the music for 'Rachel.' Years later (1950) he wrote that he had for a long time thought about writing an opera and was still thinking about it. A note to the letter adds that his earlier intention was not carried out because of the beginning of the war.

In a sense this was probably true, for in 1939 the Soviet Union was officially Germany's ally, having signed the Non-Aggression Pact with its secret protocols: in accordance with which Soviet forces were soon to occupy half of Poland. To put on an anti-German opera at this time was clearly impossible, whereas *Ivan Susanin* with its anti-Polish sentiments was far more appropriate.

With Russia's entry into the war against Germany, however, the situation changed, and Bulgakov's libretto for 'Rachel,' after his death, became patriotic. The well-known composer R.M. Glier wrote the music to it in 1942-43 and the poetess Margarita Aliger went over the text, presumably turning it into the loose verse of the final version. Its première was in 1943, on the All-Union Radio in

18 For this and further details, see 94.
19 For these letters, see 256, pp. 233, 92, 249.

Moscow. After the war it was also given a concert performance, on 19 April 1947, at the P.I. Tschaikovsky Concert Hall in Moscow, by the actors of the K.S. Stanislavsky Opera and Dramatic Studio.

We should clearly not attach a great deal of importance to Bulgakov's libretti. To examine the text of 'Rachel' and compare it with Maupassant's story tells us more about the difference between a libretto and a literary composition than about its quality. As it reads, it is direct, totally lacking in subtlety, and melodramatic in the extreme: as may indeed be suitable for a text meant only for singing. Its plot is minimal, and its patriotic language clearly to the taste of wartime Russia. Maupassant's story is certainly far richer in a literary sense, concentrating more on the German officers' party and particularly on Von Eyrik (nicknamed 'Mademoiselle Fifi'), who is killed by Rachel. The ringing of the bells has more point, since Chantavoine has refused to ring them while his land is occupied: what Von Eyrik had constantly demanded is only carried out after his death, to disguise the fact that Rachel is hiding in the belfry.

But this is hardly a criticism of the libretto, for the techniques in an opera are simply different and we cannot judge it in terms of its literary value. It is difficult to agree with Leontiev's view that Bulgakov's libretti were dramatic works in verse in their own right, which could be performed almost as they stand, independently from the music – and that they should be published alongside his plays.[20] One can imagine both 'Rachel' and 'Minin and Pozharsky' making for effective opera, but as plays they would be bound to fail – and Bulgakov did not make the mistake of trying to write plays in the guise of libretti.

He deserves credit, perhaps, for seriously trying to work within the medium. But most of all, the composition of libretti was simply a job for him, not without interest, but something which cannot be compared with his serious literary work – which, in the late thirties, despite the increasing seriousness of his illness, was not yet complete.

THEATRICAL ROMANCE (NOTES OF A DEAD MAN)

The origin of *Notes of a Dead Man*, as *Theatrical Romance*[21] was first called, goes back to the manuscript 'To a Secret Friend' of 1929 and the 'novel about the theatre' destroyed in 1930. M.O. Chudakova also suggests a connection with the early novel about the devil. Another manuscript, the beginning of what is described as a book about travels, and dating from 1934, appears too to be related

20 **187**, folio 556
21 The title may also be translated as 'A Theatrical Novel': 'Romance,' however, seems more appropriate.

to the same general theme. Bulgakov began a new version on 26 November 1936[22] and worked on it during the remainder of that and most of the following year, reading each chapter as he completed it to his friends from the Art Theatre. In 1937, however, probably in the autumn, in the face of a growing illness and other plans he considered more important, he put the work aside and never completed it. The unfinished novel was first published, as *Theatrical Romance*, in the journal *Novyi mir* in August 1965, twenty-five years after Bulgakov's death; a few months earlier one chapter had appeared in the newspaper *Literaturnaia Rossiia*. Both publications contained appreciative commentaries, by actor Toporkov and writer Simonov respectively.[23] By this time the rehabilitation of Bulgakov was well underway: the novel's appearance was marked with interest and approval by other critics. In 1966 it was published in the volume of *Selected Prose*, and in the next few years it was translated into English, French, German, and Polish. It was republished in the collection of *Novels* in 1973.

Theatrical Romance can be considered an autobiographical work to the extent that many of its details have been taken from Bulgakov's own life and from his knowledge of his contemporaries in the Moscow Art Theatre. Its narrator, Sergey Leontievich Maxudov, is employed by the *Shipping Gazette* (read *Gudok*). He writes a novel, the first part of which is published in a journal which then is closed, but later he is invited to convert it into a play, here called 'Black Snow,' for the Independent (Moscow Art) Theatre. This, he learns, has two directors, Aristarkh Platonovich (Nemirovich-Danchenko) – at present away in India (America) – and Ivan Vasilievich (Stanislavsky), who, however, have not spoken to each other for forty years. But Maxudov argues about his play with Ivan Vasilievich, who wants to make impossible changes; when finally it is decided to put it on, there are endless delays caused by Ivan Vasilievich rehearsing the actors according to the famous 'Method' he has invented. Here *Theatrical Romance* breaks off: it was, apparently, to continue with the return from India of Aristarkh Platonovich, an amusing scene of his lecture in the theatre about his travels, the further fate of Maxudov's play and criticisms of it, and an unhappy love affair.[24]

A great deal in the work is clearly identifiable. Lyovshin has pointed out how the physical descriptions of Maxudov's room correspond to Bulgakov's home on the Sadovaya, and Mikhalsky indicates the accuracy of Bulgakov's descriptions

22 Told to M. Michel Vassilieff by Yelena Sergeevna; see also **245**, pp. 226-7; **177**; and **491**, pp. 96-7

23 **157**, pp. 97-100, and **159**, pp. 16-17

24 **2**, p. 40

of the theatre.[25] But, nevertheless, *Theatrical Romance* is far from being an autobiography as such. What Bulgakov has done is to make a careful selection of details from his own life – making the fate of 'Black Snow' more similar to that of
Molière than of *Days of the Turbins* – and use them to write a work of fiction in
which, of course, many of his own attitudes are expressed.

In particular, it would be absurd to maintain that Maxudov is a picture of
Bulgakov. Rather, he is simply a narrator, somewhat reminiscent in his conversational style, particularly in his habit of addressing the reader directly, of the
earlier narrators in *Notes of a Young Doctor* and 'Notes on the Cuffs.' Maxudov
himself is weaker than his creator, less successful, less talented, and less well-
balanced. One can, of course, imagine Bulgakov frequently sharing with him
many of his depressions, his anxieties, his over-sensitivity to the criticisms of
others, even perhaps his thoughts of suicide. (In the book Maxudov steals a gun
to shoot himself – but learns just in time that his novel will be published.) But
Bulgakov had sufficient sense of purpose, and above all sufficient humour
(which Maxudov totally lacks), to rise above this and in this very novel to make
fun in exaggerated form of his own weaker side.

Our view of Maxudov's character, however, and how much importance we
attach to it, will depend to some extent on our reading of the book's preface.
This dissociates the author from the narrator who, it is explained, committed
suicide after sending the author his unfinished notes for publication. Bulgakov
further states that Maxudov himself imagined most of the events and remained a
newspaper employee – never writing plays or working for a theatre: 'Maxudov's
notes, therefore, are the fruit of his imagination, an imagination which was, alas,
morbid. Sergei Leontievich suffered from a disease with a very unpleasant name
– melancholia' (p. 190).[26] One is clearly tempted to take the preface largely as a
way of explaining the unfinished manuscript and of disclaiming any connection
with the Moscow Art Theatre. If, however, we take it at its face value, then we
must conclude that in Maxudov we are dealing with an over-sensitive, almost
pathological, dreamer, who not only attempts suicide near the beginning but
who really commits it at the end, after giving a number of indications in his
notes that he intends to do so all the time (he talks of 'leaving for ever' or of
'soon no longer existing' on at least four occasions after his first attempted suicide). Maxudov says himself he has suffered 'a crushing failure' and is 'a melancholic into the bargain' (p. 158); in his private life things constantly seem to go
wrong for him, sometimes humorously: he feels afraid, he gets stains on his

25 **349**, pp. 119-20, and **376**, pp. 39, 44
26 Page references, which are indicated in the text, are to **160**.

clothes, his bootlaces break, his friends desert him. When he enters the theatre
he becomes almost pathetic in his desire to please others – particularly Ivan Vasilievich, who just will not be pleased – even if Maxudov does attempt to explain
this as being only for the sake of his play. Seen in this light, the novel is essentially psychological, as the Soviet critic Vulis has in fact written; another critic
has referred to it as a parody of the Dostoevskian moments in Bulgakov's own
works.[27] An objectionable writer in the book (Likospastov – apparently based
on Yury Slyozkin) indeed calls Maxudov 'a bit of a Dostoevsky' and it is quite
possible to see him as a Dostoevskian character, with his over-serious view of
himself, his solitary existence, his pretensions which amount to nothing, his day-
dreams of glory.

Yet however justified such a view may be, it leaves us vaguely unhappy. The
problem is that Maxudov's 'day-dreams,' after allowing for a certain exaggeration, are very close to the truth about the Moscow Art Theatre and the literary
world: it is difficult to accept that they are only 'the fruit of his imagination.'
And this other world interests us rather more, so we are apt not to take Maxudov's own psyche very seriously. There exists, then, a certain unresolved ambiguity between the character of Maxudov on the one hand and the lifelike
descriptions of theatrical and literary life on the other. This is the principal weakness in the book, for it leaves one with a sense of uncertainty about its basic
purpose.

Not that the book is particularly realistic in its approach. Like the works of
Gogol, it can be interpreted on a fantastic as well as on an everyday level (giving
some weight to the view of its events taking place largely in Maxudov's imagination), even if Bulgakov's fantasy is not quite as well sustained. The element of
the fantastic – light-hearted enough, for there is always a rational, if sometimes
odd, explanation – is apparent largely at the beginning, with its dramatic, unexpected events and ordinary occurrences which are made to seem mysterious.
Thus when Maxudov goes to see Ilchin, who will later invite him to adapt his
novel, there is a thunderstorm: 'Somewhere far away over Moscow lightning split
the sky, illuminating Ilchin in a momentary phosphorescent flash' (p. 17); the
chapter ends with Ilchin's fateful words, 'I have read your novel.' In a flashback,
telling of how the novel was written, and of the narrator's nightmares and fears,
we learn that his cat, his only companion, has mysteriously died at the height of
Maxudov's depression. In a deliberately absurd parody of Gounod's *Faust* the
narrator reveals that the only reason he had not himself committed suicide was
because he was waiting to hear the end of *Faust* being played in a neighbouring

27 **518**, p. 251, and **161**, p. 192. For what follows, see **243**, p. 244, n 1. A complete list of
prototypes for the characters has apparently been compiled by Ye. Shilovsky.

flat: this interrupted by the startling appearance of Rudolfi (read Lezhnev), editor of *The Motherland* (*Rossiia*), actually in the guise of Mephistopheles. In a delightful piece of rational 'magic,' Rudolfi then produces an electric light bulb to replace the one that has burnt out. The only occasion which is equally mysterious later in the book is when Maxudov is summoned to Ivan Vasilievich and finds his way there by a number of 'signs' indicated by his actor friend Bombardov (Yanshin?): a courtyard with a man in a sheepskin coat who will ask what the visitor wants, a man washing a car without its wheels, a bust of Ostrovsky and a man in felt boots smoking beside a stove, a nurse in the hall. While not everything turns out exactly as Bombardov predicts, the differences are minor and all gives the impression of a mysterious, pre-ordained dream world.

Gogol's influence may be found too in Bulgakov's whimsical use of absurd or nonsensical detail for its own sake. Rudolfi, visiting Maxudov, asks him all kinds of personal questions – how many times a week he shaves, for example – but not because he has any particular reason as we would expect, but only out of his own curiosity. In Rudolfi's office a young man who has been criticizing Maxudov somehow scratches his ear on a nail at the moment he learns that Maxudov is standing before him. Some of the dialogue – in which as usual Bulgakov excels – can best be described as logical nonsense, as when Bombardov explains why Ivan Vasilievich hires a coach to come to the theatre:

'How extraordinary! Why hire a coach when he's got a car?'
'And if the chauffeur dies of a heart attack at the wheel and the car drives into a shop window, what happens then, might I ask?'
'But supposing the horse bolts?'
'Drykin's horse never bolts. It never goes faster than a walk.' (pp. 111-12)

When Maxudov then visits Ivan Vasilievich he has first to engage in an inane conversation about his father's death and homeopathic medicine, then his reading of his play is interrupted by the cat flying into the room and tearing down a curtain, followed by a neurotic actress, Lyudmila Silvestrovna, who throws herself at Ivan Vasilievich's feet. 'That cat is an idiot,' Bombardov says later in another piece of absurdity. 'It's got coronary thrombosis, myocarditis, and severe neurosis. It spends all day lying on a bed and never sees anybody so naturally it was terrified' (p. 151). All this is the result of a *nakladka*, the word used in the theatre when some little thing has gone wrong – and in a sense the whole book is a series of *nakladki*. In much of this we are scarcely removed from Gogol's world of the absurd, to which the whole of the theatre, including Ivan Vasilievich's famous 'Method,' might seem to belong. Yet Gogol's nightmarish vision is absent: there is no menace in this type of fantasy, neither for us nor for Maxudov.

We are left instead with a great deal of comedy in the situations Bulgakov creates. Bulgakov enjoys playing on the reader's – or Maxudov's – expectations, which turn out to be different from reality. (On a serious level, this might be said of Maxudov's expectations of the theatre itself.) In the first chapter, Maxudov is ashamed to invite Ilchin to his room because of his divan with a spring sticking out. After a long walk through the theatre – deliberately described in elevated language – to reach this 'lonely enigmatic Xavier Borisovich Ilchin,' Maxudov finds there is nothing elevated about him at all, and he has exactly the same divan with its spring sticking out. Later, at a literary party, Izmail Alexandrovich Bondarevsky (a writer just returned from abroad: Alexey Tolstoy) is heard arriving and in walks a shy and embarrassed man with a peaked cap. 'There seems to be a mistake here,' the narrator thinks, while the reader expects this in fact to be the famous author. But 'there had indeed been a mistake,' it is not the author, and the reader has been caught unawares (p. 42). Or, to return to Maxudov's signposted journey to Ivan Vasilievich, the reader expects the details to be exact: the slight discrepancies in the actual 'signs' only make the whole process more amusing.

Yet however exaggerated this comedy may be, ultimately it is still as a picture of actual life that *Theatrical Romance* makes its greatest impact, and much of the reader's enjoyment comes from the element of recognition of the real people Bulgakov caricatures. The book is first and foremost a satire, and the main target of this, together with the Art Theatre itself, is Stanislavsky. 'To someone, who knows why ...' is mentioned in the preface as being Maxudov's epigraph to his notes. Bulgakov, of course, had no time to complete the book before his death, but a further factor which may have discouraged any attempt to do so must surely have been Stanislavsky's death in 1938. It would hardly have been tactful at that time to publish material which was frankly critical of the revered grand old man of the Russian theatre.

The portrait of Stanislavsky, as everything else, is highly exaggerated. Stanislavsky was old and sick, tyrannical perhaps, but not quite as unyielding as Ivan Vasilievich (a name which, we may recall, with its reversed form, Vasily Ivanovich, Bulgakov had often used before for characters he satirizes). Yet as in any successful caricature we receive a vivid impression of the man himself, with his ordered life composed of the trivia of every day, his set opinions and little fads, his difficulties remembering people's names, his refusal to listen to anyone except his aunt, his secretary, and the theatre's business manager. 'Every great man has his foibles,' Bombardov tells Maxudov (p. 132). The actors, while revering and fearing Ivan Vasilievich like a god, never contradicting him, none the less try to accomplish what they want by bypassing him where possible – which leads to bickering and factionalism. Ivan Vasilievich is portrayed as stubborn, petty in his dislike of certain theatrical personalities, scheming – willing to alter Maxudov's play totally, so he may put it on without offending the founder members of the theatre. 'Your play is a good one,' he says after reading it through, 'all you have to do now is to write it' (p. 124). Even when rehearsals are underway, he still wants changes on the basis only of his personal preferences (trying, for example, to get Maxudov to write a duel scene in the play as a fight with sabres): reminiscent of Stanislavsky's attitude over *Molière*. The exaggeration is taken to the extreme in a barely disguised reference to Chekhov's *Uncle Vanya* where, because of an unfortunate gun-shot, Ivan Vasilievich is said to have insisted the hero wave a watering can instead, shouting 'I'll kill you' – since which time there have been no shots in plays he has directed.

Most heretical of all in this portrayal is Maxudov's increasing doubt about the validity of Stanislavsky's famous 'Method.' 'None of your theories are any good!' he tells Bombardov, 'that one who plays the murderer in black gloves ... he doesn't need theories – he can *act*! ... There *are* no theories!' (pp. 154-5). Later he becomes convinced that the 'Method' is actually harmful to the production of his play: 'I don't doubt for a moment that the method really is a work of genius, but the practical application of it reduced me to despair' (p. 180). Some of the most amusing scenes in the book are of Ivan Vasilievich directing, while the actress Lyudmila Silvestrovna lovingly records his every comment in an exercise book. Here he makes one actor express his love for a woman by the way he rides his bicycle for her; has everyone (including, accidentally, a stage-hand) write love letters on stage or give their own reactions to the distant glow of a fire, with totally inappropriate results. 'Part of his theory was the idea that at rehearsal the script should be completely disregarded and the play's characters had to be created impromptu' (p. 185). The result is rehearsals which never get beyond the first few lines of the scene, actors who after a while decide to fall sick with colds, and, worst of all, actors who become worse as a result of these exercises. All this is in marked contrast to Gorchakov's flattering comments about Stanislavsky at rehearsals or the actual records kept by the theatre of some of his pronouncements.

Yet the narrator freely admits Ivan Vasilievich's excellence as an actor: Bulgakov's portrait of Stanislavsky is biting but not malicious. Indeed, for a man so bitter over his treatment by the other, this humorous portrayal is remarkable and bears witness to the fact of Bulgakov the artist overcoming Bulgakov the man. The same is true of his portrait of Nemirovich-Danchenko, limited (because of his absence) to his office with its picture of him with 'the muse' and its photographs of him in the company of famous writers; to his letters containing detailed instructions for various actors in individual scenes; to the similar godlike awe with which his devotees, his secretary Polixena Toropetskaya (Olga Bokshanskaya) in particular, regard him. Pavel Markov has written of the pleasure with which he and his colleagues in the theatre listened to the novel, confirming that Bulgakov's sarcasm was hardly of the type to denigrate either the theatre or its founders.[28]

This is partly because of the book's humorous approach, but more because of the one attitude that underlies it, an undying love for the theatre. 'Who cared whether the box-office takings were good or not?' Maxudov says near the beginning, undoubtedly expressing much of Bulgakov's own feeling. 'This is my world!' (p. 59). A similar love for the theatre is illustrated in other characters too, particularly in the story of a major general, Komarovsky-Echappard de Bioncourt, who had resigned his command of His Majesty's Household Regiment of Lancers to become an actor. For Maxudov this love is further symbolized by a golden horse in a play he sees three times, which comes to represent all the glorious world of illusion which is so different from his everyday life: 'I tried to convince Bombardov how as soon as I caught sight of the horse I had instinctively grasped the secret of the stage and all its mysteries. How, long ago in childhood perhaps, or perhaps even before I was born I had dreamed of it and longed for it! And now I had arrived in that magic world!' (p. 154). His greatest disappointment is when he is not entirely accepted: something that must have been felt by Bulgakov too when he was not accepted on his own terms. But his one consolation, expressed at the end, is still that he can attend every performance.

For his love, felt by Maxudov as by Bulgakov, is strong enough to make up for all that is wrong with a world that, in fact, is far from magical. The novel satirizes a great deal of what goes on in the theatre and its personages – actors who row with each other at rehearsals, a conductor who belabours everyone with his complaints about the treatment of the orchestra, founder members who are desperate to repeat their former glories – but more than this it tries to capture something of the essence of theatrical life, with all its faults. The building itself is lovingly described, so is the special language belonging to this world. There is a love for small details or for little stories: one Gornostaev, for example, using an illness of which he is miraculously 'cured' to take a holiday in Switzerland and France every summer. Bulgakov introduces a multitude of different characters, with their own particularities: Gavriil Stepanovich who 'would not hurt a fly' but whose main concern is to get a one-sided contract signed as cheaply as possible; Misha Panin (based on Pavel Markov), whose sad eyes suggest 'he once killed a friend in a duel in Pyatigorsk'; Foma Strizh (Ilya Sudakov), whom Ivan Vasilievich does not trust; the buffet attendant, whose only concern is that not everything should be eaten. A particularly lively description is given of the house manager, Filipp Filippovich Tulumbasov (based on F. Mikhalsky),[29] to whom the public comes wanting tickets (there is even a long list of all their various professions). Here, and at rehearsals, in the offices, all is chaotic, and yet it is out of this collection of human imperfections that the illusion on stage is created. Most characters, it is true, tend to be little vignettes, without development, for indeed they play a subservient role to the daily life of the theatre itself. As the critic Lakshin has pointed out, in the book there are really 'only two heroes – the playwright and the theatre, the theatre as a many-faceted but single entity, strange and attractive in its mysteriousness.'

The literary world itself, represented by a handful of writers and critics, is satirized as well, and on the whole comes off rather worse. 'The new world had admitted me and I liked it,' Maxudov claims before going to a literary party (p. 41). The next morning his impressions have already changed: 'I saw a new world yesterday and it was repulsive. I won't belong to it. It's a strange world. A disgusting world' (p. 49). The other writers and literary figures – Likospastov, Izmail Alexandrovich, Agapenov, Lesosekov, the young man in Rudolfi's office, Volkodav who writes a lampoon on Maxudov – are largely marked by self-importance, conceit, and envy and malice towards those of talent. (The notable exception to this is the editor Rudolfi, whom the narrator describes interestingly and with respect.) One of the most hilarious incidents in the book is when Agapenov and his clique come upon a poster announcing Maxudov's play, alongside works of major world dramatists (as had happened in Bulgakov's own case) – with him in the background observing. But the greatest condemnation of this world is the fact that what these people write is trivial too, based on odd incidents they have witnessed and tell everyone about, or on characters they have met. Maxudov is shown as gaining nothing from reading their books, despairing himself, and questioning how these others manage to get into print: it is an indictment of all would-be writers, in the Soviet Union and outside, who cater simply to public taste and attitudes and their own enjoyment of cheap fame.

For one thing that sets Maxudov – and Bulgakov – apart from the others is real talent, which does not need the pretentious chatter of literary soirées. A more serious side of the novel shows something of the whole process of artistic creation: Maxudov's dreams of the civil war which started him writing his novel, then the figures growing in his imagination so that they seem to be acting out an independent life which he is scarcely able to control – the basis for his play – then simply the hard work in shortening and revising. The narrator talks several times of his youthful enthusiasm at being published or having a play performed – 'My God! How stupid it was, how stupid! But I was still young then, you

29 Told me by Vl. Lakshin. The quotation that follows is from 2, p. 39.

shouldn't laugh at me' (p. 32) – but clearly we are not meant to take his disclaimers seriously: it is such enthusiasm, combined with that for the creative act itself, that distinguishes Maxudov from the more cynical writers concerned only with public success. This was a quality which Bulgakov possessed all his life, as he wrote what he felt the urge to write, without considering how acceptable it would be.

Theatrical Romance contains many different elements: satire and descriptions of the theatre and the literary world, descriptions of the creative process, detail both realistic and fantastic, an attempt at studying the psychology of an individual. Its main fault is its lack of form, the succession of somewhat disjointed scenes, and the ambiguity over its basic purpose. On the other hand, its whimsical style reminiscent of Gogol, its lightness of touch, and the irreverent record it provides of the Moscow Art Theatre in the 1920s and 1930s make it delightful and fascinating reading. In a sense it draws on the strengths of early prose works, such as *Notes of a Young Doctor* and 'Notes on the Cuffs,' while avoiding the facetiousness of the latter. At the same time it is a worthy predecessor in its satire, although less serious in its totality, to *The Master and Margarita*. In its present form it is perhaps light-weight, and certainly untidy, not a polished work of literature – but then it is incomplete. It none the less shows Bulgakov's writing at his most mature, and we can only regret that his short life did not allow him to complete it.

DON QUIXOTE (adaptation)

'My last attempts to write for the dramatic theatres were the purest Don-Quixotism on my part. And I shall not repeat it any more. I shall be missing from the dramatic theatre front. I have experienced, and experienced too much ...'[30] So Bulgakov wrote to Veresaev on 4 April 1937, only three months before he received a letter from Vasily Vasilievich Kuza asking him to write a new adaptation for the Vakhtangov Theatre. Whether his reference to 'Don-Quixotism' is coincidental or whether he had already been thinking about the possibility of an adaptation of Cervantes' novel is uncertain: we know only that at some time or other he had had a conversation with Kuza on the subject. But Kuza's immediate suggestion in July 1937 was for an adaptation of either Zola's *Nana*, Maupassant's *Bel-Ami*, or Balzac's *Eugénie Grandet*.[31] Bulgakov was not enthusiastic, considering the first two unsuitable for the Soviet stage and Balzac too boring. It was then that Kuza took up the idea of *Don Quixote*. 'This idea,' he wrote, 'excites us no less than *Nana*. In a conversation with me you said that it would be

30 **379**, p. 162
31 This and what follows is based on **34**, pp. 273-4, and on **187**, folios 250-1.

very difficult. Dear Mikhail Afanasievich, think about it most seriously.' Bulgakov finally agreed, signing on 3 December a contract which gave him a year in
which to write the play.

He started almost immediately, but then put the play aside to work on his
most substantial version of *The Master and Margarita*, which then had to be dictated to Olga Bokshanskaya. But on 26 June 1938 he joined his wife in a house
they had rented for the summer in Lebedyan, a small town some 300 kilometres to the south of Moscow, and it was here that he essentially wrote the first
draft of the play. After a month he returned to Moscow, where he started correcting it, while reading Cervantes in the original and becoming so enthusiastic
that he even tried writing parts of his letters to Yelena Sergeevna (still in Lebedyan) in Spanish. Despite a heat-wave in Moscow at the end of July and beginning
of August he worked solidly on the play, declining Dmitriev's suggestion to visit
him in Leningrad, particularly since he was already a sick man. 'I feel terrible,'
he wrote to him, 'and I simply cannot physically carry out such a feat.' The play
was finished by the middle of August and sent to the theatre on 9 September.
Since it was rather long, several scenes were later deleted (they are now published separately[32]) and the final version is dated 18 December 1938.

Bulgakov's adaptation of *Don Quixote* takes some of the best-known incidents from the book, following Cervantes' text reasonably closely; with a few
slight changes for dramatic reasons and occasional more significant departures
from the original. At the end of the fifteenth century in Spain, Señor Alonso
Quixano, imagining himself to be a knight-errant, Don Quixote, sets out in
search of valiant deeds to perform, with a simple peasant, Sancho Panza, as
squire. After various adventures he is tricked into returning home by his niece
Antonia and some concerned friends; but he departs again and is received, for
his entertainment value, at the duke's court, while Sancho is in jest given an island to govern, as he has long desired. Don Quixote is finally persuaded to return
when he is defeated in combat by Samson Carrasco (in the play in love with
Antonia), who disguises himself as 'Knight of the White Moon.' The plays ends
with Don Quixote's death following his realization of his folly.

Don Quixote received initial approval from *Glavrepertkom* in November
1938, and it was decided to put it in the repertory of the Vakhtangov Theatre
for the following year; approval was confirmed on 17 January.[33] But now there
was a delay because of the illness of the producer, R.N. Simonov, who had to be
replaced by I.M. Rapoport. (P.V. Vilyams was now appointed as set designer.)[34]

32 **34**, pp. 274-7
33 See the versions of the play in **186**, *fond* 656, *opis* 5, folio 1030-1.
34 **255**

Doubting that the original performance deadline of 1 January 1940 could be met, Bulgakov also sent the play to the Pushkin Dramatic Theatre in Leningrad, the Griboedov Theatre in Tbilisi, and a number of provincial theatres. Kozhich, of the Pushkin Dramatic Theatre, immediately travelled to join his company then on tour in Moscow, accompanied by the outstanding actor Nikolay Cherkasov, who read the play to him on the train.[35] By August the theatre had accepted the play and a contract was signed three months later (by Yelena Sergeevna, now acting on behalf of her invalid husband) – the Vakhtangov Theatre having lost the première rights through its own failure to perform the play by the date specified. Work began on the play the following autumn, after Bulgakov's death.

It thus happened that the first major production of *Don Quixote* was at the Pushkin Theatre in Leningrad, where it opened on 13 March 1941, rather than at the Vakhtangov Theatre, for which it had originally been intended. (At least two provincial theatres staged the play earlier: the Town Theatre in Kineshma in April 1940 and the Republic State Russian Theatre of Drama in Petrozavodsk in January 1941.) The Leningrad production by V. Kozhich was an immediate success with the public, due in part at least to Cherkasov, who was playing the role of Don Quixote for the fourth time. (In 1918-19 he had doubled for Shalyapin in Massenet's *Don Quixote*; in 1922 he had taken part in L.F. Minkus' ballet, and in 1926 in Alexandra Brustein's musical comedy version of the novel. The fifth occasion would be in the famous film of 1957.) In Cherkasov's notes he indicates that for this performance he tried to stress the difference between Don Quixote's idealism and the squalor of his society; to show Quixote's profound faith in the justice of his cause. One of the funniest scenes, he recalls, was the preparation at an inn of a balsam to cure all ills – which all then drank and became violently sick. But the dominant mood of the play was none the less a sad one. The last scene, Don Quixote's death, was played as pure tragedy, 'at the top of our voices, according to all the traditions of a tragic spectacle. Particularly strong in this respect were Don Quixote's death-bed monologues.'

Critical reaction was favourable, with both Cherkasov and B. Gorin-Goryainov as Sancho Panza receiving high honours. S. Yunovich's settings and dress designs also contributed to the success of the performance.[36] It was pointed out that Don Quixote was never funny, but rather lyrical and intellectual; that the play was full of humanism, even if perhaps there was not enough emphasis on the world Don Quixote was fighting. *Izvestiia* referred to the play as 'unquestionably one of the most successful attempts at an adaptation of Cervantes' work' – a view that has been repeated in later years.[37]

35 For this and what follows, see **241**, pp. 134, 93-5; and **240**, pp. 21-7.
36 **213**, p. 82
37 **251**; also **314**, IV, p. 172; **214**; and **406**, II, pp. 207-8

Unfortunately, the play was not destined to remain long in the repertory, for the outbreak of war with Germany three months after the opening brought immediate difficulties. Fascism had of course seized Spain too, in a bitter civil war, a few years earlier: now, the performance of a play stressing personal idealism as opposed to the accepted views of society, specifically in Spain even if in a different century, must have seemed particularly appropriate. But there were only about twenty performances; the last, Cherkasov tells us, 'going on during the fascist air raids on Leningrad when one could expect alerts at any moment. In those days our shows ended at ten p.m., without the last act.' He and Kozhich wanted to renew the production later, but the sets were destroyed in an air raid, and then Kozhich fell ill and it was no longer possible.

On 8 April, three weeks after the Leningrad première, the play had finally opened too at the Vakhtangov Theatre in Moscow, with Simonov in the title role and A. Goryunov as Sancho Panza. 'Ruben Simonov,' writes Marc Slonim, 'gave a different interpretation of the Knight of the Sad Countenance. His was a gay, warm portrayal within the framework of resplendent settings by Williams.'[38] But the production was not so well received as in Leningrad. I. Anisimov, reviewing it, was more critical of the play itself, noting that Bulgakov failed to convey the ideas of Cervantes but gave instead a simply realistic portrait.[39] The play was also performed in 1954 in Kaunas, in 1966 at the Theatre of Young Spectators in Leningrad, and in 1968 – in a poor translation into Armenian – at the G. Sundukyan Armenian Dramatic Theatre in Yerevan.[40] In 1975 it was put on successfully in Rome. It was published in the 1962 and 1965 collections of plays.

Of Bulgakov's three adaptations *Don Quixote* is by far the most successful. Compared with *Dead Souls* and *War and Peace*, the novel is in any case more suitable for adaptation, with its two central characters who develop in respect to each other as the book progresses and its clearly defined plot involving Don Quixote's sorties and the attempts of his friends to get him home. Whereas Bulgakov's other adaptations inevitably become a simple succession of different scenes and rely to a great extent on the viewers' knowledge of the originals, his *Don Quixote* is far more of a play in its own right which can be appreciated without reference to the novel.

Bulgakov has been unable, of course, to include more than a few of Don Quixote's adventures, notably his battle with windmills which he takes for giants, his attack on two monks he thinks are abducting a princess, a fight with some drovers who make fun of his horse Rosinante, and various escapades in an inn he takes for a castle. He is forced to omit many other well-known scenes,

38 **485**, p. 322
39 **201**; see also **406**, II, pp. 234-5
40 **408**. Information on some of the performances is in **187**, folios 250-1.

including Quixote's freeing from their guards a group of convicts who then stone him – which at least one Soviet critic regretted because of its social significance.[41] But quite apart from this, Bulgakov has clearly not felt it necessary to make as exact an illustration of the book as in the case of the other adaptations, and while many of the scenes and much of the dialogue remain close to the original he is not afraid to make changes. Some of these are comparatively minor, necessary alterations for the sake of putting the work on the stage. Thus Don Quixote's three sorties in the book become two in the play; the three occasions when he visits an inn are combined into one, and the adventure of the wine-skins he pierces (thinking they are enemy magicians) is joined with that of the servant girl Maritornes coming to the bed of a muleteer and stumbling on Don Quixote by mistake.

There are, however, a number of more significant alterations, scenes which have no counterpart in Cervantes' original but written by Bulgakov with the purpose of making for more effective action on stage. Thus in the first and last scenes he actually shows Aldonsa Lorenzo, the girl whom Don Quixote takes to be his ideal Dulcinea but has, in the novel, never seen: illustrating Quixote's fantasies and, at the end, his realization of the truth. Sometimes the comedy is intensified. In the inn all present drink the balsam (limited in the novel to Sancho Panza and Don Quixote) with hilarious results. To entice Don Quixote home, his niece Antonia (rather than someone else in the book) disguises herself as a princess Micomicona who is in need of his assistance, with barber Nicolas playing her duenna and a priest her uncle: making possible, when they have brought Don Quixote home, an entirely invented comedy of identities, with each of them assuming two roles which they must constantly change for his benefit – a standard device for farce in the theatre.

Generally, Bulgakov tries to strengthen some of the minor characters, who in the novel have little character of their own. (Here too we may see the difference between this play and the other two adaptations, where the characters are often no more than simple stage representations.) Hence the addition of the first two scenes, with Nicolas and Aldonsa Lorenzo. In Master Nicolas' interchange with Don Quixote, not only is the play introduced with considerable economy of means, but Nicolas himself is immediately recognized as the down-to-earth barber who cannot understand why the señor Quixano should want to attack him. He also serves as the first of many foils – virtually all the 'sane' people – to Don Quixote with his imaginary world of giants and magicians: 'Brandabar ... Has our hidalgo gone totally balmy, then?! ...' (p. 366).[42] It is similar with Aldonsa:

41 214, p. 25
42 Quotations are translated from 3. Page references are given in the text.

Quixote's ideal woman arrives bringing salted pork for the housekeeper. In the inn scene Bulgakov has developed a number of characters: showing the muleteer's arrival, his banter with the servant girl Maritornes, the innkeeper interrupting them and admonishing the girl, and finally the muleteer complaining when he is put in the barn – which the audience knows is really just what he wants so he can sleep with her. The muleteer plays a part in the preparation of the balsam too; he takes a liking for Sancho Panza after the latter is tossed in a blanket when his master leaves without paying. None of this is in the original, but it is entirely in keeping with its spirit and provides necessary relief from the two central figures. Later, Don Quixote's housekeeper becomes a more important figure, another foil for her master, with her plain common sense and lack of concern about his supposedly noble guests: 'If they slaughtered this Guinean, what can you do about it! It serves him right! Surely you won't bring him to life again? I've slaughtered two of the best fat chickens in your honour to make you some soup and in truth you'll get more good from that than from the King of Guinea!' (p. 416).

The major change from Cervantes, and one which caused some critical comment, is the introduction of a love relationship between Samson Carrasco and Antonia. As was pointed out, it probably added nothing to the story itself, but we may see in it simply a fairly natural way of giving a further dimension to characters who in Cervantes are relatively colourless, and providing some motivation for Samson in his determined effort to rescue Don Quixote. The scene of Samson's reunion with Antonia after two years is further used to supply stock theatrical farce, with Antonia slipping out of the way as Samson tries to kiss her, so that he kisses the housekeeper instead.

There is indeed a certain flavour of the music hall in many of the situations in the play, created mainly by the contrast between Don Quixote's high-minded madness and the uninspiring reality of the world, with Sancho acting as intermediary. Not only their adventures but their very appearance is comic, particularly after the beatings they undergo. There is also some theatrical slapstick involving the two of them: Sancho, for example, refuses to allow his master to test his 'infallible' helmet by placing it on his head: fortunately, for Don Quixote takes his sword and smashes it to pieces with one blow. At the duke's court, Don Quixote steps back to allow the duchess to go in a door, and Sancho strides in first.

But it is really around Sancho Panza that most of the comedy revolves (representing the common-sense, worldly view, he can be ridiculed with impunity), and many of his lines give rise to a kind of music-hall repartee. Thus at the inn he explains that his master got his wounds falling over a cliff, and a typical piece of music-hall banter follows as the innkeeper asks about his own bruises, and Maritornes joins in about the battering she gets, from a different kind of combat.

Sancho can be both witty and sarcastic in his comments, as in his first meeting with Samson Carrasco or in his interchanges with the housekeeper:

Housekeeper. It's him! Yes, it's him! My poor eyes are not deceiving me!
Sancho. It's me, señora housekeeper.
Housekeeper. Yes, it's him, trouble-maker and universal tramp!
Sancho. Yes, it's her ... (p. 407)

Sancho is, of course, the most constant foil to Don Quixote's lofty ideals, and much of the comedy comes from the difference between them. It is useless for Quixote to muse on his fate and ask Sancho if he has read of more valiant knights than himself, for Sancho can only reply 'No, sir, I haven't read of them anywhere because I can neither read nor write' (p. 370). Where his master is idealistic, Sancho is materialistic, concerned with food, balsam to cure his ills (until it makes him feel worse), rewards. Becoming the governor of an island, his initial incentive to accompany his master, is the constant theme of his conversation, and he resists Quixote's attempts to interpret his motivations – such as his despair at the supposed abduction of the princess Micomicona – more idealistically: 'How should I not fall into despair when a governorship has slipped through my fingers!' (p. 427). Where Quixote is brave, Sancho is cowardly. 'Surrender!' Quixote cries at his first approach, thinking he too is his enemy Friston. 'I surrender,' he cries immediately. 'I surrender, surrender twice and three times. I surrender finally, irrevocably, once and for all' (p. 369).

Yet his admiration for his master is evident from the way he imitates him, constantly repeating his words and sometimes adding, as a form of oath, some of the names he has learnt and loves pronouncing: 'Lelilies,' 'Perez de Vargas.' When he finally returns home, he talks of it in elevated language almost worthy of Quixote himself (until he tries to use the same kind of language to talk of the housekeeper, with incongruous effect):

Oh longed-for native land! Look at your son, Sancho Panza, open your embraces to him! He returns to you not famous, but exceedingly enriched by experience received thanks to calamities, disturbances, and misfortunes of all kinds ... And lo, that governorship has flown away like smoke, the pain from the sticks' blows has passed, and the son of his native land has appeared at the place he departed from – under the canopy of these trees, to his own well! (pp. 454-5)

All this is little more than a comic parody of Don Quixote, who continues more seriously in the same style. But nevertheless his influence on Sancho Panza is profound enough for Sancho to follow him even when there are no rewards, to share his master's beatings however much he complains, and to believe a great deal of what he says. An important theme in the play is the effect of idealism – impractical when concerned only with the higher flights of fancy – on the actions of the simple but honest ordinary man. From the beginning Sancho has, despite his simple-mindedness, been marked by a certain shrewd common sense, and it is this, combined with the example of Don Quixote, which indeed makes him, on his 'island,' successful as a governor and a wise judge, despite all his discomforts.

The character of Sancho Panza is, of course, Cervantes' and Bulgakov has added little that is new. But Bulgakov has shown a great deal of skill in his selection of scenes and dialogue, to make of Sancho in particular one of his most successful stage personalities. (The relationship that develops between him and Don Quixote is reminiscent of that between Bouton and Molière or Bitkov and Pushkin, but far more intimate.) In Bulgakov, it is Sancho who gives Don Quixote his name of Knight of the Sorrowful Figure, explaining why seriously – even if this, typically, is followed by a ludicrous suggestion as to the possible cause: 'I looked at you just now in the light of the moon, and you had such a sorrowful face as I have never seen before. Perhaps you got tired in battles, or it happened because you're missing several teeth at the right and at the front. Who knocked them out for you, señor?' (p. 373). After the adventure of the windmills, when he thinks Quixote is dead, his regret for his master is tempered by practical considerations such as what the housekeeper will say to him. But later he gives Quixote his advice out of genuine concern, however comically expressed: 'My heart feels that you will be beaten, señor. Therefore during a fight spare your head in particular, don't let it be hit. Yours is full of very clever thoughts and it will be a shame if it flies apart like a clay pot' (p. 437). At the end, he is simply in despair at the death of his master.

For despite the comedy in the play, the total impression it leaves – as in Cervantes too – is rather one of sadness and pathos. Don Quixote himself is not a comic figure at all, but a struggling human being in an impossible situation, asserting his own freedom even if it involves madness. 'I fear,' he says at the end, talking of Samson Carrasco, 'that he may have cured my soul, and in curing it took it out but did not put in another ... He deprived me of the most precious gift with which man is rewarded – he deprived me of freedom! There is much evil in the world, Sancho, but there is no greater evil than captivity!' (p. 456). There is some similarity here with Bulgakov's other heroes – Molière, Pushkin – and in the figure of Don Quixote we may see something of Bulgakov's own assertion of his right to artistic freedom. In one speech in the play he actually equates the 'poet' and the 'knight' and we may recall how he himself was christened a 'knight of art' by the members of the Moscow Art Theatre. The ideal of Cervantes thus corresponds to Bulgakov's own: it becomes difficult to write of this play and keep Bulgakov and Cervantes apart.

In another respect the play reflects a concern which we find throughout Bulgakov: the whole question of what is reality. Don Quixote rejects an everyday reality which is sordid and trivial, in the name of an ideal which is a worthy one; his madness lies not in his vision but in his uncompromising dedication to it. And in a sense he is right when he sees the world as full of monsters, giants, evil magicians, with whom as a man of honour he is obliged to do battle. The sordid reality is all around him: in the inn, at the duke's court, on the 'island' where, significantly, Sancho's own wise government is based only on the personal whim of the duke, who can overthrow it. Yet his particular vision does not encompass only the evil in the world, he also finds in it what there is of beauty and ennobles this. Sancho, he says, may well see Dulcinea as an ordinary peasant girl, whereas he as knight and poet celebrates 'the woman created by his tireless fantasy,' loves her as she has appeared to him in dreams. 'I love, oh Sancho, my ideal!' (p. 373). Thus in Maritornes too he can see the fine lady rather than the common servant girl – even if she herself only finds this amusing.

His ideal world is opposed to the everyday world of cynicism in various speeches throughout the play, as he and Sancho 'fly over the world to avenge insults inflicted by the fierce and the strong on the helpless and the weak, to fight for insulted honour, to return to the world what it had lost for ever – justice!' (p. 374). It is the Christian ideal of self-denial and sacrifice which Quixote upholds, specifically to the duke's priest in perhaps the most important speech in the play:

People choose various ways. One, stumbling, clambers up the road of vanity, another crawls along the path of humiliating flattery, others climb the road of hypocrisy and deception. Am I travelling along one of these roads? No! I am travelling the steep road of knighthood and despise earthly goods, but not honour! Whom have I avenged, engaging battle with the giants who have so annoyed you? I have stood up for the weak who have been hurt by the strong! If I have seen evil somewhere, I have gone into mortal combat, to strike the monsters of malice and crime! Do you not see them anywhere? You have poor sight, holy father! My purpose is bright – to do good to all and cause evil to no one. And for this, in your opinion, I deserve condemnation? (p. 434)

Such ideals have motivated the best of men, and for them Don Quixote wins respect despite his madness – even from such people as the duchess, who admits that 'When his phantoms leave him he reasons sensibly, his thoughts are clear' (p. 448). But Don Quixote is judged mad largely by those whose own manner of life he also rejects. 'If knights considered me mad,' he concludes in his answer to the priest, 'I would be affronted to the depths of my soul, but I don't give a penny for your words, they seem comical to me.'

Compared with Quixote, the 'sane' people in the play appear trivial indeed, and if he appears mad in the world they inhabit, they appear no less mad in his: the figures in the inn concerned only with profit or sensual pleasure, scrambling to get a drink of the miraculous balsam; those at the duke's court who care only for idle entertainment. Even the more heroic characters appear no less crazy: there is nothing more absurd than Antonia, the priest, and Nicolas disguising themselves as fairy-tale characters or Samson Carrasco dressed in a suit of armour, as the Knight of the White Moon. In the final act, it is Don Quixote who first comes to his senses, while his friends seem far more reluctant to abandon the pretence: indulging their fantasies in a game which does not have the same noble basis as do Quixote's adventures. The boundary between sanity and madness is slight: Don Quixote is 'mad' because he plays his own 'game' rather than the world's less heroic ones. Yet the imaginary world has always appealed to man, whose very art is based upon it. Significantly, Quixote maintains that were he not a knight he would like to be a simple shepherd – whose life has been frequently held up in literature as an ideal, an escape into innocence from worldly concerns. It is of course a fiction, but it has entertained the imaginations of other men than Don Quixote.

But for all of this, it is everyday reality which is finally asserted, for Quixote's mistake is to flee this real world instead of attempting to fight within it: he tilts uselessly at real windmills rather than with the 'evil giants' in the world, and his ideal woman is an illusion. When vanquished by Samson Carrasco, he refuses to acknowledge a superior beauty than Dulcinea's, but already there is an element of despair and he begins to fear that she does not exist. Samson confirms this, asserting the real world over the imaginary: 'my lady lives on earth, and just because of this she is more beautiful than yours!' (p. 452).

The final scene of the play shows Bulgakov at his best, belonging to him rather than to Cervantes (who dwells more on Quixote's idea of becoming a shepherd and then, after his return to his senses, on the details of his will – with the description of his death comparatively brief and factual). It is again a total reversal of the first act, this emphasized by the same setting of the courtyard and rooms (now empty) of Don Quixote's house. Previously, we had seen there the suit of armour but now, as the two heroes appear in a fashion which reminds us of their comical appearance after their first adventures, it is seen loaded on Rosinante '*so that it appears that there rides on the horse a knight who is empty inside, with a broken lance*' (p. 454) – clearly symbolical of Quixote himself. At the beginning he had set out full of hope. Now he returns for good (not for just a year as in Cervantes); it is the end of his dreams of glory, but also the end of his sufferings. It is, too, the end of his madness, but with it comes the end of his life, symbolized by the setting sun against which the scene takes place. With the approach of Dulcinea, whom Don Quixote now recognizes as Aldonsa Lorenzo, he can at last recognize that his madness was also a form of captivity. His fulfilment comes, however, in the approach of his 'ideal' lady – 'now she has come and fills my empty armour, and enfolds me in darkness ...' – whom we understand to be death herself. Now he admits that life is better: 'Samson, you have a lady, and this lady is really more beautiful than Dulcinea ... She is alive, your lady ...' (p. 461). And so, dying, he turns significantly to call his other, live, and more true companion, Sancho Panza.

In terms of stagecraft, *Don Quixote* is not as striking as some of Bulgakov's other plays, and except for the final scene in the light of the setting sun he provides for few visual effects. But like his other plays it is full of noises – the crash of people fighting, of broken dishes, horns blowing, bells ringing, shouts, shots – and of course music. One leitmotif in the play is the guitar that Nicolas constantly plays, another the whistle used by Sancho Panza to announce his presence to Don Quixote – which was further developed in the Pushkin Theatre production of the play, where a whole system of 'call signals' between Quixote and Sancho was used whenever possible: a gentle coo from Quixote, a shrill whistle from Sancho.[43] But, in a sense, Bulgakov's lesser preoccupation with visual effects is an advantage, for in this play we are brought back to the direct impact of the text itself, which presents no such problems as *Molière* and *The Last Days*.

Although Bulgakov is indebted to Cervantes for the themes and plot of *Don Quixote*, in his treatment of it he succeeds in making the play his own. Its subject is a fantasy world existing in the mind of one man, and in this respect we might find links both with *Theatrical Romance* and with Bulgakov's most ambitious treatment of the fantastic, *The Master and Margarita*. More important, it is the culmination of Bulgakov's search for an ideal hero in opposition to the world around him. This had begun with Molière and continued with Pushkin, but in both cases there were problems because their lives were relatively ordinary compared to the godlike stature they acquired through their art – and it is difficult to depict this on stage. In Don Quixote, it is his life which is an expression of his ideal; he himself, as a fictitious character, becomes a living symbol of that reality which ordinary men can express only in their art. Thus in writing an adaptation of Cervantes, Bulgakov found his own hero, and it is perhaps not entirely a coincidence that in the novel he was now completing his last great 'artist,' the Master, his literary disciple Ivan Bezdomny, and the great prototype of an ideal world, Jesus Christ, should all, for a while at least, be considered mad by the society in which they live.

Don Quixote remains an adaptation, if a brilliant one. One can only speculate what original plays Bulgakov might have written had he lived, but, alas, *Don Quixote* was his last play in which he could develop his own themes. It is perhaps Bulgakov's tragedy that his life was interrupted at a time when, after a number of years of experimentation in the theatre, he seemed to have reached a new maturity.

12

Final years, 1938-40

At the end of the thirties Bulgakov's life hardly appeared exceptional. A neighbour of his, the film director Ye. Gabrilovich, has recalled how he thought of him as a rather untalented, ordinary writer, with whom he would sometimes chat idly on the balcony they shared: 'He and I discussed the news, pieces of scandal, the value of walks, medicines for the kidneys, divorces, extramarital affairs, and weddings.'[1] Least of all did anyone realize how ill he was - although his interest in kidney medicines was more than idle curiosity. Bulgakov may have given up the practice of medicine, but his interest in it remained: Yermolinsky recalls his fastidiousness about washing his hands, his love of chemists' shops, the care with which he would select medicines from the nearby one on the Kropotkinskaya, and his humorous plans for insisting on a urinalysis for everyone instead of passports.[2] As a doctor he could hardly remain unaware of the increasing seriousness of his own condition.

It is impossible to know for certain exactly when he became aware of it. According to one source he diagnosed sclerosis of the kidneys as early as 1937, telling his wife he would die in 1939,[3] but one may doubt if this was an exact medical diagnosis at this stage. More probably his symptoms, which must have included high blood pressure, indicated it as a possibility, which he feared because of his knowledge of kidney disorders in his family: his father had died of nephrosclerosis at forty-eight, the age he himself would reach in 1939. At all events he was certainly not well for much of 1938 and by the beginning of 1939 things were getting worse: in January he complained in a letter to the composer Dunaevsky of a prickly kind of fever.[4]

1 **281**, pp. 177-8
2 For this and much of what follows, see **266**, pp. 93-7.
3 **449**, p. 535. This also gives the date for the completion of *The Master and Margarita*, referred to below.
4 **256**, p. 233

This did not stop him working. In 1937 and 1938 he had completed three libretti and assisted on the text and production of *Ivan Susanin*, apart from writing the adaptation of *Don Quixote* and trying urgently to finish *The Master and Margarita* (largely completed by the spring of 1939). He even produced a totally insignificant unsigned 'Children's Story' for the new year of 1939.[5] On the occasion of the fortieth anniversary of the founding of the Art Theatre he had also produced a choral tribute from the Bolshoy company. And now his friends at the Art Theatre began suggesting he write a play about Stalin, and his wife encouraged him. Finally he agreed, writing his last play, *Batumi*, in June.

After the work of that year he found himself under considerable nervous strain, and it was now that his illness rapidly began to get worse. On 10 September 1939, after a pain which had attacked his eyes, he went with his wife to Leningrad, hoping for a beneficial change of atmosphere. Here, however, there was a sudden deterioration in his sight, and the doctors reported nervous hypertension, the typical indication of nephrosclerosis, which was threatening to develop into uremia – its almost inevitable final stage. On their advice, Bulgakov returned to Moscow and the next day told Yermolinsky 'the weeks, the months, and even the dates which would determine the stages of his illness.' He started final corrections to *The Master and Margarita*. On 10 October he made his will, in favour of his wife. Yelena Sergeevna took over much of his business correspondence since, as she wrote in a number of identical letters dated 26 October, 'Mikhail Afanasievich is ill for the second month now – very seriously and he is threatened with loss of his sight. The doctors have forbidden him to undertake any business connected with the theatre at all.'[6]

In the last six months of Bulgakov's life his nervousness increased to the extent that he was afraid to go out alone. He had to wear dark glasses. Yanshin recollects the last time he saw him, having difficulty in crossing the street and unable to recognize him when he helped him across.[7] Even now, it seems, he would go to the theatre occasionally, when he felt a little better: to a rehearsal of *Khovanshchina* and a performance of *The Sleeping Beauty* at the Bolshoy. To his colleagues at the theatre he smilingly expressed his optimism that he would recover: 'You see, I have managed to deceive medicine after all.'[8] But he could hardly have believed this at this stage. He was forced to go into a sanatorium, and it seems now that once again Stalin took a personal hand in his life, ordering him to be taken to one where there were better doctors than in the place origi-

---

5 **175**. In **187**, folio 287. The choral tribute is mentioned in **268**.
6 In **187**, folio 251; see also **245**, pp. 251-2
7 Told to me by Yanshin personally
8 **372**, p. 394

ginally intended.[9] Thus at the end of November he was in hospital in Barvikha, to the east of Moscow. He returned home on 18 December. To an old friend he wrote: 'To tell you frankly and in secret, the thought gnaws at me that I have come home to die. It's not to my liking for one reason: it's agonizing, drawn-out and vulgar.'[10]

Yermolinsky describes visiting Bulgakov at this time and his half-humorous 'interviews' with him for the sake of recording some of the facts of his life for posterity. The children's writer, S. Marshak, also made his acquaintance. Other visitors were artists Dmitriev and Vilyams, playwrights Boris Erdman and Fayko (Bulgakov's neighbour). They would drink together, with Bulgakov pretending things were as they had always been, until such visits became too tiring for him. Once he quoted Nietzsche, to the effect that if life has not been a success for one then death would be a success. 'But I ask you, what will become of you after death if your life has not been successful?'

By 25 January 1940 – the last day he went outside with his wife – things were becoming worse. Kachalov, Tarasova, and Khmelyov from the Art Theatre wrote to Stalin's secretary, A.N. Poskryobyshev, to ask that Stalin should be told Bulgakov was dying.[11] Yermolinsky came to stay in the flat to relieve the strain on Yelena Sergeevna. Bulgakov found it increasingly difficult to sleep and had to take increasingly large doses of drugs, which Yermolinsky would fetch for him from the shop on the Kropotkinskaya. But he still tried to work, maintaining that one should continue to do so until losing consciousness. His main concern was still *The Master and Margarita*, to which he continued to make corrections, getting his wife to read it to him, dictating changes, adding the epilogue, and finally completing it. On 4 March he told his wife: 'It's true that I'm dying – what I would have written after *The Master and Margarita*!'[12] According to Popov, he was thinking of another play for the Art Theatre: 'Richard I,' about the downfall of an all-powerful man.

'How sad the evening earth!' the final chapter (before the epilogue) of *The Master and Margarita* begins: a passage written for the most part when Bulgakov was dying. 'How mysterious the mists over the bogs! Whoever has wandered in these mists, whoever suffered deeply before death, whoever flew over this earth burdened beyond human strength knows it. The weary one knows it. And he leaves without regret the mists of earth, its swamps and rivers, and yields himself

9 Told by Yelena Sergeevna to M. Michel Vassilieff. What follows is based partly on Popov's unpublished biography in **187**, folio 556.

10 **258**, p. 29; see also **379**, p. 169, and **448**, p. 454

11 **379**, p. 160 (the date above this letter is an error, corrected in the following issue of the journal)

12 Also told to M. Vassilieff

with an easy heart to the hands of death, knowing that it alone can bring surcease.'[13]

For the last month Bulgakov's organism could not take any food, and he drank largely lemon juice. His muscles were so painful that he could not bear to move, his dry skin so sensitive that anything touching it caused him agony. He could no longer help shouting out aloud with the pain, although, groaning, he would express his appreciation when his wife and Yermolinsky had to turn him over. He lay on a couch in his study naked except for a towel over his loins. 'He observed the picture of his illness,' Popov writes 'with the sharp attention of a writer ... Loving life and seized by fits of deep melancholy at the thought of the approaching end, already deprived of sight, he would fearlessly ask to be read to about Gogol's last terrible days and hours.' He was now completely blind, and sensitive to noise, so that the curtains remained closed.[14] He talked a little, of his childhood and student days, and he prayed too. Besides his wife, her children, and Yermolinsky, Dmitriev and Boris Erdman stayed in the flat.

Sometime before his death he was visited by the secretary of the Union of Soviet Writers, A. Fadeev, who, it seems, was deeply impressed and refused to believe he was dying. Bulgakov was a member of the union,[15] but Fadeev had not even known him. 'There's been an enormous misunderstanding,' he told Yermolinsky afterwards. 'I didn't know him. I had no right not to know him!' On a couple of occasions after that, he phoned asking if the union could give any assistance. It was too late.

Bulgakov died on 10 March 1940 at 4.50 p.m.; his last words: 'Forgive me, receive me!' 'We heard from our flat how he died,' his neighbour recalls. 'Alarmed voices, screams, crying. Late in the evening we could see from our balcony a green lamp covered with a shawl and people sleeplessly and sorrowfully illuminated by it.'[16]

Yelena Sergeevna's sorrow at her husband's death, after all her patience during his illness, suddenly erupted in a fit of violent anger against God who had allowed it, as she stormed round the apartment throwing the icons on the floor.[17] That night, Bulgakov's friend Nikolay Erdman came secretly to Moscow, from where he had been banished, and sat silently for two hours in the apart-

13 **100**, p. 383; see also **245**, p. 252
14 For this and some of what follows, see **488**.
15 He thus signs himself on his autobiography written in 1937, and there is no basis to reports that he was rejected from the union. **271**, p. 731, gives 11 November 1939 as the date of Fadeev's visit; **40** gives 10 October. **245**, p. 253, which gives 15 February 1940, is probably the most reliable.
16 **281**, p. 178
17 Told personally to Irina Ivanovna Bulgakova

ment before leaving again. The following morning there was a phone call from Stalin's office: 'Is it true that Bulgakov has died?' – and then silence after the reply. There were many visitors before the body was removed.

It was taken the day following his death to the house of the Union of Soviet Writers, where a death mask was made and, at 5 p.m., a civil funeral was held.[18] Wreaths and flowers had been sent from the major Moscow theatres which had performed Bulgakov's plays. The well-known writer V.V. Ivanov spoke on behalf of the Writers' Union, mentioning the great loss to the theatre in particular and the play *Pushkin*, which the Art Theatre was preparing for production. A.M. Fayko followed for the All-Union Commission on Drama, Theatre, and Cinema, talking of Bulgakov's qualities as a dramatist, mentioning in particular his novel *The Master and Margarita*, and giving what must surely be one of the best general characterizations:

I should like to say today that one of Mikhail Afanasievich's principal qualities was an inner, tender goodness – not a sentimental goodness, not sugary, not benevolently sweet and sickly towards people, but an exacting, avid, intelligent goodness. Such was his attitude both towards the material he wrote about and towards the people who surrounded him. He was very demanding of people, but deeply affectionate and covetous of the truly human.

He concluded by mentioning the research that lay behind many of his works. V.O. Toporkov then spoke for the Art Theatre, mentioning Bulgakov's work there and the forthcoming 900th performance of *Days of the Turbins*; B.A. Mordvinov spoke for the Bolshoy. The guard of honour, which then, by shifts, took its place at the coffin, consisted of writers, actors, and artists.[19]

The next day, 12 March 1940, Bulgakov was taken first to the Bolshoy Theatre and then to the Moscow Art Theatre, where most of the company was gathered. A number of them accompanied the coffin to the crematorium, where a short ceremony was again held at 5 p.m., with Olga Knipper-Chekhova putting on the flowers for the theatre and V.G. Sakhnovsky making a short speech in which he spoke of those plays by Bulgakov which were still in the repertory, noting once more the 900th performance of *Days of the Turbins* – which took place on 24 March, a mere two weeks after Bulgakov's death.

Fairly routine obituary notices appeared in the press, and only the paper of the Art Theatre, *Gor'kovets*, gave any real prominence to the death, reporting

18 For the following details, see **232**, **272**, and **372**, pp. 391-5.
19 Namely L.M. Leonov, V.V. Ivanov, N.P. Khmelyov, V.G. Sakhnovsky, Ya.L. Leontiev, V.Ya. Stanitsyn, A.O. Stepanova, S.Ya. Marshak, Yu.K. Olesha, Ts.L. Mansurova, A.O. Goryunov, B.L. Pasternak, P.V. Vilyams, V.V. Dmitriev, B.P. Erdman, N.M. Gorchakov, M.M. Yanshin, S.A. Yermolinsky

extensively on the funeral and including an article about Bulgakov by Pavel Markov.[20] Later, Anna Akhmatova wrote a commemorative poem, which long remained unpublished.

On 15 March Fadeev wrote to Yelena Sergeevna, expressing his personal regrets, particularly for his absence from the funeral which, he feared, some people had wrongly interpreted as having a political significance. He stressed the impression that his recent meeting with Bulgakov had made upon him: 'Both political people and literary people know that he was a man who did not burden himself, in his art or in his life, with political lies, that his path was sincere, organical, and if at the beginning of his path (and sometimes later) he did not see everything as it was in fact, then there's nothing surprising in that. It would have been worse if he had falsified.'[21] A somewhat ambiguous attitude – but Fadeev was in an official position, and one feels that he had a bad conscience over Bulgakov, recognizing in him perhaps the type of literary courage which he himself did not possess.

Bulgakov's grave in the Novodeviche cemetery in Moscow is amongst those of other members of the Moscow Art Theatre: Stanislavsky is but a short distance away. For twelve years there was no stone on it, until his widow came across the one that had stood on Gogol's grave in the old Danilovskoe cemetery, before his remains had also been transferred to the Novodeviche. The shape of the stone, of Black Sea granite and brought by Aksakov with tremendous difficulty from the Crimea for Gogol's grave, is symbolical: reminiscent of that of the 'bald mountain' on which Christ was crucified. Since 1952 it has stood on Bulgakov's grave, where Yelena Sergeevna too was buried after her death on 18 July 1970.[22]

BATUMI

In 1938 Markov and the theatrical scholar Vilenkin had suggested that Bulgakov should write a new play for the Art Theatre, but at that time he was unreceptive.[23] In the spring of 1939 they had approached him again, with the idea that he should write a play about Stalin in his youth, to celebrate his sixtieth birthday that year. Bulgakov was unhappy with the idea and resisted stubbornly, but it seems that his wife joined with the others in trying to persuade him and finally he gave way – in the hope, perhaps, that it would pave the way for the performance of some of his other plays and, more particularly, for the publication of

20 **370**; see also **191**
21 **271**, pp. 158-9; also published in **296**, p. 401, and **448**, pp. 458-9
22 **339**, pp. 61-2
23 For this and much of what follows, see **448**, p. 470. I am also grateful to K.L. Rudnitsky and M.M. Yanshin for some of the information here, and to Carl and Ellendea Proffer for providing me with a copy of the play.

The Master and Margarita. Thus in June 1939 he signed a contract which gave him until 28 August to deliver *Batumi.*[24] The fact that he agreed to a mere two months for the work without allowing himself more time for revisions (even if he had basically completed *Don Quixote* in a similar period) itself suggests he was anxious to finish with it quickly so he could return to his more important concerns.

Most of the play was written within a month, and on 2 July he was able to read five completed scenes to Khmelyov, Kalishyan (director of the theatre), and his sister-in-law Olga Bokshanskaya. 'Yesterday morning a phone call from Khmelyov,' Yelena Sergeevna wrote in her diary on the 3rd. 'He asked to hear the play. An excited, joyful tone – finally a play by M.A. again in the theatre!'[25] On 9 July its art committee phoned asking Bulgakov to read to them in two days' time as much of the play as was ready. Yelena Sergeevna wrote to Vilenkin that 'It will be almost completed, bec. for him everything is very clear in his mind, and he'll now start working day and night, says, "I won't sleep, but I'll finish it, I'll set out on paper what I have found by my mind and heart."' (She indicated also that Kalishyan considered everything in the play completely correct and exact from a political and historical point of view.) A number of members of the theatre were present for the reading, which went well.[26] Now, as Bulgakov too wrote to Vilenkin, there remained ten days of intensive work to finish the corrections. He was tired, however. 'From time to time I go to Serebryany Bor, have a swim and return immediately. What will happen about a real rest – we don't know anything as yet.' *Batumi* was finished on time, and read to a special meeting of the theatre's party organization on 27 July 1939.[27]

The play opens with a scene showing Stalin in the seminary where he trained for the priesthood, and then goes on to the underground Bolshevik movement in Batumi at the turn of the century, with Stalin's subsequent imprisonment, exile to Siberia, and escape. Young Stalin is the intrepid revolutionary, but he is no more idealized than other heroes of socialist realist works. Yanshin has referred to this as a very human play, and everyone in the theatre was optimistic about its success as they prepared to put it on.

On 15 August a whole group from the theatre set out for Tbilisi and the south to study the locality. Unknown to them, however, *Batumi* had been banned the previous day, and at the first station they received a telegram with the news. All returned to Moscow in haste, except for Bulgakov and his wife,

24 See **187**, folio 542
25 Quoted in **429**, p. 27. Also translated in **9**, p. xxvii, where its authenticity is questioned.
   This is, however, confirmed by Yelena Sergeevna's letter to Vilenkin in **187**, folio 542.
26 For this and what follows, see **448**, p. 454.
27 The poster announcing this is in **187**, folio 252.

who intended to go on to the south and have a holiday – but this was cut short by Bulgakov's worsening health. Apparently, there was no formal, written ban on the play, but clearly an oral expression of disapproval was sufficient. This, according to Yelena Sergeevna, was given by Zhdanov, who said: 'A fictitious hero. While Dzhugashvili [that is, Stalin] is alive the play will not be shown.' Other reports say that Stalin had said: 'All children and all young people are alike. There's no need to put on a play about the young Stalin.'[28] Another possibility is that the play showed Stalin, in prison, denouncing conditions there – which might remind those in the know that conditions in Stalin's own prisons were far worse; or simply that the contrast between his youthful democratic ideals and his actual police state was too great.

Batumi has never been performed, and indeed for some reason – for it is now politically harmless – there is considerable hesitation in the Soviet Union about even making the manuscript available to scholars. Amongst those who have read it, it is generally accepted that it is at best mediocre and not at all typical of Bulgakov's usual style, even if he made a sincere attempt to depict Stalin realistically. It is, indeed, more of a standard socialist realist play with a strong propaganda element: showing the determination of the striking workers, Stalin's tireless efforts at agitation, the brutal suppression by the authorities. Not that it is a poor play in itself, for it is written with Bulgakov's usual professional competence – but within a genre that is itself uninspired. It is distinguished by a certain humour, particularly in scenes of the military governor receiving various perplexing telegrams about the troubled situation in Batumi; of Nicolas II discussing with one of his ministers what should be done; or, on a more personal level, of an old man who thinks Stalin is using his illegal press to print counterfeit money, and who then suggests Stalin should become a Mohammedan. But above all the play is a demonstration of a theme, the familiar one of the communist hero: dramatically effective but relying purely on outward stage action – if anything more reminiscent of Bulgakov's opera libretti than of his other plays. Its main weakness lies in its characters, who are totally uninteresting. Even Stalin is a stereotype, with no development, no conflicts, no hesitations – indeed, with the substitution of another name this could be about any revolutionary hero, for there is no real picture of Stalin himself.

Of course, Bulgakov could hardly have done otherwise: to give a sincere personal interpretation of Stalin's character might have produced fascinating results but could also have been tantamount to suicide. To what extent *Batumi* represented for Bulgakov a compromise with his artistic principles, and how much of

28 **429**, p. 27, and 7, p. xxi; other information supplied by M.O. Chudakova and
M. Vassilieff

an unsuccessful attempt it was to flatter Stalin, it is difficult to judge: it seems simply that it was something that others persuaded him was expedient to write, but which he himself did not take all that seriously.

THE MASTER AND MARGARITA

Sometime towards the end of Bulgakov's life his neighbour Gabrilovich had asked what he was writing. 'Oh, I'm writing something,' he had answered, 'just a trivial little thing.' This 'little thing' had developed over twelve years and had involved an enormous amount of research, which included the history of ancient Rome and of early Christianity.[29] Many of the books which were probably familiar to Bulgakov from his childhood in the family of a professor of theology must have been reread and studied. Eight separate versions had been produced.

The Master and Margarita, in its final, complete version, revolves around four days when Moscow is visited by the devil, referred to by the somewhat obscure name – found principally in Goethe's *Faust* – of Woland. With him are his assistants, Azazello, Koroviev (also referred to as Fagot), an enormous tom-cat, Behemoth, and a vampire maid, Hella. Among bureaucrats, petty crooks, and those simply concerned with personal gain these 'gangsters' cause havoc. But they give aid and protection to a persecuted writer in an asylum, the Master, and to his love, Margarita, after she has agreed to act as hostess for Satan's Ball. A hack poet, Ivan Homeless – who introduces us to the whole story – is brought to a deeper understanding of life and becomes a 'disciple' of the Master. Central to the book is the Master's novel about Christ and Pontius Pilate, the chapters of which form part of Bulgakov's text and conclude simultaneously with the story about the Master in the final chapter.

A fascinating account of the different stages of this work has been given by the Soviet scholar M.O. Chudakova.[30] In 1928 or early 1929 Bulgakov had begun a novel which is referred to variously as 'The Black Magician' or 'The Engineer's Hoof.' In it, the adventures of the devil in Moscow were used as a basis for satire; already, although considerably more limited in form, the book had a number of recognizable similarities with the later *The Master and Margarita*. The devil, called Woland, appeared to one Berlioz and an Antosha Bezrodny – later Ivanushka – and in the second chapter, 'The Gospel according to Woland,' related to them the story of Christ's execution (including additional material which later

29 **281**, p. 179, and **491**, p. 98; **436** attempts to list some of the books he must have read.
30 See **245**, on which I have relied considerably in what follows. See also L.Ye. Belozerskaya's unpublished memoirs and **449**, pp. 535, 561. A number of points in this section also reflect my views expressed in **524**.

disappeared). Berlioz was then killed under a tram. The fifth chapter (the fourth in a second version), which was prepared separately for publication in *Nedra* as '*Mania furibunda*' (submitted on 8 May 1929: it never appeared), later became 'The Affair at Griboyedov's.' There were other characters too – but as yet no Master or Margarita – and many individual incidents which would go into the final novel.

Bulgakov in part destroyed the two versions, such as they were, in 1930 (they have since been reconstructed). But in 1931 he evidently returned to the idea: and in his notes the name of Margarita is met for the first time, while a nameless figure accompanying her is introduced; we also find a new title 'Consultant with a Hoof.' By late 1932 or early 1933 another version was ready, with the future Master now referred to simply as 'Faust.' Further suggested titles were 'The Great Chancellor,' 'Satan,' 'Here I Am,' 'Hat with a Feather,' 'The Black Theologian,' 'He's Appeared,' 'The Foreigner's Horseshoe.' By June 1934 Bulgakov was writing, 'But in my head there roam Margarita and a cat and flights through the air'[31] – the Margarita, of course, who had been suggested by his own love affair and marriage with Yelena Sergeevna Shilovskaya. The same year he began the novel's 'conclusion,' and for the first time we find the new hero referred to as 'Master.' Work continued over the next few years, with a fourth, and then, in 1937, a fifth version (entitled 'Prince of Darkness') produced. These remained incomplete, but now, with the approach of illness, Bulgakov put aside *Theatrical Romance* and made a determined effort to complete his major work. A sixth version, with the final title of *The Master and Margarita*, was begun in 1937 and completed the following year. Most of the major changes had by now been made, the compositional form of a novel within a novel had become clearer, and by June 1938 Bulgakov was preparing it for typing, dictating it to his wife's sister, Olga Bokshanskaya:[32] the work was finished by 24 June. In November he read two chapters to his theatrical friend Vilenkin, and the following May, after another change and the completion of the epilogue, he was able to read the entire work to a number of his friends. After the onset of the last stage of his illness in September 1939, he started on the final improvements, making changes and corrections up to the time of his death, with his wife reading to him and him dictating alterations; the epilogue was included only after the manuscript had been typed and bound.

After Bulgakov's death *The Master and Margarita* remained unknown except to a handful of his friends. One copy remained with his widow, Yelena Sergeevna, another he gave for safe keeping to F. Mikhalsky, the director of the Art

31 See chapters 7 and 9; also **491**, p. 99
32 See also **34**, p. 273

Theatre museum.[33] When a newly formed commission for the publication of Bulgakov's works became active in the mid-fifties, its members decided, not unreasonably, to bring out some of his less controversial things first. The publication of *The Master and Margarita* was the height of their achievement: even after the appearance of its first part, in the November 1966 issue of *Moskva*, they feared that the second might not be allowed. But it duly followed in January 1967. According to Yelena Sergeevna (whose dressmaker was Khrushchev's daughter-in-law), it was Khrushchev himself who authorized publication. Even so, the work appeared with many deletions: most for reasons of censorship but some too, apparently, because it had to be shortened to make space for other material in the journal.

The novel's appearance created a sensation and *Moskva* was sold out immediately. The demand for it was so great that public readings were given at once. In very short order it gave rise to a whole series of reviews and critical articles, both in the Soviet Union and abroad. Whole debates started on its interpretation.[34] It was *The Master and Margarita* which overnight made Bulgakov's reputation: his rehabilitation seemed complete. Within a short time the book was translated into a number of European languages. In English it appeared in two versions, which led to some dispute between the respective publishers. Grove Press immediately translated the *Moskva* version with all its omissions; but in the meantime Collins-Harvill and Harper and Row, who had earlier secured translation rights, were offered a copy of the uncensored text of the novel, apparently obtained through the efforts of Yelena Sergeevna's nephew in Hamburg. The type was reset to produce the longer, unexpurgated volume.[35] *The Master and Margarita* has become Bulgakov's best-known work, whose popularity may be judged by the fact that the Hungarian version alone went into three editions with a total printing of 450,000.[36] In 1973 it was republished in the Soviet Union in the collection of *Novels*, in its most complete form: with the original deletions restored and even including a few minor passages which had not appeared anywhere previously. Two films have been made of it: a French-Yugoslav production in 1973 by A. Petrovic, with Ugo Tognazzi as the Master and Mimsy Farmer as Margarita – highly successful as a film but differing greatly from the book – and a more faithful rendition in Poland by A. Wajda in 1974,

---

33 For this and what follows I am grateful to Vl. Lakshin, Irina Ivanovna Bulgakova, and K.L. Rudnitsky.
34 For some of the literary arguments, see **482, 304, 338**.
35 See **422, 317**. Quotations and spellings of names are from **100**, except for the expurgated passages when **101** was used. Page references, and a reference to **101** where appropriate, are given in the text.
36 **339**, p. 58

entitled 'Pilate and Others.' A controversial stage version of the book opened on 6 April 1977 at the Theatre on the Taganka in Moscow, and (reminiscent of the old days!) was severely criticized by *Pravda*. In England, an opera entitled 'Volandt' is being prepared.

The number of critical articles since the book's appearance is staggering: for indeed *The Master and Margarita* seems to demand interpretation. Understandably, some communist criticisms have tended to tone down the religious aspects and accentuate the social ones, while a number of Western articles have taken a more religious, sometimes anti-Soviet, line. But the sum total of these commentaries is confusing: ultimately one is forced to return to the book itself and recognize that, despite the intellectual exercises it can give rise to, it is not exhausted by interpretation. *The Master and Margarita* is not a tidy work, nor does it present a logically structured argument: like many a great book, ultimately its greatness lies in its power to evoke responses intuitively from the reader. It also contains a great deal of simple entertainment, fantasy, and comedy which has no inherent significance. But despite the, at times, bewildering mass of detail, we may none the less distinguish a number of essential themes and even a basic philosphy.

At the most general level *The Master and Margarita* is concerned with the conflict of the spiritual with the material world of everyday – a theme that, in one form or another, underlies the whole of Bulgakov. Man, in society, prefers to rely on himself and thinks he can ignore spiritual issues. 'But what troubles me,' Woland says to Ivan Homeless in the first, essential conversation with him and an editor Berlioz, 'is this: if there is no God, then, you might ask, who governs the life of men and, generally, the entire situation here on earth?' 'Man himself governs it,' Homeless replies (pp. 10-11). The whole book is a demonstration of the fact that man does *not* govern the world – although he usually thinks he does. The trouble is that man is mortal, even – as Woland puts it – 'suddenly mortal,' unable to guarantee his own next day, which is demonstrated by Berlioz' dramatic death by decapitation under a tram, as Woland has foreseen. In Moscow it is Woland, the devil, who represents the spiritual; in ancient Jerusalem Yeshua-ha-Nozri, Christ himself: 'And keep in mind that Jesus existed,' Woland says. Yeshua, in the Master's novel as recounted by Woland, in fact echoes Woland's thoughts, saying – when Pilate tells him his life hangs by a hair that he can cut – 'There, too, you are mistaken ... You must agree that the hair can surely be cut only by him who had hung it?' (p. 26).

In the Soviet Union, of course, 'atheism does not surprise anyone,' as Berlioz says (p. 9), and the figure of Christ, who is at least troublesome historically, is conveniently dismissed as a myth. But in the book those who ignore the spiritual are none the less confronted with it, and its manifestations become a source of

262 Mikhail Bulgakov

discomfort and trouble. The spiritual must be either accepted or explained away, otherwise the individual remains in a state close to 'schizophrenia,' and not for nothing do many of the characters in Moscow land up in Doctor Stravinsky's psychiatric clinic until the dilemma is solved. Much as people may wish to deny it, the spiritual remains a powerful influence over men. This is evident too in the chapters set in Jerusalem. 'Surely you are not trying to tell me that all this [the military security arrangements] ... can have been evoked by that miserable thief Bar-Abba?' (101, p. 48) the high priest Kaiyapha (Caiaphas) says to Pilate, in a speech deleted in the censored version: presumably because it shows too clearly the power of religion and the futility of efforts (comparable to the Soviet anti-religious campaign) to suppress it.

In the end, it is the spiritual that triumphs, of necessity, for it is eternal. In *The White Guard* Bulgakov had written: 'Everything passes away – suffering, pain, blood, hunger, and pestilence. The sword will pass away too, but the stars will still remain when the shadows of our presence and our deeds have vanished from the earth. There is no man who does not know that. Why, then, will we not turn our eyes toward the stars? Why?'[37] The passage might almost be a description of the ending of *The Master and Margarita*, with the group of riders (the devil and his company) leaving the earth, surrounded by stars and the light of the moon, and the departure of the Master and Margarita for their eternal abode. The heroes of this novel are those who are aware of more than trivial and temporary issues. For linked with the idea of eternity is the whole question of immortality – and the kind of immortality one achieves. In this respect Pilate is an interesting hero, for he is indeed concerned with immortality: ironically his fame has come to rest not on his genuinely great deeds but on his one cowardly execution. Yet at the end he is allowed to find his fulfilment in eternity, when his desire for communion with the man he has executed is granted. The Master and Margarita too are given what they most desire: 'peace' (not 'light,' which for one reason or another they have not deserved) and sharing each other's fate. In all of this we find a fundamental optimism about the basis of the world. 'Everything will turn out right,' Woland tells Margarita. 'That's what the world is built on' (p. 386).

It will be obvious that Bulgakov's whole conception is broader than that of traditional Christianity, and indeed Yeshua-ha-Nozri is a character in his own right differing considerably from the Jesus of the gospels. Yeshua, like the Master too, is timid, does not want to die, and has no following except for his one disciple Matthu Levi (Matthew), who 'makes up' all the stories about him with the result that people are confused. 'I am beginning to fear,' Yeshua says with ironical understatement, 'that this confusion will continue for a very long time'

37 **168**, p. 297 Fatal E = Unnatural "Natural" event.
  · H of D = Reversion of Experiment
M & M · Affirmation of the Higher order.

(p. 21). Other details have also been changed, although the traditional story is referred to as well: Pilate does not wash his hands, for example, but rubs them 'as though washing them' (p. 32); the traitor Yehudah (Judas) does not hang himself but is murdered on the command of Pilate, who none the less suggests he might have committed suicide. Various possibilities have been suggested to account for the changes in the story: the fact that it is (in part, at least) told by the devil, who traditionally lies (not very convincing, for elsewhere he does not lie when talking seriously), or that it is the story seen from Pilate's point of view. Bulgakov, however, is simply using the gospels as a source, writing anew an old story and in so doing revitalizing it, establishing all the more firmly Christ as an actual, living person. Yeshua, shown as a wandering, simple-minded philosopher, is none the less an impressive figure. 'Before us,' one critic writes, 'there arises no mythologized, no legendary Christ but an ordinary man with a name which has not yet become a symbol.'[38] At the same time we have little difficulty in recognizing him as divine: indeed Pilate sees a kind of transfiguration with Yeshua appearing in a crown, although his face then becomes that of the Roman emperor, exemplifying Pilate's dilemma.

Bulgakov presents us with facts that differ in detail but ultimately do nothing to alter the fundamental message of the gospels, which essentially is set out in the first three chapters, in the all-important conversations between Woland, Berlioz, and Homeless, and between Yeshua and Pilate. Yeshua's basic philosophy involves a belief in God, the coming of the 'kingdom of truth,' and love of man. For him, all are 'good people,' even those who act cruelly, or betray him. Pilate has no such beliefs. 'The trouble,' Yeshua says, 'is that you keep to yourself too much and have lost all faith in men ... Your life is too barren, Hegemon' (p. 24). His is a philosophy, like Bulgakov's, involving the importance of the individual as opposed to the needs of the state – for which reason he is crucified. As Yeshua explains: 'every form of authority means coercion over men and ... a time will come when there shall be neither Caesars, nor any other rulers. Man will come into the kingdom of truth and justice, where there will be no need for any authority' (p. 30). Pilate represents the state and, although as a man he may hate his role, in his official capacity he can recognize only expediency. Yet ultimately all temporal power is an illusion – as Woland says, its influence 'microscopic' in comparison with his own, so that those who wield it 'become quite laughable, even pathetic' (101, p. 288). This is certainly true of Pilate who, even within the limited time of his life-span, is forced by his position to do not as he wants but as the high priest Kaiyapha has decided, and then to resort to subterfuge to take his revenge on a man he despises.

38 197. An interesting if far-fetched interpretation is given in 361.

It is in the manifestations of temporal power, as seen in the novel, that we can find most similarity between ancient Jerusalem and Moscow under Stalin: where Christ's words about authority disappearing sound like a hollow parody of a communist theory. For both societies represent dictatorships of a different kind, and the parallels are clear – however much they were toned down in the censored version. In Jerusalem it is Kaiyapha who is spokesman for political and religious orthodoxy. 'While I, the High Priest of Judea, am alive, I will allow no profanation of the faith, I will protect the people!' (p. 38). In Moscow the same attitude is expressed in different words by the Master's critics. (It was much the same argument that critics in the RAPP had used against Bulgakov himself.) Here, of course, power has its secret police, whose activities are constantly referred to: people inexplicably disappearing from the fateful apartment where Woland will take up residence; a theatrical trial of the house committee chairman (yet another!), Nikanor Ivanovich, involving foreign currency; police agents on guard outside the apartment; a paid spy, Baron Meigel. Margarita dreams that the Master is in exile, the place of which she equates with hell on earth (a deliberately vague reference none the less deleted from the *Moskva* version). But in Jerusalem, Pilate has his secret police too, in Aphranius. In both societies there are also the informers: Yehudah denounces Christ for thirty pieces of silver, while in Moscow one Aloisy Mogarych makes friends with the Master[39] only so that he may denounce him and acquire his flat.

The problem is, of course, that individuals barter away their individuality to the state, through their desire for riches, comfort, or security – or through plain cowardice, which Pilate, who epitomizes it in his relationship to Yeshua, comes to understand as the most terrible of human sins. For Yeshua's 'good people' are shown to be weak, and in the Moscow episodes their all too human vices are unmercifully satirized, providing much of the comedy in the book: Nikanor Ivanovich with his willingness to take bribes, for example, and his philistine attitude towards culture – 'Who's going to pay the rent – Pushkin?' (101, p. 190); Margarita's neighbour, Nikolay Ivanovich, with his absurd advances to his 'Venus,' her maid Natasha; or the woman who spills oil causing Berlioz to slip under the tram, Annushka, nicknamed 'The Plague' because she causes a scandal wherever she appears. 'Scraggy Annushka the Plague,' one perceptive Soviet commentator writes, 'with her invariable can and purse in her hands – the personified spirit of kitchen gossip, elusive intrigue, and all kinds of mean tricks which are wilfully performed – is the most "eternal" personnage amongst Bulgakov's satirical figures.'[40] With some of these figures, like bartender Andrey Fokich Somov, who

39 The passage making this clear is found only in **6**, pp. 560-1.
40 **364**, p. 168. The quotation that follows is on p. 166.

is left with money that has turned into just strips of paper, we can even sympathize. 'But how trivial is this paper money,' we read, 'when with Fokich there is speaking eternity itself.' For one of the themes of the book is surely that Christ is the saviour of precisely such people – and that the temporal state does not provide a substitute. Thus Woland has arrived in Moscow to find out what the Moscow inhabitants are like and if they have changed inside. Watching the audience at the Variety Theatre, where he performs, he finds their only concern is for money and material goods despite the aims of communism to transform them, although they are capable at times of compassion: 'They're ordinary people, in fact they remind me very much of their predecessors, except that the housing shortage has soured them ...' (101, p. 147).

A great deal in their behaviour can be explained by the material conditions, of a state based on materialism. The housing crisis can lead to crookery involving 'five dimensions' – changing three rooms into six (a story Koroviev tells Margarita) – or to Aloisy Mogarych and one Poplavsky doing all they can to obtain the Master's and Berlioz' apartments respectively (the latter mocked delightfully by Koroviev in his exaggerated display of the feeling that Poplavsky should have, but totally lacks, towards his dead nephew). Life, generally, is not very joyful. Sturgeon at the theatre can be 'of second freshness.' Good products are sold in shops for foreign currency (as is still the case today), to the disadvantage of those that do not have any, as Behemoth and Koroviev point out.

It is the state too which has tried to foster certain attitudes, which also receive their share of attention. Foreigners, such as Woland, are for that fact alone treated with suspicion. Busybodies like master-of-ceremonies Bengalsky and a theatrical official in the Variety Theatre can self-importantly make socially 'correct' comments and demand proper explanations, whether these are desired or not – but here the reader is allowed his sense of gratification as, in contrast to real life, these figures are put down. An office director goes overboard on instigating clubs of different kinds which the employees are forced to join – and is parodied by Koroviev, who founds a choral club and sets them all singing against their will, so that they cannot stop. Bureaucracy is such that an empty suit can continue to write resolutions, which are all approved by the suit's owner when he reappears. Official attitudes are satirized too. 'Remove the document – and you remove the man' (101, p. 329), Koroviev says, and the Master repeats it. Belief in documents is such that Berlioz' uncle Poplavsky, when ordered to produce his passport by the tom-cat Behemoth, immediately does so. Elsewhere, Behemoth parodies lip-service to a cause and well-known political phrases: '"Of course, messire," said the cat. "If you think it wasn't very grand, I immediately find myself agreeing with you"' – 'History will be my judge' (101, pp. 315, 316). The police too are constantly satirized, particularly at the end when they come up with a satisfactory 'rational explanation' for events which does not succeed in explaining anything; when cats are arrested in case they might be Behemoth; and so, too, is anyone whose name sounds like Koroviev or Woland. Such a society has neatly been summed up by the English scholar D. Piper: 'In conditions where the existence of right and wrong, of good and evil, are denied, where writers masquerading as masters cannot recognise Woland for what he is, where a concern for the blessings of existence is the accepted modus vivendi, then into this moral vacuum a figure of *zlo* [evil] will inevitably step and people will lack the spiritual equipment to combat him.'[41]

In all of this there are a number of allusions to actual persons or events, and elsewhere Piper (who regards the book as 'an aesthetic interpretation of the relationship between Bulgakov, his third wife and Stalin') tries to identify various figures: Woland – Stalin, Fagot – Molotov, Hella – his wife, Azazello – Kaganovich, Behemoth – Voroshilov, and so on.[42] All this is somewhat fanciful, but there are none the less a few deliberate allusions at least to Stalin: Pilate's toast to Caesar, for example – 'For us, for thee, Caesar, father of the Romans, most beloved and best of all men!' (p. 317), the last half significantly deleted in the censored version – is remarkably similar to those addressed to Stalin.[43] There are also a number of more veiled allusions to Soviet life: to the Lubyanka (the infamous prison and headquarters of the secret police), to the orgies which were rumoured to take place in Moscow in the late twenties and early thirties (compare Satan's Ball), and so on. And Baron Meigel is based on an actual spy, Baron Shteiger, whose job was to listen in to social conversations of foreign diplomats.

The target for Bulgakov's bitterest satire, however, is once again the literary and theatrical world. 'Dostoevsky is immortal!' Behemoth says (p. 362) – but few of the writers here are concerned with immortality, for it is those who conform who enjoy the comforts and advantages. At the 'Griboedov House,' the luxurious headquarters of MASSOLIT, the literary union, the offices seem to be devoted mainly to vacation trips, and writers squabble over getting rooms in the vacation village of Perelygino. The restaurant is renowned far and wide, and it is suggested this too is a hell on earth, presided over by its Satan, the manager Archibald Archibaldovich. What is important is not a writer's talent but his membership card, as is proved by Koroviev and Behemoth when they try to get in. Talent, they imagine, would be unwelcome. 'Can you imagine the furore when

41 **433**, p. 19
42 **432**, pp. 136, 142-51
43 See **468** and, for what follows, **216**, p. 406. (The details on Baron Meigel were also confirmed by Yelena Sergeevna in a conversation with M. Michel Vassilieff. I am grateful to Dr N.E. Andreyev for pointing out that the correct name is Shteiger, not Shteingel, as **216** has it.)

one of them will, as a starter, present the reading public with an *Inspector General* or, if worst comes to worst, a *Yevgeny Onegin*?' (p. 361). For such works, critical of the society in which they were written, are not required: the successful writers are those who have the 'correct' attitude (such as Berlioz is trying to explain to Ivan in the first chapter) or who can produce poems to order like the poet Ryukhin, who admits he does not believe in anything he writes. The Master himself is persecuted for writing a novel on an inadmissible theme, Pilate and Christ. 'In this day and age?' Woland parodies official literary attitudes. 'Couldn't you have chosen another subject?' (101, p. 326). The critics attack the Master unmercifully, even though his novel is not being published, and 'In literally every line of those articles one could detect a sense of falsity, of unease, in spite of their confident and threatening tone. I couldn't help feeling – and the conviction grew stronger the more I read – that the people writing those articles were not saying what they had really wanted to say and that *this* was the cause of their fury' (101, p. 167). Clearly, this was the same as had happened in Bulgakov's own life but here, in a perfect piece of wish-fulfilment, Margarita, as an invisible flying witch, is allowed to avenge the Master and wreak havoc on the flat of one of these critics.

For ultimately in this novel, justice triumphs, whether in Moscow or ancient Jerusalem. Ill-doers are punished, on a minor or major level according to their deserts. The greedy have their gains taken away from them. Fools and hypocrites are discomfitted. Yehuda of Kerioth and Baron Meigel are executed. Berlioz is given what he believes in – nothingness.

As opposed to all this, there stands, in Jerusalem, the eternal figure of Yeshua; in Moscow that of the Master, the eternal artist, master perhaps in the sense of a master in a masonic order, as Lakshin has suggested.[44] Here we have the same problem that is the basis for Bulgakov's plays about Pushkin and Molière, the conflict between the artist and the apparatus of state. As the American scholar Ewa Thompson points out, the Master stands apart from the pettiness which rules other people's lives because he has no time for it, being totally involved in creativity; underlying it all is 'Bulgakov's awareness of the contest between grandeur and pettiness, the truth and the lie, strength and weakness.'[45] Because of his novel, the Master – like other sincere writers – is imprisoned, and then finds himself in an asylum. As a man he is broken, cowed by the system, without dreams or inspiration, but his novel, in which he has tried to write the truth as he understands it, exists. 'Manuscripts don't burn' (p. 300), Woland says, probably the most famous line in the book. The novel is read, acted upon in the

44 337, pp. 302-3
45 503, pp. 62, 64

world beyond time. For art too is eternal, and in the same way Matthu Levi's parchment, which Yeshua wished him to burn, is saved and has become the basis for the gospels.

There are other characters, too, who stand apart from the self-seeking philistinism of the majority, realizing there is more to life than money or position, and Bulgakov here upholds the necessity for unorthodoxy and resistance to commonly accepted ideas. Margarita, the heroine, is a stronger figure than the Master: practical, romantic, sensual. Referred to from the first time we see her as a 'witch,' she willingly becomes one, is happy to make a bargain with the devil, and rejoices in her freedom from normal restraints. Her passionate nature is evident in the violence of her attack on the critic Latunsky's flat and her attempts to claw at the face of the Master's denouncer, Aloisy Mogarych; and in her admiration for Azazello: 'I like speed and nakedness .... Like a shot from a Mauser – boom! Ah, how he shoots!' (p. 374). Proud (refusing to ask Woland for favours which he does not offer), compassionate, and impulsive (begging that one of the sinners at Satan's Ball be released from her punishment, and later that Pilate too should be set free), Margarita has that independent spirit which for Bulgakov represents the height of humanity – and we may be reminded that in many ways she is based on the woman he married. (Her background, we might note – her important husband, comparative wealth – is similar to that of Bulgakov's wife before their marriage.)

The third major hero in Moscow is Ivan Homeless, who after giving up writing bad verses gains a realization of the importance of a world beyond that of everyday reality, and finally becomes a professor at the Institute of History and Philosophy. Several critics have seen in him the simple, ordinary man comparable to the 'Foolish Ivanushka' of Russian folk-tales, and we may too be reminded, on a more serious level, of Sancho Panza and his receptiveness to Don Quixote's ideals. It is indeed in Ivan that Bulgakov's optimism shows most clearly. Not outstanding, not naturally courageous, he none the less becomes the Master's 'disciple,' and the 'recorder' of his story in the same way as Matthu Levi is that of Christ's. For he is the basic link on which the book hangs: opening and closing the story, hearing Woland's account of Christ and Pilate, presenting the reader with the Master, dreaming of a further chapter in the novel, and, finally, receiving the Master's benediction and Margarita's kiss of gratitude. At the end, knowing he is 'powerless against this spring full moon,' he is first tormented by the sight of Nikolay Ivanovich (his opposite: name and patronymic reversed), who has failed to grasp his one opportunity to follow his 'Venus'; then he dreams again of Pilate walking with Christ, cf the Master and his love. We might even see the whole story as his dream, his particular insight. Or we might see the Master (historian turned poet) as a double for Ivan (poet turned historian), with the implication that the great artist is but an extension of the ordinary man – for the Master first appears at the end of the chapter suggestively entitled 'Ivan Splits in Two.' All in all, Ivan is the personification of man's susceptibility to spiritual truth.

Much of the discussion of the book has naturally centred around the role of the devil. If one accepts that, in Moscow, he is the representative of the spiritual, is he in fact the best? How can a traditional spirit of darkness, of evil, be a power of good, except perhaps unwillingly, as indicated by the epigraph taken from Goethe? It is here perhaps that there is the greatest disagreement, between the critics who consider Woland as the traditional figure of evil (maintaining that he misleads the Master and Margarita, and that good is brought about in spite of him) and those who see him as acting essentially for the good of mankind and hence not in any way an evil spirit. Here the writer must state that he belongs decisively to those who would place the devil on the side of the angels. Elsewhere I have tried to show that Bulgakov's devil is closer to the Old Testament concept of Satan rather than the New: the angel of God who tempts and tries man rather than the fallen angel concerned only with working evil. (All early Jewish writings, in fact, point to the fundamental unity of God and the devil.[46]) Thus Woland is not shown as opposed to God's will – indeed he carries it out by granting the Master peace as requested – but only as punishing, in most cases purely by temporary discomfiture, those who are guilty of greed, self-interest, and petty stupidity. Good and evil (light and darkness) as such are a fundamental philosophical problem in the novel. Woland indeed complains that Matthu Levi seems not to recognize the existence of shadows or evil, which are necessary to give meaning to light and good: 'What would your good be doing if there were no evil, and what would the earth look like if shadows disappeared from it?' (p. 368). For in Bulgakov's world good and evil are seen as two sides of a single moral problem. Woland on the one hand and Yeshua on the other are similarly part of one unified spiritual view of life: their function may be different – Woland, we might note, is unable to forgive sin since 'Every department must take care of its own affairs' (p. 296) – but the reality they represent is the same.

There are further implications in such a gnostic view of the world. After all, 'Shadows are cast by objects and people' – people who 'sin' because of their freedom gained by the 'original sin' of Adam and Eve in the Garden, when they ate of the tree of knowledge of good and evil. The more traditional view of the devil is that he too rebelled against God in much the same way, and hence becomes 'Prince of the World,' where innocence is rejected in favour of experience: at

46 See **316**, pp. 158-9

Satan's Ball Woland plays his more traditional role of master of the damned. (Thompson considers him as a devil in the romantic tradition of Lermontov.) Significantly, the most important source on which the book relies is the Faust tradition, with its obvious links to gnosticism. For Faust, of course, is the great rebel, standing for striving, rebellious man himself. Throughout the book there are constant references to Goethe's *Faust*: the names Woland and Margarita ('Gretchen'), the references to a poodle, to a homunculus, and the epigraph, to mention only a few.[47] It is possible to equate Woland with Lucifer or Satan; Azazello with his servant Mephistopheles – with whom Margarita, usurping Faust's role, makes the pact: 'Really, I would pawn my soul to the devil to find out whether he is alive or dead' (p. 242). It has been suggested that Koroviev too is based on Faust, now in the service of the devil as his 'interpreter.' In the sense that the Master is a creative artist, man's closest attempt at rivalling God's powers, he too may be seen as another incarnation of Faust.[48] And here we find the key to the whole book for, as we have seen, it is the individual non-conformists who are Bulgakov's heroes, those who rebel – whether against God or man. It is totally logical, then, that it should be the devil who aids the Master and Margarita, and at the end that they should be granted 'peace' and not 'light,' which in the traditional Christian sense they have not deserved, and probably would not desire. Healthy gnosticism, a total acceptance of good and evil as necessary for mankind, is seen as a positive force, as opposed to doctrinaire narrow-mindedness; one only need have faith that 'everything will turn out right.' There can be little doubt that this reflects Bulgakov's own religious attitude, for he has no time for orthodoxy in any area of life: it is the thinking, struggling man whom he admires, and this book is ultimately an expression of his whole life.

The essential meaning is thus relatively clear, and now it becomes apparent that many of the details – which can be discussed endlessly – are not in themselves significant. Although one can identify sources for specific references, what is important is the atmosphere that Bulgakov creates in his whole fantastic world. We have a devil with many of his traditional trappings: black coat, a sword, strange eyes, a limp, and so on. The clothes and appearance of both him and his henchmen are immediately striking – as much at times for their careless neglect of them as for what is actually worn. In these figures is to be found much of the comedy, particularly in that of Behemoth, 'the best jester who had ever existed in the world' (p. 384). In himself he is an incongruous figure: a cat who can talk, get on a tram and attempt to pay the fare, demand a visitor's passport, play

47 The most detailed comparison is **495**. As far as I know, I am the only one to equate Azazello and Mephistopheles: see my **524**, pp. 1167, 1168.
48 This is argued convincingly by **250**.

chess (and cheat) with the devil, have a gun fight with the police, dine at Griboe-dov's. His name is appropriate in more ways than one: not only is it mentioned biblically (in Job xl. 15-24) and elsewhere with possible diabolical connections,[49] it was also in the twenties the title of a humorous journal in Moscow – a reference probably more familiar to Bulgakov's contemporaries. The cat as the devil's or a witch's familiar is a well-known figure, of course; also the idea of a jester accompanying the devil. Azazello too comes originally from the Bible ('the demon of the waterless desert' in Leviticus xvi: 'Azazel' is the Hebrew word for 'scapegoat'), so too does an episodic character, the destroyer Abaddon (Revelation ix.11). Such figures have given rise to a whole tradition of witchcraft and black magic – which is drawn upon in particular for Margarita's flight as a witch and Satan's Great Ball (a somewhat toned-down version of a Black Mass).

Structurally, the book presents some interesting problems. There has been a great deal of discussion on its form, with most commentators linking it to the Menippean Satire.[50] Its different narrators have also received their share of attention, for there is a striking contrast between the seriousness and the realism of the Jerusalem narrative with the more light-hearted and fantastic descriptions of events in Moscow. Irony is frequently present, particularly in the use of common phrases referring to the devil: 'the devil knows,' 'the devil take him,' and so on. And one can feel the influence of Gogol in some of Bulgakov's whimsical detail – such as the application letters for Berlioz' apartment, thirty-two in two hours, which 'contained pleas, threats, slanders, denunciations, promises to renovate at the applicant's own expense, complaints of intolerable crowding and of utter impossibility to continue in the present apartment with thieving neighbors. Amongst other things, there were two suicide threats, a most vivid narrative describing the theft of dumplings, which the thief put right into his coat pocket, in apartment Number 31, and a confession of secret pregnancy' (pp. 105-6). Another example can surely be found in the last chapter, where the figures riding to Pilate on his mountain-top are reminiscent of the ending of Gogol's 'The Terrible Vengeance' (even if the outcome is quite different). Nor should we forget Bulgakov's sense of fun, his love of *mistifikatsiia*, which elsewhere too leads to a certain irreverence towards his sources, resulting almost in parody: one can recognize this here in attitudes towards Gogol, the Faust story, traditions of demonology and witchcraft, and even perhaps the gospels themselves.

In the book as a whole Bulgakov has managed to weave a complicated pattern of events and characters, keeping track of the individual strands and their place

49 See my own **524**, pp. 1166-8, for a discussion of the sources for Bulgakov's figures.
   Also **449**, pp. 543-5; **332**
50 See on this **97**, p. 127; **445**; **449**, pp. 536-9, 540-3; **476**

in relation to others. The actual background for the story is realistic, both in Moscow and Jerusalem. In Moscow, real street names and locations are frequently used – the Patriarchs' Ponds on the Malaya Bronnaya (only the tram line no longer exists), the Alexandrovsky Garden where Margarita meets Azazello, the Vorobiev Hills – while many other references are clearly identifiable. The Griboedov House seems to be the Gorky Literary Institute; the fateful flat (No 50, Sadovaya 302-bis) to be Bulgakov's own, No 50, Bolshaya Sadovaya 10 (the Pigit House which he had long ago written of as the Elpit House); the Variety Theatre nearby the former Music Hall.[51] Apparently experts on ancient Jerusalem can find a similar accuracy in Bulgakov's descriptions of that city. Most remarkable is the way Bulgakov links Jerusalem and Moscow, constantly stressing their similarity. Herod's Palace, where Pilate is staying, is linked to the Moscow scenes by the sultry heat of the day, the columns, and balcony much like those of Griboedov House or indeed those in the flat as converted for Satan's Ball. Both Moscow and Jerusalem have their bridges, towers, domes. Towards the end of the book, Bulgakov suggests the two cities are in fact identical, with a description that can apply to either:

The wind on the terrace freshened. Soon it was quite dark.

The cloud from the west enveloped the vast city. Bridges, buildings, were all swallowed up. Everything vanished as though it had never been. (101, p. 409)

Finally, when the Master and Margarita release Pilate from his mountain-top to go to Yeshua, the two cities rise out of the air on either side of them.

More important still perhaps are the many leitmotifs connecting the book's three levels, which have been described as the contemporary, the historical, and the fantastic. Most obvious of all are the constant references to the sun and the moon, suggesting again the theme of light and darkness. The full moon is, of course, regarded as a time when strange events take place, and here seems suggestive of that world beyond everyday reality – in Moscow and Jerusalem too. It is also used to locate in time the Moscow and Jerusalem episodes, which both take place at Easter, the time of the spring full moon: Wednesday to Saturday in Moscow, Friday to Saturday (with the events of Wednesday and Thursday referred to) in Jerusalem.[52] Fire also occurs as a frequent image; most appropriately, for, to quote Northrop Frye, 'The imagery of light and fire surrounding the angels in the bible ... associates fire with a spiritual or angelic world midway between the human and divine': note in particular the 'angelic' Behemoth, who

51 **349.** I am grateful to Mr Michael Glenny for the information on Jerusalem.
52 For a discussion of some of these leitmotifs, see my own **524**; **449**, pp. 548-55, 563; **495**, p. 318.

causes fire with a primus, virtually the symbol of dreary everyday Moscow life. Frye further points to the links between 'fire, intoxicating wine, and the hot red blood of animals' and to the 'identification of the *city* with fire.'[53] In the book wine, blood and the colour of it, are indeed further leitmotifs. Pilate, who has a blood-red lining to his cloak, spills wine in anger – symbolizing his spilling of blood, for the reddish-black liquid remains with him on his mountain-top; the blood of Baron Meigel, the spy, is spilt by the devil, who drinks it, as does Margarita; the Master and Margarita both drink of Pilate's wine, which poisons them – and the idea of poison is mentioned in connection with Pilate at the beginning, the dancing at the Griboedov House, and with Margarita herself, who thinks of taking it. There are other interconnections. Pilate's reaction to the appearance of Christ is remarkably similar to that of Berlioz to the appearance of Woland; Ivan compares Doctor Stravinsky in the clinic with Pilate, noting that he even speaks Latin. Being unmarried and alone is a motif linking Yeshua, Woland, and Ivan. Other constant themes are roses and the scent of rose oil, the colour yellow, Pilate pricking Christ's heart and the devil constantly pricking the hearts of men, storms and clouds 'boiling and tumbling on the earth, as always at moments of world catastrophe' (p. 401). Much of this can be interpreted symbolically – but its simple effect is to indicate the sameness of events in Moscow and Jerusalem, the fundamental unity of the world.

Behind *The Master and Margarita* there lies a very straightforward attitude, an optimistic insistence on the power of the spiritual in human life and on the individuality of man. Unavoidably in this framework there is a deep concern for ethical problems. But as Ewa Thompson points out, Bulgakov 'is a moralist but not a sermonist: he does not preach virtuous life, and whenever we seek to make him lead a *roman à thèse* argument he turns out to be inconsistent.'[54] Unthinking people may wish to create a hell on earth, but beyond the earth is eternity and immortality for those who desire to achieve it.

The Master and Margarita sums up the whole of Bulgakov and is a fitting conclusion to his career. As Kaverin has said, 'In its originality it will hardly find its equal in all world literature.'[55] It is indeed this that makes it Bulgakov's masterpiece, a work concerning the whole of human life, and this contrasted with human pettiness as found specifically in the Russian society of Bulgakov's own day. The book is unique – not least because of its presentation of philosophical issues in the form of comedy – and must be considered as one of the great Russian works of this century.

Here here!

53 **279**, pp. 145-6
54 **503**, p. 56
55 **324**, p. 544

13

Conclusion

Shortly before Bulgakov's death he had joked with his wife about what would happen in the future: 'When I die, they'll soon start to print me, theatres will snatch my plays from each other, and everywhere they'll start to invite you to give talks about your recollections of me. You'll come onto the stage in a black dress, attractively low-cut, you'll wring your hands and say in a low, halting voice "My angel has flown away ..."' Bulgakov and his wife had both laughed because this had seemed so unlikely. Only after twenty-five years did his words indeed turn out to be accurate – except that Yelena Sergeevna, remembering them, refused to make public appearances.[1]

Immediately after Bulgakov's death the Union of Soviet Writers set up a commission on his literary heritage.[2] Apart from securing living quarters and a pension for Yelena Sergeevna, it decided to publish a collection of his plays (*Days of the Turbins, Flight, Don Quixote, Molière, The Last Days*, and *Ivan Vasilievich*), including two articles: a creative biography of Bulgakov by his friend Popov and a general article about his works. Commemorative evenings took place six months and a year after Bulgakov's death, with speeches by members of various theatres.[3]

But the volume of plays did not appear, and the biographical article written for it by Popov remained in manuscript. The Soviet Union was soon involved in war with Germany, and publicly at any rate there was little discussion of Bulgakov. There were, of course, the two plays still in the Art Theatre repertory (*Days of the Turbins* and *Dead Souls*), and the premières of *Don Quixote* in 1941 and

1 **339**, p. 57
2 Its members were N.N. Aseev, Ye.S. Bulgakova, V.Ya. Vilenkin, S.A. Yermolinsky, V.V. Ivanov, L.M. Leonov, Ya.L. Leontiev, P.A. Markov, S.Ya. Marshak, P.S. Popov, A.M. Fayko, K.A. Fedin, N.P. Khmelyov, and S.I. Shafrov. For what follows, see the minutes of the commission for 1940 in **187**, folio 556, and **448**.
3 See **187**, folio 556, and **372**, pp. 395-8

of *The Last Days* in 1943. But except for Bulgakov's translation of *l'Avare* and an unsigned short story, nothing of his had actually been printed since 1927 – and now the public had graver matters to occupy them.

Official attitudes towards him had in any case never been favourable. The 1926-31 edition of the *Great Soviet Encyclopaedia* had regarded him solely as a defender of the old order, claimed that his plays were successful on the stage because of fine acting rather than for any artistic qualities, and accused him of showing two tendencies, realistic when describing the demise of the aristocracy and humorous when describing things Soviet: 'In the majority of his later works Bulgakov uses the shady sides of Soviet reality with the aim of discrediting and ridiculing it.' (In this edition he was also erroneously stated to have lived abroad from 1921 to 1923 – an error which at that time would have predisposed many against him.) The *Literary Encyclopaedia* of three years later is similar in tone: we read that Bulgakov hated the new order, which he did not understand, and in his works tried to avenge his class by vilifying the new age. 'The whole creative path of Bulgakov is that of a man who is a class-enemy of Soviet reality. Bulgakov is a typical representative of the tendencies of "internal emigration."' The *Small Encyclopaedia* of 1928-31 and its subsequent edition of 1933-47 is similarly hostile; so too is the second edition of the *Great Soviet Encyclopaedia* (Bulgakov entry: 1951).

The repressive post-war years in Russia were hardly conducive to the rehabilitation of a writer who had always been regarded with suspicion. It was not in fact until 1954, the year after Stalin's death, that Bulgakov's name was mentioned publicly again, by the writer Kaverin at the Second Congress of Soviet Writers. In the first volume of a new theatrical history which appeared that year, Bulgakov was again referred to, negatively.[4] But at last, with the advent of the 'thaw' in literature, a new commission on his works was created, its most active members being Yelena Sergeevna, Vl. Lakshin, S. Lyandres, V. Kaverin, K. Simonov, and S. Yermolinsky. *Days of the Turbins* was restaged, and in 1955, fifteen years after Bulgakov's death, it was printed for the first time in the Soviet Union, together with *The Last Days* (which was still being shown at the Art Theatre). By now neither play contained anything that was controversial: the commission was proceeding cautiously enough. But it was not long before indications of a fundamental change in attitude became apparent: *Flight*, banned in 1928 and 1933, was performed both in Moscow and Leningrad in 1957. The year 1962 saw the publication of *Life of Monsieur de Molière*, previously rejected, and the same year, at long last, there appeared a collection of plays which included, besides the two already published, *Don Quixote, Flight*, and *Molière*. Over the next

4 See **324**, p. 557, and **406**, I, pp. 136, 171, 174

few years there was a succession of major publications: six of Bulgakov's stories under the title of *Notes of a Young Doctor* (1963); his unfinished novel, *Theatrical Romance*, and a further collection of plays containing two as yet unpublished ones, *Ivan Vasilievich* and *Half-witted Jourdain* (1965); another play, *Bliss*, and a major collection of prose works, which included his early novel *The White Guard*, with an introduction by Lakshin (1966). A few of his shorter works had also been published by this time. More plays were performed: *Ivan Vasilievich* and *Molière* in 1966 and 1967. Also in 1966 there was an exhibition in the Central Theatrical Library to commemorate the 75th anniversary of Bulgakov's birth, with photographs of productions of his plays, reviews, and producers' comments.[5]

Gradually the official attitude towards Bulgakov had been changing, and this too is reflected in the encyclopaedia entries. That of the *Theatrical Encyclopaedia*, by K.L. Rudnitsky in 1961, is factual and avoids critical judgement; similar too is the *Short Literary Encyclopaedia* of 1962. Although negative criticism continued for a while to appear,[6] on the whole the re-emergence of Bulgakov was welcomed with enthusiasm. The real sensation, of course, was the publication, in the November 1966 and January 1967 issues of *Moskva*, of *The Master and Margarita*: if a book asserting the actual existence of Christ and frankly critical of certain aspects of Soviet life was allowed to appear, what, one might think, could not now be printed? A selection from 'Notes on the Cuffs' followed in 1967, and since that time a number of other early feuilletons by Bulgakov have appeared in journals and newspapers. A collection of novels (*Romany*), including the complete *Master and Margarita*, was published in 1973 – even if this was, in fact, intended more for the foreign than the home market. By now Bulgakov has been accepted as one of the great Soviet writers, with a most favourable reference to him appearing for the first time in the recent edition of the *Great Soviet Encyclopaedia* (1970).

At the same time, it must be added, there have been some failures too. *The Crimson Island*, which was suggested for the second collection of plays in 1965, was turned down by the editors; *Zoyka's Apartment* and *Adam and Eve*, accepted for the same edition by the editors, were later rejected by the censors (so that *Half-witted Jourdain*, a play Yelena Sergeevna did not even know existed, had rapidly to be substituted).[7] And it soon became apparent that the publication of *The Master and Margarita* did not herald any permanent change in literary attitudes. *Zoyka's Apartment*, announced for publication in 1968 in the

5 533
6 See, for example, **267**, pp. 213-16
7 I am grateful to K.L. Rudnitsky for this information.

review *Baikal*, again did not appear.[8] In the editorial offices of the 'Iskusstvo' publishing house there remains a manuscript for a book of reminiscences on Bulgakov, containing something of the order of twenty-five articles, some of which were read at an evening devoted to his memory in 1965. K. Simonov was apparently the moving force behind this, and it was proposed to publish the book in three volumes,[9] but after the Soviet invasion of Czechoslovakia in August 1968 there was a new hardening of official attitudes which prevented its appearance. L.Ye. Belozerskaya's memoirs also remain unpublished. There are still many of Bulgakov's works which are generally unavailable in the Soviet Union (*Zoyka's Apartment, The Crimson Island, Adam and Eve*, 'Heart of a Dog'), and others, notably some of the *Diavoliada* stories, which have not been reprinted since the twenties. Since the death of Yelena Sergeevna in 1970, the commission has tended to be less active, although certainly there are now a number of serious Soviet scholars working on Bulgakov.

The situation, then, is one that occurs so often in Soviet literature: a writer is admired and published but then there are second thoughts about some of his works, and further publication of his more suspect pieces is actively discouraged. One looks in vain for a commemorative plaque on any of the buildings in Moscow Bulgakov lived in. Nevertheless, we should perhaps be thankful that, if still not entirely accessible to his own countrymen, at least Bulgakov is now recognized there as one of their major writers. And in the West he has in one sense fared somewhat better, in that all his major works have been published and there have been performances of several of his plays.

It is difficult to summarize Bulgakov's achievement. A writer of great versatility, he would say that the narrative and the dramatic forms were 'equally necessary to him, like left and right hands to a pianist.'[10] He is equally at home with farce and with tragedy, with the grotesque and the realistic, with the historical and the imaginary. In his best works he tends to combine these elements: Vera Smirnova talks of 'the surprising combination of tragic and comedy, lyricism and biting satire, almost buffoonery, into which are suddenly drawn sincerely sorrowful notes, a real tragic pathos.'[11] It is perhaps this odd combination of the humorous and the serious (reminding us of Bulgakov's literary master, Gogol), at times alienating the reader from characters with whom he might otherwise identify, that is the most striking feature in Bulgakov's work. (This may perhaps reflect his own personality too − a brilliantly funny story-teller, full

8 **306**, p. 342
9 Based on information given by Yelena Sergeevna to M. Michel Vassilieff and on **239**, p. 11
10 **2**, p. 3
11 **489**, p. 322

of gaiety, he was inwardly shy, serious, and his life was basically tragic.) Yet for all his love of the fantastic, his approach to writing was basically that of a realist, who set down what he saw around him. Noted as a satirist, he is reported to have said that 'any attempts to create satire are doomed to utter failure. It cannot be created. It creates itself, unexpectedly.'[12]

The importance he attached to careful observation of actual life has been noted by Paustovsky. Bulgakov, he writes, 'was greedy for everything in surrounding life ... that stood out above the surface, whether it were a man or some characteristic of his, a surprising action, an unusual thought, a suddenly noticed trivial detail (like the candle flames of the footlights bent over at a right angle by a draught) – all this he grasped without any effort and used in his prose, in his plays, in his ordinary conversation.'[13] Bulgakov in many ways was a conservative, both in his manner of speech and dress and in his literary tastes. For this reason he stood apart from modernistic tendencies in art and literature, which he did not understand and which did not interest him nearly so much as life itself. In the context of Russian and Soviet literature, he falls clearly within the classical tradition, occupying a place somewhere between Gogol and realists such as Tolstoy: representing perhaps a synthesis between the two positions rather than, on the one hand, exploring further the irrationality of man as does Dostoevsky or, on the other, following Chekhov's path of trying to present simple and ordinary life. His most important characteristic of all, perhaps, is his utter honesty, his unhesitating expression of ideas in which he believed despite the difficult circumstances of his life.

His refusal to compromise has finally been justified in the posthumous recognition of him as one of the major Soviet writers, whose masterpiece *The Master and Margarita* must rank alongside such works as Zamyatin's *We*, Pasternak's *Doctor Zhivago*, Sholokhov's *Quiet Don*, the stories of Babel, and the novels of Solzhenitsyn. In the Soviet Union itself, for political reasons, Bulgakov is of course more appreciated than all of these except Sholokhov. Yet he too has always had a certain political significance. In the twenties, his works – *Days of the Turbins*, in particular – were a focus for the more liberal intellectuals and fellow-travellers, who shared his ideals of artistic freedom and a less simplistic understanding of the so-called class struggle, and who were concerned with literary quality rather than ideological correctness. For the émigré, too, he provided a hope that genuine literature would survive the dictates of the politicians. (In this he was not, of course, alone, but an important voice amongst a number of others.) In the thirties and forties, his few plays being performed were perhaps

12 From Popov's unpublished biography in **187**, folio 556
13 **419**, pp. 60-1

only a faint reminder of ideals which had almost disappeared – but a reminder they were, nevertheless. Unlike Fedin, another writer – and essentially a good one – Bulgakov never compromised, nor did he become part of the literary 'establishment'; unlike Zoshchenko, also critical of his society, Bulgakov did not restrict himself to superficial criticism, but dealt with underlying, basic issues. With his rehabilitation he has become a symbol of the survival of genuine talent, despite past repression. On the other hand, he has never been identified with such political dissidence as has surrounded Solzhenitsyn – since politics for him, on the surface at least, was always secondary to literature. Bulgakov had not the temperament of a genuine literary politician, nor was his age conducive to his becoming one.

And yet a lingering doubt about his motives remains. Bulgakov, resentful of the attacks of critics upon him, continued to produce works which could only be seen as provocative. Was he *really* so naïve that he did not understand this and still expected acceptance and success, or was he in a sense writing in a spirit of defiance towards a society which he found in many ways uncongenial: half-welcoming perhaps, in Dostoevskian fashion, the renewed attacks that followed? How much of his writing represented ultimately for him a deeply personal struggle against the new authorities? Such questions are unanswerable, but also unavoidable.

We are perhaps entitled to ask, as a final question, what is there of 'wisdom' in Bulgakov, what is there that is new? Of the new there is little, for he was never concerned with being an innovator as such. On the contrary, he is concerned with age-old problems, his 'wisdom' lies in reiterating eternal themes and ideas which have occupied men for centuries, in an age which is in danger of forgetting them. For this reason one can hardly doubt that he will occupy a permanent place in world literature too, where universality is a major consideration. No writer produces in isolation from his own society and Bulgakov clearly writes on problems specific to the Soviet Union of his day. But his best works – his masterpiece, *The Master and Margarita*, his other novel, *The White Guard*, his plays *Days of the Turbins* and *Flight*, his biography *Life of Monsieur de Molière*, his tales 'Heart of a Dog' and 'A Chinese Story,' even his adaptation *Don Quixote* – all deal with the problems of individuals in their struggles with the world around them. Nor can the originality of these works (with the obvious exception of the adaptation) be questioned. In addition, there is the entire body of Bulgakov's other works – plays, tales, feuilletons, adaptations – which show considerable quality even if they are not, individually, of world importance. Here we might place some of his most interesting writing: *Zoyka's Apartment, Molière*, and *The Last Days* amongst his plays; *Theatrical Romance* amongst his longer prose works; the *Diavoliada* stories, *Notes of a Young Doctor*, 'A Psalm,' and 'Fire of the Khans' among his shorter ones. Not every work of a great writer has to be a masterpiece; what is required is a consistency of purpose, a body of good writing which will contain both the trivia and the failures on the one hand and the few masterpieces on the other. It is this, surely, that Bulgakov gives us.

Yet he remains relatively unappreciated in the West, except amongst students of Russian literature. This, I would suggest, is simply a question of time, combined perhaps with the fact that he has been overshadowed by the *succès de scandale* of Solzhenitsyn. His masterpiece, after all, has been known for barely ten years. There have been few good translations, particularly of his plays, and no really major productions. His reputation is already secure in his own country, even if not all his work is known. With time for him to become better known elsewhere, it would seem likely that it will grow internationally to the same extent.

Selective bibliography

In the listing that follows I have not attempted to duplicate bibliographies already published or in preparation, and those who want more exhaustive information are referred to **306** and **311**. In my selection I have been guided first by the sources which I refer to in my text or notes (using, for simplicity, the relevant entry numbers in this bibliography); second by the need to list those places where the works of Bulgakov himself are to be found. In the latter case, I have included the most important modern reprints, which may be more accessible than the originals: and indeed in the case of the *Gudok* feuilletons, which are difficult to find outside the Soviet Union, I have listed, besides those I refer to in my text, *only* the reprints. Translations into languages other than English are included only when I have referred to these works in my text. Many secondary sources I have used are not listed here, again in order to avoid unnecessary duplication, but I have endeavoured to ensure that the major ones are all represented.

I / PRIMARY SOURCES

A / Collections of Bulgakov's works

1 *Dramy i komedii.* Intr. V. Kaverin, 'Zametki o dramaturgii M. Bulgakova,' pp. 5-15; K. Rudnitskii, 'Primechaniia,' pp. 578-96. Moscow: Iskusstvo, 1965. Contains: 'Dni Turbinykh,' 'Beg,' 'Kabala sviatosh,' 'Poloumnyii Zhurden,' 'Poslednie dni,' 'Ivan Vasilievich,' 'Don Kikhot'
2 *Izbrannaia proza.* Intr. Vl.Ia. Lakshin, 'O proze Mikhaila Bulgakova i o nem samom,' pp. 3-44. Moscow: Khudozhestvennaia literatura, 1966. Contains: 'Zapiski iunogo vracha' ('Polotentse s petukhom,' 'Stal'noe gorlo,' 'Kreshchenie povorotom,' 'V'iuga,' 'T'ma egipetskaia,' 'Propavshii glaz'), 'Belaia gvardiia,' 'Zhizn' gospodina de Mol'era,' 'Teatral'nyi roman'

3 *P'esy.* Intr. Pavel Markov, 'Bulgakov,' pp. 5-16; K. Rudnitskii, 'Primechaniia. Biograficheskie spravki,' pp. 463-80. Moscow: Iskusstvo, 1962. Contains: 'Dni Turbinykh,' 'Beg,' 'Kabala sviatosh,' 'Poslednie dni,' 'Don Kikhot'

4 *P'esy: Adam i Eva. Bagrovyi ostrov. Zoikina kvartira.* Paris: YMCA Press, 1971

5 *Rasskazy.* Leningrad: Smekhach, 1926. Contains: 'Vospalenie mozgov,' 'Zolotye korrespondentsii Feraponta Ferapontovicha Kaportseva' ('Nesgoriaemyi amerikanskii dom,' 'Lzhedimitrii Lunacharskii,' 'Van'ka durak,' 'Brandmeister Pozharov'), 'Letuchii gollandets,' 'Parshivyi tip,' 'Voda zhizni,' 'Samotsvetnyi byt' ('Sredstva ot zastenchivosti,' 'Skol'ko Brokgauza mozhet vynesti organizm?'), 'Ploshchad' na kolesakh,' 'Egipetskaia mumiia'

6 *Romany.* Intr. K. Simonov, 'O trekh romanakh Mikhaila Bulgakova,' pp. 3-10. Moscow: Khudozhestvennaia literatura, 1973. Contains: 'Belaia gvardiia,' 'Teatral'nyi roman,' 'Master i Margarita'

7 *Selected Works.* Intr. Avril Pyman, 'Mikhail Afanasyevich Bulgakov,' pp. ix-xliv. The Commonwealth and International Library. Pergamon Oxford Russian Series. Oxford: Pergamon, 1972. Contains: 'Rokovye iaitsa,' 'Psalom,' 'Belaia gvardiia' (extract), 'Beg,' 'Master i Margarita' (extract)

8 *Diaboliad and Other Stories.* Ed. and intr. Ellendea Proffer and Carl R. Proffer. Trans. C.R. Proffer. Bloomington: Indiana University Press, 1972. Contains: 'Diaboliad,' 'The Fatal Eggs,' 'No. 13. The Elpit-Rabkommun Building,' 'A Chinese Tale,' 'The Adventures of Chichikov,' 'A Treatise on Housing,' 'Psalm,' 'Four Portraits,' 'Moonshine Lake,' 'The Raid,' 'The Crimson Island'

9 *The Early Plays of Mikhail Bulgakov.* Ed. and intr. E. Proffer. Trans. C.R. Proffer and E. Proffer. Bloomington: Indiana University Press, 1972. Contains: 'The Days of the Turbins,' 'Zoya's Apartment,' 'Flight,' 'The Crimson Island,' 'A Cabal of Hypocrites'

10 *Neizdannyi Bulgakov.* Ed. E. Proffer. Ann Arbor: Ardis, 1977

B / *Individual works by Bulgakov*

11 'Adam and Eve.' Trans. Ellendea Proffer. *Russian Literature Triquarterly*, no 1 (1971), pp. 163-215

Bliss:

12 'Blazhenstvo (Son inzhenera Reina v 4-kh deistviiakh).' *Zvezda vostoka* (Tashkent), no 7 (1966), pp. 75-107

13 'Blazhenstvo (Son inzhenera Reina v 4-kh deistviiakh).' *Grani*, no 85 (1972), pp. 3-52

The Crimean feuilletons:

14 'Puteshestvie po Krymu.' *Krasnaia gazeta (vechernii vypusk)*, 3, 10, 22, 24, 31 Aug. 1925, p. 4 for all dates

The Crimson Island:

15 'Bagrovyi ostrov.' *Novyi zhurnal*, no 93 (1968), pp. 38-76 (prologue and first two acts)

Days of the Turbins:

16 *Dni Turbinykh. Poslednie dni.* Moscow: Iskusstvo, 1955
17 *Dni Turbinykh.* Russian Titles for the Specialist, no 6. Letchworth: Prideaux, 1970 (reprinted from *P'esy*)
18 'Days of the Turbins.' In *An Anthology of Russian Plays*, II. Ed. and trans. F.D. Reeve. New York: Vintage, 1963. Pp. 255-334
19 'Days of the Turbins.' In *Six Soviet Plays*. Ed. and trans. Eugene Lyons. London: Gollancz, 1935
20 *Die Tage der Geschwister Turbin, die weisse Garde.* Trans. Käthe Rosenberg. Berlin-Charlottenburg: S. Kagansky (c. 1927)
See also **40**

Dead Souls: see **91**

Diavoliada stories:

21 'D'iavoliada.' *Nedra*, no 4 (1924), pp. 221-57
22 *D'iavoliada. Rasskazy.* Moscow: Nedra, 1925. Contains: 'Diavoliada,' 'Rokovye iaitsa,' 'No 13 – Dom El'pit – Rabkommuna,' 'Kitaiskaia istoriia,' 'Pokhozhdeniia Chichikova' (reprinted by Ardis, 1976)
23 *D'iavoliada.* London: Flegon Press, 1970. Contains: 'D'iavoliada,' 'Dom no 13,' 'Pokhozhdeniia Chichikova'
24 'Luch zhizni' ('Rokovye iaitsa'). *Krasnaia panorama*, nos 19-22, 24 (1925)
25 'No 13 – Dom El'pit – Rabkommuna.' *Krasnyi zhurnal dlia vsekh*, no 2 (1922), pp. 23-7
26 'Rokkovy iaitsa.' / 'Rokovye iaitsa.' *Russkaia mysl' (La Pensée russe)*, 13 Sept. to 24 Nov. 1950 (serialized)

27 'Rokovye iaitsa.' *Nedra*, no 6 (1925), pp. 79-149
28 *Rokovye iaitsa.* London: Flegon Press, 1970
29 *Rokovye iaitsa.* Intr. Petr Pil'skii, 'Ironiia i fantastika,' pp. 5-10. Riga: Literatura, 1928. Contains: 'Rokovye iaitsa,' 'D'iavoliada,' 'Dom no 13,' 'Pokhozhdeniia Chichikova'
30 *Sbornik rasskazov.* New York: Izdatel'stvo im. Chekhova, 1952. Contains: 'Rokovye iaitsa,' 'D'iavoliada,' 'Dom no 13,' 'Pokhozhdeniia Chichikova'
31 'The Adventures of Chichikov.' Trans. Lydia W. Kesich. In *Great Soviet Short Stories.* Ed. F.D. Reeve. New York: Dell, 1962. Pp. 72-86
32 'The Fatal Eggs.' In *The Fatal Eggs and Other Soviet Satire.* Trans. Mirra Ginsburg. London: Collier-MacMillan, 1965. Pp. 51-133
   See also 8, 117, 119

Don Quixote:

33 *Don Kikhot.* Russian Titles for the Specialist, no 23. Letchworth: Prideaux, 1971 (reprinted from *P'esy*)
34 'Neizdannye stseny iz P'esy *Don Kikhot.*' (Publikatsiia E.S. Bulgakovoi.) In *Servantes i vsemirnaia literatura.* Ed. N.I. Balatov. Moscow: Nauka, 1969. Pp. 273-7

'Fire of the Khans':

35 'Khanskii ogon'.' *Krasnyi zhurnal dlia vsekh*, no 2 (1924), pp. 101-11
36 'Khanskii ogon'.' *Nash sovremennik*, no 2 (1974), pp. 114-26

Flight:

37 *Beg.* Russian Titles for the Specialist, no 7. Letchworth: Prideaux, 1970 (reprinted from *P'esy*)
38 *Flight.* Trans. and intr. Mirra Ginsburg. New York: Grove, 1969
39 *On the Run.* Ginn Drama texts. Trans. Avril Pyman. London: Ginn, 1972
40 *La Fuite. Les Journées des Tourbines.* Intr. Paul Kalinine, 'Eléments pour une chronologie,' pp. 7-50. 'Bibliographie des œuvres de Boulgakov,' pp. 51-2. Trans. P. Kalinine. Paris: Laffont, 1971

Golos rabotnika prosveshcheniia feuilletons:
All references to the above journal unless otherwise indicated.

41 'KA-EN-PE i KA-PE.' No 4 (1923), pp. 19-21
42 'V shkole gorodka III Internatsionala.' No 4 (1923), pp. 22-3

43 'Pervaia detskaia kommuna.' Nos 5 and 6 (1923), pp. 30-2
44 'Pervaia detskaia kommuna.' *Sem'ia i shkola*, no 11 (1966), pp. 38-9
45 'Ptitsy v mansarde.' Nos 7 and 8 (1923), pp. 36-8

Gudok feuilletons and similar:
All references below are to *Gudok* unless otherwise indicated. The stories
are signed Mikhail Bulgakov, M. Bulgakov, M. Bulgako, Mikhail, M., M.B.,
Em., Em. Be., Emma B., F.S.-ov., Gerasim Petrovich Ukhov, Ivan Bezdom-
nyi, M. Ol-Rait, Neznakomets.

46 'Bubnovaia istoriia.' *Literaturnaia gazeta*, 19 Aug. 1970, p. 16
47 'Buza s pechatiami.' 30 April 1925, p. 4
48 'Chelovek s gradusnikom.' 16 July 1925, p. 4
49 'Chelovek s gradusnikom.' *Sovetskii krasnyi krest*, no 1 (Jan.-Feb. 1968),
   p. 27
50 'Glav-polit-bogosluzhenie.' 24 July 1924, p. 4
51 'Glav-polit-bogosluzhenie.' Published in error in V. Kataev, *Gorokh v stenku*.
   Moscow: Sovetskii pisatel', 1963. Pp. 314-16
52 'Igra prirody.' 13 Sept. 1924, p. 4
53 'Kak Buton zhenilsia.' 28 April 1925, p. 5
54 'Kak na tetkiny den'gi mestkom podarok kupil.' 14 Aug. 1925, p. 3
55 'Karaul!' *Literaturnaia gazeta*, 4 Sept. 1974, p. 16
56 'Kogda mertvye vstaiut iz grobov.' 8 Aug. 1925, p. 3
57 'Kolybel' nachal'nika stantsii.' 24 Sept. 1924, p. 3
58 'Konduktor i chlen imperatorskoi familii.' 27 Feb. 1925, p. 3
59 'Konduktor i chlen imperatorskoi familii.' *Literaturnaia gazeta*, 7 Nov.
   1973, p. 16
60 'Letuchii gollandets.' 2 Sept. 1925, p. 3
61 'Madmazel' Zhanna.' *Literaturnaia gazeta*, 17 April 1974, p. 16
62 'Mertvye khodiat.' 25 Sept. 1925, p. 3
63 'Nalet.' 25 Dec. 1923
64 'Ne te briuki.' 16 Sept. 1925, p. 3
65 'Neunyvaiushchie bodistki.' 6 March 1925, p. 4
66 'Novyi sposob rasprostraneniia knigi.' 21 Oct. 1924, p. 4
67 'O pol'ze alkogolizma.' 15 April 1925, p. 4
68 'Okhotniki za cherepami.' 18 June 1924, p. 4
69 'Parshivyi tip.' 19 Dec. 1925, p. 4
70 'Parshivyi tip.' *Literaturnaia gazeta*, 16 April 1969, p. 16
71 'P'ianyi parovoz.' 12 June 1926, p. 3
72 'Pivnoi rasskaz.' 17 Aug. 1924, p. 5
73 'Po telefonu.' 30 Dec. 1924, p. 4

74 'Prazdnik s sifilisom.' 27 March 1925, p. 4
75 'Prikliucheniia pokoinika.' 27 June 1924, p. 3
76 'Razvratnik.' 14 July 1926, p. 3
77 'Razvratnik.' *Literaturnaia gazeta*, 10 July 1974, p. 16
78 'Re-ka-ka.' 5 Sept. 1924, p. 4
79 *Revizor* s vyshibaniem.' 24 Dec. 1924, p. 4
80 'Seriia nol' shest' no 0660243.' In *Pechatilis' v Vecherke*. Moscow: Moskovskii rabochii, 1973. Pp. 9-13
81 'Sil'nodeistvuiushchee sredstvo.' 3 Jan. 1924, p. 3
82 'Taina nesgoraemogo shkafa.' *Komsomol'skaia pravda*, 16 Feb. 1969
83 'Tri kopeiki.' 3 Sept. 1924, p. 4
84 'Vospalenie mozgov.' *Literaturnaia gazeta*, 14 Aug. 1968, p. 16
85 'Zakoldovannoe mesto.' 9 Jan. 1925, p. 4
86 'Zhelannyi platilo.' 10 Dec. 1924, p. 4
   See also 5

'Heart of a Dog':

87 *Sobach'e serdtse*. Intr. pp. 9-10. Paris: YMCA Press, 1969
88 'Sobach'e serdtse.' *Grani*, no 9 (1968), pp. 3-85
89 *The Heart of a Dog*. Trans. Michael Glenny. London: Collins, 1968
90 *The Heart of a Dog*. Trans. Mirra Ginsburg. New York: Grove, 1968

Ivan Vasilievich:

91 *Ivan Vasil'evich. Mertvye dushi*. Munich: Tovarishchestvo zarubezhnykh pisatelei, 1964

The Last Days:

92 *Poslednie dni*. Russian Titles for the Specialist, no 8. Letchworth: Prideaux, 1970 (reprinted from *P'esy*)
   See also 16

Libretti:

93 'Minin i Pozharskii.' Publikatsiia A.C. Wright. *Russian Literature Triquarterly*, no 15 (1978), pp. 325-40
94 'Rashel'.' Publikatsiia A.C. Wright. *Novyi zhurnal*, no 108 (1972), pp. 74-80

Life of Monsieur de Molière:

95 *Zhizn' gospodina de Mol'era.* Intr. G. Boiardzhiev, 'Kratkoe preduvedom-lenie,' pp. 5-8. Afterword: V. Kaverin, 'Mikhail Bulgakov i ego Mol'er,' pp. 225-32. Series Zhizn' zamechatel'nykh liudei. Moscow: Molodaia gvardiia, 1962
96 *Life of Monsieur de Molière.* Trans. Mirra Ginsburg. New York: Funk & Wagnalls, 1970

The Master and Margarita:

97 'Master i Margarita.' Part I. Intr. K. Simonov, pp. 6-7. Afterword: A. Vulis, pp. 127-30. *Moskva,* 10 (Nov. 1966), pp. 6-130. Part II. *Moskva,* 11 (Jan. 1967), pp. 56-144 (censored version)
98 *Master i Margarita.* Intr. L'Archevêque Jean de San Francisco (Shakhovskoi). Paris: YMCA Press, 1967 (as the *Moskva* version)
99 *Master i Margarita.* Frankfurt: Possev-Verlag, 1969 (integrated text)
100 *The Master and Margarita.* Trans. Mirra Ginsburg. New York: Grove, 1967 (censored version)
101 *The Master and Margarita.* Trans. Michael Glenny. London: Collins, 1967 (complete version)

'The Miser' – translation:

102 'Skupoi.' (Trans. of *l'Avare.*) Mol'er, Zh-B. *Sobranie sochinenii v 4-kh tomakh.* Ed. A.A. Smirnov and S.S. Mokul'skii. III. M-L: Academia, 1939. Pp. 363-497
103 'Skupoi.' (Trans. of *l'Avare.*) Mol'er, Zh-B. *Izbrannye komedii.* M-L: Detizgiz, 1952. Pp. 261-328

Molière:

104 *Kabala sviatosh.* Russian Titles for the Specialist, no 24. Letchworth: Prideaux, 1971 (reprinted from *P'esy*)

Nakanune feuilletons:
All references are to *Nakanune* or to its 'Literaturnoe prilozhenie' (L.p.) or 'Literaturnaia nedelia' (L.n.) unless otherwise indicated.

105 'Bagrovyi ostrov. Roman tov. Zhulia Verna. S frantsuzskogo na esopovskii perevel Mikhail A. Bulgakov.' L.n., 20 April 1924, pp. 2-6

106 'Belobrysova knizhka. Format zapisnoi.' 26 March 1924, pp. 2-3
107 'Benefis Lorda Kerzona.' 19 May 1923, p. 3
108 'Chasha zhizni. Veselyi moskovskii rasskaz s pechal'nym kontsom.' 31 Dec. 1922, pp. 10-11
109 'Den' nashei zhizni.' 2 Sept. 1923, p. 7
110 'Kiev-gorod.' 6 July 1923, pp. 2-4
111 'Komarovskoe delo.' 20 June 1923, pp. 2-3
112 'Krasnaia korona (Historia morbi).' L.p., 22 Oct. 1922, pp. 2-3
113 'Moskovskie stseny.' 6 May 1923, pp. 2-3
114 'Moskovskie stseny.' Russkaia mysl' (La Pensée russe), 22 May 1969, p. 5
115 'Moskva 20-kh godov.' Pt. I: 27 May 1924, pp. 2-3. Pt. II: 12 June 1924, pp. 2-3
116 'Moskva krasnokamennaia.' 30 July 1922, p. 2
117 'Moskva krasnokamennaia. Pokhozhdeniia Chichikova.' Sel'skaia molodezh', no 1 (1966), pp. 37-41
118 'Pod stekliannym nebom.' 24 April 1923, p. 2
119 'Pokhozhdeniia Chichikova.' L.p., 24 Sept. 1922, pp. 2-6
120 'Psalom.' 22 Sept. 1923, p. 7
121 'Putevye zametki.' 25 May 1923, p. 4
122 'Samogonnoe ozero.' 29 July 1923, p. 9
123 'Samotsvetnyi byt. Iz moei kollektsii.' L.p., 15 July 1923, pp. 1-2
124 'Shanson d'ete.' 16 Aug. 1923, pp. 2-3
125 'Sorok sorokov.' 15 April 1923, p. 2
126 'Stolitsa v bloknote.' 21 Dec. 1922, p. 2; 20 Jan. 1923, p. 6; 9 Feb. 1923, pp. 2-3; 1 March 1923, p. 5
127 Traktat o zhilishche. M-L: Zemlia i fabrika, 1926. Contains: 'Traktat o zhilishche,' 'Psalom,' 'Chetyre portreta,' 'Samogonnoe ozero'
128 'Trillioner.' Literaturnaia gazeta, 13 Sept. 1972, p. 16 (from 'Stolitsa v bloknote')
129 'V noch' na 3-e chislo (Iz romana Alyi makh).' L.p., 10 Dec. 1922, pp. 3-6 (early sketch for The White Guard)
130 'Vecherok u Vasilisy. Otryvok iz romana Belaia gvardiia.' 31 May 1924, p. 3, and 3 June 1924, pp. 2-3
131 'Zapiski na manzhetakh.' L.p., 18 June 1922, pp. 5-7
132 'Zolotistyi gorod.' 30 Sept. 1923, p. 2; 6 Oct. 1923, p. 2; 12 Oct. 1923, p. 2; 14 Oct. 1923, pp. 2-3
133 'Zolotye dokumenty (Iz moei kollektsii).' 6 April 1924, p. 3
134 'Glimpses of Our Capital.' Living Age, 31 March 1923, pp. 769-71 (second part of 'Stolitsa v bloknote')
135 'Lord Curzon Day in Moscow.' Living Age, 14 July 1923, pp. 60-2 See also 143

Notes of a Young Doctor:
All references to *Meditsinskii rabotnik* unless otherwise indicated.

136 'Ia ubil.' Nos 44 and 45 (18 Nov. and 12 Dec. 1926), pp. 13-15 and 14-16 respectively
137 'Ia ubil.' *Nedelia* (Voskesnoe prilozhenie k *Izvestiiam*), no 14, 1972, pp. 6-7
138 'Kreshchenie povorotom.' Nos 41 and 42 (1925)
139 'Morfii.' No 45 (9 Dec. 1927), pp. 11-14; no 46 (17 Dec. 1927), pp. 6-7, 10; no 47 (23 Dec. 1927), pp. 10-13
140 'Morfii.' *Russkaia mysl' (La Pensée russe)*, 12 March, 19 March, 26 March, and 7 April 1970, pp. 7
141 'Polotentse s petukhom.' Nos 33 and 34 (1926)
142 'Propavshii glaz.' Nos 36 and 37 (1926)
143 *Rasskazy*. In *Moskva*, no 5 (May 1963), pp. 141-66. Contains: 'Polotentse s petukhom,' 'V'iuga,' 'T'ma egipetskaia,' 'Sorok sorokov'
144 'T'ma egipetskaia.' Nos 26 and 27 (1926)
145 'V'iuga.' Nos 2 and 3 (1926)
146 *Zapiski iunogo vracha; rasskazy*. Biblioteka Ogonek, no 23. Moscow: Pravda, 1963. Contains: 'Polotentse s petukhom,' 'Kreshchenie povorotom,' 'Serebrianoe gorlo,' 'V'iuga,' 'T'ma egipetskaia,' 'Propavshii glaz'
147 *Zapiski iunogo vracha*. Russian Titles for the Specialist, no 1. Letchworth: Prideaux, 1970 (reprinted from *Izbrannaia proza*)
148 'Zvezdnaia syp'.' Nos 29 and 30 (12 Aug. and 19 Aug. 1926), pp. 12-14 and 12-15 respectively
149 *A Country Doctor's Notebook*. Trans. Michael Glenny. London: Collins; New York: Bantam, 1975 (contains all nine stories)
150 'An Egyptian Darkness' and 'The Blizzard.' In *The House on the Fontanka: Modern Soviet Short Stories*. Ed. Margarete Orga. London: William Kimber, 1970. Pp. 66-93
151 'From the Notes of a Young Doctor,' *Soviet Literature*, no 8 (1968), pp. 90-119. Contains: 'The Towel with the Cock,' 'The Blizzard,' 'An Egyptian Darkness'

'Notes on the Cuffs':

152 'Iz *Zapisok na manzhetakh*.' Intr. A. Vulis. *Zvezda vostoka*, 35 (March 1967), pp. 10-18
153 'Zapiski na manzhetakh.' *Rossiia*, no 5 (1923), pp. 20-5
154 'Zapiski na manzhetakh.' *Vozrozhdenie* (almanach), II. Moscow: Vremia, 1923. Pp. 5-19
155 'Zapiski na manzhetakh (Otryvki).' *Grani*, no 77 (1970), pp. 74-81
See also 131

Scenarios:

156 *'Neobychainoe proisshestvie' ili 'Revizor' (po Gogoliu).* Stsenarii Bulgakova
i Korostina. Ed. K. Iukov. S.S.P. GUKF Materialy stsenarno-proizvodstvennoi
konferentsii. Moscow: Tsedram, 1935 (republished, with introduction by
A.C. Wright, in *Novyi Zhurnal*, no 127, 1977, pp. 5-45)

Theatrical Romance:

157 'Teatral'nyi roman.' Afterword: V.O. Toporkov, 'O *Teatral'nom romane*
Mikhaila Bulgakova,' pp. 97-100. *Novyi mir*, no 8 (1965), pp. 6-100
158 *Teatral'nyi roman.* Letchworth: Prideaux, 1972 (reprinted from
Izbrannaia proza)
159 'Teatral'nyi roman.' Intr. K. Simonov. *Literaturnaia Rossiia*, 28 May 1965,
pp. 16-17 (one chapter)
160 *Black Snow: A Theatrical Novel.* Trans. Michael Glenny. Intr. M. Glenny,
'About Mikhail Bulgakov, His Novel, the Moscow Art Theatre and Stanislavsky,' pp. 5-12. London: Hodder and Stoughton; New York: Simon and
Schuster, 1967
161 *Theaterroman.* Trans. Thomas Reschke. Afterword: Ralf Schröder,
'Bulgakows Parodie und das Moskauer Künstlertheater,' pp. 187-94.
Berlin: Volk und Welt, 1969

'War and Peace':

162 'Voina i mir.' Intr. A.C. Wright, 'Mikhail Bulgakov's Adaptation of *War and
Peace*' (to be published shortly)

The White Guard:

163 'Belaia gvardiia.' *Rossiia*, nos 4 and 5 (1925), pp. 3-99 and 3-82 respectively
(first two parts only)
164 *Belaia gvardiia.* Intr. D.G.B. Piper, pp. v-viii. Rarity reprints no 7.
Letchworth: Bradda, 1969 (reprinted from *Izbrannaia proza*)
165 'Belaia gvardiia, glavy iz romana.' Publikatsiia E.S. Bulgakovoi. *Literaturnaia Rossiia*, 18 Nov. 1966, pp. 16-18
166 *Dni Turbinykh (Belaia gvardiia) roman.* 2 vols. Paris: Concorde, 1927-29
167 *Dni Turbinykh (Belaia gvardiia) roman.* Intr. Petr Pil'skii, pp. 7-10. Riga:
Literatura, 1927 (first two parts, plus a fraudulent ending based on the
play)

168 *The White Guard.* Trans. Michael Glenny. Epilogue: Viktor Nekrasov, 'The House of the Turbins,' pp. 299-320. London: Collins, 1971 (also in paperback: Collins, Fontana Books, 1973)

169 *Die Weisse Garde.* Trans. Larissa Robiné. Afterword: Ralf Schröder, 'Bulgakows Roman "Die Weisse Garde" – Der Zerfall einer Familie als weltgeschichtlicher Epilog und Prolog,' pp. 321-54. Berlin: Kultur und Fortschritt, 1969
See also 129, 130, 180

Zoyka's Apartment:

170 *Zoikina kvartira. (Okonchatel'nyi tekst).* Intr. Ellendea Proffer, pp. x-xix. Ann Arbor: Ardis, 1971

171 'Zoikina kvartira.' *Novyi zhurnal,* no 97 (1969) pp. 57-95; no 98 (1970), pp. 55-88

172 'Zoia's Apartment.' Trans. Carl R. Proffer and Ellendea Proffer. *Canadian Slavic Studies,* 4, no 2 (1970), pp. 238-80

173 *Soykas Wohnung (Zoikina kvartira). Komödie in 4 Aufz.* Trans. Erich Boehme. Berlin: J. Ladyschnikow, 1929

Miscellaneous works:

174 'Bogema.' *Krasnaia niva,* no 1 (1925), pp. 9-13

175 'Detskii rasskaz' (unsigned). *Sovetskii artist,* 1 Jan. 1939, p. 3

176 'Iurii Slezkin (Siluet).' Intr. to Iu.L. Slezkin, *Roman balleriny.* Riga 1928. Pp. 7-21

177 'Mne prisnilsia son.' *Nedelia,* no 43 (1974), pp. 10-11

178 'Neobyknovennye prikliucheniia doktora.' *Rupor,* no 2 (1922), pp. 10-12

179 'Neobyknovennye prikliucheniia doktora.' *Literaturnaia Gruziia,* no 2 (Feb. 1975), pp. 39-45

180 'Petliura idet na parad. Iz romana *Belaia gvardiia.*' *Krasnyi zhurnal dlia vsekh,* no 6 (June 1924), pp. 429-34

181 'Spiriticheskii seans.' *Rupor,* no 4 (1922), pp. 6-7

182 'Tipazh.' *Literaturnaia gazeta,* 21 Feb. 1973, p. 16

183 'Pis'mo M. Bulgakova sovetskomu pravitel'stvu.' *Grani,* no 66 (1967), pp. 155-61

184 'Writers on Trial.' *Survey,* no 67 (April 1968), pp. 122-7 (includes Bulgakov's letter to the Soviet government)

c / *Archives* (the principal sources are listed below)

185 Lenin Library – Manuscript Division (*Otdel rukopisei*). Bulgakov's major archive is *fond* 562, but at the time of writing it is still closed for cataloguing purposes. Some of the materials are listed in the various editions of the *Zapiski otdela rukopisei Gosudarstvennoi Biblioteki im V.I. Lenina*, Moscow.

186 Central State Archives of Literature and Art (*TsGALI*). Materials in *fondy* 656, 1250, 2030, 2050

187 Institute of Russian Literature, Leningrad (*Pushkinsky dom*). Materials in *fond* 369

188 Archives of the Moscow Art Theatre

189 Library of the All-Russian Theatrical Society (*VTO*): various typescripts

II / SECONDARY SOURCES

190 Abalkin, N. 'Sorok let spustia. *Dni Turbinykh* v Khudozhestvennom teatre.' *Pravda*, 8 Feb. 1968, p. 3

191 Akhmatova, Anna. *Sochineniia*. 'Pamiati M. B-va,' II, 141-2. Munich and Washington: Mezhdunarodnoe literaturnoe sodruzhestvo (Inter-Language Literary Associates), 1967-69 (poem first published in *Den' poezii*. Leningrad: Sovetskii pisatel', [1966])

192 '*Aleksandr Pushkin* M.A. Bulgakova i V. Veresaeva.' *Vakhtangovets*, no 1 (10 March 1936), p. 3

193 Allier, Raoul. *La Cabale des dévots (1627-1666)*. Geneva: Slatkine reprints, 1970

194 Alpers, B. 'Reaktsionnye domysli M. Bulgakova (*Mol'er* v filiale MKhAT).' *Literaturnaia gazeta*, 10 March 1936, p. 4

195 Al'tshuler, A.M. 'A.M. Gor'kii i problema stilevykh poiskov poslerevoliutsionnoi prozy i dramaturgii (A.M. Gor'kii o M.A. Bulgakove).' *A.M. Gor'kii i russkaia literatura*. *Uchenye zapiski Gor'kovskogo Gosudarstvennogo universiteta*, no 118 (Gor'kii, 1971), pp. 158-66

196 Al'tshuler, A.M. 'A.P. Chekov i M.A. Bulgakov.' In *Gertsenovskie chteniia: Literaturovedenie*, XXV. Ed. A. Grigor'ev. Leningrad: LGPU im. Gertsena, 1972. Pp. 57-9

197 Al'tshuler, A.M. 'Bulgakov-prozaik.' *Literaturnaia gazeta*, 7 Feb. 1968, pp. 5-6

198 Al'tshuler, A.M. '*Dni Turbinykh* i *Beg* M.A. Bulgakova v istorii sovetskogo teatra 20-kh godov.' Avtoreferat dissertatsii, predstavlennoi na soiskanie uchenoi stepeni kandidata iskusstvovedeniia. Moscow: 1972

199 Al'tshuler, A.M. 'Dramaturgicheskaia traditsiia A. Chekova i *Dni Turbinykh* Bulgakova.' In *Materialy X nauchoi konferentsii literaturovedov Povolozh'ia.* Ulianovsk 1969, pp. 144-6

200 Anastas'ev, A. *MKhAT v bor'be s formalizmom.* Moscow: Iskusstvo, 1953

201 Anisimov, I. *'Don Kikhot* v teatre Vakhtangova.' *Sovetskoe iskusstvo,* 27 April 1941, p. 3

202 Arnazi, B. 'Kamernyi teatr: *Bagrovyi ostrov.' Novyi zritel'*, no 1 (1 Jan. 1929), p. 13

203 Askol'dov, A. 'Vosem' snov (*Beg* v Stalingradskom dramaticheskom teatre).' *Teatr*, no 8 (1957), pp. 61-6

204 Averbakh, L. Review of *D'iavoliada. Izvestiia*, 20 Sept. 1925, p. 4

205 Averbakh, L., and V. Kirshon. 'Pochemu my protiv *Bega* M. Bulgakova.' *Na literaturnom postu*, no 20-21 (Oct.-Nov. 1928), pp. 48-50

206 B.G. Review of *Bagrovyi ostrov. Pravda*, 18 Dec. 1928, p. 5

207 Bachelis, I. *'Beg* nazad dolzhen byt' priostanovlen.' *Komsomol'skaia pravda*, 23 Oct. 1928, p. 2

208 Bachelis, I. 'O belykh arapakh i krasnykh tuzemtsakh.' *Molodaia gvardiia*, no 1 (Jan. 1929), pp. 105-11

209 *'Bagrovyi ostrov* v Kamernom teatre. Beseda s A. Ia. Tairovym.' *Novyi zritel'*, no 49 (2 Dec. 1928), p. 14, and *Zhizn' iskusstva*, no 49 (1928), p. 14

210 Bauman, El. 'Spektakl' kinoakterov.' *Sovetskaia kul'tura*, 21 Jan. 1967, p. 3

211 Beaujour, Elizabeth. 'The Use of Witches in Fedin and Bulgakov.' *Slavic Review*, 33, no 4 (Dec. 1974), pp. 695-707

212 Belyi, A. 'Neponiatnyi Gogol'.' *Sovetskoe iskusstvo*, 20 Jan. 1933, p. 4

213 Ben'iash, R.M. 'Cherkasov.' *Teatr*, no 2 (1970), pp. 79-90

214 Berkovskii, N. 'Rytsar' pechal'nogo obraza. *Don Kikhot* v Teatre dramy im. Pushkina.' *Iskusstvo i zhizn'*, no 4 (April 1941), pp. 23-6

215 Bern, L. *'Revizor* v kino.' *Vecherniaia Moskva*, 17 Nov. 1934, p. 3

216 Bertensson, S. *Vokrug iskusstva.* Hollywood 1957

217 Berzer, A. 'Vozvrashchenie mastera.' *Novyi mir*, no 9 (Sept. 1967), pp. 259-64

218 Beskin, E. 'Kremovye shtory.' *Zhizn' iskusstva*, no 41 (12 Oct. 1926), p. 7

219 Beskin, E. 'Nozdrev – I.M. Moskvin.' *Sovetskoe iskusstvo*, 27 Dec. 1932, p. 3

220 Beskin, E. 'Za god.' *Zhizn' iskusstva*, no 2 (11 Jan. 1927), pp. 5-6

221 'Besplodnaia politika.' *Sovetskoe iskusstvo*, 17 July 1936

222 Bezymenskii, A. 'Otkrytoe pis'mo Moskovskomu Khudozhestvennomu Akademicheskomu teatru (MKhAT I).' *Komsomol'skaia pravda*, 14 Oct. 1926, p. 4

223 Billington, Michael. 'Bulgakov Play.' *The Guardian*, Manchester, 23 March 1972, p. 10

224 Bis. *'Bagrovyi ostrov*. Novaia postanovka Kamernogo teatra.' *Komsomol'-skaia pravda*, 13 Dec. 1928, p. 4

225 Blium, V. 'Chetyre shaga nazad (*Dni Turbinykh* v Khudozhestvennom teatre Pervom.)' *Programmy gosudarstvennykh akademicheskikh teatrov*, no 54 (5-11 Oct. 1926), p. 5 ↓

226 Blium, V. 'Eshche o *Dniakh Turbinykh*.' *Programmy gosudarstvennykh akademicheskikh teatrov*, no 57 (26 Oct.-1 Nov. 1926), p. 5 ☞

227 Blium, V. 'Pravaia opasnost' i teatr.' (Illus. M. Khrapkovskii). *Ekran*, no 7 (Feb. 1929), p. 5

228 Bogoliubov. 'Eshche o *Zoikinoi kvartire*.' *Programmy gosudarstvennykh akademicheskikh teatrov*, no 64 (14-20 Dec. 1926), p. 11

229 Broide, M. 'Teatral'naia politika sovetskoi vlasti (Doklad A.V. Lunacharskogo v Kommunisticheskoi akademii).' *Programmy gosudarstvennykh akademicheskikh teatrov*, no 55 (12-18 Oct. 1926), p. 10

230 Brustein, Robert. 'Russian Evenings.' *New Republic*, 27 Feb. 1965, pp. 26-8

231 'Budushchii sezon v domakh kul'tury.' *Vecherniaia Krasnaia gazeta*, 13 July 1933

232 'M.A. Bulgakov.' *Gor'kovets*, no 11 (1 April 1940), p. 4

233 'Bulgakov i russkie pisateli (po semeinym vospominaniiam).' *Russkaia mysl' (La Pensée russe)*, 22 May 1969, p. 5

234 Bulgakov, M., and V. Veresaev. 'Perepiska po povodu p'esy *Pushkin (Poslednie dni)*.' *Voprosy literatury*, no 3 (March 1965), pp. 151-71

235 Chatfield-Taylor, H.C. *Molière: A Biography*. New York: Duffield, 1906

236 Chebotareva, V.A. 'Mikhail Bulgakov na Kavkaze.' *Ural'skii sledopyt* (Sverdlovsk), no 11 (1970), pp. 74-7

237 Chebotareva, V.A. 'Nachalo puti. K tvorcheskoi biografii M. Bulgakova (1920-1921 gg.).' *Bakinskii rabochii*, 14 May 1967, p. 4

238 Chebotareva, V.A. 'O rodine uteriannoi i vozvrashchennoi.' *Bakinskii rabochii*, 20 April 1971, p. 3

239 'Chelovek porazitel'nogo talanta.' *Literaturnaia Rossiia*, 2 April 1965, pp. 10-11

240 Cherkasov, N.K. *Chetvertyi Don Kikhot: istoriia odnoi roli*. Leningrad: Sovetskii pisatel', 1958

241 Cherkasov, N. *Notes of a Soviet Actor*. Trans. G. Ivanov-Mumjiev and S. Rosenberg. Moscow: Foreign Languages Publishing House, 1957

242 Chernoiarov, V. 'Sbornaia komanda.' *Novyi zritel'*, no 32 (9 Aug. 1926), pp. 8-9

243 Chudakova, M.O. 'K tvorcheskoi biografii M. Bulgakova 1916-1923 (po materialam arkhiva pisatelia).' *Voprosy literatury*, no 7 (1973), pp. 231-55

244 Chudakova, M.O. *Masterstvo Iuriia Oleshi*. Moscow: Nauka, 1972

245 Chudakova, M.O. 'Tvorcheskaia istoriia romana M. Bulgakova *Master i Margarita.*' *Voprosy literatury*, no 1 (1976), pp. 218-53

246 Chushkin, N.N. 'Put' khudozhnika.' *Ezhegodnik MKhAT 1948 god*, I. M-L: Iskusstvo, 1950. Pp. 573-634

247 Cusumano, Suzanne. 'Mikhail Boulgakov.' *Etudes*, 328 (1968), pp. 391-401

248 Dandrel, Louis. 'Théâtre. "L'île pourpre" de Boulgakov.' *Le Monde*, 24 Feb. 1973, p. 23

249 Darov, A. 'Voskresenie Bulgakova. *Master i Margarita.*' *Novoe russkoe slovo*, 17 March 1968, pp. 2, 5

250 Delaney, Joan. '*The Master and Margarita*: The Reach Exceeds the Grasp.' *Slavic Review*, 31, 1 (March 1972) 89-100

251 Derzhavin, K. '*Don Kikhot* (Prem'era v Gosudarstvennom akademicheskom teatre dramy imeni A.S. Pushkina).' *Izvestiia*, 20 March 1941, p. 4

252 '*Dni Turbinykh*. Anketa *Vechernei Krasnoi gazetoi.*' *Krasnaia gazeta*, vechernii vypusk, 9 Oct. 1926, p. 4

253 '*Dni Turbinykh* i *Liubov' Iarovaia* (Otchet o dispute v teatre Meierkhol'da).' *Na literaturnom postu*, no 4 (20 Feb. 1927), p. 73

254 Dobronravov, B.G. 'Avtobiografiia i stat'i.' *Ezhegodnik MKhAT 1949-50 gg*. M-L: Iskusstvo, 1952. Pp. 605-31

255 '*Don-Kikhot* v teatre im. Vakhtangova.' *Moskovskii Bol'shevik*, 4 April 1939, p. 1

256 Dunaevskii, I.O. *Izbrannye pis'ma*. Leningrad: Muzyka, 1971

257 Durylin, S. 'Moskovskii Khudozhestvennyi teatr vo vremia voiny.' *Teatr. Sbornik statei i materialov*, I (1944), pp. 80-98

258 Dychkovskii, S. 'Biografiia M.A. Bulgakova (1891-1940).' *V pomoshch' prepodavateliu russkogo iazyka v Amerike. (A Guide to Teachers of the Russian Language in America:* A Pedagogical Journal in Russian). (San Francisco). 17, 67 (1963), pp. 20-31

259 E.S-oi. 'Ubogoe zrelishche (na spektakle *Bagrovyi ostrov*).' *Trud*, 29 Dec. 1928, p. 4

260 El'sberg, Zh. 'Bulgakov i MKhAT.' *Na literaturnom postu*, no 2 (3 Nov. 1927), pp. 44-9

261 Erlikh, A. *Nas uchila zhizn': Literaturnye vospominaniia.* Moscow: Sovetskii pisatel', 1960

262 Erlikh, A. 'Oni rabotali v gazete.' *Znamia*, no 8 (1958), pp. 162-90

263 Ermakova, T.A. *'Beg* M. Bulgakova (K voprosu ob ideinokhudozhestvennom soderzhanii p'esy).' *Moskovskii oblastnoi pedagogicheskii institut imeni N.K. Krupskoi. Uchenye zapiski.* Tom 223, vypusk 9. Moscow, 1968. Pp. 101-15

264 Ermilov, V. *'Mertvye dushi* v Khudozhestvennom teatre.' *Literaturnaia gazeta*, 5 Jan. 1933, pp. 3-4

265 Ermilov, V. 'Teatr i pravda (k diskussii o *Mertvykh dushakh* na stsene MKhAT).' *Izvestiia TsIK SSSR*, 27 Feb. 1933, pp. 2-3

266 Ermolinskii, Sergei. 'O Mikhaile Bulgakove.' *Teatr*, no 9 (Sept. 1966), pp. 79-97

267 Ershov, L.F. *Sovetskaia satiricheskaia proza 20-kh godov.* M-L: Akademiia nauk SSSR, 1960

268 Eskin, A. *V nashem dome.* Moscow: Vserosiiskoe teatral'noe obshchestvo, 1973. Pp. 76-9

269 'Etakaia smeshnaia komediia.' *Sovetskaia kul'tura*, 13 Nov. 1971, p. 4

270 *Ezhegodnik MKhAT 1947 god.* M-L: Iskusstvo, 1949

271 Fadeev, A.A. *Pis'ma 1916-1956.* 'Pis'mo E.S. Bulgakovoi ot 15 marta 1940 g.,' pp. 158-9. Moscow: Sovetskii pisatel', 1967; also in *Novyi mir*, no 4 (1966), p. 227

272 Faiko, A.M. 'Rech' A.M. Faiko na grazhdanskoi panikhide po M.A. Bulgakove.' *Gor'kovets*, no 11 (1 April 1940), p. 4

273 Fedin, Konstantin. 'V poiskakh Pushkina.' *Literatura i iskusstvo*, 24 April 1943, p. 3; republished as **274**

274 Fedin, K. 'Mikhail Bulgakov o Pushkine.' In his *Pisatel', iskusstvo, vremia.* Moscow: Sovetskii pisatel', 1957. Pp. 440-6

275 Fel'dman, Z.V. 'B.G. Dobronravov v sovremennom repertuare.' *Ezhegodnik MKhAT 1949-50 gg.* M-L: Iskusstvo, 1952. Pp. 695-746

276 Fitzpatrick, Sheila. *The Commissariat of Enlightenment.* Cambridge: University Press, 1970

277 Fleming, Peter. Review of *The White Guard. Spectator*, 14 Oct. 1938, p. 603

278 Freidkina, L. *Dni i gody Vl.I. Nemirovicha-Danchenko.* Moscow: Vserossiiskoe teatral'noe obshchestvo, 1962

279 Frye, Northrop. *Anatomy of Criticism: Four Essays.* New York: Atheneum, 1967

280 Furonskii, Mark. 'Teatr M.A. Bulgakova.' *Russkaia mysl' (La Pensée russe)*, 22 May 1969, p. 8

281 Gabrilovich, Evgenii. 'Vtoraia chetvert'. Rasskazy kinematografistov.' *Iskusstvo kino*, no 2 (1969), pp. 174-85

282 Galichenko, N.V. 'Doctors as Writers: Veresaev and Bulgakov.' In *Proceedings: Pacific Northwest Conference on Foreign Languages.* Twenty-third annual meeting, 28-29 April 1972. Corvallis: Oregon State University, 1973. Pp. 273-80

283 Gellershtein, N. 'Meditsinskie novelly.' *Vecherniaia Moskva*, 24 Aug. 1963, p. 3

284 Gluzberg, Z. 'Zhan-Batist Poklen.' *Moskovskii komsomolets*, 21 March 1967, p. 3

285 Golikova, N. 'Snova i po-novomu: Mikhail Bulgakov i *Dni Turbinykh*. MKhAT, 1968.' *Literaturnaia Rossiia*, 1 March 1968, p. 17

286 Gorbov, D. 'Itogi literaturnogo goda.' *Novyi mir*, no 12 (Dec. 1925), pp. 129-48

287 Gorchakov, Nikolai A. *Istoriia sovetskogo teatra.* New York: Izdatel'stvo im. Chekhova, 1956. Translated as 288

288 Gorchakov, N.A. *The Theater in Soviet Russia.* Trans. Edgar Lehrman. New York: Columbia University Press, 1957

289 Gorchakov, Nikolai M. 'Ideia p'esy – osnovanie postanovki.' *Teatr*, no 8 (1950), pp. 55-72

290 Gorchakov, N.M. *'Mol'er* v MKhAT.' *Literaturnaia gazeta*, 10 Feb. 1936, p. 5

291 Gorchakov, N.M. *Rezhisserskie uroki K.S. Stanislavskogo: Besedy i zapisi repetitsii.* Moscow: Iskusstvo, 1951 (1st ed., 1950). Translated as 292

292 Gorchakov, N.M. *Stanislavsky directs.* Trans. Miriam Goldina. New York: Funk & Wagnalls, 1954

293 Gor'kii, A.M. *Gor'kii i sovetskie pisateli. Neizdannaia perepiska.* Literaturnoe nasledstvo, LXX. Moscow: Institut Literatury Akademii nauk SSSR, 1963

294 Gor'kii, A.M. *Letopis' zhizni i tvorchestvo A.M. Gor'kogo.* Vypusk 4 (1930-36). Moscow: Akademiia nauk, 1960

295 Gor'kii, A.M. *Perepiska A.M. Gor'kogo s zarubezhnymi pisateliami.* Arkhiv A.M. Gor'kogo, VIII. Moscow: Akademiia nauk, 1960

296 Gor'kii, A.M. and A.A. Fadeev. 'M.A. Bulgakov v neizdannykh pis'makh A.A. Gor'kogo i A.A. Fadeeva' (Publikatsiia Z.G. Mints). *Tartu Riikliku Ulikooli Toimetised. Uchenye zapiski Tartuskogo gosudarstvennogo universiteta. Trudy po russkoi i slovianskoi filologii, V.* Tartu, 1962. Pp. 399-402

297 *Gor'kovskie chteniia 1953-1957.* Moscow: Akademiia nauk, 1959

298 Gremislavskii, I.Ia. 'Pamiati P.V. Vil'amsa.' *Ezhegodnik MKhAT 1947 god.* M-L: Iskusstvo, 1949. Pp. 611-32

299 Grimarest, Jean Léonor Le Gallois de. *La Vie de Monsieur de Molière.*
Edition critique par Georges Mongrédein. Paris: Brient, 1955
300 Grinval'd, Iakov. *'Mertvye dushi* v MKhAT SSSR im. Gor'kogo.' *Vecherniaia
Moskva*, 11 Dec. 1932, p. 3
301 Grossman, L.P. 'Tvorcheskii put' L.M. Leonidova.' *Ezhegodnik MKhAT
1944 god.* Moscow: Muzei MKhAT, 1946. Pp. 349-77
302 Gruzdev, Il'ia. 'Bez Pushkina.' *Literatura i iskusstvo*, 24 April 1943, p. 3
303 Gul', R. 'Kievskaia epopeia (noiabr'-dekabr' 1918 g.).' *Arkhiv russkoi
revoliutsii* (Berlin), no 2 (1921), pp. 59-86
304 Gus, M. 'Goriat li rukopisi?' *Znamia*, no 12 (1968), pp. 213-20

305 Haber, Edith. 'The Mythic Structure of Bulgakov's *The Master and
Margarita.*' *Russian Review*, 34, no 4 (Oct. 1975), pp. 382-409
306 Hamant, Yves. 'Bibliographie de Mihail Bulgakov.' *Cahiers du monde russe
et soviétique*, XI, 2 (1970), pp. 319-48
307 Hewes, Henry. 'Lively Visitors.' *Saturday Review*, 20 Feb. 1965, p. 43

308 Ianshin, M. 'O masterstve i shtampakh.' In *Masterstvo rezhissera*. Ed. V.N.
Vlasov. Moscow: Iskusstvo, 1956. Pp. 153-202
309 Ianshin, M. 'Pouchitel'naia neudacha.' *Sovetskoe iskusstvo*, 17 March
1936, p. 3
310 Il'f, I., and E. Petrov. *The Twelve Chairs.* Trans. John Richardson, Intr.
Maurice Friedberg. London: F. Muller, 1961
311 *An International Bibliography of Works by and about Mikhail Bulgakov.*
Comp. Ellendea Proffer. Ann Arbor: Ardis, 1976
312 Isarova, Larisa. 'Primety sovremennosti i iskusheniia mody.' *Literaturnaia
gazeta*, 15 March 1967, p. 8
313 'Iskusstvo i klassovaia politika (iz doklada tov. Kerzhentseva).' *Rabochii i
teatr*, no 48 (1928), pp. 2-3
314 *Istoriia sovetskogo dramaticheskogo teatra v VI tomakh.* Ed. A. Anastas'ev
et al. Moscow: Nauka, 1966-71
315 Ivanov, Vsevolod. *Perepiska s A.M. Gor'kim.* Moscow: Sovetskii pisatel',
1969

316 Jones, Ernest. *On the Nightmare.* International Psychoanalytical Library,
no 20. London: L. and Virginia Woolf at the Hogarth Press and Institute
of Psychoanalysis, 1931
317 Jordan, F. 'Publisher's Protest (Reply to E. Pawel).' *Commentary*, 45,
no 5 (May 1968), pp. 10-11

318 K.F. 'Ispoved' Chichikova; "Serp i molot" obsuzhdaet *Mertvye dushi.'*
Sovetskoe iskusstvo, 14 Jan. 1933, p. 3

319 *Kamernyi teatr i ego khudozhniki.* Ed. A.M. Efros. Moscow: Vserossiiskoe
teatral'noe obshchestvo, 1934

320 Kannak, E. Review of *Sobach'e serdtse. Novyi zhurnal*, no 91 (1968),
pp. 300-2

321 Kapralov, G. 'V poiskakh sovremennosti.' *Zvezda*, no 9 (1958), pp. 187-95

322 Karaganov, Aleksandr. Review of *P'esy. Soviet Literature Monthly*, 33,
no 9 (Sept. 1963), pp. 191-3

323 Kataev, V. 'Trava zabveniia.' *Novyi mir*, no 3 (1967), pp. 3-129

324 Kaverin, V. *Sobranie sochinenii v shesti tomakh*, VI. 'Bulgakov,' pp.
543-54. 'Bessrochnyi dogovor,' pp. 555-8. Moscow: Khudozhestvennaia
literatura, 1966

325 Kaverin, V. 'Zametki o dramaturgii Bulgakova.' *Teatr*, no 10 (1956),
pp. 69-73

326 Khaikin, B. 'Opera *Mat'.' Izvestiia*, 23 Feb. 1938

327 Khmelev, N. 'Rabota nad obrazom.' *Ezhegodnik MKhAT 1945 god*, II.
M-L: Iskusstvo, 1948. Pp. 381-2

328 'Khronika iskusstv.' *Literaturnaia gazeta*, 20 April 1937, p. 6

329 Knebel', M. *Vsia zhizn'.* Moscow: Vserossiiskoe teatral'noe obshchestvo,
1967. Pp. 424-7

330 Kovac, Anton. 'The Problem of Good and Evil in Bulgakov's Novel
The Master and Margarita.' New Zealand Slavonic Journal (1968),
pp. 26-34

331 Krasnov, A. 'Khristos i Master.' *Grani*, nos 71-3 (1969-70), pp. 162-95,
150-92, 175-94 respectively

332 Kruzenshtern-Peterets, Iu. V. 'Diskussiia tol'ko nachinaetsia.' *Novoe
russkoe slovo*, 19 May 1968, p. 8

333 'Kuda idet MKhAT? Rabochie Khamovnikov o p'ese Bulgakova. Doloi
Beluiu gvardiiu!' Rabochaia Moskva, 20 Oct. 1926, p. 4

334 Kurbatyi, M. 'Sredi trekh sosenok.' *Programmy gosudarstvennykh
akademicheskikh teatrov*, no 54 (5-11 Oct. 1926), p. 4

335 Lakshin, Vl. 'Dve biografii.' *Novyi mir*, no 3 (1963), pp. 250-5

336 Lakshin, Vl. Review of *Notes of a Young Doctor. Soviet Literature
Monthly*, 34 (Feb. 1964), pp. 189-90

337 Lakshin, Vl. 'Roman M. Bulgakova *Master i Margarita.' Novyi mir*, no 6
(1968), pp. 284-311

338 Lakshin, Vl. 'Rukopisi ne goriat! (Otvet M. Gusu).' *Novyi mir*, no 12
(1968), pp. 262-6

339 Lakshin, Vl. 'Uroki Bulgakova.' *Pamir* (Dushanbe), no 4 (July-Aug. 1972), pp. 57-62

340 Lanina, T. 'Stanislavskii i Enukidze.' *Teatr*, no 6 (1967), pp. 9-14

341 Laville, Pierre. 'Huit songes et quelques propositions.' Dossier no 1 (accompanying the Programme to *La Fuite* at the Théâtre des Amandiers, Nanterre), 1970

342 Leonidov, Leonid M. 'Drug sovetskogo teatra.' *Sovetskoe iskusstvo*, 21 Dec. 1939, p. 4

343 Leonidov, L.M. *Vospominaniia, stat'i, besedy, perepiska, zapisnye knigi.* Moscow: Iskusstvo, 1960

344 Leonidov, O.L. 'Letopis' zhizni i tvorchestvo B.G. Dobronravova.' *Ezhegodnik MKhAT 1949-1950 gg.* M-L: Iskusstvo, 1952. Pp. 633-65

345 Leonidov, O.L. 'O.S. Bokshanskaia.' *Ezhegodnik MKhAT 1948 god*, I. M-L: Iskusstvo, 1950. Pp. 635-60

346 Less, A. *Neprochitannye stranitsy: Rasskazy.* 'K istorii *Pushkina*,' pp. 251-8. Moscow: Sovetskii pisatel', 1966

347 Levidov, M. 'Dosadnyi pustiak. (*Dni Turbinykh* v Khudozhestvennom teatre).' *Vecherniaia Moskva*, 8 Oct. 1926, p. 3

348 Levkovich, Ia.L. 'Pushkin v sovetskoi khudozhestvennoi proze i drama-turgii.' In *Pushkin: issledovaniia i materialy*, v. Nauka, 1967. Pp. 140-78

349 Levshin, V. 'Sadovaia, 302-bis.' *Teatr*, no 11 (1971), pp. 110-20

350 Lezhnev, I. *Izbrannye stat'i.* Intr. Al. Dymshits, 'I.G. Lezhnev (1891-1955),' pp. 3-7. Moscow: Khudozhestvennaia literatura, 1960

351 Lezhnev, I. *Zapiski sovremennika*, I. 2nd. ed. Moscow: Sovetskii pisatel', 1935

352 Liandres, S. '"Russkii pisatel' ne mozhet zhit' bez rodiny ..."' (Materialy k tvorcheskoi biografii M. Bulgakova).' *Voprosy literatury*, 10, no 9 (Sept. 1966), pp. 134-9

353 Lièvre, Pierre. 'Théâtre. L'appartement de Zoïka.' *Mercure de France*, 1 April 1937, pp. 141-4

354 Likhachev, D.S. 'Literaturnyi ded Ostapa Bendera.' In *Stranitsy istorii russkoi literatury*. Ed. D.F. Mirnov. Moscow: Nauka, 1971. Pp. 245-8

355 Lir. '*Dni Turbinykh* i *Liubov' Iarovaia*. Disput v teatre im. Vs. Meierkhol'da.' *Programmy gosudarstvennykh akademicheskikh teatrov*, no 7 (15-21 Feb. 1927), p. 13

356 Litovskii, O. *Glazami sovremennika: Zametki proshlykh let.* Moscow: Sovetskii pisatel', 1963

357 Litovskii, O. *Tak i bylo: ocherki, vospominaniia, vstrechi.* Moscow: Sovetskii pisatel', 1958

358 Lunacharskii, A.V. *Sobranie sochinenii v vos'mi tomakh.* Moscow: Khudozhestvennaia literatura, 1963-67

359 Lur'e, Ia. and I. Serman. 'Ot *Beloi gvardii* k *Dniam Turbinykh.' Russkaia literatura*, 8, no 2 (1965), pp. 194-203.

360 MacCarthy, Desmond. 'The Moscow Art Theatre.' *New Statesman & Nation*, 5 Dec. 1931, pp. 713-14

361 Mahlow, Elena N. *Bulgakov's* The Master and Margarita: *The Text as a Cipher*. New York: Vantage, 1975

362 Maiakovskii, V. *Polnoe sobranie sochinenii v trinadtsati tomakh*. Moscow: Khudozhestvennaia literatura, 1955-61

363 (Maiakovskii, V.) *Novoe o Maiakovskom*. Literaturnoe nasledstvo, LXV. 'Vystuplenie na dispute "Teatral'naia politika sovetskoi vlasti" 2 Oct. 1926,' Pt. I, pp. 37-42. Moscow: Akademiia nauk SSSR, 1958

364 Makarovskaia, G. and A. Zhuk. 'O romane M. Bulgakova *Master i Margarita.' Volga*, no 6 (June 1968), pp. 161-81

365 Maksimova, V. 'Vozvrashchenie k legende. (P'esa M. Bulgakova, *Dni Turbinykh* v Moskovskom Khudozhestvennom teatre im. Gor'kogo).' *Moskovskaia pravda*, 19 Jan. 1968, p. 3

366 Mandelshtam, Nadezhda. *Hope against Hope*. New York: Atheneum, 1970

367 Mandelshtam, N. *Hope Abandoned*. New York: Atheneum, 1974

368 Markov, P. 'Istoriia moego teatral'nogo sovremennika. Vospominaniia.' *Teatr*, no 5 (1971), pp. 77-94

369 Markov, P. 'Mikhail Bulgakov.' *Soviet Literature*, no 6 (1971), pp. 158-62

370 Markov, P. *Pravda teatra. Stat'i*. Moscow: Iskusstvo, 1965. 'O Bulgakove,' pp. 226-9 (article first published in *Gor'kovets*, no 11, 1 April 1940, p. 4)

371 Markov, P. 'Teatr.' *Pechat' i revoliutsiia*, no 7 (1927), pp. 130-57

372 'Materialy o M.A. Bulgakove.' Contains: Konstantin Paustovskii, 'Bulgakov i teatr,' pp. 378-88; 'Zasedanie Khudozhestvennogo soveta – chtenie *Bega* Bulgakovym (v MKhAT),' pp. 388-90; 'Stenogramma rechei, proiznesennykh na grazhdanskoi panikhide po Mikhaile Afanas'eviche Bulgakove,' pp. 391-5; 'Iz vystuplenii na vechere pamiati M.A. Bulgakova v pervuiu godovshchinu smerti,' pp. 395-8; 'Zapis' dlia teatra,' pp. 398-9; 'Pis'mo M.A. Bulgakova,' pp. 399-400. *Mosty*, no 11 (1965), pp. 378-400

373 Meierkhol'd, V.E. *Stat'i, pis'ma, rechi, besedy*, II. 'Meierkhol'd protiv meierkhol'dovshchiny (Iz doklada 14 marta 1936g.),' pp. 330-47. 'Vystuplenie na sobranii teatral:nykh rabotnikov Moskvy 26 marta 1936 goda,' pp. 348-58. Moscow: Iskusstvo, 1968

374 '*Mertvye dushi* Gogolia v Khudozhestvennom teatre.' *Sovetskoe iskusstvo*, 23 Oct. 1931, p. 4

375 Mikhailova, I. 'Pocherk teatra.' *Teatr*, no 1 (1970), pp. 39-42

376 Mikhal'skii, F. *Dni i liudi Khudozhestvennogo teatra*. Moscow: Moskovskii rabochii, 1966

377 Mikhal'skii, F. *Muzei Moskovskogo Khudozhestvennogo teatra.* Moscow: Moskovskii rabochii, 1958

378 Miliavskii, Boris. *Satirik i vremia.* Moscow: Sovetskii pisatel', 1963

379 Milne, Lesley. 'K biografii M.A. Bulgakova.' (Publikatsiia Lesley Milne). *Novyi zhurnal,* no 111 (1973), pp. 151-74

380 Milne, Lesley M. 'M.A. Bulgakov and *Dead Souls:* The Problems of Adaptation.' *Slavonic and East European Review,* 52, no 128 (July 1974), pp. 420-40

381 Mindlin, E. 'Molodoi Mikhail Bulgakov (Iz vospominanii).' *Nash sovremennik,* no 2 (Feb. 1967), pp. 98-102

382 Mindlin, E. *Neobyknovennye sobesedniki: Kniga vospominanii.* 'Nakanune,' pp. 116-43. 'Mikhail Bulgakov,' pp. 144-55. Moscow: Sovetskii pisatel', 1968

383 'MKhAT prinial k postanovke *Beg* Bulgakova.' *Pravda,* 11 Oct. 1928, p. 6

384 Mlechin, V. 'Neprochitannyi Gogol'.' *Rabis,* no 1 (Jan. 1933), pp. 25-6

385 Mokul'skii, S. 'Zametki po povodu *Dnei Turbinykh.*' *Rabochii i teatr,* no 19 (July 1933), pp. 8-10

386 Morgenshtern, M. '*Zoikina kvartira* v Teatre im. Vakhtangova.' *Programmy gosudarstvennykh akademicheskikh teatrov,* no 60 (16-22 Nov. 1926), pp. 10-11

387 Muchnic, Helen. *Russian Writers: Notes and Essays.* New York: Random, 1971

388 Mustangov, E. 'Mikhail Bulgakov.' *Pechat' i revoliutsiia,* no 4 (1927), pp. 81-7

389 N. Sm. Review of *Nedra,* kniga chetvertaia. *Izvestiia,* 9 April 1924, p. 7

390 'Nashi tvorcheskie plany.' *Sovetskaia kul'tura,* 24 July 1956, p. 1

391 Nekrasov, Viktor. 'Dom Turbinykh.' *Novyi mir,* no 8 (Aug. 1967), pp. 132-42. Translated in 168

392 Nemirovich-Danchenko, Vl.I. 'Sokrashchennaia stenogramma zamechanii Vl.I. Nemirovich-Danchenko po spektakliu *Poslednie dni (Pushkin).*' *Ezhegodnik MKhAT 1943 god.* Moscow: Muzei MKhAT 1945. Pp. 679-707

393 Nemirovich-Danchenko, Vl.I. *Teatral'noe nasledie. I: Stat'i, rechi, besedy, pis'ma.* 'Zamechaniia po spektakliu *Poslednie dni (Pushkin).* Sokrashchennaia stenogramma,' pp. 328-44. Moscow: Iskusstvo, 1952

394 'Novaia postanovka Khudozhestvennogo teatra.' *Literatura i iskusstvo,* 24 April 1943, p. 3

395 *Novatorstvo sovetskogo teatra.* Ed. A. Anastas'ev *et al.* Moscow: Iskusstvo, 1965

396 Novitskii, P. '*Bagrovyi ostrov* – dramaticheskii pamflet v 4 deistviiakh s prologom.' *Repertuarnyi biulleten Glaviskusstva RSFSR*, no 12 (Dec. 1928), pp. 9-10

397 Novitskii, P. 'N.P. Khmelev.' *Novyi mir*, no 1 (1939), pp. 234-54

398 'Novoe v rabote Glavrepertkoma.' *Vecherniaia Moskva*, 9 June 1928

399 Novoselitskaia, L. 'Zhizn' i smert' Romana Khludova.' *Teatr*, no 8 (1968), p. 113

400 Nurse, Kenneth. '"Flight" into confusion.' *Daily Telegraph*, London, 30 March 1972, p. 12

401 Nusinov, I.M. 'Put' M. Bulgakova.' *Pechat' i revoliutsiia*, no 4 (1929), pp. 40-53

402 'O fal'shi.' *Sovetskoe iskusstvo*, 11 March 1936, p. 1

403 *O Stanislavskom. Sbornik vospominanii.* Ed. L.Ia. Gurevich. V.O. Toporkov on *Mertvye dushi*, pp. 318-23. Moscow: Vserossiiskoe teatral'noe obshchestvo, 1948

404 'Obraz velikogo khudozhnika. P'esa M. Bulgakova *Mol'er.*' *Vecherniaia Moskva*, 3 Jan. 1967, p. 3

405 Obraztsova, A. 'Vosem' snov i chetyre probuzhdeniia. *Beg* M. Bulgakova v Moskovskom teatre imeni Ermolovoi.' *Moskovskaia pravda*, 11 May 1967, p. 3

406 *Ocherki istorii russkogo sovetskogo dramaticheskogo teatra.* Ed. N.G. Zograf. 3 vols. Moscow: Akademiia nauk SSSR, 1954-61

407 *Ocherki istorii russkoi sovetskoi dramaturgii.* Ed. S.V. Vladimirov and G.A. Lapkina. 3 vols. V.A. Sakhnovskii-Pankeev, 'Bulgakov,' II, pp. 122-43. M-L: Iskusstvo, 1963-68

408 Oganian, Z. Review of *Don Kikhot. Kommunist* (Erevan), 13 July 1968, p. 4

409 Olesha, Iurii. *Ni dnia bez strochki: iz zapisnykh knizhek.* Moscow: Sovetskaia Rossiia, 1965

410 'Opera *Petr I.*' *Teatral'naia dekada*, no 32 (11 Nov. 1937), p. 11

411 Orlinskii, A. 'Grazhdanskaia voina na stsene MKhAT.' *Pravda*, 8 Oct. 1926, p. 6

412 Orlinskii, A. 'Protiv bulgakovshchiny.' *Novyi zritel'*, no 41 (12 Oct. 1926), pp. 3-4

413 Orlinskii, A. Review of *Zoikina kvartira. Pravda*, 13 Nov. 1926, p. 8

414 Orlov, Alexander. *The Secret History of Stalin's Crimes.* London: Jarrolds, 1954

415 Orlovskii, Serge. 'Moscow Theaters, 1917-1941.' In *Soviet Theaters, 1917-1941.* Ed. Martha Bradshaw. New York: Research Program on the USSR, 1954. Pp. 1-127

416 Osinskii, N. 'Literaturnye zametki.' *Pravda*, 28 July 1925, pp. 4-5

417 P.B. 'Ob odnom literaturnom dispute.' *Zhizn' iskusstva*, no 44 (2 Nov. 1926), p. 12

418 Partridge, Helen H. 'Comedy in the Early Works of Mikhail Bulgakov.' Dissertation, Georgetown University, Washington, DC, 1969

419 Paustovskii, Konstantin. *Kniga skitanii.* 'Chetvertaia polosa,' pp. 23-35. 'Snezhnye shapki,' pp. 60-6. Moscow: Sovetskaia Rossiia, 1964 (first published in *Novyi mir*, no 10 (1963), pp. 63-118). Translated in 420

420 Paustovsky, Konstantin. *The Story of a Life.* Trans. Manya Harari and Michael Duncan. London: Collins & Harvill, 1964

421 Pavlov, V.A. 'Dni Turbinykh.' In his *Teatral'nye sumerki: Stat'i i ocherki ob akademizme i o MKhATe, 1926-27 gg.* Moscow: Novyi zritel', 1928. Pp. 85-91

422 Pawel, Ernst. 'The Devil in Moscow.' *Commentary*, 45 no 3 (March 1968), pp. 90-3

423 Pereverzev, V. 'Novinki belletristiki.' *Pechat' i revoliutsiia*, no 5 (Sept.-Oct. 1924), pp. 134-9

424 Pertsov, V. *Poety i prozaiki velikikh let.* Moscow: Khudozhestvennaia literatura, 1969

425 Pertsov, Victor. 'Two Novels about Nineteen-Eighteen – Alexei Tolstoy and Mikhail Bulgakov.' *Soviet Literature*, no 1 (1968), pp. 158-62 (originally published in *Literaturnaia gazeta*, 30 Aug. 1967, pp. 4-5)

426 'Pervye spektakli sezona.' *Sovetskaia kul'tura*, 29 Sept. 1956

427 'P'esa o Pushkine.' *Literaturnaia gazeta*, 9 Oct. 1935, p. 5

428 'P'esy M. Bulgakova v izdatel'stve *Sovetskii pisatel'.*' *Vecherniaia Moskva*, 11 June 1940, p. 3

429 Petelin, V. 'M.A. Bulgakov i *Dni Turbinykh.*' *Ogonek*, no 11 (15 March 1969), pp. 25-7

430 Pikel', R. 'Pered podniatiem zanavesa (Perspektivy teasezona).' *Izvestiia*, 15 Sept. 1929, p. 5

431 Pimenov, V. 'Nikolai Cherkasov.' *Literaturnaia Rossiia*, 1 Sept. 1967, pp. 6-7

432 Piper, D.G.B. 'An Approach to Bulgakov's *The Master and Margarita.*' *Forum for Modern Language Studies*, 7, no 2 (1971), pp. 134-57

433 Piper, D.G.B. 'Three Early Soviet Novels.' *Journal of Russian Studies* (Bradford), no 20 (1970), pp. 3-20

434 Pletnev, R. 'O iumore romana *Master i Margarita.*' *Novoe russkoe slovo*, 8 Sept. 1968, p. 5

435 Pletnev, R. 'O *Mastere i Margarite.*' *Novyi zhurnal*, no 92 (1968), pp. 150-60

305 Selective bibliography

436 Pletnev, R. 'Pontii Pilat i roman M. Bulgakova.' *Novoe russkoe slovo*, 22 Sept. 1968, p. 5

437 'Po planu i vne plana.' *Smena*, 3 Nov. 1955

438 Poliakova, E.I. *Teatr i dramaturg: iz opyta raboty MKhAT nad p'esami sovetskikh dramaturgov, 1917-41 gg.* Moscow: Vserossiiskoe teatral'noe obshchestvo, 1959

439 Popov, Aleksei. 'Vospominaniia i razmyshleniia.' *Teatr*, no 5 (1960), pp. 110-22

440 Popov-Dubrovskii. 'Na khudozhestvennom fronte.' *Pravda*, 25 Dec. 1928, p. 4

441 Potanina, G. 'Vstrecha v Leningrade.' *Russkaia mysl' (La Pensée russe)*, 22 May 1969, p. 5

442 Pravdukhin, V. 'Literatura signaliziruet.' *Leningradskaia pravda*, 27 Feb. 1927, p. 4

443 Pravdukhin, V. Review of *Nedra*, Book 4. *Krasnaia nov'*, no 2 (March 1924), pp. 307-10

444 Proffer, Ellendea. 'Bulgakov's Notebooks for *Last Days*.' *Russian Literature Triquarterly*, no 3 (1972), pp. 431-44

445 Proffer, E. 'Bulgakov's *The Master and Margarita*: Genre and Motif.' *Canadian Slavic Studies*, 3, no 4 (1969), pp. 615-28

446 Proffer, E. 'The Major Works of Mikhail Bulgakov.' Dissertation, Indiana University, 1971

447 Proffer, E. *Mikhail Bulgakov.* Ann Arbor: Ardis (to be published in 1978)

448 Proffer, E. 'Mikhail Bulgakov: Documents for a Biography.' *Russian Literature Triquarterly*, no 7 (1974), pp. 445-74

449 Proffer, E. 'On *The Master and Margarita*.' *Russian Literature Triquarterly*, no 6 (1973), pp. 533-65

450 Proffer, E. 'On *Zoia's Apartment*.' *Canadian Slavic Studies*, 4, no 2 (1970), pp. 281-7

451 Proffer, E. 'An Unpublished Scene from the Original *Days of the Turbins (White Guard)*.' *Russian Literature Triquarterly*, no 7 (1974), pp. 475-9

452 'Protest protiv *Dni Turbinykh*.' *Krasnaia gazeta* (vechernii vypusk), 5 Oct. 1926, p. 1

453 Pushkin, Alexandr. *Eugene Onegin.* Trans. Vladimir Nabokov. Bolligen Series LXXII. New York: Bolligen, 1964

454 'Pushkinskii sezon.' *Teatral'naia dekada*, 21 Sept. 1936

455 Puti razvitiia teatra (*Stenograficheskii otchet i resheniia partiinogo soveshchaniia po voprosam teatra pri Agitprope TsK VKP(b) v mae 1927g.*). Ed. S.N. Krylov. M-L: Knigopechat', 1927

456 Ravich, N. 'Pamiatnye vstrechi.' *Zvezda*, no 7 (1958), pp. 147-59
457 'Repertuar MKhAT.' *Sovetskoe iskusstvo*, 16 Oct. 1932, p. 4
458 'Repertuarnyi plan Bol'shogo teatra.' *Sovetskoe iskusstvo*, 25 Jan. 1938
459 Reshetar, John S. *The Ukrainian Revolution, 1917-1920: A Study in Nationalism*. Princeton: University Press, 1952
460 Rogachevskii, M.L. 'Perepiska s sovetskimi dramaturgami.' *Ezhegodnik MKhAT 1948 god*, I. M-L: Iskusstvo, 1950. Pp. 389-448
461 Rudnitskii, K. 'Mikhail Bulgakov.' *Voprosy teatra*, 1966, pp. 127-42
462 Rudnitskii, K. 'Mol'er, *Tartiuf* i Bulgakov.' *Nauka i religiia*, no 1 (Jan. 1972), pp. 84-90
463 Rudnitskii, K. *Spektakli raznykh let*. Moscow: Iskusstvo, 1974. 'Bulgakov,' pp. 227-85
464 Rudnitskii, K. 'Veshchie sny. *Beg* M. Bulgakova v teatre im. Ermolovoi.' *Izvestiia*, 21 April 1967, p. 4
465 Rudnitskii, K. 'Vozvrashchenie Turbinykh.' *Vecherniaia Moskva*, 1 Feb. 1968, p. 3
466 *Russkaia sovetskaia dramaturgiia*. Ed. A.O. Boguslavskii and V.A. Diev. I. Moscow: Akademiia nauk, 1963
467 Rybnik, Aleksandr. 'Bez poiska net otkrytii.' *Pravda vostoka*, 3 Feb. 1968, p. 3
468 Rzhevskii, L. 'Pilatov grekh: O tainopisi v romane M. Bulgakova *Master i Margarita*.' *Novyi zhurnal*, no 90 (1968), pp. 60-80. Translated as **469**
469 Rzhevsky, L. 'Pilate's Sin: Cryptography in Bulgakov's Novel, *The Master and Margarita*.' *Canadian Slavonic Papers*, 13, no 1 (1971), pp. 1-19

470 Sadko [Blium, V.]. 'Nachalo kontsa MKhAT'a.' *Zhizn' iskusstva*, no 43 (25 Oct. 1927), pp. 7-8
471 Sakhnovskii, V.G. 'Gogol's v MKhAT SSSR im. Gor'kogo. Kak i pochemu staviatsia *Mertvye dushi*. Itogi dvukhletnei raboty.' *Sovetskoe iskusstvo*, 15 Nov. 1932, p. 3
472 Sakhnovskii, V.G. 'O spektakle *Mertvye dushi*.' In *K spektakliu 'N.V. Gogol'. "Mertvye dushi." Dramaticheskaia kompozitsiia M.A. Bulgakova*.' Moscow: Muzei MKhAT, 1937
473 Sakhnovskii, V.G. *Rabota rezhissera*. M-L: Iskusstvo, 1937
474 Semanova, M. 'Snizhenie satiricheskogo zamysla (Spektakl' *Mertvye dushi* na stsene Teatra Komedii).' *Leningradskaia pravda*, 30 Oct. 1952, p. 3
475 Sharratt, Barbara Kejna. '*Flight* – A Symphonic Play.' *Canadian Slavonic Papers*, 14, no 1 (1972), pp. 76-86
476 Sharratt, B.K. 'Narrative Techniques in *The Master and Margarita*.' *Canadian Slavonic Papers*, 16, no 1 (1974), pp. 1-13

477 Sheremet'eva, E. 'Iz teatral'noi zhizni Leningrada.' *Zvezda*, no 12 (1976), pp. 192-200

478 Sheshukov, S.I. *Neistovye revniteli: Iz istorii literaturnoi bor'by 20-kh godov.* Moscow: Moskovskii rabochii, 1970

479 Shorokhov, Valerii. 'Iz pushek po vorob'iam.' *Teatr*, no 3 (1968), pp. 71-3

480 Simonov, K. *Razgovor s tovarishchami. Vospominaniia. Stat'i. Lit. zametki. O sobstvennoi rabote.* 'Posledniaia kniga Bulgakova,' pp. 181-4. 'Zhizni, knigi, rukopisi. Iz perepiski,' pp. 215-64. Moscow: Sovetskii pisatel', 1970

481 Skobelev, V. 'V piatom izmerenii.' *Pod'em*, no 6 (1967), pp. 124-8

482 Skorino, L., and I. Vinogradov. *'Master i Margarita Bulgakova.'* L. Skorino, 'Litsa bez karnaval'nykh masok (Polemicheskie zametki),' pp. 25-42, and 'Otvet opponentu,' pp. 76-81. I. Vinogradov, 'Zaveshchanie mastera,' pp. 42-75. *Voprosy literatury*, no 6 (June 1968), pp. 24-81

483 Slashchev-Krymskii, Ia.A. *Trebuiu suda obshchestva i glasnosti.* Constantinople 1921

484 Slashchov, Ia. *Krym v 1920 godu: Otryvki iz vospominanii.* Dm. Furmanov, 'Predislovie,' pp. 3-14. M-L: Gosudarstvennoe izdatel'stvo, 1923

485 Slonim, Marc. *Russian Theater from the Empire to the Soviets.* New York: Collier, 1962

486 Slonim, M. *Soviet Russian Literature: Writers and Problems.* New York: Oxford, 1969

487 Smelkov, Iu. 'Piat' sezonov Irkutskogo teatra.' *Teatr*, no 10 (1969), pp. 55-61

488 'Smert' pisatelia (zapisano po semeinym vospominaniiam).' *Russkaia mysl' (La Pensée russe)*, 22 May 1969, p. 7

489 Smirnova, Vera. *Sovremennyi portret: Stat'i.* 'Pisatel' i mir, v kotorom on zhivet,' pp. 56-106. 'Mikhail Bulgakov – dramaturg,' pp. 282-332. Moscow: Sovetskii pisatel', 1964

490 'Sovet GRK o *Bege* Bulgakova.' *Pravda*, 24 Oct. 1928, p. 5

491 *Sovetskie pisateli. Avtobiografii,* III. Ed. B.Ia. Brainina and A.N. Dmitrieva. Bulgakov, 'Avtobiografiia' (1926 and 1937), pp. 85-7. Biographical notes, pp. 87-101. Moscow: Khudozhestvennaia literatura, 1966

492 Stalin, I.V. *Sochineniia,* XI. 'Otvet Bill'-Belotserkovskomu,' pp. 326-9. Moscow: Politicheskaia literatura, 1949. Translated as **493**

493 Stalin, I.V. *Works,* XI. 'Reply to Bill-Belotserkovsky,' pp. 341-4. Moscow: Foreign Languages Publishing House, 1954

494 Stanislavskii, K.S. *Sobranie sochinenii v vos'mi tomakh,* VIII: Pis'ma, 1918-38. Moscow: Iskusstvo, 1961

495 Stenbock-Fermor, Elisabeth. 'Bulgakov's *The Master and Margarita* and Goethe's *Faust.' Slavic and East European Journal*, 13, no 3 (1969), pp. 309-25

496 Sudakov, I. 'Rannie roli N.P. Khmeleva.' *Ezhegodnik MKhAT 1945 god*, II. M-L: Iskusstvo, 1948. Pp. 33-42
497 Sudakov, I. 'Znachenie ideinogo zamysla v sozdanii spektaklia.' In *Masterstvo rezhissera, sbornik statei*. Ed. V.N. Vlasov. Moscow: Iskusstvo, 1956. Pp. 369-90

498 Tal'nikov, D. *'Mertvye dushi* v Khudozhestvennom teatre.' *Teatr i dramaturgiia*, no 1 (April 1933), pp. 55-60; no 2-3 (May-June 1933), pp. 24-9
499 Tarsis, V. *Sovremennye russkie pisateli*. Leningrad: Izdatel'stvo pisatelei, 1930. P. 45
500 Tatarinova, N. 'Vstrecha c XVI vekom.' *Sovetskaia kul'tura*, 16 Nov. 1971, p. 3
501 'Teatr. Disput o *Dniakh Turbinykh* i *Liubovi Iarovoi*.' *Pravda*, 10 Feb. 1927, p. 6
502 *Teatral'naia entsiklopediia*. Ed. S.S. Mokul'skii. Moscow: Sovetskaia entsiklopediia, 1961
503 Thompson, Ewa M. 'The Artistic World of Michail Bulgakov.' *Russian Literature*, no 5 (1973), pp. 54-64
504 Turkeltaub, I. *'Bagrovyi ostrov* v Moskovskom Kamernom teatre.' *Zhizn' iskusstva*, no 52 (23 Dec. 1928), pp. 10-11
505 'Tvorcheskii put' (1874-1946)' (on I.M. Moskvin). *Ezhegodnik MKhAT 1946 god*. M-L: Iskusstvo, 1948. Pp. 25-92

506 Uriel' [O. Litovskii]. 'Bulgakov vzialsia za NEP. (*Zoikina kvartira* v studii im. Vakhtangova).' *Komsomol'skaia pravda*, 13 Nov. 1926, p. 4
507 Uspensky, Boris. *A Poetics of Composition: The Structure of the Artistic Text and Typology of a Compositional Form*. Trans. Valentina Zavarin and Susan Wittig. Berkeley: University of California Press, 1973

508 'V khudsovete Kamernogo teatra.' *Novyi zritel'*, no 4 (20 April 1929), pp. 12-13
509 Veresaev, V. *Pushkin v zhizni*, II. Moscow: Sovetskii pisatel', 1936
510 Vilenkin, V. 'Russkaia klassicheskaia dramaturgiia na stsene Moskovskogo Khudozhestvennogo teatra, 1917-1947 gg.' *Ezhegodnik MKhAT 1947 god*. M-L: Iskusstvo, 1949. Pp. 197-250
511 Vin. *'Bagrovyi ostrov*.' *Nasha gazeta*, 14 Dec. 1928, p. 4
512 'Vneshnii blesk i fal'shivoe soderzhanie. O p'ese M. Bulgakova v filiale MKhAT.' *Pravda*, 9 March 1936, p. 3
513 'Vokrug postanovki *Mertvykh dush*. Vstrecha rabochikh s postanovshchikom i akterami MKhAT.' *Rabochaia Moskva*, 3 Feb. 1933, p. 4

514 Volkov, N.D. *Teatral'nye vechera*. Moscow: Iskusstvo, 1966

515 *Vospominaniia ob Il'e Il'fe i Evgenii Petrove*. Evgenii Petrov, 'Iz vospominanii ob Il'fe,' pp. 7-25. Iurii Olesha, 'Ob Il'fe,' pp. 26-33. Konstantin Paustovskii, 'Chetvertaia polosa,' pp. 80-92. Mikhail Stikh (M. L'vov), 'V starom *Gudke*,' pp. 93-100. Moscow: Sovetskii pisatel', 1963

516 'Vstrecha dlia vas – Mikhail Ianshin.' *Komsomol'skaia pravda*, 8 Nov. 1970, p. 4

517 *Vstrechi s Meierkhol'dom: Sbornik vospominanii*. Ed. L.D. Vendrovskaia. N. Chushkin, 'V sporakh o teatre,' pp. 415-31. L. Varpakhovskii, 'Zametki proshlykh let,' pp. 459-79. Moscow: Vserossiiskoe teatral'noe obshchestvo, 1967

518 Vulis, A. *Sovetskii satiricheskii roman: Evoliutsiia zhanra v 20-30e. gody*. Tashkent: Nauka, 1965

519 Wardle, Irving. 'Melodrama with Flair.' *Times*, London, 23 March 1972, p. 11

520 Wardle, I. 'Undisguised Truth in Drama of the Absurd.' *Times*, 1 April 1972, p. 9

521 Wrangel, General Baron Peter N. *Always with Honour*. 2nd printing. New York: Robert Speller, 1963

522 Wright, A. Colin. 'Mikhail Bulgakov and Yury Slyozkin.' *Etudes slaves et est-européenes*, 17 (1972), pp. 85-91

523 Wright, A.C. 'National and Universal Themes in the Work of Mikhail Bulgakov.' To be published in *Slawistische Studien und Texte* (East Berlin), 1978

524 Wright, A.C. 'Satan in Moscow: An Approach to Bulgakov's *The Master and Margarita*.' *PMLA*, 88, no 5 (Oct. 1973), pp. 1162-72

525 *Zadachi Glaviskusstva*. Ed. A.A. Alekseev and A.A. Gol'dman. Moscow: TsK Vserabis, 1929

526 Zagorskii, M. '*Bagrovyi ostrov* v Kamernom teatre.' *Vecherniaia Moskva*, 13 Dec. 1928, p. 3

527 Zagorskii, M. '*Zoikina kvartira* v Studii im. Vakhtangova.' *Programmy gosudarstvennykh akademicheskikh teatrov*, no 59 (9-15 Nov. 1926), p. 9

528 Zagorskii, M. 'Vtoroi opus Bulgakova – *Zoikina kvartira*.' *Vecherniaia Moskva*, 1 Nov. 1926, p. 3

529 Zakhava, B. *Vakhtangov i ego studiia*. Moscow: Akademiia, 1930

530 Zamiatin, E. *Litsa*. 'O segodniashnem i o sovremennom,' pp. 213-30. New York: Izdatel'stvo im. Chekhova, 1955 (reprinted from *Russkii sovremennik*, no 2, 1924)

531 Zavalishin, V. 'Satirists and Humorists: Mikhail A. Bulgakov (1891-1940).'
In his *Early Soviet Writers*. New York: Praeger, 1958. Pp. 329-33
532 Zemskaia, E.A. 'M.A. Bulgakov. Pis'ma k rodnym (1921-1922gg).'
Izvestiia Akademii nauk SSSR. Seriia literatury i iazyka, 35, no 5 (1976),
pp. 451-64
533 Zhdanova, K. 'Na vystavke M.A. Bulgakova.' *Teatr*, no 1 (1967), p. 124
534 '*Zoikina kvartira* v studii im. Vakhtangova (Beseda s rezhisserom A.
Popovym).' *Vecherniaia Moskva*, 26 Oct. 1926, p. 3
535 Zubkov, Iu. 'Polet v osennei mgle.' *Literaturnaia Rossiia*, 12 May 1967,
p. 20

Index of Bulgakov's works

Index of names